Postsecondary Education and Transition for Students with Learning Disabilities

Postsecondary Education and Transition for Students with Learning Disabilities

SECOND EDITION

Loring C. Brinckerhoff,
Joan M. McGuire,
and
Stan F. Shaw

Foreword by Vickie M. Barr

pro·ed
An International Publisher

8700 Shoal Creek Boulevard
Austin, Texas 78757-6897
800/897-3202 Fax 800/397-7633
www.proedinc.com

© 2002, 1993 by PRO-ED, Inc.
8700 Shoal Creek Boulevard
Austin, Texas 78757-6897
800/897-3202 Fax 800/397-7633
www.proedinc.com

Library of Congress Cataloging-in-Publication Data

Brinckerhoff, Loring Cowles.
    Postsecondary education and transition for students with learning disabilities /
Loring C. Brinckerhoff, Joan M. McGuire, Stan F. Shaw; with a foreword by
Vickie M. Barr.—2nd ed.
        p.   cm.
    Expanded ed. of: Promoting postsecondary education for students with learning
disabilities. c1993.
    Includes bibliographical references and index.
    ISBN 0-89079-872-9 (alk. paper)
    1. Learning disabled—Education (Higher)—United States—Handbooks, manuals, etc.
2. Special education—United States—Planning—Handbooks, manuals, etc.   3. Special
education—Law and legislation—United States—Handbooks, manuals, etc.   I. McGuire,
Joan.   II. Shaw, Stan F.   III. Brinckerhoff, Loring Cowles. Promoting postsecondary
education for students with learning disabilities.   IV. Title.
LC4818.5.B75   2002
371.9—dc21
                                                                    00-065314
                                                                    CIP

This book is designed in Goudy.

Printed in the United States of America

1   2   3   4   5   6   7   8   9   10   05   04   03   02   01

Contents

FOREWORD

Since the publication of the first edition of this textbook in 1993, perhaps the single best example of the gains that have been made in the broad arena of postsecondary education and students with learning disabilities is the ever increasing visibility of this "invisible" disability category. Evidence of this increasing visibility is confirmed by postsecondary enrollment statistics, name changes of national disability-related organizations, components of federal legislation, the increasing number of specialized summer precollege preparation programs, the extension of grant and scholarship opportunities to include students with learning disabilities, coverage by the mass media, and campus-wide policies and procedures.

Enrollment statistics go a long way in helping to increase the visibility of this category. Students with learning disabilities continue to represent the fastest-growing category of disability reported by first-time, full-time college freshmen. In 1998, 41% of all such freshmen identified themselves as students with learning disabilities. Ten years before, in 1988, just 15% had made such self-disclosure.

Increasing visibility is also evidenced by numerous other changes, both large and small. At least one national organization has changed its name to more accurately reflect the now equal use of its services by students with learning disabilities, including those enrolled in postsecondary institutions. The former Recording for the Blind is now Recording for the Blind & Dyslexic. The most recent reauthorization of the Individuals with Disabilities Education Act mandates that transition services now begin for students with disabilities, including those with learning disabilities, at age 14, rather than at the previously mandated age of 16. As a result, students with learning disabilities are learning about transition-related issues and postsecondary options at younger and younger ages. The self-advocacy skills and feelings of self-empowerment that often result from the attainment of such knowledge serve to increase the numbers of those who choose to go on to postsecondary education, thus contributing to the enrollment statistics stated above.

The HEATH Resource Center's annual compilation of information on summer precollege preparation programs for students with disabilities has certainly shown an increase in the number of campuses that offer such opportunities

specifically designed for students with learning disabilities. Our annual publication, *Financial Aid for Students with Disabilities,* has recently been able to list several organizations that extend scholarship opportunities to students with learning disabilities. Both such advances serve, in their own small ways, as evidence
of changes that have resulted due to the increasing visibility of students with
learning disabilities on college and university campuses.

The mass media, for good or bad, has also played a significant role. While
many positive, fair, and informative pieces have appeared in recent years focusing on the topic of students with learning disabilities in postsecondary education, several strong "backlash" pieces have also been published. Although such
backlash pieces certainly do not serve to increase the insightfulness of the uninformed regarding students with learning disabilities, it is possible that they have
indirectly enhanced the visibility of these students. If so, perhaps we can count
that as a positive outcome of a most unfortunate occurrence.

Finally, the development or fine-tuning of an array of campus-wide policies
and procedures has resulted from the increased visibility of students with learning disabilities in postsecondary education. In this 2001 edition of their textbook, my colleagues Loring Brinckerhoff, Joan McGuire, and Stan Shaw help
readers understand these policies and procedures as well as other substantive
issues related to postsecondary education and students with learning disabilities.
Along with the other contributing authors, a finer group of professionals cannot be found to lead us into the new millennium with this thorough, thought-
provoking, and user-friendly text. Now that events have led students with learning disabilities to be less invisible than previously, this text skillfully guides
readers to the next levels of understanding and action. In this revised edition,
readers will benefit from new chapters dedicated to the topics of transition planning; the provision of services for students with attention-deficit/hyperactivity
disorder (ADD and ADHD) and how such services differ from those that might
be provided to students with learning disabilities; the very current issues associated with standardized tests and eligibility requirements for testing accommodations; the promotion of our products; and the delivery of assistive technology and its use by students with learning disabilities on college and university
campuses.

Additional chapters provide readers with the very latest thoughts on topics
that serve as the foundations, or cornerstones, of our professional operations.
Relevant legislation and court cases are explained; information regarding psychosocial issues, adult development, and self-determination is presented; assessment issues are detailed; and issues regarding the definition of the population,
the provision of accommodations, and policies, procedures, and programmatic
considerations are expounded upon. Finally, in a concluding chapter, Brincker-

hoff, McGuire, and Shaw offer their thoughts on future directions for the field of postsecondary disability services for students with learning disabilities.

While I, in this foreword, have been using the terms *visible* and *invisible* to frame my points regarding the increased presence of students with learning disabilities in postsecondary education in recent years, Brinckerhoff, McGuire, and Shaw tell readers that much of the "heavy lifting" regarding the development of necessary policies and procedures has been accomplished. They muse that, over future years, the issues that will continue to advance postsecondary educational experiences and opportunities for students with learning disabilities will be much more institution based. Perhaps the next edition of their textbook will speak to proactive institutional advances—of policies, programs, and procedures that have been voluntarily developed and implemented by a collaborative cross-section of the campus community, benefiting all students, including those with learning disabilities. Hints of such movement away from the reactive to the proactive have been seen by those of us at HEATH. We will all look forward, then, to Brinckerhoff, McGuire, and Shaw ushering us through whatever future understandings emerge within the next several years, perhaps with even yet another edition of this text.

In the meantime, I am extremely honored to have been asked to prepare a few stage-setting thoughts for this edition of this cutting-edge text. As the visibility of students with learning disabilities in postsecondary education continues to escalate, I will keep my copy of this new edition within easy reach. It will serve as my guide, and I hope yours, as we all work together to foster the successful postsecondary experiences of students with learning disabilities.

Vickie M. Barr
Director, HEATH Resource Center
The National Clearinghouse on Postsecondary
Education for Individuals with Disabilities

PREFACE

The field of postsecondary education and learning disabilities has moved through adolescence and is embarking upon adulthood. Our first book, *Promoting Postsecondary Education for Students with Learning Disabilities: A Handbook for Practitioners* (1993) attempted to break new ground and provide our colleagues with a blueprint for serving students with learning disabilities in postsecondary education. As our students earn college degrees and pursue professional programs, this second edition builds upon that foundation and presents new information, taking the pulse of the field and expanding the horizons of our readership at the secondary level and beyond. Like an awkward teenager poised on the threshold of adulthood, the field of postsecondary LD is striving to find a new identity in rapidly changing times. In doing so, we need to retain the basic elements of earlier programming that have proven to be effective and shed policies and procedures that are no longer useful, or have merely continued out of tradition. Our vision should embrace excellence in service delivery and technological innovations, never losing sight of the legal foundations that have influenced the profession.

During the past 15 years, disability service providers in the postsecondary arena have established a professional identity. In 1985, the membership of the Association on Higher Education and Disability (AHEAD) was nearing 500 members. Today it has grown to nearly 2,000 members. As a profession, we now have professional and program standards, a code of ethics, and documentation guidelines for LD and ADHD to guide us. As a result, students, educators, clinicians, and service providers can access "best practice" standards from their own vantage points, using universally endorsed priorities.

Gone are the days when we were expected to be all things to all people. In the past, we may have been called upon to respond to a laundry list of consumer demands consistent with secondary school accommodation offerings, and expected to decipher the relevance of the lengthy menu of accommodation requests and implement all those services by ourselves, on demand. It was not an uncommon practice to provide students with LD and ADHD with the same accommodations across all subject areas semester after semester, regardless of the students' strengths and weaknesses documented in clinical evaluations. LD service providers often found themselves in the role of student "advocate."

Whether this meant picking up the phone and dialing the number for Recording for the Blind & Dyslexic (RFB&D) or trying to help a student plan his or her next career move, we attempted to do it all.

During the last few years, research, court cases, Office for Civil Rights rulings, and professional collaboration have helped us to refine our vision and reshape the postsecondary disability landscape. We know that there must be linkage between the nature and severity of the disability and a requested accommodation so that access is assured without fundamentally altering the technical standards of courses and programs. We recognize the necessity of addressing clinically supported accommodations and services over personal preferences in order to maintain course and academic integrity. We value the importance of self-determination and have come to expect students to participate in their own advocacy. We acknowledge that it is our job as colleagues to work with faculty to determine what is most effective. As we move into another stage, it is critical that we respect faculty as key players in serving students with LD and ADHD.

Scott (2000) points out that the concept of universal design in the planning and delivery of instruction and the evaluation of student learning is the threshold that service providers and institutions of higher education need to cross today. By applying the analogy of architectural access to instruction, she argues that all students will benefit, not just those with disabilities. In an era of changing demographics, this emphasis on a pedagogy that accommodates an increasingly diverse student population through the creation of universally designed educational settings will diminish the need to accommodate individual learning disabilities.

The authors of this text have been on the front line of service delivery as coordinators of learning disability efforts at five colleges, including 2- and 4-year public and private institutions. During the past 15 years, they have implemented state, regional, and national technical assistance and have consulted with a variety of testing and licensing agencies. Through these technical assistance efforts, some very creative solutions to service delivery have emerged from college deans and faculty and from the students themselves. Cyndi Jordan (2000) comments, "It's not the salary; it's not the benefits, but the 'elements of potential' that keep us in the field of postsecondary education and learning disabilities." It is that sense of knowing that something we do will make a difference for the students we serve. It may be assisting a student by tapping into new technology such as a personal digital accessory or a voice-input word-processing software program, or helping students recognize the types of reasonable accommodations and support they need in different academic situations, or encouraging secondary students to try out accommodations in high school before going to college. Navicky (2000) posits that professionals who work with students with learning disabilities and ADHD face the challenge of serving many students and tailoring their approach to each one. It is our hope that this volume will assist professionals at the secondary and postsecondary levels to tailor the cloth to fit the unique and changing needs of the talented students we serve.

This widely expanded version of our first book reflects the expertise and commitment of many individuals. The nine contributing authors who assiduously crafted their chapters and exhibited good humor and patience with the process merit our utmost gratitude and respect. All the appendixes have been placed on a CD-ROM, and they include numerous examples of downloadable policies, data collection forms, and useful resources, many of which were contributed by professionals from highly respected programs in the United States and Canada. Vickie Barr, the director of the HEATH Resource Center, the National Clearinghouse on Postsecondary Education for Individuals with Disabilities, has set the stage for the book content by providing a backdrop against which to consider the growth of our field. Colleagues including Patricia Anderson, Manju Banerjee, Lydia Block, Ken Chep, Lyman Dukes III, Barbara Rhein, and Louise Russell have provided us with ideas, challenges, and discussions to sharpen our focus and broaden our perspectives.

No volume of this magnitude would exist were it not for the incredible talent and tenacity of our "technical team." John Toman and Teresa Foley, colleagues at the University of Connecticut, deserve accolades for the production of the CD-ROM. Only they know the minute detail and precision that are embodied in this tool. Jamie Tilden's willingness to take on the word processing and disk management made the process manageable. Carrol Waite, our colleague and assistant extraordinaire, has worked tirelessly from the inception of this project to its conclusion. We want to also acknowledge the vision of our esteemed editor, Jim Patton, for his encouragement and creative ideas in making this text one of a kind. Finally, we want to acknowledge the unwavering support of friends, both personal and professional, and family who helped us maintain our sense of perspective during the production of this work.

LCB
JMM
SFS

C H A P T E R

INTRODUCTION

Since the publication of our first edition, *Promoting Postsecondary Education for Students with Learning Disabilities*, the field of higher education and learning disabilities has come of age. In 1993, when the book was first published, many colleges and universities were just beginning to offer comprehensive services to students with learning disabilities. Now over 1,200 campuses in the United States and Canada offer students with learning disabilities or ADHD individualized support services. Many of these changes are grounded in the legal underpinnings of the Americans with Disabilities Act (ADA), the reauthorization of the Individuals with Disabilities Education Act (IDEA), and, in Canada, the Canadian Charter of Rights and Freedoms. These laws have worked to enhance the integration and participation of individuals with disabilities in all aspects of society, including the postsecondary arena and competitive employment.

Today, students are arriving on college campuses better prepared academically and with aspirations raised by their own successful track records, as well as supportive parents and encouraging high school teachers. They have typically thrived in the "least restrictive environment" in high school, which has resulted in many more students with learning disabilities and ADHD taking sufficient academic course work to qualify for postsecondary opportunities. Increasing numbers of high school students with learning disabilities are now taught learning strategies, metacognitive awareness, and the social skills that will be necessary for college success, and they are learning those college survival skills within the regular education classroom setting with the assistance of LD support staff.

High school students, their parents, and college counselors are much more aware of the range of available college options due, in part, to the efforts of advocacy groups like the Learning Disabilities Association of America (LDA)

1

and the International Dyslexia Association (IDA), as well as the publication of several LD postsecondary college guidebooks. Students are becoming their own advocates and the coauthors of their Individual Transition Plans. Finally, colleges and universities have come to understand the potential that such students add to campus life and, in some cases, are actively recruiting these individuals.

Efforts to foster change and expand services for college students with learning disabilities have been fueled by the availability of federal and provincial monies that have promoted the development of model demonstration projects for college students with learning disabilities. In 1999, 21 U.S. colleges and universities were awarded funds from the U.S. Department of Education for innovative demonstration grants. The purpose of these demonstration projects is to provide "technical assistance and professional development for faculty and administrators in institutions of higher education in order to provide them with the skills and supports that they need to teach students with disabilities. The program will also be used to widely disseminate research and training to enable faculty and administrators in other institutions of higher education to meet the educational needs of students with disabilities." Many of the funded proposals supported in this grant initiative subscribe to the concept of "universal design for instruction" (Scott, McGuire, & Foley, 2000), a concept that promotes effective teaching approaches and techniques that will enhance the learning of all students in higher education, including those with disabilities.

In Canada, similar initiatives that are specifically designed to enhance the learning of students with disabilities in higher education are also under way. One of the most ambitious is the Learning Opportunities Task Force in Ontario. With a total budget of over five million dollars, it has been mandated to establish and then evaluate pilot projects in the postsecondary sector for students with learning disabilities through 2002. The work is primarily carried out by part-time consultants who work directly within the postsecondary sector, or who have extensive experience in learning disabilities. At the present time, eight pilot projects have been approved involving both 2- and 4-year settings across Ontario. Over 500 students with documented learning disabilities have been identified for participation in these projects. One of the outcomes of these pilot projects will be to determine those services and accommodations that are most effective in the postsecondary setting and provide the best value for the money spent. The Task Force staff hopes that these findings will "alter the way transition is managed for these students from secondary to postsecondary education and the way we support LD students in educational settings "(Eva Nichols, personal communication, December 20, 1999). Many of these model programs will likely serve as the blueprints for services offered in the United States and elsewhere in Canada.

Eight years after the publication of the first edition of this book, it is apparent that the field has made many significant advances in the areas of assessment, service delivery, use of technological aids, and accommodation of students with learning disabilities and ADHD in postsecondary settings. Those 8 years, however, have not been without controversy. Several important cases have recently begun to specifically address the identification, assessment, and accommodation of students with learning disabilities at the undergraduate and graduate levels (Elswit, Geetter, & Goldberg, 1999). The Supreme Court rulings of the late 1990s has also raised public awareness and, in doing so, has stirred a maelstrom of debate around accommodation and service issues in higher education settings.

We are living in turbulent times. Some high school guidance counselors still question whether learning disabilities and ADHD are real or simply a ticket to get an accommodation of more time on the SATs. Some college deans see priority registration, course substitutions, and the use of notetakers or taped textbooks to be crutches. Robert Sternberg, professor of psychology at Yale, has written extensively on matters pertaining to psychology and disability. He notes that in some universities, students are excused from difficult courses like math and foreign languages because they have a disability in those subjects. It's no wonder, state Sternberg and Spear-Swerling (1999), that some parents have sought to have learning disabilities diagnosed in their children to make them eligible for such benefits. Zirkel (2000) recently commented on the favoritism that college students with LD often garner, noting that the evidence points to a significant increase in "false positives" of students who do not truly qualify as having a disability. He supports this premise by noting that many of the college students with learning disabilities that he has encountered have had, on the average, "a significantly higher parental income" and "were often white." He goes on to say, "At-risk factors for disabilities are usually connected with poverty, not wealth." The observations shared by some faculty and administrators have led many observers to question whether a significant number of those students are truly learning disabled, or rather, in the words of one college official, "upper-income game players." Mark Kelman, professor of law at Stanford University, and Jillian Lester, professor of law at UCLA, underscore the skepticism shared by some in their book *Jumping the Queue: An Inquiry into the Legal Treatment of Students with Learning Disabilities* (1997):

> It is plausible that there truly are children with learning disabilities out in the world, but that our diagnostic techniques are so poor that a high proportion of children labeled as having LDs do not "really" have them, while a significant number of those who actually have LDs are not so identified. (p. 29)

Perhaps the most strident, and certainly most vocal, critic of the identification of students with learning disabilities in higher education in the 1990s was Jon Westling, then provost of Boston University. He made national headlines when he commented in a speech to the Heritage Foundation, "Enormous numbers of students in grade school and high school have been diagnosed as learning disabled. In Massachusetts, almost one in five students are crammed into this category. The national average is 12 percent. Are we in the midst of a silent genetic catastrophe?" (Shalit, 1997, p. 16). Mr. Westling was ultimately criticized by Judge Patricia Saris in her resolution of a Boston University case in which students with LD and ADHD sued the university for allegedly unfair treatment under the Americans with Disabilities Act, the Rehabilitation Act, and Massachusetts state law. Judge Saris concluded that Westling was "substantially motivated by uninformed stereotypes" about students with learning disabilities. Unfortunately, his views are undoubtedly still shared by many.

The intent of this edition is to update readers and to highlight some of the changes that have occurred during the last decade. It is hoped that this book will help to build better links between high school teachers, vocational rehabilitation counselors, parents, and future consumers, as they establish internal support with campus administrators, faculty, and staff. By effectively networking at both the secondary and postsecondary levels, LD service providers will be better able to promote postsecondary education to students with learning disabilities and ADHD. The following sections present chapter highlights.

Chapter 2: A Comprehensive Approach to Transition Planning

This chapter articulates the transition requirements specified under the reauthorization of the IDEA as it applies to adolescents with learning disabilities and ADHD who are moving from secondary to postsecondary settings. The increasingly active role of the student is examined as it relates to transition planning, including participation in the transition planning team, selecting high school classes, searching for the best postsecondary option, and enrolling in either a 2- or a 4-year setting. Transition planning is viewed as a student-centered activity and one that is both sensitive to and reflective of the developmental and educational needs of the student.

Students with learning disabilities and ADHD must be knowledgeable about the differences between high school and college, so they are better prepared for the road ahead. The inherent differences in the structure of these two educational settings are shown in a table that compares high school and college across a variety of domains. In order to make transition planning easier for teenagers with learning disabilities and ADHD, the chapter includes a variety of transition planning tools and resources that can be used by guidance counselors and special education personnel. Transition planning materials may include checklists, transition planning inventories, student workbooks, self-advocacy handbooks, and training videos. A detailed timetable for college planning across all four years of high school is included to assist students, parents, high school support staff, and guidance counselors. Some of the transition planning steps, such as applying for the SAT, are discrete and time sensitive, while others are not specific to any particular grade level. Several common themes emerge across grade levels, including learning how to describe your disability to others, fostering self-determination, learning about legal rights, selecting courses, developing an Individual Transition Plan (ITP), exploring postsecondary options, and evaluating LD support services. The chapter concludes with numerous suggestions on writing the college essay, using the common application form, tapping into Internet resources, and reflecting upon the implications of taking the SAT or ACT under nonstandard conditions.

Chapter 3: Judicial Intent and Legal Precedents

In Chapter 3, Laura Rothstein presents an overview of the IDEA, Section 504 of the Vocational Rehabilitation Act of 1973, and the ADA. She then develops some striking comparisons between the laws. Initially, each of these three legal mandates is reviewed, and implications for serving students with learning disabilities are offered. Readers should find the underlying principles of the laws to be relevant for both secondary and postsecondary service providers. A section on the 1997 reauthorization of the IDEA provides up-to-date information on guidelines for the development of the IEP, the ITP, and requirements regarding reevaluation. Since the impact of Section 504 on postsecondary settings is significant, the chapter focuses primarily on what colleges may and may not do under this civil rights legislation. Rothstein reminds the reader that, under Section 504, institutions are required to respond by making whatever modifications in academic requirements are necessary to ensure that such requirements do not discriminate or have the effect of discriminating against a qualified student with a disability. She emphasizes that the "provision of accommodations for college students with disabilities need not guarantee them equal results or achievement; accommodations must merely afford them an *equal opportunity* to achieve equal results. [emphasis in orignal]"

The impact of federal law on higher education institutions and their relationships with students with learning disabilities is substantial. Rothstein systematically discusses who is protected under the law and how these protections affect students with learning disabilities in postsecondary settings. She delineates the parameters of these laws by citing numerous court cases that serve to further shape judicial intent. These cases should give LD service providers additional insights as they seek to make informed judgments about admissions, service delivery, and academic adjustments for college students with learning disabilities and ADHD. Rothstein notes that written policies or guidelines for serving students with disabilities are often born from the legal principles discussed in these recent court cases. She concludes the chapter with several specific suggestions for university administrators on how to create policies and practices that conform to both the letter and the spirit of the law.

Chapter 4: Issues in Defining the Population

Donald Hammill (1990) states that "few topics in the field of learning disabilities have evoked as much interest or controversy as those relating to the definition of this condition" (p. 74). Chapter 4 begins by addressing those concerns and by offering some reasons it is critical for the field to adopt a definition of learning disabilities that is appropriate at the postsecondary level. One approach to defining this population is to survey current definitions and to determine which elements within them are germane to adults. The definition of the National Joint Committee on Learning Disabilities (NJCLD) is cited for its many advantages, including the fact that it has been endorsed by representatives of nine national organizations that have a major interest in learning disabilities, including the Association on Higher Education and Disability. It is suggested that if more postsecondary service providers would adhere to this functional definition, the field would not be faced with challenges to the credibility of adult learning disabilities and to accommodations to assure equal treatment and access.

Building on the work of the NJCLD, the authors of this chapter point to the need to establish an operational definition in a manner that will allow individuals with little formal training in learning disabilities and diagnosis to make clear decisions about service eligibility. Four levels of investigation are offered. Level I involves the identification of significant difficulties and relative strengths in any one of six skill areas. Level II requires verification that the learning disability is intrinsic to the individual. The disability may be the result of either central nervous system dysfunction or an information-processing problem in one of three areas: (a) executive functioning, (b) cognitive processing, or (c) a knowledge base of general information. Level III involves the identification of concomitant limitations, such as a lack of psychosocial skills or physical or sensory abilities, that must be viewed not as elements of the learning disability, but as related problems that may or may not be associated with a learning disability. Level IV addresses alternative explanations for a learning difficulty. Factors cited include a lack of motivation; environmental, cultural, or economic influences; inappropriate instruction; and the possibility that the primary disability is not a learning disability (for example, it might be a psychological disorder or a health impairment). The model is then applied and illustrated with a variety of typical college student profiles that serve to delineate the more subtle differences between individuals with learning disabilities and those classified as "slow learners" or as having attention-deficit/hyperactivity disorders or traumatic brain injuries.

Chapter 5: The Connections Among Psychosocial Issues, Adult Development, and Self-Determination

In Chapter 5, Lynda Price discusses three critical assumptions surrounding the psychosocial development of individuals with learning disabilities: (a) learning disabilities do not disappear with adulthood; (b) adults with learning disabilities require specialized services and education; and (c) psychosocial issues influence individuals with learning disabilities. Price cites numerous research articles that add support to these three assumptions. She underscores the need for ongoing psychosocial support of college students with learning disabilities who typically have difficulties such as problems starting and maintaining relationships, excessive dependency on others, less satisfaction with familial relationships, low self-esteem, lack of confidence, feelings of inadequacy, and depression. Given these three assumptions, Price proposes a new, holistic model that views people with learning disabilities as having a variety of unique psychosocial needs across their lifespans.

Price combines the fundamentals of adult learning theory with a "cross-disciplinary" focus (e.g., psychology, adult development, vocational education, and special education) to produce a new hybrid model for support. This model acknowledges the importance of adult developmental theories as equally applicable to adults with learning disabilities. She revisits the work of Malcolm Knowles and his "learner-centered" approach, which stresses the importance of participative education, in which adults are viewed as responsible and independent learners. He also stresses the concept of discovery learning to facilitate educational growth through personal insight and self-exploration and by building on past experiences. Price applies Knowles's learning principles to college students with learning disabilities and addresses the importance of self-determination within this context. Self-determination is defined as the "ability to identify and achieve goals based on a foundation of knowing and valuing oneself" (Field & Hoffman, 1994). The ingredients for self-determination include a number of interrelated components that can be specifically taught as skill areas: (a) self-actualization, (b) assertiveness, (c) creativity, (d) pride, and (e) self-advocacy. Table 5.3 in the chapter provides the reader with a succinct comparison between self-determination and psychosocial development. Salient points articulated in the text are compared and then included in the final section on effective practices.

There is no one best practice for addressing the psychosocial needs of college students with learning disabilities, but a varied approach that focuses on enhancing their self-awareness and helps them to set realistic goals with appropriate strategies is essential. One particular approach that holds promise in this regard is peer mentoring. Mentors can provide students with learning disabilities with realistic guidance about the hidden challenges of higher education. Price notes that when assisting this population, professionals in college, adult, and vocational education need to be knowledgeable about a variety of techniques and counseling approaches.

Chapter 6: Assessment of Learning Disabilities

Chapter 6, by Joseph Madaus, provides a refreshing and updated look at the controversial area of LD adult assessment. His intent is not to teach practictioners "how to" conduct an LD assessment, but rather "to provide readers with the tools and information they need so they can read assessment reports and glean information as a knowledgeable consumer." He begins by defining the terms *assessment, testing,* and *diagnosis.* Assessment is the process of "accumulating a variety of data in order to make decisions about an individual," whereas testing is administering a set of specific questions to a person to derive a score that should become one piece of the larger assessment process (Salvia & Ysseldyke, 1998). Diagnosis is "the ongoing hypothesis testing and decision making to determine the nature and scope of the problem" (Johnson, 1987). The dynamic process of assessment is viewed as an opportunity to collect information to test knowledge and skills and to determine the nature and severity of a given problem.

Madaus expands on these fundamental points and describes the components of "an ideal" LD diagnostic report. He advises readers not to be overly dependent on any one test for determining a learning disability, to consider the benefits of informal measures (such as writing samples), and to pay careful attention to the clinical observations of the examiner. He concludes this section by noting that, in the ideal world, a comprehensive LD evaluation should conclude with "a set of data-driven recommendations that suggest teaching approaches, learning strategies, auxiliary aids and, if necessary, reasonable accommodations to help the student succeed." Unfortunately, many LD reports are not comprehensive, nor are they grounded in data that support realistic accommodation decision making. Conclusions reached by Madaus are further supported by research conducted by McGuire, Madaus, Litt, and Ramirez (1996), who reviewed LD documentation from over 300 students who participated in the LD support services program at the University of Connecticut.

The chapter also includes a thorough discussion of a variety of ways that institutions have addressed the thorny issue of assessment services at the postsecondary level. Many postsecondary settings do not offer assessment services in-house because they are costly and are not required under Section 504 or the ADA. Some postsecondary institutions may feel an ethical obligation to assist students with suspected, but undiagnosed, learning disabilities and opt to provide assessment services at no cost or to assist students with the "creative financing" of LD evaluations. Madaus leads the reader through the pros and cons of providing diagnostic services on campus while sharing some creative solutions implemented by various institutions.

The section on psychometric qualities is designed to help readers become more knowledgeable about psychometric issues such as test scores, test validity and reliability, and the selection of appropriate assessment measures for use with a given population. In addition, Madaus spotlights two innovative ways for helping consumers understand their strengths, weaknesses, and the meaning of their test scores by using graphic, visual representations of the test data. These prototypes are illustrated in Tables 6.1 and 6.2 and can be replicated by service providers who want to help students assume ownership of their disability by understanding the connection between subtest scores and their need for a given accommodation.

Readers may find it reassuring that Madaus acknowledges, "It is not uncommon to read a psychoeducational assessment and be left pondering how the evaluator arrived at a specific diagnosis or a particular conclusion." One reason for this rests on the "discrepancy model" required under the IDEA, which is embraced by many evaluators at the secondary school level. It presumes that the diagnosis of a learning disability must be grounded in an observed discrepancy between actual grade placement and grade equivalency scores, or based on a comparison between a student's intellectual ability and his or her performance on achievement measures. Depending on the criteria used, the state in which one resides, and institutional practice, a difference of one or more standard deviations may be considered significant and, therefore, indicative of a learning disability. Readers are provided with several additional suggestions for scrutinizing LD documentation reports so that informed judgments can be made as to whether a given diagnosis is valid and the recommendations in the report supportable. This chapter concludes with a quick "tutorial" that profiles many of the most popular assessment measures used to document specific learning disability in adults.

Chapter 7: Determining Eligibility for Services and Testing Accommodations

Chapter 7 discusses how eligibility determinations are reached in college, in graduate school, and by testing and licensing agencies. In order to be eligible for support services or academic accommodations in higher education, students with learning disabilities and/or ADHD must have a disability that results in the inability to perform, or severe restriction in performing, a major life activity that the average person in the general population can accomplish. In order to determine a student's eligibility for protections under the ADA, postsecondary disability service providers must review the student's documentation carefully to ascertain if it verifies the stated disability. Once the disability has been established and the student is deemed eligible for accommodations, the documentation must support the necessity of the requested accommodations. Those accommodations should be provided as long as they are viewed as fair and reasonable by the institution, or testing agency, and pose no undue hardship, administrative burden, or financial burden.

At the graduate and professional school levels, it is often a challenge for evaluators to write LD or ADHD diagnostic reports that indicate that an individual is "otherwise qualified" for the rigors of a graduate, law, or medical school despite the presence of a learning disability or ADHD. Many of these individuals are also gifted and have an extensive repertoire of finely tuned compensatory strategies that can further confound the diagnosis and make it even more difficult to demonstrate the need for accommodations. Testing and licensing agencies face the additional burden of having to determine who is otherwise qualified to receive testing accommodations or auxiliary aids based solely on the paper documentation submitted, without having an opportunity to get to know the individual directly.

The complexities of LD and ADHD documentation and the lack of uniformity in the writing of reports, combined with several recent court cases that addressed postsecondary LD issues, precipitated the development of professional guidelines for the documentation of LD and ADHD. This chapter presents an overview of the Association on Higher Education and Disability LD guidelines (July 1997b), which are included in Appendix 7.2 (on the CD-ROM). A corollary to the "AHEAD Guidelines for Documentation of a Learning Disability in Adolescents and Adults" is the "Consortium Guidelines for Documentation of AD/HD in Adolescents and Adults," which can be found in Appendix 7.3 (on the CD-ROM). Readers are encouraged to tailor these documents to fit the needs of their respective settings. For example, the Educational Testing Service (ETS) adapted and modified both of these sets of guidelines and has published a set of policy statements that apply to all its test programs, including the SAT. The ETS policy statements and new guidelines for psychiatric disabilities can be viewed at its Web site (http://www.ets.org/disability).

The chapter closes with thirteen common "pitfalls and perils" for service providers to avoid when reviewing LD and ADHD documentation at the post-secondary and graduate school levels. In several instances, actual case studies are used to elaborate on a given point or to illustrate what constitutes appropriate documentation to support requested accommodations such as extended test time, use of a paper-based test format instead of a computer-based test, and the use of a reader, notetaker, or a scribe.

Chapter 8: Policies, Procedures, and Programmatic Considerations

Learning disability service providers should pay particular attention to recent court decisions and to rulings of the Office for Civil Rights that highlight the need for colleges and universities to develop written policies and procedures surrounding the provision of accommodations to students with disabilities. Heyward (1998) has noted that the most common institutional deficiencies include "failure to either develop procedures or monitor procedures to ensure that students' requests for accommodations are properly handled" (Chapter 7, p. 16). This chapter guides service providers who are addressing this important task for the first time and alerts those who are charged with monitoring the implementation of policies and procedures to variables that can affect successful enforcement.

Recognizing that there must be institutional engagement, or "buy in," in the development of disability policies and procedures on campus, the authors note that key administrators should pay careful attention to the legal underpinnings of the ADA and Section 504 that ultimately shape policy development. Clearly, institutions are better served by a proactive approach to policy development than by reacting to student complaints or legal decisions. Service providers are cautioned to take stock of the political nature of policy development and become familiar with generic institutional policies before naively embarking on what is realistically an arduous task involving numerous constituencies. Readers will find the flowchart in this chapter useful, as it pinpoints a number of important steps in the policy development process. For example, surveying comparable institutions to determine their approaches to a policy matter such as course substitution might save staff time that would otherwise be spent on crafting an original document.

Drawing on the work of Jarrow (1997a), the authors delineate a number of broad areas that lend themselves to policies and procedures, including the process for accessing such services as accommodations, documentation guidelines, confidentiality, course substitutions, full-time student status with less than a full-time credit load, and the appeal process for accommodations that are denied. It is also important for LD service administrators to ensure ongoing monitoring of policy implementation, and this chapter identifies certain organizational elements that must be in place in order to ensure successful implementation.

The progression of the field of postsecondary disability services to become a legitimate profession is addressed in this chapter as well as in Chapter 12, particularly as it relates to the development of professional standards, a code of ethics, and program standards. Readers will find the recently approved AHEAD Program Standards (Shaw & Dukes, in press) and the work of Anderson (1998a) especially helpful. Anderson's research has led to consensus among 131 experts regarding those support service components essential to service delivery for college students with learning disabilities. These 55 components across 14 categories provide a framework for LD service providers to examine the approach used on their respective campuses, bearing in mind that not every component will constitute an essential programmatic function for every institution.

Finally, Chapter 8 provides an updated discussion on the process of program development, including current thinking about program affiliation or location within the organization of the institution. The issue of services or programs is revisited, and a revised developmental continuum of service-delivery model is presented. Readers are encouraged to reflect upon changes in progress on some campuses to meet the needs of an increasingly diverse student population through an inclusionary model such as an academic skills center. Whether disability services should be a component of such a "mainstreamed" center warrants collaborative discussion. The chapter concludes with ideas for the development of a summer transition program and a charge to readers to reflect on some of the challenges facing the field as it moves into a new millennium.

Chapter 9: The Dynamic Process of Providing Accommodations

In Chapter 9, Sally Scott notes, "Determining which accommodations are appropriate and how they should be provided is not an easy task." She uses this statement as the central tenet for her chapter, as she skillfully discusses the dynamic process of actively considering the disability-related needs of students within the context of a variety of postsecondary settings. Determining what accommodations are reasonable and appropriate for any given setting is a complex process and one that varies depending on the severity of the student's disability, his or her specific accommodation needs, and the mission of the testing agency or institution. Scott examines the accommodation needs of students and test takers with learning disabilities and ADHD across these areas: (a) the college classroom, (b) testing environments, (c) learning outside the classroom, and (d) program requirements.

Scott points out that college classrooms are rapidly changing given the advent of new ways of delivering information. As a result, service providers need to find new, innovative approaches to providing accommodations to students with learning disabilities and ADHD. It is no longer sufficient to provide a student with merely a copy of the professor's overheads and notes, to permit tape recording of lectures, or to secure a student note taker. These conventional accommodations of the past are giving way to the need for accommodations that will assist students with disabilities to access the virtual classrooms of the 21st century, classrooms in which video and audio conferencing, Web site access, on-line learning, and cross-country chat room participation are the standard. For some students with learning disabilities, accommodations may include the use of laptop computers that will permit them to access a professor's lecture notes, overheads, slides, or course outlines directly from the Web before the lecture is even presented. Others may be able to hook up their laptop computers directly to that of another student in the class who is taking notes and simultaneously relaying them to other students' laptops. Some students with audio-processing disorders or ADHD may use assistive listening devices to minimize outside distractions and to hear lectures without audio interference.

Professors often view their examination procedures as sacred, but when a student with a disability requests more test time, some are willing to comply if the request is supported by documentation or, in many instances, by a letter from the ADA or the disability services coordinator on campus. More and more students with learning disabilities are requesting an "alternative test format," however, in addition to more time. Changing the content material to be covered, the mode of presentation, or the test format is often a delicate and complex matter. Scott posits that when the testing format taps into a student's learning disability, rather than his or her level of achievement, then an accommodation needs to be considered. Some of the accommodations discussed in the chapter include using a reader, placing the examination on tape, enlarging the test, hiring a scribe, and permitting students to use a word processor. Several practical recommendations are also offered as to how testing accommodation services for students with learning disabilities can be coordinated in light of security considerations and an ever increasing volume of requests.

Student learning outside of the classroom often involves the use of accommodations and/or auxiliary aids that will assist in the completion of homework assignments or job internships. The standard accommodation for many students with dyslexia is the use of audiotaped textbooks or digital audio disks from Recording for the Blind & Dyslexic in Princeton, New Jersey. The Library of Congress tapes and campus volunteers who are willing to tape on request can also be important resources for students with learning disabilities. Increasingly, many service providers are taking advantage of assistive technology with computers that have built-in optical scanning and recording devices. This technology permits students to scan classroom text materials and handouts for themselves without having to be dependent on a volunteer reader.

Additional campus resources explored by Scott include college libraries and computer labs. College libraries are often overlooked or underused by students with learning disabilities. Scott discusses two main approaches that librarians can use to assist patrons with learning disabilities to access catalog information, databases, microfiche, and Internet resources. She also discusses how these students may need some additional orientation, hands-on experience, and assistance with organizing themselves given the mountain of information surrounding them. Clear signage is a start, as well as some flexibility in check-out policies. Computer labs are another important resource for students with learning disabilities who may want to perform basic word-processing functions, register for classes, access on-line course components, or use the Internet for research.

Scott also addresses the issue of providing students with learning disabilities and ADHD with program modifications. These modifications often affect such areas as financial aid, course loads, registration, and eligibility for the dean's list. Few areas generate more opinion than course substitutions. Although the majority of postsecondary institutions provide students with documented learning disabilities an alternative for meeting the conventional foreign language or mathematics requirement, this remains a sensitive area given the *Guckenburger v. Trustees of Boston University* (1997) lawsuit. Scott notes, "In both foreign language learning and mathematics, the field is recognizing that the more learning options and accommodations available in these potentially difficult content areas, the fewer students there will be that need a course substitution."

In the final section of the chapter, Scott presents readers with additional sources of information for enhancing faculty and student understanding of learning disabilities and the process of providing accommodations. The most important message of this chapter is that, whenever possible, accommodations that promote the greatest level of student independence should be encouraged. These may involve the deployment of learning strategies by students and the use of instructional strategies by faculty, in concert with a broad array of auxiliary aids and accommodations that permit students to demonstrate their true abilities in higher education and beyond.

Chapter 10: College Students with ADHD: New Challenges and Directions

In Chapter 10, Jane Byron and David Parker from the University of North Carolina at Chapel Hill, address a broad range of topics pertaining to college students with ADHD. Specifically, they address the following issues: (a) defining the population, (b) documentation, (c) accommodation decisions, and (d) service provision options.

The reader is provided with background on the evolution of the term *ADHD*: from when it was first subsumed under the medical model and referred to as "minimal brain dysfunction" or "hyperactive child syndrome" to its present-day metamorphosis as "attention-deficit/hyperactivity disorder" (AD/HD) in the *Diagnostic and Statistical Manual of Mental Disorders–Fourth Edition* (DSM–IV) (American Psychiatric Association, 1994). There appears to be consensus that ADHD is identified by the core symptoms of impulsivity, distractibility, and inappropriate levels of concentration and attention. The authors point out that, in college, an unprecedented number of students are presenting ADHD documentation and requesting accommodations and services. These students are discovering that ADHD directly affects their day-to-day academic functioning and social skills. As a result, a large number of them are turning to medications to help them stay focused and to keep up with the increased demands of college. Unfortunately, there is also a reported trend that some of these students are experimenting with medications and "self-medicating," which has raised new concerns. Other college students with ADHD may forget to take their medication, despite a strong motivation to do so, and fall behind in their coursework because they cannot concentrate.

Byron and Parker point out that students with ADHD are a relatively new type of college student, one that has required the postsecondary disability field to revisit its thinking and, in many cases, to revise its practices with regard to service provision. They note, "Chief among these issues is the nature and role of disability documentation. Students with learning disabilities have traditionally needed to present disability coordinators with more comprehensive documentation than their counterparts with ADHD." Recently, service providers have become increasingly leery of accepting prescription pad diagnoses of ADHD from medical doctors and are beginning to require more comprehensive documentation that addresses the impact of the student's disability in a given educational setting. As a result, many service providers are looking for documentation guidelines they can use or modify on their respective campuses. In 1998, the Consortium on ADHD Documentation developed comprehensive guidelines in direct response to service providers' requests for guidance. These guidelines are discussed in further detail in Chapter 7. The Consortium guidelines helped to bring the issue of educational testing to the forefront and opened a dialogue between service providers and testing agencies as to the merits of requiring educational testing as part of the ADHD workup. The chapter authors share their concerns and describe a self-initiated program evaluation at UNC–Chapel Hill that resulted in the decision to require psychoeducational assessment data in ADHD documentation so that the current educational impact of the disability can be ascertained.

The third area discussed by Byron and Parker is the process of making accommodation decisions. In the past it was common practice for evaluators to simply recommend a quiet room, or "a distraction-free setting," for individuals with ADHD. More recently, diagnosticians have begun to recommend a cornucopia of accommodations to students with ADHD, ranging from books on tape to single dormitory rooms. A concern expressed by the authors is that college students with ADHD frequently request accommodations that are not clearly supported in the documentation.

There appears to be a lack of consensus among service providers about the methods that should be employed to determine the need for accommodations. In the realm of ADHD, most service providers depend heavily on the clinical judgment of the evaluator, the student's prior history of accommodations, and any available psychoeducational measures. Byron and Parker suggest that service providers should collect data on the students' use of extra test time in each class. That information can then be used the following semester to further substantiate the need for more or less testing time.

The final area addressed in this chapter is that of service provision options for ADHD students. In the eyes of the authors, one of the most important service options for this population is disability awareness training. Byron and

Parker note that once in college, many ADHD students develop a new aware-ness of the impact of their disability. This awareness forms a "foundation as they learn how to self-advocate successfully while developing coping skills for man-aging the impact of their disability independently." An increasingly popular method for assisting students with ADHD cope with the rigors of college life is coaching. As a result, many Offices for Students with Disabilities (OSD) have elected to add coaching services to their lists of available support services. The authors summarize the differences between a coaching model and a learning strategies intervention model used at UNC–Chapel Hill in the LD Support Services office. LD service providers, diagnosticians, and special education teachers should find the authors' discussion of the benefits and limitations of each of these popular approaches insightful. In order to synthesize the wealth of information presented in this chapter, the authors developed a case study involving a college sophomore with ADHD. They use this realistic case study as a vehicle for applying the concepts covered in the chapter by having the reader confront a variety of issues, including assessment, documentation, accommoda-tions decisions, service provision, and the use of medications. By the conclusion of this chapter, readers should feel much more prepared for serving students with ADHD in secondary and postsecondary settings and more knowledgeable about how to develop the support services and accommodations these students need to succeed in college.

Chapter 11: The Use of Assistive Technology in Postsecondary Education

In Chapter 11, Bryant, Bryant, and Rieth offer an up-to-date look at the types of assistive technology (AT) devices available to college students with learning disabilities and ADHD. Specifically, the authors address the following topics: (a) a rationale for the use of AT devices; (b) benefits of assistive technology in postsecondary education settings; (c) a brief discussion of AT service delivery systems; (d) a description of specific AT devices and their use; (e) an examina-tion of AT assessment, selection, monitoring, and evaluation procedures; and (f) a discussion of barriers to AT use and proposed solutions.

Assistive technology devices can maximize a student's abilities and poten-tial. For college students with learning disabilities, assistive technology is a nat-ural because it allows them an opportunity to actively participate in all aspects of the college curriculum by providing alternative methods of responding to the learning environment. For example, tape-recorded, Web-based lessons can be linked directly to speech synthesis devices, and optical character-recognition systems can be coupled with speech synthesis devices to enhance the reading rate and comprehension of text of students with dyslexia. Research by Vogel and Reder (1998) cited in the chapter indicates that overall, students who successfully use assistive technology tend to be more successful academically and are more satisfied with themselves and their performance. Numerous user benefits cited by the authors include enhanced self-esteem, increased motivation to learn, increased productivity, and an improvement in basic skills.

The next section describes a variety of assistive technology devices that can be used across academic domains including, reading, writing, mathematics, listening, and study skills. Reading skills can be enhanced with devices and programs that involve speech synthesis, optical character-recognition systems, and tape recorders. Optical character-recognition systems, or "reading machines," can permit users to scan text and download it into a computer and then have it read back to them. This technology is particularly helpful for those individuals who exhibit no difficulty comprehending spoken language yet may have difficulty reading conventional text.

Many college students with learning disabilities have significant problems with written expression. Assistive technology devices are well suited to assist with idea generation, spelling, grammar, and handwriting. One of the most powerful ways of getting college students with learning disabilities to write is to help them generate or organize their ideas prior to writing with the assistance of an outlining program. Outlining programs allow users to create the Roman numerals for major headings with a simple key stroke. The suggested topical areas can be moved easily and subordinate headings added. For students who relate better to pictures, there are programs that can be used to generate flowcharts, diagrams, webs, and "mind maps." These prewriting tools are a must for anyone working with students in the area of written expression. Beyond mere word processing, many of the latest software programs include word prediction software, spell checking, proofreading programs, speech recognition, and speech-reading systems. When used in conjunction with word processors, speech recognition systems help the user to convert oral language into written text. Speech synthesizers allow students to hear what they have written, providing an opportunity to catch errors that might otherwise go undetected and to make corrections. One naturally thinks of calculators as another type of assistive device that anyone with deficits in math can use. Some of the newest calculator models discussed in the chapter have a variety of functions including built-in speech synthesizers.

Other aids profiled by the authors include personal FM listening systems to help students focus on the voice of the speaker. These systems amplify the speaker's voice and carry it directly into an earplug used by the receiver. Personal data managers are becoming more and more popular for helping students plan their time and store and retrieve information. Electronic reference materials such as dictionaries, thesauruses, almanacs, and encyclopedias have opened up new opportunities for assisting students with writing term papers and reports and researching paper topics without ever leaving a dorm room.

Service providers, teachers, and consumers with disabilities will find the section on how to select appropriate assistive technology based upon individual needs to be very helpful. The authors discuss the importance of examining individual characteristics including functional strengths, functional limitations, and the most suitable types of adaptations. They refer to this process as making the "person and technology match." Once recommendations have been made and the student has an opportunity to try out the technology, it is important to monitor and evaluate its effectiveness.

The chapter concludes with a thoughtful look at barriers and solutions for using assistive technology devices. Not surprisingly, a lack of training in the use of specific AT devices is one of the top-ranked barriers to implementation. If there is no administrative commitment for ongoing staff development and training, the effectiveness of AT will be minimized.

Chapter 12: Postsecondary Disability Personnel as Professionals

This chapter describes the development of professional standards and a code of ethics, which delineate what disability professionals do and how they should act, as milestones in the professionalization of disability services. The professional standards provide a basis for training, hiring, and evaluating postsecondary disability practitioners, and a systematic process is reviewed to help professionals apply the code of ethics to guide their actions, particularly in times of crisis.

Consideration is given to the different types of training that can be offered and the professional development opportunities that need to be available to administrators, direct service personnel, and faculty. After implementing initial inservice training efforts, service coordinators may need to determine the types of additional, ongoing professional development activities that will be necessary.

Many service providers subscribe to the benefits of providing faculty with inservice training on learning disabilities, but unless training is ongoing, not a one-shot inservice event, little substantive attitudinal change will occur. The most effective training efforts are those that are conducted over time and that are tailored to the multifaceted needs of the audience. It is clear that requiring a large number of staff and faculty to attend a mandatory inservice workshop is not the most effective approach. Different constituencies at an institution of higher education have different needs depending on their entry-level knowledge and degree of involvement with students with learning disabilities. Several suggestions from a position paper by the NJCLD (National Joint Committee on Learning Disabilities, 1988) are offered on beginning a personnel development program.

The authors emphasize that the choice of postsecondary LD service-delivery models may have far-reaching implications for staff training. It is important to determine which service-delivery model would best meet the needs of the consumers. One model should not be selected over another based on the training style of initial personnel or the professional bias of an administrator. Staff should be hired who can address the impact of a learning disability by instructing students in self-advocacy skills, writing skills, and learning strategies.

Direct service personnel, whether part-time or full-time, may need training regarding the program's mission, the service-delivery model, office operating procedures, and ways to approach faculty. It is recommended that such training efforts be extended over several days prior to the start of the academic year. Suggested training topics for in-house professional development activities are also included in this section. Higher education administrators need to understand and be supportive of the frontline efforts of LD service providers. These key individuals, who set policy, address concerns about curricular modifications, and may strongly influence funding patterns, must be kept abreast of LD support service activities on a regular basis and not just at the end of the fiscal year. Finally, suggestions are offered on developing a comprehensive, multifaceted, ongoing personnel development program.

Chapter 13: Promoting Our Products

The climate in higher education has changed since the publication of the first edition of this book. Among the primary attributes of this new environment, according to Heyward (1998), are a greater number of students to be serviced and fewer resources. The need for service providers to showcase their initiatives is critical, especially at a time when reviews of programs and prioritization of resources are inherent in "strategic planning." This chapter offers practical suggestions for marketing LD services on and beyond the campus, and delineates a process for program evaluation, including an annual report (see Appendix 13.2 on the CD-ROM). The focus on performance outcomes for students is addressed as a reality that requires careful planning.

Ideas to promote campus visibility of LD services are presented here, including membership on key campus committees, institutional publications and presentations, collaboration with important campus offices such as that of human resources, and fostering connections with supportive faculty. Given the standards of practice that now exist in the field of postsecondary disability services, an opportunity to "showcase" LD programs as an essential element of institutional initiatives should be embraced, whether it be when requesting administrative support or developing policy. Creative examples of marketing LD services beyond the campus are included in this chapter.

In an era when accountability is not just a buzzword but a required indicator of performance, it is absolutely critical that service providers implement a comprehensive process of program evaluation. This chapter not only provides a detailed discussion of the elements of a model of evaluation, it also delineates the application of the model to the program of LD services at the University of Connecticut, culminating in an annual report that offers readers a concrete example of presenting evaluation data. The chapter concludes with a cautionary note for service providers. Despite the standards-based reform movement of the 1990s with its emphasis on accountability, enrollment management, and retention and graduation, postsecondary LD service providers must assume a leadership role in facilitating dialogue about the statutory regulations requiring the assurance of equal educational access for students with disabilities. No one can question the importance of successful outcome indicators, but they do not preclude the rights of qualified students to participate in postsecondary education, regardless of their success or failure.

Chapter 14: Future Directions in Postsecondary Learning Disability Programming and Service Delivery

This chapter begins with a review of the tremendous change and development that occurred during the 1990s. During that time, students with "hidden" disabilities became the largest proportion of identified college students with disabilities. Professional standards, program standards, a code of ethics, and LD and ADHD documentation guidelines provided direction and support for learning disability specialists.

Programmatic and professional change that needs to occur in the new millennium includes increased focus on self-determination for service providers, students, and faculty. Self-determined professionals model collaborative decision making and goal setting and attainment. Students are encouraged to self-advocate, become independent learners, and learn to navigate the bureaucracy that is often inherent in higher education settings. In a similar vein, faculty need to be supported to be effective instructors for *all* their students. This will reduce the need for modifications and accommodations and allow students with disabilities to be more independent within the postsecondary environment. The need for training to prepare professionals to deliver data-based services that can be empirically defended and evaluated is also presented as a challenge to the field. Finally, the authors of this book encourage the readers to become institutional leaders who apply their knowledge about effective practice to their own institutions.

Appendixes

Drawing upon advances in technology that have burgeoned since the first edition of this book, the appendixes are located on a CD-ROM. Ninety-two entries include examples of policies and procedures, numerous Web sites that describe an array of resources, and program record keeping and data collection forms, providing readers with easily accessible materials that can be downloaded for reference and use. A "Guide to the CD-ROM Appendixes" is located at the back of the book.

Throughout the book, materials that are located in the appendixes are referenced according to chapter. For example, Appendix 8.1 (on the CD-ROM), the University of Connecticut's *Policies and Procedures for Students with Disabilities*, is referred to in Chapter 8. The CD-ROM contains supplemental appendixes for Chapters 2, 8, and 9, in addition to those that are cited in the text. These resources from a number of highly recognized programs in the United States and Canada comprise reproducible materials that relate to day-to-day service provision. With the permission of the contributor, these materials can be adopted in their current form or adapted with this added notation: "Materials adopted/adapted with permission from [name of institution, name of disability office or LD program]."

CHAPTER

A COMPREHENSIVE APPROACH TO TRANSITION PLANNING

"One of the biggest frustrations in working with students with learning disabilities and attention deficit disorders is when the student has been somehow bypassed in the process of their planning all the way through school. So, in my opinion, student participation—active participation— in the process is the most important element towards students taking responsibility and becoming their own best advocates."
—Louise H. Russell, Director, Student Disability Resources, Harvard University

Effective transition planning is achieved through collaborative effort involving the student, family, school, community agencies, employers, and adult service providers (Blalock & Patton, 1996; Block, 1998b; NJCLD, 1994c). The 1997 reauthorization of the Individuals with Disabilities Education Act (IDEA; P.L. 105-17) emphasizes the importance of including students and parents as active participants in the Individualized Education Program (IEP) and transition planning, and using collaborative and interagency approaches to developing outcome-oriented plans based on the students' needs, taking into account their preferences and interests (Hasazi, Furney, & Destefano, 1999). Beginning when a student is 14 and every year thereafter, until graduation, the law requires that the annual IEP meeting include a statement of transition service needs to ensure that educational experiences in the school or community will move students with disabilities closer to their desired post-school goals or outcomes (O'Leary, 1998).

This legal mandate was in direct response to data from the National Transition Study (Blackorby & Wagner, 1996) indicating that only 13.9% of individuals with learning disabilities sought admission to postsecondary education after being out of school for two years. This percentage was lower than that for students with serious emotional disturbance (17.0%) or who were visually impaired (33.0%) or hard of hearing (28.5%). Vogel and Reder (1998) note, "In general, the statewide and national studies reported significantly lower educational attainment for adults with LD. The range in reported high school graduation rates was between 32% and 66%, whereas high school dropout rate is as high as 54%." The U.S. Department of Education (1996) reported that 42.9% of adolescents with learning disabilities drop out of high school compared with 24.4% of the general population. According to the National Joint Committee on Learning Disabilities (1994c), many high school students with learning disabilities simply do not complete high school and therefore are not in a position to consider the full array of postsecondary options available to them.

This chapter describes the transition requirements articulated under the reauthorization of the IDEA as it applies to adolescents with learning disabilities who are moving from secondary to postsecondary settings. The role of the student is examined as it relates to transition planning, including participating in the transition planning team, selecting high school classes, searching for the best postsecondary option, and enrolling in either a 2- or 4-year college setting. Practical suggestions for guidance counselors, special education teachers, and parents are included as they relate to supporting students in this transition process. Rhona Hartman, the former executive director of the HEATH Resource Center, a national clearinghouse on postsecondary education for individuals with disabilities, suggests that transition planning should be viewed as a bridge "whose size, span, strength, beauty, efficiency, and direction depend on the individual who travels it" (Hartman, 1993, p. 31). The intent of this chapter is to examine that bridge and to focus on the central role that the student with a learning disability plays in traversing it from high school to higher education.

Making the Transition

Cowen (1993) noted that college-bound students with learning disabilities must go through the same process as their peers who are not learning disabled, but because of their learning disabilities, they may face additional challenges that need to be addressed. For example, many college-bound students with learning disabilities do not understand their individual disability, how it affects their learning, and how to describe it to others in plain language (Eaton, 1996; Field, 1996b; Goldhammer & Brinckerhoff, 1992). Many high school graduates with learning disabilities have neither the content preparation necessary to succeed in college nor a repertoire of learning strategies that will allow them to circumvent the disability. Their proficiency using assistive technology that would allow them to compete equitably with their nondisabled college peers is often minimal (Bryant & Bryant, 1998; Bursuck & Jayanthi, 1993; Deshler, Ellis, & Lenz, 1996). High school students also need to become more knowledgeable about Section 504 of the Rehabilitation Act and the Americans with Disabilities Act (ADA) and their implications in higher education. Vogel and Reder (1998) point out that, unlike the "search and screen" mandate of the IDEA of 1990, Section 504 does not mandate that postsecondary institutions screen students for possible learning disabilities. Rather, students with diagnosed learning disabilities or attention-deficit/hyperactivity disorders who want support services, accommodations, or both must request services and provide documentation of their disability.

Given the complexities of learning disabilities and attention-deficit/hyperactivity disorders, many high school students need guidance on how to find a suitable college program, one with a range of LD support services that will be compatible with their specific interests, abilities, and perceived needs. Cowen (1993) observes that the "proliferation of services available in colleges and universities requires an extensive search, which requires knowledge of (1) how to read and evaluate the many guides available; (2) how to locate services in colleges not listed in the guides; and (3) how to evaluate the located services" (p. 40). The good news is that over 1,300 identified colleges and universities in the United States and Canada offer programs or services for students with learning disabilities (Kravets & Wax, 1999). The challenging news is that the plethora of postsecondary options currently available to students with learning disabilities may be very confusing, and therefore, these students need assistance in evaluating options and determining which program and setting might be right for them (Vogel & Reder, 1998). Finally, once students with learning disabilities have been admitted into college, they often need further assistance in how to stay in college so that they can graduate (Brinckerhoff, Shaw, & McGuire, 1993; McGuire, 1997; Vogel & Adelman, 1993).

This combination of factors underscores the need for systematic transition planning that should begin early in the student's high school career and continue into college. Effective transition planning must be a student-centered activity that reflects the developmental and educational needs of the student at different grades and times. It also requires collaborative efforts among parents or guardians and secondary and postsecondary personnel (NJCLD, 1994b).

The Reauthorization Act

Typically, adolescents need extra support and assistance from family, friends, and school personnel as they negotiate the transition from high school to adult life. Halpern (1994) offers a cogent definition:

> Transition refers to a change in status from behaving primarily as a student to assuming emergent adult roles in the community. These roles include employment, participating in a postsecondary education, maintaining a home, becoming appropriately involved in the community, and experiencing satisfactory personal and social relationships. The process of enhancing transition involves the participation and coordination of school programs, adult agency services, and natural supports within the community. . . . (p. 117)

The importance of transition plans and services for adolescents with disabilities is recognized in the reauthorization of the Individuals with Disabilities Education Act. The law views transition as a coordinated set of activities that are based on the needs of the individual student and that are designed to prepare students for the years beyond secondary school. To ensure that the student completes secondary school prepared for employment or postsecondary education, as well as for independent living, the law requires that an Individualized Transition Plan regarding the course of study be written for students with disabilities beginning at age 14 as part of the IEP (Individualized Education Program). Lerner (1997) notes that many school districts use an attachment to the student's IEP to indicate transition goals and activities to meet those goals. Other schools may develop a separate Individualized Transition Plan (ITP).

Judith Heumann, assistant secretary of the U.S. Department of Education, comments that "these new provisions compel us to consider more seriously the benefits of strong transition planning for students with learning disabilities, whether they plan to pursue academic courses of study, vocational courses, or a more uniquely designed program of study" (1997, p. 12). Once post-school goals are identified, the team must decide which specific activities will move the student forward toward accomplishing these goals. Furthermore, the IDEA does not require a state to provide a free appropriate public education (FAPE) beyond age 18 if it is inconsistent with state law, court ruling, or practice. Seniors who are unsure about college as a viable option may want to consider working part-time during their final year of high school (e.g., in a cooperative education program) as a transition to full-time work. Heumann suggests that some students may even want to consider co-enrolling in community college and high school to ease the transition to full-time college-level coursework after graduation.

Differences Between High School and College

In order to plan effectively for facilitating a student's transition to postsecondary educational options, all members of the transition planning team should be aware of the many inherent differences between the high school and college settings. According to Dalke and Schmitt (1987), as students with learning disabilities move from high school to college, they may be confronted with many more challenges than their peers without learning disabilities. The inherent differences in the structure of these two settings are illustrated in Table 2.1.

Two of the biggest differences between high school and college concern the amount of in-class time and opportunities for direct teacher contact. High school students are in class approximately 6 hours a day, and it is not unusual for high school students to have contact with their teachers five times a week. In comparison, college classes may meet only one to three times a week, thus, the opportunities for direct teacher contact are much more limited. Dalke (1993) points out that classroom size may also be an important variable for some students, given that high school classes typically have 25 to 30 students, in comparison to college, where some classes may be as large as 200 or 300 students.

Students in high school may spend a limited amount of time completing homework assignments, often having the opportunity to finish them during resource room time or in a study hall. In contrast, many college students spend only 12 hours per week in class, but invest 3 to 4 hours per day in studying. The emphasis on independent learning in college is substantial. Brinckerhoff, Shaw, and McGuire (1993) note that, in college, studying may mean rewriting lecture notes, paraphrasing information from reading assignments, and integrating information gleaned from a variety of sources (e.g., texts, class lectures, or library assignments). DuChossois and Michaels (1994) comment that for students with learning disabilities—who may take longer reading textbooks, taking notes on assigned work, and understanding important concepts in a given assignment—the time investment is often considerably more than for their nondisabled peers.

Another contrasting point related to homework concerns the amount and frequency of direct teacher feedback students receive on their work. In high school, homework is often assigned on a day-to-day basis, and students are expected to turn it in daily or weekly for feedback. In college, "homework"

Table 2.1
Differences in High School and College Requirements

	High School	College
Class time	6 hours per day, 180 days Total: 1,080 hours	12 hours per week, 28 weeks Total: 336 hours
Class size	25–30 students	Up to 200–300 students
Study time	Whatever it takes to do your homework! 1–2 hrs. per day	Rule of thumb: 2 hrs. of study for 1 hr. of class. 3–4 hrs. per day
Tests	E.g., weekly, at the end of a chapter; frequent quizzes	2–4 per semester; e.g., at the end of four-chapter unit, at 8:00 A.M. on the Monday after Homecoming
Grading	Passing grades guarantee you a seat. Performance evaluations may be subjective, based on level of effort or level of improvement.	Satisfactory academic standing requires grades of C or above; performance is based on mastery of course content.
Teaching	Teachers often take attendance; may regularly check notebooks and homework assignments; lecture from textbook and often use blackboard and worksheets; impart knowledge and facts.	Professors rarely take attendance and seldom check homework or monitor daily work; lecture nonstop and rarely teach the textbook; require library research; challenge students to integrate information from a variety of sources.
Freedom	Structure defines most of the time. Limits are set by parents, teachers, and other adults. High school buildings are monitored.	Managing time and personal free- dom is greatest problem college students face. Self-reliance is the key. College campuses are often extensive and security may be a concern.

Note. Adapted from "Preparing Students with Learning Disabilities for Postsecondary Education: Issues and Future Needs," by S. Shaw, L. C. Brinckerhoff, J. Kistler, and J. M. McGuire, 1991, *Learning Disabilities: A Multidisciplinary Journal, 2,* pp. 21–26. Copyright 1991 by *Learning Disabilities: A Multidisciplinary Journal.* Adapted with permission.

often consists of long-range assignments such as term papers, projects, and integrative essays. Students are expected to work independently for a grade. Instead of receiving a grade at the end of each chapter or unit, college students may receive a grade only once a month or only following mid-term and final examinations. In high school, students with LD may have been graded based on indicators such as effort or level of improvement. In college, these students may find that they are receiving significantly lower grades than in high school because grading has become less subjective and is based only on their mastery of course material (Dalke, 1993). In addition, many college students find themselves in academic environments with high-achieving high school graduates where expectations are greater and grading is even more competitive.

High school instructors are responsible for teaching a broad range of students and for teaching all students factual content, while college professors often expect students to integrate information independently from a variety of sources rather than to parrot isolated facts. College professors may also require students to think more analytically, as well as to synthesize abstract information (Shaw, Brinckerhoff, Kistler, & McGuire, 1991). Another related concern is that secondary school teachers often provide external reinforcement of students' work without ever assisting students to develop the capacity to self-monitor their progress (duChossois & Michaels, 1994). As a result, many students with learning disabilities exit high school without the ability to monitor their own work, reflect on its quality, predict academic outcomes, or adjust or adapt their approach to academic tasks in order to achieve their goals.

Life and time demands are very different in college than in high school. High school students find that their time is structured by limitations set by parents, teachers, and other adults. College environments require students to function independently by managing their time and organizing their days (and nights). Students are faced with the freedom to make their own decisions about scheduling time, choosing their own classes and majors, and conducting their social lives (duChossois & Michaels, 1994). In addition, most high schools are in one building, allowing for monitoring and control of student access by virtue of teacher supervision. College campuses may be vastly different, with dozens of buildings and offices spread over miles. Brinckerhoff et al. (1993) stress that increased levels of personal freedom constitute one of the biggest adjustments that students with learning disabilities must make as they enter college. When considered as a whole, these dramatic differences between the demands of high school settings and those that characterize higher education can create a challenging climate for students with learning disabilities and ADHD.

The Process of Transition Planning

Many high school students frequently comment that they were not included in the decision-making process or that their parents "set everything up" for them. Unfortunately, many well-meaning parents and high school personnel, in the guise of protecting these students from failure and stress, have made decisions for them. Individualized transition planning should be viewed as a golden opportunity for students to shape their own academic destinies by learning about their disabilities, asking questions, presenting ideas, and advocating for themselves. Blalock and Patton (1996) view the transition planning process as "just the opportunity needed to shape one's future in a powerful way" (p. 11). Beginning at the age of 14, if not before, teenagers with learning disabilities should be encouraged to participate actively in, and even manage the individualized transition process, supported by a multidisciplinary team (deFur & Reiff, 1994; Thoma, 1999). This team should ideally consist of the student, family member(s), critical teachers in special and general (especially vocational) education, appropriate adult agency staff, and any others tied to essential transition services. Each member has an important role to play in fostering student independence and decision making. In some districts, it may be possible to invite a postsecondary education representative to the team to discuss the realities of the college experience. In other cases, it may be more appropriate to guide students through the process of contacting postsecondary personnel, gathering detailed information, and reporting to the team what they have learned. Together, the team should craft a realistic transition plan that addresses the following questions:

1. Where is the student going? This includes the student's type of employment goals, lifestyle preferences, and education needs.

2. What is needed to help the student reach the identified goals? This includes courses the student needs to take, experiences that will help the student make decisions, and modifications or accommodations in school to better prepare the student.

3. Who needs to be involved? This could include the student, parents, special educators, vocational education counselors, vocational rehabilitation representatives, high school content-area teachers, potential employers, guidance counselors, mental health providers, and community-based organizations.

4. How will the goals be accomplished? Who will implement the activities, who will monitor the implementation and review the transition, and who will serve as case manager?

The above four points underscore the need for hiring transition coordinators or facilitators in the high school who are familiar with federal, state, and district transition policies and mandates regarding students with disabilities. Hasazi et al. (1999) point out that these positions are often funded jointly through education and vocational rehabilitation and may include the establishment of an interagency transition planning office within the high school guidance department. In any case, central office support and leadership are essential in the initial establishment and continued funding of such positions.

In school districts where a transition facilitator is not on staff, the coordination of the transition planning team often becomes an added responsibility of the LD resource teacher. This individual who is assigned to the student's case must be sensitive to cultural differences and values of the student and family when he or she recommends resources and collaborates with other high school staff. The transition team leader should insist that the student be an active participant in the process of carving out transition goals in the IEP or the Individual Transition Plan. The IEP document becomes the blueprint for service delivery and for transition planning. Students should be at the center of this process, with the LD teacher serving as the team coordinator in conjunction with school personnel and the parent(s). Ideally, student input about secondary and postsecondary goals, curriculum options, and the level of support services needed to meet these goals should be solicited by teachers in advance of the meeting. Powers et al. (1996) notes that students need preparation for the IEP planning and implementation process. They must be taught roles, duties, and responsibilities for effectively planning and implementing their IEPs throughout their high school careers. Some examples of transition activities that can be directed by the student and will ultimately support students in the IEP and the transition process include:

- scheduling the meeting;

- inviting team members and guests, including friends, to the meeting and sending reminder notices;

- preparing refreshments and name tags;

- wearing clothes appropriate for a formal meeting;

- sitting at the head of the table;

- leading the meeting—with support as needed by teachers, parents, and friends;

- implementing strategies each week to help accomplish their goals and objectives;

- meeting with support personnel each week to discuss their goal attainment process; and

- adjusting strategies, schedules, and supports (in collaboration with their teachers and family members) to help attain their goals.

During the planning meeting, students should be encouraged to express concerns, show preferences, and give opinions based on personal experience. They may also need to learn how to express their thoughts at the meeting in a way that makes others listen to them and respect their views (Eaton & Coull, 1998; West et al., 1992). The bottom line is that students need repeated opportunities to practice their self-determination skills in a supportive environment. The IEP process, including its preparation, planning, and implementation phases, provides an excellent opportunity to learn those skills. While they are learning those crucial self-determination skills, students develop a transition plan that is created for them and by them (Field, Hoffman, & Spezia, 1998, p. 121).

A successful student-directed IEP process was pioneered for the Fairfax County schools in Virginia and is outlined in two valuable guides that have been produced by the National Information Center for Children and Youth with Disabilities (NICHCY). A Student's Guide to the IEP, Helping Students Develop Their IEPs, and an accompanying audiotape are available from NICHCY, P.O. Box 1492, Washington, DC 20013, 800-695-0285. The text of the guides can be downloaded from the NICHCY Web site: http://www.nichcy.org/. The Florida Department of Education has produced a teacher and student guide entitled Dare to Dream: A Guide to Planning Your Future (Perkins, Bailey, Repetto, & Schwartz, 1995) that outlines simple steps for students and teachers to follow when addressing the issue of transition planning from high school to postsecondary placements.

Transition Planning Curriculum Materials

Teachers, administrators, parents, and other adults frequently assume that individuals with learning disabilities need no formal instruction in life skills, as they can learn those tasks on their own or from peer models. Cronin (1996) points out, "In reality, many students with learning disabilities do not learn life skills on their own. They need life skills content in high school and throughout their school careers" (p. 98). High school resource room teachers should consider using some of the latest transition planning materials to present their students with a coordinated, comprehensive approach to transition planning. Hasazi et al. (1999) reviewed five model high school transition sites in the United States and found that many of the teachers in those sites "were skilled in the use of person-centered planning processes designed to enhance student and parent participation in the IEP/transition planning process, and an increasing number were implementing curricula designed to teach students how to lead their own IEP/transition planning meetings" (p. 559).

One highly effective approach is *The Transition Planning Inventory* (TPI) (Clark & Patton, 1997). This instrument is designed for use with high school students with disabilities in planning their transition from school to adult life. The TPI is intended to "provide school personnel with a systematic way to address critical transition planning areas that are mandated by the Individuals with Disabilities Education Act (IDEA) and that are based on information regarding the student's needs, preferences and abilities" (p. 1). The form consists of three surveys, one to be completed by each student, his or her parent(s), and a school representative. The primary benefit of *The Transition Planning Inventory* and other similar systems (*Enderle-Severson Transition Rating Scale*, Enderle & Severson, 1991; *McGill Action Planning System*, Vandercook & York, 1989) is that they systematically assess a student's transition needs and abilities so that instructionally sound programming and curriculum planning decisions can be tailored to the student. A transition-referenced assessment process actively engages both the parents and the student in the educational process by having them address real-life issues. This process of asking questions often serves as a "wake-up call" to students and parents in a way that a psycho-educational achievement battery can never do (Clark, 1996).

Another example of transition-related curriculum materials is *Tools for Transition: Preparing Students with Learning Disabilities for Postsecondary Education* (Aune & Ness, 1991b). It includes units on enhancing students' understanding of learning disabilities, interpreting information from initial diagnostic reports into everyday language, understanding the IEP, and actively planning for the future in vocational and postsecondary settings. An accompanying videotape presents realistic scenes that demonstrate and reinforce many of the self-advocacy skills taught in the curriculum.

Dalke and Howard (1994) have developed a similar product called *Life Works: A Transition Program for High School Students* that is designed to comply with federal guidelines regarding transition planning. It includes two student workbooks. Book One, "Understanding Yourself," helps students discover more about their learning styles, study habits, and personal strengths and weaknesses. Book Two, "Exploring Your Options and Setting Goals," assists students in their exploration of postsecondary options like college, vocational technical schools, and employment. A companion teacher's guide supplements each unit activity in the two student workbooks with transition objectives, unit lead-in activities, discussion topics, and follow-up activities. There is also a section on working with parents that includes resources and worksheets for parents to use to help with their child's transition.

A comprehensive product designed to specifically address the transition to postsecondary settings for students with learning disabilities and ADHD has been added to the effective tools teachers can use. The Eaton-Coull Learning

Group (ECLG) based in Vancouver, British Columbia, has developed two sets of transition materials that address the unique transition needs of students with learning disabilities as they move from middle school into high school and from high school into college. The complete *Transitions to High School* (Eaton & Coull, 2000) training kit includes a teacher discussion guide, self-advocacy handbook, student workbook, and companion video. These materials are best suited for seventh and eighth graders. The companion package for older students is *Transitions to Postsecondary Learning* (Eaton & Coull, 1998). The educational video can be used as an awareness tool as well as an effective instructional tool not only for students but also for high school and postsecondary faculty. Beyond increasing awareness, the goal of the video is to emphasize the importance of self-advocacy skills and to communicate realistically through the words of real students what transition planning is all about. The practical suggestions featured in this video do much to demystify learning disabilities and attention-deficit/hyperactivity disorders for the layperson and to encourage students to take ownership of their disability so they can advocate effectively with teachers and faculty. The handbook materials and accompanying discussion guide allow teachers and facilitators to expand upon the concepts presented in the video and to tailor their presentation to a given audience.

Developing a Timetable
for Transition Planning

The National Joint Committee on Learning Disabilities has expressed its concern that "many students with learning disabilities do not consider postsecondary options (two and four-year colleges and vocational schools) because they are not encouraged, assisted or prepared to do so" (NJCLD, 1994c, p. 98). The NJCLD further stated that many students with learning disabilities *should* select postsecondary education options and that, if transition plans are well designed and implemented effectively, those students will be successful.

By developing a timetable for college planning that centers around students, it is possible to empower them into becoming active members of the transition planning team. A timetable approach that begins in eighth grade and concludes with high school graduation allows students to gradually assume greater responsibility for their own learning outcomes and to view the postsecondary planning process as a series of coordinated steps that involve input from a number of supporting players over a period of years. It also allows parents an opportunity for the gradual transfer of control and responsibility to their son or daughter as they prepare for the "empty nest" that will soon follow. Some of the steps presented are discrete and time sensitive, like applying for the SAT, and other steps should be developed early on or later in the high school experience but not necessarily at a particular grade level (e.g., writing an IEP goal).

Transition Programming Before and During High School: A Continuum

The following section presents a 5-year timetable for comprehensive transition planning that addresses the educational, vocational, and psychosocial needs of adolescents with learning disabilities as they move through middle school and high school toward graduation. Important points in this discussion are presented in Table 2.2.

In order for students with learning disabilities to be successful in high school, they need to make a carefully planned transition from middle school to high school. Guidance counselors will have a significant influence on several critical choices that will ultimately shape the futures of these students. These include: (a) the curriculum track in which students enroll, and (b) the courses students take. Unfortunately, many high school students do not seek the advice of guidance counselors and, as a result, are assigned a specified curriculum track and a roster of courses. Students with learning disabilities should actively seek the advice of guidance counselors, parents, special education teachers, and general education teachers in order to ensure their role in active decision making. These adults should encourage students with learning disabilities to take the most academically challenging program possible in the most integrated setting. Traditional resource room models that focus solely on academic remediation and content tutoring will not give these students the competencies they need when they move toward content-driven coursework (Spector, Decker, & Shaw, 1991). DuChossois and Michaels (1994) found that many high school students with learning disabilities used their resource room as "a glorified study hall." The resource room must not be "a place where students passively sit and hear reiterations of what has been presented in class," they continue. "Rather, the emphasis should be placed on developing an understanding of the way the students learn and then teaching students how to learn better and more efficiently" (p. 85). Aune (1991) interviewed high school students about what they were taught to do to compensate for their weaknesses. The most common response was "Try harder." She also found that the repertoire of study strategies routinely used by high school students with learning disabilities was extremely limited; only 15% of the students reported that they had been taught any type

Table 2.2
A Timetable for Transition Planning for Students with Learning Disabilities and ADHD

Grade 8—Preparing for High School Success

Students with learning disabilities/ADHD need to:

- Take the most academically challenging program in the most integrated setting possible.

- Consult LD teachers as needed on how to become independent learners.

- Actively participate in IEP meetings and suggest goals that focus on study skills, time management, and test-taking strategies.

- Seek opportunities that will foster self-determination and independence through increased responsibility at home and in school.

- Develop money management skills and assist in meal preparation, shopping duties, and caring for clothing.

- Expand academic interests through electives and extracurricular activities.

- Begin to identify preferences and interests.

- Keep a calendar for activities and homework assignments.

- Develop appropriate social skills and interpersonal communication skills.

- Learn about high school expectations and offerings.

Grades 9 & 10—Transition Planning Begins

Students with learning disabilities/ADHD need to:

- Continue to practice Grade 8 goals.

- Learn what learning disabilities are and are not.

- Develop an understanding of the nature of their own disability and learning style.

- Clarify the exact nature of their learning disability or ADHD by reviewing the diagnostic report with an LD specialist or psychologist.

- Learn about civil rights and the responsibilities of high schools and colleges under the IDEA, Section 504, and the ADA.

- Self-advocate with parents, teachers, and peers.

- With parent input select classes (e.g., word processing, public speaking, study skills) that will prepare them academically for college or vocational/technical school.

- Avoid temptation to "retreat" to lower-track classes, if college-bound. Select solid college prep courses.

- Be wary of course waivers and carefully consider implications of those choices.

(continues)

Table 2.2 *Continued.*

Grades 9 & 10—Transition Planning Begins (Continued)

- Use LD support and accommodations in math or foreign-language classes rather than seeking a waiver, if possible.

- Seek classroom teachers and learning environments that are supportive.

- Enroll in remediation classes if necessary.

- Focus on "strategy-based" learning with LD teacher.

- Balance class schedules by not taking too many difficult courses in the same semester, or too many classes that play into the area of weakness.

- Beware of peer advice on which classes to take and avoid.

- Provide input on who should participate in the planning team.

- Become a co-leader of the transition planning team at the IEP meeting.

- Demonstrate independence by writing some of their own IEP goals.

- Try out accommodations and auxiliary aids in high school classes that are deemed appropriate by LD teachers (e.g., taped textbooks from RFB&D, note takers, laptop computers, extra time on exams).

- Know how, when, and where to discuss and request needed accommodations.

- Learn about technological aids such as talking calculators, four-track tape recorders, optical scanners, handheld spell checkers, voice-activated software, and electronic day planners.

- Know how to access information from a large library.

- Meet with a guidance counselor to discuss PSAT registration for October administration (in the 10th grade).

- Arrange with guidance counselor to take PSAT/PLAN with accommodations if warranted.

- Register for SAT II if appropriate.

- Use "score choice" option for SAT II test, to release only those scores desired.

- Gain a realistic assessment of potential for college and vocational school.

- Consider working at a part-time summer job or volunteer position.

Grade 11—Transition Planning in the Junior Year

Students with learning disabilities/ADHD need to:

- Continue to practice Grade 8, 9, & 10 goals.

- Review IEP and ITP for any changes or modifications for the upcoming year.

- Advocate for a complete psycho-educational evaluation to be conducted by the beginning of 12th grade as an IEP goal.

(continues)

Table 2.2 *Continued.*

Grade 11—Transition Planning in the Junior Year (Continued)

- Present a positive self-image by stressing their strengths, while understanding the influence of their learning disability.

- Seek "LD role models" in school through a peer-mentor program.

- Keep grades up. Admissions staff look for upward grade trends.

- Arrange for PSATs with accommodations in mid-October. Apply for a social security number if necessary.

- Match vocational interests and academic abilities with appropriate postsecondary or vocational options.

- Explore advantages and disadvantages of community colleges, vocational technical schools, and 4-year colleges given the learning disability and/or ADHD.

- Meet with local Department of Rehabilitation Services (DRS) counselor to determine their eligibility for services. If eligible, ask counselor for assistance in vocational assessment, job placement, and/or postsecondary education or training.

- Consult several of the popular LD college guides and meet with a college advisor to discuss realistic choices.

- Finalize arrangements for the SATs or ACTs with necessary accommodations. Visit Web site for ACT (www.act.org) and College Board (www. collegeboard.org).

- Start with a list of 15–20 colleges based on the LD guides, visit the Web site for these institutions, and request specific information about LD services offered.

- When reviewing a prospective college Web site, determine how available support services are on campus. Is there specific information on the site about disabilities?

- Preview colleges with www.collegebound.net or usnews.com search site.

- Narrow listing to 8–10 preliminary choices based on competitiveness, location, curriculum, costs, level of LD support, etc.

- Request any additional information needed from college (e.g., applications to LD program, specific fee information, financial aid forms, etc.).

- Discuss with parents, counselor, regular education teachers, and LD teachers the anticipated level of LD support needed in a postsecondary setting.

- Understand the differences between an "LD program" and support services models.

- Attend "LD college nights" at local area high schools. Assume responsibility for asking questions of college representatives.

- Develop a "Personal Transition File" with parent and teacher assistance. Contents should include: current diagnostic testing, IEPs, grades, letters of recommendation, and student activity chart or résumé.

(continues)

Table 2.2 *Continued.*

Grade 11—Transition Planning in the Junior Year *(Continued)*

- Narrow options to 5 or 6 schools ranging in competitiveness and levels of LD support.

- Prepare a "College Interview Preparation Form" to use during the campus interviews.

- Arrange for campus visit and interviews in advance. Don't just drop in on the LD support services office staff and expect an interview.

- Consider sitting in on a class or arrange to meet college students with learning disabilities through the support services office. Listen to their firsthand experiences.

- Meet with the designated LD services coordinator to determine the level of support offered and to assess the nature of the services offered (e.g., remedial, compensatory, learning strategies, etc.).

- Determine how important self-advocacy is on campus. Determine how accommodations are arranged with faculty.

- Follow up with a personal thank-you note to the disability coordinator.

- Consider a private LD preparatory school or a "13th year" program if postsecondary education doesn't seem to be a viable option.

- Consider enrolling in a summer orientation program specifically for students with learning disabilities/ADHD. Contact HEATH Resource Center (800-54-HEATH) for more information.

- Apply for a summer job, volunteer position, or career-related work experience.

Grade 12—Transition Planning in the Senior Year

Students with learning disabilities/ADHD need to:

- Continue to practice Grades 8, 9, 10, & 11 goals.

- Update IEP and ITP quarterly.

- Retake the SATs or ACTs to improve scores. Note that scores may be flagged as "special" or "nonstandard." Discuss implications with guidance counselor.

- Select several colleges as "safe bets" for admission, several "reasonable reaches" and one or two "long shots."

- Consider early decision only if convinced that a particular school is the best match.

- Note all application deadlines. Complete a paper-based application to use as a model for on-line versions.

- Consider downloading applications or using the Common Application.

- Be alert to early application deadlines for some LD college programs.

- View a variety of college shopping networks: Collegenet (www.collegenet.com); Collegelink (www.collegelink.com); AppZap (www. collegeview.com/appzap).

(continues)

Table 2.2 *Continued.*

Grade 12—Transition Planning in the Senior Year (Continued)

- Carefully select people to write letters of recommendation. Give teachers and counselors plenty of time. Pick a teacher who knows their personality. Recognize that such letters may include comments about the learning disability. Keep Personal Transition File.

- Keep a listing of names, phone numbers, and addresses of postsecondary contact people and copies of all applications in their Personal Transition File.

- Role-play the college interview with guidance counselors or special education teachers.

- Decide whether to disclose their learning disability/ADHD prior to admission.

- View "Transitions to Postsecondary Learning" video and complete student handbook exercises with LD teachers (Eaton/Coull Learning Group, 800-933-4063).

- Pick up all necessary financial aid forms (FAF) for college from guidance counselor. Males who are 18 years old must register for the draft to be eligible for federal aid forms.

- Discuss financial considerations with guidance counselors and search the Web using www.finaid.org or fastweb.com.

- Tap into Department of Rehabilitation Services. If eligible for job guidance, consider enrolling in internships or job-shadowing experiences that permit "hands-on" skill building.

- Formulate a realistic career plan.

- Forward mid-year grades to colleges.

- Wait for the news from colleges. If the news is good, then:

    Rank postsecondary choices based upon their ability to successfully compete and the provision of support services to meet their unique learning needs.

    Notify all schools of their decision.

    Pay housing deposit by May 1, if appropriate.

    Arrange to have final transcript sent to the college.

    Hold an exit interview with guidance counselor and LD teachers.

    If the news is not good, then:

    Appeal the admissions decision, especially if some new "LD-relevant data" were not considered or overlooked.

    Pursue any of a variety of alternatives such as applying to a less competitive college with a "rolling admissions" policy; enrolling in a postgraduate year at an LD preparatory school; enrolling in a community college with academic support services.

    Consider taking a college course for credit over the summer at a community college or in conjunction with a summer orientation program.

Note. Adapted from "Making the Transition to Higher Education: Opportunities for Student Empowerment," by L. C. Brinckerhoff, 1996, *Journal of Learning Disabilities, 29*, pp. 135–136. Copyright 1996 by PRO-ED. Adapted with permission.

of study strategy during the past year. During eighth grade, students should be taught a variety of skills that promote better study habits, time management, test preparation, and test-taking abilities.

Middle school students should also be encouraged to participate actively in their IEP meeting and to suggest goals for inclusion in the document (Martin & Marshall, 1996; Wehman, 1998). By planning and implementing their own IEPs, students learn self-advocacy, decision making, self-evaluation, and goal attainment skills. "Rather than IEP meetings merely fulfilling a bureaucratic necessity, active student involvement, combined with a supportive team, converts the process into a meaningful celebration of a student's education" (Field, Martin, Miller, Ward, & Wehmeyer, 1998, p. 120).

Transition Programming in the Freshman and Sophomore Years

Table 2.2 incorporates the belief of Cowen (1993) that during the freshman year of high school students for whom postsecondary education is appropriate should (a) develop a clear understanding of what learning disabilities are and are not; (b) develop a general understanding of the nature of their disability; (c) learn about their legal rights; (d) select courses that will prepare them academically for college; (e) explore career options; and (f) develop greater independence. Each of these goals is discussed below as they relate to the transition planning process and the central role that the student with a learning disability plays in reaching these goals. The topic areas of learning strategies instruction and fostering self-determination conclude this section on programming during ninth and tenth grades.

Developing an Understanding of Learning Disabilities

The first step in building future self-determination skills is for students to gain an understanding of what learning disabilities are and are not (Brinckerhoff, 1993; Field & Hoffman, 1996a; Goldhammer & Brinckerhoff, 1992). LD teachers should give students a general overview of learning disabilities, discuss basic definitional issues, and explicate some common terminology (e.g., ADHD, metacognition, dyslexia). They may need to clarify that learning disabilities are not the same as "learning problems" or "learning differences" but rather, by definition, are neurologically based, intrinsic to the individual, and present throughout the life span.

Developing an Understanding of Their Own Learning Disability

The second step to building greater self-advocacy skills is to help students develop a greater understanding of their own unique learning disability (Aune & Ness, 1991b; Brinckerhoff, 1994; Eaton & Coull, 1998; Wilson, 1994). Once students understand that a learning disability is not a reflection of limited intellectual ability and that it will not be outgrown, they may be more receptive to discussing their own unique profile of strengths and limitations. Parents and LD teachers can be instrumental in helping these teenagers to understand how their learning disabilities impact their lives both academically and socially. Cowen (1993) advises that parents can be particularly helpful in assisting their child by identifying areas of cognitive strength, athletic prowess, and creative talents. Parents should encourage their son or daughter to participate in extracurricular activities that may broaden the child's horizons. Parents also can help by communicating their confidence in their child's ability to be successful in high school and by actively encouraging them to reach for postsecondary options (NJCLD, 1994b). The primary role of parents during the initial stages of the transition planning process is to encourage and support their child to reach for realistic educational goals and to help them understand their profile of strengths and weaknesses (Cordoni, 1987; Field, Hoffman, & Spezia, 1998; Koehler & Kravets, 1998).

LD specialists can further expand on what the parent addresses at home by helping students to understand the connection between their unique learning styles and their academic performances. Aune (1991) points out that the student's understanding and acceptance of his or her strengths, weaknesses, and learning disability form the foundation for all other transition activities. One way of accomplishing this heightened awareness is to have students write a brief paragraph describing their strengths and weaknesses (Dalke & Howard, 1994; Eaton, 1996; Johnson, 1989). This initial writing sample can be included in a journal and used as a baseline by LD teachers when determining how much students have learned about their learning disability over time. Koehler and Kravets (1998) have developed a reproducible handout, "Student Readiness Assessment," which is ideally suited for use by guidance counselors when conferring with students with learning disabilities about how ready they are for college (see Appendix 2.1 on the CD-ROM).

Learning About Their Rights Under the Law

Another related component of self-determination awareness that should be addressed by LD teachers involves training students about changes in their legal rights under Section 504 and the Americans with Disabilities Act once they enter postsecondary education (Brinckerhoff et al., 1993; Dunn, 1996; Scott, 1991; Vogel, 1997). Students and their parents need to understand that the prescriptive requirements of the IDEA (e.g., special education services, diagnosis, free appropriate public education) end with high school graduation. LD support staff should be prepared to discuss the ramifications of these laws in both high school and higher education settings. Emphasis should be placed on the fact that Section 504 and the ADA initially focused on physical-access issues (e.g., ramps, accessible bathrooms), but more recently have expanded to encompass programmatic access for individuals with hidden disabilities. The major components of the ADA should also be highlighted with particular emphasis placed on accommodations that are appropriate for work, such as using readers, tape-recorded materials, or laptop computers with built-in spelling and grammar checks (Latham, 1998; Latham & Latham, 1993). Students should be encouraged to "try out" various accommodations such as listening to textbooks on tape or CD, using extended time to complete exams, and using a computer to write examinations or papers. Many high school students with learning disabilities do not realize that they have a legal right to these accommodations, based on verification of the nature and severity of the learning disability, and that academic adjustments are not "favors" to be granted informally by their general education teachers but requirements under the law. Many students with learning disabilities have not yet discovered that the academic adjustments provided in high school and in college may also be offered as "reasonable accommodations" in the workplace under the ADA (Heyward, 1998). LD service providers have known for years that just because a particular accommodation is included in a "laundry list" of accommodations at the end of a diagnostic report doesn't necessarily mean that it will be effective for the student. Furthermore, the types of accommodations students receive when taking classroom tests can serve as evidence of their need for accommodations when they apply for college admissions tests or licensing examinations (Barr, Hartman, & Spillane, 1995). Therefore, these accommodations decisions need to be made carefully, as their impact can be far-reaching.

Selecting Courses That Will Prepare Students for College

Cowen (1993) states that if students enter high school with basic competencies in reading and math (e.g., functional literacy skills at the fifth- or sixth-grade level), guidance counselors should encourage them to take college preparatory courses. If they lack those basic skills, then deficits in reading or mathematics should be addressed early in the student's high school career. Guidance personnel need to also be aware that academic preparation begins with the selection of appropriate classes that will afford students with LD maximum opportunities for accessing higher educational opportunities (McGuire, Hall, & Litt, 1991). Too often, students with learning disabilities are counseled to take "modified" or simplified courses that allow academic credit toward graduation but provide only limited training and background knowledge for transition to postsecondary education or employment (Shaw et al., 1991). McGuire, Norlander, and Shaw (1990) state that "a retreat to lower-track classes at this point will limit the student's postsecondary options" (p. 72). Guidance personnel also need to be sure that the student is not scheduled to be in the resource room for assistance during the same time essential college-preparatory courses are held. If students do not select certain college prep courses such as algebra I or chemistry during the freshman or sophomore years in high school, they may find themselves woefully underprepared for the rigors of a college curriculum. Furthermore, many college admissions officers carefully consider the *quality* of the high school courses the student elected to take. College-bound students should be advised to avoid more than one or two "basic" classes (e.g., "Nutrition Today" or " Basic Math 99") each semester. Although it may look impressive on the high school transcript that a student with a learning disability has earned all As, these basic classes, or electives, do little to excite college admissions personnel, who routinely recalculate high school GPAs based on college preparatory coursework. It is better for a student with a learning disability to take a mainstreamed college-preparatory class and earn a C+ than to enroll in a basic course and earn a grade of A. High school students with LD should also be advised to steer away from advanced placement (AP) or honors classes if those courses will either result in a disproportionate amount of their study time or pull their overall high school GPA down. However, if a student with a learning disability can earn a respectable grade of B or above in an accelerated class, it could help to support his or her application to a competitive college by further indicating that he or she is otherwise qualified despite the learning disability.

A high school transcript that displays successful completion of a wide array of courses (science, history, literature, foreign language, art, math, music) is attractive to college admissions staff. Involvement in school- or community-sponsored clubs, team sports, and theatrical performances also enhances a college admission candidate's application (Barr et al., 1998). Consequently, the high school transcript should be reviewed carefully, particularly at the midpoint in the student's career, to be sure it reflects the quality of coursework necessary for entrance to college. If it does not meet that standard, then the program of study should be upgraded and adjusted accordingly. Whenever possible, waivers from mathematics or foreign language classes should be avoided in high school because they may prohibit access to certain undergraduate and graduate degree programs, where such proficiencies can be required despite the presence of a disability. Consequently, parents, as well as the student, need to be informed about the implications a waiver in high school may have in the college admissions process. If a waiver is granted in high school, it should be done only after the student has attempted a foreign language class with resource support and made a "good faith effort." Furthermore, the student's diagnostic testing should substantiate the need for the waiver based on a severe language-based learning disability with related processing deficits.

Guidance counselors and parents need to keep in mind that it may be possible for high school students to take a foreign language on a pass/fail basis, so that their grade point average will not be adversely affected. A student who is able to complete 2 years of foreign language in high school may still have to complete one intermediate-level foreign language course in college. For some students with learning disabilities the intermediate course can be a formidable barrier. An alternative is for the student to "hang in" and take 3 years of a foreign language in high school so that the foreign language requirement at college can be met.

Koehler and Kravets (1998) suggest that guidance counselors use a multiyear educational plan that lists the specific courses that will satisfy the school's graduation requirements, promote academic success in the child, satisfy his or her special interests, and accommodate future plans such as college, work, or the military. This long-range plan should be completed early in the freshman year and should include input from all relevant school professionals so the student and his or her parents can make informed decisions. Koehler and Kravets have developed several collaborative planning forms that may be useful for guidance counselors to use in planning and monitoring student progress over time (see Appendixes 2.2 and 2.3 on the CD-ROM).

Exploring Career Options

Compared to their nondisabled peers, individuals with learning disabilities are often more focused on the present, due to the disability itself, which is often characterized by problems with abstract thought and an inability to perceive the "big picture." As a result, many high school students with LD have particular problems making long-range vocational or educational plans (Michaels, Thaler, Zwerlein, Gioglio, & Apostoli, 1988; Patton & Dunn, 1998; Wehman, 1992). They may not actively choose to explore the range of options available to them after high school because they are more focused on the present. Given that postsecondary planning takes years of forethought, this lack of future direction often places such students at a disadvantage. Consequently, adolescents with learning disabilities may need assistance from parents, teachers, and guidance personnel to develop their understanding of:

- the world of work,
- the differences between the work and school environments,
- their individual strengths and weaknesses,
- ways to maximize their strengths and minimize their weaknesses,
- ways to incorporate their interests and strengths into career plans, and
- how to set short- and long-term goals (Michaels et al., 1988, p. 50).

High school guidance counselors should encourage students to participate in a career exploration program. Biller (1985) states that career exploration programs develop the following abilities:

- awareness of the need to plan ahead and the relationship between present and future events;

- awareness of information necessary for career planning and knowledge of how and where to get it;

- understanding of how to make decisions;

- knowledge of general career development information;

- knowledge of specific information about a variety of occupations and the organization of the world of work; and

- knowledge of specific information about the clusters of occupations.

For some students with LD, it may be opportune to systematically explore vocational service options through the Division of Rehabilitation Services (DRS) in addition to addressing educational services delivered through the special education system. Career exploration that includes vocational classes, field trips to work sites, and volunteer work experiences can help students identify preferences and interests in vocational areas. The School-to-Work Opportunities Act, signed into law on May 4, 1994, offers students with learning disabilities the opportunity to participate in a variety of vocational rehabilitation experiences. Through this act, funding is provided to programs such as tech-prep, career academies, school-to-apprenticeship programs, cooperative education, youth apprenticeships, and business-education compacts. The act requires the above programs to include a school-based learning component and a work-based component, as well as such activities as guidance and counseling, workplace mentoring, technical assistance for employers, and coordination with employers (Evers, 1996).

Students should also continue career exploration through participation in extracurricular activities, hobbies, and a variety of work experiences (Cowen, 1993). Identified interests, aptitudes, values, and opportunities provide a basis for tentative occupational decisions. Evaluating one's interests in such experiences contributes to career maturity. For students with LD, the learning disability itself may be an important influence in the choice of a major or career. Self-administered, self-scoring instruments, such as *The Self-Directed Search* (Holland, 1971), can be provided to the student for a cursory assessment of interests as they relate to various occupational fields. *SIGI Plus* (Educational Testing Service, 1991), an interactive computerized interest and career inventory, affords the student an opportunity to participate in a more detailed exploration of likes, dislikes, values, and goals in relation to potential majors and careers. Students may need to be cautioned not to make hasty career decisions based on an area of weakness or on what they think their parents want them to do.

Developing Greater Independence

In addition to exploring possible career areas and occupational clusters, Cowen (1993) points out that secondary students with learning disabilities need to work actively with their counselors and teachers to determine which vocational skills are considered basic for employment. Michaels (1994) notes that many of the skills described as important in postsecondary settings may also be critical in the world of work. He adds that "preparation for transition and employment must consist of a delicate balance of capitalizing on strengths while simultaneously developing compensatory strategies for weaknesses" (p. 27). One of the best ways for students to determine exactly what their strengths and weaknesses are and to evaluate their level of independence is to secure a summer job. Maintaining the discipline of working a job will afford students an opportunity to establish a work ethic by adhering to a consistent work schedule and by independently shouldering new responsibilities.

By the sophomore year, if not before, students should be able to clarify the exact nature of their learning disabilities, along with continuing to develop and refine academic skills and career options and further their independence (Cowen, 1993). One way to further students' understanding of their learning disabilities is to help them understand the psycho-educational report. This can be a formidable challenge, since all too often the diagnostic report contains terminology that is too technical or too vague for students to fully understand.

Anderson (1993) points out that analyzing diagnostic reports is frequently the most expedient method of determining appropriate academic adjustments and modifications. Consequently, students may need to be reminded that any accommodations provided by their teachers should be rooted in the findings and recommendations contained in the diagnostic report (Anderson & Brinckerhoff, 1989). Students should be encouraged by LD specialists or school psychologists to develop transition planning goals that encourage "trying out" accommodations or technological aids, such as taped textbooks, laptop computers, and extended time on exams, while they are still in the structured setting of high school. LD teachers should reassure high school students that it is to their advantage to use these accommodations in their general education and college preparatory classes rather than trying to "tough it out" without academic adjustments. During the sophomore year, the LD teacher and guidance personnel should be sure that students with learning disabilities are also aware of the range of accommodations that are available to them for the PSATs so that when they take the SAT I or ACT during their junior year, they will already have experimented with a variety of testing accommodations. However, it may be prudent to advise them that just because an accommodation is listed in the diagnostic report by the school psychologist or LD specialist, there is no guarantee that the recommended accommodation will be provided by a testing agency or disability service provider when they get to college. Vogel and Reder (1998), however, suggest that "students who have a history of using accommodations in a previous setting will have an easier time receiving similar accommodations in the new postsecondary setting if they can document the prior use" (p. 62).

Students should be given an opportunity to meet with a school psychologist or LD specialist to discuss the psycho-educational evaluation and relate those findings to their own perceptions and experiences. Important points contained in the report should be discussed, questions raised, and terminology clarified. High school support staff need to interpret these diagnostic findings in a format that enables students to understand their unique profile of strengths and weaknesses and to identify the accommodations they need to compensate for their deficits. At the high school level, it might even be appropriate to have the student "sign off" that they have read the report.

Eaton and Coull (1998) underscore the importance of encouraging students to practice describing their disability to their parents or a best friend. They advise students, "You should be able to describe your disability without pausing, choking, coughing, or turning red with embarrassment. Describe your disability with confidence. Don't be embarrassed or ashamed of having a disability. . . . Who knows, one of your professors may have a learning disability and/or ADHD" (p. 43).

Learning Strategies Instruction

High school students need to be confident about the strategies and accommodations that will work for them. If a student is lacking basic skills, then the remediation of those skills should be addressed as soon as possible. If students have mastered basic skills, then it may be appropriate to teach them a variety of learning strategies. For over a decade, researchers at the University of Kansas (e.g., Deshler, Ellis, & Lenz, 1996) have studied the benefits of a learning strategies approach for teaching adolescents with learning disabilities versus a more traditional, content-focused approach. The research literature suggests that students with learning disabilities are either "strategy deficient" or unable to spontaneously tap previously learned strategies they need for a given task (Deshler et al., 1996; Wade & Reynolds, 1989; Wang & Palincsar, 1989; Wong & Jones, 1992). The Strategic Intervention Model (SIM), developed at the University of Kansas Institute for Research in Learning Disabilities (KU-IRLD), includes a variety of strategies that have been specifically designed for these strategy deficient students. The instruction systematically moves through an 8-stage process called the SIM Instructional Methodology, which begins with a heavy emphasis on an interactive process that is guided by the teacher (focusing on discussions about rationales for the use of the strategy, specification of strategy components, and explicit modeling by the teacher) and proceeds to an emphasis on student mediation of the learning process (Ellis, 1990).

If students are empowered with new strategic approaches to learning, they will be able to break down and prioritize assignments independently. The LD specialist and the student should work together in selecting a repertoire of learning strategies for the student to master that will promote academic success (Dalke, 1991). These skills may be taught in a resource room setting or as an integral part of a study skills course. Bursuck and Jayanthi (1993) point out that a learning strategies approach is "much more comprehensive than most study skills programs, in that in addition to learning how to perform particular skills, students also learn why and when to apply these skills as well as how to monitor their implementation" (p. 179). Spector et al. (1991) note that when learning strategies, organization, and time management skills are integrated into the resource room curriculum, students become more responsible learners, and the role of school personnel can be limited to monitoring their progress. Without such skills, students with learning disabilities are often ill prepared for the transition to postsecondary education and employment.

High school guidance personnel should be made aware that traditional resource room models that feature content and basic skills tutoring approaches may not provide these students with adequate preparation to succeed in college-preparatory courses (Decker, Spector, & Shaw, 1992). Subject-matter tutoring may act as a short-term "quick fix," but it does not provide strategic learning and problem-solving skills that transfer across the curriculum (Shaw et al., 1991). Ideally, guidance personnel and high school LD support teachers should collaborate to be sure that students with learning disabilities are accessing study skills courses that have learning strategy instruction woven throughout the curriculum (Bursuck, 1991; Decker et al., 1992; Deshler et al., 1996).

Block (1993) observes that students with learning disabilities often have inadequate organizational and study skills, as well as deficits in some combination of written language, reading, and mathematical skills. They may have difficulty locating and organizing materials needed for study, allocating sufficient time for study, finding the right environment in which to study, making and adhering to schedules, and identifying the points that they need to study. Seidenberg (1986) points out that many students with learning disabilities also exhibit skills deficits in reading-related study strategies (e.g., comprehension monitoring, summarizing, outlining, and scanning). She maintains that these students can be supported in a regular academic curriculum by teaching them specific learning strategies or metacognitive skills. Explicit instruction in all these areas is critical if students are going to meet the demands of college (McGuire et al., 1991; Siperstein, 1988). Generalizable skills, such as outlining and note taking, memory techniques, test-taking strategies, and basic word-processing skills should be incorporated into the standard resource room curriculum. As a result of this kind of strategy-based training, high school students with learning disabilities can become more responsible and independent learners (Bursuck & Jayanthi, 1993; Deshler et al., 1996).

High school teachers should provide students with the multiple benefits of assistive technology that enable individuals with learning disabilities to compensate for reading, organization, memory, and math deficits (Day & Edwards, 1996; Raskind, 1998). Raskind and Scott (1993) point out the importance of choosing technologies relative to the individual, the functions to be performed, and the contexts in which the technologies will be used. The sooner that students realize that assistive technology is an essential tool for making the learning environment more accessible and for enhancing individual productivity, the better. For a comprehensive discussion of assistive technology for students with learning disabilities, readers should consult Chapter 11.

Fostering Self-Determination

Individuals with learning disabilities must be empowered with skills to advocate for themselves. Parents, high school teachers, and guidance personnel can prepare students with learning disabilities for adulthood by teaching them self-determination skills. This training typically focuses on assisting students to set goals for themselves and then to actively develop and implement a plan to attain those goals (Eaton, 1996; Wilson, 1994). In addition, young adults need to be able to monitor their progress toward their goals and "to modify the task-attack strategy and time lines for goal attainment based upon feedback from a variety of sources" (Wilson, 1994, p. 180).

The skills that are designed to enhance self-advocacy often involve assertive communication, understanding oneself as a learner, and utilization of self-monitoring techniques. Unfortunately, the research literature suggests that despite their importance, self-advocacy skills are typically not taught in high school (Aune & Ness, 1991a; Dalke & Franzene, 1988; Ryan & Price, 1992; Wilson, 1994). Students with learning disabilities need to develop personal qualities that allow for realistic self-appraisal and risk taking (NJCLD, 1994c). By being knowledgeable about themselves and skillful in knowing when and where to self-advocate, students with learning disabilities can obtain personal independence and meet success in both their educational and career goals (Brinckerhoff, 1993; Goldhammer & Brinckerhoff, 1992; Tessler, 1997).

During the beginning years of high school, consideration should be given to one intervention approach that has been particularly successful with students who have difficulties with social interactions: participation in a support group (Block, 1993; Johnson, 1989; Price, 1988). Support groups can give students an opportunity to openly discuss their personal frustrations with school, teachers, parents, and their friends in a mutually supportive environment. A trained group leader or facilitator can assist these adolescents in refining an array of social interaction skills, such as maintaining eye contact, using the appropriate voice or tone, practicing good body posture, and developing good listening skills (Johnson, 1989; Price, 1993). Michaels et al. (1988) state that "separating parents' wishes and desires from realities and abilities is one issue that must be confronted by students" (p. 72). The availability of a support group can offer a "safe" milieu in which to explore issues such as this as students grapple with the transition to adult life.

Transition Programming in the Junior Year

The junior year is perhaps the most critical year for high school students, as they lay the final groundwork for their postsecondary experience. Table 2.2 presents a detailed listing of objectives to be addressed during the junior year. The proposed academic program should be selected with considerable thought, given that college admissions officers look very carefully for any changes or trends in the educational rigors in the program of study. Depending on students' postsecondary goals, they should be advised that if they elect to take only two or three college-preparatory classes per semester, they may not appear to be prepared for a competitive college curriculum that typically consists of four or five courses. Guidance counselors should address these issues early to be sure that the student understands the ramifications of his or her choices. It is during this time that planning should focus on matching the student's interests and abilities with the most appropriate postsecondary setting. Patton and Polloway (1992) point out that a wide range of educational and vocational opportunities are now available to young adults with learning disabilities. Guidance personnel can be especially helpful in describing the diverse range of 2- and 4-year options available to students after graduation based on personal visits to those institutions. The educational alternatives available after high school include 4-year colleges and universities, junior and community colleges, vocational or technical schools, 13th-year programs, home study, and adult education. College-bound students should begin the search process by developing a tentative list of 2- or 4-year colleges, vocational technical schools, or universities that are of interest to them (Barr et al., 1998; McGuire & Shaw, 1986).

Exploring Postsecondary Options

Guidance personnel play an integral role in apprising students of a variety of postsecondary options available to them. An increasing number of high school students with LD realize that in order to be better prepared for adult life and the world of work, additional training is necessary after graduation. Some students with learning disabilities may elect to pursue careers in technical areas that deemphasize reading and writing skills and capitalize on hands-on activities. For those students, vocational training might be the most appropriate option for reaching their goals (Michaels et al., 1988). For other students, a technical college curriculum that specifically emphasizes mathematics, science, or engineering while requiring less verbal ability may be a more appropriate choice. Some students may meet more success in college settings that feature a co-op curriculum that focuses on both coursework and work experience rather than in an institution with a more traditional liberal arts curriculum.

Community colleges serve a larger proportion of students with learning disabilities than any other segment of postsecondary education (Barnett, 1993). The attraction of community colleges is greatest for students with learning disabilities who would like to attempt some college work while simultaneously maintaining the support of friends and the familiar routine of living at home. Since community colleges have open admissions policies, smaller class ratios, comparatively low tuition fees, academic and personal counseling, and a wide range of vocational, remedial, and developmental courses, they are a logical and advantageous first step for students with more severe learning disabilities. Another advantage of community colleges is that many degree programs do not require standardized entrance exams such as the SAT or ACT. As a result, many community colleges have developed effective and creative disability support practices and programs that help individuals with learning disabilities reach their fullest potential (Bursuck, Rose, Cowen, & Yahaya, 1989; Cocchi, 1997).

Students should be instructed in how to use college resource guides or directories and the latest computer-guided software to assist them in the college search process (Mangrum & Strichart, 1997). Internet sites like Collegenet.com, Collegeview.com, and CollegeLink.com allow prospective students to search for colleges based on type, region, intercollegiate sports, major, tuition, financial aid, and other factors. Students can then use hot links to go from these search results to the home pages of the school to get more information, to compare and contrast school offerings, and even to apply on line. Students with learning disabilities should pay careful attention to admissions criteria, which often vary widely from one institution to another (Cowen, 1993; duChossois & Stein, 1992). Generally speaking, information should be collected regarding minimum entry requirements based on high school class rank, grade point average, prerequisite coursework, and SAT or ACT scores. In addition to those factors, students with disabilities who are able to meet the minimum standards for admission may want to consider the academic qualifications of the "average student" for a given institution. He or she may want to eliminate those colleges that appear to be too competitive or do not provide an array of generic student support services (Cowen, 1991; Mangrum & Strichart, 1997; McGuire & Shaw, 1986).

Finding the right match between LD student characteristics, the postsecondary setting, and the LD support services offered is a complex process. DuChossois (1998, p. 77) has aptly stated the first rule to be: "Student, know thyself." To this end, she has developed a listing of useful questions that high school students can use to look at themselves as well as their study skills and habits. Included are such things as note taking, completing reading assignments and papers, preparing for exams, and managing behavior during tests.

The staff of the HEATH Resource Center suggest that prospective students with learning disabilities make a "short list" of 6–10 prospective schools:

The key point is to set aside disability-related concerns. This list should be based on what the student wants, components of various academic programs offered, admissions related requirements, cost, opportunities, financial aid, location, community resources, athletics, social activities. After the short list is created bring disability concerns back into the picture. Now work to refine the short list by becoming familiar with the services that are provided to students with learning disabilities at each of the colleges or universities on the list. (Barr et al., 1995, p. x)

Evaluating LD Support Services

Never before have there been so many options available to individuals with learning disabilities in the United States and Canada for securing a quality education in conjunction with a range of support services. The most recent edition of *Peterson's Colleges with Programs for Students with Learning Disabilities or Attention-Deficit Disorders* (Mangrum & Strichart, 1997) lists over 1,000 institutions with services for students with learning disabilities and ADHD in the United States. One word of caution is warranted, however: Although LD college guides should be viewed as a logical starting point in the college search, the information contained in them may be outdated. In regard to the increasing numbers of postsecondary institutions offering support programs, Hartman (1997, p. v) states: "As students became better prepared, as their aspirations were raised by supportive parents and teachers, and as colleges and universities come to understand the strengths and potential that such students add to campus life, the number of such programs multiplied."

By perusing college directories that are specifically targeted for students with learning disabilities, students are better able to determine the type of services they may need. The student, parent(s), and the high school guidance counselor should work closely together to determine if the type of LD services offered will be a good match given the student's needs (duChossois, 1998). Guidance counselors should help students to distinguish between comprehensive "LD programs" and those with limited support services (Kravets & Wax, 1997; Lipkin, 1993; Mangrum & Strichart, 1997). Some students with learning disabilities may do very well in a postsecondary setting that offers only limited services if they are independent self-advocates who have a repertoire of compensating strategies and already know what accommodations are effective. Students with learning disabilities or ADHD who require more structure may have difficulty anticipating their needs. Those students who do not know what accommodations they may need should seek out a more comprehensive LD program.

High school students should understand the differences between a comprehensive LD *program* and a *support services model*. An LD program is often characterized as having one person who spearheads the efforts to develop the program, who typically has expertise in the area of learning disabilities (Brinckerhoff et al., 1993; Vogel, 1987). Mangrum and Strichart (1988) identify the following as components of postsecondary programs for students with learning disabilities: diagnostic testing, individual educational programs, academic and program advising, basic skills remediation, subject-area tutoring, specialized courses, auxiliary aids and services, and counseling. Although not every component will be offered on every campus, the critical aspects of LD programs are individualization, a basis in diagnostic data, and coordination by a professional with training in learning disabilities (Brinckerhoff et al., 1993).

In contrast, *support services* at the postsecondary level may be defined as those generic activities that are carried out to ensure equal educational opportunity for any student with a disability. Brinckerhoff (1993) outlines a variety of "minimal resources" that can ensure adequate support services in a climate of fiscal austerity. Basic LD services typically include the minimal requirements mandated under Section 504, such as access to taped textbooks, tape recorders, assistance in arranging testing accommodations, readers, note takers, and provisions for arranging course substitutions. The operative word in a service approach is *generic*, meaning that the services are inclusive of and available to all students with disabilities (Brinckerhoff et al., 1993).

Members of the student's transitional planning team should refer to the continuum of postsecondary LD support services described in Chapter 8, as they anticipate how much support will be necessary in college. The model includes five points on a service continuum: (a) decentralized services; (b) loosely coordinated services; (c) centrally coordinated services; (d) data-based services, and (e) fee-based services. The points on the continuum refer to the level of support available to students at the postsecondary level. DuChossois and Michaels (1994, p. 102) aptly point out that, for a student with a learning disability, the effort involved in finding the right school is further complicated by "the requirement to find appropriate support services suited to the student's individual learning needs." This time-consuming process of college selection and "comparison shopping" for the best level of LD support services should be included as a student-generated goal in the Individual Transition Plan.

Once students have developed a tentative list of 6 to 10 colleges that seem appropriate, they should seek more detailed information regarding admissions and specific information on the range and types of LD support services available on campus. Each listing should be verified with a follow-up phone call to the designated LD contact person, since program staff and resources frequently change and directory information is not always accurate (McGuire & Shaw, 1986). Small (1996) astutely points out that the quality of any given college's response is subject to "the vagaries of funding, administrative fiat and the current image an institution is trying to promote." What was an effective, coordinated support program one year may turn into a vague assortment of academic services the next (Brinckerhoff, 1996a; Small, 1996).

SAT and ACT Preparation

Every year, about two million high schoolers take SAT exams, and almost as many take the ACTs (Rubenstone & Dalby, 1994). During the fall of the junior year and even during the latter part of the sophomore year (if requested) students may take the Preliminary Scholastic Assessment Test (PSAT) in order to prepare for the new SAT I: Reasoning Tests. As in the past, the SAT I focuses on verbal and mathematical skills. The SAT II: Subject Tests are two subject-specific examinations whose subjects include English, foreign language, history, and natural sciences. The scoring system has been recalibrated on a "re-centered scale" that increases national test score averages. However, students may need to be reminded that although the new scores are higher, the value of the scores as compared to other students' scores in the entering class remains the same.

Guidance counselors should assist students in registering for the PSAT or for the PLAN, which is a warm-up exam for the ACT. Guidance personnel and special education teachers should encourage students to take these tests with accommodations as long as the documentation supports a need that is based on the nature and severity of the disability. Testing accommodations may include a reader, a writer, a tape-recorded version, large type, large-block answer sheets, extended time, use of a private room, or multiple test days. Commencing with the 1999–2000 academic year, the College Board requires that any accommodation request in excess of 100% additional time, or any request for multiple test days must be accompanied by a copy of the student's IEP or 504 Plan. The school psychologist or the private diagnostician who wrote the student's report should be contacted to be sure the disability documentation is complete and to provide written verification of the need for alternative testing arrangements (Carlton, 1998). The College Board has adopted a set of documentation guidelines prepared by the Educational Testing Service (ETS) that provide guidance to parents, consumers, and educational testing professionals about the type of documentation necessary to verify accommodation requests for test takers with learning disabilities or attention-deficit/hyperactivity disorder. Copies of the *ETS Policy Statement for Documentation of a Learning Disability in Adolescents and Adults* and the *ETS Policy Statement for Documentation of Attention Deficit/Hyperactivity Disorder in Adolescents and Adults* are available through the ETS Web site at www.ets/disability.org/disability. For a further discussion of these guidelines and eligibility criteria, readers are advised to consult Chapter 7.

In December of the junior year, the results of the PSAT should be reviewed carefully to determine individual areas of strength and weakness. The results of this test may be helpful in determining future courses the student should select in order to prepare for college (Cowen, 1993). If students do not do well on their first attempt, then a dedicated course in test preparation or a workshop on test anxiety may be warranted, but at a price. Aviezer (2000) points out that SAT and other standardized-test preparation or coaching services have become big business, earning hundreds of millions of dollars every year. Kaplan Educational Centers and the Princeton Review, the two largest SAT preparation companies, both offer professional courses ranging from 6 to 8 weeks and practice tests for approximately $800. Considerable controversy exists between the test developers at ETS and the preparation agencies as to whether these expensive test preparation courses in fact make an appreciable difference in test scores.

If students anticipate taking the SATs with alternative testing accommodations, they should contact their guidance counselors before the first of January in that year. Students should also be informed that, should they seek certain alternative testing accommodations, such as additional test time or a change in the construct of the test, their scores will be flagged, meaning they are stamped "nonstandardized administration" when they are sent to an institution. If students request only additional breaks but no additional testing time, their SAT scores will not be flagged. Students who elect not to use documented accommodations while taking standardized tests risk underperformance on those tests and may, therefore, submit scores that negatively misrepresent their true potential to colleges. For a more in-depth discussion of flagging issues relating to the SATs, readers are advised to consult Chapter 3. Some students may be concerned that this intentional flagging of test scores may result in adverse treatment by a prospective college. Therefore, guidance counselors should be aware of which postsecondary institutions do not require SATs or ACTs at all. Fairtest (www. fairtest.org) provides a list of colleges that do not require ACTs or SATs for admission.

The Personal Transition File

Vogel and Reder (1998) recommend that students become actively involved in developing their own Personal Transition Portfolio. The parent(s) should help their child collect and maintain this ongoing personal file of school and medical records, IEPs, résumés, and samples of academic work (NJCLD, 1994c). The file should also include the most recent psycho-educational evaluation that gives the diagnosis of learning disability and the nature of the disability. Vogel (1993b) advocates that, in addition to high school transcripts and ACT or SAT I scores, students include nonconfidential letters of recommendation and even a brief autobiography along with other significant writings that highlight special talents or abilities. Students with learning disabilities should be advised to bring their transition file to campus interviews so that they can highlight their high school academic and extracurricular record as well as talk about their learning disability. This process, begun in junior high, should reflect a gradual shifting of responsibility for record keeping and decision making from a parent or guardian to the individual with LD (Vogel & Reder, 1998). The Highland Park High School (Illinois) Special Education Department has developed a "College Interview Preparation Form" (Alexander & Rolfe, 1991) that students can complete before their campus visit (see Appendix 2.4 on the CD-ROM). Eaton and Coull (1998) have developed a "Checklist at High School: Before Transitioning to College" form that helps students to inventory their preparedness for college and to address questions about the LD documentation (see Appendix 2.5 on the CD-ROM). A similar checklist for students, "Checklist: When You Are at College," reminds students about some of their responsibilities for seeking services (see Appendix 2.6 on the CD-ROM). The authors have also produced a handy glossary of commonly used terms that students should master before the IEP meeting (see Appendix 2.7 on the CD-ROM).

The "College Interview Preparation Form" (Alexander & Rolfe, 1991) can be used as an advance organizer for structuring the college interview, as an ice-breaker during the interview, and as a powerful way of showcasing the student's credentials and self-advocacy abilities. Block (1998b) has developed an excellent handout specifically for college-bound students with learning disabilities, *Questions to Ask During the College Search* (see Appendix 2.8 on the CD-ROM). These two items and the checklist by Eaton and Coull (1998) are excellent examples of how LD specialists and guidance counselors can work together to help students become better prepared so they can be central players on the transition planning team.

Ideally, this collaborative effort will be expanded to include a postsecondary LD support person who can help high school personnel and students anticipate postsecondary expectations (Aune, 1991; Dalke, 1993; Rose & Bursuck, 1989). Such ongoing communication between high school and postsecondary service providers can help to alleviate a number of common problems in the transition process including chronic difficulties in obtaining student records for the purpose of assessing student eligibility for services; lack of communication regarding the number of students who plan to attend community college after completing the senior year; new college students with disabilities registering for courses that are too difficult for them; and lack or inconsistency of methods used by high schools to inform their students with disabilities about postsecondary education options and vocational rehabilitative services. Bursuck and Rose (1992) note that each of these problems regarding the inefficiency of the transition process is particularly evident from feeder high schools to community colleges.

Narrowing Postsecondary Options

During the spring of their junior year, students should finalize all arrangements for the ACT or SAT I and write preselected colleges for application materials and information regarding their LD services, as well as seeking out college admissions representatives who visit local high schools during LD College Nights. Meetings with regional representatives from 2- and 4-year colleges at high school college nights provide students and their parents with an opportunity to discuss admissions requirements, curricular and recreational options, and the range of disability services available on campus. For many students with learning disabilities these discussions with campus representatives will be a real eye-opener as they realize that few community colleges and even fewer 4-year institutions offer the comprehensive array of special education services that are available in most high schools (Bursuck & Rose, 1992). After gathering preliminary information about a particular college or course of study, students should narrow their choices by making a phone call to the director or coordinator of LD support services to arrange for a personal interview. Too often, it is the parent who makes these arrangements, but this is one more instance in which students should be given the opportunity to refine their self-advocacy skills and assume responsibility for their academic endeavors.

The campus visit and interview may be especially important for students with LD whose qualifications look marginal on paper, but whose potential and abilities can come across in an interview. The typical campus interview may not involve the parents, so students themselves will have the opportunity to address any "irregularities" in their application, such as low ACT or SAT scores despite a strong high school GPA, or to discuss the reasons they did not participate in extracurricular activities—for example, due to outside tutoring demands. Students should prepare and organize their personal portfolio in advance and generate a list of questions regarding the admissions process, the college's curricular offerings, and specifically about learning disability support services. Given that college may be a $125,000 investment, students and parent(s) should take the time to visit the campus together and to meet with LD support staff directly. When parents have an opportunity to speak with the interviewer, they should be reminded not to overpower admissions or LD support staff with input regarding their child. Postsecondary service providers may prefer to interview the student alone without parent prompting in order to get an accurate reading of a student's level of motivation, social skills, and understanding of his or her disability. Prospective students should be encouraged to arrange to meet other college students who have learning disabilities who have used the support services on campus and to sit in on a class so they can develop a realistic view of college life (Kravets, 1999). The foreshadowing of the college experience through another peer can be very powerful.

Barr et al. (1998) encourage students with learning disabilities to visit the campus while classes are in session so they can get a realistic impression of campus life. If that is not possible, students should talk by phone with Disability Services staff who coordinate LD support services on campus. Barr et al. suggest that the following questions may be particularly helpful for prospective students who are learning to sort out options:

- Does the college require standardized admissions test scores? If so, what is the range of scores of those admitted?

- For how many students with learning disabilities does the campus currently provide services?

- What are those students' major fields of study?

- What types of academic accommodations are typically provided to students with learning disabilities on campus?

- Will this college provide the specific accommodations that I need?

- What records or documentation of a learning disability are necessary in order to arrange academic accommodations for admitted students?

- How is confidentiality of applicants' records, as well as of enrolled students, protected? Where does the college publish the Family Education and Privacy Act guidelines so that I can review them?

- How is information related to the documentation of a learning disability reviewed? By whom?

- Does the college or university have someone available who is trained in and understands the needs of adults with learning disabilities? What academic and personal characteristics have been found to be important for students with learning disabilities to succeed at this college?

- How many students with learning disabilities have graduated in the past 3 years?

- What is the tuition? Are there additional fees for learning disabilities–related services and, if so, for which services beyond those required by Section 504 and the ADA?

After visiting the campus, the student and the parent(s) should evaluate the overall campus environment across a variety of academic, social, and recreational domains. Specifically, they should evaluate the social and learning climate of that postsecondary setting, its geographic location, and the availability of housing and of financial aid, if desired. Cowen (1993, p. 49) states, "The most important comparisons will be their comfort level with the service coordinator and staff and the comprehensiveness of the needed services." Students may want to personalize their approach to the college search by writing a thank-you note to the individual who interviewed them during their campus visit. This brief note should come from the student, not the parent, if it is to have any positive impression on the admissions officer. Prospective attendees of community colleges or vocational-technical education programs should pay particular attention to how they will manage the academic rigors and social changes within a particular degree or certification program. They should also explore what they will need to do in order to be prepared for transfer into a 4-year setting or for employment. Regardless of the approach taken, students should work at developing a list of questions that may be helpful in sorting out college options.

In recent years, numerous step-by-step transition planning guides have been produced to guide high school students with learning disabilities and their parents through the decision-making process (Cowen, 1990; duChossois & Stein, 1992; Lewis, 1996; McGuire & Shaw, 1986; Vogel, 1993b). Two of these guides, *Choosing the Right College* (duChossois & Stein) and *Postsecondary Decision-Making for Students with Learning Disabilities* (Vogel), are commercially available and are specifically designed to help students with learning disabilities organize their college search. Both guides include a checklist for evaluating LD support services, as well as appendixes with a variety of resource materials and information on state and national resources. One highlight of *Postsecondary Decision-Making for Students with Learning Disabilities* is the student booklet, which includes a series of program objectives that could be incorporated directly into the IEP. Ideally, these objectives should be completed during the junior year of high school. The guide is also available with a companion teacher's guide and a set of overhead transparencies that can be used by LD specialists or guidance counselors to teach students about the college-search process. One feature of *Choosing the Right College* is a school/self-assessment chart that students can fill in themselves as they compare their unique needs with the services available in different postsecondary settings. The manual also contains a two-page listing called "Tips for College-Bound Students with Learning Disabilities," which will be invaluable to students and parents as they prepare for the college search.

Erica-lee Lewis (1996) has written a refreshing guide, *Help Yourself: Advice for College-Bound Students with Learning Disabilities*, which talks specifically to teenagers with learning disabilities. She writes the book as if she were sitting knee to knee with a teenager who is thinking about college. She addresses some delicate LD issues under the rubric of "Categorization Sucks," "Know Your Brain," How Do I Know If Accommodations Are Worth the Hassle? and "Coming Out." One of the biggest advantages of this book is the resource directory, which will make information gathering easier in a variety of areas including financial aid assistance, technological aids, legal and advocacy support networks, and online resources.

If students are interested in a more formal approach to preparing for the transition to higher education, they may want to consider a campus-based orientation program. These fee-based programs are specifically designed for students with learning disabilities and ADHD who plan to attend college. Some programs are offered prior to the senior year of high school, and others require completion of high school as a prerequisite for participation. Key features of these transition programs include opportunities for students to attend college lectures, learn self-advocacy skills, try out different types of assistive technology, and live in a dormitory. Specialty workshops on time management, active textbook reading, note-taking skills, and test preparation are often part of the programs. Examples of schools that offer such programs include the University of Michigan in Ann Arbor, Muskingum College in New Concord, Ohio, and Landmark College in Putney, Vermont. By learning firsthand in advance what skills are necessary for college, students can be better prepared for postsecondary experiences on *any* campus (Brinckerhoff, 1994). For more information regarding transition options for students with learning disabilities and ADHD, readers should contact the HEATH Resource Center in Washington, D.C. Its toll-free line (800-54-HEATH) and Web site (www.heath.ace.org) provide up-to-date information and publication materials on disability issues in higher education. Another valuable Web site for college-bound students is the LD site, www.ldonline.org. Guidance counselors, students with learning disabilities, parents, and teachers may also find a quarterly newsletter called *The Postsecondary LD Report*, by Lydia S. Block, PhD, a welcome resource to assist them in the college planning process. This newsletter features articles with college admission staff, guidance counselors, diagnosticians, and college-bound adolescents with learning disabilities. Subscription information as well as a list of related resources on transition is available on the Web site at www.ldreport.com.

Transition Programming in the Senior Year

At a recent college planning night, the director of admissions from an independent college commented to a group of college-bound students and their parents, "The good news is that you're going to run away from home, and your parents are going to help you pack!" For students with learning disabilities, this can be a double-edged sword. The future holds newfound freedoms, but it is also a time when students have to make informed decisions that may have long-term consequences.

Senior year often commences with students filling out applications and writing college essays. As noted in Table 2.2, applicants with learning disabilities should be encouraged to use a Common Application form for a variety of colleges. The Common Application is a standard format that can be photocopied and is honored by more than 120 colleges nationwide (Rubenstone & Dalby, 1994). Using it can save time, allowing students to focus on developing one or two well-thought-out essays to submit with their applications. The Common Application is available on disk or via the Internet (http://www.commonapp.org), so students can complete an application on line and either submit it electronically or mail the hard copy. For more information on the Common Application, readers should contact the National Association of Secondary School Principals (800-253-7746). Another time-saving approach is to hook up with the CollegeLink program, a service that allows applicants to complete a single application on their personal computer, which can be forwarded to about 500 institutional subscribers for a fee. Students bring their diskettes to their guidance counselors, and all transcripts and recommendations can be forwarded to up to eight member colleges (Rubenstone & Dalby, 1994).

Students should be advised to fill out applications neatly, in ink or, preferably, on a typewriter (Block, 1998a). The college essay can be a powerful "tipper" in close cases, especially if the essay is particularly strong or weak. It should be written by the student and physically prepared by him or her, not Dad's or Mom's secretary at the office. The essay is an opportunity for the student to spotlight an aspect of his or her life and to discuss a significant personal struggle, a family experience, or intellectual pursuit that reached beyond the conventional high school curriculum. Students should be advised to write about a topic that is personally exciting to them rather than something that "sounds intellectual" or is too routine (Kuperstein & Kessler, 1991). Writing about their learning disability can be a good topic if it is handled in a creative and self-affirming manner. However, students need to realize that such an essay is a form of self-disclosure that could work against their admission. Applicants should also be advised not to send more information than is requested and to avoid exaggerating their achievements—a thick file does little to impress an admissions staff. Students who provide a brief historical overview of their learning disability and then focus on just one or two events that changed their lives may come across better on paper than students who attempt to tell their life story of dyslexia in two pages. Reciting a lengthy list of extracurricular activities that have been pursued casually, deluging admissions officers with letters from "connected" people, and "sending a life preserver in the school's colors with a plea to rescue you from the wait list will not help" (Day, 1994, p. 54). Admissions people have tremendous integrity, and such ploys are frowned upon. The Learning Disabilities Association of Massachusetts (LDAM) offers a 15-minute video, "Planning for Success: The College Application Process for Students with Learning Disabilities," which includes numerous suggestions for students with LD who are beginning the application process. For more information on the video, readers should call LDAM at 781-891-5009.

Students would be well advised to choose their references carefully. Letters of recommendation from general education teachers in college preparatory classes who write that, despite a learning disability, this student is college able are likely to get more attention than a routine letter from a guidance counselor who hardly knows the student. Letters from special education teachers can shed valuable light on a student's prospects for success in college if they realistically highlight the student's abilities and address his or her level of motivation to succeed in school. If the student chooses to self-identify as having a learning disability in the admissions process, then a letter from the LD resource room teacher might be appropriate if it substantiates the student's level of motivation and achievement potential with college preparatory coursework. A letter from a supervisor at McDonald's who can speak from daily experience with the candidate carries more weight than one from a famous U.S. senator who went to school with the applicant's father (Day, 1994). Letters of recommendation from family, friends, clergy, and elementary school teachers, who know little about the student's current educational strengths, carry little weight in the admissions process. Finally, students should ask their guidance counselors to review all application forms for completeness 2 or 3 weeks prior to the application deadline.

Many students with learning disabilities and ADHD ask whether it is advisable to disclose their disability in the application process. There are several cases in which disclosure may be warranted. If, for example, students did not take or complete the core foreign language requirement in high school, then they will need to address this point in a personal statement. Marybeth Kravets (1999), a noted college consultant at Deerfield High School in Illinois, encourages students with disabilities to disclose the disability somewhere on the application. This is usually done in a personal statement in which the applicant can discuss the disability, how they have accepted it, and what compensatory skills they have developed. Kravets suggests that "students should let the college know what the disability is and when it was diagnosed, how it impacts academics and/or life" (p. 3). It is very important for students to collectively discuss with their parents and counselor how this disclosure statement will be worded. Whenever possible, it is advisable to put a positive spin on the learning disability and the accompanying abilities. Scott Lissner (1999), director of Academic Support Services at Longwood College, encourages applicants to include a discussion on the topic "what you have learned about yourself and how you have dealt with your disability." If applicants choose to reveal their disability, they should tie the disclosure in with their documentation and present a rationale as to why certain requirements weren't met, or why certain grades were lower than anticipated. It might also be useful to suggest that admissions personnel focus on some of the unique abilities in the application (e.g., superior math abilities, sports talents, leadership). Such positive attributes can paint a more complete picture of who the student is. However, all applicants, regardless of disability, need to be reminded that the high school transcript is their number one credential for establishing their potential for college success.

Louise Russell (personal communication, August 16, 1999), director of student disability resources at Harvard University, takes a different view. She believes that as long as an asterisk denotes extended time on standardized tests, students with disabilities will wonder what influence, if any, that isolated bit of information will have on their admission profiles. A student's decision on whether to elaborate on the asterisk in an essay or accompanying letter is very personal and should rest on what message, if any, that student thinks is missing in order for him or her to be considered "otherwise qualified." Students who performed unevenly throughout high school or were not diagnosed with a disability until relatively recently and so lack a track record reflecting successful remediation techniques, may wish to annotate their story, albeit briefly. However, prospective students should be advised that few colleges have learning specialists on their admission panels, and detailed clinical information may be misunderstood by otherwise learned decision makers: in some cases, it may be better to let the existing record speak for itself.

By the beginning of the senior year, it may be appropriate for students to narrow their career exploration process to a preferred area of study at the postsecondary level. Job shadowing and internship experiences should be provided to allow students to test their hypotheses about career choices and to determine if and how their learning disability may interfere with performance (Dowdy & McCue, 1994; Michaels et al., 1988; Sitlington & Frank, 1990). The student, parent(s), teacher, and guidance counselor should work together to establish a tentative career goal and to determine areas of college study that are consistent with that goal (Cowen, 1993; Wehman, 1992). In some instances, it may be appropriate to refer a student to a Department of Rehabilitative Services counselor for an initial intake interview to determine eligibility and to establish a need for services. Once an individual is determined to be eligible for services, a DRS counselor may be assigned to a student in order to gather as much information as possible about work history, education and training, abilities and interests, rehabilitation needs, and possible career goals (Dowdy, 1996; Dowdy & McCue, 1994). If finances are a consideration, students should be encouraged to ask their local vocational rehabilitation counselor if they qualify for financial assistance. The Department of Rehabilitative Services can assist with college tuition if students can demonstrate that their college program is the most cost-effective method for them to reach their vocational goal as specified in their Individual Written Rehabilitation Plan (IWRP).

Parents who are applying for financial aid may need to be reminded to file the forms early. The good news is that federal and state government educational institutions and private agencies are committed to making higher education accessible to students regardless of need. According to the College Scholarship Service, more than five million students were awarded almost $28 billion in aid for the 1993–94 school year (Rubenstone & Dalby, 1994). L. Stern (1997) encourages students to pick the colleges they want and not to rule out "high-priced spreads." She notes that "places like Amherst are nearly $28,500 a year, but almost half of the students are getting an average of $19,770 in need-based loans, jobs and grants." Students with learning disabilities may have some additional expenses that need to be factored into the financial aid request. For example, some colleges may charge an additional fee for specialized LD tutorial support; students may need to buy adaptive equipment for their computers; or they may need to purchase a four-track tape recorder for textbook reading. All such expenses should be anticipated so that the financial aid package will be adequate for the upcoming year. For additional information on financial aid and student loan information, readers are advised to consult the Nellie Mae Web site: www.nelliemae.org. It is the largest nonprofit provider of student and parent education loans in the country.

Letters of acceptance generally begin to arrive in mid-March. However, many colleges routinely hold the final acceptance notice until they have an additional quarter of high school grades. Students should not be alarmed, as this process is often standard at more competitive institutions. However, if a student has not heard within 4 to 6 weeks of the date that admissions decisions typically are made, the student, *not* the parent, should phone to check on the status of the application. It is possible that documentation is missing or transcript grades were inadvertently not sent. If a student receives several letters of acceptance, then he or she is in the pleasant position of having to rank college choices. If the student is unsure about which college to accept, then a follow-up phone call or a second visit may be appropriate (Kuperstein & Kessler, 1991; Lipkin, 1993). After carefully deciding what college to attend, based on the above considerations, the student should write a brief acceptance letter and mail in the deposit with a housing request early.

Sometimes parents are unrealistic about their child's potential for college success. DuChossois and Michaels (1994, p. 82) comment that parents may have difficulty accepting the compromise of a local community college rather than the "big name" school that they originally envisioned for their child. Families must sometimes confront feelings of disappointment if the student is not qualified to attend a school at the academic level that they would like or at the level of the student's peers. If a student with LD is denied admission, then the student and the family may need to be reminded that "not getting into college doesn't mean that your child is not bright, or is incapable of academic success or even unworthy of higher education. What it does mean is that the colleges selected may be very competitive, or that space was limited, or that the college believes your child is not ready right now" (Rubenstone & Dalby, 1994, p. 156). In such instances, it might be appropriate to consider a postgraduate year, specialized LD preparatory school, community college with strong academic supports, or time off. Of these options, the most popular alternative is a community college, since it can afford students an opportunity to mature socially, to improve their academic skills, and to select college-level courses that can be transferred to a more competitive postsecondary setting after a year or two.

Final Thoughts on Postsecondary Transition

Secondary education must be a process of moving students with learning disabilities from a state of dependency to one of independence (duChossois & Michaels, 1994). Secondary school personnel can help to prepare students with learning disabilities for the challenges of higher education by beginning to replicate some of the demands of postsecondary education while the student is in high school. Postsecondary LD service providers can help by collaborating with their secondary-level colleagues and by realistically presenting the higher education experience to applicants with disabilities. Parents can assist their sons and daughters by validating their dreams and by nurturing their social development and academic growth. However, the key ingredient to success in higher education and, ultimately, in the world of work lies within the students themselves. They are the ones who must master the critical study skills, learning strategies, and daily living and vocational skills that will enable them to traverse a life span with dignity and independence.

CHAPTER

3

JUDICIAL INTENT AND LEGAL PRECEDENTS

Laura F. Rothstein

It has been over 25 years since the passage of P.L. 94-142 and Section 504 of the Rehabilitation Act of 1973. During this period, the field of special education has witnessed rapid change, due, in part, to a variety of court cases, consumer lobbying efforts, and legal mandates that have directly altered the way services are provided to people with disabilities. The 1990 passage of the Americans with Disabilities Act, which is a further reflection of this trend, ensures that people with disabilities are granted full participation in society.

These legal advances have already affected the lives of many people with disabilities in the United States, but nowhere is the potential for empowering more people greater than in the area of learning disabilities. Given the rapid increase in the number of self-identified students with learning disabilities who are seeking services, it has become increasingly important for secondary and postsecondary teachers, administrators, and support staff to have a working knowledge of the rights, responsibilities, and subsequent policies for serving this population.

The purpose of this chapter is to (a) present an overview of the key provisions of P.L. 94-142, Section 504 of the Rehabilitation Act of 1973, and the ADA; (b) demonstrate how these three legal cornerstones compare and contrast and how they affect service delivery to students with learning disabilities at the secondary and postsecondary levels; (c) cite selected court cases that have helped to shape and define the scope of the law; and (d) lay a foundation, based on both the legislation and court cases, that can be used to develop guidelines, policies, and procedures, which are discussed in Chapter 8.

Legal Foundations

Public Law 94-142

Historically, the underpinnings of P.L. 94-142 rest in litigation involving two landmark cases: *Pennsylvania Association for Retarded Citizens (PARC) v. Commonwealth of Pennsylvania* (1972) and *Mills v. The Board of Education of the District of Columbia* (1972). These two class-action suits outlined several important substantive and procedural rights that were later incorporated into P.L. 94-142. Both were premised on the principle of "equal educational opportunity" that was first articulated by the Supreme Court in *Brown v. Board of Education of Topeka* (1954), which held that "separate but equal" was not enough. Through these early judicial mandates, future legislation evolved and culminated in the establishment of uniform standards for providing equal educational opportunity to children with disabilities.

The Education for All Handicapped Children Act (EAHCA), P.L. 94-142, was signed into law in 1975 and provides the guidelines and regulations for special education service delivery throughout the United States. The EAHCA was amended in 1990 and in 1997. Under the 1990 amendments, the title of EAHCA was changed to the Individuals with Disabilities Education Act (IDEA). The major purpose of the IDEA is:

> to ensure that all children with disabilities have available to them a free appropriate public education that emphasizes special education and related services designed to meet their unique needs and prepare them for employment and independent living. (20 U.S.C. § 1400(d)(1)(A))

It is important that postsecondary service providers become familiar with the IDEA for several reasons. Many high school students with learning disabilities and their parents expect that aspects of the IDEA, including educational programs and services offered in high school, will continue in college. Since this is not the case, it is important to note the differences between the two educational settings as they relate to legal rights, access to services, and programming options. The IDEA guarantees that all children, regardless of disability, are entitled to a free, appropriate public education in the least restrictive environment. This entitlement is supported by the use of federal funds according to a payment formula that takes into account the national average expenditure per public school child and the number of students with disabilities receiving special education in each state (Ballard, Ramirez, & Zantal-Wiener, 1987). Because the IDEA is a grant statute and since federal funds are conditional on performance and compliance, it is very specific in its requirements for service provision. Under the IDEA, two criteria must be met to establish eligibility: (a) a student must actually have one or more of the disabilities defined under the act, and (b) such a student must require special education and related services. If these two conditions are met, the student is ensured appropriate, public education in the least restrictive setting at no expense to the parent or guardian. The major underlying principles of the IDEA are the following (Rothstein, 1997):

1. *All* age-eligible children are to be provided education. This is sometimes known as the zero reject principle.

2. Education is to be provided in the *least restrictive appropriate* placement. This is sometimes referred to as the mainstreaming principle.

3. Education is to be provided *at no cost* to the parents.

4. Education is to be *individualized* for each child.

5. *Procedural safeguards* are to be available to ensure compliance.

The Education of the Handicapped Act Amendments of 1990 (P.L. 101-476) included many provisions to strengthen P.L. 94-142. Its new title, the Individuals with Disabilities Education Act, more accurately reflects the preference for emphasizing person-first terminology and the current practice of using the term *disability* instead of *handicap* (Maroldo, 1991). The 1990 amendments made many significant changes. The law now includes autism and traumatic brain injury as protected disabilities under the scope of the IDEA. Initial plans for also including attention-deficit disorder (ADD) as a disability category under the act were amended following public comment and clarification by the Office of Special Education and Rehabilitative Services (OSERS). Current policy stipulates that children with ADD who require special education and related services can meet eligibility under already existing categories such as "other health impaired" (Davila, Williams, & MacDonald, 1991). Related services, such as rehabilitation counseling and social work services, are also covered in the revised legislation.

Of particular relevance to the postsecondary arena is the emphasis the 1990 and 1997 amendments place on providing for transition services. Transition services are a set of coordinated activities designed to facilitate the student's move from high school to a variety of postsecondary activities, including, but not limited to, higher education, vocational training, and adult education.

The IDEA amendments of 1990 mandated that the Individualized Education Program (IEP) include a transition plan for students no later than age 14 with respect to the child's course of study, and at age 16 (or younger if appropriate), a transition plan including a statement of interagency responsibilities or any needed linkages (20 U.S.C. § 1414(d)(1)(A)(vii)). Under the 1997 amendments, beginning when a student is 14, and annually thereafter, a student's IEP must contain a statement of his or her transition service needs (National Information Center for Children and Youth with Disabilities, 1997). Additionally, under the 1997 amendments, beginning at least 1 year before the student reaches the age of majority under state law, the IEP must contain a statement that the student has been apprised of his or her legal rights that will transfer upon reaching the age of majority. These significant changes in special education law will facilitate the transition from high school to college for many students with learning disabilities. Since the IDEA requires that students have a transition plan, it is important that the plan be a realistic reflection of the rigors and realities of college life. The previous chapter includes a detailed transition planning timetable that addresses the critical components in preparing students for life after high school (Table 2.2). Because the IDEA applies only to individuals with disabilities between the ages of 3 and 21 (or until high school graduation) who are receiving special education or related services, close coordination has not been maintained by the courts between the provisions in the IDEA and the regulations under Section 504 of the Rehabilitation Act of 1973, which is more typically applied to adults.

The IDEA amendments of 1997 (P.L. 105-17) are accompanied by regulations that were published in the *Federal Register* in March 1999 after a lengthy and contentious period of discussion (20 U.S.C. § 1400 *et seq.*). In addition to the changes pertaining to transition, of particular significance to the postsecondary arena are the parameters regarding reevaluation. At least every 3 years, the IEP team must review existing evaluation data and additional information needed to determine eligibility, educational needs, and modifications to enable a student to participate in general education. However, this reevaluation does *not* have to include any new testing of the student. If the team determines that no additional data or tests are needed to determine continued eligibility, the local educational agency must notify the student's parent(s) of the determination and the reasons for it, and the right of the parent(s) to request an assessment. In light of the movement among colleges and universities to require documentation that meets specified guidelines (see Chapter 7 for a discussion regarding the development of guidelines for documentation of learning disabilities and ADHD), college LD service providers should communicate to parents the importance of reviewing the most recent testing of a college-bound secondary student to ensure that it will comply with the guidelines of colleges. In most cases, it is in a student's best interest to be reevaluated in the junior or senior year of high school since the documentation serves as the foundation for making decisions about reasonable accommodations in a postsecondary setting. Frequently, parents mistakenly believe that a high school IEP follows a student into a postsecondary setting, whereas it is the assessment report that colleges use in the determination of eligibility for services including accommodations.

Section 504 of the Rehabilitation Act of 1973

Section 504 of the Rehabilitation Act of 1973 (P.L. 93-112) was the first federal civil rights legislation designed to protect the rights of individuals with disabilities. Unlike P.L. 94-142, which is very detailed in its provisions, Section 504 is brief in actual language, yet the statute applies to both children and adults with disabilities from preschool through adult education. The statute states in part: "No otherwise qualified individual with a disability . . . shall, solely by reason of his or her disability, be excluded from participation in, be denied the benefits of, or be subjected to discrimination under any program or activity receiving Federal financial assistance . . ." (29 U.S.C. § 794).

The statute applies to people with disabilities who are viewed as "otherwise qualified" to participate in and benefit from any program or activity that is receiving federal financial assistance. Recipients of federal funds may include state education agencies, elementary and secondary school systems, colleges and universities, libraries, vocational schools, and state vocational rehabilitation agencies. In order to be granted protections afforded to a person with a disability under Section 504, individuals must meet the following eligibility criteria: they must (a) have a physical or mental impairment that substantially limits one or more major life functions, (b) have a history of such impairment, or (c) be regarded as having such impairment, and (d) be deemed to be "otherwise qualified" despite the disability.

The specific classes of people protected under Section 504 include anyone with a physical or mental impairment that substantially limits one or more major life activities, such as caring for oneself, performing manual tasks, walking, seeing, hearing, speaking, breathing, learning, or working. Determination of a "substantial limitation" could be documented by the history of a disability, or by the belief on the part of others that a person has such a disability. For example, a college student with a history of treatment for a psychiatric disability in junior high school might still be considered as disabled because he or she was previously identified and treated as "disabled." A person born with a cleft palate or a burn victim is probably protected under Section 504 because he or she would be perceived by others as having a disability.

The intent of Congress in including both individuals with a record of an impairment and those who are regarded as having a disability as part of the definition was to extend the statutory protections beyond the actual existence of an impairment. There are a number of conditions that often lead to discrimination because of subjective attitudes. These include alcoholism, cancer, diabetes, epilepsy, HIV-positive status, learning disabilities, and speech impairments. Whether these conditions will all be considered disabilities has been called into question by 1999 Supreme Court decisions that are discussed later in this chapter.

Substance use and abuse is treated specially in the definitional portion of the Rehabilitation Act. Individuals who are engaging in the illegal use of drugs are not protected. Individuals who have successfully completed drug rehabilitation and who are no longer using illegal drugs are protected, however, against discrimination based on the past status. While alcoholics are considered to be disabled, a person whose current use of alcohol prevents him or her from performing the duties of the job or whose alcohol abuse constitutes a direct threat to the property or safety of others is not considered to be a protected individual. While this definition refers only to employment, it seems probable that a similar definition would apply to students in higher education.

Impact of Section 504 on Postsecondary Settings

All federal agencies that have oversight over federal financial assistance have promulgated regulations to implement Section 504 of the Rehabilitation Act. The model regulations include a section specifically devoted to postsecondary education (34 C.F.R. § Part 104, Subpart E). This section provides guidance on issues related to admissions and recruitment, treatment of students, academic adjustments, housing, financial and employment assistance to students, and nonacademic services.

Subpart E of the Section 504 regulations is applicable to all postsecondary educational programs and activities that receive federal funding. Any college or university that receives federal financial assistance "may not, on the basis of handicap, exclude any qualified handicapped student from any course, course of study or other part of its education program or activity" (34 C.F.R. § 104.43[c], 1989). College students with learning disabilities are clearly protected under

Section 504 and must be granted an opportunity to compete with their non-disabled peers. Furthermore, these students may expect to be provided modifications or "academic adjustments" that will assist them in compensating for their learning disability (Rothstein, 1986).

Section 504 also stipulates that "a recipient shall operate each program or activity . . . so that the program or activity, when viewed in its entirety, is readily accessible to handicapped persons" (34 C.F.R. § 104.22[a]). Not only does this provision apply to physical facilities on campuses, but it also covers all aspects of student life including admissions, recruitment, academic programs and adjustments, treatment of students, and nonacademic services (34 C.F.R. § 104.42–104.44, 104.47). In brief, colleges and universities must be free from discrimination in their recruitment, admissions, and treatment of students. Treatment of students can take many forms, including access to housing, student health services, financial aid, athletic or cultural facilities, and campus transportation systems.

The impact of Section 504 on postsecondary settings is significant and extensive. Under its provisions, a college or university may not:

1. limit the number of students with disabilities admitted;

2. make preadmission inquiries as to whether or not an applicant has a disability;

3. use admission tests or criteria that inadequately measure the academic level of applicants with disabilities, unless the measures used have been validated as a predictor of academic success in the education program or activity in question;

4. give students with disabilities access to examinations that are not administered with the same frequency as tests given to nondisabled students; in addition, any admission test given to an applicant with a disability must be in an accessible location;

5. give tests and examinations that do not accurately reflect the applicant's aptitude and achievement levels without the interference of disability-related factors (e.g., providing additional time on exams or the use of a reader);

6. limit access or excuse a student with a disability who is otherwise qualified from any course of study solely on the basis of his or her disability;

7. counsel students with disabilities toward more restrictive careers than are recommended for nondisabled students; however, counselors may advise students with disabilities about strict licensing or certification requirements in a given profession;

8. institute prohibitive rules that may adversely affect students with disabilities, such as prohibiting the use of tape recorders or laptop computers in the classroom; auxiliary aids, such as four-track tape recorders and hand-held spell checkers, must be permitted when they are viewed as appropriate academic adjustments that will help to ensure full participation by students with disabilities if they do not fundamentally alter the program;

9. refuse to modify academic requirements that would afford qualified students with disabilities an opportunity for full educational participation; permitting additional time to meet degree requirements and allowing a student to receive a course substitution for a foreign language requirement are examples of such actions;

10. provide less financial assistance to students with disabilities than is provided to nondisabled students, or premise financial aid decisions on information that is discriminatory on the basis of disability, thereby limiting eligibility for assistance;

11. provide housing to students with disabilities that is not equivalent and accessible and at the same cost as comparable housing available to nondisabled students;

12. prohibit full participation in campus services or activities that are nonacademic in nature, such as physical education, athletics, or social organizations (Brinckerhoff et al., 1993).

The program may, however, deny the accommodations if it can demonstrate that they fundamentally alter the program, lower standards, or are unduly burdensome financially or administratively.

Under Section 504, institutions are required to respond by making modifications in academic requirements as necessary to ensure that such requirements do not discriminate or have the effect of discriminating against a qualified applicant with a disability (34 C.F.R. § 104.44[a]). Many of the modifications or adjustments listed above are readily achievable without being too time consuming or costly. It should be noted that the provision of accommodations for college students with disabilities need not guarantee those students equal results or achievement; accommodations must merely afford them with an *equal opportunity* to achieve equal results.

The Americans with Disabilities Act

Senator Robert Dole commented upon the signing of the ADA by saying, "Forty-three million disabled Americans deserve to be brought into the mainstream of American life—to enjoy a meal at a restaurant, to see their favorite movie, to travel to a job on public transportation, to communicate by telephone, or to cheer at a ball game. The ADA's message to America is that inequality and prejudice are unacceptable. The ADA's important message to people with disabilities is that the time has come to live independently with dignity and to exercise the right to participate in all aspects of American life" (Bureau of National Affairs, 1990).

The ADA was signed into law on July 26, 1990, as P.L. 101-336. Its intent is to provide equal opportunities for people with disabilities. The ADA does not replace Section 504, but it draws much of its substantive framework from both Section 504 and the Civil Rights Restoration Act of 1987. The ADA expands the provisions in Section 504 to the private sector. Essentially, it prohibits discrimination against the same population and in many of the same areas as Section 504 but includes areas that were not covered under Section 504, such as private businesses, nongovernment-funded accommodations, and services provided by state or local governments.

The definition of an individual with a disability under the ADA is identical to the definition previously outlined in Section 504. This individual is one who has a physical or mental impairment that substantially limits one or more major life activities, has a record of such an impairment, or is regarded as having such an impairment—even if he or she does not, in fact, have such an impairment. Specific learning disabilities would be considered to be an impairment under the ADA, since learning is viewed as a major life activity. It is also unlawful to discriminate against an individual, whether disabled or not, because of a relationship or association with an individual with a known disability. The ADA treats individuals with substance and alcohol problems similarly to Section 504. Like Section 504, this treatment seems to apply to employment, but it is probable that it would apply to students in higher education as well.

The ADA is divided into five sections, or "titles," which are concerned with nondiscrimination on the basis of disability within a certain scope of activities. The five sections cover employment; public services (state and local, not federal); public accommodations (privately provided); telecommunications;

and miscellaneous provisions. These sections have varying degrees of impact on the issues affecting students with learning disabilities in higher education.

Title I: Employment

Title I covers the area of employment. It specifies that an employer with 15 or more employees may not discriminate against an individual with a disability in hiring, promotion, benefits, or any other employment-related activity if the person is qualified to perform the essential functions of the job, with or without accommodations. All higher education settings, both public and private, are bound by this title, except for entities that are wholly owned or operated by the U.S. government. As a result, the postsecondary service academies (e.g., the U.S. Naval Academy, Air Force Academy, and Military Academy) are not covered under ADA regulations. Under the ADA, a prospective employee must be able to meet the employer's requirements for the job, such as level of education, employment experience, or licensure. Employers may ask about an applicant's ability to perform a job, but they cannot ask if an applicant has a disability or subject the applicant to tests that tend to screen out people with disabilities. An employer cannot require a prospective employee to take a medical examination before being offered a job. An employer cannot refuse to hire an applicant because the disability prevents that individual from performing duties that are not essential to the job. It should be noted that the ADA does not require an employer to hire an applicant with a disability over other applicants merely because the person has a disability. It only prohibits discrimination on the basis of a disability.

Once an individual with a disability is hired, the employer is required to provide "reasonable accommodation" in the workplace. This may include job restructuring, part-time or modified work schedules, modification of exams or training materials, taped texts, provision for readers or interpreters, and modification of equipment so that it is readily accessible. The costs associated with the needed accommodations are assumed by the employer. However, employers need not provide accommodations that are of a personal nature or that impose an "undue hardship" on business operations. An undue hardship is defined as "an action requiring significant difficulty or expense" when it is considered in light of a variety of factors, which include the nature and cost of the accommodation in relation to the size, resources, nature, and structure of the employer's operation. If the cost of the needed accommodation would be an undue hardship, then the employee must be given the choice of providing the accommodation or paying for the portion of the accommodation that causes the undue hardship.

In general, a larger employer would be expected to make accommodations requiring greater effort or expense than those required of a smaller employer. However, an employer may require that applicants or employees not pose a "direct threat" to the health and safety of themselves or other persons. A direct threat must include evidence that there is a significant risk of substantial harm to the individual or others that cannot be eliminated or reduced by reasonable accommodation. The direct threat must be shown to be real and must be based on present abilities, not conjecture about future circumstances. Such determinations must be made on an individual basis in light of reasonable medical judgment.

Title II: Public Services and Transportation

Title II is divided into two subparts. Subpart A requires that state and local governmental entities and programs be accessible to individuals with disabilities, and Subpart B addresses transportation services provided to the general public. Virtually all state colleges and universities and local governmentally operated institutions (such as community colleges) would be subject to Title II of the ADA (Rothstein, 1997). Subpart A of the act also requires institutions to conduct a self-evaluation plan. In a higher education setting, a self-evaluation plan must have been conducted by January 26, 1993. The purpose of the plan is to determine what programs or activities on campus need to be made accessible and to establish a time frame for change (up to 3 years). If modification is necessary, the institution must develop a transition plan. If modification is not going to occur, then people with disabilities must be provided with alternative ways to effectively access the program. Institutions already covered under Section 504 that have previously conducted a self-evaluation need only do another self-evaluation to reflect any changes in policies and procedures since the initial evaluation (56 Fed. Reg. 35718 [1991]). However, the Department of Justice strongly encourages public entities to review their full range of programs and services, since most Section 504 self-evaluations were conducted more than a dozen years ago and few have been monitored on an ongoing basis. For specific suggestions on how to conduct a self-evaluation plan in a postsecondary setting, readers are encouraged to consult *Title by Title—The ADA's Impact on Postsecondary Education* (Jarrow, 1992b).

Subpart B requires public entities that purchase or lease new buses, railcars, or other vehicles to ensure that those vehicles are accessible to and usable by individuals with disabilities, including people in wheelchairs. While these requirements have an impact on campus transportation systems, detail about these requirements is not included here because of its limited applicability to students with learning disabilities.

Title III: Public Accommodations

Title III of the ADA applies to 12 categories of privately provided programs of public accommodation (Rothstein, 1997). This title ensures that goods, services, privileges, advantages, and facilities of any public place be offered "in the most integrated setting appropriate to the needs of the individual," except when the individual poses a direct threat to the health or safety of other people. Private entities such as restaurants, hotels, retail stores, places of education, parks and zoos, and recreation sites such as bowling alleys, health clubs, or golf courses may not discriminate against individuals with disabilities. Private institutions of higher education are clearly covered under the protections of Title III unless they are wholly owned and operated by a religious organization. This exemption applies to entities controlled or operated by religious organizations, such as day-care centers or nursing homes, that are open to the public. Although this exemption may relieve an institution from Title III of the ADA, Section 504 of the Rehabilitation Act would still apply if the institution receives federal financial assistance.

Auxiliary aids and services must be provided to individuals with disabilities unless an "undue burden" would result. Auxiliary services may include access to qualified interpreters, readers, assistive listening devices, audio recordings, large-print materials, or speech synthesizers or the modification of equipment. In a postsecondary setting, attendant care, personal readers, specialized equipment for independent-study purposes, or individually prescribed devices such as wheelchairs or hearing aids would not need to be provided by the institution.

As a result of the ADA, all new construction and alterations of existing facilities must be accessible. Physical barriers in existing facilities must be removed if removal is "readily achievable." "Readily achievable" means "easily accomplishable and able to be carried out without much difficulty or expense" (U.S. Department of Justice, 1991, p. 5). Examples include the simple ramping of a few steps, installation of grab bars, lowering of telephones, or other modest adjustments. Institutions are required to engage in readily achievable barrier removal whenever and wherever instances of architectural, communication, or transportation barriers are identified. If barrier removal is not readily achievable, institutions must make the program and activities available through alternative methods to ensure full participation by individuals with disabilities (Rothstein, 1997).

One of the most complex issues faced by postsecondary service providers involves the licensure of students with disabilities for the professions. Title II and Title III of the ADA contain sections that pertain to testing, licensing, and certification that may be particularly relevant to postsecondary service providers. Both state and local governments, as well as private entities, are barred from discriminating against qualified individuals with disabilities in licensing and certification programs. The ADA requires examinations (and the application process leading to examination) for licensure and certification to be accessible to people with disabilities, regardless of who is doing the actual test administration. The agency administering the exam must provide any modifications or auxiliary aids at no expense to the test taker. If the test is administered by a state or local government, discrimination on the basis of disabilities is prohibited under Title II; if it is administered by a private entity, it is covered by Title III.

The ADA regulations offer two standards for licensing boards to use in decisions about accommodations for eligible board candidates. One standard defines the limit of accommodations to allow boards to reject an examination accommodation request if it will result in an undue burden to the board because of additional expense or effort in creating and/or administering the modified examination. The second standard allows boards to reject an accommodation if it will fundamentally alter the measurement of skills or knowledge that the examination was designed to measure (Americans with Disabilities Act, 1990, § 309[b][31]).

Titles IV and V: Telecommunications Relay Services and Miscellaneous Provisions

Title IV requires that telecommunications services be made accessible to people with hearing and speech impairments. Title V contains miscellaneous provisions that apply to all of the other titles and ensure that the ADA does not limit or invalidate other federal or state laws that provide equal or greater protection for the rights of individuals with disabilities. These sections have limited application to the issue of students with learning disabilities, except to the extent that a state might have greater obligations with respect to these individuals.

Although there are several sets of regulations implementing the various titles of the ADA, no new regulations were promulgated under the ADA relating to postsecondary education. The intent that the ADA and Section 504 were to be read consistently is probably the reason additional regulations were not viewed as necessary under the ADA. The litigation and regulatory enforcement in postsecondary education seems to indicate, however, that there are a number of areas in which it would be useful for federal agencies to provide additional guidance in the form of regulations. These areas include the issue of learning disabilities, including who is entitled to protection, what accommodations are to be provided, obligations following academic failure, and how standardized testing scores should be used. These issues are discussed more fully in sections that follow.

Comparing the IDEA, Section 504, and the ADA: Implications for Higher Education

The IDEA, Section 504, and the ADA

The IDEA, Section 504 of the Rehabilitation Act, and the Americans with Disabilities Act complement each other in a variety of ways to ensure equal access to educational opportunities. The IDEA is very precise in its regulations and offers few opportunities for broader interpretation, while Section 504 and the ADA have regulations that are less detailed with respect to higher education. Table 3.1 provides a comprehensive overview comparing the IDEA, Section 504, and the ADA in a number of areas.

The definition of "qualified individuals with disabilities" is much narrower under the IDEA, which includes a specific listing of the disabilities covered under the act. Under the IDEA, students from 3 to 21 years of age are eligible for services. Section 504 regulations do not refer to a specific age group per se, but to public elementary, secondary, and postsecondary education. Section 504 is deliberately broad, resulting in more children being referred for services. For example, children with HIV or orthopedic impairments are protected under Section 504 but may not be viewed as "educationally impaired," which would allow them to receive special education services under the IDEA. For a student to be served under the IDEA, he or she must be of an age for which persons without disabilities are provided services or be of an age for which it is mandatory under state law to provide such services to a person with a disability (Maroldo, 1991). Although the definition of an "appropriate education" under the IDEA is tightly bound to the need for special education services, Section 504 and the ADA are not restricted to special education.

The IDEA is primarily concerned with issues in the elementary and secondary arenas and has no impact on postsecondary service delivery, with the possible exception of community colleges that may be subject to public school system jurisdiction. Unlike the IDEA, neither Section 504 nor the ADA imposes an obligation on postsecondary institutions to provide a free appropriate education to all qualified people with disabilities. Section 504 simply states that institutions may not discriminate against qualified individuals with disabilities.

Table 3.1

Comparison of the IDEA, Section 504, and the ADA

	IDEA	Section 504	ADA
Mission	To provide a free, appropriate, public education (FAPE) in the least restrictive environment.	To provide people with disabilities, to the maximum extent possible, the opportunity to be fully integrated into mainstream American life.	To provide all people with disabilities broader coverage than Section 504 in all aspects of discrimination law.
Scope	Applies to public schools.	Applies to any program or activity that receives federal financial assistance.	Applies to public or private employment, transportation, accommodations, and telecommunications regardless of whether federal funding is received.
Coverage	Only those students age 3–21 who need special education and related services because of their disability.	All qualified people with disabilities regardless of whether special education services are required in public elementary, secondary, or postsecondary settings.	All qualified people with disabilities, and qualified nondisabled people related to or associated with a person with a disability.
Disability defined	A listing of disabilities is provided in the act, including specific learning disabilities.	No listing of disabilities is provided, but criteria including having any physical or mental impairment that substantially limits one or more major life activities, having a record of such an impairment, or being regarded as having such an impairment.	No listing of disabilities is provided. Same criteria as in Section 504.
Identification process	Responsibility of school district to identify through "Child Find" and evaluate at no expense to parent or individual.	Responsibility of individual with disability to self-identify and provide documentation. Cost of evaluation must be assumed by the individual, not the institution.	Same as Section 504.

(continues)

Table 3.1 *Continued.*

	IDEA	Section 504	ADA
Service delivery	Special education services and auxiliary aids must be stipulated in the Individualized Education Program.	Services, auxiliary aids, and academic adjustments may be provided in the regular education setting, arranged for by the special education coordinator or disabled student services provider.	Services, auxiliary aids, and accommodations arranged for by the designated ADA coordinator; accommodations must not pose an "undue hardship" to employers.
Funding	Federal funds are conditional on compliance with IDEA regulations.	No authorization for funding is attached to this civil rights statute.	Same as Section 504.
Enforcement agency	Office of Special Education and Rehabilitative Services in U.S. Department of Education.	Office for Civil Rights in the U.S. Department of Education.	Primarily the U.S. Department of Justice, in conjunction with the Equal Employment Opportunity Commission and Federal Communications Commission. May overlap with OCR.
Remedies	Reimbursement by district of school-related expenses is available to parents of children with disabilities to ensure a FAPE.	A private individual can sue a recipient of federal financial assistance to ensure compliance with Section 504. Attorney fees and costs may be ordered.	Same as Section 504 with monetary damages for some violations. Attorney fees and litigation expenses are also recoverable.

Note. Adapted from *Handicapped Requirements Handbook*, January 1993, Washington, DC: Thompson Publishing Group. Copyright 1993 by Thompson Publishing Group. Adapted with permission.

Consequently, Section 504 regulations are quite different in their specifications regarding identification, assessment, and service delivery.

The IDEA requires local education agencies to identify, assess, and serve students with disabilities at no cost to the parent. In contrast, college students with learning disabilities have the responsibility to identify themselves by notifying the appropriate institutional representative or LD service provider of their disability. The student also has the responsibility for providing documentation of the learning disability and for working with the LD service provider to determine what academic adjustments may be necessary to compensate for the learning disability (Brinckerhoff, Shaw, & McGuire, 1992). Students who were not actively involved in decision making under the IDEA often find themselves ill prepared for assuming their new responsibilities under Section 504 and the ADA, such as contacting the professor and making arrangements for accommodations independently. Jarrow (1992a) emphasizes that both the request for accommodation and the provision of support must be "appropriate and timely and the institution is not required to jump through hoops" to meet the needs of students who fail to give adequate notice of their accommodation needs.

Scott (1991) points out that one major difference between the IDEA and Section 504 concerns the manner in which accommodations are secured in higher education settings. Support services and auxiliary aids are mandated requirements under the IDEA. In higher education, support services and auxiliary aids are viewed as an array of options that may or may not be utilized by students with disabilities. Jarrow (1991) states that Section 504 requires students with disabilities to receive appropriate accommodations upon request. However, if students choose not to identify themselves as disabled, the institution is under no obligation to search them out and offer support. Neither Section 504 nor the ADA imposes any obligation on colleges to admit and rehabilitate students with disabilities who are not otherwise qualified, or to make major changes in an academic program in order to accommodate a student with a disability. As a practical matter, however, colleges may find benefits in being proactive in encouraging students with disabilities to identify themselves in order to receive services.

Heyward, Lawton, and Associates (1991a) point out that one of the most common mistakes made at the elementary and secondary levels is assuming that a student who is not entitled to protections under the IDEA is also not protected under Section 504. In fact, many states or school districts have sought to avoid complying with Section 504 by arguing that the IDEA is the exclusive remedy for those alleging disability discrimination in the elementary and secondary arenas. School districts must comply with the ADA, Section 504, and the IDEA. This was substantiated under a congressional action in 1986 with the Handicapped Children's Protection Act of 1986 (P.L. 99-372), which indicates that all the rights, protections, and remedies provided under Section 504 and other federal statutes are also available to students covered by the IDEA. Another major difference between the IDEA, the ADA, and Section 504 concerns the availability of supportive personnel. Students with learning disabilities in elementary and secondary schools are often surrounded by a team of special educators, speech and language specialists, counselors, and teachers. Institutions of higher education are not required to provide special programs, and few higher education settings have the luxury of providing comprehensive support services to students with learning disabilities (Brinckerhoff, 1991). Consequently, students entering college for the first time must learn the differences between these three pieces of legislation so they can act responsibly and effectively advocate for the services they need.

Section 504 states that postsecondary institutions cannot discriminate on the basis of disability, but it does not detail what needs to be accomplished for an individual to achieve meaningful access. Heyward, Lawton, and Associates (1991b, p. 2) point out that in seeking to interpret the "reasonable accommodation standard" under the Rehabilitation Act, courts have noted that "no standard for determining the reasonableness of an accommodation has been formulated" (*Dexler v. Tisch*, 1987). The determination of what academic adjustments are appropriate must be made on an individual case-by-case basis and are not typically included in a formal document such as an IEP. At the postsecondary level, testing accommodations or other selected academic adjustments should provide the institution with a measure of the students' knowledge and skills that is equivalent, or at least similar, to those used to assess all other students. It is important to keep in mind that the faculty members' right to academic freedom may not outweigh the students' right to a needed accommodation (King & Jarrow, 1991).

The following list includes a variety of considerations used in determining action under Section 504 and/or the ADA in postsecondary settings:

1. Is the institution public or otherwise covered by state accessibility or accommodation statutes?

2. Is the institution a recipient of federal funds?

3. Does the applicant have a disability that is protected under Section 504 and the ADA?

4. Is the applicant "otherwise qualified" for admission? Despite the disability, are the academic and technical standards for admission to the institution being met?

5. Once admitted, does the proposed accommodation represent an appropriate academic adjustment?

   a. Can the student perform the essential functions that the program requires?

   b. If not, would there need to be a fundamental change in an essential element of the program in order to accommodate the student?

c. Does the proposed accommodation pose an "undue hardship" (either financially or administratively) on the institution?

d. Does the proposed accommodation pose health or safety concerns to others?

Unlike the IDEA, Section 504 and the ADA are civil rights statutes that merely include some general compliance guidelines. They contain no authorization for funding. The major difference between the ADA and Section 504 is that the ADA is broader in its application and covers more programs and services than Section 504 (Rothstein, 1991). Under Section 504, no specific mention is made regarding the eligibility for disability-related support services of people with temporary disabilities.

Another critical difference between the IDEA, Section 504, and the ADA concerns enforcement and procedures for addressing alleged discrimination claims. The Office for Civil Rights (OCR) within the Department of Education is charged with enforcing Section 504, while OSERS is the agency charged with enforcing the IDEA. Depending on the title, the ADA is enforced both publicly and privately by the Department of Justice or the Equal Employment Opportunity Commission (EEOC). The U.S. attorney general has the authority to institute lawsuits when there is "reasonable cause" to believe that "any person or group of persons is engaged in a pattern or practice of discriminating against individuals with disabilities, or to institute a suit when any person or group of persons has been discriminated against under (Title III) and such discrimination raises an issue of general public importance" (42 U.S.C. § 12188[b][1](B)).

Under Section 504, if an applicant believes that he or she has been discriminated against on the basis of disability in a program that is receiving federal financial assistance, a complaint can be filed with the OCR through the regional office that services the state in which the discrimination allegedly took place (see Appendix 3.1 on the CD-ROM). The complaint must be in writing and must be filed within 180 days of the date the alleged discrimination occurred. The complaint should be specific in its scope; otherwise, a simple complaint investigation can turn into an overall compliance review visit (Section 504 of the Rehabilitation Act, 1991). An extension for filing may be granted by the regional OCR director for good cause. The letter of complaint must be signed and should explain who was discriminated against, by whom or by what institution, when the discrimination took place, who was harmed, and who can be contacted for further information about the alleged discriminatory act. The OCR regional office may be contacted for assistance in preparing a complaint. The ADA adopts all of the power, remedies, and procedures in Title VI of the Civil Rights Act of 1964.

Impact of Federal Laws on
Postsecondary Education

The impact of federal law on higher education institutions and their relation-ship with applicants and students with learning disabilities has been substan-tial. There is a significant body of judicial attention to this issue as well as numerous Department of Education Office for Civil Rights opinions that have developed since the 1973 passage of the Rehabilitation Act. While some issues have been more clearly resolved, others remain unsettled, leaving institutions and individuals with learning disabilities unsure of their respective obligations and rights. The following subsections discuss by topic area the general direction that the law has taken with respect to these issues. It is essential to keep in mind that unless the Supreme Court has definitively ruled on an issue, the guid-ance inherent in legal decisions may be accepted by courts only in the partic-ular jurisdiction of the ruling. Nonetheless, some likely interpretations appli-cable in most, if not all, jurisdictions can be predicted.

Who Is Protected?

Substantial Impairment and Mitigating Measures

Section 504 and the ADA provide protection to individuals with impairments that substantially limit one or more major life activities (29 U.S.C. § 706[8][B]; 42 U.S.C. § 12102[2]). It also protects individuals who are regarded as having such an impairment and those who have a record of such an impairment. Major life activities are defined as "functions such as caring for one's self, performing manual tasks, walking, seeing, hearing, speaking, breathing, learning and work-ing" (34 C.F.R. § 104.3[j][2][ii]). Until 1999, there was a dispute as to whether the substantial limitation should be considered with or without mitigating mea-sures or other compensating factors. For example, should an individual with a visual impairment be evaluated as substantially limited if eyeglasses correct the impairment? In 1999, the Supreme Court, in a trilogy of cases that have been much criticized, held that the impairment should be evaluated with mitigating measures (*Sutton v. United Airlines*, 1999). While the cases all involved employ-ment settings, not higher education, the Court sent a signal that may affect higher education by remanding a case involving a learning disability and a pro-fessional licensing exam for reconsideration in light of its decision.

The case of *Bartlett v. New York State Board of Law Examiners* (1998) is the first instance in which a federal appellate court addressed the issue of accommodations on a bar exam for a student with a disability. Marilyn Bartlett is a middle-aged college professor who, by all reports, struggled through school with an undiagnosed learning disability. It was not until she was enrolled in law school that Dr. Bartlett was formally identified as having a learning disability and was granted accommodations. When she applied for accommodations for the New York State bar examination, based upon a learning disability, her request was denied for these reasons: her documentation was deemed to be too old (18 months); she was late to register (the deadline for applicants with disabilities was 60 days earlier than the deadline for other applicants, a policy later changed on the advice of the U.S. Department of Justice); and her scores on two subtests of the *Woodcock Reading Mastery Tests–Revised* (Woodcock, 1994) were viewed as being too high to reflect a substantial learning impairment. After being denied accommodations by the New York State bar examiners on two more occasions, she brought suit in July 1993.

Dr. Bartlett was granted time and one-half and a reader-scribe who could record her answers on the next administration. During the 21-day trial that ensued, it was determined that she did have a learning disability that affected her reading despite the testimony of the Bar Examination Board's expert witness, who claimed that she did not have a disability since she scored at the 30th percentile on the decoding subtest of the *Woodcock Reading Mastery Tests–Revised*. The court determined that Dr. Bartlett read "slowly and without automaticity" and that the diagnosis of a learning disability must be made "on the basis of clinical judgment and identified in the context of an individual's total processing difficulties" (*Bartlett v. New York State Board of Law Examiners*, p. 1099). The court further held that Dr. Bartlett's learning disability was covered under the ADA because she was substantially limited in the major life activity of reading. The fact that she had self-accommodated, so that she could function adequately and competently enough to complete a law school education, did not prevent her from being covered. The court held that such "self-accommodations" or mitigating or corrective measures should not be considered when deciding whether she met the definition of disability.

This appellate court decision has been called into question by the *Sutton* decision. Indeed, the Supreme Court in *Sutton* specifically referred to the *Bartlett* decision, a case that was to have been considered by the Supreme Court but subsequently has been sent back to the circuit court for reconsideration in light of *Sutton*. The *Bartlett* case is interesting because it falls between the context of higher education and employment. A professional licensing exam is generally necessary for reasonable employment options within a particular profession. Thus, it could be viewed as an employment exam. On the other hand, it is also akin to an exit exam from an educational program, thus focusing on the major life activity of learning. It is not clear whether the major life activity of working is the only relevant life activity to be considered in a case such as this.

It is possible that the lower court may still decide that Dr. Bartlett is substantially limited in the major life activity of reading, which is not specifically listed, but could easily be considered a major life activity. The fact that she had self-accommodated sufficiently to be able to "learn" at a reasonable level would not leave her unprotected, because she is still affected in reading speed and automaticity, areas where her impairment is not sufficiently affected by mitigating or self-accommodating measures especially in a timed condition such as the bar examination.

In any case, it is unwise for disability service providers and higher education administrators to take a path of not accommodating learning disabilities based on the *Sutton* case until this issue is more clearly resolved. The better avenue is to ensure that the learning disability is appropriately documented.

Documentation Issues

Several issues arise in the context of documentation. The first centers on why documentation is required at all. Other issues are the qualifications of those evaluating the individual, how recent that evaluation must be, and what deference the courts will pay to different evaluations. The obligation of a student to provide documentation in a timely manner has also been addressed by courts and the OCR. In addition, the question of who must pay for documentation falls into this area.

Documentation is required for disabilities only in cases where the individual wishes the disability to be considered for purposes of accommodation. It might also be required in cases where the individual requests that the disability be taken into account in making an admissions decision initially. For example, an applicant might have poor high school grades and want to have the admissions decision maker consider the fact that the learning disability was not identified and accommodated until his or her senior year of high school. Another example is a student who has difficulty taking standardized tests (even with accommodation) because of a learning disability and who wants the admissions decision makers to know about that. However, it is important to note that few college admissions offices have the personnel on staff who can adequately review disability documentation. It can be a challenge under the best of circumstances to review disability documentation in order to determine the potential impact of the learning disability on an applicant's future academic performance. It is even more difficult when dealing with documentation that is limited in scope or content, which is frequently the case with attention-deficit disorder or psychiatric documentation.

In cases where a student wants special consideration because of the disability, it is the obligation of the student to make known the disability and to provide appropriate supporting documentation (*Dubois v. Alderson-Broaddus College, Inc.*, 1997; *Kaltenberger v. Ohio College of Podiatric Medicine*, 1998; *Salvador v. Bell*, 1986). This is particularly true in the case of learning disabilities and related disabilities as compared to certain orthopedic impairments. For example, a student with quadriplegia who asks for a note taker will probably not be expected to provide a physician's documentation of the inability to write. The student with a learning disability, however, who makes the same request is in a different situation. Legal mandates allow the educational agency to require that individual to provide justification for accommodation.

An evaluation for the presence of a learning disability is expensive. The full battery of tests may easily cost in the $1,000 range. Unlike evaluations under the IDEA, for which the school pays, in most instances the postsecondary student seeking the accommodation will be required to assume the cost of assessment because the burden is on that individual to make known the disability and to document it.

Courts have just begun to address the issue of who is qualified to diagnose a learning disability and to recommend accommodations. One of the few cases to address the credentials issue is *Guckenberger v. Boston University* (1997), a case that received a substantial amount of media attention. The standard set in *Guckenberger* is that evaluations of a learning disability need not be made by someone with a doctoral degree, so long as the evaluator is a trained and experienced professional in the area of learning disabilities. The court in *Guckenberger* was more stringent, however, for evaluations of ADD and ADHD, requiring that the evaluator have a PhD or an MD What is probably of major importance is that any evaluator in a higher education context have experience in assessing adults with learning disabilities and related disabilities because of differences in this population as compared with children.

Guckenberger also addressed the issue of how often or how recent such evaluations should be. Boston University had changed its policy to require that documentation be within the past 3 years. The court held that such a rigid standard was not appropriate in the case of a learning disability, and that where qualified professionals deem retesting not to be necessary, documentation need not meet the 3-year currency requirement. Again, what seems critical is whether there is a significant reason the past documentation is no longer valid. If so, more recent documentation would be justified. This is a potential area for dispute about payment. Where there is a dispute about the validity of the documentation, there are questions as to whether the individual claiming the disability should be obligated to pay for a new evaluation. There is no clearly settled answer to that question. It seems that institutions would be on solid legal ground to require the student or applicant to pay if there were a good-faith reason for challenging older documentation.

Judicial precedent does not address to any great extent the components that should be included in the documentation. Good practice would seem to dictate, however, that the documentation indicate not only the diagnosis and the instruments used to render the diagnosis, but also the appropriate accommodations for the disability. The test instruments used to measure various skills should be appropriate for their use (see Chapter 6 for a comprehensive discussion of assessment) (*Bartlett v. New York State Board of Law Examiners*, 1998). Unfortunately, evaluators do not always know enough about the particular academic discipline to make appropriate recommendations. For this reason, the individual might want to request the academic program to provide to the evaluator information to help clarify. For example, does the program have lengthy reading assignments? Does the work involve calculations or analytical reasoning? What types of exams are usually given—multiple choice, essay, etc.? How long are the exams? Without such information, evaluators can make only the most general of recommendations. It may be necessary for the individual to ask the evaluator who made a diagnosis in the past to update and supplement that diagnosis with accommodation recommendations based on information about the academic program.

The appropriateness of accommodation requests in various settings has been a matter of concern in the area of professional licensing exams. It is currently common practice for state boards of law examiners to request information about accommodations given in the law school attended by an individual requesting accommodations. Typically, law school exams are 3 to 4 hours, spaced out over a couple of weeks at the end of the semester. A bar exam is usually all day for 2 to 3 consecutive days. Both law school exams and bar exams usually include both multiple-choice and essay components. It is for this reason that postsecondary service providers may become cynical about the all too common practice of some evaluators of simply recommending unlimited or double time, perhaps as a negotiating starting point. The problem with such a recommendation is that it adversely affects the credibility of the evaluator. While it may initially be more burdensome to obtain this more specific documentation, the ADA requires an interactive process in determining appropriate accommodations, and requesting specific additional information would certainly be deemed part of such a process.

Another question regarding documentation is the deference that the courts must give to the evaluators who write the recommendations for either party about the validity of an accommodation request. There is not yet a definitive answer, but the *Bartlett* case seems particularly well reasoned on this. In that case, the court noted that bar examiners are not experts on learning disabilities.

For that reason, it is not appropriate to give automatic deference to the determination by the bar examining authorities regarding the eligibility of an applicant for an accommodation on the basis of a learning disability. The court did, however, indicate that neither should a presumption one way or another be given to the treating physician's or another qualified professional's evaluation of a learning disability. There is an obvious potential for bias by the experts of either party, and, therefore, the court should consider such evaluations in that light as well as considering the direct knowledge of the person requesting the accommodation and the relevant experience and expertise of the evaluator. It should be noted as a general concept, however, that the historical "automatic" deference to educational institutions is no longer the rule (*Wynne v. Tufts University School of Medicine*, 1991).

Application and Standardized Test Scores

In the admissions process for undergraduate, graduate, and professional schools, certain practices regarding the applications of people with learning disabilities must be carefully considered. These include the requirement of standardized tests and other criteria used for admission, and the practice of flagging test scores. The model regulations under Section 504 of the Rehabilitation Act establish the framework for these issues. Of relevance are the prohibitions on using tests or other criteria that have a disproportionate, adverse effect on individuals with disabilities unless these criteria have been validated as a predictor of success in the education program or activity in question and alternatives with less disproportionate impact are not available (34 C.F.R. § 104.42[a][2]). Admissions tests must also be selected and administered in such a way as to ensure that the results reflect the aptitude, achievement level, or other skills purported to be measured, rather than reflecting impairments.

It should be noted that most entities that oversee and administer standardized test programs, such as the Educational Testing Service, are private providers that receive no federal financial assistance. As a consequence, these private enterprises are not directly affected by the Section 504 regulations. Because most of the users of their tests (i.e., colleges and universities) are recipients of federal financial assistance, these programs began developing appropriate reasonable accommodations for disabilities even before the 1990 Americans with Disabilities Act required them to do so.

At present, virtually all of the standardized testing services, as well as the professional licensing examiners, provide accommodations to individuals with disabilities. Nonetheless, disputes still arise as to whether these programs have impermissibly denied requested accommodations. Most of the disputes with college entrance test providers have been resolved informally and have not reached judicial resolution. The professional licensing examiners, however, have not always reached informal resolution, and in a number of cases denials of accommodations have been addressed by the courts (*Bartlett v. New York State Board of Law Examiners*, 1998; Rothstein, 1997; Simon, 1998).

Assuming that the standardized test required in the admission process provides accommodations for individuals with disabilities, it will generally be permissible to require applicants to have taken those tests. It seems quite clear, however, from litigation involving the National Collegiate Athletic Association (NCAA), that it is essential that higher education institutions take care in how standardized test scores are used in the admission process. Clearly, such scores should never be the sole criterion for admission. Nor should they be used as the sole criterion for minimum competency. A brief overview of the issues involving the NCAA is helpful. Over the last several years, the NCAA has been a subject of scrutiny because of its role in determining freshman-year eligibility for high school students wishing to participate in Division I or II college athletics. The association required that students register and apply for certification based upon these criteria: (a) graduation from high school; (b) successful completion (with at least a grade of D) of at least 13 core-curriculum academic courses; (c) a GPA of at least 2.00 (or higher, depending upon SAT or ACT scores); and (d) a combined score on the SAT verbal and math sections, or a total score on the ACT, that met a "qualifier index" (Hishinuma, 1999, p. 363). Eligibility for college athletic scholarships based on a mandated minimum SAT score established by the NCAA was questioned, and several students with learning disabilities filed complaints against the association, claiming that its criteria, particularly (b) and (d), discriminated against athletes with LD and constituted unfair roadblocks. A recent landmark consent-decree settlement was reached between the NCAA and the U.S. Department of Justice (*United States of America v. National Collegiate Athletic Association*, 1998; "NCAA Alters Policy," 1998) that addresses a number of points of particular relevance to student athletes with LD: (a) courses that are designed specifically for students with LD will be considered as "core" courses if the curriculum provides the same type of skill and knowledge as courses for students without disabilities; (b) students can initiate their own application for waiver; and (c) in the event that a college freshman with LD does not meet NCAA initial eligibility criteria, he or she can earn a fourth year of eligibility based upon academic success while participating in athletics. The implementation of these changes is subject to close scrutiny, and the NCAA is required to file an annual report to the Department of Justice on its efforts to comply with this consent decree, which is in effect until 2003.

Currently, it seems impermissible not to have an individualized assessment of qualification for college-level work when there is an indication that the standardized test scores do not accurately represent the applicant's ability because of a disability. This might be the case when there is a significant disparity between test scores and grades. Similar challenges to the validity of standardized test scores on the basis of race are also in the midst of controversy. What would seem to be the safest practice, and the one that makes the best sense for sound policy, would be to consider standardized test scores, but to take care that they are never used as the sole criterion or overweighed for academic admission.

A more difficult question involves the practice of flagging standardized test scores of individuals who have been given accommodations. The permissibility of this practice is currently the subject of discussion among federal policy makers and providers of standardized testing services. In the interim, the original policy of the Office for Civil Rights and the U.S. Department of Education, which allows flagging seems to be permissible. It states:

> The Office for Civil Rights will not find an institution out of compliance if that institution requires submission of test scores by applicants, even though there is a strong possibility that the tests do not reflect a handicapped applicant's ability. However, to ensure that it is in compliance, the institution must guarantee that the admissions decisions take into account other factors such as high school grades, recommendations, etc. This policy is, in fact, recommended by testing services. Until such time as more viable policy can be worked out, the testing services will be allowed to continue to notify their users that tests were taken under nonstandard conditions. *This is an interim policy only* [emphasis in original].

Further input from the Department of Justice may help to determine under what instances, if any, score recipients should be notified that a test was taken under nonstandard conditions. Psychometricians have argued that without the flagging, the score does not accurately reflect that the test was given under "nonstandard" conditions. Most testing services have eliminated the practice of flagging except where additional time has been provided, although even that remains a subject of debate. Some testing services have begun to engage in evaluation of accommodated tests to determine their validity and comparability, so that flagging can be eliminated without compromising sound psychometric practice.

The first lawsuit to directly address the issue of flagging was recently settled in federal district court in San Francisco, entitled *Breimhorst et al. v. Educational Testing Service* (Case No. c-99-3387 WHO). The plaintiffs were Mark Breimhorst, an individual with a physical disability; Californians for Disability Rights, a grassroots membership organization of people with disabilities in California; and the International Dyslexia Association. Disability Rights Advocates, a nonprofit law center in Oakland, California, represented all plaintiffs. The sole defendant in the case was Educational Testing Service (ETS). The complaint alleged that ETS's practice of flagging violated (a) the Americans with Disabilities Act of 1990; (b) the Rehabilitation Act of 1973; (c) California's Unruth Civil Rights Acts; and (d) California's Unfair Business Practices Act. ETS denied the allegations contained in the complaint and denied having violated any law.

In February, 2001, ETS announced in the *New York Times* that it "had made a significant step forward in resolving the controversial issue of 'flagging' (Lewin, 2001). Mark Breimhorst, an individual with no hands who took the Graduate Management Admissions Test (GMAT) with the accommodations of a trackball mouse and additional testing time, won the right to have the "non-standardized administration" notation dropped from his score report. As part of the ETS settlement, the testing agency agreed to stop flagging for the accommodation of extended time on the GMAT, the Graduate Record Examinations, the Test of English as a Foreign Language, and many other tests that it administers as of October 1, 2001. The parties are still in the process of resolving the issue for tests administered by ETS but owned by the College Board. A panel of experts will consider the extent to which accommodations of extended time affect comparability of scores between people with disabilities and those without. The findings of the experts are expected to be released in Spring, 2002.

Accommodations

The model regulations under Section 504 of the Rehabilitation Act contemplate a variety of accommodations and modifications that should be considered for students with disabilities in postsecondary education (34 C.F.R. § 104.44). Contemplated adjustments include academic adjustments (e.g., length of time for degree completion, course substitution, and adaptation of the manner in which specific courses are conducted), permission to use tape recorders in the classroom, exam modifications, and ensuring the availability of auxiliary aids (e.g., taped texts and similar services). The ADA regulations add note takers, transcription services, and written materials to the examples of auxiliary aids and services that might be provided (28 C.F.R. § 35.104). Programs are not required to provide individually prescribed devices or services for personal use by a student. These regulations do not require modifications that would change the fundamental or essential aspects of a program.

These regulations do not directly address cost and administrative burden issues, nor has judicial attention to this issue been entirely conclusory. Generally speaking, the judicial interpretation of Section 504 and the ADA establishes that programs are not required to provide accommodations or modifications that are unduly burdensome either financially or administratively, as part of the definition of what is considered to be "reasonable" (*Southeastern Community College v. Davis*, 1979; *United States v. Board of Trustees for University of Alabama*, 1990). Such a decision requires an individualized assessment of not only the person requesting the accommodation, but also the impact on the resources and staffing of the program providing the accommodations.

In the early years after the passage of the Rehabilitation Act, there was confusion about whether state vocational rehabilitation agencies had the primary or sole responsibility for paying for auxiliary aids. Currently, based on judicial and agency interpretation, it seems that while those agencies can be looked to as sources of funding, and the educational program can facilitate the provision of services to students from those agencies, the postsecondary institution remains ultimately responsible for such services (Rothstein, 1997).

Substantial judicial and regulatory agency attention has been devoted to the individualized assessment of when specific requested accommodations are to be provided. In addition to the issue of whether the student has a disability for which accommodations are to be considered (an issue addressed previously in this chapter) is the question of whether the requested accommodation is unduly burdensome and whether it fundamentally alters the program.

Undue Burden

The issue of undue burden can refer to both administration and finance. Administrative burdens might be raised in the case of a student who requests that a tape recording of each class be transcribed by the program's staff. The institution might well be able to demonstrate that the time to transcribe every class lecture and discussion in a timely manner would place an enormous burden on the institution. In addition, the cost burden is likely to be high in such a case. Given the array of accommodation possibilities, many of which are discussed in Chapter 9, and the advances in the area of technology, an institution would do well to engage in an interactive process to determine other methods of accommodations (e.g., the use of carbonized note-taking paper) that do not constitute either an undue administrative or an undue financial burden.

Undue administrative burdens are likely to arise also when a student fails to request an accommodation in a timely manner. The OCR opinions have been particularly unsympathetic to students who do not make their requests in a reasonable amount of time, particularly when the process for requesting accommodations is clearly communicated to students. Administrative burden could also be raised in cases involving requests to take exams with additional time. In order to schedule rooms, arrange for proctors, and ensure exam security, institutions need to determine definite time frames for exams. For this reason alone, it would probably be difficult to make a case for allowing a student to take an exam with unlimited time.

There is no magic formula for assessing undue financial burden. This determination depends on the resources of the institution, the cost of the specific accommodation, the number of requests for such an accommodation, and whether the accommodation would benefit more than one person. For example, while installing a ramp may be expensive, it would usually have significant benefit for a large number of people. A note taker for one student would benefit only that student, and so the resources of the program become more relevant. What is unresolved is how to assess the resources of the program. Is an institution to look to the departmental budget, the college budget, the entire institution's budget, or whose? Perhaps the reason this issue has not received more attention is because most institutions are reluctant to open up their discretionary budgets to review, which is likely to be required in litigation.

Study-abroad programs, off-campus programs, and noncredit courses can raise both administrative and financial burden issues. It may be difficult to find the personnel to provide certain services for programs offered abroad. Off-campus programs (e.g., internships) and noncredit courses can sometimes be an administrative burden because of the timing of the request for accommodations. This issue can often be resolved to some degree by ensuring that student handbooks, registration materials, and other communications make clear the mechanism for requesting accommodations. In the case of internships, there is often a need for interactive communication between the internship placement provider and the education program facilitating the internship. Questions as to whose obligation it is to pay for such accommodations between these parties have not really been addressed by the courts or OCR to any great extent. There has been some indication, however, that the institution has the initial burden of facilitating the accommodation.

With respect to noncredit courses, more notice may be needed to ensure accommodations because of the opportunity to sign up with little advance registration time. The other issue, of course, is whether the programmatic budget for the noncredit coursework is the only budget to consider for determining undue financial burden. The courts have not clearly addressed this issue. Although the ADA regulations seem to prohibit different deadlines for signing up for any coursework or examinations, the need to have reasonable time to identify personnel or make other arrangements for certain accommodations would seem to dictate the need to at least encourage students to give as much notice as possible of the need for accommodations.

Fundamental Alteration

The law seems clear that programs are not required to make fundamental alter-ations to their programs or to lower standards. The application of that premise to individual situations has been the subject of numerous judicial decisions and OCR opinions. The first issue that an institution must address in responding to a challenge in this situation centers on the determination of what constitutes an essential aspect of its program. It is clear that the burden is on the institution to address this, although substantial deference is generally given to higher education institutions on this issue (*Wynne v. Tufts University School of Medicine*, 1991).

This standard has been applied to the use of standardized test scores for admission; requirements related to academic standing for admission generally; the requirement to maintain a certain grade point average to remain enrolled; requests for course waivers or substitutions; reduced course loads; extensions of time for graduation; additional exam time; the use of calculators and other devices for exams; and a variety of other situations. It is impossible to give broad-brush guidance about how these cases are likely to be decided, but a few well-reasoned cases give some sense of the direction the courts will take.

The *Wynne* decision is one of the best sources of guidance. The case involved a request by a medical student with a learning disability to have a cer-tain test given in a different format. The court required the institution to show that "relevant officials" within the institution had considered alternative means, their feasibility, cost and effect on the program, and had come to a "rationally justifiable" conclusion that the alternatives would either lower aca-demic standards or require substantial program alteration. This deliberative process requires a determination of who the relevant officials are and the mech-anism by which they determine the essential requirements of a program. These relevant officials must then rationally assess whether the requested accommo-dation would fundamentally alter the program or be too financially or adminis-tratively burdensome.

Thus, an individual faculty member may not be the appropriate source to determine that a request for additional time on an exam should be denied. While that faculty member's opinion should perhaps be considered, it should not be dispositive in all situations. A denial of additional time would require the faculty member to demonstrate that speed is an essential component of what is being tested or that for some other legitimate reason additional time should not be provided.

The issue of course substitution received substantial judicial attention in the case of *Guckenberger v. Boston University* (1997). The court basically applied the burdens set out in *Wynne* and found that the relevant officials within the institution had made a rationally justifiable determination that waiving foreign language and math requirements was a fundamental alteration of the program ("BU Decision a Ringing Affirmation," 1998). Generally speaking, most institutions that have been challenged on course substitution and waiver issues have been successful in demonstrating that they were justified (*Bennett College [NC]*, 1995). Since the *Wynne* decision, some institutions have been successful in demonstrating that their course-load requirements were justified, as in *Zukle v. The Regents of the University of California* (1999). In that case, the 9th Circuit Court of Appeals upheld a medical school's refusal to permit a student to enroll in clinical rotations out of sequence. The *Zukle* case contrasts with another case that was recently decided—*Wong v. The Regents of the University of California* (1999)—which also involved a medical student seeking adjustments in clinical rotation scheduling. Andrew Wong was allowed to take 8 weeks off to read before his pediatric clerkship because the school had allowed him to take rotations out of order in the past, and he was able to demonstrate, based on his past history, that the additional preparation time was an effective accommodation. A court remanded the case for a determination in light of *Zukle* and *Wynne* and held that the University of California had an obligation to "submit a factual record indicating that it conscientiously carried out" its statutory obligation and had not provided such a record.

With respect to the use of standardized test scores and other criteria for admission, the results of judicial and OCR opinions have provided some general guidance. The OCR has reviewed a number of complaints by applicants that they were denied admission to an institution because of a learning disability. In most, if not all of these cases, the OCR investigation has led to a finding that the individuals' *overall* record indicated ability that was substantially lower than the requirements for admission. In many cases, the OCR found that the institution had admitted other applicants with learning disabilities, and that the complaining applicant had an overall academic record substantially below that of admitted applicants (*Gent v. Radford University*, 1997; *University of Minnesota*, 1995). These court and OCR rulings are based on the regulations of Section 504 that postsecondary institutions are not required to substantially alter their standards including academic requirements. Students who have not maintained the requisite grades to remain enrolled fall under the category of "not otherwise qualified."

The area where institutional standards have been called into question is in the use of a minimum standardized test score as a criterion for admission. This has been the focus of several challenges to NCAA requirements related to academic eligibility for athletic scholarships. Although it is legitimate to set admission standards that require an applicant to demonstrate ability to succeed in higher education, rigid adherence to a specific minimum standardized test score and absolute requirements about specific coursework may not always be the only way to demonstrate that ability (*Bowers v. NCAA*, 1997, 1998).

Institutions should take care in placing sole or undue weight on standardized test scores or any one factor for admission or scholarship eligibility. This is sound practice even without disability discrimination law, and it helps to avoid some of the challenges to criteria based on race.

Obligations After Performance Deficiencies

One area of activity for postsecondary institutions with respect to students with learning disabilities involves the obligation to the student who fails to meet the academic or other performance requirements and then requests readmission. In cases where the student had already been provided appropriate accommodations, that student will be unsuccessful in challenging the denial of readmission, generally speaking.

The situation is somewhat more complicated in cases where the student had not been receiving reasonable accommodations. Because the burden is initially on the student to make known the existence of the disability, with supporting documentation, in order to obtain reasonable accommodations, there must generally be compelling reasons for the student to be excused from that requirement. In some instances, the student may not have been evaluated and diagnosed. In others, the institution may not have policies and procedures that facilitate requesting accommodations. In either case, the burden will probably be on the student to demonstrate why accommodations were not requested in a timely manner. If that burden has been met, the denial of readmission might still be upheld if the institution can demonstrate that the student would not have succeeded even with the accommodations. Generally, good practice would probably be to allow the student to petition for readmission. The decision maker could then consider the diagnosis, the reason for not making known the disability, and the likelihood of success with accommodations, in determining whether to readmit. If that has been done, the courts and OCR will probably support the decision of the institution. The fact that the disability might affect academic performance will not require the institution to waive academic performance standards, such as minimum grade point average to graduate (*Betts v. Rector & Visitors of University of Virginia*, 1996; *DePaul University*, 1993; *Ellis v. Morehouse University School of Medicine*, 1996; *Kaltenberger v. Ohio College of Podiatric Medicine*, 1998; *Leacock v. Temple University School of Medicine*, 1998; *McGuinness v. University of New Mexico School of Medicine*, 1998; *Milani*, 1996; *Tips v. Regents of Texas Tech University*, 1996).

It also seems that in instances where a student has been readmitted after performance deficiencies and there are still reasonable questions about meeting the standards, the institution has the discretion to make readmission subject to conditions not applicable to students who are newly admitted (*Haight v. Hawaii Pacific University*, 1997).

Relationship of Institution to Professional Licensing Process

Because this book is predominantly focused on postsecondary education rather than professional licensing, the details of those cases involving accommodations on standardized tests such as teacher's exams, bar exams, and medical licensing exams are not discussed here. It should be noted, however, that at this point the licensing authorities in many jurisdictions seem to be more stringent in terms of documentation and accommodation granting than is the current practice in higher education. For that reason, graduate and professional higher education programs that prepare students for entry into a profession would do well to provide counseling to their students about the burdens they will need to meet in order to receive accommodations on professional licensing exams. These students should also be encouraged to begin as early as possible to ascertain whether they will be eligible for the accommodations they request. Negotiations on these issues can sometimes take months to resolve. Beginning early can avoid stressful debates at the last minute when the student wants to be focused on preparation for the exam instead of appealing to administrative bodies regarding the denial of accommodations.

Higher education programs should also maintain a thorough record on accommodations provided to students because many professional licensing exam authorities request information about previously used accommodations. The postsecondary administrator responding to these inquiries should take care to emphasize that the fact that accommodations requested for professional licensing were not provided in the education program should not be dispositive of the need for the accommodations. The administrator should clarify the types of examinations given in the educational program and distinguish those from exams given for professional licensing (Rothstein, 1997).

Developing Practical Guidelines
Based on Legal Precedents

Many postsecondary service providers are concerned about developing written policies or establishing guidelines concerning service provisions for students with learning disabilities. Chapter 8 provides a thorough examination of the development of policies. This process should involve careful planning and must be rooted in the legal principles discussed in this chapter in light of the IDEA, Section 504, and the ADA. As policy decisions are shaped on campus, new court cases can offer service providers additional guidance as to the parameters of the law.

The following are some suggestions for university administrators to ensure that their policies and practices conform with the letter and spirit of the ADA and Section 504:

General

- Conduct a self-evaluation and prioritization if one has not already been done. If it has, it is a good idea to periodically review the self-evaluation to see if the goals have been met and if new goals should be delineated.

- Involve students, faculty, and staff with disabilities in the self-evaluation and review processes.

- Share relevant self-evaluation information with the appropriate staff and with the faculty.

- Ascertain who in the institution has been designated to coordinate ADA compliance and who handles services for students with disabilities. Ensure that they are fully trained on ADA issues.

- Ensure that appropriate training occurs on a periodic basis. Change-over in staffing means that regular re-training should be done.

Students

- Faculty and staff should be provided with training on the requirements related to students regarding disability discrimination law.

- Faculty should be encouraged to indicate on their syllabi and orally how to go about obtaining reasonable accommodations.

- Admissions materials should indicate nondiscrimination policies and where to obtain information for applicants with disabilities.

- Application forms should not include impermissible questions about disabilities. University counsel should be consulted on this issue.

- Admissions professionals should be aware of disability discrimination legal requirements.

- Student services and academic and student affairs administrators should have policies in place regarding accommodations for coursework, exams, and auxiliary services. Communication via student handbooks, Web sites, etc., about these policies is essential.

- Policies to ensure appropriate confidentiality protection for students with disabilities should be in place and should be made known to appropriate staff and faculty and to students affected by these policies.

- A process should be in place to encourage students to self-identify as early as possible when accommodations are required.

- A record of accommodations should be kept in the student's file to demonstrate compliance.

Programmatic

- Relevant publications (such as admissions materials, student handbooks, etc.) should provide information about how to receive reasonable accommodations and about grievance procedures.

- A grievance procedure to resolve disputes about accommodations and discrimination should be in place and should be made known to affected parties in appropriate publications and other communications.

Conclusion

It has taken over 2 decades to bring legislative intent more in line with practice for individuals with disabilities in higher education. The laws and court cases discussed in this chapter should give service providers the background they need to make informed judgments about admissions, service delivery, and accommodation standards for students with learning disabilities. By carefully balancing the institutional mission with the rights of these students, along with the rights of faculty members, guidelines can be established that will foster academic freedom in a climate of nondiscrimination. Given the controversies surrounding these issues, it is likely that there will be substantially more litigation before these issues are clearly resolved.

CHAPTER

ISSUES IN DEFINING THE POPULATION

The problem of defining the term *learning disabilities* has challenged the field since Sam Kirk's first attempt in 1962. The fact that the definitional controversy has not been resolved is evidenced by topical issues of journals such as *Learning Disability Quarterly* (Swanson, 1991a) and *Journal of Learning Disabilities* (Rosenberg, 1997), which were devoted to articles on definitions of learning disabilities. Although most definitions have been developed primarily for children in public schools, some have sufficient breadth to make them relevant to adults (Mellard, 1990; Smith, Dowdy, Polloway, & Blalock, 1997). It would, therefore, be counterproductive to attempt to develop a new definition at the postsecondary level. Institutions of higher education must establish criteria for eligibility under provincial laws or Section 504 and the Americans with Disabilities Act based on an operational definition of learning disabilities.

This chapter will address the following definitional issues regarding the adult postsecondary population:

- identifying appropriate definitions of learning disabilities;

- establishing an operational model for determining the presence of a learning disability;

- differentiating learning disabilities from other disabling conditions or other learning difficulties; and

- deciding when and whether to label students with learning disabilities.

Challenges in Defining Learning Disabilities

Institutions of higher education must recognize the population of students who are guaranteed protection under Section 504 of the Rehabilitation Act and the ADA. Although these laws do not define learning disabilities, they do specify that if an individual has a physical or mental impairment that substantially limits one or more major life functions or has a history of such an impairment or is regarded as having such an impairment and meets the academic and technical standards required for admission or participation in a college's programs or activities, then that student must be ensured equal educational opportunity.

Students with apparent sensory disabilities or physical limitations are relatively easy to identify. It is more difficult to make a determination of eligibility for students with hidden disabilities such as a learning disability. In communicating with prospective and current students, as well as with faculty and staff, it is necessary to specify the process by which eligibility for protection is determined. As indicated in Chapter 3, institutions are in compliance when they request documentation of a specific learning disability. Despite its lack of specificity, the concept of specific learning disabilities enjoys considerable support among professionals in the field. Tucker, Stevens, and Ysseldyke (1983), in a survey of 199 professionals, reported that 83% considered the category viable and 88% believed that students with learning disabilities were clinically identifiable by specific symptoms or a constellation of symptoms that distinguished them from students with other problems in learning. More recently, Swanson and Christie (1994) demonstrated that children and adults, experts and novices, all had an implicit notion of what constitutes a learning disability. Nonetheless, this support and understanding has traditionally given way to dissension when it comes to operationally defining the disability. In addition, clearly defining the population is essential when attempting to garner administrative support (political and fiscal) and differentiate "protected" students from students who are not guaranteed equal access under the law.

Hammill (1990) conducted a comprehensive discussion and review of 11 major definitions of learning disability. The conceptual elements identified in those definitions include:

1. *Existence throughout the life span:* This is a critical element for those working with adults. Many early definitions focused on children, since manifestations of a learning disability were typically seen in school. It was then hoped that the learning disability would be remediated or "cured," or would disappear by adulthood. Instead, we see a growing number of adults with LD seeking support services or accommodations in postsecondary education (Blackorby

& Wagner, 1996; Henderson, 1999), adult education (Newman, 1994), and employment and vocational rehabilitation (Smith et al., 1997).

2. *Intraindividual differences:* This phrase is used to describe differences in performance within an individual (i.e., an individual might be above average in math, below average in writing) rather than an aptitude-achievement discrepancy. The latter descriptor may be problematic in identifying college students, since they may have learned to successfully compensate for learning difficulties, thus diminishing any discrepancy. In addition, many diagnostic instruments are not scaled beyond high school or normed on adults, making the determination of an aptitude-achievement discrepancy problematic with adults.

3. *Central nervous system dysfunction:* Some definitions cited by Hammill (1990) indicate that a problem in the central nervous system (CNS) is the cause of learning disabilities. Although this may be the case in many with severe learning disabilities, it has not yet been proved across the entire spectrum of individuals with learning disabilities (Hynd, Marshall, & Gonzalez, 1991).

4. *Problems with learning processes:* Some definitions suggest that disruptions in the processes of memory, attention, or cognition make proficient performance in some skill or ability areas difficult for students with learning disabilities. This is a critical component for definitions regarding adults, since poor teaching, diminished motivation, or educational disadvantage can also cause learning problems.

5. *Specification of academic, language, or conceptual problems as potential learning disabilities:* Most definitions specify that academic problems (e.g., problems in reading, writing, spelling, or math), language problems (e.g., problems listening, speaking, or writing), or conceptual problems (e.g., problems thinking or reasoning) can be manifestations of learning disabilities.

6. *Other conditions as potential learning disabilities:* Some definitions have identified difficulties with social skills, spatial orientation, or integration of motor abilities as learning disabilities. Controversy has persisted over the years regarding the relevance of defining these problems as learning disabilities (Myers & Hammill, 1990).

7. *Coexisting or excluded disabilities:* Some definitions distinguish between primary and secondary disabilities (e.g., a learning disability may be the primary disability while a psychological disorder could be a secondary disability). Many adults with learning disabilities do have coexisting disabilities. Psychological problems may manifest themselves as social misperceptions or in ongoing frustration in individuals with learning impairments, health problems, or psychiatric disorders (Rosenberg, 1997).

Keeping these seven points in mind will help professionals as they attempt to determine an appropriate definition of learning disabilities.

The definition of learning disabilities used in public schools was promulgated under the Education for All Handicapped Children Act (now the Individuals with Disabilities Education Act):

> The term "specific learning disability" means a disorder in one or more of the basic psychological processes involved in understanding or in using language, spoken or written, which may manifest itself in an imperfect ability to listen, speak, read, write, spell, or to do mathematical calculations. The term includes such conditions as perceptual handicaps, brain injury, minimal brain dysfunction, dyslexia, and developmental aphasia. The term does not include children who have learning disabilities which are primarily the result of visual, hearing, or motor handicaps, or mental retardation, or emotional disturbance, or environmental, cultural, or economic disadvantage. (U.S. Department of Education, 1977, p. 65083)

Documentation of a learning disability provided by a public school will typically be based on some form of this definition. Although the definition does imply that learning disabilities occur at all ages, its use of the term *children* makes it inappropriate for use with adults. Other concerns include the use of the ambiguous term *psychological processes*, inclusion of "an imperfect ability to" spell as possible evidence of a learning disability, and use of obsolete terms such as *perceptual handicap* (Myers & Hammill, 1990).

The major problem with the public school definition of learning disabilities is the use of the *aptitude-achievement discrepancy*. Problems with discrepancy formulas have included confusion as to the nature and/or reality of the condition of LD. This is because the symptom is confused with the problem; that is, low achievement relative to overall ability (the supposed outcome of a learning disability) is confused with a specific cognitive deficit (the supposed cause of the achievement delay) (Mather & Roberts, 1994). Meltzer (1994) contends that "product-oriented measures, including aptitude (IQ) and standardized achievement tests, have been the cornerstone for the diagnosis of learning disabilities" (p. 580). She aptly points out that "these measures emphasize the end product of learning while largely ignoring the processes and strategies that students use to approach various learning and problem-solving situations" (p. 581). This is particularly problematic for college-bound students with LD who may have severe processing problems but do not demonstrate a discrepancy because they have learned to compensate for their disability. This relates to the issue of "functional limitations" dealt with in the Price case discussed in Chapter 7.

Concerns about discrepancy formulas have also been expressed by clinicians, who argue that they leave little room for professional judgment.

Although the association between LD and aptitude-achievement discrepancies seems logical, problems emerge in the operationalization of this association (Fletcher et al., 1998). One major drawback is that, in some cases, a learning disability adversely affects performance on both the aptitude and the achievement measures used to diagnose it, resulting in a profile that does not meet discrepancy criteria but nonetheless is LD (Mather & Healey, 1990; Swanson, 1993). Diagnostic inferences are further complicated by (a) the frequency with which severe discrepancies occur in the nondisabled population (Brackett & McPherson, 1996), and (b) the significant overlap that exists between commonly used measures of intelligence and achievement, thus calling into question the assumption that they measure discrete skills (Kaufman, 1994). In summary, research conducted by the National Institute of Child Health and Human Development indicates that the aptitude-achievement discrepancy is *not* a clear diagnostic marker for learning disabilities ("Whole Language," 1996).

The National Joint Committee on Learning Disabilities (NJCLD), composed of nine organizations with a major interest in learning disabilities, including the Association on Higher Education and Disability (AHEAD), American Speech-Language-Hearing Association, Council for Learning Disabilities, and National Association of School Psychologists, developed its own definition:

> Learning disabilities is a general term that refers to a heterogeneous group of disorders manifested by significant difficulties in the acquisition and use of listening, speaking, reading, writing, reasoning, or mathematical abilities. These disorders are intrinsic to the individual, presumed to be due to central nervous system dysfunction, and may occur across the life span. Problems in self-regulatory behaviors, social perception, and social interaction may exist with learning disabilities but do not by themselves constitute a learning disability. Although learning disabilities may occur concomitantly with other handicapping conditions (for example, sensory impairment, mental retardation, serious emotional disturbance) or with extrinsic influences (such as cultural differences, insufficient or inappropriate instruction), they are not the result of those conditions or influences. (NJCLD, 1994a, pp. 65–66)

The NJCLD definition addresses many of the conceptual issues cited in Hammill's review (1990) in a way that is appropriate for adults. It is important to reiterate that use of the aptitude-performance discrepancy model is not advisable because:

1. Diagnostic instruments are often not normed or scaled adequately for adults, neither do they include items to assess skills approaching college level.

2. Adults may have had years of training to help them gain proficiency or compensatory strategies in problematic skill areas.

3. At the postsecondary level, learning disabilities often manifest themselves in ways other than deficiencies in basic skill levels.

4. Some non-learning-disabled college students have superior aptitude scores that could result in a discrepancy when skill levels are determined by norm-referenced tests.

Shaw, Cullen, McGuire, and Brinckerhoff (1995, p. 591) note that the NJCLD definition would seem to be the definition of choice at the postsecondary level because:

- it is the most descriptive definition of learning disabilities;

- it is in line with the concept of intraindividual differences across areas;

- it specifies that learning disabilities exist throughout the life span;

- it deals with learning disabilities as the primary condition, while acknowledging possible concomitant disabling conditions;

- it does not rule out the possibility that learning disabilities can occur in people who are gifted and talented; and

- it has support from a broad range of professional constituencies.

In the conclusion of his review, Hammill (1990, p. 82) notes that the NJCLD definition "is probably the best descriptive statement about the nature of learning disabilities." Based on an extensive review of the research, Doris (1993) agrees that the NJCLD has the essential elements described in the literature for a definition of LD.

Subsequent to the first NJCLD initiative to address the issue of definition in 1981, the Interagency Committee on Learning Disabilities (ICLD), which included personnel from a range of federal agencies, put forth a definition that was intended to be similar to but an improvement on the NJCLD definition. Social skills are identified as a specific manifestation of learning disabilities in the ICLD definition (Interagency Committee on Learning Disabilities, 1987). Although there is no doubt that the recognition of concomitant social-skills deficits is important (Greenspan, Apthorp, & Williams, 1991), including social skills in the definition would cause considerable overlap with the category of individuals with psychological disorders. For that reason, the ICLD definition should be considered with extreme caution. The revised NJCLD definition, on the other hand, reflects current research that indicates that although individuals with LD may demonstrate problems with self-regulation and social interaction, those characteristics do not constitute a learning disability in and of themselves. The New Jersey Special Needs Regional Centers for Learning Disabilities (1998) use the NJCLD definition with college students. They use a clinical model developed at the University of Georgia that "weighs the impact of gender, severity of disability, ethnicity, age, motivation, experience, correlation between intelligence measures or achievement and the reliability, as well as the validity of psychometric instruments" (p. 2).

Each postsecondary institution needs to first adopt a definition of learning disabilities, and the NJCLD definition is clearly the one to choose. Professionals at each institution of higher education must then determine how to identify "significant disabilities" that are "intrinsic to the individual" so that they can obtain an operational definition to assist them in determining which students are entitled to equal access in postsecondary settings. The following section will attempt to provide some guidance.

An Operational Definition of Learning Disabilities

As noted by Shaw et al. (1995), the LD field is struggling to cope with a definitional crisis in which there is considerable disagreement over essential criteria and appropriate diagnostic practices. Nowhere is this more apparent than at the postsecondary level, where an adequate operational definition for LD is especially critical, because practitioners must establish eligibility for services under Section 504 and the ADA, not the IDEA. Because these two pieces of legislation contain no conceptual or regulatory definition of LD, many postsecondary practitioners are confused as to the appropriate criteria to apply in the case of a student who is referred for and suspected of having LD but was not diagnosed in childhood. Since most postsecondary personnel do not have training or expertise in LD classification and diagnosis, it is particularly important for them to have a clear and functional operational definition. In addition, although some recently developed assessment tools are appropriate for adults, many of the psychometric tests commonly used to diagnose LD are not normed for adults and often do not include items that are appropriate for assessing college-level skills (see Chapter 6).

Therefore, a viable operational definition must first and foremost describe criteria that apply across the age range. It must also address the logical association between achievement and aptitude in a way that allows for early identification and is not subject to error because of limitations of the examiner or the instrumentation. In addition, an improved operational definition must encompass a broader perspective of LD by defining achievement as more than just academics and providing criteria that address the information-processing dimension and the various exclusionary factors mentioned in most conceptual definitions. Furthermore, it must provide for the exercise of informed clinical judgment throughout the eligibility process. Other features of a viable operational definition include the following: (a) it must result in what Kavale, Forness, and Lorsbach (1991) describe as an ordered, sequenced decision-making process; (b) it must produce what Semmel (1986) refers to as improved educational outcomes; and (c) it must give attention to such dimensions as problem severity, pervasiveness, and chronicity (Adelman, 1989).

Figure 4.1 presents an operational interpretation of learning disabilities based on the NJCLD definition. This model, proposed by Shaw et al. (1995), incorporates four levels of investigation to determine if an individual has a learning disability. We strongly advocate the use of the four-step process but acknowledge the need for review, debate, and possible modification of the descriptors used *within* each level of the process. The model begins with the most critical issue: identifying intraindividual discrepancies.

Level I

Level I (intraindividual discrepancy) involves two steps: identifying a significant difficulty in any of the specified skill areas listed and identifying successful performance in several other skill areas. Information gleaned at Level I may be used to identify a learning problem and to eliminate students with mental retardation or who are slow learners. Yet Level I alone is not sufficient to determine the presence of a learning disability.

A change has occurred in the original model proposed by Brinckerhoff et al., 1993. A subject matter area has been removed from Levels I and II based on the following Tomlan and Mather (1996) critique:

> We question whether difficulties in a subject area should be used in determining intraindividual discrepancies. Would a weakness in geography or chemistry have the same viability as a weakness in listening or writing? Surely the specificity of the acquired knowledge in the various content domains is different from the more global skills encompassed in the other

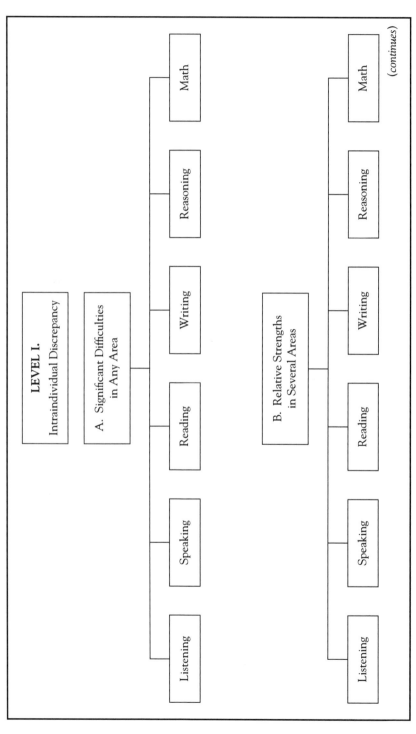

Figure 4.1. An operational definition of learning disabilities in higher education. *Note.* Adapted from "Operationalizing a Definition of Learning Disabilities," by S. Shaw, J. Cullen, J. McGuire, and L. Brinckerhoff, 1995, *Journal of Learning Disabilities, 28,* p. 592. Copyright 1995 by PRO-ED. Adapted with permission.

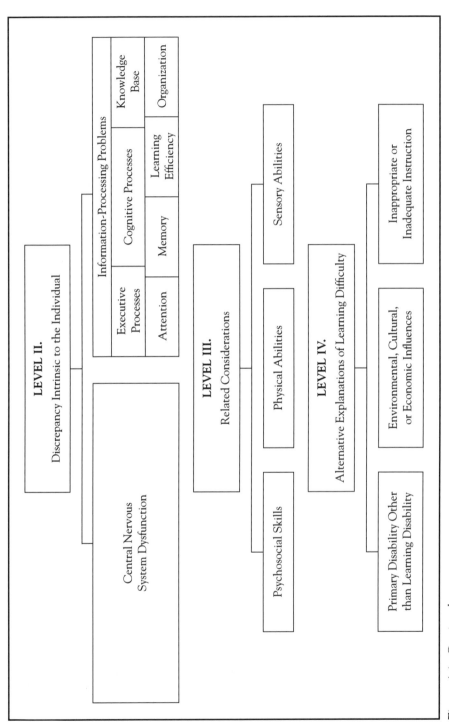

Figure 4.1. *Continued.*

areas presented. Furthermore, weaknesses in content area domains may be more indicative of limited exposure and educational opportunities than of learning disabilities per se. (p. 222)

Level II

Level II (discrepancy intrinsic to the individual) requires verification that the learning difficulty is intrinsic to the individual. This could involve a determination of CNS dysfunction or specification of deficits in information processing (Kolligian & Sternberg, 1987; Swanson, 1987) that are related to the skill deficits identified in Level I.

At this time, it is difficult to identify specific areas of CNS dysfunction in most individuals with learning disabilities. Only those with the most severe problems or with apparent organic impairment will be identified in this way. On the other hand, students with learning disabilities are seen as having deficient information-processing mechanisms. In addition, identifying CNS dysfunction typically requires a medical orientation, while identifying information-processing problems in memory, organization, or learning efficiency is within the province of educators. Therefore, an information-processing perspective can help us "understand students' learning processes and the factors that affect learning processes" (Ariel, 1992, p. 196). Information processing is conceptualized as an individual's acquisition, storage, and utilization of information (Swanson & Watson, 1982).

The three major components (Mercer, 1991; Rock, Fessler, & Church, 1997; Swanson, 1987) of information processing are described in a very basic fashion as:

1. *executive processes*—higher-order processes used to plan, monitor, and evaluate learning and performance;

2. *cognitive processes*—strategies or processes that enable students to learn and solve problems (e.g., verbal rehearsal, classification memory, summarization, and integration); and

3. *knowledge base*—available information in long-term memory applied to help learn new information (e.g., select, integrate, or compare information).

Information-processing theory suggests that learning problems are caused by individuals' inability to organize their thinking skills and systematically approach learning tasks (Swanson, 1987). In other words, these students need to learn how to learn. Deshler, Ellis, and Lenz (1996) have demonstrated that students who have a learning disability can profit from instruction that teaches them how to learn. Individuals with learning disabilities have exhibited difficulties in short- and long-term memory (Swanson & Cooney, 1991), attention to task (Hallahan & Reeve, 1980), strategic production (Torgeson, 1994), strategic learning (Swanson, 1987), and development of automaticity of skills and strategies (Kolligian & Sternberg, 1987). Students with learning disabilities also experience difficulties in executive control or self-regulation, resulting in poor selection, monitoring, evaluation, and modification of strategies (Wong, 1991).

Level II allows for any one or more of a broad spectrum of factors that may explain or account for the deficits identified in Level I. The model does not focus exclusively on any single element, such as CNS dysfunction, however, as a required condition of a learning disability. Assessment data must provide an *intrinsic* explanation for the learning difficulty. Chapter 6 will discuss the issues and instruments for this kind of assessment. The interaction between Levels I and II yields the most critical data for identifying a learning disability because it demonstrates that the learning difficulties are, in fact, a result of an information-processing problem within the individual. The final critical piece of information is in Level IV—determining whether there is an alternative explanation for the intrinsic learning difficulties identified in Levels I and II that can be attributed to non-LD (extrinsic) factors.

Level III

Level III (related considerations) involves the identification of concomitant limitations in areas such as psychosocial skills and physical or sensory abilities. These are not elements of a learning disability but may be viewed as related to a learning disability. Although a student can be identified without any related deficits, this level has two important purposes:

1. It provides for the specification of additional problems that may need to be addressed for program planning purposes.

2. It may identify deficits that relate to the determination of alternative explanations for learning difficulties identified in Level IV.

For example, the area of psychosocial deficits is often a problem for college students with learning disabilities. Deficiencies may stem from lack of social skills, learned helplessness, or negative self-concept (Price, 1993). If psychosocial problems have become predominant, however, classification in another category of disability (psychological disorder) may be more appropriate.

Level IV

Level IV (alternative explanations of learning difficulty) addresses exclusions or alternative explanations for a learning difficulty. Application of this level provides an opportunity to specify a primary disability other than a learning disability or to identify an alternative explanation of the deficits identified in Level I. For example, a student who is not motivated to learn (i.e., who does not complete homework or attend class) may have learning difficulties that are not related to a learning disability. A more complex example is that of a student who is under the influence of drugs. That student's intraindividual discrepancy may not be intrinsic if it occurs only while he or she is under the influence of drugs, or it may be intrinsic if permanent damage has resulted from drug abuse. In either case, the diagnostic process may result in the determination of a primary disability of "other health impaired" or "psychological disorder." These determinations will require professional judgment based on this model so that non-LD factors can be ruled out.

Postsecondary administrators, service-delivery personnel, and related services personnel required to render eligibility or classification decisions can apply this model to review available data or implement diagnostic procedures in order to make consistent, valid, and defensible decisions about which students have learning disabilities, which do not qualify for services, and why. This model is presented to stimulate discussion (Coutinho, 1996; Smith et al., 1997; Tomlan & Mather, 1996) and alternative approaches to providing operational definitions of learning disabilities at the same time that it gives practitioners a basis for action.

Figure 4.2 is provided to illustrate the heterogeneity that is characteristic of students in postsecondary settings. In addition to depicting the range of strengths and weaknesses indicated by the term *learning disabilities*, the figure exemplifies the divergent ability levels that may characterize students in various postsecondary settings. The profile depicting a student with a learning disability at an open-enrollment community college indicates average skills in math and reasoning, below-average skills in listening and reading, and significant deficits in writing and speaking. The profile of a student with a learning disability at a 4-year college demonstrates below-average scores in math that are significantly discrepant from the student's average and above-average scores

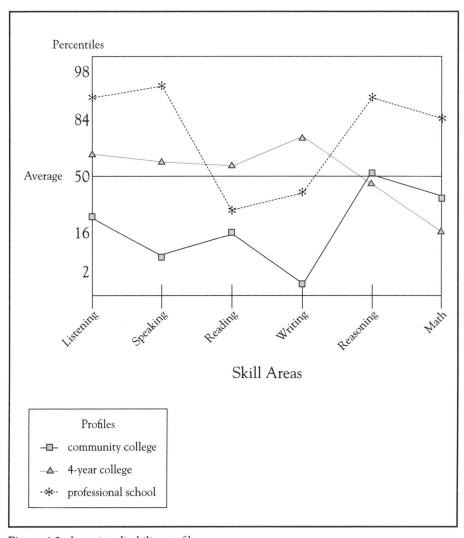

Figure 4.2. Learning disability profiles.

in all other skill areas. The profile of a student with a learning disability at a professional school indicates reading and writing scores in the average range that are significantly discrepant from all other scores, which are above average or well above average. In spite of the variability in the range and level of abilities in these three profiles, they all demonstrate the intraindividual discrepancy necessary for Level I consideration as a student with a learning disability.

Differentiating Learning Disabilities from Other Conditions

Learning Disability or Other Disability?

Given the heterogeneous nature of learning disabilities, the problem with definition, and the difficulty of determining eligibility, labeling has been a concern for a long time (Dunn, 1968; G. O. Johnson, 1962). Over several decades, public schools have seen a dramatic increase in the percentage of students identified as having learning disabilities and a concomitant decrease in the percentage of students identified as having many other disabling conditions (U.S. Department of Education, 1990). Of particular note is the "disappearance" of many students with mild mental retardation during the time of the sharpest growth in the LD population (MacMillan, Gresham, & Bocian, 1998). In a similar vein, huge discrepancies have occurred from district to district and state to state in the ratio of students with learning disabilities compared to those with emotional disturbances (U.S. Department of Education, 1990).

Postsecondary institutions need to be particularly careful about classification because of the differences between the IDEA and Section 504/ADA. The former provides a free, appropriate education for all students with disabilities, while the latter requires access only for "otherwise qualified" students with disabilities. It is also important to note that regulations regarding the IDEA define a learning disability, while regulations for Section 504/ADA do not. Recent research has demonstrated that public schools fail to follow the IDEA requirements in more than half the cases, often inappropriately identifying students with mental retardation under the category of learning disability (MacMillan et al., 1998). Therefore, it is even more imperative that postsecondary institutions specify their operational definition.

Mental Retardation or Learning Disability?

Many laypeople, including some college faculty, perceive anyone with a learning disability as having mental retardation. In order to maintain the integrity of support services and justify the presence of students with learning disabilities in postsecondary education, particularly competitive settings, differentiation from students with limited intellectual ability is critical. In Figure 4.1, Levels I and IV provide the information necessary to differentiate students with learning disabilities from those with mental retardation. At Level I, college students with learning disabilities typically demonstrate several areas of significant difficulty and many areas of relative strength. Students with mental retardation often demonstrate many areas of significantly below-average performance without particular strengths. As indicated in Figure 4.3, students with learning disabilities demonstrate an uneven profile with significant peaks and valleys, while students with mental retardation typically demonstrate a rather flat profile with weaknesses that extend across skill areas.

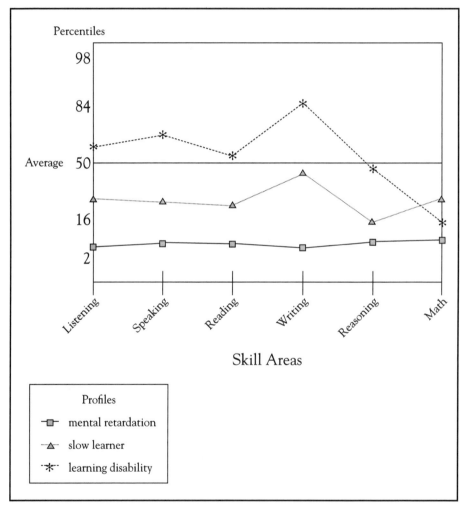

Figure 4.3. Profile of intraindividual differences for students with special needs. *Note.* From "Operationalizing a Definition of Learning Disabilities," by S. Shaw, J. Cullen, J. McGuire, and L. Brinckerhoff, 1995, *Journal of Learning Disabilities, 28,* p. 593. Copyright 1995 by PRO-ED. Reprinted with permission.

According to the model, Level I would not yield evidence of intraindividual differences for a student with mental retardation. Level IV stipulates exclusions including the student's having a primary disability other than a learning disability. The diagnostic data alone or classification indicated by diagnosticians could exclude a student from identification as one with a learning disability because of significantly below-average performance across most indicators.

Psychological Disorder or Learning Disability?

Students with psychological disabilities are seeking access to postsecondary institutions in ever greater numbers (Unger, 1991). Differentiating students with learning disabilities from students with psychological disorders at the postsecondary level creates the same difficulties that public school personnel have dealt with for many years. This is not to suggest that the problem is just a bureaucratic issue of labeling. It can often be critical for the student, faculty, and staff to understand the primary disability in order to determine appropriate services and accommodations.

If we use the operational interpretation in Figure 4.1 on students with psychological disorders, Level I might not differentiate a learning disability from a psychological disorder, since both have a similarly uneven profile. However, Level II might differentiate the two diagnostic categories, because it is likely that none of the intrinsic impediments to learning would be apparent in students with psychological disorders. Level III provides an opportunity to consider other problem areas. Indications of significant psychosocial deficits will usually become evident as major conditions, leading to Level IV and an alternative explanation for learning difficulties.

Learning Disability or Learning Difficulty?

There is little doubt that many postsecondary institutions, particularly those with open-enrollment policies, are experiencing increasing numbers of students at risk for encountering learning problems. Some of these students have learning disabilities, but the majority are slow learners because of less than average ability or limited educational opportunities. Others may have presumed or documented CNS dysfunction. Some students with *presumed* CNS dysfunction are now described as having an attention-deficit disorder (ADD) or attention-deficit/hyperactivity disorder (ADHD). Those with *documented* CNS dysfunction may have an impairment called traumatic brain injury (TBI) or acquired brain injury, which may result from an external event (accident or fall) or an internal event (tumor or disease). Table 4.1 provides a framework, using the four levels of operational interpretation, for determining whether students with these learning problems are also qualified students with learning disabilities.

Slow Learners

Slow learners (i.e., students with less than average ability) may appear to have learning disabilities, but upon careful analysis they can be distinguished rela-

Table 4.1
Differentiating Learning Disabilities from Other Learning Difficulties

Learning Disability	Slow Learner	Attention-Deficit Disorder	Traumatic Brain Injury (TBI)
Level I Intraindividual Discrepancy	Few intraindividual differences; flat profile.	May have typical LD profile.	Likely to have pronounced LD profile of strengths and weaknesses.
Level II Intrinsic	No indication of specific learning problems other than limited ability.	Will typically have attention, perceptual, and/or learning dysfunctions.	Obvious central nervous system dysfunction and possibly other significant problems.
Level III Related Considerations	Usually no specific related conditions.	Psychosocial deficits are likely.	Many related conditions including physical and emotional concerns.
Level IV Alternative Explanations	May be excluded because of environmental, cultural, economic, or educational disadvantage. Slow learner is *not* a disability under the law.	Primary disability may be "ADHD," "other health impaired," or "seriously emotionally disturbed" (psychological disorder).	Primary disability could be TBI or "other health impaired" depending on the severity of the conditions identified in Level III.

tively easily. Table 4.1 indicates that both Level I and Level II demonstrate clear differentiations. Slow learners typically have a flatter profile, indicating primarily below-average performance in most areas, unlike the significant peaks and valleys of students with learning disabilities (see Figure 4.2). Nor do they exhibit specific learning deficits other than limited intellectual aptitude to explain their performance. As indicated in Figure 4.3, slow learners can be differentiated from individuals with mental retardation because their ability level is not as low and they tend to demonstrate more variability than is seen in the extremely flat profile of individuals with mental retardation. Slow learners are not a protected class under disability law.

Attention-Deficit Disorder

Students with ADD have been identified under a variety of names. These students were first discussed more than a half century ago (Strauss & Lehtinen, 1947). Diagnostic labels used to identify this group have included Strauss syndrome, brain damage, minimal brain dysfunction, and hyperactivity. The condition was last described in *DSM–IV* as attention-deficit/hyperactivity disorder (American Psychiatric Association, 1994). Children with ADHD are typically impulsive, hyperactive, and inattentive (Reeve, 1990). Adults with ADHD are more likely to demonstrate disorganization, restlessness, problems with authority, frustration, poor self-esteem, and relationship problems (Nadeau, 1995b). Table 4.1 indicates that many students with ADHD will fulfill Levels I, II, and III of the operational definition of learning disabilities. As noted in a policy decision from the Office of Special Education and Rehabilitative Services, they may have a primary disability other than a learning disability (Davila, 1991), thus meeting the criteria for "other health impaired" or "seriously emotionally disturbed" as their primary disability, which would make them eligible for the IDEA services under those categories. In postsecondary settings, they may be eligible as individuals with a disability under any of those classifications if they meet the other criteria (e.g., otherwise qualified; substantial limitation to a major life function). An extensive discussion of ADHD and postsecondary disability services is provided in Chapter 10.

Traumatic Brain Injury

Students with TBI have had a severe injury involving parts of the brain, which often creates physical, mental, and emotional difficulties (Bigler, 1990). As indicated in Table 4.1, they may also fit the operational definition of learning disabilities with one notable exception. At Level I students with TBI will most often demonstrate severe deficits that are likely to result from areas of injury, and strengths in areas that were not affected. Application of Levels II and III will yield evidence of significant CNS dysfunction that may affect many learning processes and cause related problems in a variety of areas. However, students with TBI may be distinguished from students with conventional learning disabilities in Level IV, where they may exhibit any of a variety of other disabilities depending on the nature of their injuries. Other primary disabilities could include sensory impairments or chronic health problems. These students will be eligible for accommodations under any of these definitions if they meet the other criteria of the law(s).

Should We Label?

After defining learning disabilities, providing an operational interpretation of that definition, and distinguishing learning disabilities from other conditions, it is logical to ask if and when it is appropriate or necessary to label students. The issue of labeling is not new (Dunn, 1968; G. O. Johnson, 1962). Some professionals focus on the benefits to a protected class whose members receive special programs and services (Kauffman, 1989). Others have documented the stigma, isolation, and lack of utility associated with the use of categorical labels (Reynolds, 1984; Ysseldyke, 1987). In a special education planning effort in Connecticut, it was determined that categories of disability need to be maintained to protect students but that labels were not productive in determining service delivery or types of accommodations (Campbell & Shaw, 1992).

At the postsecondary level it is necessary to determine which students have learning disabilities, whether or not that information is important for service delivery. Every institution must know who is protected under the law, but given the many at-risk students in addition to those with disabilities, institutions may meet the needs of all students and provide equal access without categorical programs that separate students with disabilities from other students. This may be possible at open-enrollment, 2-year colleges where significant numbers of students will be in need of generic accommodations and support from generic learning centers. Programs that serve only students with documented disabilities, on the other hand, will need to focus on eligibility requirements. One of the key outcomes of the Boston University decision is that we must be able to substantiate our determination of who is eligible for protections under Section 504/ADA on the basis of a learning disability (Shaw & McGuire, 1996).

Conclusion

Coutinho (1996), Smith et al. (1997), and Tomlan and Mather (1996) have noted that the model in Figure 4.1 provides the basis for a more specific and effective method of identifying students with learning disabilities. The NJCLD definition and its operational interpretation should provide personnel at institutions of higher education with the tools to determine which students have learning disabilities. Personnel at postsecondary institutions should develop policies and procedures to formally implement this four-level process:

Level I: Determining whether there is an intraindividual discrepancy.

Level II: Identifying elements indicating whether the discrepancy is intrinsic to the individual.

Level III: Specifying related considerations.

Level IV: Determining possible alternative explanations of the learning difficulties.

Subsequent chapters provide detailed information on the diagnostic data used to make that decision and the process required for documentation.

THE CONNECTIONS AMONG PSYCHOSOCIAL ISSUES, ADULT DEVELOPMENT, AND SELF-DETERMINATION

Lynda Price

Exploring the ramifications of learning disabilities in adults often depends a great deal on one's own personal perspective. You may feel like a traveler with a brand-new passport ready to explore a new country. As with a journey to a new country, the more you think you know about this area, the more you realize that you still have much to learn. Perhaps part of the paradox is that learning disabilities are as unique as the individuals who have them. For instance, listen to how three people describe their personal perspectives on their disabilities:

> PAUL—Twenty years ago this country was fighting a war in Viet Nam. During this same time, I was just in the beginning stages of my own personal war. The battleground was the classroom. For me, the weapons were numbers, letters, reading, and writing. The blows of these weapons contorted the way I saw myself and the way I went about school for the next 14 years of my life. . . . [When] I was in the third grade, it didn't bother me to be labeled dyslexic. However, I knew I was different because of the type of people who were in my [special education] class. On the outside I seemed happy, but on the inside I felt shame and embarrassment. My perception of

how my friends saw me changed also. Even though all the kids appeared to like me, deep inside myself I always felt like they were feeling sorry for me. . . . At Landmark College, I learned about my disability. . . . [They] taught me not to go around the disability, but to go through it. Today, I'm not bound to student notetakers and tape recorders. That's the difference between remediation and empowerment. (Ryan & Price, 1992, p. 17)

ANGELA—My story begins in Miss Coe's sixth grade classroom. I had just read a paragraph from the previous night's history assignment for the third time. I heard my name being called, "Angela, we're waiting. . . . Well class, it seems Angela doesn't think she has to study like the rest of you. I guess she thinks that she's so smart she can just do everything without reading the book." [The teacher] was telling them I was different. . . . I was beginning to believe everything that was being said about me. Maybe I was lazy. Maybe I didn't try hard enough. Maybe I was just stupid. . . . I married and years later . . . a friend suggested that I get tested for learning disabilities. It was the first time this possibility had been suggested to me. When it was verified that I had learning disabilities, I let go of tears that had been held back for many years. The examiner said she understood how upsetting it must be to learn so late in life that I had Dyslexia. "No," I said, "I'm so relieved! Now I know that it has a name. I'm not lazy, or stupid. Now I can do something about it! Where do we start?" (Assenza, 1994, pp. 3, 4)

MARY—I thought about beginning this [college] paper with an amazing and thought-provoking quote from a student with a learning disability. A quote that would motivate the reader to understand the complexities of what it is like to have a learning disability, the day-to-day awakenings of the sometimes far-reaching effects of their disability and the emerging awareness of realizing the magnitude and innumerable coping skills they use to hide their disability from the world around them whether in their school, workplace, home, or relationships. I know the effects a learning disability has on an individual because I live with them, and as each day passes, I learn something new about how my disability affects so much of my life. . . . Before I just thought that it was me. I couldn't do something right or I was just dumb. These have been very common feelings for me. . . . I [now] accept that there are some things I cannot do or will always struggle doing because of my disability, but that does not make me a bad person. It just makes me a person with a mild learning disability. (anonymous personal communication, May 11, 1997)

Obviously, these people are unique individuals with their own stories to tell about the journey from childhood to adulthood. However, these three individuals also have a great deal in common. They all have learning disabilities. They all have lived with their disabilities since they were children and continue to feel the impact into adulthood. All three describe a variety of feelings and psychosocial issues (e.g., shame, anger, frustration, low self-esteem, lack of self-awareness) that have surrounded their learning disabilities throughout their lives. As they matured into adulthood, all three experienced significant changes in self-perception about their learning disabilities, especially in terms of personal control and disability self-awareness. In addition, each adult's comments illustrate a number of critical connections among three important areas for individuals with learning disabilities across the lifespan: (a) the psychosocial ramifications of learning disabilities; (b) the different stages of adult development; and (c) the value of self-determination skills.

The purpose of this chapter is to define a major paradigm shift into a new, previously unexplored area that crosses the boundaries of special, vocational, and higher education. This shift may create new attitudes, beliefs, and best practices that result when two educational models (adult development and self-determination) are combined with current knowledge about psychosocial issues and adults with learning disabilities.

Ideas presented in this chapter clearly underscore a significant theme that emerges through the examination of the relationships among psychosocial issues, adult development, and self-determination. The concept of autonomy, or the degree of control individuals have over their own lives, becomes a focal point. While the concept of control may have different labels depending on the training or professional perspective of the author (i.e., locus of control by psychologists; internal motivators by adult specialists; knowing and valuing oneself by educators), the importance of this concept is paramount for adults both with and without disabilities as they cope with the myriad challenges of adult life.

Underlying Assumptions About Learning Disabilities

One cannot discuss the connections among psychosocial issues, adult development, and self-determination without first understanding three critical assumptions found in the extant literature base on learning disabilities.

Learning Disabilities Do Not Disappear with Adulthood

After more than three decades of research, many professionals now admit that children with learning disabilities continue to carry the ramifications of their disabilities into both adolescence and adulthood. As Smith et al. (1997) explain, "We now know that learning disabilities are not outgrown in childhood. Learning disabilities continue and, in fact, may even intensify in adulthood as task and environmental demands change" (p. 258). Such changes are reflected in the critical adult areas of employment and postsecondary education.

For instance, when students with learning disabilities move into these new, challenging settings, they often still show difficulties in perception, reading, math, written communication, and psychosocial skills. It must be emphasized that such observations may or may not describe all children who become adults with learning disabilities. However, many professionals agree that these difficulties are frequently observed in their students and will continue to require attention, understanding, and support in adulthood (Adelman & Vogel, 1993a; Smith et al., 1997).

Adults with Learning Disabilities Require Specialized Services and Education

Because the ramifications of learning disabilities are permanent, it follows that some individuals with this hidden disability will also require specialized services, education, and support throughout their lives. To support this position, Kavale (1988) stresses that one key component of the successful, long-term adjustment of adults with learning disabilities is the use of intensive, ongoing, educational interventions geared specifically to meet their needs.

Examples of these services were described by adults with disabilities in a study by the Learning Disabilities Association of America (LDA) in 1994. The adults surveyed had requested these specific services: evaluation (66%), tutoring (60%), psychological therapy or academic support (47%), vocational counseling (33%), language therapy (27%), and medical services (25%). They also believed that the following services would be useful to them in the future: job placement assistance (28%), social or vocational skill training (24%), vocational counseling, support groups, job coaching, peer support services, and advocacy services ("Adults with Learning Disabilities," 1994).

Psychosocial Issues Influence Individuals with Learning Disabilities

The previously discussed LDA study underscores the need for ongoing support services in the psychosocial area. This request seems reasonable, as many professionals now believe that there is a strong relationship between learning disabilities and psychosocial issues throughout one's life (Brier, 1994; Fox & Forbing, 1991; Lombana, 1992; VSA Educational Services, 1991).

Some authors recognize that psychosocial issues and learning disabilities go hand in hand, because they have seen that children with learning disabilities are more vulnerable to emotional disturbances (Brier, 1994; Bryan, 1989; Cohn, 1998; Epstein, Cullinan, & Neiminen, 1984; Silver, 1984). Even as adults, these same individuals tended to report many problems in a variety of psychosocial areas, such as starting and maintaining relationships, excessive dependency on others, less satisfaction with familial relationships, low self-esteem, lack of confidence, feelings of inadequacy and depression, and less participation in recreation and community activities (Smith et al., 1997).

A New Model for Adults with Learning Disabilities

When the three previous assumptions are viewed together, they validate a new paradigm for learning disabilities in adults. The holistic model to be presented has a number of characteristics that make it particularly relevant to the education of people with learning disabilities in the new millennium.

First, such a holistic model does not regard adults with learning disabilities as grown-up children, but instead reveals them to be individuals with unique profiles that are different from those of children. Second, the new paradigm is not limited to one setting, age group, or profession, but is holistic and elastic enough to apply to different methods of service delivery for people with learning disabilities throughout their life span. Third, this model acknowledges the importance of adult developmental theories (i.e., self-directed learning, learning readiness contingent on adult/societal roles, reflection as it promotes self-knowledge) as equally applicable to adults with learning disabilities. Fourth, it applies the most up-to-date trends in special education (e.g., inclusionary education, transition, and self-determination). Last, it builds on best practices within a "cross-disciplinary" focus (e.g., psychology, adult development, vocational education, special education).

Adult Developmental Models

One way to use a cross-disciplinary focus to approach adult service delivery for people with disabilities is through an adult-oriented framework. A number of credible adult theoretical models (e.g., Erikson, 1959; Levinson, 1986) currently exist in the professional literature. Malcolm Knowles is the individual considered by many to be the father of Adult Learning, however (Bell, 1989;

Daly, 1980; Feuer & Geber, 1988; Fisher & Podeschi, 1989; Tennant, 1986). In his two classic texts from the 1970s, *The Modern Practice of Adult Education* (1970) and *The Adult Learner: A Neglected Species* (1978), Knowles laid the groundwork for what adult educators use every day as an instructional model in a variety of settings.

His theme was a simple one. Adult students have traditionally been taught within a pedagogical paradigm, the "teacher-centered" approach, that is the foundation for all learning in the elementary and secondary school systems throughout the United States. While this approach may be advantageous for young children who require extensive guidance and structure in every aspect of their educational experience, it is frequently inappropriate for teaching adults, who come to the classroom bringing a different set of challenges and strengths.

As a result, Knowles proposed a European model of instruction called *andragogy*, which was specifically formulated to address the needs and strengths of adult students. This humanistic approach was less teacher-centered and more learner-centered (Bell, 1989; Daly, 1980; Fisher & Podeschi, 1989; Rada, 1980). In addition, Knowles hypothesized that adult learners differed from children in their innate learning style. These differences became the five key principles that underly andragogy. They are summarized as:

1. Adults tend to be self-directed learners.

2. Adults bring to the classroom a rich base of experience that should be tapped as part of their learning.

3. Adults have a more "problem-centered" orientation in terms of learning specific tasks in contrast to the "subject-matter orientation" of children.

4. Adult learning readiness is triggered by what they need to know to be responsible adults and citizens in their home and society.

5. Adult learning motivation is internal, or intrinsically based; whereas the motivation of children is due to external or extrinsic factors (Knowles, 1984; Rada, 1980).

Knowles also described the concepts of control and discovery, two themes that continually run through his work on andragogy (Bell, 1989). For instance, he emphasized the importance of participative education, in which adults are viewed as responsible and independent students. He also stressed the concept of discovery learning to facilitate educational growth through insight and early opportunity for application in adult-oriented settings (Bell, 1989).

Knowles argued the traditional public school system had failed most adults in those two critical areas because teaching methodology did not address differing learning styles of adults and children. He posited that most college classes were still taught with the pedagogical, teacher-centered approach more applicable to children, while adults required a more flexible, participative, experience-based form of instruction (Feuer & Geber, 1988). Knowles also argued that the natural tendencies of people as learners were often undermined by the ways society and the school system shape human nature. As he said:

> Typically by the time people have finished school, gotten a job and a family, they come to see themselves as fully responsible for their own lives. But the minute they walk into a situation labeled training or education, they hark back to their previous experience in school. They put on their dunce caps, sit back, fold their arms in front of them and say, "OK, teach me." We've been conditioned to see the role of learner as a dependent one. Adults emerge from their schooling with set notions about what education is all about, and this conflicts with their evolving needs to be self-directing. (Feuer & Geber, 1988, pp. 33, 35)

It is interesting to note a recurring theme in both Knowles's work and that of others in adult development. Many adult educators believe that life is a continuing, dynamic process in which adults formulate a body of knowledge, beliefs, perceptions, and ideas of self-identity through various tasks and challenges in differing environments (Knowles, 1984; Rada, 1980). But if this is true for all adults, does it have special significance for adults who carry the dual challenge of learning disabilities?

Andragogy and Learning Disabilities in Adults

While Knowles never directly referred to people with learning disabilities when discussing andragogy (i.e., the unique learning system based on adult development), a number of innovative connections can be found between these two critical topics. They are summarized in Table 5.1.

The relationships between learning disabilities in adults and andragogy also underscore an important theme that is directly applicable to service delivery for this rapidly growing population. Educators have found that adults do not grow out of their learning disabilities, while Knowles simultaneously observed that adults are lifelong learners. Consequently, both Knowles and adult disability service providers stress that adult-oriented support must be available wherever

Table 5.1

A Comparison of Learning Disabilities in Adults and the Principles of Andragogy

Adults with Learning Disabilities	Principles of Andragogy
1. Adults do not grow out of learning disabilities.	1. Adults are lifelong learners.
2. Adults require specialized assistance: • teaching • support/services • disability awareness	2. Adult instruction must be focused on the needs of the learner (i.e., "learner centered").
3. Adults need authentic survival skills: • coping techniques • learning strategies	3. Adult instruction must build on the students' "teachable moments."

and whenever it is requested. Both have emphasized the value of specialized education and support for their target populations.

The disability literature has demonstrated that adults with learning disabilities clearly require a particular type of assistance that is personalized to build on their unique strengths and to compensate for their weaker areas, such as cognitive and perceptual difficulties, language problems, academic weaknesses, and psychosocial deficits (Adelman & Vogel, 1993a; Cosden & McNamara, 1997; Gregg & Ferri, 1998). Such specialized support echoes a key component of andragogy.

Knowles also encouraged a personalized approach to teaching adults that clearly was more "learner centered" and less "teacher centered" than the traditional, pedagogical instruction used in settings from elementary school to university (Daly, 1980; Knowles, 1984; Rada, 1980; Tennant, 1986). He stressed that adults learn best when their learning is structured around these five critical principles: (a) it should be self-directed; (b) it must build on their life experiences; (c) it must be problem centered (e.g., dealing with everyday issues or new knowledge that they must have to move forward in their lives) instead of subject centered (i.e., driven by a standardized curriculum that does not reflect their needs); (d) it should be triggered by what individuals need to know as functioning citizens and adults in their home communities; and (e) it must be internally motivated (i.e., have an internal locus of control) versus externally motivated.

It is interesting to note that special educators have unknowingly talked about the principles of andragogy in describing successful adults with learning disabilities. For example, Hallahan and Kauffman (1997) state, "Successful individuals have a realistic acceptance of their weaknesses coupled with an attitude of building on their strengths. They compartmentalize their learning disability and see it as only one aspect of their identity. . . . [They] build on their strengths by selecting occupations that match their abilities and minimize their difficulties" (p. 195). Gerber and Reiff (1991) echo these principles in their concept of reframing as a positive way to view one's disability.

Knowles and other educators have stressed the importance of learning based on authenticity. Knowles felt that no concept was more important to adult success than the use of all types of life experiences to figure out exactly what individuals need to learn and why they want to learn it. He believed that all adults learn best when they focus their attention on solving genuine, personal problems that they encounter in their everyday lives. This concentrated attention on specific, prioritized issues triggers the adult learning process, while at the same time, facilitating further cognitive skill development. Hence, the results of this process become significant, long-term benefits for adult learners.

Adults should use all of their life experiences (successes and failures) to turn current challenges into fruitful learning experiences (Gerber & Reiff, 1991). As Knowles says, "To adults, education is a process of improving their ability to cope with the life problems they face now" (1984, p. 53). Therefore, professionals need to capture those "teachable moments" (as Knowles describes them) on an ongoing basis to enhance survival skill development for adults with disabilities.

Self-Determination and Individuals with Learning Disabilities

A second critical area in the new paradigm shift concerning adults with learning disabilities is the concept of self-determination (Benner, 1998; Field, 1996a; Field & Hoffman, 1994; Field, Hoffman, & Posch, 1997). Self-determination has received wide attention in the special education literature during the last few years. It has been defined as "the ability to identify and achieve goals based on a foundation of knowing and valuing oneself" (Field & Hoffman, 1994, p. 164). Self-determination encompasses a number of interrelated components that can be specifically taught as skill areas: (a) self-actualization, (b) assertiveness, (c) creativity, (d) pride, and (e) self-advocacy. These components also can be the focus of transition-based instruction to facilitate the successful entry from adolescence into adulthood (Field, 1996b; Field & Hoffman, 1994; Field et al., 1997; Ward, 1992).

Transition for individuals with disabilities and self-determination have always gone hand in hand. While effective transition skills have been discussed in the professional literature since the mid-1980s, they were examined from a new perspective with the reauthorization of the Individuals with Disabilities Act (IDEA) in 1990 and 1997. This key legislation underscored the importance of full participation for adolescents with disabilities in all aspects of transition planning (i.e., setting short- and long-term personal goals, understanding one's own strengths and weaknesses, taking necessary classes for high school graduation, starting career exploration, exploring various community resources, and writing the Individual Transition Plan). The language of the IDEA mandated not only that students with disabilities be actively involved during the annual planning, but that their preferences, interests, and concerns be included in the Individual Transition Plan as much as possible. While such lofty goals seemed laudable, many professionals and parents were confused about how to actually do what was required to achieve them (see Chapter 2).

To address those concerns, the U.S. Department of Education, Office of Special Education and Rehabilitative Services (OSERS), funded 26 model demonstration projects to flesh out definitions, conceptual frameworks, and intervention techniques for self-determination (Field et al., 1997). While each project had its own perspective on self-determination, all were in agreement about the major skill areas necessary to facilitate growth in this critical area for secondary youth with disabilities: problem solving, self-development, self-advocacy, and life skills. Various interventions tested by the model projects included: self-determination curricula; specific mentoring and modeling strategies; community-based, experiential learning/generalization across different settings; and planning for the future with as much direct student participation as possible (Field et al., 1997; Ward & Kohler, 1996).

Because of its strong links to secondary transition planning as delineated in the IDEA, most of the current knowledge about self-determination has been linked to adolescents with disabilities and their experiences in secondary education. At first glance, this makes a great deal of sense. Adolescence is traditionally seen as a time of extreme psychosocial, physical, and educational change. In addition, difficulties with common developmental tasks associated with youth (e.g., creating a sexual identity, integrating social and ethical values, identifying personal interests, developing self-confidence in social situations) seem to become larger hurdles for youth with disabilities (Deshler et al., 1996; Smith, 1997).

However, the successful resolution of these developmental tasks may be problematic for adults with disabilities as well as adolescents. Field, Hoffman, and Posch (1997) explain: "Adolescence is characterized by a progressive movement toward increased self-awareness and personal independence" (p. 288). Testimonials from adults with learning disabilities, along with the literature on adult development as conceptualized by such leaders as Erikson and Knowles, illustrate that issues of independence, identity, and exploration are critical milestones for adults as well. For example, adults (as well as teenagers) may need assistance when they change jobs, move to a new area, or find themselves diagnosed after struggling throughout their childhood years with unidentified learning disabilities. Because self-determination clearly applies to individuals with disabilities across the lifespan, the rest of this chapter delineates critical connections among adult developmental stages, self-determination, and various psychosocial issues observed in some adults with learning disabilities.

Psychosocial Issues and Adults with Learning Disabilities

Before discussing the types of psychosocial issues that can have such a significant impact on the daily lives of some adults with learning disabilities, it is necessary to understand exactly what psychosocial issues are. The term *psychosocial* concisely summarizes two integral areas of the everyday lives of individuals with learning disabilities: the psychological aspects (i.e., how one sees oneself or feels about oneself), and the social aspects (i.e., how one relates to others in one's everyday environment and how one communicates with others). These characteristics are discussed in the professional literature under the related categories of: self-concept, social skills deficits, dependency issues, stress, anxiety, and negative feelings or behaviors.

Five Categories of Psychosocial Issues of Adults with Learning Disabilities

Perhaps the one counseling issue that repeatedly emerges for individuals with learning disabilities is the lack of a positive self-concept (Cohn, 1998; Cosden & McNamara, 1997; Gerber & Reiff, 1991; Gregg & Ferri, 1998; Hoy et al., 1997; Margalit, 1998; Weiner, 1998; Wilchesky & Minden, 1988). For instance, the significant impact of low self-esteem on the lives of adults with learning disabilities is illustrated in the case studies by Gerber and Reiff. Through extensive interviews with successful adults with learning disabilities, the authors describe how the hurdles of individual learning disabilities often leave adults angry, frustrated, and stressed out because they can't do certain tasks easily or efficiently. These negative feelings are often turned inward and reinforce low self-esteem, self-confidence, and self-respect. But the interviews also showed that the reverse can be true. These negative feelings can be used to motivate individuals to try one more time or to look for new ways to jump the hurdles. It is this creativity and persistence that can feed feelings of competence and self-respect. As Gerber and Reiff (1991) observe, "In a sense, the hard knocks of past experience offer a source of strength" (p. 26).

A second psychosocial issue that repeatedly emerges in the literature about adults with learning disabilities is inappropriate or ineffective socialization skills (Cohn, 1998; Denckla, 1986; Hoy et al., 1997; Jackson, Enright, & Murdock, 1987; Margalit, 1998; Renick & Harter, 1989; Weiner, 1998). B. K. Smith (1986) emphasizes the importance of social relationships for adults with learning disabilities and explains that these individuals may have missed the opportunity as children to develop such critical socialization skills as interpreting social clues, recognizing subtle signals from facial or body language, being aware of a speaker's vocal tonality, understanding time constraints, and interpreting other people's moods. His thesis is supported by Margalit's study of preschoolers with learning disabilities who demonstrated more loneliness and maladjustment, had fewer friends, and received lower acceptance peer ratings than children without learning disabilities. Kroll (1984) summarizes other studies and concludes that socialization seems to be a consistent problem area for many adults with learning disabilities throughout their lives.

Difficulties with socialization and a poor self-concept may lead to over-dependence in adulthood on significant people in one's life (e.g., teachers, parents, spouses, roommates, or counselors). Many authors have described individuals with learning disabilities as having difficulty making decisions that shape their lives on a day-by-day basis (Cohn, 1998; Cosden & McNamara, 1997; Hill Top Preparatory School, 1988; Hoy et al., 1997; Price, 1988; Weiner, 1998). One reason people with learning disabilities may often be overly reliant on others is that they do not trust their own judgment (Cohn, 1998; Gregg & Ferri, 1998; Michaels, 1997). Due to a pervasive sense of failure and inadequacy based on memories of past experiences, they lack a sense of personal strength and competency (Cohn, 1998; Michaels, 1997; Ryan & Price, 1992). Michaels describes this lack of self-confidence as it affects "the belief in one's ability to positively effect change in one's own life" (p. 189). Many individuals with learning disabilities not only deeply internalize their failures, but also attribute their successes to chance or to others. Consequently, they continue to nourish the twin demons of feelings of incompetence and excessive dependency on others in their environment. As Michaels explains, "The result is an individual with a poor sense of personal competency who lacks the will to try in pre-anticipation of failure. [Such people] have been described as having difficulty taking responsibility for oneself, separating from parental control and values, separating from the control of the school system, and developing an internal locus of control . . ." (p. 189).

Low self-esteem, inadequate social skills, and dependency issues usually result in a great deal of ongoing stress and anxiety for adults with learning disabilities. Many authors have observed physical and emotional signs of stress and anxiety for this population, some of which are severe enough to be similar to posttraumatic stress (Cohen, 1985; Cohn, 1998; Gerber & Reiff, 1991; Gregg & Ferri, 1998; Hall & Haws, 1989; Hayes & Sloat, 1988; Hoy et al., 1997; Payne, 1997; Rourke, 1989). For instance, when Freils (1969) observed students with learning disabilities, she found these common characteristics: physical mannerisms such as tics, red eyes, bleeding fingernails; general physical health problems (e.g., long-term colds, coughs, stomach disorders), and conversations that repeatedly focused on stress or anxiety. Hoy et al. explored the levels of stress, anxiety, and depression seen in adults with learning disabilities and found similar results. For example, the college students in the sample demonstrated high levels of anxiety. Also, some of the female subjects showed "significant signs of depression" (p. 278).

Excessive stress and anxiety can be significant contributors to a range of negative behaviors and feelings. For instance, Cohn (1998) describes himself and others with learning disabilities by saying, "For those with learning disabilities, recognizing unexpressed negative feelings is often extremely difficult because of years of repression. . . . Unfortunately, they frequently transform their feelings of shame, resentment, and frustration into anxiety" (p. 514).

But perhaps these psychosocial issues were summarized best when an instructor from Hill Top Preparatory School (1988) described her students as being:

> shy, egocentric, inflexible, immature, and lacking in social skills. They may display poor impulse control, excessive frustration, anxiety, denial, projection, anger, depression, strong dependency needs or health problems because of the difficulty with an energy drain in coping in school and/or stressful social situations. They misunderstand and are misunderstood. (p. 3)

It should be stressed that this comment may not describe all children who become adults with learning disabilities. However, it does point to areas of concern for some individuals that may require ongoing attention, understanding, and support in adulthood, as discussed in depth later in this chapter.

Caveats About Psychosocial Issues

One cannot discuss the psychosocial ramifications of learning disabilities without keeping a few critical comments in mind. It is important to remember that one should not generalize all of the previously described psychosocial characteristics to all adults with learning disabilities. The preponderance of the professional literature clearly demonstrates that many adults with learning disabilities may exhibit one or more of these characteristics over time (Cosden & McNamara, 1997; Gerber & Reiff, 1991; Hayes, 1993; Ryan & Price, 1992; Telander, 1994; Weiner, 1998; W. J. White, 1992). However, each individual with learning disabilities is just that—a unique individual.

For instance, the previous material obviously does not represent the complete profile of unique strengths and weaknesses for each adult with learning disabilities. People with disabilities, like people without disabilities, demonstrate many positive psychosocial traits as well as negative ones. Many individuals with learning disabilities are highly motivated, creative people with a strong desire to be successful, despite the many setbacks that they have faced (Gerber & Reiff, 1991; Hallahan & Kauffman, 1997; Ryan & Price, 1992). Some have a great sense of humor; some show positive coping mechanisms that allow them to reach their goals; and some are outstanding problem solvers who find unique solutions to problems that no one else has imagined. In summary, it is vital to look at an individual's psychosocial strengths as well as his or her weaknesses when providing assistance to adults with learning disabilities in postsecondary settings.

Numerous testimonials and articles in professional journals have described in dramatic terms various psychosocial issues that seem to be the long-term ramifications of learning disabilities for adults (e.g., high levels of disability-related stress and anxiety, loneliness or an ongoing sense of isolation from one's peers, disability-induced frustration, and an inability to communicate one's needs to others). However, it is difficult, if not impossible, to determine the generalizability of this information. Most of it probably contains at least a grain of truth. But, given the state of the current research base on both psychosocial issues and learning disabilities in adults in general, we still must proceed with caution in discussions of this complex, multifaceted area.

Connecting Adult Developmental Theory, Psychosocial Issues, and Self-Determination

A new way to approach effective service delivery for adults with learning disabilities that is based on the relationship among andragogy, self-determination, and psychosocial issues has been examined. The remainder of this chapter continues that cross-disciplinary focus by suggesting practical hints and applications for professionals in various adult-oriented settings. These ideas fall into two interrelated categories: the connections between self-determination and andragogy, and the connections between self-determination and the psychosocial attributes of some adults with learning disabilities.

Self-Determination and Andragogy

Both self-determination and andragogy focus on personal freedom and choices. Choices often involve defining personal goals and then figuring out how to achieve them (Field & Hoffman, 1994, 1996a; Knowles, 1984; Ward, 1992). The freedom to make such choices is often a critical factor in the lives of adults with learning disabilities because many children with learning disabilities have come to see themselves as being incompetent and helpless. Because such a negative self-image carries a pervading sense of low self-esteem, these children grow into adults who continue to view themselves as passive failures who are incapable of achieving their dreams (Smith et al., 1997).

But how does this apply to postsecondary service delivery? As seen in Table 5.2, the connections between self-determination and andragogy provide important clues about how to teach valuable strategies to adult students in a variety of settings. For example, Field and Hoffman (1994) list five major components that have become the foundation for self-determination. As displayed in the left column of Table 5.2, this set of personal skills, ideas, and beliefs can also be taught as specific skills in problem solving, self-determination, self-advocacy, and life skills (Ward & Kohler, 1996).

Andragogy also provides professionals with suggestions to tap into adult learning processes, as seen in the right-hand column of Table 5.2. Knowles guided adult educators with these principles, which he felt drove the andragogical style of instruction for all adult learners (Knowles, 1984; Rada, 1980). When one compares the two columns in Table 5.2, it becomes apparent that these adult principles say exactly what and how adults with learning disabilities should be taught, mirroring the five components of the self-determination model.

For instance, the self-determination principle called "Know yourself" is another way to describe learners who are internally motivated through andragogical instruction. The self-determination principle of "Value yourself" implies that these individuals have examined the rich body of experience that is part of their total life history, especially in the areas of their unique strengths, deficits, needs, and preferences. Both knowing and valuing oneself assume that the adult learner understands from the beginning how any new knowledge will

Table 5.2

A Comparison of Self-Determination and the Principles of Andragogy

Five Model Components of Self-Determination	Principles of Andragogy
Know yourself	Foster self-directed learning, highlight learning readiness
Value yourself	Accentuate life experiences, facilitate internal motivation
Plan	Focus on personal goals, stress personal achievement
Act	Solve authentic problems, stress personal experiences
Experience outcomes and learn	Reflect to learn new ideas, emphasize self-evaluation

Note. Adapted from "Development of a Model for Self-Determination," by S. Field and A. Hoffman, 1994, *Career Development for Exceptional Individuals, 17,* pp. 159–169. Copyright 1994 by *Career Development for Exceptional Individuals.* Adapted with permission.

be useful in implementing personal choices. All of these areas subsumed in Field and Hoffman's model of self-determination (1994) reflect the best practices of andragogy as delineated by Knowles.

In addition, these life choices then become goals that constitute a road map for future learning and adult instruction. While Field and Hoffman (1994) describe choices as "Planning" and "Acting" in their self-determination model, the principles of andragogy expand those concepts further for learners. Knowles stresses that adults must be involved in "mutual planning" with instructors or support staff to design their own learning objectives and activities (Feuer & Geber, 1988). This ownership is a critical component for adults to carry out their learning plans. Knowles also emphasizes that adults want ideas and skills that are applicable to the real-life problems and challenges that they face every day. The mutual planning process, as described by Knowles, then leads to risk taking, dealing with conflict and criticism, and accessing resources, just as Field and Hoffman anticipated in their model of self-determination.

According to Knowles, during the final stage of andragogy, adults should evaluate their own learning. He emphasizes reflection as a way to foster new knowledge from both past and present experiences. He visualized this process as a form of discovery learning, with growth through new insights about oneself and one's environment (Knowles, 1984). Such discoveries have strong parallels in Field and Hoffman's final component of self-determination (Field, 1996a; Field & Hoffman, 1994). It is here that learners are encouraged to compare their outcomes and performance in terms of personal expectations, to realize their successes, and to make any necessary adjustments for their next set of goals and activities.

Table 5.2 illustrates another important point for professionals. Each model component emphasizes active learners who know themselves well and can build on life experiences to achieve goals that they themselves have chosen. As Field et al. (1997) explain, "Acceptance of a focus on self-determination requires a fundamental shift in the way educational planning and implementation are conducted. It also holds the potential for increasing both the effectiveness and relevance of education for youth with and without disabilities" (p. 292).

Self-Determination and Psychosocial Issues

Although the educators who discussed self-determination never framed its components in psychosocial terms, many connections are still apparent that provide important insights into each topic. For example, Field et al. (1997) could have been discussing psychosocial development when they described the importance of teaching self-determination skills to youth with learning disabilities who struggle as part of normal adolescent development to find their own identities, become independent, and mature into self-aware individuals.

As illustrated in Table 5.3, self-determination can be conceptualized as the result of positive psychosocial skill development. For example, the self-knowledge that Field et al. (1997) stress as an important consequence of self-determination skill development could be viewed as similar to the psychosocial area of disability self-awareness. Whether it is called valuing and knowing oneself or disability self-awareness, such critical self-knowledge is the foundation for a variety of positive psychosocial traits (e.g., increasing self-confidence, decreasing dependency on others, developing effective social skills, and decreasing excessive stress and anxiety). However, the question again arises: How does this information apply to postsecondary disability service delivery?

Many examples can be found in Table 5.3 to answer this question. For instance, Field et al. (1997) explain that "knowing yourself" implies the following actions: "Dreaming; knowing your strengths, weaknesses, needs, and preferences; knowing the options; and deciding what is important to you" (p. 287). Such identity exploration, as defined by these actions in the self-determination process, can in turn, dramatically shape how one sees oneself (i.e., one's self-concept).

Adults with learning disabilities can learn to further appreciate their uniqueness by accepting and valuing themselves; admiring the strengths that come from their uniqueness; recognizing and respecting their rights and responsibilities; and taking care of themselves. These actions, which clearly describe various forms of identity exploration, internalization, and psychosocial development, are listed by Field et al. (1997) as the sub-steps to "Valuing yourself," a second step in self-determination.

Table 5.3

A Comparison of Self-Determination and Psychosocial Development

Five Model Components of Self-Determination	Principles of Psychosocial Development
Know yourself	Identify strengths and weaknesses
Value yourself	Increase self-confidence and disability self-awareness
Plan	Decrease dependency behaviors
Act	Foster effective social skills and independence
Experience outcomes and learn	Decrease stress and anxiety; replace negative behaviors and feelings with positive ones; increase self-confidence; learn disability self-awareness; foster effective social skills and independence

Note. Adapted from "Development of a Model for Self-Determination," by S. Field and A. Hoffman, 1994, *Career Development for Exceptional Individuals, 17*, pp. 159–169. Copyright 1994 by *Career Development for Exceptional Individuals*. Adapted with permission.

The other three self-determination areas listed in Table 5.3 can be linked to positive psychosocial development in the same way. These provocative links then create combinations of support and growth potential for adults with learning disabilities that can be easily adapted to service delivery in many postsecondary or adult-oriented settings.

Recommendations and Conclusion

The connections between andragogy, self-determination, and psychosocial issues have many thought-provoking implications for adults with learning disabilities. However, one important question remains to be addressed: How can professionals use this information on a practical, daily basis with students who have learning disabilities?

One caveat is also important to remember when applying these new ideas to adult-service delivery. While this information can be used by professionals with a wide variety of expertise, it has been conceptualized to be part of a "smorgasbord" approach for adults with learning disabilities. Professionals should purposefully choose and then refine a mixture of these suggestions to fit the specific needs and resources of their institution or agency. Also, each practitioner is strongly encouraged to personalize these suggestions to his or her own expertise, values, and beliefs as an effective postsecondary disability service provider.

Effective Practices Suggested by the Connections: Disability Self-Awareness, Authenticity, and Independence

The first suggestion emanating from the relationships among andragogy, self-determination, and psychosocial issues is the facilitation of disability self-awareness. This foundation concept usually implies specific, in-depth knowledge about one's personal strengths and weaknesses in a variety of areas (i.e., academics, communication, social skills, physical abilities, vocational interests and expertise, etc.). Disability self-awareness also may include knowledge of how one reacts to variables in different environments (e.g., school versus home) and how one can internalize these insights into positive, proactive strategies to meet the everyday challenges of adulthood.

Such crucial information, however, is rarely available to the people who need it the most, individuals with learning disabilities. As Michaels (1997) says, "Currently both special and general education programs treat 'learning disabilities' as something not to be discussed or acknowledged. Students leave school for college, employment, and/or vocational training with no personal ownership of their learning disabilities or knowledge of how their learning disabilities affect them on a day-to-day basis. More importantly, they also lack self-awareness or strategies they can employ to negotiate successfully in a variety of adult settings" (pp. 199, 200).

To avoid this serious omission, Michaels advocates counseling students with learning disabilities about disability self-awareness in a structured, ongoing manner. He conceptualizes this personalized instruction in three related stages: intellectual awareness (I received special education because I had problems in school); emergent awareness (I know that I have these specific strengths and weaknesses); and anticipatory awareness (I feel competent because I know myself well and know what strategies I need to employ to be successful). Such focused instruction about disability self-awareness is valuable because adults with learning disabilities struggle with those disabilities in two areas of their lives: at home and at work.

A second important best practice is authenticity. The importance of real-life experiences when counseling or teaching adults with learning disabilities cannot be underestimated. For example, Knowles stresses repeatedly in his work on andragogy that educators must set up tasks and learning experiences that fulfill a number of important criteria. Adult education must build on previous knowledge and past history. It should also be "problem centered" to reflect the broader lives of responsible adults and citizens in our society versus only "subject-matter" material to pass specific courses or tests.

As part of the authenticity of instruction, Knowles (1984) also talks about a concept he calls "readiness to learn":

People become ready to learn something when they experience a need to learn it in order to cope more satisfyingly with real-life tasks or problems. The educator has a responsibility to create conditions and provide tools and procedures for helping learners discover their "need to know." And learning programs should be organized around life-application categories and sequenced according to the learners' readiness to learn. (p. 44)

But how can postsecondary disability service providers use authentic instruction for students with learning disabilities? First, professionals can assist students with learning disabilities to express and prioritize two or three problems that they consistently face every day (e.g., I avoid talking to my peers because I can't think of what to say; I'm always failing essay exams). Next, professionals should assist, but not direct, students to set realistic goals with appropriate strategies for each one. As part of this process, disability service providers should continually encourage new, personal insights about disability self-awareness. Finally, extensive support and feedback should be provided as students actually try out strategies and evaluate the results. (This process again reflects the best practices of both self-determination and andragogy, as illustrated in Table 5.2.)

Using mentors for adults with learning disabilities is another powerful approach to teaching with authenticity. Mentoring in this case can be broadly defined to encompass a variety of social relationships, such as college friends, teaching assistants, faculty, staff, and other students with or without learning disabilities. These individuals are usually already in the environment where the student is experiencing difficulties. They also may have struggled with similar issues themselves. As a result, the realistic guidance that mentors can provide offers a gold mine of useful information about hidden and overt expectations, challenges, and college experiences for students with learning disabilities.

Mentoring has other long-term benefits as well. Close, productive relationships with mentors definitely promote social skills, self-determination, and psychosocial strengths for students with learning disabilities (see Table 5.3). Peers and supportive faculty both clearly can help students with disabilities to successfully navigate the often bewildering complexity of the everyday college environment (Michaels, 1997; Ryan & Price, 1992; Telander, 1994). In addition, personal mentorships have been shown to promote academic success and retention in postsecondary settings (Weiss & Repetto, 1998).

A third suggestion that emerges from the relationships among andragogy, self-determination, and psychosocial issues is the importance of facilitating independence and self-directed learning for adults with learning disabilities.

Well-meaning parents and teachers have frequently reinforced children with learning disabilities to be dependent on others. The very support system that was meant to help them often has handicapped them instead. For example, Weiss and Repetto (1998) note that support services such as subject-matter tutoring continue the dependency of students with learning disabilities on others instead of encouraging them to develop their own study skills and knowledge base in academic settings.

Consequently, all adult instruction and services for students with learning disabilities must have individual student empowerment as the primary focus in its overall programmatic philosophy and mission. This implies that whether adult education takes place on an assembly line, in a literacy center, or in a college classroom, the psychosocial characteristics of personal control and independence must always be blended with academic and vocational learning.

How can student independence and self-determination be promoted in adult settings? One way is through ongoing, metacognitive instruction (i.e., scaffolding, direct instruction, or specific learning strategies) in college tutoring centers to facilitate the often underdeveloped and overlooked concepts of personal control, optimism, belongingness, self-efficacy, and self-esteem for students with learning disabilities (Deshler et al., 1996; Smith et al., 1997). Another method is to formally teach independence and autonomy through curricula that specifically promote self-determination (for specific suggestions, see the work of Field and Hoffman, 1996a). A third, more indirect approach may be chosen by some professionals if time and resources are not available in their settings to formally teach self-determination on a daily or weekly basis. This method involves consistently infusing the ability to make choices and personal decisions into every area of the instructional environment (e.g., time management, study skills, course selection).

The total instructional or counseling environment, where adults with learning disabilities receive daily accommodations and assistance, definitely promotes either dependency or independence in students. For instance, Field and Hoffman (1996a) assert, "Self-determination is promoted or discouraged by environmental variables (e.g., opportunities for choice making, attitudes of others, supports in the environment) and by the knowledge, beliefs, and skills of the individual (e.g., awareness of one's strengths and weaknesses, valuing of the self, and planning and communication skills)" (p. 171).

These opportunities should be available to adults with learning disabilities through a range of options and activities in postsecondary settings. Students must be encouraged to make as many choices as possible, whether they involve which friends to spend time with or which classes to take for electives. Students should learn how to set short- and long-term goals for themselves through the co-creation of an action plan developed specifically for postsecondary education.

Adults with learning disabilities should be encouraged to be mentors or peer tutors. Students could also intern in a future career field or volunteer their time if service learning projects are available.

All of these concepts promote the best practices of andragogy, positive psychosocial development, and self-determination because postsecondary disability personnel can facilitate or impede these critical concepts in a variety of subtle, or not so subtle, ways. Whether they are conscious of it or not, disability personnel are instinctually teaching students with learning disabilities every day to be more independent or dependent through student-teacher interactions, through environmental variables, and with specific instruction and support that either models or ignores the ideas of independence and self-determination (Deshler et al., 1996; Field & Hoffman, 1996a).

Reconfigure Traditional Secondary Educational Models

The fourth suggestion is a group of ideas that go beyond a single practice to encompass a totally new way of delivering education and disability support to students in secondary settings. It demands that professionals, students, parents, and administrators use the previously discussed information to rethink or reconfigure secondary education and curricula. Such a new vision forces all stakeholders to see the education and support of individuals with learning disabilities as a truly lifelong process of integrated, enriching experiences instead of as a set of isolated IEPs, teaching plans, and activities.

This radical paradigm shift can happen in a number of ways including the following: (a) stress more effective, realistic transition planning (as discussed in the previous section and in Chapter 2) that relies on authenticity whenever possible; (b) move away from using subject-matter tutoring and remediation in resource rooms as the only secondary model for instruction and assistance; (c) emphasize and integrate learning strategies into all aspects of secondary education to promote independence and self-determination skill development; (d) readjust accountability for all stakeholders (e.g., educators, parents, teachers, administrators, counselors, students) in terms of equality, roles, and responsibilities; and (e) make sure that the overall secondary educational model accurately reflects the IDEA and its intention for a more active student role throughout all high school activities and instruction.

Changing Roles of Professionals

The last decade has seen the creation of a rapidly growing body of knowledge about individuals with learning disabilities as they mature into adulthood.

However, one vital element is still missing in these activities and theories. The vast majority of these ideas are just that—commonsense ideas without a central, well-documented core of best practices that have been corroborated by empirical evidence. But how can education for adults with learning disabilities have professional credibility and validity if it is not founded on other unifying, well-respected educational paradigms, such as a model of adult development? This is where connections among andragogy, self-determination, and psychosocial skills become especially valuable. The examples found in Tables 5.1 and 5.2 clearly underscore Knowles's theories and educational philosophies. In addition, these new relationships strongly enhance and clarify the extant knowledge base concerning adults with learning disabilities.

Under the unifying theme of adult development, the knowledge base concerning the needs and strategies of adults with learning disabilities can continue to grow and flourish. For example, Patton and Polloway (1996) report that in 1985 only 3% of the articles published in *Learning Disabilities Quarterly* concerned adult issues. By 1990, this figure had increased to 28%. It follows that expanding this information base to encompass articles or studies on the connections among andragogy, psychosocial issues, and self-determination skills will enrich and enlarge it even further.

In addition, as the specialty area of support services for adults with disabilities grows during the next decade, professionals who specialize in serving adults with learning disabilities will clearly benefit from knowledge and methods organized around a core set of adult developmental principles. The current alternative is a hodgepodge of ideas that apply to one setting or meet the needs of one group of educators. However, it is clearly preferable to use information from this chapter as a beginning point to explore such questions as: How should adults with learning disabilities implement discovery learning? Can adults with learning disabilities use reflection for disability self-awareness? Should mutual goal planning and self-evaluation be used with students with learning disabilities in postsecondary education? These are only a few of the myriad questions that could provide valuable ideas and tools for adults with learning disabilities.

Furthermore, these questions point to an area that definitely needs a great deal more discussion in the professional literature. Both special and adult educators must ask themselves: How should we train professionals, especially postsecondary disability service providers, to effectively meet the needs of adults with learning disabilities? One answer is already available from the discussion of andragogy and self-determination. Both subjects point to a theme that is often repeated in this chapter. Students with learning disabilities who hope to become self-determined adults must be taught by self-determined professionals.

Knowles supported this thesis 3 decades ago when he admitted that his own teaching style drastically changed through his use of andragogy: "I have found in my role as a teacher of adults I have spent less and less of my time deciding what students should learn . . . and more and more of my time helping them discover for themselves what they need to learn and then helping them find the most effective resources" (1970, pp. 37–38). Benner, not an adult educator but a special educator, echoed Knowles nearly 30 years later when she described her rapidly changing role:

> Today, there is a positive paradigm shift emerging in special education and other disability service professions, involving professionals changing their roles from helpers to enablers. . . . Rather than setting up services that are done to and for students with disabilities and their families, the students and their families collaboratively plan and implement the services that are needed. . . . Students who are allowed to influence the goals of their program have opportunities to gain control of their lives rather than being controlled externally while a teacher's goals are imposed on them. (1998, p. 213)

Here is another place where andragogy provides valuable insights for professionals. Knowles advocated for the importance of lifelong learning for adult students, but he clearly meant it for their instructors as well. He believed that professionals would benefit from discovery learning as much as their students, that they should teach and implement for themselves the areas of mutual goal setting, experience-based activities, and self-directed evaluation. Here we find the final paradox of andragogy. Such a powerful teaching philosophy can be learned only when it is mutually practiced by both adults with learning disabilities and those who educate them.

This may not be as challenging as it sounds. There are many ways to be a "self-determined" educator. Suggestions for professionals include the ideas that: (a) postsecondary disability service providers should try a new role as a facilitator, not a director, who functions within an equal partnership among stakeholders in a college setting (e.g., parents, students, administrators, and other staff); (b) disability service providers in higher educational settings should practice as much professional monitoring and self-reflection as possible; (c) disability personnel should participate in ongoing professional training and development applicable to their role with postsecondary students who have disabilities; and (d) postsecondary disability service providers should use both formal and informal networks and resources, particularly those from local Offices for Students with Disabilities.

In conclusion, professionals have seen dramatic changes in the last 2 decades in the knowledge base concerning adults with learning disabilities. All indications from the literature show that this trend will continue. But where exactly is this journey taking us? As the testimonials from the beginning of this chapter illustrate, most of the journey depends on one's point of view. So little is known, but the field is in the process of learning so much about what happens to children with learning disabilities when they grow into adulthood. As if they were traveling through an unexplored country, many disability professionals are not quite sure where they are going. But the language, the ideas, and the insights into andragogy, self-determination, and psychosocialization may prove to be a valuable road map that directs the efforts of those who teach adults with learning disabilities.

CHAPTER

Assessment of
Learning Disabilities

Joseph W. Madaus

Given that the regulations of Section 504 of the Rehabilitation Act of 1973 and the Americans with Disabilities Act of 1990 (ADA) do not require that postsecondary institutions provide assessment services to students with previously diagnosed or suspected learning disabilities, most institutions depend on documentation submitted by students to determine eligibility for services, individually appropriate accommodations, and auxiliary aids. Thus, although postsecondary LD service providers are not required to become knowledgeable in the administration of standardized tests, they are faced with the formidable challenge of "deciphering" assessments on a daily basis to determine student eligibility and appropriate accommodations (Brackett & McPherson, 1996, p. 69).

Service providers' perceptions of this challenge have been corroborated in two studies that occurred nearly a decade apart. In a national survey of postsecondary LD service providers conducted in 1988 by Norlander, Shaw, and McGuire, 299 program administrators and direct service personnel were asked to rate both their present and their desired level of competence in a variety of skill areas. Results indicated that competencies falling in the area of assessment were ranked "most desired" by learning disability specialists. In addition, the authors found that learning disability specialists identified the need for additional training in nine specific areas related to LD assessment, ranging from the ability to evaluate the psychometric properties and usefulness of assessment instruments, to the ability to interpret standardized tests of intelligence, academic achievement,

157

and information processing (Norlander et al., 1988). In fact, the authors reported that the ability to interpret tests of academic achievement was the most desired skill and received the highest possible ranking.

Nearly a decade later, Madaus (1997) surveyed 567 disability service personnel in North America regarding perceptions of the importance of 54 job roles and functions. Items related to the interpretation of disability documentation were determined to be essential skills, and because of this high level of perceived importance, were included in the Professional Standards set forth by the Association on Higher Education and Disability (1997a). Despite the fact that these skills have been determined to be a standard of the profession, the challenge of interpreting reports may be compounded by the fact that less than 25% of disability service providers report special education or psychology as their primary area of training and education. As a result, many professionals entering the field may have minimal background in educational assessment and psychometrics (Madaus, 1997).

This chapter is based on two major premises: First, "It's Not You—It's the Report." In an ideal world, LD evaluations would be comprehensive and would naturally lead to recommendations for interventions and accommodations, as well as improved student self-understanding. This ideal is presented in order to provide a backdrop for what service providers and consumers of educational assessments *should* be able to expect. Of course, the ideal often does not match reality. Many reports submitted to postsecondary institutions are of questionable technical validity, are poorly written, are incomplete, or incorporate recommendations and conclusions that are not substantiated by testing data. Much of the confusion and uncertainty regarding decision making based on these reports stems from the poor quality of the reports themselves. Through a discussion of the weaknesses found in many reports, the ideal will be contrasted with the reality of current practice.

The second major premise of this chapter is that reading and understanding assessment reports are skills that can be developed with some understanding of basic psychometric concepts and knowledge of commonly used instruments. Novices may be surprised to learn that many instruments are used improperly or imprecisely, and that a test or subtest name is no guarantee of its quality or validity. Further, two subtests from different instruments might have the same name but measure a stated concept very differently. This chapter presents information related to basic measurement concepts, major diagnostic methods (e.g., severe discrepancy model, clinical model), and knowledge helpful in "cracking the code" of diagnostic assessments. The chapter concludes with reviews of instruments commonly submitted to postsecondary institutions to verify eligibility and the need for accommodations.

Thus, the intent of this chapter is not to teach practitioners *how* to conduct an LD assessment, which is beyond the scope of this text. Rather, the intent is to provide readers with the tools and information they need to read assessment reports and glean information as a knowledgeable consumer.

It's Not You—It's the Report: Issues in Definition and Practice

Historical Perspective on LD Assessment

Since its inception, the field of learning disabilities has been beset with controversy related to definition (Hammill, 1990; Stanovich, 1999; Swanson, 1991a). While the field was initially dominated by physicians and psychologists (Hammill, 1993), a shift occurred in the mid-1960s with the rise of school programs and the involvement of parents and educators. The impact of these influences is noted by Lyon and Moats (1993), who explain that the "field, as we know it today, emerged not from initial scientific discoveries about difficulties learning to read or write, but because many children who ostensibly should have been able to learn in school could not" (p. 3).

The LD field has thus evolved as a combination social, political, and educational movement, resulting in a multidisciplinary profession with several theoretical and conceptual perspectives and definitions (Gregg & Ferri, 1996; Lyon & Moats, 1993). These varying perspectives have resulted in "pervasive and, at times, contentious" disagreements about definition, diagnostic criteria, and assessment practices (Lyon & Moats, 1993, p. 1). The assessment and remediation of LD has been considered the domain and interest of many disciplines and professions, including but not limited to education, psychology, school psychology, speech and language pathology, neurology, psychiatry, ophthalmology, optometry, social work, and occupational therapy (Hammill, 1993; Lyon & Moats, 1993; Mercer, Hughes, & Mercer, 1985). Diagnosticians from any of these disciplines look at a student "through his or her idiosyncratic clinical lens" (Lyon, 1996, p. 59) and may focus on different aspects and attributes of the person (Lyon & Moats, 1993; Morris, 1993). The ensuing result is that "different clinicians may evaluate the same child and classify him or her completely differently, even though they obtained congruent information" (Morris, 1993, p. 78). The fact that some professionals within the same disciplinary circle may also disagree about how to define and assess LD (Hammill, 1993) creates additional confusion and adds to the controversy.

While debate has raged both across and within professional disciplines, much of what has forged day-to-day practice has been political and governmental legislation. Lyon and Moats (1993) state that "the concept of unexpected underachievement as operationalized by a discrepancy between IQ and achievement has served as the driving clinical force in the diagnosis of LD" (p. 5). This discrepancy approach, which was adopted and outlined with the passage of the Education for All Handicapped Children Act (P.L. 94-142) and continued via the Individuals with Disabilities Education Act (P.L. 105-17; Fletcher et al., 1998), is the primary method for determining eligibility at the secondary level (Brackett & McPherson, 1996).

Researchers have argued that although these inclusionary and exclusionary guidelines have been accepted, they are superficial and lack consistency and empirical validity (Connell, 1991; Morris, 1993; Reynolds, 1985). However, because there are no national standards for diagnosis and eligibility criteria, and because federal guidelines and other diagnostic guides such as the *Diagnostic and Statistical Manual of Mental Disorders–Fourth Edition* (American Psychiatric Association, 1994) do not set specific guidelines for determining what constitutes a significant discrepancy between ability and achievement, definitions and criteria can vary from state to state, and in many cases, from district to district (Brackett & McPherson, 1996; Doris, 1993; Hawks, 1996; Lyon, 1996; Lyon & Moats, 1993; Mercer et al., 1985). Further compounding the issue is the fact that the determination of a severe discrepancy can be a direct result of the test battery chosen, and not the student's performance (Salvia & Ysseldyke, 1998).

The consequence of these factors is the imprecise or incorrect use of the LD label, which results in overidentification and misclassification of students, and, in general, many students are poorly served (Brackett & McPherson, 1996; Doris, 1993; Reynolds, 1981). By extension, because the secondary schools are one of the primary tributaries for LD assessments at the postsecondary level, the lack of clear definitions and practice has left colleges and universities, and in particular, LD service providers, constantly confronting ambiguity with the LD documentation they inherit (Siegel, 1999).

What Is Assessment, Testing, and Diagnosis?

In the postsecondary arena, the terms *assessment*, *testing*, and *diagnosis* are sometimes used interchangeably. Programs may advertise the existence of "diagnostic services." Students may be referred by faculty in order to undergo "testing."

The imprecision in terminology may be the result of a perspective described by Anderson (1993) in which assessment of students with learning disabilities has traditionally been "viewed as a single evaluation in which students perform a set of formal tasks or tests, the results of which are used to make decisions about instructional strategies or program selection" (p. 103).

However, *assessment* is the process of accumulating a variety of data in order to make decisions about an individual. Testing is one portion of this process. In *testing*, a set of specific questions is administered to a person to derive a score (Salvia & Ysseldyke, 1998) that should then become one piece of the larger assessment process. Salvia and Ysseldyke explain the breadth necessary in a comprehensive assessment, stating that "when we assess students, we consider the way they perform a variety of tasks in a variety of settings or contexts, the meaning of their performance in terms of the total functioning of each individual, and the likely explanations for these performances" (p. 6). They also stress consideration of the specific demands of the test or task, stating that "high-quality assessment procedures take into consideration the fact that anyone's performance on any task is influenced by the demands of the task itself, by the history and characteristics the individual brings to the task, and by the factors inherent in the context in which the assessment is carried out" (p. 6).

As testing is part of the assessment process, so too, is diagnosis. Johnson (1987) describes *diagnosis* as "a complex process that involves a search for patterns . . . ongoing hypothesis testing and decision making to determine the nature and scope of the problem" (p. 9). The learning process is examined as completely as possible, with a recognition that problems in learning in one area may affect or "mask" performance in another (Johnson, 1987). Thus, assessment is more than the administration of a single test or a battery of tests; it is rather an ongoing process that involves obtaining an educational history, performing formal and informal testing, observing behavior, analyzing error patterns, and making a differential diagnosis that rules out other possible conditions or factors that impede learning.

Although the exact components of a comprehensive evaluation will vary, the following section presents a broad overview of components that should be included in a typical report. Service providers may find this information helpful in situations where more data are needed on a student and an evaluator or school must be contacted. Because the specific components will vary from report to report, and because some school districts may abbreviate the ideal report format (McLoughlin & Lewis, 1994), service providers should use professional judgment in determining which missing information is critical and which can be overlooked.

Current Practice: The Ideal

Identifying Information

A report should begin with basic information including the student's name, age, gender, and grade (if relevant). Furthermore, the date of present testing is critical, as is the student's age at the time of testing.

Reason for Referral

The specific reason that the student was referred for assessment should be clearly stated at the outset of the report. This statement should then serve as the rationale for test selection and specification of the nature of the problem so that appropriate interventions can be planned (Bradley-Johnson & Johnson, 1998).

Background Information

A critical portion of any assessment process should start with an examination of the student's educational or case history. This information can be gleaned from structured or semi-structured interviews or through the completion of questionnaires or rating scales by the student or other significant individuals. Such data can shed light on factors that may have led to current problems, the student's perceptions of academic difficulties, specific areas of strengths and weaknesses, strategies used (or not used) to compensate for difficulties, and other factors that might be interfering with learning (Behrens-Blake & Bryant, 1996; Bradley-Johnson & Johnson, 1998; Johnson, 1987). If available, past school records and previous testing should also be reviewed with relevant information incorporated into the present results. The manual of the *Wechsler Individual Achievement Test* (WIAT; Psychological Corporation, 1992) stresses the importance of background information, warning test users of their "special responsibility for accuracy and thoroughness, which are accomplished to a great extent by placing WIAT results in a context encompassing the total history of the child as opposed to using the test results in isolation" (p. 4). Such an analysis of the larger context is especially important in the assessment of college-age students and adults, as the individual is likely to have a long history of difficulties in learning, some of which may be attributable to causes other than a learning disability.

Formal and Informal Measures

Due to the subtleties of learning disabilities and the heterogeneity of the adult population, the assessment of these problems requires careful selection of a range of measures (Johnson, 1987). Selection of instruments must include consideration of the nature of the referral question and the demands of the task. Most tests require multiple skills, both implicit and explicit, some of which are beyond what the tests claim to measure (Johnson, 1987; Sternberg, 1999). For example, in taking a verbal analogies test, a student must demonstrate explicit knowledge of vocabulary and reasoning, but must also demonstrate implicit knowledge of how to take a test, including working under time constraints and selecting an appropriate answer (Sternberg, 1999). Likewise, the Digit Span test on the *Wechsler Adult Intelligence Scale–Third Edition* (WAIS–III; Wechsler, 1997a) requires auditory perception, memory, and articulation (Johnson, 1987).

There is no standard battery for use in evaluating learning disabilities (Sattler, 1992). Likewise, no single test can properly assess the complexity of the learning process and the central nervous system (Hartlage & Golden, 1990). Therefore, a combination of measures, generally called a test battery, are employed in order to provide a comprehensive evaluation that answers the referral question and measures general cognitive functioning or intelligence, academic achievement, and information processing. This last component is especially important in the evaluation of college students and adults, as numerous researchers have pointed to differences and deficits in the processing skills of students with learning disabilities (Meltzer, 1994; Schuerholz et al., 1995; Swanson, 1987, 1991a, b; Wong, 1991) and have posited that information-processing variables may, in fact, be better predictors of academic success than achievement scores (Schuerholz et al., 1995). Examination of information-processing abilities permits analysis of the efficiency, flexibility, and accuracy by which students solve problems and learn new information (Meltzer, 1994), including the manner by which they access, organize, and coordinate multiple mental activities. Because there are multiple mental components involved in all learning tasks, LD is "not simply a deficiency in a certain cognitive area, but rather represents poor coordination of several mental components and/or cognitive areas involved in information processing" (Swanson, 1987, p. 7). Thus, information-processing data are of value to the college-age and adult learner in that they provide insight into strengths and weaknesses in such areas as memory, sequencing, visual processing, auditory processing, verbal processing, and fluid reasoning (Anderson, 1993; Behrens-Blake & Bryant, 1996; Gregg & Hoy, 1990). For the college service provider, this information is also extremely useful in validating requests for accommodations related to tasks that depend on processing skills, such as taking notes or learning a foreign language.

In addition to these formal measures, informal measures such as writing samples and curriculum-based work samples can provide rich data. The structure of a formal measure may not tease out certain types of difficulties that may instead be exposed through informal measures. Furthermore, examination of how the student tries to write and learn, including exploring, questioning, hypothesizing, organizing, and remembering information, may reveal problems more directly related to limited learning opportunities or poor learning habits than to a learning disability (Johnson, 1987).

Observation of Behaviors

The evaluator's informal observations of the student during testing can provide valuable data. Especially useful are comments related to behaviors and strategies that either help or interfere with the student's performance. In addition, conditions such as fatigue or extreme anxiety may impede performance and result in scores that are not true indicators of the student's ability. Without such clinical observations, the inferences made from test scores will be invalid.

Results and Differential Diagnosis

A well-written evaluation report should weave standardized test results, informal measures, past history, and current observations into a clear and concise picture of a student's strengths and weaknesses. Statements about strengths are often overlooked by evaluators, but they are critical to planning effective interventions (Bradley-Johnson & Johnson, 1998) and presenting a more balanced view of the student. Consumers should also be alert for the use of a rule-out rubric in making a differential diagnosis of learning disabilities. Because problems in learning can be the result of a number of factors, it is critical for the evaluator to examine and rule out such factors as insufficient or inadequate prior educational experiences, depression, medical conditions, poor motivation, English as a second language, the impact of cultural factors, and physical or sensory problems with vision, hearing, or speech.

Recommendations

The report should conclude with a set of data driven recommendations that suggest teaching approaches, learning strategies, auxiliary aids and, if necessary, reasonable accommodations to help the student succeed. Siegel (1999) stresses that a comprehensive assessment should "make clear which accommodations are being recommended and how they relate to the learning disability in question" (p. 314). Service providers should understand that postsecondary institutions are not bound to recommendations made by private evaluators or previous teachers and should consider such recommendations only as hypotheses (Bradley-Johnson & Johnson, 1998). Private evaluators and secondary teachers may not have a realistic understanding of the requirements of postsecondary institutions in general, or of the specific requirements and technical standards of a particular institution or program of study. It is the service provider who must bring this perspective and understanding to the decision-making process.

Current Practice: The Reality

Shortcomings in LD Assessments

Documentation of LD serves as the bedrock for decisions related to determining eligibility for protection from discrimination and for services on the basis of disability, determining individualized academic adjustments and auxiliary aids, and promoting student self-advocacy (McGuire et al., 1996). For that reason, comprehensive and quality assessment reports are an essential starting point for all programming decisions. However, recent research (Madaus & Madaus, 1998; McGuire et al., 1996; McGuire, Fresco, Foley, Madaus, & Owen, 1999) has indicated that information submitted to postsecondary institutions varies widely in quality and scope and often falls far short of its intended purpose in program planning. Likewise, in describing a review of documentation involved in a recent high-profile legal case, Siegel (1999) observes, "These evaluations resembled a patchwork quilt in which none of the squares were the same. Each evaluation used different tests, different terminology, and different labels for LD" (p. 314). The following discussion will highlight the differences between the "ideal" report and the reality of current practice.

Identifying Information

Madaus and Madaus (1998) provide examples of reports in which the student's name, age, or gender did not match other available records, and in which the date of testing was incorrectly reported. While these are often typographical errors, they blur important information about the student and raise immediate questions about the quality of the report and thoughtfulness of its preparation.

Background Information

Despite the importance of background information in relation to current performance, McGuire et al. (1996) found that only 58% of submitted reports contained this crucial information. Results of a follow-up analysis by McGuire et al. (1999) indicated that this figure has remained consistent.

Tests Used

One of the major concerns put forth by McGuire et al. (1996) relates to problems with instrumentation, in terms of both a set of comprehensive measures and the technical adequacy of the instruments employed. Nearly half (45%) of the reports provided results of only an aptitude test, generally the *Wechsler Adult Intelligence Scale–Revised* (WAIS–R; Wechsler, 1981) or the *Wechsler Intelligence Scale for Children–Revised* (WISC–R; Wechsler, 1974). When more than one test was given, the typical battery consisted of the WAIS–R and the *Bender Visual Motor Gestalt Test* (Koppitz, 1963, 1975). These findings illustrate that despite calls from professional organizations and researchers, and even statements in federal legislation, there is a disconnect between practice and theory. For example, the Learning Disabilities Association of America (LDA) stated clearly in its position paper on eligibility that "the diagnosis of the Specific Learning Disabilities Condition requires clinical judgement derived from multiple data" (1990, p. 2a). The National Joint Committee on Learning Disabilities called for comprehensive assessments that include "a variety of activities and procedures intended to ensure a comprehensive set of data for determining an individual's status and needs" (1994b, p. 52). Federal guidelines in the Individuals with Disabilities Education Act state: "No single procedure is used as the sole criterion for determining whether the child is a child with a disability" (34 CFR § 300.532[f]). In the McGuire et al. (1996) study, only 49% of the reports included a discussion of academic achievement, and the authors note that these discussions were usually very generic in nature, providing "vague and incomplete information" that offered "limited insight into a college-bound student's strengths, weaknesses, and level of functioning" (p. 302). Likewise, Siegel (1999) reports that in some cases, no achievement tests were reported, and instead, an LD was inferred from a discrepancy between the verbal and performance scales of an IQ test.

One area of optimism relates to the discussion of information processing. McGuire et al. (1996) found that only 19.1% of the reports submitted in the late 1980s and early 1990s discussed the area of information processing. However, a follow-up analysis of reports from the mid-1990s found that over 70% of the reports contained such a discussion, and that rate was steadily rising over the 3-year period that was studied (McGuire et al., 1999).

Another major weakness found by McGuire et al. (1996) relates to the instrumentation used by evaluators. Researchers have noted a dearth of standardized, reliable instruments suitable for use with an adult population (Anderson, 1993; Lyon & Moats, 1993). In fact, Lyon and Moats state that "fewer than one third of the psychometric tools used in the diagnosis of learning disabilities meet criteria for adequate norms, reliability, and validity" (pp. 5–6). Likewise,

McGuire et al. (1996) report the use of tests such as the *Bender Visual Motor Gestalt Test* (38.1% of the reports noting its use) and the *Wide Range Achievement Test–Revised* (WRAT–R; Jastak & Wilkinson, 1984; 11.5% reporting use). Both of these instruments have serious flaws that limit their utility in decision making (described in a subsequent section of this chapter). Results of a follow-up analysis (McGuire et al., 1999) indicate a rapid growth in the use of the *Woodcock–Johnson Psycho-Educational Battery–Revised* (WJ–R; Woodcock & Johnson, 1989; from .06% reporting use in 1996 to 50.5% reporting use in 1999), but also an increase in the use of the WRAT–R (from 11.5% in 1996 to 21.4% in 1999). Madaus and Madaus (1998) cite cases of examiners using instruments that are improperly normed for a college-age or adult student, and extrapolating scores from established norms. As discussed later in this chapter, such scores are not valid, and, furthermore, they violate the American Psychological Association's standards for test use (APA, 1985).

Results and Differential Diagnosis

Madaus and Madaus (1998) cite examples of reports in which the stated test results did not match the accompanying computer-scored results, and in which two different sets of scores were presented on the same student. The common use of only computer-generated scoring sheets without analysis is also problematic. As Sattler describes, computerized reports "usually do not take into account either the examinee's unique clinical history or the complete assessment results" (1992, p. 790) and thus cannot replace clinical judgment. Madaus and Madaus describe the case of a computer-scored report that indicated that a student diagnosed with LD had "no significant strengths and no significant weaknesses." Clearly, this contradicts the fundamental nature of a learning disability. In terms of a specific diagnosis, Gregg and Hoy (1990) report that of 110 cases of students requesting LD services at the University of Georgia, only 15 possessed reports containing a specific diagnostic statement of a learning disability. Nearly a decade later, McGuire et al. (1999) found that only 55% of submitted reports contained a specific diagnosis of LD. While the authors accurately state that this might be due to the multidisciplinary team approach used by public schools, they also note the importance of a specific diagnosis that rules out alternative explanations for learning problems such as "learning differences" or "a unique learning style," which in and of themselves are not sufficient for the diagnosis of LD.

Recommendations

Despite the importance of a solid set of data-based recommendations that tie together assessment results and a specific intervention plan, McGuire et al.

(1996) found that nearly half (48%) of the reports offered no recommendations. Siegel (1999) notes that in the reports she reviewed, "there was, at best, a tenuous connection between the evaluator's 'findings' and the recommendations for accommodations" (p. 314). This observation was verified by McGuire et al. (1999), who discovered that only 15% of submitted reports had recommendations that were specifically linked to test results. Of course, the reverse side of this coin is that frequently recommendations are made with little understanding or unrealistic expectations of the demands and requirements of a postsecondary setting, or they are read as "thou shalt" edicts that parents and students may expect to receive. Thus, the omission of recommendations can actually be fortuitous for service providers!

Summary: The Need for Comprehensive Assessments

On a humanistic level, the importance of a comprehensive assessment with the use of tentative hypothesis testing was illustrated by Stracher (1996), who presented the compelling case of a college-level student who was diagnosed in high school as having borderline mental retardation. Analysis of past records and discussions with the student revealed that in fact the student had a language-based learning disability and thus was improperly diagnosed and served. Although the student was successfully moving through her college program, she expressed feelings of inadequacy and incompetence to college personnel. As this case poignantly illustrates, psychoeducational evaluations have the potential to influence readers' perceptions of students, and to ultimately affect educational outcomes (Bradley-Johnson & Johnson, 1998). Unfortunately, the state of the art in educational testing appears to lag far behind these lofty yet necessary ideals.

On an institutional level, the importance of a multifaceted assessment process with comprehensive evaluations was stressed by Gregg and Hoy (1990), who note that unless there is a data-based link between the assessment report and a request for accommodations or modifications, academic standards risk being devalued. Certainly, this link has been the center of a maelstrom of recent legal challenges related to the balance between academic standards and individualized accommodations. The next section discusses a variety of methods that postsecondary institutions can adopt in an attempt to establish a fulcrum for this sometimes delicate balance.

LD Assessment: The Role of Postsecondary Institutions

Should Postsecondary Programs Offer LD Assessments?

Although there is no specific reference to documentation in the regulations of Section 504, it is reasonable for an institution to request that a "student provide supporting diagnostic test results and professional prescriptions for auxiliary aids" (U.S. Department of Education, 1991, p. 3). In cases where the student does not have a prior diagnosis, or in cases where the student's prior documentation has become outdated, assessment may obviously be required before services can be initiated. However, unlike the regulations of the Individuals with Disabilities Education Act (P.L. 105-17, 1997), which govern secondary schools, the regulations of Section 504 do not require postsecondary institutions to offer diagnostic testing services to students with suspected LD.

Perhaps as a direct result of the lack of specificity in the law, there is variation in the provision of assessment services at the postsecondary level. Depending on institutional mission, program objectives, and available resources, assessment services can range from no services at all to a panel that reviews submitted diagnostic information, to full assessment services (Anderson, 1993; Behrens-Blake & Bryant, 1996). Within those programs that offer assessment services, the rationale can also vary widely. Some programs feel an ethical obligation to assist students with suspected but undiagnosed LD, for example, to alleviate the potentially prohibitive cost of obtaining an external evaluation ("Offering Campus LD Testing," 1996; Madaus, 1998). Assessments may also be provided for the purpose of evaluating a previously undiagnosed LD, confirming or updating existing testing, or to determine strengths and weaknesses in specific content areas, such as mathematics or foreign language.

Other programs have instituted assessment services to ensure that students who receive services do so on the basis of clear and consistent eligibility criteria (Behrens-Blake & Bryant, 1996). For example, the University of Georgia requires that all students requesting specific modifications or substitutions on the basis of a learning disability undergo a complete psychoeducational battery. Gregg and Hoy (1990) state that such an approach provided consistency in determining which students were eligible for services, maintained academic integrity in making program decisions, and minimized the impact of those private evaluators "who 'sell' the label learning disabled and some who identify everyone as learning disabled due to their lack of knowledge of learning disabilities" (p. 33). The authors argue that the real financial cost to postsecondary institutions comes in providing ongoing services to students who are not entitled to them, and that the proactive approach of filtering out students who are misdiagnosed was cost effective in the long term.

Conversely, some institutions cite the high costs, extensive professional staff time, lack of a trained staff diagnostician, and potentially low rate of diagnosis among students undergoing assessment as reasons for not providing assessment services (Madaus, 1998). Other institutions fear a conflict of interest in basing decisions about eligibility and accommodations on the results of an in-house evaluation, or in cases where the in-house evaluation does not match the results of a private evaluation ("Offering Campus LD Testing," 1996). Thus, for a variety of reasons, diagnostic and assessment services were rated by a sample of over 500 service providers to be a nonessential component of a disability support program (Shaw & Dukes, in press).

Reasons for Assessment

There are generally three main types of students who refer themselves or are referred to disability service offices with questions related to assessment. Behrens-Blake and Bryant (1996) describe the first group as nontraditional students who attended public schools prior to the enactment of P.L. 94-142. Some of these students may have graduated from high school after great difficulty, while others may have dropped out of school and entered the workforce. The student may have an undiagnosed LD and be returning to school for a degree or advanced training. A second group are traditional-age students who are encountering difficulty in the postsecondary arena. These students may have been high achievers in high school, seeking an explanation or validation of their newly experienced learning problems (Behrens-Blake & Bryant, 1996; Stewart, 1994). A third group of students (which may include members of the first two groups) are those seeking assistance in completing courses or obtaining a course substitution in a specific content area, such as math or foreign language. Regardless of group affiliation, referral patterns are likely to be heaviest just after exam periods, particularly fall mid-terms and winter finals (Madaus, 1998; Stewart, 1994).

Before proceeding to an LD assessment or recommending to the student that an assessment be pursued, service providers can attempt to obtain preliminary information related to the difficulties experienced by the student. This may be facilitated through the use of a structured questionnaire such as the one found in Appendix 6.1 (on the CD-ROM), with follow-up questioning to probe significant responses. Such a process may help illuminate which problems may be due to cognitive processing difficulties, such as memory, and which may be due to other factors such as an insufficient amount of time spent on academics, unrealistic expectations, poor study habits, anxiety, medical conditions such as depression and illnesses, or substance abuse. Through this process, the service provider can also ascertain if there are existing campus resources that may be of value, such as academic advisors, learning centers, assistive technology labs, tutoring centers, or counseling services. If so, the student could be referred to or be encouraged to access and exhaust those resources, revisiting the issue of an LD assessment only if serious learning problems persist.

In addition, a referral for assessment should be held until the student is clear regarding the ultimate purpose of the testing. Confusion may exist in the minds of some students regarding the purpose of obtaining an LD assessment.

They may expect, based upon experiences with the medical model, that "*the* LD test" will provide information and a solution to problems in learning. It is critical to explain to students that while the primary purposes of an LD assessment are to establish a profile of learning strengths and needs and to determine the impact of a possible disability upon that profile, a "cure" for these difficulties is not possible. The student should clearly understand the purpose and potential outcome of the assessment, such as to determine eligibility for an intensive LD support program or for reasonable academic adjustments such as extended test time or a course substitution. Another plausible rationale is the case of a student who is planning to pursue an advanced degree and may be in need of accommodations on tests such as the GRE, LSAT, or other certifying exams. Unless such a rationale can be clearly established, the student should be encouraged to think carefully about the time, energy, and cost that will be incurred in the evaluation process. Finally, service providers should stress to students that the mere fact that the assessment process is pursued does not guarantee either the diagnosis of a learning disability or the provision of services or accommodations.

Facilitating the Assessment Process

Since the cost of an LD evaluation can vary from several hundred to several thousand dollars, service providers can provide invaluable assistance to students who must become consumers of a complex product. Many students do not know what tests to ask for when working with an evaluator and, hence, may be "sitting ducks in the marketplace" ("Offering Campus LD Testings," 1996). It may be beneficial to provide the student with a list of the specific documentation required by the institution, or with a copy of the AHEAD *Guidelines for Documentation of a Learning Disability in Adolescents and Adults* (Association on Higher Education and Disability, 1997b). The student can then bring this information to the evaluator to ensure that he or she receives testing that is both comprehensive and valuable.

In addition, service providers can help by compiling a list of local or within-state evaluators, which can be provided to students as a starting point for locating a qualified evaluator. A notation on the form indicating that the LD office does not endorse any particular evaluator and that the student is not limited to the names on the form may help avoid confusion and any perceived conflicts of interest. Because cost is often ultimately the mitigating factor in whether a student is evaluated, service providers may inquire if the evaluator is willing to work on a sliding scale for students. The student should also be instructed to check whether health insurance will cover all or a portion of the costs. In any case, it is important to note to the student that cost is not a guarantee of quality, and that he or she must be a vigilant consumer.

Instituting an Assessment Service

Before instituting an assessment service, LD service providers should carefully consider the implications in terms of staff time and resources. For example, Trueba (1991) describes the efforts of the Disability Resource Center at the University of Wisconsin–Madison to provide a comprehensive psychoeducational assessment to students. Within 4 years, over 200 students had been evaluated, but only 17% were identified as having a learning disability. Because the assessment battery required up to 15 hours per student to complete, and because of the low hit rate, the Center reduced the availability of assessment services.

In order to conserve resources, the University of Connecticut instituted an intensive screening component prior to its assessment process (Madaus, 1998). This was intended to be a first-sort to determine those students who should pursue additional diagnostic testing and to "tease out" those students whose difficulties might be related to other factors, including motivation, illness, or poor study skills. In one academic year, 12 students were screened out, while 13 were referred for additional testing. Of the 13, 8 (32%) were subsequently diagnosed as having a learning disability. This first-sort allowed the program to reallocate resources that would have been required to fully evaluate all 25 students (Madaus, 1998). The screening battery and procedures undergo continual evaluation and refinement, including the addition and removal of particular instruments, and the establishment of a maximum grade-point-average cutoff of 2.0 to ensure that those students who are experiencing the most serious academic difficulties receive higher priority.

Other Options

Service providers should be creative in developing solutions on their campuses. Are there existing resources such as psychology, school psychology, or teacher-training programs with whom the disability office could collaborate? Are there interested or knowledgeable faculty available on campus or at a nearby college? Finally, service providers should check with local professional organizations and advocacy groups, who may be aware of existing and helpful resources.

Reading Psychoeducational Assessments

It is estimated that students in American public schools take more than 250 million standardized tests per year, including tests to measure achievement, to measure the performance of schools, and to make educational decisions about individuals (Salvia & Ysseldyke, 1998). Testing has become so pervasive (APA,

1985) that it is an accepted and expected component of the lives of students (and their families) and has led some to contend that it is a "major life function."

Given the impact and importance of testing, two critical points must be made. First, test results should be considered to be a "snapshot" of a student at one point in time, and to be only a portion of the student's entire profile. Morris (1994) notes that one of the primary purposes of evaluation instruments is to translate and "compress" concepts and skills such as reading into smaller, quantifiable values that allow comparisons and manipulations. In order to do this, the test can measure only a sample of a domain of interest, which in turn is directly related to how the domain is defined and operationalized. Thus, it is essential to remember that each student has a variety of skills and interests that cannot be captured by the narrow domains measured by standardized tests.

Second, test scores, in and of themselves, are meaningless. Rather, it is the way in which the scores are used to make inferences and decisions about individuals that is of importance. Decisions and judgments that are made without a clear understanding of the content of the measurement instrument are invalid at best and have long-range harmful consequences at worst.

For example, what decisions might be made about a student's reading skills and reasonable accommodations if an evaluation report purports to measure a student's reading comprehension via the WRAT–3 (Wilkinson, 1993)? Would the decision be different if the report contained scores from a WJ–R (Woodcock & Johnson, 1989) or a WIAT (Psychological Corporation, 1992). As Siegel (1999) indicates, there are seemingly infinite ways to assess reading, spelling, and arithmetic, and the choice of test(s) can directly determine whether a disability will be identified. Thus, knowledge of a subtest name is not enough; knowledge of the specific demands of the subtest and how the subtest measures a given skill is critical.

Furthermore, it is not unusual for a diagnosis to be made on the basis of one discrepant subtest score. Is this acceptable practice, and can individual subtests be evaluated in isolation, or should composite scores be used? For example, the WAIS–III consists of 14 subtests that seem to measure a range of skills and abilities. Can these skills be isolated and used in decision making, or should the test be considered as a whole? Should the various subtests of the WIAT or the WJ–R be used in isolation, or should the broad or composite scores be employed?

In the American Psychological Association's *Standards for Educational and Psychological Testing*, the term *test user* is defined not only as the person who administers the test, but also as a person who "requires the test results for some decision making purpose" (APA, 1985, p. 1). The *Standards* further state, "The ultimate responsibility for appropriate test use lies with the test user. The user should become knowledgeable about the test and its appropriate uses and also communicate this information, as appropriate, to others" (p. 41). This is indeed a heavy responsibility, and it is hoped that the following sections can help point postsecondary LD service providers toward answers to these everyday challenges.

Psychometric Qualities

Norms

Most tests of educational achievement, aptitude, and information processing are *norm referenced*. In other words, the performance of the student is compared to the average performance of a specific group of people on whom the test was standardized, or normed. This provides insight into the student's relative standing within the specified group. Of course, it becomes critical to understand the norm group for whom the test developers intended the instrument to be used. These norms can be national or local, but they must be representative of the person being tested (APA, 1985; Hammill, Brown, & Bryant, 1992). Factors to be considered when examining norm groups include age, gender, race and ethnicity, levels of education, occupation, family income, native language, geographic dispersion, and disability status (Hammill et al., 1992; McLoughlin & Lewis, 1994; Sattler, 1992). The importance of this information is stressed by McLoughlin and Lewis, who state, "Many of the psychological variables of interest in educational assessment differ by gender and across age groups and grade levels. Thus, it is incorrect to administer a test to a student beyond the age or grade of the norms and then use the closest age or grade group to estimate the results" (p. 54). Therefore, such instruments as the WIAT (upper age limit of 19.11) or the Bender Gestalt test (upper age limit of 11.11) do not provide accurate norm-based information for interpretation of scores if the tests are administered to adult students. The recency of the norm development must also be considered and should reflect current standards of student performance (McLoughlin & Lewis, 1994).

Raw Scores

The total number of items answered correctly on a subtest constitutes the student's *raw score*. Two terms used in this computation are the *basal* and the *ceiling*. A *basal* is either the recommended starting point or the point at which the examinee answers either a consecutive number or a set number of items correctly. It therefore can be assumed that he or she has mastered the content of the items to that point, resulting in credit for all items below that point and eliminating the need to administer those items. Conversely, a *ceiling* is either the last item on the subtest or the point at which the examinee incorrectly answers either a consecutive number or a set number of items, and it can be assumed that he or she would be unable to answer subsequent items. Testing is discontinued and the student receives no credit for subsequent items. Because most norm-referenced instruments attempt to measure a broad range of skills across a broad range of ages, use of the basal and ceiling allows the examiner to target the appropriate range of items to be administered, thereby reducing time required for testing and examinee frustration. A raw score is computed based on the number of correct responses. The raw score has no independent value but is converted into a derived score in conjunction with the student's age or grade level.

Derived Scores

Derived, or normative scores, are established when the test developer initially converts the raw scores of the members of the normative sample into scores that are normally distributed. When these scores are established, a specific raw score obtained by a student can then be converted in order to facilitate comparisons to the norm group. Three types of derived scores that are of interest are equivalency scores, percentile scores, and standard scores.

Equivalency Scores. The two most commonly used scores of equivalency are age-equivalent and grade-equivalent scores. These scores are determined by computing the average raw score obtained by members of various strata of the norm sample. For example, if the average performance of 18-year-old examinees on a test of achievement is 25 items correct, and a student answers 25 items correctly, he or she has an age equivalent score of 18.0 (age equivalencies are expressed in age and months). Similarly, if the mean score of 12th graders on the test is 25 items correct, a student who answers 25 items correctly receives a grade equivalency score of 12.0 (grade equivalencies are expressed in grade and tenths of grade level; Salvia & Ysseldyke, 1998; Sattler, 1992). Scores that do not fall exactly on an obtained mean value are estimated through the use of interpolation and extrapolation; thus a student may obtain an age-equivalency score of 19.5 even though students of that age were not included in the norming sample (Salvia & Ysseldyke, 1998).

Age- and grade-equivalency scores provide information that is seemingly simple to report and easy for students, parents, and practitioners to understand. It seems to make intuitive sense that a student who earns a grade equivalency of 11.1 is functioning at the beginning 11th-grade level (Hishinuma & Tadaki, 1997). Perhaps because of this simplicity, grade-equivalency scores are often incorrectly interpreted as if they had the same psychometric qualities as standard scores (Reynolds, 1981). However, age- and grade-equivalency scores should be used with great caution for a variety of reasons including these:

• Because equivalency scores are based on an ordinal measurement scale, the distance between points on the scale may not be equal. Therefore, the scores may not represent equal units, and the difference between 2nd- and 3rd-grade scores may not be equal to the difference between 11th- and 12th-grade scores (Sattler, 1992). Furthermore, because different academic skills are learned at different rates, a deficient grade-equivalency score in one content area (e.g., reading) may indicate a more severe problem than the same grade-equivalency score in a different content area (e.g., science; Reynolds, 1981). Finally, because equivalency scores are on an ordinal measurement scale, they cannot be mathematically manipulated, limiting comparisons to other scores for research and program evaluation purposes.

• Equivalency scores can be dramatically affected by minor raw-score changes (e.g., 2 or 3 points), and thus exaggerate small differences in performance (Reynolds, 1981).

• Equivalency scores can vary from test to test and even within subtests on the same battery, making accurate comparisons between and across instruments complicated (Sattler, 1992). At the postsecondary level, it is difficult to accurately compare the performance, skills, and weaknesses of a student on several tests if only equivalency scores are reported. These scores may be truly equivalent in name only.

• Using equivalency scores in the determination of learning disabilities can be extremely problematic, especially if the criterion for diagnosis is an achievement score a given number of years or grade levels lower than an aptitude score or grade placement. In a review of age- and grade-equivalency scores on the WIAT, Hishinuma and Tadaki (1997) found that derived standard scores were substantially higher than derived age- and grade-equivalency scores on three subtests, especially at the lower and upper age levels of the norm group. The authors hypothesize that the items included on the subtests may not have been suitable for students at the extreme ends of the age level, resulting in a need to adjust the standardization data. When this occurred, the equivalency scores departed from the corresponding standard scores. As a result, if those scores are used in the determination of a learning disability, there is likely to be improper diagnoses (generally overdiagnosis). Although the authors limited their conclusions to the use of the WIAT, they note that "with all standardized tests, grade and age equivalents should be interpreted with caution" (p. 223).

Likewise, Reynolds (1981) demonstrated that on four major reading tests, students in lower grades who score two grade levels below placement actually have more serious reading problems as indicated by below-average standard scores. In contrast, the standard scores of students in upper grades who score two grade levels below placement do not depart significantly from the mean. In summary, although both groups of students score two grade levels below placement, they have very different standard scores, and therefore, varying severity of problems in reading.

Thus, despite appearing easy to interpret, equivalency scores have many limitations and should be used with great caution, if at all (Hammill et al., 1992; NJCLD, 1987; Reynolds, 1981; Salvia & Ysseldyke, 1998). In order to make more accurate comparisons and decisions, postsecondary service providers should be certain to stipulate in documentation guidelines that standard scores (described below) must be presented for all results.

Percentile Scores. Through the use of percentile scores, the student's standing relative to the standardization sample can be determined (Sattler, 1992). A percentile score is not the percentage of items that the student answered correctly but rather the percentage of people or scores occurring at or below the student's score. Two advantages to percentile scores are that they are relatively straightforward and easy to explain and interpret, and they provide accurate information about a student's relative standing in respect to the norm group (Salvia & Ysseldyke, 1998; Sattler, 1992). In addition, if percentile scores are the only type of scores presented, a consumer of the report can use the properties of the normal curve distribution to estimate standard scores from a percentile score (if the norm sample is normally distributed, as is the case with most popular instruments). A disadvantage is that, like equivalency scores, percentile scores cannot be mathematically manipulated, limiting the value of those scores in making comparisons to other instruments, and for research and program evaluation.

Standard Scores. Like percentile scores, standard scores provide information about an examinee's relative standing within the norm group. However, standard scores provide additional information by describing the distance of the examinee's score from the mean of the norm group in terms of standard deviation units (Fraenkel & Wallen, 1996). Through the use of statistics related to the mean and the standard deviation of the norm group, standard scores on a given instrument are transformed to a measurement scale that has a predetermined mean and standard deviation. Although there are a variety of standard scores (e.g., t scores, Z scores), among the most commonly used in educational assessment is the *deviation IQ* score. A deviation IQ score has a mean of 100 and a standard deviation of 15. Standard scores on instruments such as the *Wechsler*

Adult Intelligence Scale–Third Edition, the *Wechsler Individual Achievement Test*, and the *Woodcock–Johnson Psycho-Educational Battery–Revised* are based on deviation IQ scores, allowing comparisons to be made within and across instruments. In addition, performance on subtests of the WAIS–III is reported as a *scaled score*. Such scores have a mean of 10 and a standard deviation of 3.

As a way to facilitate the interpretation of standard scores and percentile ranks, Figure 6.1 (Madaus, 1999) offers a method of plotting a student's scores to establish a visual profile of strengths and weaknesses. Although there is no single way to use the chart, it might be helpful to group subtests that measure similar domains (e.g., reading, written language) across the top horizontal axis. Note that the vertical axis has both scaled scores and standard scores, with the corresponding percentile rank. Figure 6.2 (McGuire, 1992c) offers a different technique for plotting student strengths and weaknesses. The horizontal boxes offer spaces for the various domains commonly discussed in LD documentation, while the vertical axis provides ranges of scaled scores, standard scores, and percentile scores, as well as the various descriptive ranges. It should be noted that these scores and ranges could be deleted in cases where results are being explained in terms of intraindividual strengths and weaknesses, rather than in comparison to a national sample. While such visual displays of strengths and weaknesses can assist a novice service provider in interpreting test scores and in beginning to make accommodation determinations, they can also be of great value when explaining test results to students, a key to increasing student self-awareness.

Although standard scores are more difficult to explain to students and parents, they offer many advantages. First, because they place scores on a common metric, equal weight can be given to various test components and subtests. Standard scores thus offer a more accurate and precise measure of a student's performance (Reynolds, 1981). Second, because standard scores are measured on an equal-interval scale, the individual strengths and weaknesses of a student can be more accurately analyzed. This attribute also makes standard scores useful for research and program evaluation purposes, as these scores can be mathematically manipulated. Third, if the distribution of scores on the instrument is normal, standard scores can be converted easily into percentile ranks, providing useful information to students and families (Reynolds, 1981; Salvia & Ysseldyke, 1998). The value of standard scores in making inferences about a student's performance was underscored by the fact the AHEAD *Guidelines for Documentation of a Learning Disability in Adolescents and Adults* (1997b) specifically noted, "Standard scores and/or percentiles should be provided for all normed measures. Grade equivalents are not useful unless standard scores and/or percentiles are also included" (p. 3). These guidelines provide service providers with solid ground to stand upon when a submitted report contains equivalency scores alone and an evaluator questions the need for additional data.

Student Name: _____   Date of Testing: _____

Directions: Place the various subtests in the top row. Then plot that score in the appropriate box. Connecting the dots will provide a graphic illustration of strengths and weaknesses.

Scaled Score	Standard Score	Percentile
19	145	>99
18		
17		
16	130	98
15		
14		
13	115	84
12		
11		
10	100	50
9		
8		
7	85	16
6		
5		
4	70	2
3		
2		
1	55	<1

Figure 6.1. Analysis of student profile. *Note.* From *The University of Connecticut Program for College Students with Learning Disabilities: Administrative Procedures,* by J. W. Madaus, 1999, unpublished material, University of Connecticut, Postsecondary Education Disability Unit, Storrs. Copyright 1999 by J. W. Madaus. Reprinted with permission.

Student: _____ Date of Testing: _____

Directions: Place scores in appropriate grid. Be sure to state test and subtest names and corresponding scores.

	Reading	Written Language	Math	Information Processing
Strengths 4 percentile; SS = 115, 13				
Average Skills 50 percentile; SS = 100, 10				
Weaknesses 16 percentile; SS = 85, 7				

Figure 6.2. Analysis of student strengths and weaknesses. *Note.* From *The University of Connecticut Program for College Students with Learning Disabilities: Administrative Procedures,* by J. M. McGuire, 1992, unpublished material, University of Connecticut, Storrs. Copyright 1992 by J. M. McGuire. Reprinted with permission.

Validity

As noted previously, test scores in and of themselves are meaningless. Rather, the inferences and decisions that are made about individuals from the scores are what is of critical importance. The extent to which these inferences are appropriate, meaningful, and useful is a measure of a test's validity. Test validation then is "the process of accumulating evidence to support such inferences" and "always refers to the degree to which that evidence supports the inferences that are made from the scores" (APA, 1985, p. 9). Because of the consequences of the inferences made from test scores, the *Standards for Educational and Psychological Testing* (APA, 1985) clearly state that "validity is the most important consideration in test evaluation" (p. 9).

It is the inferences from test scores, not the test instrument itself, that are validated since a test is valid only for a specific purpose. Test developers attempt to validate the most common inferences that can be made for typical students in the norm sample (Salvia & Ysseldyke, 1998), and they should be expected to provide consumers with information related to the validity of the inferences made. A variety of methods and statistical procedures can be used to provide evidence of validity, and this evidence should be accumulated over time (Hammill et al., 1992). Test users should be able to find evidence to support the validity of the instrument in the test manual and in objective reviews of test instruments.

There are three main types of validity: construct validity, content validity, and criterion-related validity. It is important to note that although the three major types of validity can be broken out for descriptive purposes, they are in fact not discrete categories (APA, 1985; Hammill et al., 1992). *Construct validity* provides evidence that a test measures a psychological or theoretical human trait of interest (APA, 1985; Salvia & Ysseldyke, 1998). Support for construct validity can come from a variety of sources, including intercorrelations among items; relationships with other, established measures that purport to measure the same construct, and a lack of relationship with tests that measure different constructs; and sufficient evidence of other content and criterion-related validity (APA, 1985).

Content validity refers to the extent to which the items on the test describe the intended defined universe or domain of content, or in other words, the content, traits, abilities, or skills that the instrument purports to measure (APA, 1985; Salvia & Ysseldyke, 1998; Sattler, 1992). Critical questions include how the test developer defines the universe of content, whether the items are appropriate and do indeed adequately span the domain of interest in a representative manner (Borg & Gall, 1989; Sattler, 1992). This is an especially important consideration in the assessment of adults, as many instruments lack technical adequacy in the upper norm limits. Content validity is generally measured by expert professional judgment and statistical analysis during the test development stage. Borg and Gall note that determining content validity is a systematic set of operations that should not be confused with face validity, which is "a subjective judgement that the test appears to cover relevant content" (p. 250) made by the test user.

Criterion-related validity relates to the extent to which a person's performance on another related (criterion) measure, can be predicted from scores on the measure being validated (APA, 1985). Two main types of criterion-related evidence are predictive validity and concurrent validity. *Predictive validity* is a measure of how well the instrument predicts performance on a criterion at a later date (e.g., the use of the SAT to predict freshman year GPA). *Concurrent validity* is also a measure of performance on a criterion variable but is determined by relating the scores to another criterion measure administered at the same time (e.g., an anxiety inventory is administered to a group of college students in the LD program and then compared to a specialist's ratings of student self-esteem collected at the same time) (APA, 1985; Fraenkel & Wallen, 1996).

While ensuring validity of test results is primarily the responsibility of the test developer and the test administrator, Salvia and Ysseldyke (1998) point out that "all questions of validity are local, asking whether the testing process leads to correct inferences about a specific person in a specific situation for a specific purpose" (p. 166). Thus, individuals who review test results must also consider questions of validity, and not rely solely on the test developers' claims, or on the title of the test or subtest. Factors that must be considered include the content of the items, the manner in which the student is expected to receive information and respond, and the background and instructional history of the student. For example, does the student have a sensory disability that would affect or prohibit responses to test items? Would an item with a picture of a snowman be a valid measure of the knowledge of an immigrant from the Caribbean? Likewise, would a test that measures the decoding and word-attack skills of a student who received reading instruction via a strict whole-language approach be appropriate? Consider the plausible case of such a student who obtains a significantly lower score in reading decoding and is subsequently recommended for reading assistance and a foreign-language substitution on the basis of a severe language-related deficit. The disability service provider must then question the validity of such an inference, pointing directly to the importance of obtaining a detailed history of the student's educational experiences in combination with test results.

Reliability

Reliability "refers to the degree to which test scores are free from errors of measurement," according to the *Standards for Educational and Psychological Testing* (APA, 1985, p. 19), or to "the level of internal consistency or stability of the measuring device over time" (Borg & Gall, 1989, p. 257). For a variety of reasons, a person's score will differ from one test administration to the next, though it should not fluctuate wildly. These differences are called errors of measurement (APA, 1985) and are inherent in all obtained scores. Tests that are said to be reliable contain less error, and thus provide more consistent scores, allowing more confidence to be placed in the obtained results (Hammill et al., 1992). Conversely, tests with lower reliability contain more measurement error and offer less consistency and generalizability.

Although there are several types of reliability, the most important for consumers of test instruments are internal consistency reliability, alternative form reliability, and test-retest reliability. *Internal consistency reliability*, or split-half reliability, refers to the consistency among items on the instrument to measure the impact of error in item sampling. Typically, the instrument is administered and is then split in half. Both halves are then analyzed to determine if the items are related and in fact measure the same construct (Hammill et al., 1992). Since some tests offer alternate or parallel forms, *alternate form reliability* is a measure of the extent to which these forms can be used interchangeably. All forms of the measure are administered to the same group and results are correlated (McLoughlin & Lewis, 1994). *Test-retest reliability* is a measure of a test's stability. The instrument is administered to a sample, and then readministered to the same sample after a determined period of time. The scores on the two administrations are correlated to determine test stability (Borg & Gall, 1989).

The reliability of an instrument is generally stated as a correlation coefficient, ranging from .00 (no reliability) to 1.00 (perfect reliability, unobtainable in practice) (Borg & Gall, 1989). There is some debate in the literature related to minimally acceptable levels of reliability for decision making. Sattler (1992), McLoughlin and Lewis (1994), and Hammill et al. (1992) set .80 as a minimally accepted level for reliability. Salvia and Ysseldyke (1998) propose .60 as a minimum for group tests, .80 as a minimum for tests used for individual screening purposes, and .90 as a minimum for tests that will be used to make diagnostic and placement decisions about individuals. Hammill et al. (1992) also state that .90 is the preferred level.

In determining if a test has minimal levels of reliability, Borg and Gall (1989) state that "if no specific information on reliability is provided in the test manual, you may safely assume that the reliability of the test is low" (p. 258). It is also important to note that reliability is directly affected by the length of the test and the homogeneity of the items (Sattler, 1992). This can be an important factor when considering tests that offer a variety of subtest scores in addition to a total score. Subtests can range in reliability from some that are as reliable as the total instrument, to others that are too low to be used with confidence. Therefore, great caution must be taken when examining scores from subtests on instruments, especially if specific reliability measures are not available (Borg & Gall, 1989). Because of this reduced reliability, the amount of error variance in the score rises, increasing the potential that a particular score is more the result of random chance, and less an accurate measure of performance. Some researchers (Bray, Kehle, & Hintze, 1998) have argued that the practice of profile or subtest analysis on the Wechsler scales is ineffectual, not empirically based, and perhaps unethical in high-stakes decision making and therefore should be discontinued. Postsecondary disability service providers should be cognizant of these debates as they review documentation and consider the technical challenges inherent in being an informed consumer.

Standard Error of Measurement

A person's obtained score contains two components, a true score (which is never obtained) and an error score. The *standard error of measurement* (SEM) is a mathematical formula used to determine the distribution of error around the true score, thus allowing a range of scores, or a confidence interval, to be determined in which the individual's true score probably lies (Borg & Gall, 1989). The SEM is inversely related to reliability: the more reliable the test, the lower the SEM. The importance of this statistic was captured by Borg and Gall, who state, "Standard error of measurement helps us to understand that the scores we obtain on educational tests are only estimates and can be considerably different from the individual's 'true score.' With this in mind, we can avoid the blind faith in test scores that many educators seem to have" (p. 263).

Major Approaches to Diagnosis

With an understanding of psychometrics and the meaning of test scores, attention can be focused on the next step in the assessment process, diagnosis. It is not uncommon to read a psychoeducational assessment and be left wondering how the evaluator arrived at a specific diagnosis or particular conclusion. Knowledge of the more common approaches to diagnosis can assist LD service providers to be better able to understand the route to diagnosis and, of great importance, to be able to critically examine this route and identify potential flaws in the diagnostic process.

The Discrepancy Model

Although there are multiple methods of assessing LD, most are based on the assumption of depressed achievement (Hawks, 1996). While some researchers propose abandoning the use of intelligence tests and examining achievement scores alone (Siegel, 1999; Stanovich, 1999), the most prevalent method is the use of a discrepancy model, by which the student's level of achievement is compared to his or her level of ability, typically represented by an intelligence score. There are a variety of discrepancy models available, all of which have engendered some controversy and debate.

Deviation from Age or Grade Level

One method of assessing the existence of an LD is to examine a discrepancy between actual grade placement and grade equivalency scores received on a measure of achievement. Although this practice seems to make logical sense and to provide consistency and objectivity, it is laden with inadequacies and limitations (Reynolds, 1981; Sattler, 1992), many of which relate to problems with the use of grade-equivalency scores in general, which were described previously in this chapter. Reynolds demonstrates that more than 30% of a random sample of high school–age students would be classified as having a reading disability through the use of this method.

A variation of this practice is the use of a grade-equivalency score in comparison to an aptitude score, or intelligence quotient (Connell, 1991). However, as noted previously, because these scores are on different measurement scales, comparisons and mathematical manipulations are rendered meaningless.

Discrepancy Between Standard Scores

The discrepancy-between-standard-scores method, also called the simple-difference method (Psychological Corporation, 1992), compares and contrasts a student's measured intellectual ability with his or her measured ability in one or more areas of academic achievement. Depending on the criteria used, a difference of one to two standard deviations (i.e., 15–30 standard score points) between the two measures would be considered significant. It is important to note that the scores used for calculating the discrepancy must be based on the same standard score distribution (Sattler, 1992).

While this approach is simple to explain and use, it is flawed. It attempts to predict academic performance from measured ability (Connecticut State Department of Education, 1999) and assumes that ability and achievement have a perfect correlation ($r = +1.0$ or $r = -1.0$). However, because this is not the case, the method does not account for a statistical phenomenon called regression to the mean (Reynolds, 1985; Sattler, 1992). Thus, a student who scores particularly high or low on one measure (e.g., ability) is likely to score closer to the population mean on the other measure (e.g., achievement). As a result, this method is likely to overidentify students with above-average intelligence scores who may be underachieving, and underidentify students with below-average intelligence scores (Brackett & McPherson, 1996).

Other problems with this approach include the fact that a learning disability may depress a student's performance on an aptitude test, resulting in nondiscrepant scores (Connecticut State Department of Education, 1999; NJCLD, 1987). In addition, unless the derived difference is tested for significance, error in measurement is ignored (Psychological Corporation, 1992). As a result, measured differences may be a function of error and chance, rather than differences of practical significance. Thus, although the practice of the simple-discrepancy approach often results in diagnosis by "statistical mistake," it persists and remains what Stanovich (1999) terms "one of the most pernicious practices in our field" (p. 355).

An additional simple-discrepancy method that should be noted is the use of a discrepancy between the verbal and performance portion of an intelligence test (Sattler, 1992). This practice was also discussed by Siegel (1999) and is unacceptable for several reasons. First, it violates federal regulations as set forth in the IDEA and the standards promulgated by the American Psychological Association (1985), both of which clearly state that diagnosis should not be made on the basis of a single measure or test. Second, reliance solely on a measure of intelligence to determine whether a learning disability exists might discriminate against minority students or non-English speakers. Third, a verbal-performance split of 11 points is statistically significant on the *Wechsler Intelligence Scale for Children–Third Edition* (WISC–III), yet it occurs in 40.5 % of the population (Wechsler, 1991, cited in Bray et al., 1998). Just as making a diagnosis solely on this discrepancy is unacceptable, it is also unacceptable to infer a diagnosis from the verbal-performance split and then verify the finding with other measures.

Mathematical Equation Models

A number of assessment models use mathematical formulae to increase the precision of measurement and to account for various psychometric issues. The *regression model* adjusts for regression to the mean and attempts to account for the standard error of measurement that is inherent in all tests and measures. The equation requires knowledge of the correlation between the two measures being used (found in the test manual). The *reliability model* accounts for the reliability of the instruments used in an attempt to control for instrument error (Schuerholz et al., 1995). A third method, the *predicted-achievement method*, accounts for both regression to the mean and errors in measurement used (Psychological Corporation, 1992; Schuerholz et al., 1995).

Discussion of Discrepancy Models

As is evident, there are a variety of approaches to the discrepancy model. Advocates of these frameworks advance the statistical advantages and improved preciseness of a particular model. However, not surprisingly, researchers have found that the method used has a direct impact on the number of people diagnosed with learning disabilities (Brackett & McPherson, 1996; Connell, 1991; Reynolds, 1981; Schuerholz et al., 1995).

Discrepancy formulae have other significant limitations. First, while the various formulae have advantages to researchers, they are cumbersome to use and may be impractical in clinical and postsecondary settings (Darden & Morgan, 1996). Second, strict use of discrepancy formulae and the accompanying focus on IQ scores offer limited information about a student, including the underlying processing deficits that may lead to the existence of the discrepant skills (Darden & Morgan, 1996; Stanovich, 1999) or that may be impaired but not identified by a discrepancy model (Sattler, 1992). These information-processing skills may in fact be better predictors of academic success (Schuerholz et al., 1995). Third, because many commonly used test instruments for measuring achievement lack normative data on adults, they may inadequately portray performance in areas of achievement in adults, resulting in misdiagnosis (Darden & Morgan, 1996). Finally, in arguing against the use of intelligence tests, Siegel (1999) observes that the determination of LD can depend strictly on which IQ scale score (e.g., verbal scale, performance scale) was used in the discrepancy calculation, noting that "the difference between good and poor readers can be significant or not significant depending on which IQ score was used" (p. 312). For these reasons, Reynolds (1990) warns that "determining a severe discrepancy does not constitute the diagnosis of LD; it only establishes that the primary symptom of LD exists" (as cited in Psychological Corporation, 1992, p. 574).

Strict adherence to a formula excludes the role of clinical judgment, which should be an essential component of any evaluation. Because of the multiple problems inherent in discrepancy models, particularly when used with adult populations, some researchers (Brackett & McPherson, 1996; Hawks, 1996; Hoy et al., 1996; Sattler, 1992) have argued that skilled clinical judgment incorporating a variety of measures and data sources is an essential component of an LD diagnosis.

At the start of this decade, Gregg and Hoy (1990) warned of the potential long-term implications if postsecondary institutions allowed the discrepancy approach to serve as the sole criterion in determining eligibility for services. They forecasted that "if such a model is allowed to dominate the identification process, the chance for over-identification of the learning disabled population is increased" (p. 32). Unfortunately, because most school districts continue to rely on the discrepancy approach and continue to serve as the chief source of LD evaluations, the model likely dominates at the postsecondary level. Not surprisingly, questions, controversy, and concern about the over-identification of students with LD not only persist, but are on the rise nearly a decade later.

The Clinical Model

Under the clinical model advanced by Johnson (1987), Brackett and McPherson (1996), and Hoy et al. (1996), no diagnosis is made on the basis of a single score or discrepancy formula. Instead, this model uses a comprehensive test battery that combines a number of valid measures (Hawks, 1996) and integrates quantitative data, qualitative data (e.g., work samples, error analysis), self-reports, and background information. In addition, test-score scatter is analyzed to determine deficit patterns (Brackett & McPherson, 1996; Hoy et al., 1996). Finally, the model seeks to rule out any secondary problems (e.g., short attention span, cultural differences, insufficient instructional background) as the primary cause of the current deficit (Bracket & McPherson, 1996). Hawks (1996) describes a comprehensive diagnostic battery that is particularly appropriate for use with adults and addresses the areas of cognitive processing, academics, language, psychological adjustment, balance and coordination, and vocational skills. The breadth of the battery allows the assessor to initially obtain a broad view of the student's characteristics, and then to "zoom in" to view characteristics more specifically (Hawks, 1996, p. 151). Likewise, Johnson (1987) describes a comprehensive process that offers flexibility depending on the needs of each client, and that examines relationships among derived data to arrive at a differential diagnosis.

Such models offer many advantages, most notably the ability to measure a range of functions in an integrated approach. This allows the clinician to identify the nature and extent of the impairments caused by the learning disability (Hawks, 1996), and thus provides information not only about eligibility, but also about the specific interventions that might be useful to both the student and to the disability service provider (Darden & Morgan, 1996). Additionally, the systematic examination of information-processing functions allows discrimination between a student with a learning disability and a student who may be underprepared or of low ability (Gregg & Hoy, 1990).

However, this approach also has limitations. First, it is time and labor intensive. Second, because of the reliance on clinical judgment, the approach may not be psychometrically objective (Darden & Morgan, 1996). Furthermore, Tomlan and Mather (1996) note that because of limited training opportunities, some professionals lack the necessary diagnostic skills to use such a model. The authors warn that "although we value clinical judgement highly, without improved teacher training programs, sole reliance on clinical judgement could result in more chaos than already exists" (p. 222).

Diagnostic Models: Summary

Although most of the common models for diagnosing LD have some merit, all have shortcomings. Additionally, it is clear that there is great variation in the specific diagnostic approach used and, thus, in the reports received by postsecondary institutions. As noted previously, because school districts serve as the primary source of evaluations, the discrepancy model most likely dominates at the postsecondary level. However, depending on state and, more often, district guidelines, it may or may not be clear which model was used (e.g., a regression formula or the simple-difference model). In any case, service providers should be *extremely* critical of reports that arrive at a diagnosis on the basis of one test or even on the basis of one discrepant subtest, and remember that a discrepancy in and of itself does not signify LD. A clear and specific diagnosis should be stated, and statements that allude to learning differences, to learning difficulties, or even to specific discrepancies (without a diagnosis) are not in and of themselves diagnoses (AHEAD, 1997b; McGuire, Anderson, & Shaw, 1998). Whether service providers should choose to challenge a specific diagnosis and the resulting recommendations or to "work with" the material at hand is an institutional issue; however, in either case, being knowledgeable regarding models of diagnosis is essential for justifying decisions.

Common Assessment Instruments

While the LD field continues to grapple with the thorny issue of diagnosis, perhaps the most compelling day-to-day challenge for LD service providers is determining what to do with the data in a submitted report. Once documentation has been globally reviewed to ensure that it meets institutional guidelines as outlined in the discussion of policies in Chapters 7 and 8, more specific information is required to take the next steps. In order to examine a set of scores and make careful inferences and decisions related to a student's eligibility, need for accommodations, and strengths and weaknesses, it is critical that postsecondary LD service providers become familiar with the general content of the instruments from which the scores were derived. Understanding particular content, in conjunction with information on psychometrics and models of diagnosis, can assist service providers to be more judicious in making accommodation and programming decisions. The following section provides brief reviews of the instruments most commonly submitted in LD documentation to postsecondary institutions (McGuire et al., 1999). Interested readers are also encouraged to review such classic texts as *A Consumer's Guide to Tests in Print* (Hammill et al., 1992), Salvia and Ysseldyke's *Assessment* (1998), and Sattler's *Assessment of Children* (1992). Additionally, comprehensive reviews of specific tests can be located in *The Thirteenth Mental Measurements Yearbook* (Impara & Plake, 1998) and in such journals as the *Journal of Psychoeducational Assessment*, *Diagnostique*, *Journal of Learning Disabilities*, *Journal of Special Education*, and *School Psychology Review*.

Wechsler Adult Intelligence Scale–Third Edition

The *Wechsler Adult Intelligence Scale–Third Edition* (Wechsler, 1997a) is the latest version of the Wechsler scales of intelligence. The original version was called *Wechsler-Bellevue Intelligence Scale* (1939), and the *Wechsler Adult Intelligence Scale* was first published in 1955. The test was revised in 1981 as the WAIS–R, and again in 1997 as the WAIS–III (Sattler & Ryan, 1999). The WAIS–R became one of the most popular instruments in general use and is cited as the most frequently used measure of intellectual functioning. It is expected that the WAIS–III will continue this popularity (Kaufman & Lichtenberger, 1999).

The WAIS–III is based on the same foundation as the WAIS-R but has undergone some significant structural changes (Kaufman & Lichtenberger, 1999). While approximately 70% of the items have been retained from the WAIS–R, items that were considered biased or outdated were eliminated, and additional items were added on the lower end to help obtain a more complete score for individuals who may be functioning below average (Kaufman & Lichtenberger, 1999; Overton, 2000; Sattler & Ryan, 1999). Other notable changes include the renaming of the Digit Symbol–Coding subtest (previously called Digit Symbol) and the addition of three subtests, Matrix Reasoning, Letter-Number Sequencing, and Symbol Search. Object Assembly is now an optional subtest and has been removed from the calculation of the standard Performance Scale.

The WAIS–III contains 14 subtests, 6 of which constitute the standard Verbal Scale (Vocabulary, Similarities, Arithmetic, Digit Span, Information, and Comprehension) and 5 of which constitute the standard Performance Scale (Picture Completion, Digit Symbol–Coding, Block Design, Matrix Reasoning, and Picture Arrangement). There are three supplemental subtests, one on the Verbal Scale (Letter-Number Sequencing) and two on the Performance Scale (Letter-Number Sequencing and Symbol Search). These three supplemental subtests are used in the determination of Index Scores (Kaufman & Lichtenberger, 1999; Sattler & Ryan, 1999).

Another major change in the WAIS–III is the addition of a fourth Index Score. The four Index Scores are Verbal Comprehension, Perceptual Organization, Working Memory, and Processing Speed. The construct that each is thought to measure, as well as the subtests that constitute each index, is described below.

Index Scores

Verbal Comprehension. Verbal Comprehension is thought to be a measure of acquired verbal-related knowledge and verbal reasoning. The index comprises scores on the Vocabulary, Information, Comprehension, and Similarities sub-tests (Sattler & Ryan, 1999).

Perceptual Organization. Perceptual Organization is thought to be a measure of nonverbal reasoning, attentiveness to detail, and visual-motor integration. The index comprises scores on the Block Design, Matrix Reasoning, Picture Completion, and Picture Arrangement subtests (Sattler & Ryan, 1999).

Working Memory. The Working Memory Index relates to the memory-related ability to retain relevant information while performing manipulations or calculations. Sattler and Ryan (1999) refer to this process as a "mental scratch pad" (p. 1215). The index comprises the Arithmetic, Digit Span, and Letter-Number Sequencing subtests.

Processing Speed. This index is thought to measure quickness in processing visual information, as well as speed in psychomotor performance. The index comprises the Digit Symbol–Coding and Symbol Search subtests (Sattler & Ryan, 1999).

Verbal Subtests

Vocabulary. The student is presented with a word both orally and in print and is asked to orally explain the meaning of the word. The subtest contains 33 words in increasing difficulty, 8 of which are new items (Sattler & Ryan, 1999). This is a measure of word knowledge and may be affected by experiences, education, outside reading, and cultural opportunities (Kaufman & Lichtenberger, 1999). Additionally, the subtest correlates with a student's ability to learn and to accumulate information (Sattler, 1992).

Similarities. Pairs of words are read to the student, and he or she is asked to explain the similarity between the words in each pair. There are 19 items, 8 of which are new. The subtest may measure the student's auditory perception of simple words (Kaufman & Lichtenberger, 1999), as well as the ability to group objects and events, including the ability to organize and note relationships (Sattler, 1992). Results may also be affected by cultural opportunities, interests, flexibility, overly concrete thinking, outside reading, and memory (Kaufman & Lichtenberger, 1999; Sattler, 1992).

Arithmetic. This subtest contains 20 items that measure the student's ability to solve problems involving arithmetic operations. All responses are timed, and the student must complete all problems mentally. Six new items have been added to the 14 used in the WAIS–R (Sattler & Ryan, 1999). Seventeen of the items are presented orally, and 3 employ blocks with oral directions. Although the subtest measures numerical reasoning ability, it also requires concentration and attention. Prior education, interest, level of anxiety, ability to work under timed conditions, and the presence of an LD or attention-deficit/hyperactivity disorder (ADHD) may also affect performance (Kaufman & Lichtenberger, 1999; Sattler, 1992).

Digit Span. This subtest consists of two parts, which are scored together. In the first part, Digits Forward, the student listens to a series of digits (increasing from two to nine digits in length) and is asked to immediately repeat the series orally. In the second part, Digits Backward, the student listens to a series of digits (from two to eight digits in length) and is asked to immediately repeat the series in reverse order. This subtest measures short-term auditory memory and attention. Sequencing abilities, levels of anxiety, flexibility, and the presence of an LD or ADHD may also affect performance (Kaufman & Lichtenberger, 1999; Sattler, 1992).

Information. The student is asked questions about a broad range of events, objects, places, and historical and geographic facts. The content of the questions is based on information that the student is expected to have learned in both formal and informal educational settings (Salvia & Ysseldyke, 1998). The subtest contains 28 items, 9 of which are new. Of the new items, 2 are considered easy and 7 are more difficult (Sattler & Ryan, 1999). The subtest is designed to sample the knowledge that an average person with average opportunities should be able to accumulate through home and school experiences. Scores may provide a measure of the student's general fund of information, alertness to her environment, and social and cultural background (Sattler, 1992).

Comprehension. The student is asked questions that cover a range of situations, laws, proverbs, customs, and social mores. The subtest contains 18 items, including 6 new items, 2 of which are considered easy and 4 of which are considered more difficult (Sattler & Ryan, 1999). The subtest is designed to measure the student's knowledge of conventional standards of behavior, social judgment, and common sense. Cultural experiences, flexibility, and overly concrete thinking may also affect scores (Kaufman & Lichtenberger, 1999; Sattler, 1992).

Letter-Number Sequencing. The student is asked to sequentially order a series of numbers and letters that are presented orally in random order. This is a new supplementary subtest designed to measure attention, short-term memory, and information processing. According to the manual, it is a measure of working memory, a short-term memory storage system that is used to hold information that is being processed (Sattler & Ryan, 1999). Scores may be affected by attention, anxiety, concentration, flexibility, the presence of LD or ADHD, and levels of negativism and persistence (Kaufman & Lichtenberger, 1999).

Performance Subtests

Picture Completion. A picture missing various details is presented to the student, who has 20 seconds to name or point to the missing portion. There are now 25 instead of 20 items, 10 of which have been modified and 15 of which are new (Sattler & Ryan, 1999). The subtest is designed to measure visual discrimination and also requires concentration, reasoning, visual organization, and long-term visual memory (Sattler, 1992). Alertness to the environment, the ability to work under time pressures, and the ability to respond when uncertain may also affect performance (Kaufman & Lichtenberger, 1999).

Digit Symbol–Coding. The student is presented with a key that consists of nine boxes, each of which contains a number in the upper space and a symbol beneath it. The test box contains a number in the upper section and is empty in the lower section. In the empty box, the student must draw the symbol that was paired with the number in the key. Changes include the renaming of the subtest, the addition of one row, enlargement of the symbols, and expansion of the time limit from 90 seconds to 120 seconds (Sattler & Ryan, 1999). The subtest assesses the ability to learn an unfamiliar task and relies on speed, attention, visual scanning, cognitive flexibility, and short-term memory (Sattler, 1992). Scores may also be affected by ability to work under time constraints, anxiety, distractibility, the presence of LD or ADHD, motivation, persistence, and obsession with accuracy and detail (Kaufman & Lichtenberger, 1999).

Block Design. The student is shown a two-dimensional, red and white picture of an abstract design and must assemble an identical design using three-dimensional red and white blocks (Sattler & Ryan, 1999). The student's response is timed. The subtest now contains 14 items instead of 9. Nine of the items have been retained, and 5 new items have been added, 4 of which are easy and 1 of which is more difficult (Sattler & Ryan, 1999). The subtest is a nonverbal concept formation task and involves perceptual organization and spatial visualization. Performance may also be affected by vision, level of motor activity, and ability to work under time constraints (Kaufman & Lichtenberger, 1999; Sattler, 1992).

Matrix Reasoning. This is a new subtest that replaces Object Assembly in the computation of the Performance IQ score. The student is presented with a colored matrix that is missing a part and must determine the missing element from five choices that are presented at the bottom of the page. The subtest is untimed and is designed to measure perceptual reasoning ability. Additionally, visual perception problems, attention to detail, concentration, the ability to respond when uncertain, flexibility, and motivation may affect scores (Kaufman & Lichtenberger, 1999; Sattler & Ryan, 1999).

Picture Arrangement. The student is presented with a series of pictures in an incorrect, specified order and is asked to rearrange the pictures in proper order to produce a story. The subtest now contains 11 instead of 10 items, 5 of which have been modified and 6 of which are new (Sattler & Ryan, 1999). The subtest measures comprehension, sequencing, and identification of relationships (Salvia & Ysseldyke, 1998), as well as the ability to interpret social situations (Sattler, 1992). Scores may be affected by creativity, cultural opportunities, exposure to comic strips, and the ability to work under time constraints (Kaufman & Lichtenberger, 1999).

Symbol Search. The student is required to look at two symbols and then decide if either symbol is present in a group of five symbols. The subtest has 60 items and a time limit of 120 seconds. This is a new supplementary subtest that can replace Digit Symbol–Coding in the computation of an IQ score (Sattler & Ryan, 1999). The subtest relies on perceptual discrimination, speed and accuracy, attention and concentration, short-term memory, and cognitive flexibility (Sattler, 1992). Scores may also be affected by anxiety, motivation, persistence, obsessive concern with detail or accuracy, and the presence of LD or ADHD (Kaufman & Lichtenberger, 1999).

Object Assembly. The student is required to put jigsaw pieces together to form complete and common objects. There are five puzzles, each of which is administered. The student has varying time limits of either 120 or 180 seconds, depending on the puzzle. This subtest is optional and can be substituted for any Performance subtest for examinees 16–74 years of age. The task involves the ability to put parts together to form familiar objects and requires visual-motor coordination. Performance may be affected by rate and precision of motor activity, persistence, flexibility, experiences with puzzles, the ability to respond when uncertain, the ability to work under timed conditions, and long-term visual memory (Kaufman & Lichtenberger, 1999; Sattler, 1992).

Technical Characteristics of the WAIS–III

The WAIS–III was normed on 2,450 individuals in the United States during the early 1990s. Demographic characteristics were stratified to 1995 census data and included age, gender, race and ethnicity, educational level, and geographic region. An additional 200 African-American and Hispanic individuals were included in the sample in order to assess item bias, and individuals from five clinical samples (neurological disorders, alcohol-related disorders, neuropsychiatric disorders, psychoeducational and developmental disorders, and deaf and hearing impaired) were also included (Overton, 2000). The age range was extended 15 years to cover individuals from 16.0 to 89.11 years of age. The WAIS–III was co-normed with the *Wechsler Memory Scale–Third Edition* (WMS–III; Wechsler, 1997b), and a sample of 142 individuals aged 16 to 19 years old was linked to the *Wechsler Individual Achievement Test* (Psychological Corporation, 1992). Overall standardization procedures are considered excellent (Sattler & Ryan, 1999), and, according to Kaufman and Lichtenberger (1999), the revisions have made the WAIS–III a "much stronger instrument" (p. 164).

Reliability. The overall reliability of the WAIS–III is considered excellent, with internal consistency reliability of .93 or above for each of the three scales across all age groups in the sample (Kaufman & Lichtenberger, 1999; Sattler & Ryan, 1999). Reliability coefficients for the subtests range from .70 for Object Assembly to .93 for Vocabulary. The six standard Verbal subtests show reliabilities from .84 to .93, while the five standard Performance subtests range from .74 to .90. Standard errors of measurement in IQ points are 2.30 for the Full Scale, 2.55 for the Verbal Scale, and 3.67 for the Performance Scale. Thus, as Sattler and Ryan (1999) note, more confidence can be placed in the Full Scale score than in either the Verbal Scale score or the Performance Scale score, and more confidence can be placed in the Verbal Scale score than in the Performance Scale score.

Validity. The manual for the WAIS–III presents more evidence about studies measuring content, construct, and concurrent validity than did the manual for the WAIS–R (Kaufman & Lichtenberger, 1999). Sattler and Ryan (1999) caution that "because the WAIS–III is a newly published test, relatively little is known about its validity" (p. 1210), but they also point out that since approximately 70% of the items have been retained from the WAIS–R, it seems plausible that the adequate evidence of validity on that measure can be applied to the WAIS–III.

Derived Scores. Deviation IQ scores with a mean of 100 and standard deviation of 15 are available for the Full Scale, Verbal Scale, Performance Scale and each of the Index Scores. Standard scores for each of the subtests have a mean of 10 and a standard deviation of 3.

Summary

Because the WAIS–III is a newly published test, relatively few critical reviews have been published to date (e.g., Kaufman & Lichtenberger, 1999; Sattler & Ryan, 1999). As noted, despite numerous modifications, the WAIS–III retained nearly 70% of the items from the WAIS–R, and items that were considered biased or outdated were eliminated. Additional items were added to the lower end of the subtests. The Digit Symbol–Coding subtest has been renamed, and three subtests have been added (i.e., Matrix Reasoning, Letter-Number Sequencing, and Symbol Search). The WAIS–III also offers four Index Scores, as opposed to the three Index Scores on the WAIS–R (Verbal Comprehension, Perceptual Organization, and Freedom from Distractibility). Standardization procedures and reliability evidence are considered excellent. Evidence of validity is presented, but additional studies are required to bear out these claims. Thus, primary support for validity of the WAIS–III comes from its similarity to the WAIS–R, which is considered to have adequate validity (Overton, 2000; Sattler & Ryan, 1999).

Although scores are available for three scales, four indexes, and for each of the 14 subtests, caution must be noted in regard to the practice of profile analysis, or examining scores in isolation based on the skill or abilities that each purports to measure. First, as noted previously, the scale scores are the most reliable scores available, because they are derived from a number of subtests and, thus, more heterogeneous items. Accordingly, reliabilities for each of the subtests vary and are less than the reliability for the scale that each is a part of. Therefore, caution must be taken in making decisions about these scores in isolation, as such partitioning reduces the overall reliability and increases the overall presence of error in measurement (Bray et al., 1998; Sattler, 1992). Second, the total number of scaled-score points available may vary across subtests and age ranges. As Sattler and Ryan (1999) strongly warn, *"Applying profile analysis uniformly to all subtests would be misleading in some individual cases because the examinee cannot obtain the same number of scaled-score points on all subtests"* (p. 1220, emphasis in original). Third, despite the apparent logic in breaking down subtest scores according to content or skills measured to make predictions and design interventions, each of the subtests actually predicts the same concept, general intelligence or *g*, rather than unique processes (Bray et al., 1998; Sattler, 1992).

Finally, it is possible to derive differences in subtest and scaled scores that are statistically significant but lack practical significance because of the frequency in which they occur in the general population (Sattler & Ryan, 1999). For example, Maller and McDermott (1997) employed profile analysis techniques to the WAIS–R profiles of 194 college students diagnosed with LD, and found that nearly 94% of the sample matched the profile in the WAIS–R standardization sample. Furthermore, the authors reported that the subtest scatter profiles for the college students with LD did not explain a significant proportion of variance in performance on the SAT or ACT, and, thus, they questioned the validity of using profile analysis to determine typical profiles of students with LD.

Thus, despite the apparent logic of profile analysis of WAIS–III scores, practitioners are urged to observe caution when analyzing subtest results in an isolated fashion to make programming decisions such as the need for a note taker because of a low Digit Span score or a math course substitution on the basis of a low Arithmetic score. Detailed techniques for conducting a systematic profile analysis are outlined by Sattler (1992) and by Kaufman and Lichtenberger (1999). It is not appropriate for a diagnostic label to be applied on the basis of observed subtest scatter alone, for as Sattler (1992) strongly cautions, *"Ideas generated from profile analysis must be viewed simply as hypotheses to be checked against other information about the examinee"* (p. 166, emphasis in original).

The Woodcock–Johnson Psycho-Educational Battery–Revised

The *Woodcock–Johnson Psycho-Educational Battery–Revised* (WJ–R; Woodcock & Johnson, 1989a) is designed to be "a wide range, comprehensive set of individually administered tests for measuring cognitive abilities, scholastic aptitudes, and achievement" (Woodcock & Johnson, 1989a, p. 1). According to the manual, it is intended to a be multipurpose instrument, appropriate for diagnosis, determination of psychoeducational discrepancies, program placement, planning individual programs, program evaluation, and research (Woodcock & Johnson, 1989a). The battery comprises two major components: the *WJ–R Tests of Cognitive Ability* (WJ–R COG; Woodcock & Johnson, 1989c) and the *WJ–R Tests of Achievement* (WJ–R ACH; Woodcock & Johnson, 1989b). Each component contains a standard and a supplemental battery, and the WJ–R ACH contains equivalent forms, A and B. Originally released in 1977, the 1989 edition featured an expanded set of subtests, an expansion of the normative sample from 24 months to over 90 years of age, and the inclusion of college and university students in the normative sample. Furthermore, the WJ–R COG was grounded in the Horn-Cattell theory of information processing in response to criticisms that the original Tests of Cognitive Ability lacked a theoretical framework (Cummings, 1995).

Because of the length of the entire battery (39 subtests), examiners are encouraged to select tests based on the specific requirements of a given assessment situation (Woodcock & Johnson, 1989c). Thus, examiners might use the standard battery initially and then employ selected supplemental tests to provide a more in-depth analysis of a specific skill (Cummings, 1995).

Tests of Cognitive Ability

The WJ–R COG consists of 21 subtests. The first 7 tests listed make up the standard battery, while the supplemental battery consists of the remaining 14 subtests. The following descriptions come from materials in the WJ–R COG manual (Woodcock & Johnson, 1989c, reprinted with permission).

Memory for Names. The subject is shown a picture of a space creature and is told the creature's name. The subject is then shown a page of nine space creatures and is asked to point to the space creature just introduced, as well as to other previously named creatures. The student receives instruction for errors or nonresponses. The test is designed to measure the student's ability to learn associations between unfamiliar auditory and visual stimuli and long-term retrieval.

Memory for Sentences. The subject is asked to repeat single words, phrases, and sentences. The stimuli are presented through the use of a tape recorder. The test is designed to measure short-term memory and attention.

Visual Matching. The subject must identify and circle two identical numbers in a row of six numbers. The subtest has a 3-minute time limit and is designed to measure processing speed.

Incomplete Words. The subject hears a tape recording of words that have one or more phonemes missing and must identify the complete word. The test is designed to measure auditory processing.

Visual Closure. The student is shown a drawing or picture of an item that is distorted, has missing lines, or has a superimposed pattern and is asked to identify the item. The subject has 30 seconds to respond to each item. The test is designed to measure visual processing.

Picture Vocabulary. The student is presented with a picture and asked to identify or name the item or features of the item. The test is designed to measure comprehension-knowledge or crystallized intelligence.

Analysis-Synthesis. This is a controlled learning task in which the subject is presented with a "key" of patterns and an incomplete puzzle. The student is asked to use the information in the key to identify the missing components of the puzzle. Additionally, the subject is given feedback on his or her response. The test is designed to measure reasoning, or fluid intelligence.

Visual-Auditory Learning. The student is presented with a new visual symbol and is told a familiar word to associate with the symbol. The student must then translate a series of symbols into sentences. This is a controlled learning task, and the student receives instruction after errors or nonresponses after 5 seconds. The test is designed to simulate a learning-to-read task and to measure long-term retrieval.

Memory for Words. The student is presented with a series of unrelated words of increasing length and is asked to repeat the list in exact order. The test is designed to measure short-term memory and attention.

Cross-Out. The student is presented with a row of 20 drawings and must scan and mark the 5 drawings in the row that are the same as the first drawing in the row. There is a 3-minute time limit. The test is designed to measure visual processing speed.

Sound Blending. The student listens to a tape recording of words that are broken into parts and must state the whole word. The test is designed to measure auditory processing.

Picture Recognition. The student is presented with a set of pictures of the same variety. The pictures are presented for 5 seconds and then removed, and the student looks at a blank page for 5 seconds. He or she must then select the stimulus items from a field of distractor items. The number of both stimulus items and distractors increases in length as the test proceeds. The test is designed to measure visual processing.

Oral Vocabulary. The student is read a stimulus word. In Part A, Synonyms, he or she must state a word that is similar in meaning, and in Part B, Antonyms, he or she must state a word that is opposite in meaning. The test is designed to measure comprehension-knowledge or crystallized intelligence.

Concept Formation. This is a controlled learning task in which the subject is presented with a visual stimulus set and must state the rule(s) that governs the pattern presented. The test is designed to measure reasoning or fluid intelligence.

Delayed Recall—Memory for Names. The subject is asked to recall the names of the space creatures presented in Test 1, Memories for Names, after a lapse of 1 to 8 days. The student is not told that this subsequent testing will occur. The test is designed to measure long-term retrieval.

Delayed Recall—Visual Auditory Learning. The subject is asked to recall the symbols presented in Test 8, Visual-Auditory Learning, after a lapse of 1 to 8 days. The student is not told that this subsequent testing will occur. The test is designed to measure long-term retrieval.

Numbers Reversed. The student listens to a series of numbers of increasing length from an audiotape and must repeat the numbers in opposite order. The test is designed to measure short-term memory and attention.

Sound Patterns. The student listens to a series of pairs of complex sound patterns from an audiotape. The student must state whether the pairs are the same or different. The test is designed to be a measure of auditory processing.

Spatial Relations. The student views a geometric shape and must select from a series of shapes the components that make up the whole shape. The test is designed to be a mixed measure of fluid intelligence and visual processing.

Listening Comprehension. The student listens to a short sentence or passage on an audiotape and must provide a single word that is missing from the end of the passage. The test is designed to measure comprehension-knowledge or crystallized intelligence.

Verbal Analogies. The student is read a phrase that indicates analogies between words. The student must state a single word to complete the phrase. The test is designed to measure reasoning or fluid intelligence and comprehension-knowledge or crystallized intelligence.

Cluster Scores. Scores are available for each of the 21 subtests, as well as for several clusters. The Broad Cognitive Ability Score is based on the scores from either the seven tests of the standard battery or the standard battery and tests 8–14 from the supplemental battery. Additionally, Cognitive Factor Cluster scores can be derived for each of the seven areas of intellectual ability measured. The seven factor clusters and the subtests that describe them are: *Long-Term Retrieval* (Memory for Names, Visual-Auditory Learning, Delayed Recall— Memory for Names, Delayed Recall—Visual-Auditory Learning); *Short-Term Memory* (Memory for Sentences, Memory for Words, Numbers Reversed); *Processing Speed* (Visual Matching, Cross-Out); *Auditory Processing* (Incomplete

Words, Sound Blending, Sound Patterns); *Visual Processing* (Visual Closure, Picture Recognition, Spatial Relations); *Comprehension-Knowledge* (Picture Vocabulary, Oral Vocabulary, Listening Comprehension, Verbal Analogies); and *Fluid Reasoning* (Analysis-Synthesis, Concept Formation, Verbal Analogies).

In addition to the seven Cognitive Factor Clusters, four Scholastic Aptitude Clusters can be determined. These clusters are based on an examinee's expected or predicted levels of achievement and are recommended by the test authors as the most appropriate scores to use when determining an aptitude/achievement discrepancy (Woodcock & Johnson, 1989c). The four Scholastic Aptitude Clusters and the subtests that they comprise are as follows: *Reading Aptitude* (Memory for Sentences, Visual Matching, Sound Blending, Oral Vocabulary); *Mathematics Aptitude* (Visual Matching, Analysis-Synthesis, Oral Vocabulary, Concept Formation); *Written Language Aptitude* (Visual Matching, Visual-Auditory Learning, Sound Blending, Oral Vocabulary); and *Knowledge Aptitude* (Memory for Sentences, Visual Closure, Sound Blending, Concept Formation). Finally, two Oral Language Clusters are available that are intended to be broad measures of verbal ability (Woodcock & Johnson, 1989c).

Tests of Achievement

The WJ–R ACH comprises 14 subtests. The standard battery consists of the first 9 tests listed, while the supplemental battery consists of the remaining 5 tests. The following descriptions come from materials in the WJ–R ACH manual (Woodcock & Johnson, 1989b, reprinted with permission).

Letter-Word Identification. The subject must identify both letters in isolation and complete words. Knowledge of word meaning is not assessed.

Passage Comprehension. The subject is asked to read a short passage and then identify a missing key word through a modified cloze procedure. The subtest measures a variety of comprehension and vocabulary skills.

Calculation. The subject is given a pencil and a set of mathematical problems that range in difficulty from basic mathematical calculations to examples of geometry, trigonometry, logarithms, and calculus. The subject is not required to decide what operation to conduct or what data to include.

Applied Problems. The subject must analyze and solve practical mathematical word problems. The subject must determine what information is relevant and what mathematical operation to employ.

Dictation. This test is administered in the form of a traditional spelling test and measures the subject's knowledge of letter forms, spelling, punctuation, capitalization, and word usage.

Writing Samples. The subject must respond in writing to a series of statements and questions. Responses are scored relative to the difficulty of the item and the comprehensiveness of the student's answer. Responses are generally single sentences, and the student is penalized for errors in grammar and word use only if they are considered "severe" and fundamentally alter the meaning or construction of the sentence.

Science. This subtest measures the student's knowledge of biological and physical sciences. The subject responds to the first eight items by pointing and responds orally to the remaining items, which are read by the examiner.

Social Studies. This subtest measures the student's knowledge of history, geography, government, and economics. The subject responds to the first six items by pointing and responds orally to the remaining items, which are read by the examiner.

Humanities. This subtest measures the student's knowledge of art, music, and literature. The subject responds to the first five items by pointing and responds orally to the remaining items, which are read by the examiner.

Word Attack. The student must apply phonetic and structural analysis skills to pronounce nonsense and low-frequency words from the English language.

Reading Vocabulary. The student is asked to read a word and supply either a one-word synonym or an antonym. The student is not penalized for mispronouncing the stimulus word or for supplying an answer that differs in tense or number from the correct answer.

Quantitative Concepts. The student replies to orally presented questions that measure knowledge of mathematical concepts and vocabulary. The student is not required to perform any calculations or to determine which mathematical operations to employ.

Proofing. The student must read a typewritten passage, identify an error in punctuation, capitalization, word usage, or spelling and indicate orally how to correct the error.

Writing Fluency. The student is presented with a stimulus picture and three words and must write a simple descriptive sentence that incorporates the words. There is a 7-minute time limit.

Cluster Scores. While scores can be derived for each subtest, the subtests can also be combined into the following five Achievement Clusters: *Broad Reading* (Letter-Word Identification, Passage Comprehension); *Broad Mathematics* (Calculation, Applied Problems); *Broad Written Language* (Dictation, Writing Samples); *Broad Knowledge* (Science, Social Studies, Humanities); and *Skills* (Letter-Word Identification, Applied Problems, Dictation). If the supplemental tests are administered, six additional cluster scores can be derived, including: Reading Skills, Reading Comprehension, Basic Mathematics Skills, Mathematics Reasoning, Basic Writing Skills, and Written Expression (Woodcock & Johnson, 1989b).

Technical Characteristics of the WJ–R

Derived Scores. Derived scores can be calculated by either age or grade for each of the subtests and for each of the cluster scores, and include W scores, standard scores (mean = 100; *SD* = 15), percentile ranks, age and grade equivalencies, and a Relative Mastery Index (RMI). The RMI compares the performance of the student to the average student in a given age or grade level. It is expressed as a fraction, with a denominator of 90 (which indicates the percentage of mastery of average students, 90%), while the numerator indicates the percentage of mastery attained by the student being tested (McLoughlin & Lewis, 1994; Woodcock & Johnson, 1989b). In all, more than 80 scores can be calculated (Costenbader & Perry, 1990), and the test developers warned test users to be selective about which scores are used and to give "careful consideration to the potential value of all interpretation options" (Woodcock & Johnson, 1989b).

Three types of discrepancies can be determined, including Aptitude/Achievement discrepancies, Intra-Cognitive discrepancies, and Intra-Achievement discrepancies. The test manual cautions users to become familiar with the assumptions and "unresolved issues" related to discrepancy information in the field of LD (Woodcock & Johnson, 1989b, p. 7).

Reliability. Internal consistency reliability coefficients for the subtests range from .756 (Writing Fluency) to the low .90s, with most subtests falling in the .80 range. Each of the cluster scores obtained reliability coefficients in the mid-.90s. Although the overall reliability of the instrument is viewed favorably by test reviewers (Costenbader & Perry, 1990; Cummings, 1995; Lee & Flory

Stefany, 1995), it is recommended that the broad cluster scores be used when making decisions about individual students (McLoughlin & Lewis, 1994; Salvia & Ysseldyke, 1998).

Validity. Evidence of validity is considered to be generally adequate (Salvia & Ysseldyke, 1998). However, Costenbader and Perry (1990) questioned the content validity of the Writing Fluency and Handwriting subtests, especially when used with special populations, and the validity of the Broad Knowledge Cluster when used with culturally diverse students.

Norms. Norming procedures are considered excellent (Costenbader & Perry, 1990; Lee & Flory Stefany, 1995). The WJ–R was normed on 6,359 subjects and was stratified to reflect 1980 census data. Of special interest to postsecondary disability service providers is the inclusion of 916 college and university students (77.72% public, 22.31% private, 62.10% 4-year, 37.89% 2-year) and 1,493 adult nonschool individuals. Students with learning disabilities were also included in the norming sample.

Summary

The WJ–R is considered to be a comprehensive assessment of both achievement and cognitive ability (Costenbader & Perry, 1990; Cummings, 1995; Lee & Flory Stefany, 1995; McLoughlin & Lewis, 1994; Salvia & Ysseldyke, 1998). Specific strengths of the instrument include its general psychometric qualities and its applicability to individuals from 24 months to over 90 years of age. Cummings (1995) notes that a strength of the WJ–R is that unlike many other measures of achievement, broad domains such as reading are measured through the use of more than one subtest, and that supplemental measures are available if an examiner wishes to obtain a more in-depth perspective of a particular skill. However, reviewers (Costenbader & Perry, 1990; McLoughlin & Lewis, 1994) caution that because there are few items per subtest at each grade or age level, results from the WJ–R should not be used in determining individual instructional programming.

The Woodcock–Johnson III

Like its predecessor, the WJ–R, the *Woodcock–Johnson III* (WJ III) (Woodcock, McGrew, & Mather, 2001a, 2001b) consists of two batteries, the *WJ III Tests of Cognitive Abilities* (WJ III COG) and the *WJ III Tests of Achievement* (WJ III ACH). The stated purpose of the WJ III is to provide "a wide age-range, comprehensive system for measuring general intellectual ability (g), specific cognitive abilities, oral language, and academic achievement" (McGrew & Woodcock, 2001, p.1). The two batteries can be used individually in either a standard or extended format, or they may be used together in a variety of interpretive fashions (McGrew & Woodcock, 2001).

The WJ III has undergone extensive renorming, and several new subtests, clusters, and interpretative procedures have been added. For example, the WJ III includes an expanded normative sample based on over 8,800 subjects aged 2 years to over 90 years from over 100 geographically diverse communities in the United States (Mather & Woodcock, 2001a, 2001b). The appendixes of the Examiner's Manual for both the WJ III ACH and the WJ III COG also identify several Canadian school systems that were used in the standardization of the instrument. The sample includes a college/university cohort of 1,165 undergraduate and graduate students and an adult cohort of 1,843 individuals (McGrew & Woodcock, 2001). Additionally, the WJ III COG and the WJ III ACH are now conormed, which allows direct comparisons among and within a subject's scores that have a degree of accuracy not possible when comparing scores from separately normed tests (Schrank, McGrew, & Woodcock, 2001).

Tests of Achievement

The WJ III ACH consists of 22 tests organized into a Standard Battery (Tests 1 through 12) and an Extended Battery (Tests 13 through 22). The WJ III ACH includes seven new subtests, including measures of reading speed (Reading Fluency), numerical facility (Math Fluency), listening ability (Story Recall, Story Recall-Delayed, Understanding Directions), and phonetic coding (Spelling of Sounds, Sound Awareness). As noted previously, the oral language subtests from the WJ–R COG have been moved to the WJ III ACH.

As a result of these revisions, the subtests can be combined into a variety of interpretive combinations or clusters. For example, the tests in the Standard Battery can be combined to form 10 cluster scores, including Broad Reading, Oral Language-Standard, Broad Math, Math Calculation Skills, Broad Written Language, Written Expression, and Total Achievement. When the tests in the Extended Battery are used, 9 additional clusters can be derived (Mather & Woodcock, 2001a). Of the total clusters available, 8 are new, including Oral Language-Standard, Oral Language-Extended, Listening Comprehension, Oral Expression, Phoneme/Grapheme Knowledge, Academic Applications, and Total Achievement. Each broad achievement cluster consists of tests that measure basic skills, fluency, and application in a particular area. Mather and Woodcock (2001a) note that cluster scores should be the primary basis for score interpretation, stating that "cluster interpretation results in higher validity because more than one component of a broad ability comprises the score that serves as the basis for interpretation" (p. 11). They also point out that an examiner seldom needs to administer all of the tests or complete all of the interpretative options for a single person.

Technical Characteristics

In additional to the wide range of interpretive clusters available, the WJ III also provides two sets of discrepancy information, ability/achievement discrepancies, and intra-ability discrepancies. The discrepancy norms allow examiners to evaluate the significance of a discrepancy in the population by inspecting either the percentile rank of the discrepancy or the difference between the achievement score and the predicted achievement score in standard error of measurement units. The new *WJ III Compuscore and Profiles Program* (Schrank & Woodcock, 2001) calculates all derived scores and discrepancies and reports them in a table of scores. Hand scoring is no longer permitted. In addition, a summary narrative report, age/grade profiles, and standard score/percentile rank profiles can be generated. The relative mastery index (RMI) from the WJ–R has been renamed the relative proficiency index (RPI) (Mather & Woodcock, 2001b). The WJ III ACH is available in two forms (Form A and Form B) that reflect the same content.

Because the individual subtests are combined to form clusters, each of which has a reliability that exceeds .90 (Salvia & Ysseldyke, 2001), the reliability of the WJ III appears adequate for making individual programming decisions. Salvia and Ysseldyke (2001) state that both the norms and the validity of the WJ III are adequate. Given the recent publication date of the WJ III, limited reviews of the technical characteristics of the instrument are currently available.

Wechsler Individual Achievement Test

The *Wechsler Individual Achievement Test* (Psychological Corporation, 1992) is an individually administered battery designed for use with students in grades K–12 and aged 5 years, 0 months, to 19 years, 11 months. It was co-normed with the Wechsler scales of intelligence, including the *Wechsler Preschool and Primary Scale of Intelligence–Revised* (WPPSI–R; Wechsler, 1989), the *Wechsler Intelligence Scale for Children–Third Edition* (WISC–III; Wechsler, 1991), and the *Wechsler Adult Intelligence Scale–Revised* (WAIS–R; Wechsler, 1981). The subtests of the WIAT were designed to measure the areas covered in the definition of learning disabilities in the Education of All Handicapped Children Act (Public Law 94-142), namely oral expression, listening comprehension, written

expression, basic reading skills, reading comprehension, mathematics calculation, and mathematics reasoning. Furthermore, according to the manual, the
test was designed to "match many of the curriculum elements found in school
instructional programs" (Psychological Corporation, 1992, p. 2) and to be used
"in school, clinic, and residential treatment settings to make recommendations
for the placement, classification, diagnosis, and treatment of children" (p. 4).
To this end, the manual notes that "one of the major uses of the WIAT is to
compare a child's general ability level with his or her level of achievement"
(p. 185), one of the common methods of diagnosing learning disabilities in students, which was discussed earlier in the chapter.

Subtest Descriptions

The seven areas noted above plus the spelling subtest make up the eight subtests
of the total composite battery. Subtests can be combined to form four composite
scores: Reading, Mathematics, Language, and Writing. Furthermore, the Basic
Reading, Mathematics Reasoning, and Spelling subtests can be used as a Screening Composite. The following descriptions of the eight subtests come from the
WIAT Manual (Psychological Corporation, 1992, reprinted with permission).

Basic Reading. The student is presented with a series of pictures and printed
words and is required to point to responses (for early items) or read the response
aloud from a group of words. The student is given about 1 minute to respond to
each item.

Mathematics Reasoning. A question related to mathematics reasoning is read to
the student (the text also appears in the student's Stimulus Booklet), and,
depending on the item, the student is required to respond orally, point to a
response, or write his or her response. The student is given about 1 minute to
respond to each item.

Spelling. Dictated words are read to the student, who must spell the word in the
Stimulus Booklet. The student is given approximately 10 seconds to respond to
each item.

Reading Comprehension. The student must read a passage, listen to a question,
and respond orally to the question. The student has 1 minute to read each passage and 15 seconds to respond to the question.

Numerical Operations. The student must solve computation problems that involve a variety of operations and simple algebraic equations. The student must

write the response in the Stimulus Booklet. The problems are presented in sets, and the student has either 5 minutes or 7 minutes to complete the set.

Listening Comprehension. The student is presented with a stimulus picture, and a passage related to the picture is read orally to the student. The student must respond orally to one or more items related to the passage. The student is allowed 15 seconds to respond to each item.

Oral Expression. Initially, the student is presented with a picture illustrating a word, and then is provided orally with the definition of the word. The student must use both the picture and the definition to respond to a question with an appropriate word. In subsequent items, the student is presented with a picture and asked to describe a scene, give directions on a map, or explain steps in a process.

Written Expression. The student is provided with a topic that is presented as a prompt both orally and in writing. The student must write about the topic for 15 minutes. The response is scored according to both an analytic method (e.g., ideas and development, organization, vocabulary, sentence structure, grammar and usage, capitalization and punctuation) and a holistic method (e.g., viewing the response as a whole).

Technical Characteristics of the WIAT

Derived scores for the WIAT include standard scores (mean = 100; $SD = 15$), percentile ranks, age and grade equivalencies, normal curve equivalencies, and stanines. Each score can be reported both by age and by grade (Psychological Corporation, 1992). Two types of discrepancy formulas, Simple Difference and Predicted-Achievement, are provided to calculate discrepancy in performance on the eight WIAT subtests with the Full Scale IQ derived from the appropriate Wechsler intelligence scale. The manual states that while each WIAT subtest can be examined for deviation from ability, the use of composite scores offers "a slightly higher level of reliability" (p. 169). However, the manual recommends that the total composite score not be used in computing an ability-achievement discrepancy. Additionally, the manual urges caution in the interpretation of scores for students in the upper range of the norm group, due to a minimum of advanced items in the subtests. This is particularly true of the Spelling, Basic Reading, and Numerical Operations subtests, where the manual warns against the ceiling effect of the subtests and recommends "supplemental diagnostic testing" (p. 169) for students in this range of the norm group.

The WIAT was normed on 4,252 children in grades K–12 and was stratified to reflect 1988 census data. Approximately 6% of the sample were identified as

having a learning disability, speech–language impairment, emotional disturbance, or physical disability. The sample linking the WIAT and the Wechsler
intelligence scales included 1,284 students, although the sample for ages 17–19
was of marginal size (Ferrara, 1995). Evidence of validity is considered generally
positive (Cohen, 1993; Ferrara, 1995; Salvia & Ysseldyke, 1998), while evidence of reliability is adequate, with age-based subtest coefficients ranging from
.81 (Written Expression) to .92 (Basic Reading).

Summary

The WIAT is generally considered to be a good measure of academic achievement (Ackerman, 1995; Cohen, 1993; Salvia & Ysseldyke, 1998). However,
some reviewers have urged caution in using the WIAT as the sole method for
the diagnosis of learning disabilities, one of the major purposes of the instrument
(Cohen, 1993; Ferrara, 1995). While the manual notes a study of expected
ability-achievement score discrepancies for a sample of students with learning
disabilities, the sample was small ($n = 48$), with only 24% females. Although
the study indicated that 77.1% of the sample of students with LD exhibited significant discrepancies, approximately one out of four individuals (23.8%) in the
general standardization sample also exhibited significant discrepancies (Cohen,
1993; Psychological Corporation, 1992). An additional concern for postsecondary personnel is the upper norm age range of 19 years, 11 months, which
limits the use of the WIAT with most postsecondary populations (Flanagan,
1997). The WIAT is currently being revised (notably with greatly expanded age
norms, including postsecondary specific strata) and the WIAT–2 is expected to
be available in 2001 (Psychological Corporation, personal communication,
September 8, 1999).

The Wide Range Achievement Test–3

The *Wide Range Achievement Test–3* (WRAT–3) is an individually administered
achievement test designed to "measure the codes which are needed to learn the
basic skills of reading, spelling and arithmetic" (Wilkinson, 1993, p. 10). The
manual states that when used in conjunction with a measure of general intelligence, the WRAT–3 can be "a valuable tool in the determination of learning
ability or learning disability" (p. 10).

The WRAT–3 consists of three subtests: Reading, Spelling, and Arithmetic.
The Reading subtest measures skills in letter recognition, letter naming, and
pronunciation of isolated words. There is no measure of reading comprehension, as the test author states that when assessing learning disabilities, "it is

a grave mistake to emphasize comprehension if the person lacks the coding skills to learn the mechanics of reading" (Wilkinson, 1993, p. 10). The Spelling test assesses skills in copying marks onto paper, spelling one's name, and spelling single words. The Arithmetic subtest measures skills in counting, reading numerals, solving orally presented problems, and computing arithmetic problems presented in writing.

Originally published in 1936, the WRAT was updated in 1984 and again in 1993, although some reviewers (Flanagan et al., 1997; Marby, 1995; Ward, 1995) charge that the test remains outdated. It is designed to be administered to individuals from ages 5 to 75 years and to take approximately 15 to 30 minutes to administer. Each of the subtests has time limitations, either for response time (e.g., 10 seconds per item) or for the entire subtest (e.g., Arithmetic, 15 minutes). However, data related to the inclusion of people with disabilities in the norm group are missing, making the timed nature of the test a potentially confounding variable if it is used with a person with LD (Marby, 1995). Because of this flaw, Marby questions the diagnostic capacity of the test, labeling claims that the test can help determine a learning disability "ludicrous" (p. 1109). Furthermore, Ward (1995) cautions that the size of the nonwhite groups in the norm sample are insufficient to ensure that the test is unbiased.

Evidence of the validity of the WRAT–3 is suspect (Marby, 1995; Salvia & Ysseldyke, 1998; Ward, 1995), due to insufficient coverage of items across the domains measured (e.g., restricting a measure of reading to recognition, using single items to measure a math concept) (Flanagan, 1997; Flanagan et al., 1997; Marby, 1995) and failure to identify the construct on which the test is based (Ward, 1995). Reliability estimates are acceptable (Flanagan, 1997; Salvia & Ysseldyke, 1998).

Despite these limitations, the WRAT series has been rated as the most popular measure of general achievement among psychologists and school psychologists, possibly due to the speed of administration (Flanagan et al., 1997). Its frequent use in combination with the Wechsler scales led Flanagan et al. to label this combination the "dynamic duo" of intelligence and achievement testing among many practicing psychologists" (p. 100). However, because of the limitations noted, the true value of the WRAT–3 is as an academic screener and not as a primary measure of achievement (Flanagan et al., 1997; Overton, 2000).

The Bender Visual Motor Gestalt Test

The *Bender Visual Motor Gestalt Test* (BVMGT, or Bender Gestalt; Koppitz, 1963, 1975) is an individually administered, paper-and-pencil task that consists of nine geometric figures. Each figure is presented individually, and the examinee is required to copy the design onto paper (Salvia & Ysseldyke, 1998; Sattler, 1992). The design is placed directly in front of the examinee and remains visible until the entire pattern has been copied. Although there is no time limit, all nine designs should be completed in about 5 minutes (Sattler, 1992). Additionally, the amount of time needed to complete each design is noted by the administrator to determine whether it is diagnostically significant (Groth-Marnat, 1997). In addition to this standard administration, there are two variations to assess short-term, visual motor memory skills. In the first, the examinee is asked to complete all nine designs in standard format and then to reproduce as many designs as possible from memory. In the second variation, each card is presented for 5 seconds, and then removed, at which time the examinee must complete the reproduction from memory. However, these procedures have not been standardized, and results therefore rely solely on clinical judgment, a significant limitation to these procedures (Groth-Marnat, 1997).

Although several scoring procedures exist for the Bender, the most common is the Koppitz Developmental Bender Scoring System, which was originally created in 1963 and updated in 1975. It is critical for consumers and readers of psychological assessments to note that the Koppitz system is restricted to use with children aged 5.0 to 11.11 years (Salvia & Ysseldyke, 1998; Sattler, 1992). Some research has indicated some value in the use of this scoring system with children ages 12 to 18 (Groth-Marnat, 1997). However, this must be viewed cautiously, as the manual notes that most children obtain perfect performance after 8 years of age (Koppitz, 1964, cited in Sattler, 1992).

Although the original purpose of the Bender Gestalt was as a screening measure of brain damage and development, its use has evolved to be widely encompassing, including as a test of nonverbal intelligence, a screening test of school readiness, a predictor of school achievement, a means to diagnose reading and learning problems, a means to evaluate emotional difficulties, and a projective test for various personality disorders (Groth-Marnat, 1997; Sattler, 1992). However, due to outdated norms and questionable validity and reliability (Salvia & Ysseldyke, 1998), results from the Bender Gestalt should be viewed extremely cautiously at the postsecondary level. Furthermore, given the restricted norm range of the Koppitz scoring system, the applicability of the Bender Gestalt to a postsecondary-age population is dubious at best. However, despite these limitations, the Bender Gestalt continues to be one of the most popular and commonly used instruments by psychologists and neuropsychologists (Groth-Marnat, 1997; Salvia & Ysseldyke, 1998). Its popularity may stem from its simplicity, leading the developer of the Koppitz scoring system to write, "The very fact that the Bender Test is so appealing and is easy to administer presents a certain danger. Because it is so deceptively simple, it is probably one of the most overrated, most misunderstood, and most maligned tests currently in use" (Koppitz, 1975, p. 2; cited in Salvia & Ysseldyke, 1998, p. 590).

Pulling It Together and Making It Work

This chapter has presented a wide range of technical and specific information related to assessment and to specific testing instruments. It will hopefully provide a baseline of information and a host of references for further exploration to assist service providers in interpreting documentation data that are received. Additionally, the information can help service providers to become more critical consumers of assessment data. By understanding the fundamentals of assessment, being conversant in assessment terminology, and having a working knowledge of the domains and skills measured by various instruments, service providers can stand on firm ground when making or justifying decisions related to programming and reasonable accommodations, when speaking to an evaluator or a school district to clarify information or request additional data, and when explaining why a given set of documents is not acceptable. As with other issues of transition, it may be incumbent upon service providers to open a dialogue with private evaluators and school districts regarding the assessment and documentation needs of students in their transition to postsecondary settings. The promotion of a clear, reasoned, and rigorous process in the use of assessment data at the institutional level may eventually spill into other areas of professional practice and help to curb current shortcomings.

Perhaps a more fundamental and day-to-day use for the information covered in this chapter is in determining specific reasonable accommodations and auxiliary aids. For example, the practice of diagnosing a "spelling disability" or requesting accommodations such as note takers or scribes on the basis of a discrepant score on the Dictation subtest of WJ–R (Woodcock & Johnson, 1989), unfortunately, is not uncommon. Knowledge of the specific skills measured by this subtest can assist service providers in arriving at reasoned responses to such requests. Such knowledge may also be valuable in helping a student to understand the specifics of his or her learning disability, a fundamental step in the development of self-advocacy skills and in promoting success in the postsecondary arena and beyond.

Conclusion

While the LD field continues to debate issues related to definition and assessment practices, the number of students requesting services and the stakes related to the complexity of accommodations are rising. The already wide chasm among researchers and professional organizations, between research and practice, and between science and social policy also appears to be growing and will continue to divide the profession. Until uniform definition and objective practices for identification are delineated, a challenge of monumental proportion, the assessment process will be compromised by subjectivity and variability. Professionals from other disciplines will understandably continue to question and challenge the prevalence of learning disabilities and accompanying requests for accommodations and services. Perhaps the day will come when the field will heed recent warnings and "wake-up calls" (Stanovich, 1999, p. 359) and resolve these debates. Until that occurs, however, LD service providers may find themselves challenged by campus personnel, especially faculty, about an array of complex issues plaguing the field (Williams & Ceci, 1999).

This chapter has covered specific topics related to documentation, many of which are incorporated into the AHEAD guidelines (see Chapters 7 and 8), and includes practical information on how to understand the results of assessments. This information might be used to explain assessment results to a student, to make individualized decisions, and to justify decisions to administrators, students, and, increasingly, parents. Furthermore, it is hoped that the information will increase the confidence of practitioners who must converse with private or school-based evaluators about submitted reports that are incomplete or of questionable quality. Ultimately, it is hoped that the information in this chapter will allow practitioners to bridge the gaps between research, theory, and day-to-day practice.

CHAPTER

DETERMINING ELIGIBILITY FOR SERVICES AND TESTING ACCOMMODATIONS

Perspectives on Determining Eligibility

Heyward (1998) notes that the key to disability assessment is evidence not merely of the existence of an impairment but of the effect that the impairment has on the individual's life. Simply stated, not every impairment qualifies as a disability protected under the Americans with Disabilities Act because not every impairment is substantially limiting or handicapping. In order for a person to be eligible for support services or academic accommodations, the ADA stipulates that his or her disability must "substantially limit" a major life activity. Factors that may be considered in determining whether there is a substantial limitation include: (a) the nature and severity of the impairment; (b) the duration of the impairment; and (c) the permanent or long-term impact of the impairment (29 C.F.R. § 1630.2[j]). Within the realm of higher education or at a testing agency, this means that the individual with a disability must demonstrate that he or she is unable to perform, or is severely restricted in performing, a major life activity that the average person in the general population can accomplish.

The intent of this chapter is to (a) discuss how eligibility determinations are reached in college and graduate school and by testing and licensing agencies; (b) highlight several higher-education court cases that have shaped our thinking about how eligibility may be determined; (c) discuss the use of guidelines for the documentation of LD and ADHD in adolescents and adults; and (d) describe the process of reviewing LD and ADHD documentation for accommodations.

Determining Eligibility in College

In order to determine a student's eligibility for protections under the Americans with Disabilities Act, the postsecondary disability service provider must conduct a two-pronged assessment of the documentation. First, the student's documentation must support the stated disability. In most cases, the pivotal question is whether the student's "learning and working" are substantially limited when compared to that of most people in the general population. Some would argue that the measuring stick should be that of the *relative* peer group, while others contend that it is simply that of the average person on the street. Readers should step back and ask themselves, Would you feel better knowing that the surgeon, attorney, or architect with a learning disability you just hired was granted accommodations in graduate school by the office of student disability services (OSD) so they could perform at a level commensurate with their peers at a given graduate institution, or that the individual you hired received accommodations in graduate school for their LD after being compared with a hypothetical average 28 year old in the street? Gordon and Keiser (1998) state that establishing the "general population norm against which to judge impairment has profound implications for determinations of disability in postsecondary education" (p. 7). In any case, it points to the need for students at the postsecondary, graduate, and professional school levels to be aware of these contentious matters in order to prepare themselves to address documentation issues early in their training programs before they face licensing agencies. Furthermore, postsecondary disability service providers and advisors from secondary school onward need to counsel students about the realities of the educational "potholes" down the road.

Once the disability has been established and the student is considered to be eligible for services, the service provider must determine if the individual is "otherwise qualified" to carry out the duties of the program of study, and if so, whether the student's documentation supports the need for the requested accommodations. Heyward (1998) provides a very useful "Checklist of Basic Principles" for determining "otherwise qualified" status (see Appendix 7.1 on the CD-ROM). McGuire (1998) adds that disability service providers often have to "search for an equilibrium between the student's right to accommodations and the institution's right to maintain the integrity of its programs" (p. 25). If the documentation supports the requested accommodations as reasonable, and there is no undue hardship to be assumed by the institution or testing agency, then the requested accommodations should be granted. If, however, upon reviewing the documentation, the disability service provider or testing agency determines that the documentation is inadequate, limited in scope and content, or outdated, then corrective action must be taken. Depending on the nature of these inadequacies in the documentation, the student may have to undergo a complete reevaluation supporting the disability at his or her own expense. Frequently, it is possible for the student to submit a new, partial update that can address any deficiencies in the previous evaluation, including the current levels of achievement and anticipated functional limitations within the designated setting. In any case, testing administrators have a duty to establish informed and nonarbitrary procedures to review requests for reasonable accommodations. According to Konecky and Wolinsky (2000), this means that "application requirements and decision making must meet generally accepted standards in the field, and not result from ignorance, prejudice or stereotypes, concerning the nature and effect of learning disabilities" (p. 82).

The decision of whether the student should be provided with any reasonable accommodations during this interim period while the assessment is being updated or completely readministered is up to the disability service administrator (DSA) and program policy and procedures. Most college campuses have a provision that permits students who have a previously diagnosed disability that is supported by a long history of accommodations to continue to receive at least minimum accommodations for a semester while the testing is updated. Prudent practice would dictate that any provisional accommodation offerings should be backed up by written correspondence with the student explaining the basis of the provisional service and the expectation for updated, acceptable documentation in order to extend services into another semester.

A number of disability service providers and faculty members are functioning under the mistaken belief that they have to accept the fact that the student has a disability, and that any accommodations requested by the student or written in the report by the evaluator must be provided. The sense of expectation by students with disabilities, as well as by evaluators who view their word as final, is often challenging for disability service providers who find themselves having to turn down limited or outdated documentation while they try to educate students and evaluators about the fundamental assumptions underlying the ADA (McGuire, 1998). It is important to keep in mind that despite the existence of a qualifying disability, the requested accommodations may be denied if they are determined to be unreasonable or inappropriate. However, if the testing entity does not agree with the requested accommodations, "it can not simply reject the accommodations recommended by the clinician, but has a legal obligation to work cooperatively with the applicant (and the applicant's clinician) to determine the appropriate accommodation" (Konecky & Wolinsky, 2000, p. 77).

Determining Eligibility at the Graduate and Professional Levels

To the surprise of many graduate school faculty and administrators, a large proportion of LD and ADHD students in graduate and professional programs may not be identified until they experience the rigors of the graduate or professional school curriculum. Many of these individuals are able to manage an undergraduate education because of their giftedness, meticulous organization, verbal abilities, and work ethic, all of which contribute to innate strategy development that they themselves may not recognize as such. They often exhibit significant abilities and creative talents despite some fundamental problems with reading, written language, or mathematical reasoning and problem solving. This group of students is often misunderstood, in part, because their unique abilities have tended to mask their disabilities (Brinckerhoff, 1999). In medical school or law school, individuals with previously undiagnosed learning disabilities often struggle to adjust to the rigors of the professional school curriculum. Unlike students who have known about their learning disabilities for many years, these young graduates are at a disadvantage because they lack the coping skills and the study strategies they need in postgraduate settings. Their repertoire of previously used compensatory abilities at the undergraduate level is not sufficient, and they become overwhelmed (Frank-Josephson & Scott, 1997; Perreira & Richards, 2000; Takakuwa, 1998).

Like their undergraduate LD counterparts of a decade ago, graduate students with learning disabilities and ADHD must combat the idea that "these students" do not belong in graduate school. Jordan (1995) comments that "many believe that the term learning disabled graduate or professional student is an oxymoron which just cannot exist." Her point is well taken. Despite high aptitudes, these students often have a history of performing relatively poorly on standardized tests and in-class exams. This history of uneven test performance is often discordant with the performance of written assignments that are completed outside of the classroom, such as term papers, or the performance in areas where these students can demonstrate clinical skills on the job.

Disability service providers, not to mention graduate school admissions officers, may find it especially difficult to assess on paper which students with LD or ADHD are otherwise qualified for a medical or law school curriculum. They may realize that "standardized test measures don't tell it all," but they are often unclear as to how a learning disability or attention-deficit disorder would affect future performance in the graduate school curriculum. In such instances, it may be useful for graduate school admissions staff to confer with the Office for Students with Disabilities coordinator, an LD specialist, or a psychologist who is knowledgeable about and versed in working with LD adults in order to gain further insight about a given applicant's prospects for success. Admissions officers must determine whether an applicant meets the requirements for admission (by means of undergraduate GPA, standardized test scores, letters of recommendations, etc.) and if so, whether the applicant can meet the technical standards of the institution with or without reasonable accommodations without directly asking if he or she has a disability.

Frances Hall (1995), the director of student programs for the Association of American Medical Colleges (AAMC), points out that "we need to evaluate *ability* not their status as being disabled while keeping in mind that we must not fundamentally alter the program, or pose a threat to public safety [emphasis in original]." Ultimately, this means that faculty have to define "essential standards" of their discipline and to determine the procedures for applying standards uniformly to all students (Association of American Medical Colleges, 1993). Important questions to include are these (Hall, 1995): What can be done to ensure that we evaluate the student's true ability without the confines of disability-related factors? How can service providers, faculty, and support staff address the psychosocial issues that are often inextricably intertwined with academic concerns? What elements of the graduate school curriculum are nonnegotiable or viewed as integral to the program of study? In some instances, a graduate student who has been recently diagnosed with a learning disability and is considering medical school or a doctoral program in medical sciences should be encouraged to reflect on opting for the medical sciences program so as to avoid the stringent timed licensing tests given to medical students, which offer fewer accommodation options. In any case, graduate and professional schools need to work with disability service staff to develop consistent policies regarding requirements for admission of self-identified students with LD and ADHD and the subsequent provision of accommodations.

Determining Eligibility from a Testing Agency Perspective

The sheer volume of requests for nonstandardized testing received by testing agencies can be daunting. Testing agency personnel do not have the luxury of being able to meet directly with students, talk with their parents, or track down evaluators for additional information on each case they review. While requests must be viewed on a case-by-case basis, unlike disability service providers testing agency personnel must depend almost entirely on the quality of the written documentation an applicant submits, plus the integrity of the professional who certifies the existence of a qualifying disability and the need for the requested accommodations.

In 1998–99, over 60,000 candidates requested "nonstandard administration" of the PSAT/NMSQT, SAT, AP, PRAXIS, GRE, GMAT, and TOEFL tests from the Educational Testing Service (J. Radlinsky, personal communication, December 6, 1999). Many of these individuals were repeat test takers who had been approved for accommodations in the past. The SAT program alone accounted for over 49,000 of these requests. As might be expected, the vast majority were from individuals with learning disabilities and ADHD who wanted additional testing time and a "low-distraction setting." These figures are reflective of a national trend across other testing agencies, including the American College Testing Program (ACT), Law School Admission Test (LSAT), and the National Board of Medical Examiners (NBME). For example, in 1998, the NBME received over 500 requests for alternate testing accommodations as a direct result of documented disabilities. LSAT administrators experienced more than a threefold increase in requests from 1994 to 1996.

Although testing agencies may vary in their procedures for processing requests, the bottom line is that, in order to qualify for testing accommodations, the test taker must have a disability that necessitates the requested accommodations and have recent documentation (such as an IEP, 504 plan, or professional evaluation) on file at the secondary school or college that supports that need given the standardized testing format. Some agencies require that in order to qualify for accommodations, the test taker must have previously received the identical accommodations for school-based tests. If the test taker does not have a history of receiving accommodations for school-based tests he or she may still be eligible for accommodations, but the documentation provided to the testing agency by the student must be reviewed by qualified professionals or external consultants to determine if the requested accommodations are both reasonable and appropriate given the nature of the test.

The vast majority of students requesting accommodations for the SAT are routinely approved if the applicant has a history of the same school-based testing accommodations and an IEP, 504 plan, or professional evaluation is on file. In such cases, a qualified school staff member (e.g., guidance counselor, school psychologist) must support the requested accommodations by completing the documentation review form. Students applying for accommodations for other similar admissions or licensing exams may follow a similar protocol. Returning students or older adults who have been in the workforce for years may find it easier to have certification of the disability completed by the director of disability services at a postsecondary setting they attended, a certified vocational rehabilitation counselor, or the human resources representative at the applicant's place of employment.

Some testing agencies, like the College Board, have established a review panel consisting of a cross-section of qualified professionals throughout the country who routinely review disability documentation. The panelists are typically asked to review documentation from test takers who have no history of accommodations or who have just recently been identified as having a disability, or to consider requests in complex cases in which co-morbidity factors, such as ESL, depression, or ADHD, may cloud the diagnosis. Cases may also be reviewed in instances where the requested accommodation is "unusual" such as a 2-day test administration of a 3-hour exam. During the 1998–99 school year, less than 20% of such requests were approved. Of those denied, the vast majority were due to limitations in the documentation (B. Robinson, personal communication, November 22, 1999). For example, the evaluator may have used the *Wide Range Achievement Test–3* as the sole measure of reading achievement to diagnose a specific learning disability in reading, or an ADHD diagnosis may have been supported exclusively through the test taker's self-reporting without corroborating data from other parties. The developers of these high-stakes examinations, like OSD providers in higher education, want to be sure that test takers who are approved for accommodations (e.g., extended test time, a reader, a scribe, or a separate testing room) are, in fact, legitimately entitled to them.

Determining Eligibility in the Courts

Heyward (1998) notes that "Section 504 by its terms does not compel educational institutions to disregard the disabilities of handicapped individuals or to make substantial modifications in their programs to allow disabled persons to participate" (Chapter 2, p. 9). Instead, it requires only that an "otherwise qualified handicapped individual" not be excluded from participation in a federally funded program "solely by reason of handicap," indicating only that mere possession of a handicap is not a permissible ground for assuming an inability to function in a particular context. In the *Southeastern Community College v. Davis* case (1979), a student with a hearing impairment was denied admission to a nurses' training program because the college held that she could not safely participate in the clinical training program that was required. On the basis of the audiologist's report, the court held that the respondent was not an otherwise qualified student since her performance was dependent on lip reading, which was not sufficient in clinical settings, such as an operating room, that might necessitate the use of a surgical mask. Davis suggested that a reasonable accommodation would be to allow her to substitute additional academic courses for the clinical component or to provide her with the individual attention of a nursing instructor. The case was initially reviewed by the federal district court, then by the 4th Circuit Court of Appeals. The court concluded, "Section 504 imposes no requirement upon an educational institution to lower or to effect substantial modifications of standards to accommodate a handicapped person" (pp. 410–412).

McGuire (1998) notes that determining whether an individual has a disability that substantially limits one or more major life functions is usually the most challenging task that confronts a disability service administrator. This process has become even more complex given the recent holding of the United States Supreme Court regarding the intended protections of the ADA with respect to the impact of mitigating measures (see Chapter 3). Disability service providers and testing agency administrators should look to the Supreme Court rulings for guidance, but they should not "overreact," according to Kincaid (1999b), an attorney who specializes in disability law. Kincaid believes that "ultimately it will be the lower courts which set the standards and who interpret Supreme Court language" (p. 6). Regardless, one fact remains: each case needs to be judged on its own merits.

State courts have addressed this issue of "substantial limitation" on a case-by-case basis as it relates to requests for accommodations on standardized tests administered by various testing agencies. In *Price v. The National Board of Medical Examiners* (1997), three students with ADHD sought testing accommodations for the Medical Licensing Examination similar to those they had been receiving in medical school—additional time and a private room. The National Board of Medical Examiners turned down their requests, and the medical students sought an injunction from the court, requiring that the NBME grant their requested accommodations.

The court reasoned that the impairments, specific learning disabilities and ADHD, did not substantially limit a major life activity because each of the student's past academic history reflected significant academic accomplishments without accommodations. Specifically:

• Student one graduated from high school with a 3.4 GPA and from undergraduate school with a 2.9 GPA, and there was no medical evidence of ADHD until 1994, after his enrollment in medical school.

• Student two was in a gifted program from second grade through high school, graduated from high school with a 4.2 GPA (on a 5-point scale); was state debate champion, was admitted to the Naval Academy, and graduated from Vanderbilt University with a degree in physics. All of the above were accomplished without accommodations.

• Student three was a National Honor student in high school, graduated from VMI, and maintained a 3.5 GPA at Shepard College, which he attended to satisfy the science requirements for medical school. All of the above were accomplished without accommodations (*Section 504 Compliance Handbook*, 1999).

The court concluded that the three test takers were not substantially limited since they did not exhibit "a pattern of substantial academic difficulties" when compared to the average person in the general population. Although the plaintiffs may have had a disability that was protected under the ADA, the court felt that, in light of the plaintiffs' significant academic achievements without accommodations, the disability simply did not substantially limit the major life activity of learning.

A recent case, *Gonzalez v. National Board of Medical Examiners* (1999), involved a University of Michigan medical student with a diagnosed learning disability in reading and writing who failed Step I of the Medical Licensing Examination twice. He then proceeded to sue the National Board of Medical Examiners, which denied his request for additional time because it determined that he did not have an ADA-defined disability. The NBME noted that the student had a verbal IQ that was average and a performance IQ that was in the high average to superior range. He graduated from high school with a 4.3 GPA on a 5.0 scale and obtained a grade of A in all advanced placement courses. He also received a 1050 on the SAT without accommodations and a GPA of 3.15 on a 4.0 scale from the University of California–Davis. Furthermore, Gonzalez had no history of accommodations prior to entering the University of Michigan. As in the Price case, this medical student's attempt to show that he was disabled in the major life activity of working was not supported. The court determined that Gonzalez was not entitled to additional time because the scores in his LD documentation did not clearly establish that he had an impairment that substantially limited his learning, or his reading abilities, when compared to the average person in the general population.

These cases affirm the premise that there must be clear evidence of substantial limitations or adverse treatment based on the existence of an impairment that imposes substantial limitations. Heyward (1998) notes, "The mere reporting of a disability or limitations and/or presentation of documentation that discloses a history of an impairment is not sufficient. There must be evidence of a present impact on a major life activity" (Chapter 3, p. 11). In both these cases, the courts were not swayed into believing that the learning disability or ADHD was so pervasive that it affected day-to-day functioning sufficiently to be covered by the safeguards afforded by the Americans with Disabilities Act.

A slightly different spin on how eligibility may be determined in the eyes of the courts emerges from the findings in *Bartlett v. New York State Board of Bar Examiners* (1998). In 1999, the U.S. Supreme Court remanded this case to the 2nd Circuit (see Chapter 3). The appellate court had held that, even though she self-accommodated her disability through law school, Bartlett was substantially limited in her ability to read and to learn and, therefore, had a disability under the ADA. In this case, the lower court took a more expansive view of the term *substantial limitation*, as well as major life activity, in concluding that "test taking is a major life activity and that the applicant had successfully proven that she was substantially limited in her ability to read as compared to the average law school graduate" (Heyward, 1998, Chapter 3, p. 12). Delaney (1999), an attorney with the Office for Civil Rights, notes that it was Ms. Bartlett's lack of automaticity with the reading process that was "the key factor" in determining that she was substantially limited. Ms. Bartlett had some diagnostic tests that showed reading scores below the 5th percentile, compared to college freshmen, on the reading speed subtest of the *Diagnostic Reading Test*. The attorney representing Ms. Bartlett, JoAnne Simon, noted that her client used readers, her finger to follow along the page, and an index card with a rectangular hole to stop her eyes from jumping. Simon (1999) comments that testing agencies are "going hog-wild over the Supreme Court rulings, but the self-accommodations Bartlett used certainly did not mitigate her disability." Simon points out that the court specifically ruled that "a person's ability to self-accommodate does not foreclose a finding of disability." Kincaid (1999a) concurs, saying, "It's not uncommon for a student to self-accommodate a disability throughout his undergraduate studies, but come law school, he falls apart" (p. 6).

The Supreme Court remanded the Bartlett case to the 2nd U.S. Circuit Court of Appeals. Until the appellate court rules, OSD staff will have to look to the Supreme Court rulings for guidance. Certainly, the Bartlett case is important because it expands the ADA coverage by allowing a comparison to the "average person" in a highly educated group as opposed to the general population. However, at the graduate school and professional school level, it appears that "the further a student has progressed in educational level without accommodations and the higher his or her pertinent diagnostic scores, the more difficult it may be to establish substantial limitation in learning, thinking, or concentrating in comparison to most people" (Latham, 1997, p. 43). Kincaid (1999) fears that "individuals seeking a post graduate education may suffer a backlash" from the recent rulings of the U.S. Supreme Court, since many students with disabilities earn college degrees without academic accommodations. It will be important to watch closely as the courts determine who is, and who is not, disabled under the ADA particularly as this relates to students at the graduate and professional school levels.

Guidelines for Documentation of LD and ADHD

For some years, disability service providers, diagnosticians, and licensing agencies have been challenged by the inconsistencies that often exist in documentation supporting a diagnosis of learning disabilities and/or ADHD at the postsecondary level. McGuire et al. (1996) reviewed 415 reports submitted by students to a large research university with a comprehensive LD support program to establish their eligibility for services and accommodations on the basis of a learning disability. McGuire et al. noted some serious problems and inadequacies. In nearly half of the psychological evaluation batteries, only one test was administered, and that was in the domain of intelligence. Selection of technically adequate test instruments was also problematic in that the second most frequently administered test was the *Bender Visual Motor Gestalt Test* which is designed for ages 5 to 11. The *Wide Range Achievement Test–Revised* (Jastak & Wilkinson, 1984), noted in the literature to be an initial screening instrument to estimate achievement levels, was the most frequently used measure of achievement. Only 19.1% of the diagnostic reports addressed the area of information processing. McGuire et al. delineated guidelines for use by consumers and evaluators to assure the adequacy of documentation for the purpose of establishing eligibility in postsecondary settings.

In 1996, in response to these concerns, the board of directors of the Association on Higher Education and Disability formed the Ad Hoc Committee on Learning Disabilities with the task of developing guidelines to provide "students, professional diagnosticians and service providers with a common understanding and knowledge base of those components of documentation which are necessary to validate a learning disability and the need for accommodation" (p. 1). Crafting the document was a lengthy process involving members of the ad hoc committee and dozens of AHEAD members, as well as psychologists. The final version of the LD guidelines was approved by the AHEAD Board of Directors and published in July 1997. One practical feature of these guidelines is an appendix, "Recommendations for Consumers." Students often need a starting place with suggestions on how to find a qualified professional who can do testing and provide the follow-up. The intent of this appendix is not to endorse any class or group of specialists but, rather, to support the informed decision making of consumers. For a complete copy of the AHEAD *Guidelines for Documentation of a Learning Disability in Adolescents and Adults* (1997b), readers should consult Appendix 7.2 on the CD-ROM.

As a corollary to the AHEAD Guidelines, the members of the ad hoc committee met in the fall of 1997 at Dartmouth College to develop a set of guidelines for documenting ADHD under the rubric of the Consortium on ADHD Documentation. The primary purpose of this group was to develop a second set of guidelines that could be used by both testing agencies and colleges, as well as consumers, to determine whether ADHD documentation is sufficient to support the disability claim and the accommodations being requested in a particular setting. As in the process used in the development of the LD guidelines, there was an open comment period for colleagues in the United States and

Canada to offer suggestions on the initial drafts of the document. The final draft of the ADHD guidelines was sent out for further review to some of the leading medical doctors, neuropsychologists, postsecondary disability service providers, and university scholars in the field.

Recognizing that there was no definitive diagnostic tool that established ADHD, the Consortium on ADHD Documentation developed guidelines to include: qualifications of the evaluator; recency of the documentation; comprehensive documentation components, including evidence of early and current impairment; relevant testing; identification criteria from the *Diagnostic and Statistical Manual of Mental Disorders, 4th Edition* (*DSM–IV*; American Psychiatric Association, 1994); a specific diagnosis and interpretive summary; ruling out disorders that can exhibit similar symptoms; and a rationale for the recommendation(s).

The ADHD guidelines were developed for two reasons: (1) in reaction to the number of postsecondary disability service providers who felt they should no longer be placed in a position of having to accept "incredibly insufficient little notes on a prescription pad" as documentation for an attention-deficit disorder (Kincaid, 1998); and (2) to minimize misconceptions regarding the validity of ADHD in adolescents and adults by promoting the use of professionally endorsed guidelines for documentation. The guidelines were not designed to be a boilerplate, but to be tailored to the needs of the settings in which they are used with flexibility. For a complete copy of the *Guidelines for Documentation of Attention-Deficit/Hyperactivity Disorder in Adolescents and Adults* (Consortium on ADHD Documentation, 1998), readers should consult Appendix 7.3 on the CD-ROM.

At the secondary level, it is hoped that guidance counselors, school psychologists, special education personnel, and parents will find both the AHEAD and the Consortium guidelines helpful as they prepare for IEP meetings, mapping-out of Individual Transition Plans for students, and submitting documentation to licensing and testing agencies. Given that the number of ADHD students alone has almost doubled during the last decade (Gordon & Murphy, 1998), secondary school personnel and consumers need to be aware that testing agencies and postsecondary disability service providers are reviewing LD and ADHD documentation with greater scrutiny in light of the ADA regulations. Evaluators, high school personnel, and parents need to be reminded that the assessment of an adolescent with a suspected LD or ADHD must not only establish a diagnosis of the disability but also demonstrate that the disability results in a substantial functional limitation. Adherence to these guidelines should help high school professionals and parents plan ahead by requesting comprehensive documentation that validates the need for the requested accommodations. All requests for accommodations should be supported by the evaluator's clinical observations, supported with diagnostic data and a history of accommodations if appropriate, and further corroborated by parents, teachers, and the students themselves.

ETS Policy Statements on LD and ADHD

In order to improve the quality of the documentation submitted by test takers with disabilities, ETS and other college testing agencies, like the ACT and LSAT, adapted the *AHEAD Guidelines for Documentation of a Learning Disability in Adolescents and Adults* (1997b) and the *Guidelines for Documentation of Attention-Deficit/Hyperactivity Disorder in Adolescents and Adults* (Consortium on ADHD Documentation, 1998) to suit their unique needs. Generally speaking, the standards established by these testing entities are more specific than those originally embraced by the AHEAD Board of Directors or the ADHD Consortium.

There are a few changes and additions to the final version of the ETS ADHD Policy Statement that should be noted. In order to substantiate the current impact that the ADHD may have on an individual, test takers requesting accommodations must provide documentation that includes psycho-educational testing, in addition to the neuropsychological data. Many reviewers felt that, without a clearer picture of how the attention-deficit disorder affects concentration and learning, it is difficult to determine if the requested accommodations are appropriate. Consequently, ETS's ADHD Policy Statement (1998a) notes:

> The assessment of the individual must not only establish a diagnosis of ADHD, but must also demonstrate the current impact of the ADHD on an individual's ability to take standardized tests. In addition, neuropsychological or psycho-educational assessment is important in determining the current impact of the disorder on an individual's ability to function in academically related settings. (p. 6)

This issue concerning the inclusion of psycho-educational data as a part of the ADHD documentation is discussed more extensively in Chapter 10.

A second change in the ETS ADHD Policy Statement is the inclusion of an appendix entitled "Assessing Adolescents and Adults with ADHD." This was added in order to provide test takers and evaluators with additional guidance regarding the types of formal and informal measures that may be useful in the diagnosis of an attention-deficit disorder. It includes five broad assessment domains that are frequently explored when arriving at an ADHD diagnosis:

(a) the clinical interview; (b) rating scales; (c) neuropsychological and psycho-educational testing; (d) medical evaluation; and (e) collateral information from third-party sources. In addition to this appendix, the ETS ADHD Policy Statement includes three other appendixes: "DSM–IV Diagnostic Criteria for ADHD," "Recommendations for Consumers," and a listing of "Resources and Organizations" to help consumers and parents network to find additional resources.

Readers may access the most recent versions of the ETS *Policy Statement for Documentation of Attention-Deficit/Hyperactivity Disorder in Adolescents and Adults* (1998a), ETS *Policy Statement for Documentation of a Learning Disability in Adolescents and Adults* (1998b), and the newest addition, *ETS Guidelines for Documentation of Psychiatric Disabilities in Adolescents and Adults* (2001) directly through the ETS Web site: http://www.ets.org/disability.html.

Generally, the dissemination of these policy statements by testing entities has elicited praise from disability service coordinators, learning disabilities specialists, high school psychologists, and parents of teenagers with LD, who see these standards as providing order to what was an otherwise chaotic experience. They have noted that, at least now, the expectations for documentation are clearly delineated in advance, so that when it comes time for testing for the SAT, ACT, LSAT, GRE, or another similar test, they can be proactive and provide the documentation that is necessary.

It is the responsibility of testing agencies to ensure that these documentation standards are well publicized and applied evenly across all their programs so that the approval of requests for accommodations is based on criteria that are equitably implemented. In addition, testing agencies need to be sure that the application process for nonstandard testing accommodations is as easy and straightforward as possible, so test takers with disabilities can request accommodation information on their own either from the Internet or through the test program bulletins.

Reviewing LD and ADHD Documentation for Accommodations

Few issues raise more consternation in the world of learning disabilities and higher education than the issues surrounding the use and interpretation of disability documentation. Provost Jon Westling at Boston University (Elswit, Geetter, & Goldberg, 1999; Shalit, 1997) noted that the disability documentation he reviewed on file at the LD Support Services (LDSS) office was written by "snake-oil salesmen" who overdiagnose the disability. In a memo to the director of the Disability Services Office, Mr. Westling instructed the LD Support Services staff to review student files and to provide him with "scientific or medical evidence of the claimed disability, a statement of the requested accommodation(s), and scientific or medical proof that the requested accommodation(s) will enable a student to compensate for his/her disability (p. 2)." Needless to say, this was a tall order and would create challenges for most DSO staff. The field of learning disabilities, and adult assessment in particular, is not as refined or as exacting a science as Mr. Westling might have hoped.

In many ways, disability documentation is the cornerstone of effective service delivery and testing accommodations. Lorry (1998) points out that clinicians who have never submitted documentation for ADA accommodations are sometimes surprised by the "diagnostic rigor" required by colleges, universities, and testing agencies. She adds that "reports that might well have passed muster to justify classifying elementary or secondary students may be dismissed by institutions or by licensing groups" (p. 146). McGuire (1998) adds that these reports vary widely in sophistication, relevance, and credibility. Quality documentation must not only be comprehensive, but also should support the accommodations requested by the student or test taker. The assessment process as it relates to diagnosing a learning disability at the adult level is covered in Chapter 6.

The following section highlights 13 common pitfalls and perils to consider when reviewing LD and ADHD documentation at the postsecondary level. In several instances actual examples from LD and ADHD documentation as well as verbatim excerpts from psycho-educational reports are included to further illustrate the caveat under discussion. It is hoped that these observations, which complement the information in Chapter 6, will be useful to postsecondary service providers and testing agency personnel who review documentation and provide accommodations, as well as diagnosticians who have a responsibility to maintain diagnostic rigor and to report test information accurately.

Appearance of the Documentation

LD and ADHD documentation should be typed or printed on letterhead, dated, signed, and be legible with the name, title, and professional credentials of the evaluator; additionally, it needs to include information that specifies the evaluator's license or certification area of specialization. The report should be comprehensive (at least 3–5 pages) and should include an attachment delineating all tests that were administered and the subtest scores for each test.

Pitfalls and Perils: Documentation that is handwritten on one page of a medical form, prescription pad (see Figure 7.1), or copy paper does little to inspire confidence that the disability is, in fact, legitimate and that a comprehensive

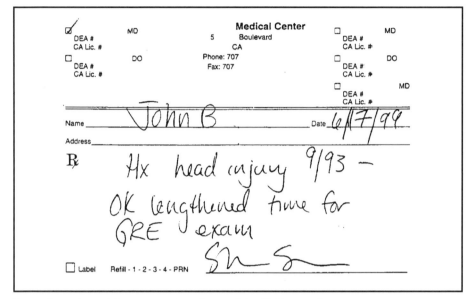

Figure 7.1. Actual documentation submitted for GRE test taker.

assessment was conducted to determine the functional limitations of the disability.

Recency of the Documentation

Documentation should be no more than 5 years old for a learning disability and no more than 3 years old for ADHD. Objective evidence regarding psychiatric disabilities, TBI, and other disabilities that are more changeable or fluid, should be updated at least annually. This is particularly true in situations where medications have been prescribed or changed. Although a learning disability is lifelong, accommodations are granted or denied based on the current impact of the disability and should not be premised merely on the historical record of a diagnosis or a self-report. Depending on the individual case, it may be possible to merely update some aspects of the psychoeducational report and thereby save the test taker both time and money. For example, if the test taker was first identified with a learning disability as an adult based in part on an assessment that included the WAIS–III, it may not be necessary to repeat a test of aptitude merely because the testing is more than 5 years old. What may be more relevant in such instances is a request for a specific achievement testing in reading, writing, or mathematics, depending on those areas where the learning disability manifests itself. Jordan (2000) reminds us that "while it might be much easier for those who are reviewing documentation to have some *magic formula* or cut-off stating how old documentation could be, it's not that easy. One must look at the purpose for which the documentation is being reviewed to determine the current need in the anticipated academic setting" (p. 39).

Pitfalls and Perils: Documentation that is slightly over 5 years old may be considered by some disability services offices, depending on how comprehensive it is and if the status of the student and the educational setting are apparently unchanged. Whenever possible, it is prudent for consumers to provide the DSO office or the testing entity with an updated version of the document that supports the current need for accommodations.

Reason for Referral

The documentation should clearly state the reason for referral. This should include information on who referred the student, the rationale for the referral, and supporting reasons for conducting a comprehensive neuropsychological or psycho-educational assessment. If this is a new evaluation to determine whether a disability exists, then the presenting problem should be plainly stated. If there is a history of a documented disability, then the purpose of the documentation may be simply to update the testing and to establish an ongoing need for accommodations.

Pitfalls and Perils: The credibility of the documentation is lessened if it does not include referral information. If the sole reason for seeking an evaluation is to secure testing accommodations just in time for a standardized test the second Saturday in October, the underlying rationale for testing may be suspect. Although this can be the sole rationale for conducting the testing, it is much more likely that the documentation will be credible if the disability affects functioning across a variety of domains within a broader context of performance areas.

▶ **One evaluator's inappropriate rationale for initiating a referral:**

REASON FOR REFERRAL: Marty is being evaluated so she can take the SATs untimed.

Evaluation Measures

It is imperative to include a listing of all the tests that were used to document the disability and to support the accommodation requests. Evaluation measures selected for the assessment battery should be reliable, valid, and age appropriate and have current normative data to support their use.

Pitfalls and Perils: Many evaluators fail to include a comprehensive listing of all the assessment measures used to reach a diagnosis, or they neglect to mention clinical observations, portfolio assessment, or the use of informal assessment measures. If the evaluator has used a diagnostic instrument that is not age appropriate, and a rationale for its use is not provided, his or her training and expertise are subject to question.

▶ **One evaluator's use of inappropriate tests to document a learning disability in an adult:**

TESTS ADMINISTERED:

Wechsler Adult Intelligence Scale–Revised (WAIS–R)
Wide Range Achievement Test–3 (WRAT–3)
Harris Test of Dominance
Bender Visual Motor Gestalt Test

Relevant Developmental, Educational, and Medical Histories

The report should include background information on the student, his or her family, early schooling, recent educational experiences, and any medical information that is pertinent for building a case. The diagnosis of ADHD in the *DSM–IV* requires evidence of an early impairment and evidence of presenting problems with inattention, impulsivity, and/or hyperactivity across two or more settings. Evaluators need to keep in mind that a self-report from the student does not make for a definitive diagnosis.

Pitfalls and Perils: Many evaluators tend to gloss over this section of the report as being tangential. However, it is important to clearly establish whether the disability was identified early on in the student's learning experience and, if so, how it manifested itself. If there is no historical evidence of a presumed disability, it will be more difficult to provide a rationale as to why the student is eligible for accommodations under the ADA.

▶ **One evaluator's limited developmental, educational, and medical history:**

BACKGROUND INFORMATION

Mr. B. reported a close and supportive relationship with his family. He is the youngest of two brothers. Notable medical history, including significant alcohol and drug use, was denied. Reportedly, there were no complications regarding Mr. B.'s birth, and his developmental milestones were achieved on time.

He was held back in the 1st grade and was placed in special reading and study groups for learning problems throughout grade school.

Statement of the Disability

Is the student's intellectual functioning in the average–to–above-average range? Is there subtest scatter or an interplay between subtests? If so, what do these patterns suggest? It is important to look carefully at processing input measures and output measures. They can often provide an indication as to how the learning disability or ADHD may affect memory functioning, visual and auditory perception, abstract reasoning and problem solving, executive functioning, and attention. Additional data (based on clinical observation) that describe the student's language; speech quality, rate, and fluency; handwriting speed; and coordination may be helpful. In sum, the testing should carefully examine areas of concern and weakness as well as areas of strength so that a complete profile of the individual can be developed.

Pitfalls and Perils: Evaluators need to be cautious about overinterpreting test results or jumping to diagnostic conclusions. A 15-point discrepancy between verbal and performance measures does not automatically mean that the student has a learning disability. Evaluators often make interpretations about uneven functioning based on differences between subscales that are "essentially trivial" (Lorry, 1998, p. 147). Lorry rightly points out that a difference of 3 points or fewer between subtests does not constitute a strength or a weakness and goes on to say, "Only when the scaled score is at least 3 points higher or lower compared to the mean of the Verbal or Performance subscale is it appropriate to consider it a relative strength or weakness" (p. 148). Nor should the WAIS–III or WISC–III be used as the sole criterion for the diagnosis of learning disabilities.

The diagnosis of a learning disability should be based on an analysis of the individual's strengths as well as his or her weaknesses. Terminology such as "learning differences" and statements like "performance is suggestive of a possible ADHD" are of little value in substantiating a diagnosis. Sometimes evaluators need to be reminded that the problem of test anxiety or a slow reading rate is not a learning disability. Finally, the presence of a medical prescription does not, in and of itself, legitimize a diagnosis.

▶ **An example of an inappropriate statement of the disability:**

Ms. D's variable attentional performance is most likely reflective of her anxiety during testing, rather than a disorder in attention per se.

However, anxiety does not explain the decrement in her reading skills under timed conditions or her mild deficit in verbal production. Rather, impairment in these areas, together with her history and clinical presentation, is most likely indicative of a mild specific reading disorder or some other learning problem.

A "Rule-Out" Statement

Intellectual limitations; sensory impairments; adverse educational, emotional, social, or environmental conditions; or ESL issues may be the primary cause of low achievement and should not be confused with a learning disability. Data that can rule in, or rule out, a disability in the presence of other concomitant factors are essential. Atypical behaviors (e.g., problems with directionality, pencil grip, pressure applied to the paper, fatigue, frustration level, direction following, excessive motor activity, etc.) should also be noted by the evaluator. These observations often provide some important clues regarding the underlying nature of the student's problems.

Pitfalls and Perils: Some evaluators fail to address contributing issues such as motivation, lack of educational opportunities, cultural and language differences, and the impact of medications on student performance. A report containing a strong rule-out statement can be helpful in establishing a clearer diagnosis.

▶ **This evaluator neglected to include a rule-out statement with the ADHD diagnosis:**

> Laura completed two behavioral checklists to assess her attentional skills as compared to same-age peers. The results of the Brown ADD Scales indicated clinical significance on the Attention Scale, a measure of consistent attention.

> The results of the second instrument, the Adult ADDES, indicated clinical significance on the Hyperactive-Impulsive Scale. The Overall Score revealed clinical significance at the 6th percentile. This means that Laura reports hyperactive and impulsive behavior seen in only 6% of her peers. Laura reported as true for her one or several times per day. "I interrupt others," "I feel restless," and "I move about unnecessarily."

Appropriate Measures of Achievement

It is surprising how many evaluators think that a WRAT–3, alone, is sufficient to document the achievement levels of students with LD and ADHD. The current levels of achievement are essential for establishing a credible diagnosis of a learning disability. The *Woodcock–Johnson Psycho-Educational Battery–Revised* (WJ–R) (Woodcock & Johnson, 1989a, 1989b, 1989c) or the recently published *Woodcock–Johnson III* (Woodcock, McGrew, & Mather, 2001a, 2001b) are either used as the assessment battery of choice by diagnosticians. If significant problem areas surface in reading, written language, or mathematical calculation on that test, then additional diagnostic measures, or informal assessments, may be warranted. It may be helpful to have a written language sample included in the diagnostic battery. Information regarding the student's reading rate, decoding, and comprehension should be standard in situations where reading and time are considerations.

The *Nelson–Denny Reading Test* (NDRT; Brown, Bennett, & Hanna, 1981) is an example of a popular screening test that is designed to measure vocabulary knowledge, reading rate, and reading comprehension under timed and extended time conditions. Mapou (2000), a clinical associate professor of neurology at Georgetown University School of Medicine, notes that "the NDRT is described in the manual as a 'screening test,' and this statement has been used by some organizations administering entrance or licensing examinations to challenge its validity as an indicator of dyslexia" (p. 23). If, however, the test is part of a comprehensive battery given by the evaluator and if the dyslexia diagnosis is based on the entire pattern of test results from a variety of reading measures, the evaluator should be able to counter that challenge. Mapou further notes that "a large improvement in the NDRT score with extended time can help the clinician argue the need for the client to have additional time on tests" (p. 23).

Mathematical functioning across both the computational and problem-solving domains should be addressed. Mapou (2000) adds that, along with neuropsychological measures, subtests from the WJ–R achievement battery (Woodcock & Johnson, 1989a, 1989b, 1989c) can provide a thorough assessment of mathematics skills. The results of the calculation subtest can give the clinician a sense of the client's mathematics proficiency, and the applied problems subtest can show how well the client can solve mathematical problems. Finally, the quantitative concepts subtest can provide useful information on mathematical knowledge. The *Key Math–Revised* (Connolly, 1988) is sometimes used in the diagnostic reports for college students to confirm diagnosis of a specific learning disability in mathematics. However, given that the *Key Math–Revised* is designed to measure the mathematical achievement of individuals in grades K–6, it has little utility in an adult assessment battery.

Often it is helpful if the evaluator includes information from a high school and/or college student's transcript to further support the impact of the disability on academic functioning. The bottom line is that achievement testing, when viewed in light of the student's intellectual and processing abilities, should reflect a substantial limitation to learning.

Pitfalls and Perils: Requests for accommodations are often denied because the evaluator used inappropriate tests or procedures. For example, evaluators should not use the WRAT–3 as the primary measure of student achievement. A broad array of measures should be used for this purpose. For suggested measures, readers should consult the listing from the AHEAD Guidelines in Appendix 7.2 on the CD-ROM. Lorry (1998) says "When all scores on the WJ–R are within one standard deviation of each other, except for a single subtest [e.g., dictation], some examiners will identify a learning disability because of one outlier. Discrepant scores from one or even two subtests are insufficient evidence on which to base a diagnosis"(p. 149).

▶ **One evaluator's short list of achievement measures to support an LD diagnosis:**

WRAT–R
Language Fundamentals–Revised

Test Results

Reports are more difficult to read when test scores are embedded in the narrative text rather than included in a table at the end of the report for a quick review. Some evaluators frown on the practice of including the actual scores, fearing that they may be misinterpreted by students. Some parents of college students have voiced concerns about their son or daughter seeing the scores and misinterpreting them. As a result, some evaluators prefer to describe performance levels as "below average" or "superior" rather than stipulating an actual score. Nonetheless, all standardized measures should be represented by standard scores or percentile ranks based on published norms. Informal assessment measures should not be overlooked, as they often provide valuable insights into the student's day-to-day functioning.

Pitfalls and Perils: Some evaluators appear to be overly reliant on test scores and fail to look at the "big picture" before arriving at an LD or ADHD diagnosis. Others appear to rely too heavily on student or parent self-reports and then merely parrot those conclusions as gospel truth without offering their own clinical observations or support. In some cases, it may be more appropriate for the evaluator to discuss the social-emotional status of the student than actual performance deficits in academic areas. A final concern is the role some evaluators assume as an advocate or cheerleader for the student they are evaluating. This bias in reporting can result in a loss of credibility, compromising the validity of the entire report.

▶ **This evaluator reaches diagnostic conclusions based only on a WAIS–R:**

Verbal Scale	Scaled Score	%	Performance Scale	Scaled Score	%
Information	9	37	Picture Completion	6	9
Digit Span	11	63	Picture Arrangement	9	37
Vocabulary	8	25	Block Design	10	50
Arithmetic	8	25	Object Assembly	9	34
Comprehension	8	25	Digit Symbol	8	25
Verbal Scale IQ	95	37%	Performance Scale IQ	86	18%

Although Mr. Roff has average verbal and nonverbal cognitive reasoning skills, as evidenced by his scores on the information and block design tests, he does not perform well on the highly academic scales (Vocabulary and Arithmetic scales). He is not sensitive to nuances in the environment and does not always respond to social cues (Picture Completion). He depends largely on a good recent memory (Digit Span) to sustain himself in an academic environment.

Mr. Roff's decoding skills (Digit Symbol) are not well developed, and his vocabulary development appears to be compromised by poor decoding deficits. These learning deficits or disabilities have interfered with Mr. Roff's academic growth.

Clinical Summary

Keiser (1998) posits that a well-written summary based on a comprehensive evaluative process is a necessary component of the diagnostic report. Assessment instruments and the data they provide do not diagnose; rather, they provide important information that "must be integrated with background information, historical information, and current functioning" (Keiser, 1998, p. 68). The clinical summary needs to recap the high points discussed in the report. The evaluator should use the summary section to rule out alternative explanations for the observed learning difficulties and to discuss how patterns of cognitive ability, achievement, and information processing are used to determine the presence of a learning disability. It is essential that the evaluator recap how learning may be substantially limited.

Pitfalls and Perils: The summary statement is a golden opportunity for the evaluator to "connect the dots" for the consumer and to highlight the functional limitations of the disability and the compensatory aids or accommodations that may be helpful in addressing the underlying disability. Unfortunately, many evaluators do not take advantage of this opportunity and merely cut and paste a previously derived conclusion and drop it into the summary section.

▶ **One evaluator's summary comments that have limited utility:**

> Ms. Eldridge is a personable young lady. It is apparent that she suffers from severe learning disabilities but her potential is quite high. One could only speculate as to the reasons she wasn't properly served in Iowa, but current testing indicated that accommodations are necessary and important if one hopes to truly evaluate her abilities and potential. Testing in an untimed format that allows her to work at her own pace and to visually check and recheck her work in order to develop patterns and learn from previous problems is recommended in order to provide an accurate assessment of Ms. Eldridge's ability to respond to cognitive challenges.

Support for Requested Accommodation(s)

Recommendations for accommodations must be tied to specific test results and clinical observations. It is very helpful for the evaluator to be familiar with postsecondary or graduate school curricula and/or with the item types of a particular admission and licensing examination (e.g., multiple choice, constructed response, or essay). For example, if a student has a specific learning disability in written expression, and the admission test is all multiple choice, then presumably the effect of the disability will be minimal. If the student has a specific learning disability in mathematical functioning and is planning on petitioning her institution for a course substitution for the Arts and Science mathematics requirement, it is critical to determine if the requested accommodations are supported in the evaluation data. Evaluators should be cautioned not to recommend a "one size fits all approach" to accommodations in their reports. Accommodation recommendations should be individualized and tailored to the particular courses and standardized test that the student is planning to complete. Evaluators who present a laundry list of accommodations may not be working in the student's best interest. Blanket accommodations do little to build on a student's strengths or compensate for specific weaknesses, or ultimately to equip the student to meet challenges after graduation in the world of work.

Many evaluators also falsely assume that a student with a history of accommodations and a previous 504 plan or IEP has sufficient justification for the recommended accommodations. This is not necessarily the case. The role of the evaluator is to provide a detailed explanation as to why each accommodation is recommended, correlating it with the student's functional limitation(s) (Keiser, 1998). If no accommodations were provided in the past, and they appear to be warranted now, the evaluator must develop a strong rationale as to why the accommodations are necessary at this time.

Pitfalls and Perils: The clinical summary at the end of the report can be a wellspring of useful information for the professional who is reviewing the documentation and for the consumer. A well-written clinical summary should constitute the punch line: a brief recap of the diagnostic conclusions that were reached in the report that support the accommodations. Clinical report summaries that merely rehash a few points verbatim or don't build a case for the recommended accommodations are of little value.

▶ **This evaluator reaches conclusions and makes accommodation recommendations not supported in the data:**

> Sally was clinically evaluated for the possibility of attention deficit/ hyperactivity disorder and she does not meet any of the criteria; in fact, Sally has excellent concentration abilities. This then goes back to the scores on digit span and arithmetic on the Wexler [sic] Adult Intelligence Scale Revised; when an individual normally gets this kind of low score it is because of short term memory and this is then felt that he needed more time in order [to] express the correct answers with these particular subtests.

> Diagnosis:

> AXIS I: No diagnosis
> AXIS II: 1. (315.31) Expressive language disorder, severe.
>   2. (315.00) Reading disorder, severe.

> Recommendations:

> • Sally should be tested using an untimed format.

> • She should use a tape recorder to record lectures and then again review her notes against the tape to help to further understand what she is getting.

▶ Figure 7.2 displays one evaluator's approach to "tailoring" accommodation recommendations using a checklist format without establishing the relationship between the disability and the recommendations.

Support for Extended Testing Time

Additional testing time is probably the most frequently requested accommodation from students with learning disabilities or ADHD. In order to determine whether additional test time is an appropriate accommodation, a number of factors need to be considered. If additional testing time was granted in the past, who granted it and how much was granted and/or subsequently used by the test taker? What was the format, length, and nature of the test to be taken? Does the test taker's disability presently directly affect his or her processing speed, reading rate, and/or visual motor integration? Does the evaluator provide corroborating evidence of processing-speed deficits based on direct observation? Does the evaluator report how medication may or may not affect the test taker's performance? Additional factors that may be relevant include whether the test taker depends on certain strategies for reading, such as reading aloud or using a reader, a scribe, or some adaptive equipment. The documentation should not only support the need for extended testing time, but also provide some evidence as to how much additional time is fair and reasonable given the nature and severity of the disability.

Pitfalls and Perils: Evaluators need to be careful not to recommend "unlimited" time to testing agencies or higher-education institutions. This is simply not an option. The standard for extended time is time and one-half at most colleges if the documentation supports the request; double time or more may be considered if warranted. However, evaluators should not overlook the possibility that, for some students, more test time may be a detriment. This is particularly true for some college students with ADHD. It may be more appropriate, in such cases, to recommend more frequent rest breaks and a low-distraction environment than to recommend more testing time. In rare instances, a 2-day administration of a test may be the most appropriate accommodation. Finally, evaluators need to be aware that testing agencies do not have to grant additional test time for individuals who simply have a generalized anxiety disorder that is limited to specific stressful situations, like taking an admissions or a licensing exam.

Learning disabled individuals are legally entitled to special education services and/or reasonable accommodations for learning and testing under the Education of All Handicapped Act (PL 94-142) of 1975 and its more recent amendment, the Individuals with Disabilities Education Act (PL 101-476) of 1990, and Section 504 of the Rehabilitation Act of 1973.

The cognitive processing disorders inherent to learning disabilities can significantly affect a person's ability to process information. These services and accommodations will allow the student to have the same access to learning course material as others and will make sure that exams test the student's knowledge of the material and not his or her learning disability.

Under the Americans with Disabilities Act of 1992, individuals with a specific learning disability are also protected from discrimination in employment and various public services, and may be entitled to reasonable accommodations to a job or work environment.

Testing Accommodations:

___ extended time limits ___ time and one-half
_X_ double time ___ triple time
_X_ private, quiet testing room
___ extra breaks during testing: every ___ minutes
___ test reader or audiotaped test
___ scribe to write examinee's test answers as the examinee dictates
___ large print edition of a test

_X_ use of colored lenses or overlays to reduce glare and/or visual distortions, or test printed on colored paper
___ use of calculator
___ use of a typewriter instead of writing answers
___ other: _____

Learning Accommodations:

___ taped textbooks
___ note-takers for classes
___ tape record classes and /or tutoring sessions (use recorder with tape counter)
___ preferential classroom seating
_X_ reduced course load: _9_ hours
_X_ extended time for assignments
_X_ calculator
_X_ word processor
_X_ Franklin Language Master 6000
_X_ use of colored lenses, overlays, or paper to reduce glare and/or visual distortions
___ large print books and enlarged handouts
_X_ course substitution for ___ foreign _X_ math ___ other _____

Recommended Support Services and/or Classes:

___ multisensory structured language phonics therapy such as Orton-Gillingham for word recognition and spelling
___ visualization/verbalization techniques for comprehension of oral and written language
___ Class or tutoring for study skills, test-taking strategies, time management, and organizational skills

(continues)

Figure 7.2. Postsecondary accommodations plan. *Note.* Adapted from "Postsecondary Accommodations Plan," source unknown, 1997.

___ prevocational or developmental education classes to improve basic skills: ___ reading ___ English _X_ math
___ tutoring for content area subjects as needed
___ develop keyboarding skills and learn to use a word processing program
___ speech/language therapy
___ since college level work may be very difficult for the client, consideration should be given to vocational assessment and training as an alternative to college
___ counseling: ___ personal ___ career ___ vocational ___ behavior management ___ family
___ other: _____

Additional Recommended Assessments:

_X_ Attention Deficit Disorder
___ neuropsychological evaluation
___ psychological evaluation
___ hearing exam
___ Central Auditory Processing
___ speech/language assessment
___ visual acuity and functional vision exam
_X_ Scotopic Sensitivity Syndrome ___
___ other: _____

Figure 7.2. *Continued.*

▶ **One evaluator's inappropriate rationale for additional testing time:**

As this candidate is learning disabled, he will also require extended time to compensate for his attention difficulties. Furthermore, it is recommended that James be allowed to take the Scholastic Aptitude Test and/or any other college admissions or achievement test on an untimed or extended time basis.

Support for Paper-Based Test Accommodations

Many individuals with learning disabilities or ADHD may find that the computer-based delivery mode that is being used more and more frequently by testing agencies has some distinct advantages over traditional paper-and-pencil test administrations. Such testing is typically conducted in a cubicle at a testing site or institutional center so distractions are fewer and sounds are muffled by the dividers between cubicles. Typically, only one test item appears on the screen at this time, so the test taker does not have to contend with competing stimuli. Most computer-based tests (CBT) have a countdown feature and a built-in clock to assist test takers with pacing. (If they do not want to see the clock, it can be hidden from view until the last 5 minutes of the test.) However, the biggest advantage of computer-based tests is that many are "computer adaptive tests." A computer adaptive test (CAT) allows the test taker to answer fewer items in order to obtain a score. As the answers are given, the computer scores the questions and uses the information to determine which question will be presented next. When the test taker answers the question correctly, the computer selects a question of greater or equal difficulty. When the question is answered incorrectly, the computer selects a question of lesser or equal difficulty. As a result, actual testing time is reduced. Computer-based tests are presently being developed that will include real-time video questions, self-voicing text, and a highlighting feature.

Test takers should be aware that in a CAT they are not permitted to return to an earlier part of the test. Once an answer is confirmed, there is no scrolling back. Typically, testing programs will provide additional scratch paper or a white board with colored markers on request. Since many test takers with learning disabilities and ADHD are conditioned to using a paper-based test format, they may find it difficult to adjust to this new technology. While some test takers with disabilities may prefer to take a paper-and-pencil test for a variety of reasons (e.g., discomfort using a mouse, desire to write on the test booklet, desire to flip backward and forward through the test), a personal preference alone or general anxiety about using a computer is not a sufficient basis for requesting accommodations. In order to be considered for a paper-based accommodation, the student must have a documented disability covered under the ADA that *substantially limits* his or her ability to take a computer-based test.

Agencies that offer computer-based tests should develop guidelines regarding the adequacy of documentation to support paper-based accommodation requests. For example, if a test taker has recent documentation from a qualified professional regarding *significant* visual impairments, chronic pain, migraines, TBI, or seizure disorders and has had a history of significant difficulties with a computer monitor due to functional limitations, a paper-based request may be appropriate. For some students with long-standing learning disabilities and significant visual-processing deficits, a reader may be an appropriate accommodation, or perhaps a scribe who can serve as keyboard entry aide. It may also be relevant for the evaluator to note in the diagnostic report if the test taker had "vision training" or reading remediation or used audio books as a compensatory tool in the past. In some cases, it may be more appropriate for the evaluator to recommend a special computer monitor with an LCD screen (no flickering), a nonglare screen, or a larger monitor as an alternative to a paper-based test. Additional breaks may be a more appropriate response in situations where the diagnosis is simply "eye fatigue."

Pitfalls and Perils: If a test taker has a well-documented learning disability and a visual-processing problem has recently been identified, the evaluator should mention why the disability was not identified earlier. As with other accommodation requests, there should be a compelling rationale for the accommodation that is supported by clinical observation as well as data in the documentation (e.g., processing speed, visual or spatial perception) to support the rationale for a paper-based format.

It should be noted that a paper-based accommodation will most likely not be approved on the basis of a student's claim that his or her test-taking strategies will only work with a paper-based format. Requests from individuals who are nearsighted or have learning disabilities who might prefer to use a paper-based test so that they can use highlighting or because they would like to go forward and backward through the test are unlikely to be approved. A testing accommodation is not appropriate simply because it would "benefit" the test taker. It is appropriate if it mitigates the effect of an impairment (Keiser, 1998). Disabilities are accommodated; strategy preferences are not.

▶ **One evaluator's inappropriate rationale for supporting a paper-based accommodation for a CBT:**

It is suggested that Zelda take the GMAT in paper-based format rather than on a computer. Her problems with attention and visual spatial organization make it difficult for her to work on a computer, especially in a testing situation. She doesn't like using a mouse and would like to be able to skip answers and return to them later.

Final Thoughts

The intent of the ADA in regard to testing is not to give people with disabilities an "edge" but to provide them with an opportunity to compete without interference from disability-related factors. In order to have that opportunity, people with disabilities should be proactive by securing documentation that substantiates their disability and their need for accommodations or support services. Students with learning disabilities and ADHD should be prepared to articulate their needs to Disability Resource Center staff or to testing agencies. They should also embrace some of the new technologies, like computer-based testing, and learn new strategies that will assist them with computer-generated tests.

In addition, psychiatrists, psychologists, and other qualified professionals who prepare reports to document ADHD and LD should understand the legal framework within which they are operating. Reports cannot be written in "a clinical vacuum where the goal is simply to establish a diagnosis" (Keiser, 1998, p. 53). Latham (1997) adds that evaluators "must be sure to use tests that are appropriate for the purpose and, where necessary, be able to explain why a student may have performed well in a prior setting while still being significantly restricted in the manner of learning, thinking, or concentrating" (p. 46). Keiser (1998) concurs, noting, "Clinicians who prepare reports for ADA determinations must be familiar with how the law defines disability. They must also understand the nature of the program or task for which the accommodations are being sought" (p. 53). In the new millennium, secondary, postsecondary, and graduate school personnel need to foster a dialogue with testing and licensing agencies through conferences and professional associations regarding the development of consistent policies and procedures for documenting and accommodating students with learning disabilities and ADHD. Through this collaboration consumers with disabilities will be better informed and prepared by having LD and ADHD documentation that is complete and transferable across subsequent educational and employment settings.

POLICIES, PROCEDURES, AND PROGRAMMATIC CONSIDERATIONS

As the field of postsecondary services for students with learning disabilities advances and issues regarding equal access to educational opportunities become more complex, it behooves postsecondary institutions to engage in ongoing review of their disability policies and procedures. Gajar (1992) notes that the wide range of services and models to meet the needs of college students with learning disabilities have, for the most part, evolved spontaneously. Since Brinckerhoff et al. (1993) addressed the issue of program development, a number of challenges, most notably reflected in litigation and Office for Civil Rights rulings, have underscored the critical need for clearly articulated policies and procedures as a component of every postsecondary institution's compliance. Jarrow (1997a) advises that "one of the most urgent lessons we have learned in the last five years is the importance of written policies and procedures for the institution to use in guiding its response to students with disabilities and the ADA" (p. 7).

Regardless of the manner by which services are provided for students with learning disabilities, colleges and universities are on tenuous ground if they have not established policies and procedures that address the statutory responsibilities stipulated in the regulations for Section 504. The purpose of this chapter is to examine the following topics: (a) policy development; (b) areas that warrant policies; (c) policy implementation and monitoring; (d) program standards; (e) administrative considerations in the provision of services for students with learning disabilities; and (f) service delivery options.

Policy Development: An Ongoing Process

"Like organizations, policies are constantly changing" (Majone, 1989, p. 150). Not only should postsecondary disability service providers keep their ears to the ground with respect to institutional climate, they should also assume a leadership role in the development and periodic review of policies and procedures that apply both across the institution and within their respective offices. Policy is not a static commodity. It is a dynamic road map that periodically should be reviewed within the context of legal precedents, evolving developments in the field, and emerging "best practices."

The backdrop for the development of policy consists of the legal underpinnings delineated in the ADA and, specifically, Section 504. As noted in Chapter 3, institutions must assure nondiscriminatory treatment of qualified students with disabilities in their recruitment, admissions, and academic programs and nonacademic services. Academic adjustments and auxiliary aids must be available on a case-by-case basis to enable students with learning disabilities to compete more fairly with their peers who do not have disabilities. At the same time, colleges and universities are not required to compromise or lower technical standards, nor are they required to fundamentally alter programs or specific degrees by changing essential requirements (Heyward, Lawton, & Associates, 1995b). Regardless of the area for which policy development is occurring, the regulations for both statutes must be revisited to assure compliance. Furthermore, every policy should be reviewed by an institution's legal counsel before it is officially adopted.

The process of policy development is often triggered by what may appear to be a routine inquiry (McGuire & Brinckerhoff, 1997). For example, a student may ask about her eligibility for dean's list status since the current policy of her school requires full-time enrollment, defined as carrying no fewer than 12 academic credits in a semester. As an accommodation for her learning disability, she often enrolls in fewer credits than 12 in a semester so that she can invest the additional preparation and study time required to compensate for her disability. Should she be restricted from this academic recognition of excellence if she' meets the standards with respect to grades but falls short of the credit requirements by virtue of the accommodation for her learning disability?

Legal decisions may precipitate the development of policy. As discussed in Chapter 3, the case at Boston University stands as a major impetus for the development of institutional policy with respect to course substitutions. To date, "courts appear to defer greatly to the decisions of academic administrators, even where discrimination on the basis of disability is at issue" (Tucker, 1996). Despite this deference, postsecondary disability service providers should heed the observations of Judge Saris in the Boston University case that an institution must be able to demonstrate that it has engaged in an objective, thorough, and reasoned process in articulating policy.

Other factors may serve as the springboards for policy development. For example, complaints by either students or their parents may underscore the need to have a clearly articulated policy about eligibility for services and the procedures for accessing such. A policy regarding access to services would be relevant in the case of a student who argues that she was not provided with testing accommodations when, in fact, she identified herself to the disability office during the final week of a semester requesting that she "get what I need for finals" without having provided the institution with documentation of a disability. The postsecondary disability service provider also has an opportunity to assume a leadership role on campus by proactively initiating the process of policy development based on his or her wisdom, professional experience, and knowledge of research and litigation in the field.

Jarrow (1997a) has delineated the difference between policy and procedure. If a statement tells *what* must be done, it is policy. If a statement tells *how* it must be done, it is procedure. Both elements are important to promulgate. To present a policy about student responsibilities for accessing services and accommodations without a description of how and with whom to obtain these services results in an information void. Clear, concise policy statements accompanied by explicit directions on steps to be taken by a student and/or faculty member will eliminate confusion and delays in ensuring access.

Before determining specific areas for which disability policies should be developed, it is advisable to engage in a variety of activities to ensure familiarity with generic institutional policies as well as the campus climate. A wise disability service provider will reflect on the tenor of campus politics and proceed judiciously in proactively initiating policy development. Policymaking is often a political process marked by conflicts in values where issues of power and its distribution are at stake. For example, the issue of defining a "liberal arts" degree is fraught with strong opinions. To naively begin the task of crafting a course substitution policy in the curricular area of foreign language for students with learning disabilities without first engaging in dialogue with administrators and faculty may be tantamount to unwittingly fostering an adversarial climate.

It is also advisable to determine the process by which institutional policy is officially developed. Is there a formal mechanism or committee structure in place by which policy is constructed? Is there an administrative body responsible for sanctioning policy? Are there different procedures for the adoption of programmatic policies and institutional policies? Do institutional policies require the approval of a board of trustees, or can a high-ranking administrator such as a provost or vice president authorize the adoption of policies? What is the role of legal counsel in the review of institutional policy? These issues bear heavily on the time frame required for all the stages in policy development, from determining the responsible personnel for working on policy to soliciting input and feedback from essential parties to the official approval and implementation of new policy. Other factors, such as the distribution of policy throughout the campus community and assuring its "visibility" in appropriate campus publications and on Web sites, must be a part of the planning process. Depending on the scope of policy development, it is not unusual to plan on at least a full academic year to achieve this task.

Steps in Policy Development

When a need for developing or revising policy is apparent, disability service providers should consider a systematic approach. Figure 8.1 (McGuire & Brinckerhoff, 1997) portrays numerous activities that are comprised in this arduous task, beginning with a determination of what is currently done on a specific campus as well as on similar campuses. The proverbial advice not to "reinvent the wheel" is well taken, since many institutions of higher education have engaged in the process of policy development for students with disabilities and can provide examples that may serve as prototypes.

A critical step involves the determination of key campus personnel who should assist in the process of creating or revising policy. The process of crafting policy should be pluralistic. Goggin (1987) opines that "if, during policy formulation and adopting, policy makers with dissenting views would air their differences and come to agreement about what are acceptable programmatic ends and what are the best means of achieving them, then policy implementation would have a much better chance of succeeding" (p. 79). According to Majone (1989), rhetoric, a component of policy development, "is the craft of persuasion, the study of all the ways of doing things with words" (p. 7). Although as a field, postsecondary disability services in the United States have the "clout" of laws from which to advocate (e.g., under Title II of the ADA, public institutions are required to develop and publicize grievance policy), it is more effective to promote discussion among various stakeholders (i.e., administrators, faculty, students, and disability personnel). Attitudes can loom as powerful impediments to achieving the "spirit of the law." Astutely identifying key players or facilitating the appointment of a committee that can work through challenges is well worth the time and effort of the disability service provider. In fact, in a recent survey of administrators of postsecondary services for students with disabilities in North America, respondents validated their critical role in serving "on

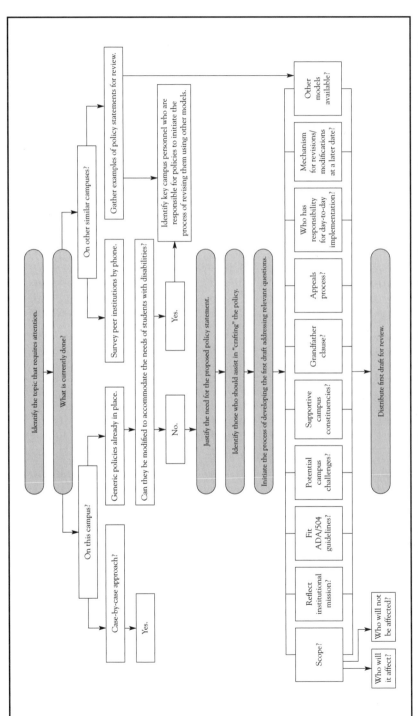

Figure 8.1. Steps in the policy development process. *Note.* From *Crafting Campus Policies: Facing Ongoing Challenges to Access and Equity*, by J. M. McGuire and L. C. Brinckerhoff, 1997, Strand presentation at the 9th annual Postsecondary Learning Disability Training Institute, Saratoga Springs, NY. Copyright 1997 by J. M. McGuire. Reprinted with permission.

campus committees to develop institutional policies and procedures regarding students with disabilities" (Shaw, McGuire, & Madaus, 1997).

The first draft of a policy should encompass a number of the elements in Figure 8.1. In some areas, an institution's mission is integral in developing a document that reflects the underlying philosophy of the college. For example, a community college that serves a nontraditional population including adults who may not have comprehensive and recent documentation of a learning disability, may develop more liberal requirements for documentation than might a professional graduate school. If a change in existing policy is anticipated, consideration should be made for incorporating a grandfather clause. Thought should be given during this stage of policy development to the nuts and bolts of daily implementation. For example, if the institution deems a course substitution policy to be a reasonable accommodation, who will bear responsibility for making such a determination? Does a policy of this nature come under academic affairs, and, if so, what are the implications if disability services are under the organizational structure of student affairs? Disability service providers are often both policymakers and policy managers. Recognizing potential conflicts of interest is important so that alternative mechanisms are in place in the event OSD personnel have a professional and ethical obligation to turn decision making over to a third party.

Areas for Policy Development

Noting that there can be no uniform list of policies and procedures that will fit every campus, Jarrow (1997a) points out that each institution must determine the level and scope of its policies. She lists these broad areas as useful though not exhaustive for policy development: (a) institutional responsibility to assure equal access; (b) responsibility for the determination of reasonable accommodations; (c) confidentiality; (d) course substitutions; (e) full-time student status with less than full-time credit load; and (f) appeals of accommodation decisions. At the University of Connecticut, the policies and procedures for students with disabilities incorporate these components (see Appendix 8.1 on the CD-ROM for the full text): (a) rights and responsibilities of students and the institution; (b) specific policies for academic accommodations, eligibility for financial aid, dean's list status, and course substitutions; (c) procedures for accessing services; (d) procedures for resolving disagreements relating to specific requests for academic accommodations; and (e) discrimination complaint procedures.

At a minimum, the following areas should be covered in disability policies and procedures:

- *Eligibility for services*. It is critical that colleges and universities establish policies and procedures that are widely distributed (e.g., via all relevant campus publications such as catalogs and programmatic materials, Web sites, etc.) and delineate the steps required to access services including accommodations. Rights and responsibilities of both the student and the institution should be addressed. Specific reference to an institution's responsibility to assure equal educational opportunity under federal or provincial statutes establishes the legal requirement for nondiscriminatory treatment on the basis of disability. The institution's policy with respect to the confidentiality of disability-related information should be stated. Regarding student responsibilities, the following topics are essential: (a) timely identification when seeking an accommodation, and (b) documentation of disability. Students wishing to receive accommodations or adjustments must provide documentation of their disability that meets the guidelines of the institution. With the widespread distribution and use of guidelines for documentation of a learning disability (AHEAD, 1997b; ETS, 1998b) and guidelines for documentation of attention-deficit/hyperactivity disorder (Consortium on ADHD Documentation, 1998; ETS, 1998a) (see Appendixes 7.2 and 7.3 on the CD-ROM for guidelines), postsecondary institutions have access to comprehensive materials that should be incorporated into policy and procedure statements. Students must bear the cost of such documentation, which should be fairly recent, come from an appropriate expert, and be sufficiently comprehensive (Tucker, 1996).

- *Procedures for obtaining reasonable and appropriate accommodations*. Given the wide array of approaches that exist in postsecondary settings for the provision of accommodations, especially in the area of testing accommodations, explicit instructions for accessing these should be included in disability policies and procedures. More institutions are now stipulating that a timely request for accommodations is part of a student's responsibility (Kincaid, 1998). It has been pointed out by Jarrow (1997a) that institutions should be guided in their decision by the notion of making a "good faith effort" to comply with the ADA. If the nature of the accommodation is relatively easy to arrange (e.g., extended test time) and there are mitigating circumstances surrounding a student's delay in requesting such an accommodation (e.g., wishing to attempt tests in the same manner as other students or initially believing that accommodations are not necessary), a college or university should always work to ensure access for eligible students.

- *Course substitutions.* The institution's policy on course substitution should be addressed. If there has been a determination that curricular requirements such as foreign language are essential components of an institution's programs and constitute technical standards that apply for all students, a statement to that effect will clearly alert consumers about the institution's policy in an area that is particularly contentious. The legality of setting such standards will surely continue to be the subject of debate and ongoing litigation, so disability service providers should pay close heed to developments in case law and rulings of the OCR.

If a course substitution policy has been adopted, the procedures a student must follow as well as the responsibilities of the institution should be delineated. It is also helpful to list the type of information and documentation a student must provide so that students can plan and prepare accordingly in anticipation of requesting such an accommodation.

• *Determination of full-time status.* The institution's policy and procedures regarding full-time status should be addressed. For example, if a student carries fewer than the stipulated number of credits required for full-time status in a given semester as a disability accommodation, what is the institution's policy regarding a student's eligibility for the services that accrue to full-time status? In the process of seeking this designation, responsibilities of both the student and the institution should be clearly spelled out, along with a statement indicating the rights and privileges afforded to a full-time student (e.g., financial aid awards, opportunity to achieve dean's list status, access to campus housing).

• *Procedures for resolving disagreements regarding specific accommodation requests.* In cases where there is disagreement about a requested accommodation, it is advisable to articulate a process by which a review of the request can occur. Timelines for accessing the process, personnel involved in the review, and the institution's response to the requested accommodation during the review process should be outlined. Appendix 8.2 (see the CD-ROM) delineates the approach developed by the University of California at Berkeley as a result of the litigation in *Campbell A. Dinsmore v. Charles C. Pugh and the Regents of the University of California* (1990). The functions of the board in addition to its composition and the time frame for resolving disagreements are described in detail.

• *Grievance policy.* Institutions may incorporate the grievance policy and procedures for disability-related discrimination claims into existing policy for investigating other areas of possible discrimination (e.g., those of race, age, or gender). Including the more universal discrimination policy and procedures specifically within publicized disability policies and procedures will ensure the availability of information. Obviously, disability service providers play an ongoing role in trying to negotiate resolutions to disputed accommodation requests, but conflict of interest precludes them from serving in a key role in a formal grievance procedure.

Implementation and Monitoring of Policy

Policy implementation occurs over time, varies from setting to setting, and is affected by a number of factors. The attributes of the policy, the nature of the organization or administration that is responsible for putting policy in place, and the talents and personalities of the individuals responsible for making the policy work all affect successful policy implementation (Goggin, 1987). Applying these points to disability policy implementation in postsecondary settings makes it clear that disability service administrators play a key role.

If implementation is to be successful, certain organizational elements must be in place, including procedures for campus-wide distribution, funding, and staffing. For example, inclusion of disability policies and procedures in campus publications requires advanced planning. The page layouts may require adjustment because of the additional space needed to incorporate this information. It is also important to proofread the proposed text for accuracy and accessibility, especially with the increasing use of Web sites to communicate information. Generic institutional Web sites (e.g., home pages with information about the college, its location, student characteristics, etc.) should be linked to more specific sites that include disability information including policies and procedures (for an example of such linkage, go to http://www.uconn.edu/administrative .html and click on "Students with Disabilities"). Budget planning may be involved if policies and procedures are included in LD program materials. If procedures such as review of documentation to determine eligibility for a course substitution require the participation of other campus staff (e.g., associate dean), the implementation of policy requires collaboration with them as well.

Training is critical in the process of implementation. Faculty not only must be apprised of their rights and responsibilities to ensure educational access, they should also understand the procedures that students with disabilities must follow in specific areas such as arranging for testing accommodations. Reports by students with learning disabilities of "handing over" their confidential test reports to individuals including faculty who have no expertise or training in this area raise grave concerns about privacy and the potential misuse of privileged information. Close contact and collaboration between disability services and the ADA compliance office or administrator are important not only as they relate to policy implementation but also to ensure that key administrators remain abreast of emerging issues on campus that may warrant a new or revised policy.

Appendix 8.3 (on the CD-ROM) is an excellent example of one institution's response to an emerging campus need. At the University of California at Berkeley, it became apparent that a mechanism was needed to deal with requests for accommodations for departmental programs such as invited lectures (e.g., the provision of sign language interpreters for a deaf community member attending a lecture). A policy and procedure are now in place for requesting and allocating funding for such expenses.

Evaluation of the process of policy implementation should be planned to examine outcomes. For example, if course substitutions are permitted in the area of foreign language, can the disability service administrator respond to a dean's query regarding the extent to which students with learning disabilities are availing themselves of this accommodation? Given the critical role faculty play, particularly in providing testing accommodations, how will the policy and procedures in this area be monitored in the event that a student subsequently files a complaint contending that she was not provided with an accommodation? Finally, Goggin (1987) points out that "a policy maker or manager must know when to and when not to redesign a policy" (p. 201). It is incumbent upon the disability service administrator to devise methods for monitoring the implementation of disability policies so that objective data are the catalyst for decisions to revise or refine policy or to assuage faculty or administrative concerns about accommodations. Formative evaluation procedures, discussed in Chapter 13, constitute one approach for monitoring policy implementation.

Finally, regardless of the administrative configuration or type of disability support services, policies and procedures constitute an integral component of an institution's response to ensuring equal access. Proactively addressing this element is an example of both professional and programmatic standards setting.

Programmatic Considerations

Program Standards

Recognizing that there is no universal administrative model for the delivery of learning disability services, the field has nonetheless progressed to a point where essential elements in the ensurance of access should serve as the underlying foundation for *all* program development. Given the growth in the number of students with LD enrolled in higher education and the ever evolving clarification of responsibilities of colleges and universities to this cohort, service providers, seasoned veterans and newcomers alike, should engage in the proverbial "pulse taking" regarding office functions. Testimony to the forward movement of the postsecondary disability services profession is evident in the initiatives begun in 1994 by AHEAD. Task forces were organized to develop professional standards (see Chapter 12), program standards, and a code of ethics (Shaw, 1997a). With the support of AHEAD, rigorous methods have been used to empirically validate the standards of our daily performance and practice (Shaw et al., 1997) as well as the service components that are fundamental in ensuring equal access (Shaw & Dukes, in press). The time has come for the field to embrace and put into practice these hallmarks of a profession.

In 1998, 563 out of 800 randomly selected members of AHEAD responded to a survey (70% response rate) sent out under the auspices of the AHEAD Program Standards Task Force Committee for the purpose of identifying essential service components of Offices for Students with Disabilities. These components were gleaned from a review of the literature and the input of content experts. Regardless of the "personality" of an institution, 27 program standards have been identified as fundamental by the AHEAD membership and recommended by the task force to the AHEAD board of directors to "set parameters for essential postsecondary disability services and assert the credibility and unique responsibilities of the OSD" (Shaw & Dukes, in press). These standards have been identified as essential for OSDs regardless of the type of school (2- or 4-year), funding source (public or private), location (U.S. or Canada), or competitiveness (open enrollment or competitive).

The AHEAD program standards stipulate that the office that provides services to students with disabilities should include functions in nine areas: (1) consultation, collaboration, and awareness; (2) information dissemination; (3) faculty and staff awareness; (4) academic adjustments; (5) instructional interventions; (6) counseling and advocacy; (7) policies and procedures; (8) program development and evaluation; and (9) training and professional development. Table 8.1 displays these categories with their 27 service components. Notably, policies and procedures are identified as an essential program standard (items 7.1–7.5).

Another major contribution to the field occurred with the completion of a Delphi survey by Anderson (1998a, b) that resulted in the identification of support service components essential to service delivery for students with learning disabilities. A panel of 131 experts from North America engaged in the Delphi technique, which is designed to elicit consensus through an iterative process of repeated survey responses. A questionnaire was developed that consisted of 113 service components identified through an extensive review of the literature and input from content experts. This questionnaire was then distributed to a panel of experts who were asked to rate each item with respect to how essential it was for the office providing services to students with LD. The Delphi procedure consisted of three rounds of responses from the 131 experts from the United States and Canada, a process of gathering their opinions, comments, and judgments. Rounds two and three reflected reasoned consensus obtained by systematically aggregating individual judgments. Panel experts validated 55 components as essential for the office providing services for students with LD. Table 8.2

Table 8.1
AHEAD Program Standards

To facilitate equal access to postsecondary education for students with disabilities, an office that provides services to those students should:

1. Consultation, Collaboration, and Awareness

1.1 Serve as an advocate for students with disabilities to ensure equal access.

1.2 Provide disability representation on relevant campus committees (e.g., academic standards, policy development).

2. Information Dissemination

2.1 Disseminate information through institutional publications regarding disability services and how to access them.

2.2 Provide services that promote access to the campus community (e.g., TDDs, alternative materials formatting, interpreter services, adaptive technology).

2.3 Provide referral information to students with disabilities regarding available campus and community resources (e.g., assessment, counseling).

3. Faculty and Staff Awareness

3.1 Provide consultation with faculty regarding academic accommodations, compliance with legal responsibilities, as well as instructional, programmatic, physical, and curriculum modifications.

3.2 Provide consultation with administrators regarding academic accommodations and compliance with legal responsibilities, as well as instructional, programmatic, physical, and curriculum modifications.

3.3 Provide individualized disability awareness training for campus constituencies (e.g., faculty, staff, administrators).

3.4 Provide feedback to faculty regarding general assistance available through the office that provides services to students with disabilities.

4. Academic Adjustments

4.1 Maintain records that document the plan for the provision of selected accommodations.

4.2 Determine, with the student, appropriate services and accommodations consistent with the student's documented disability.

4.3 Have final responsibility for determining academic accommodations.

(continues)

Table 8.1 *Continued.*

5. *Instructional Interventions*

5.1 Advocate for instruction in learning strategies (e.g., attention and memory strategies, planning, self-monitoring, time management, organization, problem solving).

6. *Counseling and Advocacy*

6.1 Assist students with disabilities to assume the role of self-advocate.

7. *Policies and Procedures*

7.1 Develop written policies and guidelines regarding procedures for determining and accessing "reasonable accommodations."

7.2 Establish guidelines for institutional rights and responsibilities with respect to service provision (e.g., documentation of a disability, course substitution or waiver).

7.3 Establish guidelines for student rights and responsibilities with respect to service provision (e.g., documentation of a disability, course substitution or waiver).

7.4 Develop written policies and guidelines regarding confidentiality of disability information.

7.5 Encourage the development of policies and guidelines for settling a formal complaint regarding the determination of a "reasonable accommodation."

8. *Program Development and Evaluation*

8.1 Provide services that are based on the institution's mission or service philosophy.

8.2 Coordinate services for students with disabilities through a full-time professional.

8.3 Collect student feedback to measure satisfaction with disability services.

8.4 Collect data to monitor use of disability services.

8.5 Report program evaluation data to administrators.

9. *Training and Professional Development*

9.1 Provide disability services staff with ongoing opportunities for professional development (e.g., conferences, credit courses, membership in professional organizations).

9.2 Provide services by professional(s) with training and experience working with college students or adults with disabilities.

9.3 Adhere to the Association on Higher Education and Disability Code of Ethics.

Note. From *AHEAD Program Standards*, by Association on Higher Education and Disability, 1998, Columbus, OH: Author. Copyright 1998 by AHEAD. Reprinted with permission.

displays these 55 support service components across 14 categories. Given the multiple responsibilities of LD service providers, many of these essential support service components address areas that can be particularly challenging. For example, the issue of documentation is a vexing one. These experts agreed that it is essential to require documentation that is thorough (item 3.4, i.e., addresses at a minimum the areas of aptitude, achievement, and information processing); includes more than one test instrument (item 3.3); clearly identifies the nature of the LD (item 3.1); and has been completed by a qualified professional (item 3.2). Notably, the criteria identified by these 131 experts are reflected in the AHEAD *Guidelines for Documentation of a Learning Disability in Adolescents and Adults* (1997b).

Other essential service components validated by the Anderson study include the coordination of services by a professional with training in LD (item 5.1), an emphasis on assisting students to determine appropriate compensatory strategies based upon documentation (item 11.3), instruction in learning strategies (item 14.1), and collaboration with other campus resources regarding ways to work with students with LD (items 10.1–10.3). Anderson (1998b) has recommended that the identification of these essential LD support service components and procedures will "facilitate institutional planning and help students identify the support services that can rightfully be expected in any setting" (p. 1). Whether an institution is in the beginning stages of program development or engaging in the important step of periodic program review and evaluation, these two sets of essential program components offer critical, objective data to guide practice. The manner by which a college or university incorporates these program standards will vary according to a number of factors including administrative considerations, operational procedures, and institutional mission. As Anderson so aptly points out, steps to "identify and validate components and procedures essential to the delivery of services to postsecondary students with LD will serve as a critical step toward developing a more cohesive service delivery system for this growing population" (p. 1).

Program Development

The organizational "positioning" of programs for students with learning disabilities bears heavily on issues such as funding, staffing, and visibility on campus. Ideally, decision making should emanate from a structured, systematic process of weighing the benefits and limitations of program alliances across a variety of settings within an institution (e.g., OSDs, learning centers, and campus departments). In reality, it is more likely that planning for serving the needs of students with learning disabilities occurs informally or evolves in response to the

Table 8.2
Essential LD Support Service Components

It is essential that the office responsible for providing services to students with learning disabilities . . .

1. Admissions

1.1 provides guidelines regarding the type(s) of documentation required by the institution to applicants wishing to submit additional information to be reviewed.

1.2 encourages the institution to include a statement on the acceptance letter to all students through which a student with a learning disability may self-identify to the office that provides services to students with LD or other disabilities.

2. Assessment

2.1 provides referral information to students regarding resources for diagnostic evaluations for which the students must pay the cost.

3. Verification/Certification of Eligibility of LD

3.1 requires documentation that clearly states the nature of a student's learning disability.

3.2 requires documentation that has been completed by a licensed or certified professional with experience diagnosing adolescents or adults with LD.

3.3 requires documentation that includes more than one test instrument.

3.4 requires documentation that addresses at a minimum the areas of aptitude, achievement, and information-processing abilities.

4. Consultation/Collaboration/Advocacy

4.1 provides representation on a campus-wide disability advisory committee consisting of faculty and administrators.

4.2 provides representation on a campus-wide disability advisory committee consisting of faculty, administrators, and students.

4.3 consults with faculty and administrators regarding compliance with legal responsibilities.

4.4 consults with faculty and administrators regarding reasonable accommodations, and instructional, programmatic, and curriculum modifications.

4.5 consults with representatives from campus departments (e.g., library, health services, residential life, counseling services).

4.6 functions as a liaison between students with LD and faculty to ensure equal access.

4.7 encourages self-determination and self-advocacy in students with LD.

(continues)

Table 8.2 *Continued.*

5. Coordination of Services

5.1 coordinates services for students with LD through a professional with training and experience working with college students or adults with LD.

5.2 provides services for students with LD that are coordinated through a full-time professional.

6. Policies & Procedures

6.1 promotes the development of written policies and guidelines for faculty regarding procedures for determining and accessing "reasonable accommodations."

6.2 develops written policies and guidelines for students regarding procedures for determining and accessing "reasonable accommodations."

6.3 promotes the development of policies and guidelines for determining the full-time or part-time status of students with LD who require a reduced courseload as a "reasonable accommodation."

6.4 promotes the development of policies and procedures for settling a dispute regarding the determination of a "reasonable accommodation."

6.5 develops written policies and guidelines regarding the confidentiality of a student's disability information.

6.6 develops policies and guidelines regarding acceptable documentation for students with LD.

7. Program Development

7.1 provides services that are consistent with the institutional mission.

7.2 provides services that are based on the specific mission or service philosophy of the office or program providing services to students with LD.

7.3 develops specific goals and objectives for the program or office that provides services to students with LD.

7.4 provides services for part-time and nontraditional students.

7.5 provides services for graduate and professional students.

7.6 initiates efforts to increase funding from institutional resources for mandated services.

7.7 assists other campus resources that provide special workshops to meet the needs of students with LD (e.g., career services, counseling center, academic skills center, writing or math center).

8. Program Evaluation

8.1 collects data to monitor use of LD services.
8.2 collects student feedback to measure satisfaction with LD services.
8.3 collects data to measure effectiveness of LD services.
8.4 reports program evaluation data to administrators.

(continues)

Table 8.2 *Continued.*

9. Outreach Services

9.1 disseminates written information to faculty and staff regarding available LD services and how to access them.

9.2 disseminates written information to incoming students regarding available LD services and how to access them.

9.3 disseminates written information to administrators regarding available LD services and how to access them.

9.4 disseminates written information to the community (e.g., high schools, vocational rehabilitation) regarding available LD services and how to access them.

9.5 provides information in institutional publications regarding available LD services and how to access them.

9.6 provides information in alternate formats (e.g., audiotape, videotape, large print, computer disc) regarding available LD services and how to access them.

10. Counseling and Academic Advising

10.1 assists other campus resources that provide individual personal counseling to work with students with LD.

10.2 assists other campus resources that provide career counseling to work with students with LD.

10.3 provides academic advising in conjunction with faculty and other academic personnel to students with LD.

11. Academic Adjustments

11.1 works collaboratively with students to determine appropriate academic adjustments for course examinations based on documentation.

11.2 works collaboratively with students to determine appropriate auxiliary aids based on documentation.

11.3 works collaboratively with students to determine appropriate compensatory strategies based on documentation.

11.4 collaborates with faculty and students to determine appropriate academic-related accommodations.

12. Training and Professional Development

12.1 provides LD awareness and sensitivity training opportunities for faculty, staff, and administrators.

12.2 provides LD awareness and sensitivity training opportunities for staff in campus offices (e.g., residential life, financial aid, health services).

(continues)

Table 8.2 *Continued.*

12. *Training and Professional Development* *(continued)*

12.3 provides training opportunities for faculty, staff, and administrators regarding instructional modifications, testing accommodations, and strategies for students with LD.

12.4 provides regular staff meetings and training for LD service providers.

12.5 provides opportunities for professional development for LD service providers (e.g., conferences, credit courses).

13. *Subject-Area Tutoring*

13.1 assists other campus resources that provide content tutoring to work with students with LD (e.g., academic skills center, writing or math center, academic departments).

14. *Learning Strategies Instruction*

14.1 provides instruction on learning strategies (e.g., attention and memory strategies, planning, monitoring, regulating, time management, organization, scheduling, problem solving) through LD services.

14.2 assists other campus resources that provide instruction on learning strategies (e.g., credit courses and seminars, academic skills center, writing or math center) to work with students with LD.

14.3 promotes learning strategies instruction as a viable approach for students with LD.

Note. From *Essential Support Service Components for Students with Learning Disabilities at Postsecondary Institutions in North America: A Consensus-Based Determination*, by P. L. Anderson, 1998a, unpublished doctoral dissertation, University of Connecticut, Storrs. Copyright 1998 by P. L. Anderson. Reprinted with permission.

increasing demands from this growing cohort. Whether services are designed from scratch or refined to include the essential components identified by Shaw and Dukes (in press) and Anderson (1998a), familiarity with the organizational structure of the institution is critical, since change may be inherent in the process of program development.

Institutional Mission

An institution's mission must be considered as the foundation or underpinning for the development of LD programs. Bloland (1991, p. 28) wisely cautions that we cannot "discuss the culture of higher education as if it were a single, monolithic entity. We have major research universities, community colleges, freestanding professional schools, denominational colleges, trade schools, and liberal arts colleges." A corresponding caveat applies to LD programs at the postsecondary level. No single model or approach will fit every institution, given the diversity that is a hallmark of the American system of higher education.

Consider the following examples of mission statements that portray qualitatively divergent environments. The mission statement of Middlesex County College, a public community college in New Jersey, states that it is "committed to serving all those who can benefit from postsecondary learning and creating an environment responsive to the educational needs of individuals" (*Middlesex County College Catalog*, 1997, p. 26). The statement from the University of Utah reflects the teaching, research, and service functions of large, publicly financed universities when it says that its mission is:

> to educate the individual and to discover, refine, and disseminate knowledge. As a major teaching and Research University, the flagship institution of the Utah State system of higher education, the University of Utah strives to create an academic environment where the highest standards of scholarship and professional practice are observed and where responsibilities to students are conscientiously met. It recognizes the mutual relevance and interdependence of teaching and research as essential components of academic excellence. It welcomes students who are committed to learning and who conform to high academic standards. The right of free inquiry is zealously preserved; diversity is encouraged and respected; critical examination and creativity are promoted; and intellectual integrity and social responsibility are fostered. The University is fully committed to the goals of equal opportunity for full, unhampered, and responsible participation in every aspect of campus life. (University of Utah home page, http://www.admin.utah.edu)

LeMoyne College is a 4-year, liberal arts, Catholic college that describes its mission as follows:

> The institution offers higher education in a 450-year-old intellectual and religious tradition. The more than 300 Jesuit schools, colleges, and universities throughout the world stress academic excellence, preparation for life in the professions or workplace, education of the whole person, respect for the integrity and freedom of all persons, the formation of clear goals in life based on solid religious or philosophic principles, an emphasis on ethics and values, the development of a concern for others, especially those most in need, and service to the local and regional community. (*LeMoyne College Catalog*, 1998–99, http://www.lemoyne.edu/catalog_98-99/general.htm)

How an institution envisions its mission and institutes activities to put it in operation will have profound implications for many facets of campus life including support services. For example, in smaller, less academically competitive settings, the institutional mission may imply a commitment to a holistic education where teaching, learning, and student development are equally valued. In large, research-focused universities, functions may center more on research productivity and scholarly initiatives with less emphasis on the service aspect of student development.

In the process of LD program development, there must be a "good fit" between program goals and objectives and the institution's mission. To push for institutional change or improvement, which is often what happens when one advocates for essential LD service components, without reflecting on whether such change is consistent with the institutional mission, is to jeopardize one's credibility and long-term effectiveness. As an example, requesting LD program staff to address remediation of basic skills deficits in an academically competitive research setting could be construed as dissonant with institutional purpose.

Understanding the Organizational Structure

Many colleges and universities have been formally serving students with disabilities as required under Section 504 since the early 1980s, in varying degrees and through divergent approaches. It was suggested by Jarrow in 1986 that 90% of the progress in service delivery for students with disabilities had occurred between 1975 and 1985. Given this history of service delivery for students with physical disabilities, it is more likely to be the exception than the rule to have the opportunity to create services for students with learning disabilities from the ground up. However, as the demand for LD services has increased due to the number of these students accessing postsecondary education, existing OSD support staff have often been instrumental in shaping the development of services to meet the needs of this cohort. Collaborative planning with personnel from other campus student support services affords an opportunity to promote disability awareness and avoid duplication of services. However, sensitivity to "turf" issues and the employment of tact in working with veteran campus support staff are paramount.

In most instances, the organization of a postsecondary institution is clearly established, with divisions and units delineated according to the organizational chart. According to Sandeen (1989), higher education organizations are typically composed of divisions that address academics, finances, student affairs, and development. Results of a nationwide survey of postsecondary disability service programs substantiated the location of the majority of these programs within the division of student affairs. Clark (1990) reports the following results based on a response rate of 37% from 700 surveyed postsecondary institutions: 62% reported organizational location within student affairs, 20% within academic affairs, 7% in other college units, 4% within departments; the remaining 7% indicated divergent affiliations. In another study of 18 large state universities with comprehensive LD services, 69% of the 13 institutions that responded reported that LD services were located within the disabled student services unit (Woods, Sedlacek, & Boyer, 1990). Shaw and Dukes (in press) found that 90% of 563 AHEAD members participating in a survey to identify essential program components reported that their office served all students with disabilities. It appears, then, that the location of LD services rests predominantly in OSDs under the organizational umbrella of student affairs (with services located under academic affairs a distant second).

Whether LD services or programs have evolved from already existing offices (e.g., OSDs) or are developed through a comprehensive planning process (e.g., a component of academic skills centers), careful consideration needs to be paid to the *benefits and constraints* inherent in the student affairs and academic affairs models. Table 8.3 illustrates a comparison between the two organizational approaches to housing the LD service function.

Under academic affairs, policy making is a function that often rests within the unit. As more critical issues such as reasonable accommodations in testing, course substitutions, and the delineation of essential course components are raised by students with learning disabilities, postsecondary institutions can expect challenges to policies and procedures of the academic realm. Faculty may identify more strongly with a program within academic affairs, and there is the potential for LD programs to serve as a practice site for graduate students in special education, educational psychology, counseling, or clinical psychology. At the same time, limitations of the academic affairs model include lack of fiscal support and space, dissonance between the responsibilities of an LD service provider and those of faculty, and contractual arrangements that are usually not of 12-month duration.

The traditional mission and activities of the student affairs division are well suited to service delivery. If a constellation of support services is already in place, there is an opportunity to centralize them under a generic office such as a learning and academic support center. For example, at the Mont Alto campus of Pennsylvania State University, services for students with LD are incorporated into the Academic Skills Center (N. Hatzes, personal communication, January 20, 1999). Additionally, the student-focused nature of the division of student affairs may promote the visibility of LD services on campus. On the

Table 8.3

A Comparison of the Organizational Structures of Academic Affairs
and Student Affairs: Benefits and Limitations

Considerations	Academic Affairs	Student Affairs
Benefits	• Mission of the division—academic matters—and LD program goals and objectives may be congruent.	• Mission of the division—student support—subsumes the traditional function of the OSD.
	• Access to key administrators (e.g., deans, vice president; president in the case of small colleges) may be more feasible within the organizational hierarchy.	• Specific functions within the division are often related to needs of students with LD (e.g., admissions, housing, registration, orientation).
	• Policies and procedures (e.g., foreign-language substitutions) that impact students with LD are often generated by Academic Affairs.	• Potential exists for developing a centralized, comprehensive system of services using a center or cluster model (e.g., campus learning center with computers, tutorial assistance, note takers, adaptive equipment, etc.).
	• More opportunities for program research exist given emphasis on data and productivity.	• Retention is a major concern, which relates to outcomes for students with LD.
	• Possibility of developing practicum site for graduate assistants and interns exists.	• Fiscal needs can be justified within the context of "student support services."
	• Funding may be more predictable and secure with options for work-study students.	• Position of administrative staff is often a 12-month one.
	• Faculty attitudes may be more supportive given Student Affairs' "perceived lack of status" (Bloland, 1991).	• Campus-wide visibility exists by virtue of student-based focus.
Limitations	• Fiscal support may be problematic given the "teaching" function of this division.	• Division is vulnerable to budgetary cuts in eras of limited funds.
	• Space allocation is a concern.	• Space allocation is a concern.
	• Role and responsibilities of LD services coordinator may be inconsistent with traditional faculty responsibilities.	• Credibility of OSD initiatives to promote reasonable accommodations may be devalued by some faculty concerned with lowering standards.

(continues)

Table 8.3 *Continued.*

Considerations	Academic Affairs	Student Affairs
	• Nine-month contract is the traditional employment arrangement. • Budget constraints exist in areas such as equipment, supplies, etc., since these are not perceived as integral to the academic function. • If faculty status is to be allocated to LD coordinator, obtaining such a position is extremely challenging.	• Competencies of staff may not include expertise in LD, thus requiring ongoing staff training dependent upon staff roles. • Salary levels may be problematic in attracting well-qualified LD personnel. • Participation in decision making regarding academic policies may be limited. • Dependent upon the organizational structure, there may be more hoops to jump through regarding decision making.

Note. From *Academic Affairs or Student Affairs: Pros and Cons,* by J. M. McGuire, 1992, unpublished material, University of Connecticut, A. J. Pappanikou Center on Special Education and Rehabilitation, Storrs. Copyright 1992 by J. M. McGuire. Reprinted with permission.

other hand, the question of status should be considered, since it has been suggested that student affairs and its supporters are typically not seen by faculty as particularly important (Bloland, 1991). This has implications with respect to faculty attitudes and openness to change that are critical to ensuring equal opportunity for students with learning disabilities. Funding for student affairs personnel can become problematic in times of fiscal crisis. Barr and Fried (1981, p. 81) sum up the dichotomy succinctly: "Academic affairs, with its cadre of faculty, and student affairs may constitute two distinct subcultures on many campuses."

This is not to suggest a simplistic approach to deciding the optimal location of LD programs on campus. Jarrow (1999b) has addressed this question of program affiliation:

> The age-old question among disability service providers is always, "Where is it best for my program to be housed administratively? Academic affairs? Student affairs? Human Resources?" The answer is simple . . . whenever possible, you want your program to be housed and/or in some way associated

with whatever administrator or unit holds the most power and respect within the institution. (p. 3)

Jarrow has also spoken of the politics inherent in effective service delivery. Without keeping an ear to the ground regarding the political climate and key campus players, disability service providers are "likely to find that your issues, and your effectiveness on behalf of the population you serve, will remain on the sidelines of the institutional agenda" (p. 2). Jarrow wisely counsels against competing with other campus programs. Bearing in mind that the LD program or the OSD fulfills a legal mandate for the institution in ensuring equal access for students with disabilities, it is imperative that a collaborative approach underly the work of the disability service provider, especially when there is competition for fiscal resources.

By understanding the culture of an institution and its impact on service delivery, the LD service provider can draw upon an awareness and knowledge of the unique character and climate of a setting in order to advocate effectively regarding programmatic concerns and divisional affiliation. Since the culture of an institution affects its decision-making process as well as its formal and informal organization, sensitivity on the part of LD program personnel has the potential to serve as a powerful tool in effecting change regardless of organizational placement.

Key Questions

In laying the groundwork for developing or expanding LD programs, additional points should be considered in juxtaposition to the institutional mission and organizational structure. Table 8.4 outlines a series of questions that can promote a planned process for program development.

Areas such as admissions, eligibility criteria for services, and access to and assurances of reasonable accommodations all imply a need for explicit policies and procedures to be in place within the LD program unit. As campus awareness of LD services broadens, referrals to the program will increase, underscoring the importance of defining the scope of activities such as assessment. Because of the pivotal role played by faculty members in the area of reasonable accommodations, planning should address their need for information and technical assistance with respect to classroom accommodations that promote access yet do not compromise standards. Finally, systematically planning for program evaluation will ensure expedient data collection so that program and student outcomes can be monitored and serve as a basis for program planning and modification.

Table 8.4
Questions To Be Addressed in Program Development

- Is there a clear, concise statement of philosophy or mission for LD services?

- Is there detailed information on procedures for accessing LD services?

- What role, if any, will staff from LD services assume in the admissions process?

- What criteria will be used to determine student eligibility under Section 504?

- What documentation will be required from students seeking services?

- Will assessment or evaluation services be offered by the LD program?

- What procedures will be used to determine reasonable accommodations, and how will accommodations be efficiently and effectively provided?

- How will policies and procedures relating to equal educational opportunity for students with LD (e.g., course substitutions) be developed?

- What range of services will be offered by the LD program (e.g., diagnostic assessment services, counseling, learning strategies instruction, career and vocational guidance, self-advocacy training)?

- How accessible to students with LD are generic services offered to nondisabled students?

- What mechanisms will exist for promoting faculty and staff awareness and knowledge regarding LD?

- How will program evaluation be conducted? For whom? By whom?

Service Delivery Issues

Services or Programs: A Definitional Maze

Depending upon the institution, students with learning disabilities are assisted in their pursuit of postsecondary education through offices that are often described either as providers of services or providers of a program. On the surface, this may seem like semantic hairsplitting. In reality, this dichotomy can create confusion on the part of consumers, parents, and professionals seeking information, resulting in a lack of clarification that can be seen in the literature on types of services available to college students with learning disabilities (Bursuck et al., 1989; R. Nelson & Lignugaris/Kraft, 1989). In a nationwide survey,

Bursuck et al. found that three categories of postsecondary support services were typical: Section 504 access services, special services, and remedial services. In Nelson and Lignugaris/Kraft's research, only 14 of the 31 articles that were reviewed reported on surveys of *services* to support students in postsecondary settings; evaluations of specific *programs* were described in 6 articles. Guides such as *Peterson's* (Mangrum & Strichart, 1997) and *The K&W Guide* (Kravets & Wax, 1999) contain detailed information, including size of the institution, number of staff, availability of diagnostic testing, and types and extent of support services offered. In some states, resource guides are available that provide an overview of the disability services on each college campus (K. Jackson, personal communication, February 8, 1999; Anderson, Halliday, & McGuire, 1997). In order to avoid ambiguity in terminology, a brief discussion of terms is warranted.

Comprehensive college LD *programs* are characterized by a planned process that includes the support of key campus administrators. Often one person spearheads the efforts to develop the program (Vogel, 1982); that individual typically has expertise in the area of learning disabilities. A program at the postsecondary level should be based on the specific individual needs of students. Determination of needs should proceed from reliable and valid documentation that often is gathered through in-house assessment services. Programs are coordinated in a centralized location (Brinckerhoff, Shaw, McGuire, Norlander, & Anderson, 1988). A range of services is available, and a diagnostic-prescriptive approach is often used to select appropriate services tailored to match each student's unique needs. Vogel (1993a) identifies the following as components of comprehensive postsecondary programs for students with learning disabilities: program information in university publications; well-developed policies and procedures; faculty and staff awareness training; current and comprehensive testing; director and staff with expertise in LD; individualized direct services; frequent monitoring of academic progress; and ongoing program evaluation. Although not every component will exist on every campus, the critical aspects of LD programs are individualization, a basis in diagnostic data, and coordination by a professional with training in learning disabilities. In some instances, because of the specialized nature of services provided by trained staff, LD programs offer a limited number of "slots" for students with learning disabilities and charge a fee. This enhanced model is permissible only if generic disability services are also available at no cost.

Services at the postsecondary level can be defined as those generic activities that are carried out to ensure equal educational opportunity for any student with a disability. Brinckerhoff (1991) outlines a variety of "minimal resources" that can ensure adequate support services in a climate of fiscal austerity that may preclude formal programs. Again, the critical distinction between programs and services centers on the qualifications of the personnel and the degree to which individualized interventions are available. Brinckerhoff states that an LD service provider can have training in broader areas such as counseling or student affairs, rather than in learning disabilities and assessment.

Basic LD services typically might include provision of taped textbooks; assistance in arranging testing accommodations; auxiliary aids such as tape recorders, readers, note takers; assistive technology; and provisions for making course substitutions. The operative word in a service approach is *generic*, meaning that the services are inclusive of and available to all students with disabilities.

Brinckerhoff (1991) describes another type of service as "user-fee services," which are more like programs since they typically include diagnostic services, a trained LD specialist, individualized tutoring, and counseling. This level of support includes a fee that is usually assessed every semester. The legitimacy of charging a fee for specialized programs was initially discussed by Rothstein in 1986, who pointed out that, at that time, neither case law nor the regulations seemed to require special training programs. Subsequent rulings by the OCR ("Offering Campus LD Testing," 1996) have confirmed that enhanced programs beyond the basic requirements of Section 504 can be offered for a fee, but it is critical that students be apprised of the availability of services mandated under Section 504 at no cost. As long as a student with a learning disability can access generic support services at no cost, user-fee services are not deemed discriminatory because specialized support programs are above and beyond the Section 504 requirements for reasonable accommodations.

It is also important to bear in mind that institutions must offer services to all students with learning disabilities regardless of their status as full- or part-time students. A recent survey by the 11th U.S. Circuit Court of Appeals affirmed the responsibility of an institution to provide auxiliary aids without consideration of a student's enrollment in a regular program (Heyward, Lawton, & Associates, 1991c). The implications of this ruling for settings that offer flexible class scheduling, such as evening and weekend courses, are significant since provisions for reasonable accommodations cannot be constrained by the parameter of traditional "office hours."

Rather than becoming bogged down in semantics, we can simply state that there is a value for every institution in clearly delineating its approach to ensuring equal access to students with learning disabilities. It is very possible for an OSD to assist students with learning disabilities in a programmatic way. Staff can be expanded to include a part-time or full-time LD specialist. Tutorial services can be developed to focus on areas that are typically a problem for students with learning disabilities, using a learning-strategies approach (Deshler,

Schumaker, Lenz, & Ellis, 1984) and emphasizing student independence and autonomy (Brinckerhoff et al., 1992). In an inclusionary model of student support services a campus Academic Skills Center or Office of Learning Assistance may incorporate disability services as one of several functions such as skills development and academic advising. No one approach will fit the needs of every student. Support services may provide a suitable match for some, whereas a comprehensive, highly structured program may offer the intensive intervention required by others (Shaw, McGuire, & Brinckerhoff, 1994).

A "Developmental" Continuum of Service-Delivery Models

Twenty years ago, only a handful of colleges and universities were addressing the needs of students with learning disabilities in a programmatic way (Vogel, 1993a). Seven years ago the field of postsecondary LD services was emerging as a vital area in response to consumer needs (Brinckerhoff et al., 1993). Today, the picture has come into sharper focus. Using the revised continuum originally conceptualized by McGuire and Shaw (1989), which highlights various types of support services, administrators and service providers should carefully consider components of each level of service in determining which conceptually fits with the overall institutional mission.

The notion of a continuum (see Table 8.5) also captures the evolution of approaches for serving students, since increasing demands have often served as a catalyst for moving in the direction of increased program specialization. In some settings, decentralized services may be available as represented by Level 1 on the continuum. As pressure for services increases in both scope and the number of students requesting them, an institution may move to centrally coordinated or data-based services. In his study to identify the essential job functions of administrators of OSDs, Madaus (1996) found that nearly 80% of the 549 AHEAD members who responded described their institutional support services as data based or centrally coordinated. It is also important to bear in mind that there may not be a one-to-one correspondence between elements noted on the continuum and those of an actual service or program. Regardless of where on this continuum an institution falls, the threshold question remains the same: Are qualified students with learning disabilities provided equal educational opportunities in a nondiscriminatory fashion through access to academic adjustments and auxiliary aids? An annual review based on the goals and scope of the services offered should be conducted to address this question and facilitate planning for future needs (McGuire et al., 1990). The next section discusses considerations to bear in mind about administrative support, whether

Table 8.5
Continuum of Postsecondary LD Support Services

Decentralized Services	Loosely Coordinated Services	Centrally Coordinated Services	Data-Based Services	Fee-Based Services
Disability contact person(s) has multiple responsibilities and responds to student needs on an ad hoc basis	Disability contact person provides services to students and consults with other campus personnel	Full-time learning disability specialist	Full-time learning disability director or coordinator	Full-time learning disability director and learning disability specialists
Basic services as mandated under Section 504	Generic 504 support services available	Services often housed in Office for Students with Disabilities or available as a component of an office for learning assistance or academic skills center	Learning disability specialist(s)	Comprehensive policies and procedures strategy based
Few formal policies	Procedures in place for accessing services	Full range of accommodations provided	Services either free standing or a component of OSD	Optional personalized services above and beyond what is required by law
	Peer tutors available for all students	Formal policies and procedures across areas including eligibility for accommodation	Full range of accommodations provided	Enhanced services often housed in an office other than OSD
	Students referred to other campus services (e.g., counseling and/or career services, residential life)	Strong emphasis on student self-advocacy	Comprehensive policies and procedures in place	Services often include diagnostic assessment, basic skills remediation, and subject-area tutoring
		Peer support groups sometimes available	Strong emphasis on student self-advocacy	Individualized instruction based on comprehensive documentation
		Specially trained LD tutors may be available	Development of individualized support plans based on current documentation	Services required under Section 504 and the ADA available at no cost
			Tutoring in learning strategies available from trained staff or graduate-level interns	Usually requires a separate application to determine eligibility for specialized program
			Data-based contact records and service-use profiles generated for annual report	Student participation in intensive program services is monitored
				Fee structure may vary depending on amount of services

Note. From *Resource Guide of Support Services for Students with Learning Disabilities in Connecticut Colleges and Universities*, by J. M. McGuire and S. F. Shaw (Eds.), 1989 (rev. 1996, 1999), Storrs: University of Connecticut, A. J. Pappanikou Center on Special Education and Rehabilitation. Copyright 1999 by J. M. McGuire and S. F. Shaw. Reprinted with permission.

program development occurs from the ground up or evolves from already existing services.

Garnering Administrative Support

After the mission and organizational structure of the institution have been studied, it is important to find the best fit along the continuum of LD support services. As pointed out in the previous section, the process of finding the right niche for LD services can have long-term implications and may change in times of administrative restructuring and organizational change. In this section, the issue of garnering and maintaining administrative support will be viewed from two vantage points: that of service providers who are initiating LD support services and that of veteran service providers who are trying to maintain services or perhaps develop new programming initiatives in response to escalating requests for services or changing organization patterns. Later in this chapter, the issue of support services in graduate and professional programs will be discussed.

Initiating LD Support Services

A common mistake of many well-meaning campus support staff is to try to develop LD services overnight. This process takes at least 6 months of careful, comprehensive planning to become established. During the early stages, it is important to determine which key players on campus are most likely to support efforts for developing LD services. Similarly, the question of who is most likely to be resistant to or threatened by the development of LD services should be posed early on. A campus-wide survey of an array of stakeholders should be conducted in order to determine what is currently done on campus for students who are at risk, and by whom. Survey data can be helpful in identifying allies, determining the scope of services to be offered, and creating an interface between LD services and existing campus resources (e.g., the academic assistance center or counseling center).

After conducting campus fact-finding initiatives, the LD contact person should survey what other peer institutions are doing regionally and across the country. Many 2- and 4-year institutions have notable services for students with learning disabilities. Learning disability specialists at peer institutions are valuable resources when discussing future plans and pinpointing roadblocks and triumphs. Telephone discussions, e-mail correspondence, fax exchanges, and other means of information sharing are very useful for fact finding to build a rationale for establishing services on campus. If feasible, after the LD service provider conducts an informal telephone survey, he or she should target one or two institutions for a site visit. A half-day site visit with a veteran LD service coordinator can be very beneficial for the neophyte. Such meetings are enhanced if one or two key players from the visiting campus have the opportunity to meet with a variety of administrative staff, LD service personnel, and students. Fact-finding meetings can focus on a variety of issues ranging from eligibility criteria to service-delivery options. It is often helpful for the newcomer to review and collect sample service-delivery forms that can be adapted for future use. Additional service-delivery forms and suggestions for standard operating procedures can be found in resource books by McGuire, Madaus, and Plaia (1998) and Vogel and Adelman (1993). In addition to site visits and telephone contacts, articles cited in "References" at the end of this book contain a wealth of valuable information pertinent to creating services. The HEATH Resource Center in Washington, D.C., is another valuable resource for gathering information on higher education and disability issues (800-54-HEATH). National conferences, such as the annual Postsecondary Learning Disability Training Institute (sponsored by the University of Connecticut–Storrs) and the annual AHEAD conference offer in-depth topical information and opportunities for future networking.

To ensure that the planning process becomes a collaborative effort and not the sole initiative of any one individual, it is best for planning efforts to emanate from a cross-section of campus constituencies. An advisory board or ad hoc committee can provide further direction and shape the newly emerging services. This group can often make more inroads with members of the administration than any one individual could. The committee may be tightly focused on LD issues or it may have the broader mission of addressing the needs of students with any disability. In either case, it should be composed of representatives from a cross-section of the entire campus community, including faculty, staff, deans, and, possibly, alumni, students, consulting psychologists, speech and language clinicians, and parents. These individuals can offer insights into developing a workable plan of action. Involving staff from the psychology department, special education department, or other campus disciplines may result in suggestions for hiring of future personnel and the development of intern training sites. Faculty, staff members, or alumni who have a family member with a learning disability or have a learning disability themselves may be particularly supportive of these efforts. Members of the advisory group can serve as a "political action committee," which can strategize on how to approach the campus administration with a broad-based proposal that is likely to attract support. Using the CIPP model of program evaluation (see below), McGuire,

Harris, and Bieber (1989) offer a format for a proposal for creating specialized services for students with LD. Drawing upon their suggestions, the following decision-oriented approach can guide the program planning process:

Context

- What is the context in which the program will operate (e.g., within OSD; as part of an academic or learning support center)?

- What needs (e.g., growth in student enrollment; institutional commitment to retention; student requests for specific services) underlie program development?

- What resources already exist?

Input

- What program services are needed to meet program goals?
- What are the personnel requirements for program implementation?
- What are the budgeting considerations?
- What are space and facility needs?

Process

- What methods and activities will be implemented to put program goals and objectives into operation?

Product

- What are the outcomes to be achieved through program implementation (e.g., student retention; student graduation; training of graduate students)?

The proposal should begin with a strong rationale for services and should emphasize that existing campus resources cannot effectively meet the needs of a growing number of students with learning disabilities. Data collected on service requests and numbers of campus students with learning disabilities make the case more convincing. Even the most resistant administrators will take note of the fact that in an age of enrollment management, it is important to attract "otherwise qualified" students and to retain them. Therefore, the proposal can be strengthened by promoting LD services as a marketing tool to attract additional qualified students. Coordinated efforts with the admissions office can help to sell these services to a broader high school audience. Arguing that LD support services are only another aspect of the institution's retention efforts can be a convincing idea. Finally, service providers can use the legal justifications for providing these services as a powerful rationale for a proposal. Avoiding costly litigation and addressing issues of institutional compliance with Section 504 and the ADA are additional motivators that catch the attention of administrators. Drafting a program proposal provides an opportunity to create a document tailored to attract seed money from corporate sponsors, internal grant sources, and alumni. One often overlooked consideration is the potential impact that parents may have on helping to expand fledgling services. Parents are often very appreciative of efforts to ensure access through support services and may be willing to commit some of their own financial resources to get these services off the ground. If a fee is charged for specialized tutorial support, then the possibility of scholarship funds needs to be addressed during these early planning stages.

There are a variety of ways of presenting the proposal to the department head or dean who is most likely to be responsible for overseeing the operations of the proposed LD support services. It might be useful to invite that person to a meeting where the proposal can be showcased by several members of the planning or advisory team. This initial meeting should clearly stipulate the rationale for providing the services. Supporting testimony from faculty and students may also be appropriate. The proposal should include the overall goals and objectives for the program, the range of services to be offered, staffing considerations, operating expenses, suggestions for the location of the services, and a projected time line. An executive summary of the proposal could be used as an outline for the meeting. A more low-key approach is for the designated LD contact person to approach the dean or department head privately to discuss the proposal informally, while concurrently soliciting his or her support. The new LD service provider should be prepared to demonstrate to the dean of student affairs or academic affairs how the mission of the LD support services interfaces with the overall mission of the institution.

For the vast majority of service providers, the luxury of offering a comprehensive LD program has often been impossible due to funding limitations, inadequate space, or a lack of institutional commitment. Brinckerhoff (1991) points out that it is not easy to garner administrative support for new initiatives in challenging fiscal times. Consequently, colleges and universities may want to develop a "core of generic support services" for students with learning disabilities and not attempt a comprehensive program until long-term institutional support is ensured. By starting small, LD service providers can take a systematic approach that will give them the opportunity to gradually gain the attention of campus administrators over the competing demands of other campus personnel.

Another consideration for starting small is noted by Mangrum and Strichart (1988), who point out that not all students with learning disabilities need the support and services of a comprehensive program.

LD coordinators must realize that their ground-breaking efforts may not be received warmly by all constituencies on campus. Administrators may not be as receptive to the idea of providing educational opportunities to students with learning disabilities as they are to providing services for students with physical disabilities or vision or hearing impairments. Faculty members may be concerned that admitting students with learning disabilities will lower academic standards or require them to water down their curriculum. Some may fear that academic adjustments will infringe upon their academic freedom in the classroom. Mangrum and Strichart (1988) surveyed LD college program directors and found that there generally was no change in a college's image as long as the population of students with learning disabilities did not exceed 10% of the base population. They also observed that many college administrators and faculty still think that "the learning disabled have insufficient intelligence to succeed in college" (p. 220). Consequently, one of the first priorities for LD service providers is to build awareness and to assure faculty and administrators that serving college students with learning disabilities does not devalue the professional stature of the institution. Convincing the faculty is probably one of the most challenging jobs an LD program director will face. Attending departmental faculty meetings, meeting with individual faculty members, and making presentations to heighten awareness can all help to win faculty support for the idea of LD services on campus. Follow-up meetings with key administrators and faculty will depend on a number of factors, including the amount of perceived backing behind the LD services office, the level of training and experience of the LD service provider in working with college students with learning disabilities, and available financial resources.

Once the proposal for establishing specialized LD support has been accepted by the administration, staffing needs must be addressed. Mangrum and Strichart (1988) note that the person who serves as the "initial catalyst" for the college LD program often becomes the first program director. This individual is formally charged with the responsibilities of establishing services and negotiating, on their own turf, with the campus support staff who have already been working with these students. These initial meetings often take place in the academic development center or learning assistance center. The meetings should be non-threatening, and the LD service provider should be humble in proposing an expanded service model that may initially appear to be an infringement to the director of the campus peer-tutoring program or to an academic-skills counselor.

As institutions of higher education engage in strategic planning to move into a new millennium characterized by increased diversity in student populations, the time may be right to propose an inclusive model of service delivery. It is possible for LD services to become a component of generic campus academic support centers or to expand the mission of existing offices to serve students with learning disabilities. For example, at Boston College, LD services have been incorporated into the Academic Development Center in the college library. In that setting, LD services are viewed as one type of service among many that are readily available and visible to both students and faculty. A similar model is used at the Mont Alto campus of Pennsylvania State University, and numerous examples can be found by searching Web sites that describe campus academic resources. Institutions with federally funded student services programs such as TRIO that are charged with serving first-generation college students, members of minority groups, and students with physical disabilities may consider adding an LD specialist to the staff who can work with students who have learning disabilities.

Once the LD support services are well defined and funded, it is time to market services to the campus community. Brinckerhoff (1991) offers several suggestions for publicizing LD services and for enhancing program visibility. Dalke (1991) presents a variety of suggestions for service coordinators on ways to develop program literature and materials, offering specific ideas for developing a program brochure and an informational videotape, as well as suggestions on marketing program information to potential students and the general public. She also notes that people do not become informed overnight and that "it will take time to disseminate information about the services, but perhaps more importantly, it will take time to help everyone become more aware and appreciative of the unique needs of students with disabilities as they pursue their careers in higher education" (p. 77). With the rapid expansion of Web sites to "market" colleges and their services, links from generic campus home pages to disability-specific sites hold great promise for information dissemination.

The guidelines and suggestions presented in this section should lay the foundation for establishing a well-defined set of core services for students with learning disabilities. By keeping the first-year plan manageable in scope, service providers can be responsive to the changing needs of the administration, faculty, and staff and, most important, the students they serve. The following section will address many of the administrative challenges that veteran LD service providers may face as they seek to ensure program viability and stability.

Veterans: How to Maintain and Enhance LD Support Services

One of the best ways to ensure the future security of LD services is to make them an indispensable and *visible* entity on campus. This can be achieved in

several ways. Service providers need to keep deans and other college administrators informed about the activities of the office. These individuals should
receive annual updates about the services being offered, including demographic
information, retention figures, and other related data that will help to underscore the impact of these services on students. An executive summary of the
annual report should also be distributed to other campus resource personnel
and deans. College administrators should be invited to sponsored events and
workshops that focus on the LD office's activities. Memos from faculty and letters of appreciation from parents, students, and alumni are also useful in expanding awareness. The role of the LD support services office can also be promoted by holding volunteer or faculty awards receptions each spring. Such
annual gatherings afford an opportunity to spotlight faculty, staff, or volunteers
who have been supportive of college students with learning disabilities. Administrative superiors and college deans should be on hand for these events. Such
small-scale, low-cost publicity efforts should be covered by campus reporters,
who can heighten awareness through the campus newspaper. By letting key
administrative players know about services throughout the year, and not just at
the beginning of the next funding cycle, the attitudinal support base can be
strengthened. A newsletter with a special column featuring LD issues could be
sent to all faculty, staff, and students who have contact with the LD student services office. Private consultants, community contact people such as rehabilitation counselors, Learning Disabilities Association of America parent groups,
and local high school teachers could receive invitations to an LD open house
at the beginning of each semester. If the college admissions office sponsors
information workshops for regional high school personnel including guidance
counselors, the LD program director can be a part of the agenda, highlighting
services offered to students with learning disabilities. Middlesex County College (http://www.middlesex.cc.nj.us/) in Edison, New Jersey, sponsors a high
school guidance counselors' breakfast each year to enhance the awareness of
high school personnel about a variety of postsecondary LD issues. Another successful technique for expanding outreach efforts is to establish an LD speakers'
bureau on campus. This group might be composed of three or four college students who are willing to talk with high school students, speak at college fairs,
and give talks to departmental faculty (Brinckerhoff, 1991).

Second- or third-year veterans should contact the chairs of less supportive
departments on campus in the spirit of building bridges. It may be useful for the
program director, rather than a member of the staff, to personally meet with the
department chair to discuss mutual concerns about the LD support services on
campus. A successful student with a learning disability from within the department may be a powerful contributor at such meetings. Faculty development
efforts can expand in areas that are often more complex and sensitive, such as

the appropriateness of course substitutions or policies regarding withdrawal from a course beyond the standard deadline without penalty. Other key departments on campus, including athletics or minority affairs, may be prepared to "join forces" with the LD support services office, once the office is respected and accepted as a critical campus resource.

LD service providers must monitor the rate of expansion of services in subsequent years to prevent an erosion in the level of personal service available to students who are already being served. Providing personal service means appreciating faculty and consumers who drop in unexpectedly to see the office, unflinchingly repeating information to parents of prospective students over the telephone, and dropping current work for a student who needs immediate attention. These actions convey the message that even though the LD support services office may be expanding in the number of students being served, personal contact has not been sacrificed. A related concern as services expand is support staff burnout. Professional stress can be minimized by ensuring reasonable schedules for daily appointments, providing meetings for staff on a weekly basis, and supplying opportunities for ongoing professional training. As the staff expands to address the changing needs of students, the LD service provider may seek to share some job duties with staff so that they can assume control of some aspect of the LD support services office. This might involve cofacilitating a peer support group, or conducting interviews with all prospective students and their parents.

It is important to note that heightened campus awareness and a professional image are not enough to guarantee future services. Supplemental funds must be sought out by LD service providers so that services can be maintained and expanded where needed. When it is not possible to achieve a strong internal institutional commitment to funding, it may be possible to raise funds through additional user fees. Some LD support services offices are now charging additional fees for summer orientation programs, specialized tutorial support, or diagnostic testing. Even in times of fiscal restraint, opportunities exist to secure additional funding through fund-raising activities or by soliciting the support of alumni or parents of students with disabilities. For example, the University of Wisconsin–Madison was able to fund a tape-recording studio in the Disabilities Resource Center solely through the contributions of alumni. The 25th and 50th class reunions may be looking for projects to support, and disability services are often a good prospect. Service providers should keep in mind that potential donors are much more likely to donate to a cause that is supported by a track record of success than to a trial balloon. The adage that "people give money to people" bears careful thought. By personalizing the services that are offered, service providers give potential donors an opportunity to view first-hand, or through the eyes of their son or daughter, the effect that these supports can have on their child's academic progress and self-esteem.

Services for Students in Graduate
and Professional Programs

As students with learning disabilities experience success in their postsecondary programs, they are increasingly enrolling in graduate and professional schools. Data from the recent report from the National Center for Education Statistics (Horn, Berktold, & Bobbitt, 1999) verify that the proportions of college graduates with and without disabilities who enrolled in graduate school within a year after earning their bachelor's degree were similar. Having demonstrated their qualifications and successfully navigated the competitive waters of admission to graduate school (e.g., law school, medical school, business administration program, allied health program), these students arrive on campus with varying perceptions of their needs. Brinckerhoff (1997) notes, "Many first-year graduate students believe, now that they are in their areas of specialty (i.e., international banking, special education, or pediatrics), their learning disabilities won't affect them. Others believe that all they need to do is 'buckle down' and study harder to get the results they desire" (p. 153). Few of the graduate and professional schools these students attend offer services analogous to those they may have had access to in their college or university. Although reasonable accommodations must be provided for eligible students, learning specialists are a limited to nonexistent resource in most graduate schools. The notion that LD support services should be offered at this level is often met with negative reactions, especially in more competitive settings, because of the perception that generic campus services can address student needs.

The approach to service delivery at the graduate level often begins on an ad hoc basis, with no central coordination. Students may approach generic disability support services, academic support service personnel, or assistant deans with concerns about their studies or requests for accommodations. Just as the transition from high school to college frequently is challenging for students with learning disabilities, so, too, is the transition to graduate school, where the learning demands change and the competition escalates. Brinckerhoff and McGuire (1999) identify a number of attributes of the academic environment and delineate the differences in demands between the undergraduate and graduate levels. As illustrated in Table 8.6, opportunities for feedback at the graduate level are less frequent and often hinge on a student's ability to assertively seek it out. Given the concerns graduate students harbor regarding self-disclosure, often because of fear that the information may be used against them or not regarded as confidential, they may be reluctant to approach faculty who are the gatekeepers to maintaining rigorous standards. On the other hand, some attributes of the graduate learning environment may constitute a strong match for some

Table 8.6
Graduate School and Beyond

Factors To Consider	Undergraduate Level	Graduate Level
Reading	Moderate load	Moderate to overwhelming
Writing	Term papers (15 pages)	Thesis and/or dissertation (150–250 pages)
Studying	As needed	Must be self-directed with close monitoring to avoid snowballing effect
Organizational skills	Important and challenging, but variety exists depending on courses	Critical because of demand to organize large quantities of technical material and balance due dates
Courses	Broader overview of content	Specific and technical in nature, often assuming extensive knowledge base
Feedback	More frequent via tests, papers	Expectations for student-initiated discussions regarding feedback and performance
Grades	More frequent	Less frequent
Deadlines	Short-term (4–8 weeks)	Often long-term (8 months–2 years)
Class time	2 or 3 times a week	Once a week, often at night
Study groups	Common	Isolated learning, self-directed
Group work	Not typical	More group work
Advising	For registration purposes once or twice per semester	Ongoing contact for guidance
Disclosure	Willingness to do so more common	Fear of disclosure not unusual
Support	OSD/LDSS office	Academic support services
Accommodations	Extended test time a frequent request	Extensions for papers are common

Note. From *Factors Differentiating Undergraduate and Graduate Study,* by L. C. Brinckerhoff and J. M. McGuire, 1999, unpublished material, University of Connecticut, Storrs. Copyright 1999 by L. C. Brinckerhoff and J. M. McGuire. Reprinted with permission.

students with learning disabilities. In medical school, lecture notes are typically available to all students, as are taped versions of class lectures. Smaller class size and frequent discussion, particularly in seminars, constitute an excellent venue for highly verbal students who can demonstrate their strengths in oral presentations and debates. Depending on the graduate program, the format of student evaluation may require consideration as it relates to reasonable accommodations. Requesting an extension for a lengthy paper may not be viewed as unreasonable, whereas requesting an alternate test format may raise issues around technical standards and essential components of a program of study.

As service providers in graduate institutions can expect to experience a trend toward enrollment of more students with learning disabilities, it behooves them to engage in collaborative conversations with administrators about "universal" elements of service delivery that are essential, whether at the graduate or undergraduate level: policies about eligibility for accommodations including guidelines for documentation; procedures for accessing services including the designated disability contact person; mechanisms for educating faculty about their rights and responsibilities; and procedures for addressing grievances. The following are accommodations that graduate schools might reasonably be expected to make for students with learning disabilities: course load modification and extended time for the completion of examinations, courses, thesis requirements, and degree(s) (Association of American Medical Colleges, 1993; Stone, 1996).

As Brinckerhoff (1997) points out, the key players in the process are the students, who must be willing to take risks, to realistically assess their strengths and weaknesses, and to request academic accommodations that will allow them to compensate for their disabilities. Students should also be apprised that testing and licensing agencies such as the National Board of Medical Examiners and state bar examining committees are not bound to approve the same accommodations for examinations as were provided in graduate school. The horizon is expanding for successful students with learning disabilities, and the diversity they will bring to graduate and professional programs can only enrich the fabric of the nation's increasingly diverse educational community.

Developing a Summer Transition Program

Another approach to increasing revenues for program services is to develop a summer orientation program. Transition programs attract the interest and attention of prospective students with learning disabilities, thereby increasing the number of students who visit the campus and ultimately apply for admission. In an age of aggressive marketing to assure stable enrollment patterns, this benefit alone could help garner additional administrative support. Another advantage of a summer transition program is the opportunity it provides for campus personnel to gather both formal and informal data on new students. Observational data obtained from new students can be very useful to service providers in planning future services for those students.

According to Dalke and Schmitt (1987), transition programs should accomplish the following:

- provide students with an educational experience similar to that expected in higher education;

- assist students in obtaining a clear picture of their strengths and weaknesses and needs as they relate to the demands of the postsecondary environment;

- provide opportunities for students to explore and address issues related to the emotional factors involved in losing a familiar support system of family, friends, and teachers;

- provide opportunities for students to practice self-advocacy skills;

- familiarize students with the physical environment of the campus and community;

- identify and explain campus and community organizations, agencies, and related support services that are available to students;

- provide instruction to students in areas such as study skills, time management, note taking, test-taking strategies, and library use;

- provide direct instruction to students in academic areas such as reading comprehension, written language, and basic math skills; and

- provide staff with formal and informal student performance data.

The activities planned to meet these goals will vary from campus to campus depending on the availability of financial resources, qualified staff, and the location of the institution. Dalke (1991) notes that ideally the program should occur during the summer prior to the semester that students enter as first-year students. In order for the program to achieve the breadth and scope of its goals, it should last between 4 weeks and 2 months. Finally, although the summer is the logical time for service providers to offer such a program, the summer months are not a prized time for students with learning disabilities to attend still more school. Some may be looking for freedom after high school graduation or a special vacation with friends before setting off for college. Others may depend on summer employment to generate funds to finance their education. With these factors in mind, marketing efforts must be assertive and address both the desire of parents to boost their son's or daughter's scholastic achievement before college and the student's desire to enjoy the summer. Promoting the possibility of earning college credits and adjusting the course load in the student's first semester also hold promise for selling the idea of a summer program.

Many direct service providers underestimate the amount of advance planning time it takes to develop, publicize, and implement a summer orientation program for students with learning disabilities. Planning should begin at least 6 months in advance. Initially, the LD service provider must assess the amount of administrative support that the institution is willing to provide. Drawing up a brief proposal concerning the program to share with unit directors and deans is a good starting point. The proposal should include a rationale for the services, expected duration, range of services to be offered, staffing and space considerations, and projected income and expenses. The LD service provider may need to "sell" this transition program idea to the administration (Brinckerhoff & Eaton, 1991). It is important to anchor the purpose of the program within the overall mission of the college or university. Service providers may need to assure the administration that this outreach effort will not devalue the academic stature of the institution and will ultimately provide many benefits, such as improving the retention of students with learning disabilities, generating additional tuition income, and enhancing institutional recognition. These preliminary planning sessions should take place in early fall so that dates can be set and publications and mailings can occur in a timely manner.

In the planning stages, such matters as the availability of facilities for summer programs are critical. Some colleges and universities run summer institutes and specialized programs (e.g., Elderhostel) that may preclude access to key facilities such as the computer center or library. Staffing should be well thought out including the availability of faculty and the types of courses relevant to the needs of the students enrolling in the program. Without careful attention to such issues well in advance of advertising, a summer program can be jeopardized and at risk for problems.

The development of a pilot program with a small cohort of students may be one effective technique for garnering administrative and faculty support. This approach has several distinct advantages. A small group permits greater flexibility in altering services in response to changing and unanticipated needs. Also, convincing adjunct campus staff (e.g., residential life, food services, and library services staff) to provide support the first time through is easier if the numbers are manageable. Similarly, up-front publication costs can be kept to a minimum when only a small number of slots are to be filled. Future marketing efforts can build upon preliminary efforts so that target audiences can be more clearly defined and feeder networks established.

Start-up funds for summer program efforts may be sought from a variety of sources, both on and off campus. If the administration is supportive of the idea but unable to provide monetary backing, corporate underwriting or private foundations are another possibility. Foundations are often interested in providing seed money for efforts such as this that have a good potential for becoming self-supporting in a short period of time. Service providers should also explore the possibility of securing scholarship funds for students, since these programs are often staff intensive, which necessitates additional tuition charges. Fees typically range from a few hundred dollars for state-funded programs to over $7,000 for the highly specialized 7-week summer skills development program at Landmark College in Putney, Vermont. Regardless of the cost, marketing considerations should focus on what makes the orientation program unique.

Some campuses direct themselves exclusively to an LD audience, while others cater to any high school student who is at risk. Some programs are exclusively designed for students who will be attending the sponsoring institution; others are open to students who will be attending any postsecondary institution; a few are designed for high school sophomores and juniors who have the goal of attending college and wish to focus on learning strategies beforehand. The HEATH Resource Center in Washington D.C., publishes a useful resource list of summer precollege programs, and consumers would be well advised to contact advocacy organizations such as the Learning Disabilities Association of America (LDA) and its local affiliates for updated sources.

Admission criteria for most LD college orientation programs at competitive 4-year colleges often reflect the admissions standards of the respective school and require a high school diploma for admission and a high level of motivation to succeed. Supporting documentation typically includes a high school transcript, a copy of the high school IEP, if applicable, and a current psychoeducational evaluation that clearly indicates the diagnosis of a learning disability. Personal interviews and brief essays are other ways to determine the level of maturity and motivation that potential participants may have for attending the program. Especially during the first year or two of such transition programs, service providers should be very careful in selecting appropriate candidates. Enrolling a student with mild mental retardation, or one who has a history of psychiatric problems, may quickly dilute the targeted purpose of the program, which is solely for students with *learning disabilities*, not just students who have problems with learning. Some parents overlook this point as they desperately seek summer options for their son or daughter after high school graduation. Conversely, learning that college is not a good match for a student over a

6-week summer session rather than a 15-week semester can minimize emotional stress and serve as a catalyst for reflective planning and counseling.

Determining Transition Program Content

The content of summer orientation programs varies from institution to institution. Nearly all summer programs include a strong emphasis on refining study skills, enhancing academic performance, and addressing the components of successful transition. Training may be conducted either on a one-to-one basis or in small groups. The characteristic goals of these programs are to make students more aware of their strengths and weaknesses and to teach them how to compensate for their learning disability, manage time more effectively, enhance interpersonal and self-advocacy skills, and familiarize themselves with campus and community resources. Some programs are offered for course credit, others offer credit toward graduation, and some are noncredit. The program at Adelphi University in New York addresses the following components: how to use college texts; note taking; memory skills; listening, reading, writing, and thinking skills; vocabulary building; and library use. Other institutions may also provide specific instruction on researching and writing a term paper, using adaptive computer equipment, learning anxiety reduction techniques, exploring career goals, and developing public-speaking skills. In some settings, a special workshop for parents focuses on how to let go and how to respond from a distance to the continuing support needs a son or daughter may have.

Support services provided during the summer have the potential to assist students in evaluating both their educational and their psychosocial needs. As noted in Chapter 2, the key to academic success in college often rests on psychosocial adjustment. One option for facilitating this adjustment is to hire peer support leaders who can participate in an "icebreaker" panel discussion the first night of the program. Peer support leaders are often juniors, seniors, or graduate students with learning disabilities who can help new students by modeling active student participation and independent decision making in all facets of the college program. Such student leaders often have an interest in human service professions and find this summer work experience valuable for building up their résumés. The increase in credibility that comes from employing successful young adults with learning disabilities to model appropriate college behavior as opposed to hiring a staff member to handle crisis situations cannot be underscored enough. However, professional staff may be used for conducting mock interview sessions with faculty members, leading small-group discussions on college adjustment, and role playing how to ask for accommodations from faculty. Instructional and video materials such as *Transitions to Postsecondary*

Learning (Eaton & Coull, 1998) can provide students with an opportunity to articulate their own strengths and weaknesses. In addition to workshops and guided discussion groups, the program should provide ample opportunity for a variety of prearranged social activities such as swimming, picnics, sporting events, and day trips to vacation spots. Dalke (1991) points out that social activities provide students with yet another setting where they can make new friends and begin to build a support network.

Evaluation of the Transition Program

Chapter 13 presents a comprehensive overview of methods for conducting an evaluation of services. However, a few points that may be unique to a summer orientation program warrant mentioning here. The relatively brief duration of these programs gives service providers an ideal opportunity to gather formal and informal observational data on this "captive" student group. This information can be used to evaluate the effectiveness of the services offered in order to plan for students' service needs in the fall and to improve the overall content of the program for future years. Dalke (1991) emphasizes that any transition program should include a mechanism for recording and summarizing student data. McGuire et al. (1990) state that until college personnel systematically identify the interventions that facilitate positive outcomes for college students with learning disabilities, we will continually ask ourselves whether we are not simply stringing together services that have limited potential for fostering success among this group.

Before the transition program is completed, it is essential to collect a variety of outcome data from participants. A satisfaction questionnaire can provide important feedback from student consumers that can be used for revision of program services. Coupled with this could be exit interviews with a sample drawn from participants who can share personal insights and suggestions for future planning. Preparing for follow-up of students who enroll in postsecondary programs should include gathering data on how to contact them to "debrief" on the quality of their transition and their perceptions about the benefits of having enrolled in a summer transition program. Reports of consumer satisfaction including quotes constitute a powerful marketing tool when advertising in subsequent years. Summer transition program coordinators should also build in mechanisms to solicit input from program staff, including the faculty who offer courses, dorm counselors, and learning specialists. An approach to the evaluation of summer transition programs that incorporates all stakeholders can yield valuable information for key administrators who often examine the value of offering such discretionary services only from a cost-benefit perspective.

Ideally, the transition to college for students with learning disabilities should begin years before enrollment and should follow a sequence of activities such as those presented in Chapter 2. Through summer programs, veteran service providers can help to bridge this transition by providing the necessary training in social and academic skills before the student becomes fully immersed in the college environment. The philosophy of a summer orientation program should not be one of holding students' hands or raising false expectations, but one of building awareness and empowerment so that students with learning disabilities can begin the fall term confident that they are equipped with a variety of strategies and techniques that will foster college success.

Challenges in Service Delivery

The new millennium provides an opportunity for people in our field to reflect on changes in the arena of higher education and to engage in dialogue and debate about the way we do business. As Vogel (1993a) suggests, retrospective activities provide "the opportunity to identify trends, similarities, and contrasts among programs . . . and to place them within a framework that may prove useful to both consumers, present and future program directors, and service providers" (p. 85). It is imperative that we be vigilant in remaining abreast of research in the area of effective interventions so that our models of service delivery, as heterogeneous as they may be, do not become stagnant and can be said to be reflective of "best practice."

In addition to adopting empirically validated standards of practice, service providers should consider the research on effective interventions at the secondary (Deshler, Warner, Schumaker, & Alley, 1983; Wong, Butler, Ficzere, & Kuperis, 1997) and postsecondary levels (Butler, 1995) as they make decisions about tutorial interventions at the postsecondary level. Students with learning disabilities are often characterized by difficulties in some aspect of information processing (Swanson, 1987; Swanson & Hoskyn, 1998). To compensate for these deficits, instruction in "learning how to learn" and in monitoring one's approach to the learning task offers an alternative to the traditional content-tutoring model. Rather than tutoring to "remediate, placate and suffocate students while intending to be supportive and empathetic" (Ellis, 1990, p. 61), the goal should be to foster the development of academic self-sufficiency, clearly a goal that is critical to success at the postsecondary level. Strategy instruction for students with LD is related to optimal performance. Research has also indicated that instruction at the skills level may be critical for students with LD, particularly since performance in higher-order thinking tasks that would typically be required in many college-level courses cannot occur without some minimal threshold of skills (Swanson & Hoskyn, 1998). Some students with basic skill deficiencies may require remedial courses, which requirement would have implications for their choice of a postsecondary setting. The LD service provider is in a position to investigate the availability of remediation through other campus services (e.g., the academic skills center) but should not try to be all things to all students.

Finally, it is important for service providers to create links on campus with personnel in other support offices so that fragmentation of services and lack of coordination can be avoided. Albert and Fairweather (1990) used a case study methodology to examine the array of services offered and methods of service delivery in a large, public research university. In addition to the Office for Students with Disabilities within the general administrative organization, a comprehensive LD program was available through academic affairs within departments such as special education, educational psychology, and counseling. Feedback gathered from students pinpointed the confusion that can emerge because of differences in functions between offices offering assistance. Lack of communication and coordination among service providers (e.g., disability services personnel, financial aid, and the LD program) resulted in uncertainty in some students with learning disabilities as to where they should seek assistance. The authors concluded that a horizontal organizational structure can contribute to unclear administrative roles and lines of authority as well as to ambiguity regarding the locus for accessing services.

Conclusion

In their essay addressing the political nature of student affairs, Mamarchev and Williamson (1991, p. 77) sound a vibrant chord: "No matter how competent you are, no matter how much you believe in yourself, no matter how much integrity you may have, if you do not understand the politics of your institution, you will not last." Extrapolating from this, it is reasonable to conclude that regardless of the locus of LD programs, an overriding goal of every LD coordinator must be to "network" and monitor the political pulse on campus. Despite the legal foundations underpinning institutional responsibilities to students with learning disabilities, changing instructional milieus and diminishing resources underscore the critical importance of developing LD programs that complement, rather than duplicate, other campus initiatives.

CHAPTER

9

THE DYNAMIC PROCESS OF PROVIDING ACCOMMODATIONS

Sally S. Scott

Extended time on tests: *"It took the pressure off so that I didn't freeze up worrying about the time"*

(Murphy, 1992, p. 50)

Books on tape: *"I was watching the words as I was listening to the tape, and it was the first time I ever read a book and understood it cover to cover; and I was 27 years old"*

(Murphy, 1992, p. 53)

Note takers: *"Note takers are great because I can't write fast in class while I am trying to hear what the teacher is saying and to try to write it down, I miss half the lecture"*

(Finn, 1998, p. 50)

The student comments listed above provide insight into the power of accommodations in the college environment for students with learning disabilities. Yet determining which accommodations are appropriate and how they should be provided is not an easy task. Federal laws, the Americans with Disabilities Act (ADA) and Section 504 of the Rehabilitation Act of 1973, have established broad parameters clarifying that colleges and universities may not discriminate against individuals with learning disabilities and that they must provide meaningful access to the institution's services, programs, and activities. Chapter 3 discussed the legal requirements of this federal mandate. Policy considerations, discussed in Chapter 8, provide the infrastructure for making the college or university accessible. This chapter presents considerations in operationalizing these mandates and policies—or the procedural aspects of assuring nondiscrimination through the accommodation process.

Accommodations are often discussed as a list of services that must be available to students with learning disabilities (e.g., distraction-free testing environment, note taking, or use of a word processor). However, central to the provision of services for students with learning disabilities is the understanding that nondiscrimination comprises more than a menu of services. It is a dynamic process of actively considering varying individuals' disability-related needs within the context of the specific postsecondary setting.

In this chapter, examples of accommodations and accommodation decision making are discussed. However, college LD services are not "one size fits all." Accommodations will certainly vary by individual student, based on the student's learning disability profile and disability-specific needs. Services and procedures for accommodation will also appropriately vary by institution, in keeping with such defining factors as the mission of the institution for all students and the specific role of the LD support services. (See Chapter 8 for a more in-depth discussion of these factors.)

Since the provision of accommodations will vary somewhat to fit individual campuses, it is important to approach discussion of accommodations from an understanding of the principle behind the process, or the spirit of the law. The ADA and Section 504 have mandated that regardless of variation in mission or structure, colleges and universities must provide *equal access* for students with learning disabilities to the full range of college programs and services. Often the term "access" creates images of physical barriers that are discriminatory against individuals with disabilities. For example, access to a building for a student in a wheelchair may entail a ramp; or access to a lecture for a student who is deaf may require use of a sign language interpreter. Since learning disabilities are cognitive disabilities—that is, they affect student thinking and learning—"access" issues may not always be quite so apparent. However, the potential for discrimination based on disability and the mandate for equal access are just as real.

This chapter highlights the access needs of college students with learning disabilities in order to provide guidance for service-provider decision making in structuring accommodations. A variety of accommodations and services are described, as well as options and considerations in service delivery. Issues in matching accommodations to individual students' needs are examined, as well as the interactive nature of disability-based accommodations, student learning strategies, and faculty instruction.

Providing Accommodations and Services

One of the primary functions of the LD support office is to provide and monitor the accommodations and services available to students with learning disabilities on campus. In the 1980s, when LD services were first becoming widespread, it was common for LD services to be highly centralized and for the LD support office to be viewed as the sole provider of LD accommodations. As the field has evolved, its professionals have come to recognize that while strong leadership is needed from the LD support office, true access to the full range of college programs and services must involve the expertise and efforts of many departments on campus.

Accommodation needs of students with learning disabilities must be viewed in terms of access to the entire college environment. For students with learning disabilities, access issues fall primarily into four broad areas: (1) the college classroom; (2) testing considerations; (3) learning outside the classroom; and (4) programmatic requirements. Each of these contexts is examined for the thinking and learning demands expected of all students. Characteristics of learning disabilities that may result in barriers to access in each setting are highlighted in addition to suggestions for accommodations and services that, in many cases, involve collaboration between the LD support office and other departments on campus. Though not all accommodations discussed are provided on all campuses, it is incumbent on each institution to determine how equal access to each of these four broad areas is assured for students with learning disabilities. (See Heyward, 1998, for an extensive discussion of legal requirements.)

The Classroom Environment

The classroom environment has traditionally been the core of college teaching and learning. To consider access to this environment for students with learning disabilities, it is important to examine how instruction is delivered and the instructor's in-class expectations of students. Service providers also need to keep in mind that the "classroom" in higher education is rapidly changing. Academic courses are increasingly being taught with an online component and distance-learning courses and programs are rapidly growing. Consideration must be given to accommodations for students with learning disabilities in both traditional and emerging classroom environments.

Traditional Classrooms

In the traditional college classroom, instruction is most frequently provided through a lecture format (Carrier, Williams, & Dalgaard, 1988; Suritsky, 1992). Information is conveyed orally, and students are expected to record and remember key lecture information. Cowen (1988) notes that 72% of college students with learning disabilities indicated difficulty in taking adequate notes. Suritsky found that students with learning disabilities reported difficulties in such important aspects of note taking as writing fast enough, paying attention, making sense of notes taken, and choosing information to include in notes. Indeed, many college students with learning disabilities will need alternative ways to acquire notes in a lecture-based setting because of auditory-processing problems, fine-motor deficits affecting handwriting, or short-term memory problems, for example, that make note taking difficult. There are a variety of ways to provide this accommodation.

Providing a *note taker* is a frequent accommodation. Students who are presently enrolled in the course and who are committed to learning the material are often the best resource for effective notes. Campuses may choose to coordinate this accommodation through a volunteer or reimbursement system (University of Massachusetts, 1994). For example, Florida Atlantic University provides note takers through an extensive volunteer program. The school recruits student note takers, provides carbonless note paper (paper that allows the student to take notes in duplicate), and coordinates the drop-off of notes for students with disabilities. Volunteers are thanked for their services with a personal letter of recommendation, a certificate of achievement, campus credit for service reflected on their transcripts, and gift certificates donated by local businesses ("Recruit Volunteer Staff," 1999). At the University of Georgia, a reimbursement system is used. Students with learning disabilities who are eligible for a note taker are encouraged to discuss this accommodation with the instructor within the first 2 weeks of class and provide him or her with an announcement to be read to the class to recruit a note taker. The note taker completes university employment paperwork and obtains carbonless note paper at the LD support office. The student with the learning disability makes arrangements with the note taker for the drop-off and pick-up of notes. At the end of the term, the note taker is reimbursed by the university for services. (For additional suggestions for service delivery options, see Dalke, 1991. To obtain lined carbonless note-taking paper, contact the bookstore, Rochester Institute of Technology, Rochester, NY, http://finweb.rit.edu/bookstore.)

Regardless of the system used, note takers must be dependable, familiar with the subject matter, and have legible handwriting. Service providers must ensure that the accommodation is effective, provided in a timely way, and made available at no cost to the student with a learning disability (Heyward, 1998). If notes are inadequate or there is a delay in providing this accommodation, service providers need to promptly consider a backup plan. Often the instructor of the class can be of assistance by identifying a qualified note taker in the class and specifically recruiting his or her assistance, or by providing a copy of the instructor's notes while other arrangements are coordinated. (See Appendix 9.1 on the CD-ROM for suggested guidelines for note takers.)

Based on individual disability profiles, some students with learning disabilities may find *tape-recording* lectures to be a more effective means of access to lecture content. Dalke (1991), however, aptly points out that this accommodation should be used strategically. For example, if a student has twelve 50-minute class sessions a week, it is highly unlikely that he or she will have an additional 10 hours of study time per week to listen to the lectures again. Recordings of lecture notes should be listened to immediately after class for clarification purposes and not depended on as a fruitful exam preparation technique. It may be more beneficial for students to selectively tape-record lectures. The counter on the tape recorder allows students to use taped notes as a backup at places where the lecture material becomes too dense or is presented too rapidly. Students should jot down the counter number in the margin of their notes for easy reference. The pause button should be used during breaks and general class discussions. Instead of recording an entire 50-minute lecture, students can return to 10–15 minutes of tape-recorded high points and problem areas from the lecture to help fill in gaps in their notes and guide their future studying.

Service providers may need to remind students to ask professors, as a courtesy, for permission to tape-record lectures. Most professors are comfortable with being recorded, but for some it may be considered intrusive. In such situations it is important that students not be confrontational but inform the professor of the learning disability that affects their note-taking abilities. They should make an appointment during office hours to discuss the situation privately. Many colleges have a standard agreement form that can be signed by both parties to indicate that the tapes are for a student's personal use and will be erased at the conclusion of the course (see Appendix 9.2 on the CD-ROM).

Laptop computers are becoming more and more popular as note-taking aids for students with learning disabilities. For students with fine-motor deficits or extensive spelling difficulties, a laptop computer may be the best means of access to note taking. In addition to circumventing specific learning disability deficits, a laptop also permits access to other tools that promote student independence, including the use of a spell check or screen reader for reviewing or editing notes after class. Small laptops, such as the Alpha Smart (www.alpha smart.com; 888-274-0680), are popular with some students for note taking. As more and more students bring their own computers to campus, they may wish to use their personal laptops for note taking in class. Some campuses provide laptop computers on loan from the LD support office or through library check-out. In some situations, the state Office of Vocational Rehabilitation may fund the purchase of a laptop for a student if it is integral to the student's career objectives (e.g., journalism, business, or education).

Access to lectures and the process of note taking are by far the most fre-quent classroom barriers experienced by students with learning disabilities (Lewis & Farris, 1999). However, based on the individual profile of the student, other instructional aspects of the classroom may need to be considered as well. For example, in a large lecture class, the instructor may assign student seating in order to match names with faces. For a student whose learning disability involves attention issues, sitting in the back of a large lecture hall may severely limit note taking or listening ability. He or she may need an *FM assistive listen-ing device* to enhance concentration or *preferential seating* at the front of the class. In a class with heavy use of overhead transparencies for conveying graphs and charts, a student with visual-processing deficits may need *copies of overheads* rather than having to rely on accurate perception and copying to obtain infor-mation. In a seminar class, instructional methods may involve class discussion. For a student whose learning disability affects oral language, allowances may need to be made for class discussion if participation is not essential to the course.

There are myriad examples of how traditional class instruction and expec-tations may interface with the deficits of a specific student's learning disability profile and warrant creative accommodations. Many of these accommodations will be infrequent and possibly specific to one instructor's class structure. When considering these less common classroom accommodations, it is important to discuss the essential requirements of the course with faculty in order to deter-mine when these accommodations exceed the concept of "reasonable" and result in a fundamental alteration of the classroom environment and/or course requirements. When nonessential classroom elements pose a barrier to the stu-dent with a learning disability, creative accommodations should be considered.

Emerging Classrooms

College faculty are increasingly incorporating various online components into classroom instruction. Some instructors choose to incorporate the use of the Internet into their traditional classroom courses by such means as posting the syllabus, class notes and overheads, and notices about upcoming classes on the course Web page, as well as being available for question-and-answer sessions via e-mail. Other faculty are adapting classroom pedagogy in response to the new learning options created by the Internet, asking students to complete interactive assignments; form collaborative workgroups on the Web; and work with supplemental course material including multimedia items for audio, video, or slide shows, for example. Students may be expected to post and discuss their work on line, form individual portfolios on line, or participate in chat groups. With the introduction of such online course components, LD service providers should be aware that emerging classroom environments may present new opportunities and new barriers for students with learning disabilities.

Some students may experience difficulties with various aspects of online learning. Carmela Cunningham, coordinator of the Disability and Computing Program at UCLA, notes that access barriers in Web sites may range from visual-processing difficulties with frames, color, or text, to attention difficulties with flashing items, to auditory problems with speech synthesis (personal communication, September 16, 1999). Regardless of the extent to which faculty are incorporating online components, the new sites need to be fully accessible to students with disabilities. As Jarrow states, "Every time a faculty member throws up a web page for Intro 101 that is not accessible for individuals with disabilities, he or she has created one more barrier to full participation and pushed your institution a little further in the direction of noncompliance" ("Computer Labs," 1999, p. 2).

Currently, no Web accessibility standards have been mandated. However, a comprehensive set of guidelines for meeting the Web access needs of people with disabilities has been developed by the Web Accessibility Initiative (WAI, http://www.w3.org/WAI/) as a working group of the World Wide Web Consortium (W3C). Online services can also help Web-site designers build accessible pages. A program called Bobby (www.cast.org/bobby) was created by the Center for Applied Special Technology to check pages and point out potential problems of access.

Because online instruction continues to evolve, LD service providers are encouraged to develop a systematic method for informing campus employees who design or select Web pages about Web access ("Computer Labs," 1999). Carl Brown, director of the High-Tech Center Training Unit for the California Community College System, concurs that it is essential for colleges to offer technical support so accessibility can be built into courses while they're being created ("Colleges Strive," 1999). Carmela Cunningham notes that the UCLA Disability and Computing Program offers a two-person team to conduct Web access evaluation as educators begin to design their Web pages. She suggests, for campuses just beginning the process of technology access, that LD service providers become familiar with the latest technology guidelines, communicate with the instructional technology staff on campus, and proactively discuss the "usability" of Web sites for everyone (personal communication, September 16, 1999).

Distance Learning

Another emerging classroom environment is distance learning. According to the U.S. Department of Education (1996b), 33% of all 2-year and 4-year institutions of higher education offered some form of distance education to their students in 1995. This number jumped to 44% in 1997, with over 1.5 million students taking distance education courses.

Distance learning is a generic term for an educational environment where teacher and learners are separated by physical distance and the delivery of instruction is mediated electronically. Different technologies are used for delivery, including print media, voice technologies (such as real-time, voice mail, and audio conferencing), video technologies (such as videotapes, live telecasts, cable television, and video conferencing), surface mail, and computer technologies (such as computer-assisted instruction, the Internet and the World Wide Web).

The novelty in distance learning is that it is not a replication of the traditional classroom experience in a different setting. Rather, it is a different learning prototype in which space and time are learning continuums rather than discrete entities. Students can access the information to be learned on their own time and at a location of their convenience. Furthermore, since teaching and learning are based on a digital exchange of information, three options become possible: (a) information can be transformed from one format into another, (b) information can be manipulated with significant ease and efficiency, and (c) vast amounts of information can be accessed from a single site almost instantaneously. Depending on format and instructional demands, students with learning disabilities may experience barriers in distance learning. However, Carl Brown, one of the leaders in the field, points out that "the goal is that virtual classrooms should be held to the same standards as conventional classrooms" ("Colleges Strive," 1999, p. A69).

Although proponents claim that distance learning is particularly helpful to students in remote geographic areas, to nontraditional students, and to students with disabilities, that claim has been challenged by others, who question the ease of access to on-line courses for such students (American Council on Education, 2000). Distance learning can be difficult for students with learning disabilities to access for several reasons:

1. *Distance learning requires a certain level of technological competence as a prerequisite.* In other words, students must already have a basic level of technical awareness or must quickly become familiar with the various technicalities of information exchange (Phipps & Merisotis, 1999). For some students who are not abstract thinkers, this can be a problem.

2. *Technology is constantly changing, and this can give rise to technical incompatibility in communication.* One limitation of technology is that even the most advanced hardware and software are not 100% guaranteed and will on occasion break down (Coombs, date unknown). It is the student's responsibility to know what to do or whom to reach when a technical problem arises. Often, technical assistance is not immediately available, or is available only during traditional office hours at the main campus, or is itself a distance student service requiring the student to explain the difficulty and follow instructions to fix it over the phone. This can pose a challenge for students with learning disabilities who have difficulty with oral directions and information processing.

3. *When there is limited opportunity for face-to-face interaction with the teacher, students must rely on technical or virtual communication to bridge the gap separating teacher and class participants.* For those students who need "live" classroom discussions and experiential learning, this can become a challenge. Willis (1995) notes the difficulty of carrying on a stimulating teacher-class discussion when spontaneity is altered by technical requirements and distance. Where class discussions are asynchronous (i.e., delayed) and in written format, an additional hurdle exists for students with written language disabilities.

4. *In a traditional classroom, instructors often use different visual and nonverbal cues to get the student's attention.* Such cues also help instructors to differentiate between students who are attentive and following instructions and those who are distracted, bored, or confused. They can then adapt their teaching accordingly. Such visual cues are usually lacking in distance learning courses. The instructor is unable to identify students who may be struggling with the material, and the student is similarly disadvantaged by not being able to convey understanding, or a lack thereof, through non-overt means. Some of the nuances of communication are lost for these students.

5. *Students taking distance learning courses need to be effective time managers.* The ability to adhere to a schedule is particularly important when face-to-face instruction is not available. "While an on-line method of education can be a highly effective alternative medium of education for the mature, self-disciplined student, it is an inappropriate learning environment for more dependent learners" (Reid, 2000). Instruction that occurs asynchronously places an additional responsibility on students with learning disabilities. They have to be organized, self-motivated, and have established study habits to participate successfully in distance learning courses (Illinois Online Network, 2001).

These reasons beg the questions "Is distance learning for students with learning disabilities?" and "What impact does distance learning have on traditional accommodations and support services for these students?"

Distance-learning formats differ based on instructional and curricular objectives, as well as by size of institution. Each delivery format has advantages and disadvantages for students with learning disabilities. For example, with video conferencing, if the channel that carries the transmission among sites does not have the necessary capacity, students may observe "ghost images" when rapid movement occurs in real time. This can be very distracting, especially for students with learning disabilities and ADHD (Reed & Woodruff, 1995).

Distance-learning courses for students with learning disabilities pose a new set of challenges for service providers. Some previously used accommodations, such as preferential seating or spell checkers, become obsolete. In determining accommodations, service providers must take into account not only the individual student's needs as stated in the psycho-educational evaluation report, together with the requirements of the curriculum and the expectations of the teaching faculty, but also the learning environment in terms of its delivery format, mode of communication, and student readiness. Currently, few LD diagnostic reports provide any recommendations for accommodations for distance-learning courses. Academic adjustments in the virtual classroom are a relatively new ADA compliance area. The implication is a changing paradigm for LD services (Banerjee, 1999). Instead of the traditional personal contact of the LD support office, services must be provided to distance-learning students through limited direct contact, alternate means of communication (typically e-mail), and off-site personnel. In this new environment, service providers may need to have an understanding of the different courseware that is available and used by faculty to deliver courses. They need to be knowledgeable about the accessibility of the courseware. They must have an understanding of the various Web-based instructional techniques in use, their benefits and their limitations. In response to this need, the California Community College System has developed guidelines for access to various formats of distance education (see "Guidelines" at http://www.rit.edu/~easi/dl/disccc.html). The guidelines note that students with learning disabilities may need accommodation in distance-learning formats requiring the processing of text information. The guidelines suggest that correspondence, CAI, and Web courses might require the availability of large-print, audiotape, or e-text versions of text material, as well as the proactive application of the W3C guidelines for Web design. The HEATH Resource Center (Payne, 1993) suggests that taping of video or audio conferencing might be appropriate to allow students to review material and learn at their own pace. In addition, traditional classroom accommodations such as extended time for tests or provision of a note taker may be appropriate. Rapp (1998) has developed suggestions for educators who are providing distance learning to students with learning disabilities (see Appendix 9.3 on the CD-ROM).

Michele Thomas, of Disability Services at Northern Arizona University (NAU), provides the following helpful recommendations for service providers beginning to address distance-learning accommodations (personal communication, October 10, 1999). She suggests (a) LD service providers should retain the responsibility for ADA compliance. At NAU, the Disability Service Office provides all information on how to access services on its Web site, including a "Request to Self-Identify" form. Disability documentation is submitted to Disability Services and reviewed to determine eligibility and accommodations. Staff of the Disability Service Office then enlist the distance-learning site coordinator's assistance in providing accommodations; (b) Whenever possible, LD service providers should collaborate with colleagues across the state. Many of NAU's distance-learning sites are located at community colleges that assist in providing services; (c) LD service providers should offer training in and education about learning disabilities. NAU has hosted a day-long training with an outside consultant and has provided manuals and brochures to distance-learning staff. In addition, Disability Services staff attend major meetings about distance learning to promote awareness of needs and issues.

The following principles for accessibility compliance and accommodations for students with learning disabilities in distance-learning courses serve as an additional guide for disability service providers (California Community Colleges, 1999).

1. Distance-education courses should be designed to allow students with learning disabilities the maximum opportunity for access to information without the need for external assistance.

2. Distance-learning courses should have built-in accommodations, such as enlarged print, content layout that is not text heavy, and visuals that are self-explanatory, whenever possible.

3. As far as possible, information should be available in an alternate format. For example, for students who are auditory learners, visual information should be available in an audio version as well.

4. Accommodations should focus on increasing the inherent accessibility of the content and the mode of its delivery and communication, rather than on adding hardware and software after the fact.

5. Complete access to distance-learning courses means access to all the resources, materials, media of communication and exchange, and various formats for interaction and course delivery. Accessibility cannot be restricted to only some technologies.

6. Distance-education courses, resources, and materials must be designed and delivered in such a way that the level of communication and the course-taking experience is the same for students with and without disabilities.

7. Where distance-learning courses involve lease or purchase of resources from a third party, the college must provide "in-house" modifications, if necessary, to ensure access, unless doing so fundamentally alters the nature of instruction or imposes undue financial and administrative burdens on the college.

8. Colleges are encouraged to develop LD service policies and procedures for distance-learning courses and to review them to make modifications for accessibility as needed.

9. Making sure that accessibility to distance-learning courses, materials, and resources is a shared college responsibility. All appropriate campus constituencies, such as LD services, distance-learning centers, instructional technologies, and the media center, must be involved in making this happen.

Testing

Testing and evaluation of student knowledge are common in higher education. Accommodation of classroom tests is the service most frequently requested by and provided to students with learning disabilities (Bursuck et al., 1989; Lewis & Farris, 1999; Yost, Shaw, Cullen, & Bigaj, 1994). It is also one of the most often cited areas in allegations of discrimination made by those filing complaints with the Office for Civil Rights (Gephart, 1998), which speaks to the sensitive nature of these accommodations.

Classroom tests that are constructed and provided by college instructors vary widely in such areas as format, length of time required, content coverage, and mode of presentation (visual or auditory). Each of these components of classroom tests has the potential to interface with the specific deficits of an individual student's learning disability. Some college students with learning disabilities may have difficulty with reading rate or decoding, understanding test questions, writing under pressure, organizing thoughts, or remembering the mechanics of spelling, punctuation, and syntax. Others may have difficulty with math calculation, fine-motor skills, memory, or language (Alster, 1997; Dalke, 1991; Patton & Polloway, 1996). It is little wonder, therefore, that some aspect of a learning disability may interfere with a testing demand that may have little to do with mastery of the content the instructor is attempting to assess.

Because of the sensitive nature of academic assessment, test accommodation requests must always be clearly supported by the student's disability documentation and considered in the context of the specific class. The guiding legal principle for test accommodations delineated in Section 504 of the Rehabilitation Act is that the "results of the evaluation must represent the student's achievement in the course rather than reflecting the student's impaired sensory, manual, or speaking skills (except where such skills are the factor that the test purports to measure)" (34 CFR, Subpart E, § 104.44[c]). In other words, a test accommodation should not compromise the purpose of the test. The need for test accommodations should be considered in three areas: the format of the test, the environment of the test, and the time demands of the test.

Test Format

Every test format has inherent sensory and cognitive demands outside the content material under examination. For example, a print test measures visual-processing and reading skills; written responses tap fine-motor and written-language abilities—all in addition to subject matter mastery. Similarly, an oral test reflects such factors as the student's auditory-processing, attention, and short-term memory skills. When the testing format reflects the student's learning disability rather than the student's achievement, accommodation must be considered.

Judicial guidance for this process of weighing the essential skills that are assessed in a test in juxtaposition with a student's learning disability is provided in the case of *Wynne v. Tufts University School of Medicine*, a case that was heard in the 1st Circuit U.S. District Court of Appeals in April 1990 and was remanded in April 1992. The case involved a first-year medical student who, after failing eight out of fifteen courses, was tested at university expense and found to be dyslexic. He claimed that after he was identified as having a learning disability, the university unlawfully discriminated against him based on his handicap, in violation of Section 504, when it refused to modify testing methods to accommodate his learning disability (Jaschik, 1990). The student requested that he be given an alternative type of test, preferably an oral exam, but his suggestion was rejected by school administrators. He also sought unsuccessfully to take a reduced course load during his second attempt at the first-year program.

The Tufts Medical School did take some steps to address Wynne's difficulties. He was permitted to repeat the first year and received special tutoring in all subjects he had failed, the use of note takers in his classes, and assistance with a learning-skills tutor to improve his study habits. In his second attempt in the first-year program, he passed all but two of the subjects he had previously failed.

He was permitted to retake those two examinations, passing one but failing bio-chemistry for the third time. Following the third failure, he was dismissed from the medical school. He filed suit, claiming that because of his learning disabili-ties he was unable to demonstrate his knowledge of course content with a con-ventional multiple-choice format. Specifically, he argued that a different for-mat of the test would "give him meaningful access to the medical education" (*Handicapped Requirements Handbook*, 1992, App. IV, p. 254). Tufts attempted to dismiss Wynne's claim, comparing it to the decision in *Southeastern Commu-nity College v. Davis* (1979), by pointing out that because Wynne was unable to meet an essential requirement for a Tufts medical degree (e.g., passing all of his courses), he was not otherwise qualified.

Initially, a decision in Tufts's favor was issued by the district court without a trial. Subsequently, the case was appealed and the full bench of the court of appeals granted Tufts's request for a rehearing and permitted other institutions to participate as *amici curiae*. The court concluded that the district court erred in granting summary judgment for Tufts and said that the present record demon-strated that "Tufts may not select the one technique that poses an insurmount-able barrier to dyslexic students."

The court of appeals remanded the case to the district court and concluded that the university had failed to adequately support its position that altering its test format would fundamentally alter the program of medical education it offers (Heyward, Lawton, & Associates, 1992). On remand, Tufts submitted additional explanations to the district court to support its position that changing the for-mat of the exam from multiple-choice to a written essay would be burdensome. With this information at hand, the court agreed that altering the test format would in fact compromise the test's ability to show a future doctor's "ability to make subtle distinctions based on seemingly small but significant differences in written information." The court also added that Tufts had reasonably accom-modated the dyslexic medical student by permitting him to repeat the first-year curriculum and by paying for note takers, tutors, and taped lecture material. This case underscores the importance of the process by which decisions are ren-dered about the essential elements of a test and the nature of accommodations.

Depending on the student's learning disability profile, there are numerous ways to circumvent barriers in test format. For students with reading decoding deficits, this may involve *providing a reader* for the test (someone to simply read aloud test questions) or having the *exam material on tape* (allowing the student to work independently and have the questions repeated as many times as needed). New technology, such as the Quicktionary Reading Pen (a hand-held electronic device that scans and reads single words) may be an appropriate accommodation for a student who needs only an occasional word read aloud (www.readingpen.com; 877-344-4040).

Students with visual perception or tracking problems may need an *enlarged-print* copy of the test with ample space for responses. Others may require *permission to write directly on the test* as opposed to filling in a computer-scored answer sheet. Students with deficits in written language may need to *dictate test responses* either to a proctor or onto a tape recorder for later transcription. Assistive technology, such as voice input, would allow the student to work independently. Alternatively, various aids such as a *word processor, spell check,* or *thesaurus* may prove to be effective. Hand-held computer versions of spell check and thesaurus such as the Franklin Language Master (www.franklin.com; 800-266-5626) are often helpful. For students with deficits in math calculation, a *calculator* may be an appropriate accommodation. "Speaking" calculators that provide both visual and audio output are especially helpful to students who have a tendency to reverse numbers (see, for example, www.bossertspecialties.com; 800-776-5885).

More controversial accommodations include the use of a *word bank* (a list of terms including distraction terms approved by the instructor that may be used during a test) for students with specific word-retrieval deficits; a *formula sheet* (a list of relevant formulas approved by the instructor to be used during a test) for students with memory deficits or extensive number and letter reversals; an *interpreter* (someone to clarify questions not related to test content) for students with reading comprehension deficits; and *alternate test formats* (such as an oral exam rather than a written exam) for students with a particular combination of learning-disability deficits that limit the effectiveness of other forms of accommodation. Each of these accommodations should be considered with caution because of the risk of compromising an essential aspect of the test. Service providers should be particularly vigilant in relying on recent documentation of the learning disability, the student's previous test-taking history, and a collaborative discussion with faculty about the fundamental knowledge the test is intended to measure before recommending accommodations. With the emergence of computer-based testing, particularly for standardized tests such as the GRE, GMAT, and PRAXIS, new challenges present themselves (e.g., the relationship between the nature and severity of the LD and a requested accommodation such as a paper-based version). Chapter 7 includes a discussion of this issue.

Test Environment

For students with learning disabilities who are easily distracted by either visual or auditory stimuli, the test environment itself may impose potential barriers. A *distraction-reduced setting* (free from phones, copiers, or student traffic) may be all a student needs to circumvent the disability. Since quiet testing space is often at a premium on college campuses, *sound suppression earplugs* or the use of a *sound screen* (a small electrical machine that produces "white noise") may further ensure a distraction-reduced test environment (see for example, www. marpac.com/sound_cond.asp; 800-999-6962). Some students may require a *private testing room* in order to apply successful test-taking strategies such as reading the test aloud, talking through test responses, or pacing.

Time Demands

The most frequently requested test accommodation is *extended time* (Bursuck et al., 1989; Yost et al., 1994). The case of *Campbell A. Dinsmore v. Charles C. Pugh and the Regents of the University of California* (1989) is one of the first examples of litigation involving the accommodation of extended test time. This was a civil suit involving a mathematics professor at the University of California, Berkeley, who refused to provide a dyslexic student with additional time on an examination. When the student requested accommodations in testing, the professor rejected the request on the grounds that "there was no such thing as a learning disability" (W. Newmeyer, personal communication, December 10, 1990). Essentially, the professor maintained that the student was using the disability as a ruse for securing additional time on the examination. Additional negotiations with the professor proved to be unsatisfactory, resulting in the student filing suit against the professor and the Regents of the University of California, Berkeley.

The plaintiff acknowledged that the Disabled Students Program and the university had attempted to rectify the problem but were "powerless" to change the professor's mind. The student demanded that the university develop policies and procedures to address future situations in which a faculty member might refuse to provide academic adjustments despite adequate documentation of a disability. The student also sought monetary damages against the professor for not providing the accommodations requested and for the emotional distress caused by making the case public. The professor was directed by members of the university's administration to provide the student with additional time to take the final examination in class, but the professor ignored the directive and would not permit the examination to be administered with the accommodations. The professor contended that granting extra time was unfair to the other students in the course. He said, "There are fast students and slow students. . . . I think all students should be tested equally" (Link, 1989, B-2). He also maintained that his academic freedom was being encroached upon.

The university promptly settled the case out of court and developed a comprehensive policy for accommodating the academic needs of students with disabilities. The professor's claim of having his academic freedom usurped was not supported, and he was required to pay monetary damages. The UC-Berkeley policy, which includes the establishment of an Academic Accommodations Policy Board for handling disagreements of this kind, is included in Appendix 8.2 on the CD-ROM. Developing a policy board similar to the one at the University of California at Berkeley may be an approach worthy of adaptation as a mechanism for resolving disagreements over what accommodations are appropriate. For a more complete discussion of policy development and procedures that campuses can establish in light of current litigation, readers should consult Chapter 8.

Studies conducted on the effects of extra time on reading comprehension (Runyan, 1991) and algebra (Alster, 1997) test scores of university students with and without learning disabilities have provided support for the equalizing process of this accommodation for students with learning disabilities. In providing this accommodation, the standard allocation is time and one-half, though service providers are encouraged to use this as a starting point for individual assessment of need rather than a categorical cap. (See for example, *Corning Community College*, 1997.) Gephart (1998) notes that determining the amount of extended time entails clinical judgment on the part of the disability service provider. The need for extended time as a test accommodation would be suggested by deficits in such areas as processing speed, reading rate, or writing fluency. However, beyond basic fluency factors, additional considerations may need to be given to student experience with the accommodation (e.g., is the student newly diagnosed and using an accommodation for the first time?), the purpose of the test (e.g., is it intended to be a speed or power test?), and the cumulative time demands of additional accommodations (e.g., use of a tape-recorded test as well as spell check and thesaurus) ("Extra Exam Time," 1995; *Measuring Student Progress*, 1995). *Scheduled breaks* may also need to be considered when students are provided additional time for testing. In addition to addressing fatigue, breaks may also serve to alleviate test anxiety and provide opportunities to implement stress reduction techniques.

Campuses structure test accommodation services in a variety of ways ranging from providing all test accommodations in a centralized fashion through the LD support office to completely decentralizing test accommodations by having each individual faculty member or department responsible for ensuring the accommodation of students. Each approach has advantages and disadvantages.

In a centralized system of test accommodation, the LD support office is able to ensure that quality accommodations are provided to students in an appropriate way (e.g., that the accommodation of a distraction-reduced room is truly a quiet and distraction-free environment). Accommodations can be monitored by staff to ensure that they are proving to be effective for students (e.g., is time and one-half adequate for a particular student or does she consistently fail to complete tests?). Other student needs, such as extreme test anxiety, may be observed, and students can be referred to appropriate support services on campus. This is a service that also can benefit faculty by relieving them of the responsibility of finding test proctors or additional testing space.

In order to provide centralized test services, however, the LD support office must have administrative support to meet the extensive labor and space demands such accommodations require. For example, at the University of Georgia, approximately 80–85% of students with learning disabilities who request accommodations use test accommodations. During the 1998–99 academic year 2,500 tests were proctored by the LD support office. During exam week alone, approximately 30–40 tests per day were facilitated. On such campuses where quiet space is at a premium, scheduling test space, keeping track of exams in transit between faculty and the LD support office, and ensuring that the proper academic adjustments are provided can be a monumental task. The test coordinator at the University of Arizona (cited in Gephart, 1998) accommodates 9,000 tests annually. He recommended that test coordinators build strong relationships with faculty, establish a detailed system for administering tests, and hire trustworthy student workers (for a complete description of services, see Gephart, 1998).

Conversely, some institutions decentralize their test accommodations for students with learning disabilities. This certainly allows for shared labor in this time-intensive task and access to space across campus for providing accommodations. Faculty have more "hands-on" exposure to how tests are accommodated and can more directly monitor the integrity of the test. A philosophical benefit of this approach is that a broader range of the campus is involved in the shared responsibility for providing access for students with learning disabilities. However, in this decentralized approach, it is more difficult to monitor the effectiveness of accommodations provided, and students may need to be strong self-advocates in order to ensure reasonable accommodations.

Consequently, many LD service providers now consider that providing these accommodations should be a shared responsibility among students, faculty, and service providers. At the University of Connecticut, students may take examinations in the department under the supervision of the faculty or a teaching assistant, or they may arrange to take their examinations in the campus library. The examination is delivered to a central location and arrangements are made in advance for a quiet testing location and coordination of the test pick-up. For a comprehensive overview of ways to provide testing accommodations for students with disabilities, readers are encouraged to consult *Testing Accommodations for Students with Disabilities* (King & Jarrow, 1990) and *Testing Accommodations in Higher Education* (Gephart, 1998).

Though classroom tests make up the large majority of testing required of students with learning disabilities, there are typically a number of other tests students must pass in order to be eligible for entry to academic programs or graduation from college, including, for example, placement exams, proficiency exams, departmental entry exams, and so forth. The same principles of providing access apply to this broad range of institutional tests. If test format, environment, or timing appears to discriminate against the student based on the individual learning profile, then accommodation that will not compromise essential requirements of the test must be considered.

Learning Outside the Classroom

Higher education is an environment focused on learning. In addition to instruction in the classroom, students are expected to acquire information and learning experiences in a number of settings outside the classroom. When the university provides these outside learning environments, such as a library or computer lab, or requires participation, such as reading textbooks and journals, as part of its academic program, these components must also be accessible to students with learning disabilities. Of note, universities are not required to provide services of a personal nature such as readers for personal use or study or other personal services or devices (Section 504 Compliance Handbook, 1999).

Books on Tape or E-Text

A major source of learning outside the classroom consists of knowledge and information attained from textbooks, journals, and other printed matter. Since access to the academic program hinges on such reading material being accessible, the college or university is responsible for providing accommodations based on individual student need, through such means as tape-recorded text.

The largest repository of tape-recorded textbooks is Recording for the Blind & Dyslexic in Princeton, New Jersey. RFB&D is a national, nonprofit, volunteer-driven organization that provides recorded educational books on loan to people who cannot read printed materials because of a visual impairment or physical or learning disability. Currently, over 60% of its users are people with learning disabilities. RFB&D has more than 80,000 books on tape, and over 3,000 new titles are added every year to the collection. RFB&D also offers some materials on e-text (electronic books created from publishers' computer files by optically scanning the print copy). E-text is available for purchase rather than loan. In order to access the services of RFB&D, students must have detailed documentation of their disability, attested to by a certifying authority, indicating the nature of the disability and how it affects reading. A disability statement must be signed by someone who either is certified medically, such as a neurologist, or is a specialist such as a neuropsychologist, special education counselor, or LD specialist. Individual memberships are $25 per year plus an initial registration fee of $50. Institutional membership at varying levels is also available to colleges. Levels depend on the number of students requiring books on tape through the LD support office. Materials are available on loan for up to a year, or longer if an extension is requested. Book requests may be made in writing, by telephone, or by fax. RFB&D's toll-free member services number is 800-221-4792. For information on institutional memberships, call 800-772-3248.

The recorded tapes must be played on a specially adapted tape recorder that is capable of playing four-track cassettes at 15/16 inch per second at variable speeds. Compact four-track recorders, similar in appearance to a Sony Walkman, may be purchased directly from RFB&D. The American Printing House for the Blind, in Louisville, Kentucky (502-895-2405) also has standard desktop recorders with two-speed operation and rechargeable AC-DC power sources, which are available for purchase. Some students may prefer to try out a tape recorder on loan to determine if they derive a benefit from tape-recorded materials. Applications for the loan of a tape recorder are available from most local public libraries and from the Library of Congress (202-287-5100).

Currently, RFB&D is piloting the digital recording of textbooks. It is anticipated that sound quality will be much better than traditional analog recordings. In addition, there will be improved accessibility to the recorded material, making it easier to locate specific pages or items of information. The "digital audio books" may potentially be accessed through a standard multimedia computer equipped with a CD-ROM or through a portable CD playback device. RFB&D anticipates that a limited number of books will be available for use by the fall of 2001.

The Library of Congress is also a source for over 45,000 books and 70 magazines. The books in the collection consist of recreational and informational reading and do not include standard textbooks. In order for people with disabilities to borrow materials, they must provide documentation of their disability by a certified doctor of medicine or a doctor of osteopathy. Since many medical doctors are unfamiliar with the educational ramifications of having a learning disability, they are encouraged to consult with colleagues in the fields of psychology or special education.

Despite these national resources for recorded textbooks, it is important for LD service providers to have some alternative means of recording materials. It is not unusual for professors to make last-minute decisions about textbook selections or to assign volumes of handouts that require prompt attention. Most campuses have established a cadre of support staff or volunteers who can attend to taping requests. One of the best ways to attract volunteers is to solicit the expertise of retired faculty, who may welcome the opportunity to read current materials in their discipline. For additional information on how to establish a volunteer reader-taper service on campus, readers are encourage to consult the *Volunteer Reader/Taping Service Handbook* (Lendman, 1991).

In addition to relying on human readers, many service providers are also taking advantage of emerging assistive technology and meeting some recording needs through the use of optical scanning and recording devices (see for example, the Omni 3000, www.LHSL.com/education; 781-203-5000). By scanning text into the computer and having an electronic voice read the text, students can be provided with either discs or audiotapes of the text in a relatively short time. In many cases, the students themselves can be taught to scan material, thus increasing student independence in accommodations. However, for some students with learning disabilities, the editing required in finalizing scanned materials may make this option inappropriate.

Another source of books on tape for service providers is the growing number of e-text sites on the Internet that provide free access to some materials. The Texas Text Exchange is a consortium of disability service providers who share e-text. They have created a Web-based digital library of electronic books to be used exclusively for accommodating students with disabilities. Currently 228 books are on line, and there are 59 active member institutions. There is no cost for membership in the consortium. Information can be obtained at http://tte.tamu.edu. Appendix 9.4 on the CD-ROM contains additional Web sites for e-text materials.

Library

The library is often considered the core of learning at a college or university. Weingand (1990) describes the library as a "window to the world of information" (p. 77). Yet, in a library setting that is predominantly a print-based environment, there are numerous potential barriers to students with learning disabilities. Depending on individual profile, students with learning disabilities may encounter difficulties with hard copy or electronic text—affecting their access to everything from books to journals, to reference materials, to databases on line. In addition, students with learning disabilities may have a variety of information-processing deficits that could inhibit access to a library's resources. For example, problems with sequencing could make locating books on the shelf very difficult; memory deficits could impede learning the system for accessing materials; and visual-processing deficits could make using microfiche impossible.

The Office for Civil Rights notes that "accessibility barriers in any text in existing university publications, computers, or library resources must be removed, if barrier removal is readily achievable." Specifically, libraries must ensure that "library catalogues, archived microfiche, daily newspapers, the internet, and any other resource available to non-disabled patrons are accessible" ("Library Resources," 1998, pp. 7–8).

Academic librarians recommend addressing the needs of college students with learning disabilities through two main approaches: the use of assistive technology and awareness of library logistics and policies. A range of assistive technology is rapidly emerging and should be considered in a variety of areas based on the access needs of students. Optical character-recognition scanners and screen readers such as the Omni 3000 and Arkenstone WYNN systems provide access to a broad range of print materials. Speech synthesis equipment for automated card catalogs and reference databases, enlarging software, and speech input or assistive-writing software should be considered (Green, 1999; Hilton-Chalfen, 1992; Jax & Muraski, 1993). Green notes that microfiche and microfilm readers with automatic page finders can promote access for students with learning disabilities; providing printer hookup with on-line catalogs can circumvent difficulties in spelling or visual motor skills; and securing text enhancements such as text magnification, bold print, underlining, and arrows may assist with on-line catalogs or other library reference tools.

When considering what assistive technology is appropriate on an individual campus, Heyward (1998) notes that an important indicator will be the extent that the campus provides technology in the education of all students. "The more technology that has been purchased by a public library to serve non-disabled patrons, the more reasonable the expectation that it will employ technology to serve disabled patrons" (p. 7:23).

In addition to assistive technology, access may entail awareness of library logistics and policies. One area in which students with learning disabilities may experience difficulties is library orientation. Lenn (1996) and Mendle (1995) recommend that library-generated print materials such as brochures and orientation literature should be available in alternate formats such as enlarged print, disc, and audiotape. Adler (1989) describes a special orientation program for college students with learning disabilities, consisting of teaching basic library tools with hands-on experience; using a learning strategies approach to encourage future problem solving; and emphasizing memory strategies.

Some students with learning disabilities experience difficulty with directionality or spatial orientation. As Lenn (1996) notes, "Maps and shelf labels are notorious for being confusing to patrons; add to this equation an LD and it escalates from frustrating to antagonistic" (p. 17). Clear signage and identification of staff service points are suggested. The use of color coding of the physical layout and a visual diagram of resources has been recommended to supplement orientation tours and individual instruction (Michael, 1988; Weingand, 1990). Other considerations may include the use of the library media center in offering multisensory instruction (Adler, 1989); the need for special listening areas or quiet study carrels; or accommodations of library policies such as providing extended time for reserve-reading checkout (Weingand, 1990).

Weingand (1990) notes that many libraries are not aware of the access needs of students with learning disabilities because often students choose not to disclose their accommodation needs. Indeed, Bishop (1995) conducted a survey of libraries at public 4-year institutions of higher education in Alabama and found that only 27% of respondents reported that programs were in place to meet the needs of students with LD. To help ensure that the needs of patrons with learning disabilities are addressed, academic librarians recommend that one person on the library staff be designated as the coordinator of disability issues and serve as a link with the campus community, including closely communicating with the LD support office. This person should keep abreast of disability needs and resources, recommend policies and procedures, and oversee staff training. Input on the direct-service needs of students with learning disabilities should be actively sought through such mechanisms as student focus groups, surveys, and other opportunities for feedback about library accessibility (Bishop, 1995; Green, 1999; Hilton-Chalfen, 1992; Jax & Muraski, 1993; Lenn, 1996; Weingand, 1990).

Computer Labs and Technology Access

Computer labs are another important source of learning outside the classroom that are playing an increasingly central role in higher education. Student uses of computer labs and technology range from basic word processing and completion of class assignments to registration for classes, access to on-line course components, and using the Internet for research. When provided with accommodations to circumvent deficits in reading, writing, or processing speed, for example, students with learning disabilities have equal opportunity to explore and use this growing resource for all students.

In addition to the specific assistive technology appropriate for college students with learning disabilities that is described in Chapter 11, colleges also need to intentionally consider how access to the broad range of computer labs and technology on campus will be coordinated. Raskind and Higgins (1998) note that colleges have approached access in different ways. Some campuses have provided assistive technology for students with disabilities at a centralized location such as the Disability Services Office or the library. However, as noted by OCR, "sole reliance upon a single centralized location (when not limited to adaptive technology training, but instead used for instructing disabled students in course subject matter) may run counter to the strong philosophy embodied in Title II and Section 504 regarding the importance of fully integrating students with disabilities into the mainstream educational program" ("Computer Labs," 1999, p. 1). Programs with a centralized approach to computer and technology access are cautioned that separate labs for students with disabilities must be comparable in the hours of operation and the range of software programs available to all students (*Contra Costa College,* 1996).

Other campuses have approached access to computing resources by using a distributive model, in which assistive technology is available throughout campus at existing computer sites (Raskind & Higgins, 1998). Increasingly, educators have recommended this approach to technology access as more in keeping with federal mandates for full integration into the range of campus computing resources. As noted by Day and Edwards (1996), "By accommodating students in this way, existing services are not duplicated, and accommodation becomes an integral part of the academic support network available to all students" (p. 489).

Campus responses to computer access needs have emerged based on institutional structures and resources. Raskind and Higgins (1998) note variation in such factors as the department charged with managing assistive technology (typically disability services or the computing department), the range of technology available, the amount of training and technology support available to students, and the background and expertise of staff. (See Raskind & Higgins, 1998, and Day & Edwards, 1996, for a complete description of programs and existing models.) If support services are not in place for ensuring the accessibility of computer labs and technology, the LD support office should initiate collaborative discussion with other relevant departments on campus such as academic/departmental computing services or the central computing department.

Other

Across campus other access needs may arise for students with learning disabilities. For example, sometimes students with learning disabilities request accommodation in *housing* such as a private dorm room to allow for a quiet study environment free from distractions. To determine the appropriateness of this accommodation, the institution should first consider the specific purpose of the residence hall program on campus for all students and then assess whether there are barriers to access for students with learning disabilities.

Jarrow (1999a) notes that typically the purpose of campus housing is to provide a place for students to live and sleep, and to provide access to campus. Small private schools may also focus residential hall programming on the growth and development of students, including an emphasis on learning to coexist with others. Providing study space, however, is typically not the purpose of residential programs or activities. Indeed, most institutions offer study locations and options that are much quieter than dorms, such as all-night study rooms, computer labs, and libraries, because of the noise, distractions, and interruptions from neighbors (not just roommates) inherent in college dorm life. Since the purpose of disability-based accommodations is equal access to college programs, the institution is not obligated to enhance the student's likelihood of success by creating private study space in the dormitory. However, if providing a study environment is one of the purposes of residential life on an individual campus, a student with a learning disability may indeed experience a barrier to that activity. If the student's disability documentation indicates difficulties with paying attention or perhaps the need for compensation strategies such as reading aloud or verbalizing thoughts to keep focus, a private dorm room may be an appropriate accommodation ("Students with Attention," 1998).

Some students with learning disabilities may arrive on campus with the expectation that content *tutoring* will be provided. Again, in determining whether this is an appropriate accommodation, a campus must reflect on what is required to provide equal access to the institution's educational programs and services. If the campus provides content tutoring for all students, the LD service provider should consider whether any existing policies may create barriers for students with learning disabilities. For example, at the University of Georgia, the Tutor House provides tutoring in a range of subject areas for all students. Because many students with learning disabilities have deficits in processing speed or academic areas, an approved accommodation is to permit extended tutoring sessions with Tutor House tutors. The LD support office provides occasional training of tutors on characteristics of learning disabilities and is available for consultation on individual student situations (with the student's written release). For campuses that do not offer tutorial services, there is no obligation to create those services to meet the needs of students with learning disabilities. The implementing regulations of Section 504 (34 CFR, Subpart E, § 104.44[d][2]) and subsequent OCR rulings have specifically stated that institutions are not responsible for providing services for a student's personal use or study. As Heyward (1998) notes, "Section 504 specifically excluded services of a personal nature from the range of auxiliary aids required. Because tutoring is associated more closely with individual study aid, Section 504 does not require the provision of tutoring as a necessary academic adjustment" (p. 7:20).

Programmatic Requirements

Sometimes programmatic requirements of the institution or academic department may provide barriers to students with learning disabilities. Program modifications should be addressed through policy statements or guidelines. Accommodations in such areas as financial aid, reduced course load, priority registration, and eligibility for the dean's list are discussed in Chapter 8 as policy considerations. Other programmatic requirements, however, may involve the provision of auxiliary aids or services in addition to policy guidelines. The areas of course substitutions, internships or field placements, and study abroad are programmatic areas that sometimes require dynamic problem solving and creative accommodation in addition to institutional policies for nondiscriminatory treatment.

Course Substitutions

Institutions typically have required core courses for completion of a degree or for fulfilling the requirements of a specific program of study. Sometimes required courses such as foreign language or mathematics present a range of accommodation needs or perhaps insurmountable barriers for students with learning disabilities. For example, students with language-based learning disabilities or dyscalculia (specific deficits in mathematics learning) by definition experience the impact of their learning difficulties in such required courses.

Institutions need to carefully and proactively assess how they will provide equal access to such programmatic requirements. Because of the nature of foreign language and mathematics learning and the potential overlap with aspects of learning disabilities, traditional accommodations may not be sufficient. Section 504 suggests an alternative accommodation by listing substitution of courses as a possible academic adjustment (34 CFR, Subpart E, § 104.44[1] and [d][1]). Though this accommodation is provided by the majority of postsecondary institutions (Lewis & Farris, 1999), it remains a sensitive area that has been part of highly visible and legally contested debates, most recently addressed in the case of *Guckenburger v. Boston University*, 1997.

According to Wolinsky and Whelan (1999), *Guckenberger v. Boston University* is "arguably the most important case ever litigated to a conclusion on behalf of students with learning disabilities" (p. 286). The case addressed four major substantive issues: (a) BU's newly implemented policies requiring retesting every 3 years for students with learning disabilities; (b) BU's revised requirement that a learning disability evaluator must be a "licensed psychologist, clinical psychologist, neuropsychologist, or reputable physician"; (c) BU's newly implemented policy requiring extensive documentation from evaluators and secondary schools; and (d) BU's refusal to continue allowing course substitutions in lieu of math and foreign language requirements for students with documented learning disabilities (Wolinsky & Whelan, 1999).

In June 1995, Provost Jon Westling informed the vice president and dean of students, "Boston University's unwillingness to recognize a learning disability that prevents students from meeting either language or mathematical requirements extends to the substitution of these requirements with alternative courses. For example, it is not acceptable to permit students who are required to take a foreign language to take a foreign culture course or to permit students to meet a calculus requirement with a statistics course" (memorandum to W. Norman Johnson, June 30, 1995). Up to that point, BU had been granting a handful of course substitutions to students with documented learning disabilities for the core academic requirements in math and foreign language.

At the conclusion of the trial, Judge Patricia Saris stated that "although Westling was also inspired by a genuine concern for academic standards, his course substitution prohibition was founded in part, on uninformed stereotypes." She later wrote that "a substantial motivating factor in Westling's decision not to consider degree modifications was his unfounded belief that learning disabled students who could not meet degree requirements were unmotivated . . . or disingenuous." Judge Saris directed BU to implement a "deliberative procedure" for considering whether course substitutions in foreign language in the College of Arts and Sciences would "fundamentally alter the nature" of a Boston University liberal arts degree. A Dean's Advisory committee was established to study this question. In December 1997, the committee completed its eight-page report and submitted it to then President Westling. After an extensive review and deliberation, the committee announced: "The foreign language requirement is fundamental to the nature of the liberal arts degree at Boston University. The [committee] therefore recommends against approving course substitutions for any student as an alternative to fulfilling the foreign language requirement" (memorandum and order, United States District Court, 96-11426-PBS). To assist students with this requirement, Boston University established a Foreign Language Enhancement Program that provides students with learning disabilities with one-on-one instruction, "spelling accommodations," additional time on tests, distribution of lecture notes in advance, "replacement of written with oral exams," and student tutoring at no additional cost (Report 10-11).

Rather than addressing equal access to required core courses as a dichotomous debate of whether to allow substitution or not, however, many institutions are combining sound policy with creative instruction and working with faculty to create a range of learning options for students with learning disabilities. A recent letter of finding from the Office for Civil Rights (Docket no. 09-96-2151, May 1997) pertaining to a request for a mathematics course substitution provides helpful guidance on when a course substitution may be appropriate and when other accommodations should perhaps be considered for three groups of students with learning disabilities: (1) Students whose assessments show an insurmountable barrier to their ability to succeed in math; these students should be provided with a course substitution unless the institution can demonstrate that the course is essential to the program of study. (2) Students whose assessments fall into a gray area indicating difficulty but not a clear prediction of failure; these students should attempt the course and be provided with well-tailored accommodations such as flexibility in pacing, nature of assignments, and test strategies. (3) Students whose assessments do not indicate a profile of learning disabilities that would predictably preclude success in mathematics when provided with reasonable accommodations.

Addressing the learning and accommodation needs of the second group, those students with learning disability profiles that fall in the gray area, will vary by individual institution. The "well-tailored accommodations" referred to by OCR require collaboration between faculty and the LD service provider. In the area of foreign-language learning, there has been a relatively long history of examination and research into the effect of learning disabilities, including possible accommodations and instructional options (see R. Shaw, 1999, and Ganschow, Sparks, & Javorsky, 1998, for a thorough discussion). Scott and Manglitz (2000) implemented a process for consistently reviewing requests for foreign-language course substitutions and working with foreign-language faculty to broaden accommodations and learning options for students with learning disabilities. Their goal was to decrease the need for foreign-language course substitutions on their campus. (See Appendixes 9.5 and 9.6 on the CD-ROM for the course substitution review form and a list of accommodation and learning options within foreign language.)

Similar initiatives are also emerging in the area of mathematics. For example, at Southern Connecticut State University, designated sections of mathematics are designed collaboratively by the Disability Services Office and the math instructor ("Math Class Offers," 1998). The course uses the same curriculum as other math classes, but supports such as a tutor, note taker, and test accommodations (a calculator and one page of notes) are available to all students. Students must commit to regular and punctual attendance, completed homework, and weekly tutoring if grades drop below a C average.

In both foreign-language learning and mathematics, the LD field is recognizing that the more learning options and accommodations available in these potentially difficult content areas, the fewer students that will need a course substitution. As Paul D. Nolting comments, "If study skills training is complemented by appropriate accommodations, disability service providers will find the need to substitute or waive a math course to be 'very rare' " ("Developing Study Skills," 1997, p. 5).

Internships and Field Placements

Some programs of study are structured to include an internship or field placement as an integral part of degree attainment. Many areas of study consider this hands-on experience in the field to be essential in preparing future professionals. As Heyward (1998) notes, the institution has the right to insist that students meet requirements that are "reasonably necessary to the proper use of the degree conferred" (p. 6:8).

Once again, given the range of individual profiles of students with learning disabilities, students may or may not experience barriers in field placement settings. For example, a student with dyslexia who is doing student teaching may face issues such as the need for accurate spelling on the blackboard, accurate reading of directions when conducting evaluations, or exemplary grammar and mechanics in letters to parents. In health sciences, a student with a learning disability may experience difficulty with writing legible patient case notes, following sequences, or making accurate measurements.

Students must be otherwise qualified to participate in clinical and field placement settings including meeting academic requirements for participation such as a minimal grade point average or specific technical requirements. When a student is otherwise qualified, however, the institution has the obligation to provide equal access to this aspect of educational programming. Whose responsibility is it to accommodate the student in a field or clinical setting? The ADA clearly states that the responsibility of colleges and universities to provide equal access extends to contractual arrangements. In other words, colleges and universities must ensure that other educational programs or activities not operated wholly by them, but benefiting their students, are accessible to students with disabilities (Wells & Hanebrink, 1998, p. 44). Some institutions clarify this responsibility with clinical sites through a signed agreement (see Appendix 9.7 on the CD-ROM for a sample).

Though the institution is responsible for students participating in its programs, the internship setting generally provides accommodations on site ("Attorneys Create," 1999). Institutions are cautioned, however, to monitor the effectiveness of these accommodations in order to ensure that the student is being provided equal access ("Administrators Debate," 1998; Heyward, 1998). In coordinating accommodation needs in field placement sites, Wells and Hanebrink (1998) recommend that discussion of accommodations should take place *prior to* field placement and include the student, the LD service provider, and academic and clinical educators. Further, they recommend that site accessibility and general accommodation information should be maintained in central files along with other information about the field site to help guide future students' requests for placement. If a placement site is advised of a student's disability and accommodations are provided but the student is not successful, the site may terminate the placement as it would for any other student (Kincaid, 1997a).

Study Abroad

Study abroad offers many learning opportunities for students. Some students participate as part of an academic program of study at their home college; others take the opportunity to experience a new culture or to assist in learning another language (Matthews, Hameister, & Hosley, 1998). Once again, because study abroad is an aspect of an institution's educational programming, the college or university must ensure that study abroad is accessible to students with learning disabilities ("Study Abroad Creates," 1998).

A number of excellent resources are available in this emerging area. Mobility International USA is a nonprofit organization that provides training, publications, and referrals about international exchange programs and generic disability resources (www.miusa.org/miusa.htm). Access Abroad, a 3-year model project conducted at the University of Minnesota, has focused on expanding recruitment, advising, orientation, and support services for students with disabilities, including learning disabilities, wishing to study abroad. Barbara Blacklock, of Disability Services at the university, notes that the greatest number of students accessing their study abroad program are students with learning disabilities (personal communication, October 16, 1999). The Access Abroad Project recommends a coordinated process for considering accommodations between the student, the home campus, and the study-abroad site. A site assessment form has been developed to gather information on the disability-specific needs and accommodations of each participating location and is kept on file for student reference (see Appendix 9.8 on the CD-ROM). A student needs assessment checklist is also available (see Appendix 9.9 on the CD-ROM). Blacklock notes that the checklist is a useful reference point for college service providers working with students with learning disabilities. The tool assesses academic accommodation needs but also looks broadly at accommodations that may be needed in the living environment that are essential to a successful study experience abroad. For example, students may need to be aware of whether refrigeration is available for medication, if quiet study space will be available in a home stay, or if it is culturally acceptable for a female student to be out after dark at the library.

In coordinating accommodation needs, Blacklock recommends that a team approach be used, involving the student, the LD service provider, and study-abroad office personnel. The team should assist the student by presenting possible scenarios and solutions, encouraging the student to talk about the learning disability in ways others can understand (including phrases in the second language), and providing the name and contact information of support personnel at both the home campus and the study-abroad site.

Considerations in Matching Accommodations to Individual Student Needs

The preceding section discussed procedural considerations for structuring a range of services and accommodations. No one student with a learning disability will receive all the accommodations that have been discussed. Since the purpose of providing accommodations is to ensure equal access for people with disabilities, "it is important to remember that modifications should not be made based on generalization regarding categories of disability, but should be made on a case-by-case basis" (Section 504 Compliance Handbook, 1999, Section 9, p. 64). How are such individualized accommodations determined?

Since learning disabilities are "invisible disabilities," service providers must rely on thorough documentation of both the presence and the impact of the learning disability in order to identify verified limitations that need to be accommodated. Brinckerhoff et al. (1992) advise that "there should always be a data-based connection between the student's learning strengths and weaknesses and his or her eligibility for specific types of accommodations" (p. 419). Chapter 7 discussed the importance of thorough documentation and hazards to be avoided in determining eligibility. Heyward (1998) cautions that not paying enough attention to enforcing or following through on documentation guidelines is a major pitfall facing college disability service providers.

Yet, though comprehensive documentation is essential and provides an important foundation for accommodation-decision making, determining accommodations for an individual student on a specific campus is much more than a clerical task of implementing evaluator recommendations. There will, at times, be gray areas where test scores or observations don't provide clear direction about accommodations needed in a specific context. At other times, professional judgment will be called for in choosing among accommodation alternatives. In the following section, additional sources of information for accommodation-decision making are discussed and confounding factors that may influence accommodation decisions are presented.

Additional Sources of Information

In a training manual produced by the Meighen Centre and the Learning Disabilities Association of Canada, the question is posed "What does a learning disability feel like?" And the suggested answer is "Ask someone who has one" (Drover, McMillan, Owen, & Wilson, 1996, p. 5). Similarly, when looking for additional information on the functional impact of the learning disability of a specific student in a specific college setting, the student is a viable source of supplemental information. Indeed, AHEAD *Program Standards*, adopted in 1999, specifically direct service providers to "*determine with the student* [italics added], appropriate academic adjustments consistent with the student's documentation." (See Chapter 8 for the AHEAD standards.)

Campuses structure student input in accommodation decision making in different ways. On some campuses students participate in an intake interview in which specific accommodations are requested by and discussed with the student. Other campuses review students' documentation separately and inform students that if they have any concerns about the approved accommodations, they should make an appointment to discuss that with the service provider.

At the University of Georgia, an accommodation review process is used. Accommodations for individual students are based on the LD documentation. However, at any point in the semester, if a student believes that he or she needs revised or additional accommodations, the student discusses that with the LD service provider and completes an accommodation review form (see Appendix 9.10 on the CD-ROM). In an accommodation review, the student is first asked to state what accommodation is being requested and to describe why he or she believes it is necessary based on the disability. Articulating that need has led to many constructive discussions between students and the LD service provider and has created opportunities for students to learn more about their own LD profiles. The service provider then relates any clinical observations made while working with and observing the student. For example, in working with a student on reading comprehension strategies, the service provider may have observed that decoding specialized vocabulary is a slow and tedious process for the student, supporting a request for books on tape that may not have been clearly documented in standardized assessment information. A third party on the LD services staff reviews the accommodation request for compelling evidence of a functional limitation that may only be hinted at in formal documentation. An accommodation request is not approved if it runs counter to information in the formal LD documentation.

At the Regional Center for College Students with Learning Disabilities in New Jersey, a system of "controlled observation" has been developed. This informal assessment of accommodation needs involves designing a simulated situation and directly observing student performance. Direct observation of the simulated task provides supplemental information for informed accommodation decisions.

Though the use of student self-reporting and informal data collection can be invaluable in supplementing standardized documentation and in grounding accommodation decisions in the specific demands of the environment, it also places great responsibility on the LD service provider to apply sound professional judgment. Accommodation decisions must still be based on a preponderance of evidence that the accommodation is needed for the student to have equal access to the college environment and not an unfair advantage. More sensitive accommodations requests (such as a request for a course substitution or for an alternate format for tests) would require more extensive documentation of the functional limitation.

Confounding Factors

Learning is a complex task. Influences including goals of the student, study skills, and instructional strategies have long been identified as essential and interactive components of effective student learning (e.g., Armbruster & Anderson, 1981; Scruggs & Wong, 1990). Logically, these same components interact with equal access to learning for college students with learning disabilities and may influence selection of accommodations for individual students in specific classrooms.

Promoting Student Independence

Brinckerhoff et al. (1992) have challenged the field with the statement "If the goal of postsecondary services for students with learning disabilities is to prepare them for adult life, then training for independence should become the focus of every activity" (p. 425). Nowhere is this statement more applicable than in the selection of appropriate accommodations with students.

There are frequently several ways to accommodate a specific deficit area experienced by a student. For example, for a student whose learning disability results in significant impairments in reading decoding, accommodations might consist of a reader, books on tape, or assistive technology to scan and produce e-text. Similarly, a student with a learning disability in written expression may have extreme difficulty organizing and composing an essay. A databased accommodation might be to provide a scribe and a proofreader, or to teach the student to use specific computer software for organizing and planning material and subsequent proofing through voice output, spell check, and grammar check. In both of these examples, the accommodations are designed to address the functional limitation of the student and to provide equal access. Yet the accommodations convey very different messages to the students about self-determination and independence.

Though deficit areas can frequently be accommodated in multiple ways, or in a combination of ways, all options are not always feasible. Sometimes the student's total profile will provide direction. For example, there may be specific areas of information processing to avoid, or particular strengths to tap into that are part of the comprehensive profile of the student (Anderson, 1993). Other times, staff and resources (such as time, expertise, and assistive technology) will influence what accommodations are available in providing access. Service providers are encouraged, however, to consider the range of accommodations that can provide access for a student as existing along a continuum ranging from those that are high in student dependency (such as use of a scribe or personal reader) to those that promote future independence (such as use of technology or acquisition of skills). Whenever possible, accommodations that promote the greatest level of independence for a student should be encouraged.

Interaction with Strategic Learning

In a college setting, accommodation must be provided based on the current functional impact of the disability (Heyward, 1998). However, as noted previously, strategic learning and study skills instruction can, at times, either change the functional impact of the disability or allow the limitation to be accommodated in a more independent way. For example, for a student with a learning disability that results in significant difficulty taking class notes, accommodation might consist of providing a note taker for the duration of the student's college career. Alternatively, the student could work with the LD service provider to improve note-taking skills and, over time, diminish the functional impact of the learning disability in this skill area.

There is a considerable body of research supporting the teaching of learning and memory strategies to children with learning disabilities (e.g., Scruggs & Wong, 1990). Similarly, research has indicated that college students with learning disabilities benefit from instruction in such areas as time management, test taking, organization of written language, textbook reading, and problem solving (Bursuck & Jayanthi, 1993). Typically, in a college setting, skill instruction is available through a general-study skills course. Though skills are an important component of independent learning, students with learning disabilities also frequently exhibit difficulties in monitoring strategy usage and generalizing and adopting skills to different contexts. A learning strategies approach in which students learn why and when to use study skills as well as how to monitor performance is essential (e.g., Deshler, Warner, Schumaker, & Alley, 1983).

AHEAD program standards (Shaw & Dukes, in press) specifically encourage that service providers "advocate for instruction in learning strategies (e.g., attention and memory strategies, planning, self-monitoring, time management, organization, problem-solving)." Depending on campus mission and resources, LD support offices may choose to structure this student support in different ways. Typically, such support is provided through one-to-one sessions with an LD specialist or through class instruction. The structure of one-to-one sessions varies and may range from impromptu counseling and monitoring to a structured model of services. Though impromptu sessions are constructive in that they address the immediate concerns of the student, it is important to examine the effectiveness of these sessions for strategy instruction over time. Students with learning disabilities typically need explicit support to generalize strategies and direct encouragement and goals to become independent. (See Brinckerhoff et al., 1992, for a model program structuring student independence over time.)

A study strategies course is another common way of providing strategies training. Such courses may be taught collaboratively, with an academic skills office on campus or specifically through LD services staff. Sometimes strategies courses are implemented as part of freshman orientation seminars and incorporate awareness of campus resources such as library research assistance. Some campuses have found a study skills support group to be an effective ongoing structure after completion of a strategies course as well as a positive means of improving student learning and independence by working with peers. There are numerous references and resources for structuring learning strategies instruction available to service providers. Bursuck and Jayanthi (1993) recommend the following steps in promoting independent and strategic use of study strategies for college students with learning disabilities:

1. assess the student's current levels of performance;
2. clarify teaching and learning goals;
3. demonstrate strategy usage;
4. provide drill and practice;
5. continue guided and independent practice in controlled situations;
6. practice in real-life situations; and
7. provide a post-test of skills and strategic use.

(Appendix 9.11 on the CD-ROM provides a list of Web sites with resources on study strategies and strategic learning.)

Interaction with Instructional Strategies

A final influence on accommodation selection is classroom instruction. Logically, what has more influence on access to learning than the structure and content of the class? Ruhl and Suritsky (1995) call for the development of empirically validated instructional strategies for use by faculty who teach college students with learning disabilities. Outcomes of preliminary research (Ruhl & Suritsky, 1995; Ruhl, 1996) have shown a link between faculty instructional strategies and note taking by college students with learning disabilities. These findings provide empirical insight into the interaction of instruction and student accommodations as well as a provocative future direction for improving access to learning for college students with learning disabilities.

In addition, AHEAD program standards acknowledge the importance of faculty awareness by encouraging service providers to "provide consultation with faculty regarding academic accommodations . . . as well as instructional, programmatic, physical, and curriculum modifications" (Shaw & Dukes, in press). Service providers typically provide this training through various formats, including large cross-campus workshops, departmental meetings, or individual consultation (Scott & Gregg, 2000). Many resources have been developed to provide general tips for faculty instruction. AHEAD distributes a brochure entitled "College Students with Learning Disabilities," which includes specific teaching suggestions for faculty and staff (see www.ahead.org). *College Students with Learning Disabilities: A Handbook* (Vogel, 1997) is a useful resource for faculty instruction. Many LD service providers have adapted and developed their own faculty guidebooks for encouraging instructional strategies that are effective with students with learning disabilities. (See, for example, www.ods.ohio-state.edu or www.csus.edu/sswd/sswd.html for samples.)

Training materials generally concur that many clerical tasks in classroom management facilitate accommodations for students with learning disabilities:

- A comprehensive syllabus that details the structure and expectations of the class is helpful to students who have difficulty with organization and allows students to implement time management strategies. All syllabi should include a statement encouraging students with learning disabilities to identify themselves. Wording such as the following is recommended: "If you need course adaptations or accommodations because of a documented disability, please make an appointment to discuss this with me during my office hours." Some campuses also encourage faculty to specify that all requests must be accompanied by a letter from the LD support office.

- An announcement should be made orally during the first week of class inviting students with learning disabilities to meet privately about accommodation needs.

- Faculty should make reading lists available and order materials early to allow for books on tape to be ordered or prepared.

- A written description of assignments, projects, and due dates helps students to clearly understand expectations and manage time.

- Faculty should permit taping in class; assist in finding a note taker or reader if requested; and otherwise facilitate the provision of appropriate accommodations as structured on the individual campus.

In addition to organized and structured classroom management, teaching strategies themselves are influential in access to learning. Key factors in effective instructional strategies have been identified in secondary and postsecondary settings. Recommendations (Bursuck & Jayanthi, 1993; Drover et al., 1996; Gadbow & DuBois, 1998; Gersten, 1998) include:

- Provide explicit instruction, using a clear structure for all learning concepts, linking topics across class sessions and to the overall purpose of the course. Provide advanced organizers for the whole course, each section of the course, or each lecture.

- Introduce new material in reduced segments and at a reasonable pace.

- Provide different ways of learning. Present material in more than one mode. Frequently verbalize what is being written on the board or overhead. Use different audio, visual, and tactile methods such as models. Structure group and team projects, oral presentations, experiential activities.

- Allow time for learning and processing through, for example, pauses in lectures for note taking and questions, review questions and summary statements; monitor the pause time between questions and calling on students for a response.

- Monitor class progress and provide opportunities to clarify questions.

- Encourage students to develop a personal learning style within the discipline through cognitive strategy instruction. Model study strategies such as mind-mapping of concepts; presenting relationships of ideas (e.g., hierarchical, cause and effect, chronological) both visually and verbally; demonstrating acronyms, numbered lists, rhymes, slogans, etc.

• Encourage students to monitor their own learning and progress.

Conclusion

Providing accommodations for students with learning disabilities is a dynamic process. LD service providers and their institutions need to carefully consider the full range of educational programs offered, anticipate potential barriers for students with learning disabilities, and structure accommodations and services to provide access. Some campuses will choose to structure services that closely align with minimal legal requirements. Other institutions will define *access* in broader terms and provide a greater range of accommodations and services. Regardless of access philosophy, LD service providers need to recognize that accommodation is required in the full range of educational programs and services offered by the institution. Emerging areas of distance learning and study abroad highlight the importance of working collaboratively with other departments to assure accommodations and services.

In addition to campus variation, accommodations for individual students must be decided on a case-by-case basis. Thorough documentation is essential for identifying disability-based needs. However, it is important for LD service providers to recognize that gray areas of the disability profile frequently exist and sound professional judgment is needed in accommodation-decision making. Recognizing the importance of student input and emphasizing accommodations that promote student independence are recommended considerations in sound accommodation-decision making. Similarly, service providers are encouraged to examine student learning strategies and faculty instruction as factors that mutually define the learning environment. Support and collaboration in both areas may prove fruitful to explore in minimizing the impact of a student's learning disability and thus influencing the degree and extent of accommodation required for access to the college classroom.

C H A P T E R

10

COLLEGE STUDENTS WITH ADHD: NEW CHALLENGES AND DIRECTIONS

Jane Byron and David R. Parker

Until fairly recently, conventional wisdom held that a majority of children with attention-deficit/hyperactivity disorder would outgrow their symptoms during adolescence (Conners et al.,1999); however, the recent influx of students with ADHD into offices that work with college students with disabilities signals new thinking about this earlier belief. In the past, few Offices for Students with Disabilities or programs for students with learning disabilities served individuals with a primary diagnosis of ADHD. Instead, those students may have been served under the broader term of "learning disabilities" or gone undiagnosed altogether. More recently, changes in public awareness and the refinement of assessment practices have led to a striking increase in the number of students with ADHD on campuses today. These students have been highly instructive in shaping the direction of service delivery in higher education by virtue of their experiences and needs. Their insights have helped to answer some of the questions about "best practices" for students with ADHD within the field of postsecondary disability services. Service providers have initiated innovative and effective responses while continuing to seek clearer answers to persisting questions about students with this disability.

This chapter addresses a broad range of topics pertaining to college students with ADHD. The authors hope to shed new light on this rapidly evolving adult disability by summarizing research and current practices in response to concerns raised by disability personnel in higher-education settings. Much of the information in this chapter may change in the near future as we become more knowledgeable about this disability and its impact on learning. The authors wish to acknowledge the seminal work that was published in the fall–spring 1995 edition of the *Journal of Postsecondary Education and Disability*, which appears to have been the first publication about college programming for students with ADHD specifically for service providers. It incorporated recent findings from the educational, medical, and therapeutic communities whose members had begun to work together more closely to address the multifaceted needs of students with ADHD.

Recognizing that each institution must develop practices and policies best suited to its own mission, constituencies, and resources, it is important to acknowledge that no one approach works best for all offices or, indeed, for all students. Service providers are encouraged, therefore, to adapt any information in this chapter that may apply to their setting. Specifically, this chapter addresses four areas:

- *Defining the population.* What is ADHD? Is ADHD the same thing as a learning disability? What is known about this disorder in adults and, specifically, in college students?

- *Documentation issues.* How is ADHD assessed in a manner that meets the dual purposes of disability documentation for postsecondary settings (i.e., establishing eligibility and determining reasonable accommodations)? Which instruments can be used in a comprehensive assessment? How do diagnosticians address issues of co-morbidity and their impact on academic issues?

- *Accommodations decisions.* What types of accommodations might be needed by students with ADHD? How can disability service providers use a wide range of ADHD documentation to make these important decisions?

- *Service provision options.* For campuses that provide interventions beyond accommodations, what services are uniquely helpful to students with ADHD? Do students with this disability benefit from the same services that assist students with LD? What is "coaching," and why are some colleges beginning to offer it?

Finally, the chapter concludes with a case study that illustrates the application of these areas to determine individualized accommodations and services for a college student with ADHD.

Defining the Population

As recently as the early 1990s, many professionals questioned the validity of an ADHD diagnosis in adults. Silver (1992) commented on the professional debate about this topic when he wrote:

> Few physicians who work with adults on health-related issues are aware of ADHD. Similarly, few psychiatrists or other mental health professionals who work with adults think of this disorder as a possibility when making a diagnosis. Thus it is often missed. These adults may be recognized when a clinician establishes the diagnosis in a child or adolescent and a parent says, "That's me. I have the same problems. . . ." (p. 138)

Because awareness that ADHD can be a disorder across the life span is quite recent, there is a limited amount of empirical data about adults with this disability. Even fewer studies have been conducted thus far with college students. Therefore, current attempts to understand the impact of ADHD on post-secondary students by necessity must rely upon extrapolation from the broader research on adults and, at times, even from studies about children. Bearing these limitations in mind, the next section presents definitions of ADHD, describes emerging trends relating to college students with this disability, and discusses implications for professionals.

Evolving Terms and Theories

Definitions

Early research on ADHD used a medical model to study children who primarily manifested hyperactivity and oppositional behaviors. Terms such as *minimal brain dysfunction, brain-injured child, hyperkinetic reaction of childhood,* and *hyperactive child syndrome* were among those employed to identify children who could not sit still and demonstrated significant degrees of antisocial behavior, yet seemed bright and capable of learning (Barkley, 1998; Marshall, Hynd, Handwerk, & Hall, 1997; Wender, 1995). More recently, revised editions of the *Diagnostic and Statistical Manual of Mental Disorders* (DSM; American Psychiatric Association) have continued to reflect the evolving nature of what is known about this disability and how it came to be named. The *DSM–III* (1980), for example, identified the categories of Attention Deficit Disorder with Hyperactivity and Attention Deficit Disorder without Hyperactivity. Less than a decade later, the *DSM–III–R* (1987) replaced the latter category with Undifferentiated ADD. The current edition, *DSM–IV* (1994), uses the single term Attention Deficit/Hyperactivity Disorder but has revived the use of subtypes, given the increased empirical support for this type of classification scheme (Marshall et al., 1997). The *DSM–IV* also returned to the earlier use of the term AD/HD but added the slash mark to indicate that not all individuals with this disability demonstrate difficulties with hyperactivity (Brown, 1995b).

Few disorders have undergone such an extensive revision in nomenclature in such a brief period of time. As Barkley (1998) notes, "The frequent name changes reflect how uncertain researchers have been about the underlying causes of, and even the precise diagnostic criteria for, the disorder" (p. 67). This evolutionary cycle may have contributed to a delay in American public schools' recognition that ADHD can qualify as a disabling condition under the Individuals with Disabilities Education Act. Such recognition did not occur formally until the Department of Education issued a clarification memorandum in 1991 (Latham & Latham, 1994) that classified ADHD under the category of "otherwise health impaired."

While numerous definitions of ADHD have been presented in the past, most are quite similar today. The *DSM–IV* (1994), which provides the most widely accepted diagnostic criteria for this disorder ("Directors Need," 1998; Scott, Gregg, & Davis, 1998), also offers what is considered the "gold standard" definition: "The essential feature of Attention-Deficit/Hyperactivity Disorder is a persistent pattern of inattention and/or hyperactivity-impulsivity that is more frequent and severe than is typically observed in individuals at comparable levels of development" (p. 78). As noted, the *DSM–IV* identifies three subtypes based on the current level of symptoms that have created clinically significant impairment for at least 6 months: (1) Combined Type, identified as the most common subtype, in which individuals have at least six symptoms of both inattention and hyperactivity-impulsivity; (2) Predominantly Inattentive Type, in which individuals have at least six symptoms of inattention but fewer than six symptoms of hyperactivity-impulsivity; and (3) Predominantly Hyperactive-Impulsive Type, in which individuals have at least six symptoms of hyperactivity-impulsivity but fewer than six symptoms of inattention. Clinicians must establish a history of impairment from some of these symptoms back to the individual's childhood, identify current areas of functional impairment in two or more settings, and rule out various psychiatric disorders as a better explanation for the current presentation of symptoms. The degree of severity can vary with the individual.

A National Institutes of Health (NIH) consensus paper (1998) expresses agreement with the core symptoms identified by the *DSM–IV*, citing inappropriate levels of attention, concentration, activity levels, distractibility, and impulsivity as defining characteristics. As in the case of learning disabilities, current explanations of the cause of ADHD describe a central nervous system dysfunction believed to be primarily hereditary in nature. This view centers on the failure of neurochemical activity in the brain's frontal lobe regions, which are thought to coordinate executive functioning skills such as planning, impulse delay, and organizational skills (Hallowell & Ratey, 1994; A. Stern, 1997; Wender, 1995; Wilens, Spencer, & Biederman, 1995).

Current Research Adds New Insights

Investigations into the etiology of ADHD have added to the current definition of this disability. Zametkin et al. (1990) report the results of positron-emission tomography testing (PET scans) that demonstrated reduced glucose metabolism in the brains of individuals with ADHD during the performance of tasks that required sustained attention. The brain areas most affected were those that controlled attention and motor activity (Wilens et al., 1995). Other investigations using magnetic resonance imaging (MRI) technology have identified structural differences in specific brain regions in individuals with this disorder ("Groundbreaking Study," 1999; Hynd et al., 1993; Semrud-Clikeman et al., 1994). Studies investigating the educational implications for children with ADHD have pointed to an attentional "preference" for novel tasks and active responding by students who are less able than their non-ADHD peers to ignore changes in their environments (Zentall, 1993). Other studies have depicted ADHD as a deficit in cognitive and behavioral disinhibition. This view holds that individuals with ADHD are less able to delay an immediate response, to reflect upon past experiences and use inner language in order to problem solve, and to persist at goals over time. Thus, ADHD has been conceptualized as a deficit in self-control (Barkley, 1997; Lavenstein, 1995). Further, Barkley identifies the recent hypothesis that the inattentive subtype of ADHD may be a distinctly different disorder than the Hyperactive-Impulsive subtype.

With increasingly sophisticated tools for investigating neurochemical activity and brain structure, future researchers may offer further empirical information about the causes and manifestations of ADHD. Until such time, disability service providers continue to explore fundamental issues that arise from uncertainties about the nature of this disability. As Scott et al. (1998) recently noted:

> An important aspect of the debates pertaining to ADHD for college service providers is the question of whether ADHD is a behavioral or a cognitively-based disorder. That is, is ADHD a manifestation of behavioral breakdowns (such as inhibition and self-regulation) or due to specific deficits in

underlying cognitive processes (such as selective attention)? Professional opinions and current practices vary widely. (p. 22)

Despite continuing questions about the cause, nature, and treatment of ADHD, a decade of research has solidified the public's awareness that this disability can affect children and adults alike (Tzelepis, Schubiner, & Warbasse, 1995; Wilens et al., 1995). As was true for students with learning disabilities in the period from the mid-1980s to the mid-1990s, students with ADHD are entering colleges today in sufficient numbers to create a widespread debate about this "hidden" disability. Do these students truly have a disabling condition? Is overdiagnosis a rampant problem? What accommodations, if any, are truly necessary to level the playing field for these students? Before addressing such questions and examining emerging trends relating to the college population with ADHD, it is important to remember how rapidly these concerns have emerged. As A. Stern (1997) writes:

> Long unrecognized or ignored, Attention-Deficit/Hyperactivity Disorder (AD/HD or simply ADHD) in adults has only recently gained public awareness. This national attention was jump-started by two events: a lay monograph devoted a chapter to Adult ADHD (Wender, 1987), and a first-person account of an adult with ADHD was published in *The New York Times Magazine* in 1987. In 1990, adult ADHD support groups began forming, and, by early 1995, over 150 such groups had sprung up all over the country. A national conference on adult ADHD was held in Ann Arbor, Michigan, in 1993. It drew some 360 participants that year and more than triple that number the next year. Within the last 3 years, several popular books on adult ADHD, including a textbook for professionals, have been published, and wide media coverage has followed. In 1993, ChADD—the national parent support organization for children with ADHD—changed its name to Children and Adults with Attention Deficit Disorder in recognition of the fact that ADHD was not just for children. (p. 25)

College Students with ADHD

Three trends are emerging among postsecondary students with ADHD. First, these students are presenting documentation and requesting accommodations and services in unprecedented numbers. Second, they report a growing number of academic and affective difficulties caused by their disability. Finally, a large number of college students with ADHD use medications but also report prob-

lems with this form of treatment, particularly during the transition to independence in college.

A Rapidly Growing Population

To date, there is limited empirical information about the frequency of ADHD
in adults, much less in college students. Earlier research tended to focus only on
children at a time when ADHD was believed to primarily affect boys. Additionally, the *DSM* has made changes over time in how ADHD is diagnosed.
These changes have complicated researchers' ability to follow any one group of
subjects longitudinally, since the disability-related characteristics that defined a
study group continued to change. Consequently, estimates of the incidence of
ADHD in adults have emerged from a relatively small number of studies of
adult populations as well as from an extrapolation of the research on children.
Current estimates (Barkley, 1998; Feifel, 1996; Richard, 1995a) range from 1%
to 3%, although a meta-analysis of 21 studies in seven countries, dating back to
1958, reported a range of between 2% and 7% (Wender, 1995). Both Barkley
(1998) and CHADD (1993) reported that roughly one-half to two-thirds of
children with ADHD continue to demonstrate the disorder in adulthood.

In the ADHD topical issue of the *Journal of Postsecondary Education and
Disability*, Nadeau wrote that college students "who need services for ADD are
growing in such numbers that they may soon equal those with learning disabilities" (1995c, p. 1). In the same publication, Richard (1995a) reported that 1%
to 3% of the college population may be diagnosed with attentional disorders,
although she noted the absence of data on this group. More recently, the LD
Special Interest Group (SIG) of the Association on Higher Education and Disability (AHEAD) published a survey entitled "Postsecondary Students with
ADHD: Current Practices" to learn more about trends in college programming
issues. Service providers from 21 campuses, representing an even distribution of
4-year and 2-year institutions, responded. Based on survey results, Parker (1998)
reports that these campuses had seen a 52% increase in the number of eligible
students with ADHD just between 1996 and 1998. Parker and Byron's (1998a)
informal survey of service providers in fall 1998 identified a similar trend for the
same time period. Of the 26 campuses that reported changes in the number of
eligible students with ADHD, 92% reported an increase.

With respect to the rapidly growing population of postsecondary students
with ADHD, service providers have observed that many of these students are
requesting accommodations and services for the first time. Parker (1998)
reports, for example, that nearly one-fourth (21%) of the students with ADHD
who were eligible for services on 21 campuses had been diagnosed for the first
time while in college. These findings mirror an earlier report of a similar trend

(Richard, 1995b). The issue of late diagnosis may cause service providers and administrators to ask, "Does this student really have a disabling condition, if he or she hasn't required accommodations in the past or is just being diagnosed now?"

A number of explanations may help to answer this important question. First, several factors may help younger students manage the impact of their disability to such an extent that any need for diagnosis and treatment is minimized. High intelligence, a milder degree of severity, and a structured environment at school and home may all provide a prophylactic effect that diminishes as the individual grows up and encounters increased demands on organization and attention in college or the workplace (Nadeau, 1995c; Tzelepis et al., 1995). Second, increased media attention to ADHD and refined diagnostic procedures may contribute to an increase in referrals and accurate diagnoses (Parker & Byron, 1998b). Moreover, as Richard (1995a) reports, nontraditionally aged students may have gone to school at a time when teachers had less information about ADHD. At that time, schools were not required to refer for educational assessment unless a student experienced significant discrepancies between aptitude and academic performance. These factors may have contributed to a lack of diagnosis among older, nontraditional college students.

A final explanation for the increase in diagnoses at a later age may relate to gender differences. The *DSM–IV* (American Psychiatric Association, 1994) reports that ADHD "is much more frequent in males than in females, with male-to-female ratios ranging from 4:1 to 9:1, depending on the setting (i.e., general population or clinics)" (p. 82). The next paragraph notes, however, that "data on prevalence in adolescence and adulthood are limited" (p. 82). Many of the earlier studies on ADHD focused on boys, since, historically, boys have been diagnosed with this disorder much more frequently than have girls. Turnock (1998) reports that these studies often followed the same groups of children (e.g., boys) as they matured into adolescence, thereby reinforcing the view that ADHD affected males more frequently than females. A review of these studies led Barkley (1998), for example, to note that "boys are at least three times as likely as girls to develop the disorder . . . possibly because boys are genetically more prone to disorders of the nervous system" (p. 67). A growing number of authors, however, question these conclusions (Richard, 1995b; Shea, 1998). Ratey, Miller, and Nadeau (1995) present the following explanation for what they view as an inaccurate perception about gender ratios and ADHD:

Attention Deficit Disorder (ADD) in women can be like the wolf in sheep's clothing. The recognition of attentional problems and the diagnosis of ADD in women escapes even the best clinicians, because these women often lack the typical symptoms of hyperactivity and impulsivity in childhood or adulthood, and because the social filters through which we view women's behavior often are brought to bear upon our interpretation of symptoms. (p. 260)

This perspective highlights several issues that researchers are beginning to investigate. Shea (1998) and Richard (1995b) summarize research that concluded that girls are referred for public school special services less frequently than boys are. This trend was due in part to the greater likelihood that girls would demonstrate an increased level of inattentive-type symptoms compared to the more disruptive hyperactive-impulsive behaviors found in boys. Ratey et al. (1995) summarize related research that found that girls are much older than their male counterparts when first diagnosed with this disorder.

Differences in how boys and girls are socialized may contribute to the finding that males with ADHD are more likely to develop co-morbid disorders such as conduct disorders, while females with ADHD are diagnosed with higher levels of internalized mood disorders such as depression and anxiety (Berry, Shaywitz, & Shaywitz, 1985; Faraone, Biederman, Keenan, & Tsuang, 1991; Gaub & Carlson, 1997). Ratey et al. (1995) report a growing belief that ADHD–Predominantly Inattentive Type is more common in females than in males and note that this subtype can be more difficult to diagnose than the subtypes that include greater levels of hyperactivity and impulsivity. Solden (1995) presents the view that society expects females to be more organized than males, particularly with respect to household activities such as food shopping and paying bills. Organizational impairments caused by primarily inattentive–type ADHD, consequently, are more likely to produce secondary feelings of underachievement and depression in women. These findings may suggest that female students are even less likely than their male counterparts to come to college with a history of receiving accommodations and services. In addition, they may be more likely to be diagnosed with the inattentive subtype of ADHD as well as with a higher incidence of mood disorders.

Areas of Impact for College Students with ADHD

Given the rapid increase in the number of college students with ADHD, what is known about this disability's impact on students' educational experiences? A number of articles have reported on the functional limitations that ADHD can create in a college student's ability to learn. Findings about the impact of ADHD in academic areas are discussed first, followed by issues pertaining to social-emotional functioning. In a description of general problems associated with ADHD that can lead to academic difficulties in adults, Feifel (1996) notes a pattern of avoidance that many service providers have observed in students:

> Adults with ADHD become aversively conditioned to activities requiring sustained attention to ordered steps. Behaviorally, this is expressed as a strong tendency to avoid such activities. Thus, adults with ADHD are consummate procrastinators and are often perceived as lazy or lacking self-discipline. If they *do* find the fortitude to begin such an activity, they have to battle with themselves to see it to completion because of their proclivity to distraction and their profound inability to organize tasks that require sequential steps. The inability to complete started projects is in itself a hallmark of ADHD. (p. 208)

Even when students with ADHD have been diagnosed and treated in childhood, the impact of the difficulties described above can create new and significant problems during the transition to postsecondary settings. In general, a college experience demands greater concentration abilities and organizational skills, and offers more lifestyle distractions, than the high school experience (Gersh, 1994). These changes in the environment challenge many new college students, including those without disabilities. Richard (1995b) points out that many nondisabled college students struggle with developmental issues at this point in their lives, which can cloud the impact of ADHD. She notes, however, that students with ADHD "experience these problems more intensely and with greater frequency than other students" (p. 289). Not surprisingly, a growing body of literature reports a number of academic difficulties commonly associated with college students with ADHD.

One such difficulty that has broad academic implications is the inability to plan and use time in an organized manner (Nadeau, 1995c; Quinn, 1994; A. Stern, 1997). Students with ADHD may find it extremely difficult to break a project into realistic stages and even to know where to begin, to shift from one study assignment to another at an appropriate time, or to take on a realistic number of commitments in a given day. Working-memory deficits create additional problems for some students with ADHD (Nadeau, 1995c). These students may lose their train of thought frequently, or forget information during exams that they had known just before the test, or forget a topic for a new paragraph before they can type it into their draft. Reading college textbooks can be particularly difficult for students with ADHD, particularly when the interest level is low (Feifel, 1996; Nadeau, 1995c; Quinn, 1994). Students may report that distractibility, boredom, physical restlessness, and difficulty distinguishing main points from nonessential details are chronic problems, and that they need to reread material numerous times in order to absorb it. Following a lecture can also present unique challenges for students with ADHD (Feifel, 1996; Quinn, 1994; Richard, 1995a; Willis, Hoben, & Myette, 1995). Students often report being easily distracted as they try to write everything into their notes in an effort to remain focused, and fighting the onset of intense boredom after 30 minutes of sitting still. Written assignments may create challenges for some students with ADHD (Feifel, 1996; Nadeau, 1995c; Quinn, 1994; Willis et al., 1995). They might encounter difficulty with the planning and organization of a paper, with developing a point sufficiently, and with editing for details such as the use of proper punctuation. Gersh (1994) notes that difficulty finding a quiet place to study may compound the problem of academic performance. Willis et al. (1995) suggest that students should use earplugs or soft music to filter out extraneous distractions. Research has determined that ADHD can, by itself, create educational difficulties for students (Marshall et al., 1997; Zentall, 1993).

These academic difficulties can be complicated by the coexistence of learning disabilities. Most studies have reported that approximately 25% of students with ADHD also have learning disabilities, while a slightly higher percentage of students with learning disabilities, roughly 33%, also have ADHD (Javorsky & Gussin, 1994; Semrud-Clikeman et al., 1992). Fletcher, Shaywitz, and Shaywitz (1994) report that between 26% and 80% of students with one disability also have the other. Other studies have documented a significant co-occurrence of ADHD and math disabilities, particularly in individuals with ADHD–Predominantly Inattentive subtype (Marshall et al., 1997; Nussbaum, Grant, Roman, Poole, & Bigler, 1990; Semrud-Clikeman et al., 1992; Zentall, 1993), as well as reading disabilities (August & Garfinkel, 1990; Dykman & Ackerman, 1991; Marshall et al., 1997). A recent survey of 21 campuses indicated that an average of 34% of students with ADHD also had a diagnosed learning disability (Parker, 1998). The relatively common co-occurrence of ADHD and learning disabilities in the same individual can complicate the diagnostic process and, as Scott et al. (1998) note, make the process of determining reasonable and effective accommodations for these college students even more challenging.

In addition to academic difficulties, college students with ADHD may experience affective problems that stem from their disability. Gersh (1994) reports that impulsivity and emotionality, such as interrupting conversations or being overly sensitive to criticism, can undermine the relationships students try to form and sustain. Controlling anger toward a professor or teaching assistant or expressing disagreement with a roommate in a tactful manner may be problematic for some students with ADHD. Willis et al. (1995) report frequent examples of diminished self-esteem and higher levels of stress in students with ADHD at George Washington University, particularly in students who were reluctant to accept and develop coping strategies for their disability. Students with ADHD may need to develop these strategies for the first time while in college if they were diagnosed relatively late in life. Solden (1995) has identified several affective issues emerging from her work with female college students with this disability:

> Most of them, by the time they were adults (especially if not diagnosed early on), had some deeply-embedded notion that a character defect or fatal flaw was at the source of their problems. And even *after* they were diagnosed and treated, they still often berated themselves with words like "irresponsible, lazy, unmotivated, slob, failure." Even *after* they were on medication, and had some idea that a neurobiological condition was at the root of these difficulties, they still were unable to automatically wipe away the years of low self-esteem and feelings of failure. (p. 37)

Substance abuse is a related area of concern for some college students with ADHD, particularly those who experience affective issues. Kilcarr (1998), citing Weiss and Hechtman (1993) and others, reports higher levels of substance abuse in the population of adults with ADHD. Javorsky and Gussin (1994) and Tzelepis et al. (1995) report similar findings. This trend may be due to experimentation with "self-medicating" practices or impulsive behaviors. As Kilcarr notes, students with ADHD who come to college unprepared to cope with their disability may be at particularly high risk for resorting to alcohol and drugs to relieve their feelings of being underprepared and overwhelmed. A recent study offers hope that boys who were accurately diagnosed and treated for ADHD face fewer risks of problems of this nature later in life. Biederman, Wilens, Mick, Spencer, and Faraone (1999) found that adolescent and adult males with ADHD who had used pharmacological treatments as children were 85% less likely than untreated peers to develop substance abuse disorders.

While the affective issues noted above may create significant difficulties for college students with ADHD, an even greater concern is the frequency with which these students are diagnosed with coexisting (co-morbid) psychiatric disorders. Indeed, mood disturbance is now widely seen as common in adults with ADHD (Feifel, 1996; A. Stern, 1997). Stern observes, "Co-morbidity is the rule rather than the exception in adults with ADHD" (p. 26). In reviewing earlier research, Barkley (1990) estimated that nearly 60% of boys diagnosed with ADHD also exhibited conduct or oppositional defiant disorders. Other studies have found the incidence of coexisting ADHD and psychiatric disorders to be as high as 50% (Brown, 1995b; Shea, 1998; Tzelepis et al., 1995). The recent AHEAD LD SIG survey of 21 campuses noted that an overall average of

17% of students who were diagnosed with ADHD also reported a psychological disorder (Parker, 1998).

The *DSM–IV* calls for a differential diagnosis of ADHD, pointing out that other disorders such as learning disabilities or psychological disorders may be present but do not cause the symptoms that are more accurately diagnosed as ADHD. This distinction is both critically important and, perhaps, uniquely challenging in individuals with ADHD, given the frequency with which the disability leads to damaged self-esteem and interpersonal difficulties that do not rise to the level of clinical impairment. The Utah Criteria for ADHD in Adults, for example, includes affective lability, a hot temper, explosive short-lived outbursts, and emotional overreactivity as core characteristics (Wender, 1995). Similarly, the Brown Attention Deficit Disorder Scales (BAADS) identify moodiness, irritability, and sensitivity to criticism as common symptoms (Brown, 1995a). As Shea (1998) notes, many college students with ADHD do, in fact, have diagnosed co-morbid disorders, thus making it difficult to discern whether educational difficulties stem from the ADHD, other psychiatric disorders, or both. For example, a student with ADHD and obsessive-compulsive disorder may find it difficult to finish editing a paper in order to move on to another task, while a student with ADHD and depression may find it difficult to start writing the paper at all. This combination of cognitive and affective impairments commonly experienced by many individuals with ADHD presents a new challenge to service providers. College students with ADHD who are dually diagnosed may experience more complicated diagnostic, referral, accommodation, and services needs than students with other types of disabilities.

Medications: Answers Plus New Questions

By far, the most common treatment for ADHD involves the use of stimulant medications, including methylphenidate (Ritalin), dextroamphetamines (Dexedrine, Adderall), and Pemoline (Cylert) (Faigel, 1995; Quinn, 1998; A. Stern, 1997; Wender, 1995; Wilens et al., 1995). Wilens et al. further report, however, that between 30% and 50% of adults with ADHD do not respond to stimulant medications, struggle with significant side effects, or experience increased symptoms of coexisting mood disorders. These individuals are more likely to respond to nonstimulant medications, including tricyclic antidepressants (Desipramine, Imipramine), selective serotonin reuptake inhibitors (SSRIs) (Prozac, Zoloft, Paxil), and antihypertensive medications (Quinn, 1998). Since both classes of medications increase the brain's ability to produce and utilize neurotransmitters such as dopamine and norepinephrine, which are produced at lower levels in the brains of individuals with ADHD, Wender (1995) compares treatment using stimulant and nonstimulant medications to treating a scurvy patient with a vitamin C regimen as "replacement therapy" (p. 153). Barkley (1997), in summarizing earlier research, confirmed the ability of stimulant medications to improve deficits in behavioral inhibition, verbal working memory, self-directed speech, rule-governed behavior, aggression control, and persistence in individuals with ADHD. While it is unclear why approximately 20% of the ADHD population appear to be "non-responders" to either class of medications, Silver (1992) suggests that this may be due to a misdiagnosis or to attentional problems that are located in other areas of the brain and are not effectively treated by these medications. The AHEAD LD SIG survey of 21 college campuses reported that, on the average, 67% of students with ADHD used at least one prescription medication to treat their disorder (Parker, 1998).

Despite overwhelming empirical data that support the effective use of medications, some adults with ADHD report ongoing difficulties with pharmacological treatments. Public concern about the potential misuse of drugs to treat ADHD has been reported in the media (Brink, 1998). This type of reporting can cloud research findings and add an additional stigma to the use of these medications. A second difficulty relates to the correct dosage for adults as well as to the most effective combinations of medications to use with individuals who have ADHD and co-morbid disorders. Wilens et al. (1995), in discussing combined pharmacotherapy, notes that "whereas specific individual agents have been evaluated for safety and efficacy, the use of multiple agents simultaneously for adult ADHD remains unstudied" (p. 182). Some adults do not experience benefits from any type of medication. Finally, some adults may feel uncomfortable about depending on medication to function successfully and choose to not use medications at all or to explore the use of alternative approaches such as daily exercise, carefully regulated diets, and homeopathic remedies.

A growing number of college students are discussing these concerns with service providers. The relative lack of structure and increased personal freedom in a postsecondary setting can exacerbate the difficulties students encounter when using medication to treat their ADHD symptoms. Students may forget to take their medication despite a strong motivation to do so. This may be particularly likely to happen when a student's class schedule varies from day to day. Quinn (1998) notes that some students with ADHD go off to college hoping that they have "beaten" their disability and will no longer need to take medications. Quinn (1994) also reports that some college students may resist using medications due to concerns about the "dampening effect" that stimulants can have on their personalities. Solden (1995) discusses concerns that women have raised about the interplay between these medications and PMS, menopause, pregnancy, sexual functioning, eating disorders, and obsessive-compulsive disorder. After reviewing a number of studies, Wilens et al. (1995) argue that adults may need to use higher dosages of stimulants than some physicians are comfortable prescribing, particularly doctors who primarily work with children. Finally, Garber, Garber, and Spizman (1996) report a number of common side effects to stimulant medications, such as headaches, loss of appetite, insomnia, and a period of increased irritation at the cessation of the drug's activity (known as the "rebound effect"), and to antidepressants (dry mouth, increased blood pressure, and heart rate). These side effects can discourage college students from continuing to use their medications on a daily basis, particularly if they feel their only options are to use the current prescription or not use any medication at all.

Implications for Professionals

Differences Between ADHD and Learning Disabilities

An important issue for many service providers is the question of similarities and differences between ADHD and learning disabilities. This topic is complicated by the significant number of students with both disabilities. Some service providers have noted distinctions between the impact of a learning disability and ADHD in the students with whom they work. H. Steinberg (1998), for example, reports that admissions personnel at American University began to observe distinctions between the high school records of students with LD and ADHD. She notes an increase in applications from students with ADHD, beginning in 1992. In contrast to students with LD, these students were more likely to exhibit:

> inconsistent grades in the same subject, poor performance in elective courses (e.g., physical education) and teacher reports detailing lack of motivation and follow-through. The academic profiles that students with AD/HD were presenting had more to do with application of skills than academic aptitude. (pp. 9–10)

Barkley (1997) agrees that LD and ADHD are distinct disabilities. Problems with disinhibition reduce the ability of the individual with ADHD to engage in reflective thinking "on demand." This impedes the individual's ability to identify, select, and persist with the implementation of previously developed skills in order to succeed with an academic task. He notes: "AD/HD is not a disorder of knowing what to do, but of doing what one knows. . . . AD/HD, then, is a disorder of performance more than a disorder of skill: a disability in the 'when' and 'where' and less in the 'how' or 'what' of behavior" (pp. 15–16).

Parker and Byron (1998b) report the implications of this distinction for a comprehensive LD program at the University of North Carolina at Chapel Hill. Learning Disabilities Services (LDS) worked with students with ADHD as well as students with LD and witnessed a fivefold increase in the number of students with ADHD between 1992 and 1998. Students with ADHD, who constituted 60% of the population served by LDS in 1998, were as likely as their counterparts with LD to request services in addition to accommodations. The service providers at LDS found that a traditional learning strategies model, while helpful for many students with LD, often failed to address the performance needs of students with ADHD. The strategies model helped students who needed to develop skills and who could then implement those skills fairly successfully on their own. It did not address the needs of students who, in contrast, had often developed academic skills but encountered chronic difficulty employing those skills when they needed them. In addition, many students with ADHD sought assistance with attentional disorders, questions about medications, and psychological needs, whereas students with LD usually did not request help with those matters. Figure 10.1 depicts data collected by the LDS staff in order to better understand this rapidly growing population and to discern similarities and differences between them and their peers with LD. A broad consensus about these distinctions was voiced at a professional meeting of disability service providers in July 1998. In recognition of the emerging differences between students with these related disorders, the Learning Disabilities Special Interest Group of the Association on Higher Education and Disability formally revised its name to the LD-ADHD SIG in 1998 ("Notes from," 1998).

Programmatic Considerations

The widely reported increase in students with ADHD who are now seeking accommodations and services raises a number of programmatic issues. These issues emerge as service providers and other professionals develop a clearer understanding of the differences between ADHD and LD and the unique needs of college students with ADHD in general. In an earlier discussion about the development of college LD services, Brinckerhoff et al. (1993) noted that programmatic goals and practices must be congruent with the mission of each institution. They observed, "No single model or approach will fit every institution, given the diversity that is a hallmark of the American system of higher education" (p. 170). The same is true for serving college students with ADHD. Many campuses are finding the need to address unique answers to the following questions: Are documentation guidelines helpful to clarify the need for accommodations for students with ADHD? Do students with this disability benefit from services in addition to accommodations? If so, what services address their needs

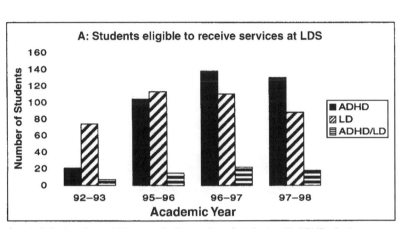

Graph A depicts the rapid increase in the number of students with ADHD who became eligible for services at UNC-CH during a 5-year period. The number of students with ADHD increased more than fivefold, replacing students with LD as the largest subgroup of the LDS student population.

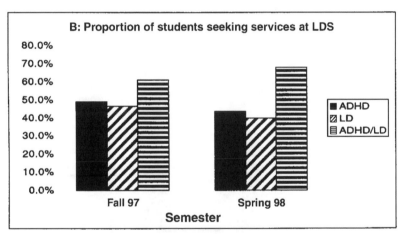

Graph B compares students' use of services (defined as three or more sessions to address issues other than accommodations). Percentages are based on the total number of students within each disability classification who are eligible to seek services and actually did so. A greater percentage of students with ADHD sought services (e.g., coaching, strategies instruction, disability awareness) compared to students with LD.

(continues)

Figure 10.1. Demographic profile of students with ADHD who are eligible for services at the University of North Carolina at Chapel Hill.

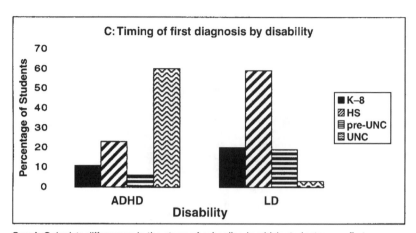

Graph C depicts differences in the stage of schooling in which students were first diagnosed, by disability type. The majority of students with LD were diagnosed prior to entering college. Most students with ADHD, on the other hand, were diagnosed for the first time after graduating from high school.

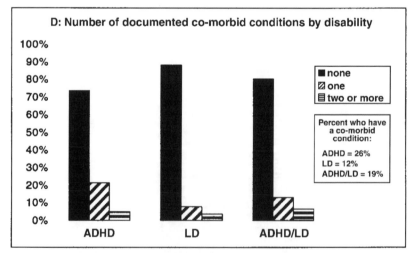

Graph D depicts the frequency with which students also reported a co-morbid psychiatric disability, such as depression or an anxiety disorder.

Figure 10.1. *Continued.*

most effectively? Are these students more appropriately served through an OSD office, a more specialized "LD" program, the counseling center, or elsewhere on campus? Would staff members benefit from additional training and information about students with ADHD? If so, who should conduct this training?

Both AHEAD'S *ALERT* survey (Parker, 1998) and Parker and Byron's (1998a) informal survey conducted in fall 1998 found that the majority of students with ADHD worked primarily with the campus OSD office (81% and 59%, respectively). Students with ADHD often encounter a need for support services in addition to accommodations, including more in-depth assessment, assistance with medication management, and therapeutic interventions. Some of these services may be new to disability service providers, including LD specialists. These issues point to the need for service providers to collaborate with other professionals on and off campus. By establishing or strengthening a network of support services for students with ADHD, service providers may feel less pressure to be a "one-stop shop" for students with a multitude of needs. Shea (1998) notes that college students with ADHD may make such a partnership a necessity:

> It is rare that a learning specialist, for example, has training in identifying and treating emotional disorders, or that a counselor has training in recognizing undiagnosed learning disabilities. The outcome is that a student who presents difficulties associated with AD/HD may have a major component of his or her difficulties overlooked in the process of seeking and receiving services. (p. 58)

P. Steinberg (1998) recently identified four universities in the Washington, D.C. area (American University, Catholic University, Georgetown University, and the University of Maryland) that have developed coordinated services that respond to the concerns noted by Shea. Each institution now has increased its links between the learning services office and the counseling center. This arrangement allows psychiatrists, psychologists, and service providers who work with students with ADHD on each campus to coordinate services more effectively. Such examples of collaborative services may become more widespread as campuses continue to explore effective programming that meets the needs of college students with ADHD within the constraints of limited budgets.

Documentation Issues

College personnel have witnessed a rapid increase in students with ADHD who request accommodations and services. This relatively new category of college students seeking assistance has required the field to revisit its thinking and, in many cases, revise its practice with regard to service provision. Chief among challenging issues is the nature and role of disability documentation. Until quite recently, many campus service providers were comfortable accepting a prescription pad note from a physician as acceptable documentation of ADHD (Byron & Parker, 1997; Scott et al., 1998).

During this time of rapid growth, service providers have typically required more comprehensive assessment from students with learning disabilities than from students with ADHD. The specific impact of an individual student's "invisible" LD could not be ascertained by the mere confirmation of a diagnosis. As service providers began working with more students with ADHD, the dichotomy between having an LD assessment report, which most campuses required, and a doctor's note for students with ADHD, began to raise some important questions. Many OSD offices routinely provide students with ADHD with a quiet test room and additional time when taking exams. Typically, testing accommodations for students with ADHD were based on the confirmation of the diagnosis alone, without any additional information about how the disability was affecting their educational experiences. Discussion in the field, however, challenged service providers to examine what essentially emerged as different standards for making accommodations decisions.

Many service providers have turned to existing knowledge about disability law to find answers. Jarrow (1997a) notes that, by law, disability documentation serves two purposes:

1. to establish that the individual has a disability and is thus protected by the law, and

2. to establish that the individual needs some accommodation in order to have equal access to opportunity. (p. 23)

As the field debates these issues, a growing number of service providers have moved away from accepting doctors' notes as the sole source of ADHD verification. Campuses have begun to require ADHD checklists, often based on DSM–IV criteria, as their next level of documentation guideline. However, some have concluded that even such checklists fail to meet the second parameter as outlined by Jarrow, since this form of documentation rarely includes information about the current impact of a student's disability in an educational setting. Scott et al. (1998), in reporting the concerns of many service providers about this type of documentation, notes that "the question remains, as to what documentation is needed in order to make individualized accommodations decisions for students with ADHD" (p. 23).

Many personnel in postsecondary institutions are now beginning to recognize the need for ADHD documentation that both verifies the disability and identifies its current educational impact on the student in question. As this shift occurs, numerous questions remain. First and foremost is a lack of understanding in the field about the actual nature of ADHD in adults. Service providers understandably have questions, therefore, about what type of documentation might clarify the accommodation needs of college students. Other concerns have to do with placing an unreasonable burden on students, who, under the law, are required to provide the documentation in the first place. What type of documentation is sufficient yet affordable? What type of assessment can be obtained in a timely manner? What types of professionals are trained to conduct the type of assessment that will provide information about current impact in an educational setting?

Richard (1995a), in surveying the field's position on these issues, described a comprehensive approach to assessment that was no longer possible for most general practitioners to carry out in their medical practices. As she reported:

> A multi-disciplinary evaluation is important in the diagnosis and treatment of ADD. Clinicians from psychology and medicine should look into a number of domains including cognitive, affective, motor, academic, work and study habits, social and general health. Recommendations in the summary report should focus primarily on academic needs that are related to the findings. (p. 20)

This approach to assessment reflected a shift from a medical view of the disability to one that included educational and psychological domains, among others. Although a multidisciplinary approach to ADHD assessment may appear burdensome, the nature of the disability requires the input of a variety of professionals. Ultimately, it is the student who benefits most from this approach, which should produce clear evidence of strengths, weaknesses, and the rationale for accommodations.

Changes in Documentation Practices

Once students with ADHD become eligible for services, they often request a wider range of accommodations than simply a quiet test room. Service providers struggle with how to respond to these requests because, in most cases, students' ADHD documentation offers little support for such accommodations. Scott et al. (1998) describe this limitation in discussing the need for documentation that elucidates the functional impact of "hidden" disabilities such as LD and ADHD. ADHD documentation that primarily offers a diagnosis, without objective evidence of functional impairments in an educational setting, often makes it difficult for service providers to determine reasonable, individualized accommodations. As Scott et al. (1998) have pointed out:

> We must ask whether the current reliance on *DSM–IV* criteria alone provides enough information for accommodating academic areas in higher education or whether additional cognitive and language assessment is reasonable to request in a college setting when trying to weigh accommodations requests of an academic nature. (p. 23)

Byron and Parker (1997) describe the frustrations that staff and students alike felt when encountering this increasingly common experience as "trying to fit a square peg into a round hole" (p. 2). This concern is shared by many service providers. Scott et al. (1998) report, "Discussion on the DSSHE-Listserv [Disabled Student Services in Higher Education–Listserv] and in articles in publications such as the *Disability Compliance for Higher Education* speak to the field's frustration when a prescription pad note is received as the sole ADHD documentation" (p. 22).

The lack of a clear consensus on the exact nature of this disability in adults produces understandable confusion when service providers begin to develop documentation guidelines. A consortium of postsecondary service providers in Colorado, for example, encountered this difficulty head on. As Fink (1998) writes:

> The initial task was to develop a draft of ADHD guidelines—perceived to be the most difficult challenge in that there was a paucity of examples available as well as a lack of information about the specific disorder and its impact on the major life activity of learning in postsecondary education. (p. 21)

Compounding the lack of a clear understanding of ADHD and its impact on college students is the training that most disability service providers share. Rarely does professional development, even for LD specialists, include specific training in the nature, assessment, and treatment of ADHD. The earlier conceptualization of attention-deficit disorder as a medical condition that primarily affects children explains this gap in many service providers' knowledge and skills.

Despite the emergence of the *DSM–IV* as the gold standard of diagnostic criteria, various authors have identified concerns about this approach to diagnosis. A. Stern (1997) points out that the *DSM–IV* ADHD criteria lack normative data for adults. Other researchers have called for a lower threshold in *DSM–IV* symptomology for adults, which currently requires that at least six symptoms (out of nine) be endorsed in either of the two categories. Barkley

(1995), for example, suggests the following revised set of guidelines: for 17 to 29 year olds, four of the Inattentive symptoms and five of the Hyperactive-Impulsive symptoms; for 30 to 50 year olds, four of each category of symptoms; and, for those older than 50, three symptoms from each of the two lists. Brown (1995b) argues that the *DSM–IV* criteria are too narrow to fully describe how the disability can manifest itself in adults. More recently, a group of researchers developed the Conners' Adult ADHD Rating Scale (CAARS) as a proposed improvement over the symptom criteria included in the *DSM–IV* (Conners et al., 1999).

In addition to understanding the nature of ADHD in adults and the degree of impairment necessary to diagnose it, another complicating factor for college students is the frequency of coexisting disorders. Given the overlapping symptoms of ADHD and these related disorders, Tzelepis et al. (1995) maintain that "a good differential diagnosis is important because the symptoms of ADHD are very nonspecific and can be symptomatic of other psychiatric illnesses" (p. 36). Mapou (1998) agrees, calling for a thorough neuropsychological assessment battery in order to clarify the actual presenting problems of an individual. Careful assessment that distinguishes among ADHD, LD, and other psychiatric disorders is necessary, according to Mapou, in order to initiate appropriate interventions for the various difficulties that an adult may be experiencing. The authors of this chapter agree, based on their work with students on the UNC-CH campus. Documentation that accurately diagnoses and informs students and service providers alike as to the often multiple needs of students with ADHD is critically important to developing effective interventions.

As the diagnosis of ADHD shifts from the exclusive purview of the medical community to a broader range of professionals, the authors' own professional experiences may have some bearing. While serving on a statewide task force with other university service providers to develop ADHD documentation guidelines, they shared the opinion of fellow task force members that medical doctors would resist providing more information if asked. This concern abated, however, as medical practitioners began routinely referring students to psychologists and other professionals for an educational assessment once the university adopted new guidelines.

ADHD Documentation Guidelines

Different Approaches to Developing Guidelines

To more fully address the need for more thorough disability documentation at the postsecondary level, professionals who work with college students with

ADHD have developed a range of responses. Jarrow (1998) notes on her Web site that service providers share the need for documentation but disagree over the type and specificity that is required. She writes:

> Some service providers have developed guidelines for documentation that vary with the disability of the student. Others have developed more generic policies that provide guidance to students and diagnosticians as to the kind of information necessary to support a request for consideration as a person with a disability at the institution.

Many service providers work with others on their own campus to develop institutional documentation guidelines. Some guidelines created to serve the needs of an individual campus are general enough to apply to all types of disabilities. As Jarrow notes, other campuses develop specific guidelines for different types of disabling conditions. Some institutions, however, prefer to work with other campuses in the same system or state to develop guidelines for that region to promote continuity among campuses as students move from one to another. At the time of this writing, campus systems within California, Colorado, Georgia, and New Jersey all use statewide ADHD guidelines.

At the national level, the Consortium on ADHD Documentation has developed comprehensive guidelines in direct response to requests from service providers (McGuire & Brinckerhoff, 1998). These guidelines, created by the same group of professionals who earlier created LD documentation guidelines for the Association on Higher Education and Disability, use the same format and represent a comprehensive approach to assessment and reporting. The consortium's guidelines have been adapted by various testing and licensing agencies (e.g., the Educational Testing Service, the Law School Admission Council, and the National Board of Medical Examiners) and are included in Appendix 7.3 on the CD-ROM.

The results of two recent, informal surveys about current campus practices suggest that the consortium's comprehensive guidelines for ADHD have had a wide impact. Parker (1998) reported the results of the LD SIG survey conducted during the spring of 1998. Eighty-one percent of the respondents noted that they would accept the *DSM–IV* checklist and a diagnostic statement as adequate ADHD documentation. Only 19% of respondents, in contrast, required more comprehensive assessment reports. By fall of 1998, however, Parker and Byron's (1998a) survey of an additional 26 campuses indicated a strikingly different practice. Only 11% of the respondents indicated that a *DSM–IV* checklist and diagnostic statement would be accepted. Nearly half of the respondents (48%) reported that they required more comprehensive documentation than simply a checklist based on the *DSM–IV* criteria. These two samples cannot be compared directly, and the results represent anecdotal information. Nevertheless, the latter figures may reflect an emerging trend in the field toward more comprehensive documentation for ADHD following the distribution of the consortium's guidelines in the summer of 1998.

Reasons for Comprehensive Assessment

Campuses that accept a diagnosis of ADHD based simply on the results of checklists (e.g., of *DSM–IV*, the Wender Utah Rating Scale, or the Brown Attention Deficit Disorder Scales) typically receive a one- or two-page form that provides limited information. Such reports usually identify the number of ADHD symptoms that the student has demonstrated or currently experiences. Further, this level of documentation often clarifies that other, "look-alike" disorders (e.g., coexisting psychiatric disorders) are not the cause of those symptoms, but such disorders may be named as additional diagnoses. Recommendations for accommodations, if any, are rarely accompanied by supporting data.

Campuses that have decided to request more comprehensive assessment reports, on the other hand, typically receive additional information that might include:

- details about the specific criteria that have been met in whichever checklist has been used (often reported in narrative form);

- a summary of the student's medical, educational (including any prior need for, or use of, academic accommodations), and, if appropriate, vocational history;

- the results of any psychoeducational assessment used to evaluate academic impact issues (including the possible presence of a coexisting learning disability);

- information about the student's current psychological functioning; and

- an interpretive summary that clarifies how the diagnosis was reached and what data are being used to support any recommended accommodations.

Clearly, the role that psychoeducational and neuropsychological assessments play in the delineation of ADHD's effect on a student dealing with the demands of an academic setting is open to debate. While many service providers recognize the potential value of educational testing, few campuses at this time appear to require it as a part of their documentation guidelines. The fact that educational testing is being discussed at all, however, may reflect the recent recognition that ADHD by itself can create cognitive and learning difficulties for college students. What is still debated widely, however, is the specific type of testing (e.g., cognitive, achievement, neuropsychological) that can best measure functioning that can affect academic performance. A growing number of researchers have argued that a neuropsychological assessment of an individual's executive functioning skills provides the most accurate measure of cognitive and academic difficulties associated with ADHD (Barkley, 1997; Brown, 1999; Mapou, 1998; Sydnor-Greenberg, 1998).

For many campuses, the catalyst that has led to further consideration of educational testing is the common practice of providing extended test time to students with ADHD. Exchanges on the Disabled Student Services in Higher Education–Listserv (DSSHE-L), legal opinions, and recommendations from ADHD researchers all add to the discussion of whether this disability, in and of itself, creates the need for additional test time when attentional concerns can often be minimized by a separate test room alone. In addition, a growing number of students with ADHD, like their counterparts with LD, are requesting a range of accommodations. These issues have led many to believe that educational testing may be necessary to clarify the current functional limitations that a student's ADHD poses. In the meantime, many campuses continue to provide additional time and a quiet test room based primarily on the diagnosis alone.

Some sources *are* clear in supporting the use of educational assessment. Marshall et al. (1997) and Zentall (1993), among others, have demonstrated that ADHD, by itself, can lead to significant educational impairments that can be measured through psychoeducational assessment. Biggs (1995) also has noted the benefits of educational assessment for college students in identifying academic impact areas and developing individualized interventions. More recently, Mapou (1998) has advocated for this position so that college service providers can individualize their intervention efforts with students:

> Because intellectual, academic and cognitive deficits persist into adulthood, most individuals with ADHD will have weaknesses in these skills. Adding an IQ test, such as the *Wechsler Adult Intelligence Scale–III* (WAIS–III) and measures of academic achievement, such as the *Woodcock–Johnson Tests of Academic Achievement* [sic], to a psychological evaluation will provide additional information. (p. 20)

The chapter authors worked with colleagues on their campus at UNC-CH to develop more comprehensive ADHD guidelines that include educational assessment. Following a self-initiated program evaluation, the decision was made to *require* psychoeducational assessment in order to provide information about the current educational impact of a given student's disability. In addition, it was felt that this level of documentation could address a number of other issues commonly reported by students with ADHD: the effect of co-morbid (and frequently undiagnosed) learning disabilities, specific difficulties in foreign language and/or math classes, and difficulty with academic tasks such as completing reading assignments (Parker & Byron, 1998b). Finally, the authors decided, based on recent trends in the field and the advice of legal experts, to move away from automatically providing extended test time to students with ADHD based merely on the existence of the disability. Comprehensive assessment is now required to provide more information about the need for extended test time or other accommodations on a case-by-case basis.

Several factors contributed to the decision to require comprehensive assessment. As more and more students with ADHD accessed the LDS office and requested a greater variety of accommodations, the staff witnessed the significant problems presented by ADHD documentation that failed to address current impact issues. Students' self-reported history of difficulties in learning was not considered sufficient evidence, by itself, of the need for accommodations. Staff members also grew increasingly concerned about the amount of time typically required to refer the student for additional assessment before an accommodations decision could be made. Students were failing classes while waiting to be tested. At the same time, two benefits were anticipated by virtue of requiring ADHD documentation that addresses current functional limitations in an educational setting: (1) the ability to respond expeditiously to students' accommodations requests, and (2) the availability of individualized information that could help students understand their strengths and weaknesses as learners. The LDS staff will continue to evaluate the impact of this documentation requirement and its implications, which went into effect in the fall of 1998.

Concerns Regarding More Comprehensive Assessment

One major concern about the requirement for more comprehensive testing for ADHD involves the additional cost to the student. P. Steinberg (1998) warns that the requirement of educational or psychological testing in addition to an ADHD diagnosis may lead to ADHD becoming a de facto "rich man's diagnosis" that exceeds the affordability of the average person. Jordan (1998) voices a similar concern, specifically with regard to nontraditionally aged students who are working while attending college. She also questions whether updated IQ testing is needed for adults who were previously evaluated, given the widely held belief that IQ scores usually remain stable in adulthood. Related to this topic is the fact that many insurance carriers do not cover the costs of ADHD assessment, much less a neuropsychological evaluation.

Disability service providers and administrators are beginning to investigate options to help students address these financial concerns. One approach involves coordinating an "in-house" arrangement with the financial aid office to include the cost of assessment in a student's total educational expenses when determining financial aid. California State Polytechnic University–Pomona, is an example of a campus that has done that successfully. Other colleges and universities have implemented an incremental increase in all students' health fees so that the standard student insurance plan covers the cost of an ADHD evaluation. A third approach entails identifying diagnosticians who will charge students a sliding-scale fee. Finally, some campuses (such as the University of North Carolina–Greensboro) have continued to provide free or low-cost assessment to full-time students, which is obviously more affordable than private practice-testing.

An additional concern involves the flexible use of guidelines to make individualized decisions. The advent of national guidelines such as the *Guidelines for Documentation of a Learning Disability in Adolescents and Adults* (AHEAD, 1997b) and the *Guidelines for Documentation of Attention-Deficit/Hyperactivity Disorder in Adolescents and Adults* (Consortium on ADHD Documentation, 1998) has created some concern that service providers, particularly those who are new to the field, will be influenced to adopt rigid standards rather than review documentation on a case-by-case basis. The chairperson of the ADHD Consortium anticipated this concern in the *Guidelines'* cover letter when he wrote:

> Furthermore, we realize that these guidelines are "not carved in stone" but are meant to be a starting point for institutions, licensing or testing agencies, and others who are trying to craft policies regarding ADHD. We encourage you to modify or adapt these guidelines to suit the unique needs of your school, institution, or agency.

A final concern that has emerged during the debate about ADHD guidelines is the issue of recency. In reflecting on the use of AHEAD's LD guidelines, Jordan (1998) argues that concerns about the age of the documentation may be misguided, particularly if an arbitrary cutoff was applied to all individuals:

> Would information about a 12-year-old tell me all I need to know about a 19-year-old? I doubt it, given the developmental and educational changes which take place during these years. Would information about a 21-year-old tell me all I need to know about a 40 year old? Probably, unless there have been significant medical occurrences which have changed the individual's cognition. (p. 13)

The Boston University case (Kincaid, 1997b), on the other hand, distinguished between LD and ADHD documentation with regard to the issue of recency. Judge Patricia Saris upheld BU's requirement that ADHD documentation be fairly current, given the fluid nature of the disorder and the role of medications in minimizing some of its effects. In responding to the need to make individualized decisions about the age of documentation, the Consortium on ADHD Documentation (1998) offered wording that many service providers have since adopted: "Flexibility in accepting documentation which exceeds a three-year period may be important under certain conditions if the previous assessment is applicable to the current or anticipated setting" (p. 2). Service providers need to continue following the debate about recency issues while focusing on the best way to develop documentation guidelines that will meet the needs of students on their campuses.

Accommodations Decisions

Recent advances in knowledge about ADHD and its potential impact on a college student's academic performance have a direct bearing on the process of determining reasonable accommodations. As noted, students with this disability have increased the number and types of accommodations they request. At the same time, many diagnosticians have begun to recommend more than just a quiet test room. Numerous sources have suggested that college students with ADHD may require note takers, books on tape, proofreaders, tutors, extended time to complete assignments, computers for exams, reduced course loads, single dormitory rooms, and foreign-language course substitutions (Bramer, 1996; Gersh, 1994; McCormick & Leonard, 1994; Quinn, 1994; Richard, 1994; "Students with Attention Deficit Disorder," 1998). As with learning disabilities, service providers must look to documentation that speaks to the current impact of a student's specific disability in order to make informed and individualized decisions.

The delays and complications that can present themselves during accommodations-decision making, however, are richly depicted by the following experience that one service provider, who requested anonymity, shared with the authors:

> Frequently students [with ADHD] request accommodations that are not clearly supported by the initial documentation. The information provided is often initially limited, and we may have to do quite a bit of follow-up with the diagnosing professionals to get all the information required to

document eligibility for some of the requested accommodations. For example, although our policy specifies the need for a psycho-educational evaluation to support requests for accommodations such as readers, or note takers, students don't always provide this when first requesting support. Or, the process of fully documenting the disability sometimes occurs in layers, e.g., initially the student requests a quiet room, later a request is made for readers and the student needs to provide additional documentation to support that eligibility. (Personal communication, January 5, 1999)

The Role of Medications

Drawing upon the earlier discussion of the importance of comprehensive assessment, this section explores the role of medications and the rationale behind the requests for extra time on tests that disability service providers must consider. Researchers continue to debate the role that medication plays in the diagnosis of ADHD. Frequently, an initial psycho-educational or neurological assessment that measures the impact of a student's attentional disorder is conducted before a student begins a pharmacological treatment. Therefore, test results typically do not reflect how a student's medication might mitigate the impact of the disability. Subsequently, when a student requests an accommodation and is benefiting from a medication, service providers may be uncertain about the current impact of that student's disability. Without an understanding of the effects of medication, the need for accommodations can be unclear. This concern has led a growing number of professionals to request that students with a diagnosis of ADHD take their medication prior to reevaluation (which should be noted in their report) for the purpose of clarifying the current impact of their disability.

An article in *Disability Compliance for Higher Education* ("Testing Accommodations for Students," 1998) reported the practice of most courts in determining that mitigating factors such as medication should not be taken into account when identifying a person's disability, saying, "Thus, chances are good that the student's use of medication would not disqualify him from the protection of the ADA" (p. 5). More recently, however, the U.S. Supreme Court sided with employers in three ADA cases by agreeing that the employees involved were able to self-accommodate such that their disability no longer created a substantial limitation to the major life activity of working ("Supreme Court Rulings," 1999) (see discussion in Chapter 3). Some service providers read these rulings as a suggestion that students with ADHD who take medications may, in a similar fashion, no longer need accommodations. Two noted disability law experts have evaluated the impact of these Supreme Court decisions on our work with college students. Kincaid has urged caution by noting, "Schools need to focus on the point that the court underscored the fact that each case must be decided on a case-by-case basis" ("Supreme Court Rulings," 1999, p. 6). Simon (1999) has gone to even greater lengths to distinguish between the issues involved in these cases and the experiences of students with ADHD:

> The court had before it impairments that when mitigated by eyeglasses or blood pressure medication were completely corrected or controlled, and the plaintiffs neither sought or needed reasonable accommodations. Thus, students who have attention deficit hyperactivity disorder and take Ritalin, but still have difficulties which require reasonable accommodations, would still be covered by the ADA. (p. 8)

This caution from the legal community is reinforced by a closer inspection of what stimulant medications can, and cannot, do to minimize the impact of this disability. Garber et al. (1996) note that stimulant medications fail to teach students reflective thinking skills or even to know what to focus on. Both of these cognitive skills can be significantly affected by ADHD and are required in many academic activities, including taking tests, following lectures, completing long reading assignments, and writing papers. As the authors note, "Even if medication decreases overt impulsive behavior, it does not teach internal reflective thinking. Some situations require what is known as 'convergent' thinking, in which all effort is directed toward one solution for quick decision making" (p. 144). This illustration may help to explain, for example, why many college students with ADHD express difficulty with multiple-choice exams even when they have taken their medication. They remain unable to focus on the essential question being asked and thus are unable to discriminate among choices.

Questions About Testing Accommodations

Richard (1995b) refers to ADHD as "the new kid on the block" (p. 284) in describing why faculty members and service providers share many questions about how to meet the emerging needs of these students. For many service providers, determining the need for testing accommodations is more straightforward for students with LD than for those with ADHD. Most LD assessment reports, for example, include standardized testing data and observational data about a student's processing speed, reading and writing abilities, and word fluency. The current range of documentation for students with ADHD might suggest that the testing accommodations typically provided vary widely among campuses.

Interestingly, the *ALERT* survey would suggest otherwise. All of the 21 campuses reported providing both extended test time and a quiet test room to students with ADHD (Parker, 1998). This may reflect a general understanding that, like LD, ADHD can by definition impair a student's processing speed skills due to problems with sustained attention. Despite this apparent consensus, opinions vary about appropriate test accommodations for students with this disability. Murphy and Gordon (1996) argue for the importance of objective documentation to support the need for additional test time:

> Frankly, in the case of ADHD, it is hard to prove either in individual cases or by citing research that extra time on an exam necessarily would be helpful. Our bona fide ADHD patients often commented that they fail because they finish too quickly, before checking their work. (p. 11)

Service providers express an equally divergent view about methods they can use to determine the need for test accommodations. An exchange of opinions on the DSSHE-L noted these viewpoints. On the one hand, Brian Rose of Rutgers University (personal communication, June 2, 1997) argued that determining the amount of necessary additional test time on a case-by-case basis is arbitrary at best. He then described a decision-making model he employs to make such decisions in as individual a manner as possible: "When all is said and done, I never feel like I have reached the 'right' or even a 'fair' result. I just feel like I have created a position I wouldn't be embarrassed to defend." Scott Lissner of Longwood (VA) College (personal correspondence, June 5, 1998) and Ruth Fink of the University of Colorado at Boulder (personal correspondence, June 5, 1998) argued that it *is* possible to determine this accommodation case by case. Lissner maintained that this entails using clinical judgment and described a four-step process that includes a review of the student's history of using this accommodation, plus any psycho-educational measures of the student's processing and motor speeds. Fink reinforced the value of using clinical judgment and the interpretation of psycho-educational testing results to determine the need for testing accommodations on a case-by-case basis.

Other service providers have discussed the importance of tracking students' actual use of testing accommodations over time to make decisions. In another posting to the DSSHE-L, David Sweeney from Texas A&M University (personal communication, June 4, 1998) noted the practice on his campus of collecting data on students' use of extra test time, class by class. These data are then used the following semester when discussing a student's need for test accommodations. A similar practice is now used at the University of North Carolina at Chapel Hill. Data are collected on the amount of additional test time used by each student, in each class, as well as the format of each exam.

This type of record keeping is possible because most students take their exams in a testing room within the LDS office. After one year, the authors have found that these data can be very helpful in determining the need for additional test time, particularly when a student's documentation fails to fully clarify that need. Ongoing collection and evaluation of these data will also assist the authors in reviewing the benefits and limitations of their campus's new requirement of psycho-educational assessment for students with ADHD.

A final venue for the discussion about testing accommodations for students with ADHD has been the courts and national testing agencies. In *Price v. The National Board of Medical Examiners* (1997) (see Chapter 7), medical students with ADHD were denied testing accommodations on the United States Medical Licensing Examination (USMLE). This decision of the court was based in part on the expert testimony of Barkley, Gordon, and Murphy, well-known researchers in the field, who testified that the students in question should be compared to the "average person in the street" in determining whether any disability impact issues rose to the level of protection under the ADA. The court was also persuaded to rule against the plaintiffs, in part, due to their past academic success (Latham & Latham, 1998). Rothstein (1998), author of Chapter 3, as well as dean, professor, and disability expert at the University of Louisville, Louis D. Brandeis School of Law, discussed this issue from the point of view of college administrators. She articulated the concern that students with hidden disabilities might expect accommodations on exams such as the USMLE simply because they had a history of such accommodations as undergraduates.

As service providers creatively address the challenges of a "new" type of college student, they can develop practices for making informed, case-by-case accommodations decisions by following some of the same procedures that have worked well for students with LD and other disabilities. Emerging data add to our understanding of the educational impact that ADHD can have on students. Such research has aided in the development of various guidelines calling for comprehensive testing that can provide useful information for students and service providers in this increasingly common situation.

Service Provision Options

As discussed in Chapter 8 on program development, service provision takes various forms on different campuses. Some campuses offer accommodations only, in compliance with the law. Practices on those campuses that offer services to students with disabilities, in addition to accommodations, vary widely. Services may be available to all students on the campus or may be designed for students with specific disabilities (e.g., LD, hearing impairments, psychiatric disabilities). Questions about services to students with ADHD parallel much of the earlier discussion in the field about students with LD. This section summarizes the benefits of services that promote disability awareness, in addition to exploring the questions of coaching, assistance with medications, and effective counseling services.

Benefits of Disability Awareness

Like many students with LD, a head injury, or psychiatric disorder, students with ADHD may confront issues related to having a "hidden" disability. These students, like all postsecondary students with disabilities, need to self-advocate in order to obtain accommodations. This process may result in interactions with faculty members and administrators who struggle with whether the student has a legitimate disability. Recent media attention may reinforce concerns about misdiagnosis and the "fairness" of providing testing accommodations to students who have achieved academic success in the past without any accommodations (Lewin, 1998; Shalit, 1997). While these campus-wide issues may lead service providers to address disability awareness at an institutional level, it is important to remember that students with ADHD can have a need for this information as well.

Many college students with ADHD report no access to, or little need for, accommodations in elementary and high school. A growing number of students are diagnosed for the first time in college, when the demands for organization, time management, sustained attention, and mastery of facts intensify. As Katz (1998) notes:

> Students with ADHD are often some of the brightest ones we may encounter in a classroom, with an unusual ability both to link ideas across traditional categories and to recognize the unexpected, to grasp ideas quickly and manipulate concepts facilely. However, they falter scholastically when in-depth study becomes the requirement for success over general knowledge and problem solving agility. (p. 3)

Many students with ADHD in college share a need to develop a new awareness about the impact of their disability. This awareness forms a foundation as they learn how to self-advocate successfully while developing coping skills for independently managing the impact of their disability.

In studying the factors that contributed to occupational success and personal adjustment in adults with LD, Gerber, Reiff, and Ginsberg (1996) identified a "reframing" process in which individuals came to understand their disability within the context of their overall strengths and weaknesses. Increased understanding and acceptance of their disability empowered these adults to make successful occupational choices and to view challenges as opportunities. Many students with ADHD share a similar need to reframe their understanding of their disability while in college or graduate school. In discussing how he addresses this issue with newly diagnosed adults, Murphy (1995) explains the importance of helping the individual rethink the impact of ADHD:

> Patients need to have at least a general understanding that they have a neurological condition, not a character defect or moral shortcoming. Often they have internalized negative messages from parents, teachers, spouse, and employers and have come to believe they are either dumb, lazy, incompetent, or unmotivated. (p. 139)

Service providers can offer direct assistance to students who want to learn more about their ADHD or can refer them to other professionals who provide this type of service. Such efforts can promote students' personal growth and lead to a more realistic, proactive approach to utilizing necessary accommodations. In addition, Richard (1995a) and McCormick (1998) have identified increased retention and higher graduation rates as additional outcomes of services that promote effective self-advocacy.

Coaching Services

During a time of rapid growth in research and clinical practice with adults with ADHD, coaching has emerged as an intervention that has attracted much attention. Since no empirical evidence is available yet to evaluate the efficacy of coaching, many service providers understandably have questions about its validity. Conversely, some service providers mistakenly believe that "coaching" is merely the current name for the same time management strategies they have taught to students with LD for many years. The emergence of coaching as a fee-based service offered by private practitioners has rekindled a debate, analogous to the earlier debate about LD, that ADHD is a "rich man's" diagnosis. Several organizations within the burgeoning field of coaching are beginning to develop training protocols, standards of practice, and certification requirements. Nevertheless, the current ability of individuals to advertise coaching services, regardless of their training, raises additional questions among many professionals in higher education. Despite these concerns, a growing number of college students with ADHD are inquiring about the availability of coaching services in a post-secondary setting.

Coaching has evolved through at least four developmental stages. Initially, adults who may not have had disabilities sought out individuals in the corporate world who could offer mentoring and assistance with job and personal performance goals. Favorite (1996) identifies personal trainers, executive coaches, and career consultants as examples of these early coaches. This type of assistance is in the process of being codified by such organizations as the Coaches' Training Institute (CTI) and the International Coaching Federation (ICF), which now offer structured training programs and are developing certification standards for personal and professional coaches in private practice (Whitworth, Kimsey-House, & Sandahl, 1998). A number of individuals simultaneously developed similar techniques but refined them in order to be particularly effective with adults with ADHD. Working within the National Attention Deficit Disorder Association (ADDA), several of these leaders began to offer training for coaches who specialized in working with adults with ADHD ("Interview with an ADD Coach," 1998). Most recently, some service providers (including the authors) began encountering students with ADHD who had received private coaching assistance that was more helpful to them than the learning strategies instruction traditionally offered to students with LD. Service providers from a number of campuses have begun to seek training in coaching techniques in order to adapt the private-practice model to a campus setting (Parker & Byron, 1998b).

What Is Coaching?

Jaksa and Ratey (1999) recently defined ADD coaching as "an ongoing relationship between a coach and client that is very goal-driven, structured, and focused on helping the clients create practical strategies to be more effective in their daily lives" (p. 3). Given the newness of coaching services and the numerous settings in which coaching has been offered, however, no one definition has yet achieved universal acceptance. Still, a range of descriptions identifies several common themes. Whitworth et al. (1998) describe a "co-active" partnership that forms the basis of a private-practice coaching relationship:

> In a co-active coaching relationship the agenda comes from the client, not the coach. . . . The relationship is entirely focused on getting the results clients want. They set the agenda. The coach's job is to make sure the agenda doesn't get lost. . . . This is different from consulting, for example, where the consultant brings specialized expertise and very often sets the

agenda for the relationships. Co-active coaching is not about the coach's content, or the coach's expertise, or giving solutions. (pp. 4–5)

Hallowell and Ratey (1994) used a sports analogy to provide an early definition of an ADD coach. They explained that "the coach keeps the player focused on the task at hand and offers encouragement along the way" (p. 226). In the brochure of the American Coaching Association (undated), an organization founded by Susan Sussman, coaching is discussed as an intervention that helps individuals with ADD by focusing on structure, skills, support, and strategies. The brochure notes:

ADD coaches help individuals to set goals, accept limitations and acknowledge strengths, develop social skills, and create strategies that enable them to be more effective in managing their day-to-day lives. They do this by establishing a pattern of frequent communication with clients to make sure they are focused and working steadily toward their goals.

Implicit in these descriptions are a number of beliefs and practices. First, coaches use questioning as their primary communication tool. ADD coaches, in particular, pose questions to model the use of self-control strategies for individuals who find it difficult to engage in reflective thinking. Second, coaches believe that clients and students usually know the answers to their own questions. This helps to explain the method of inquiry that characterizes coaching and contrasts it with the more didactic model used in learning strategies instruction. A third practice shared by many corporate, ADD, and college coaches is the overt development of mutually agreed upon ways to communicate. This is done explicitly in order to individualize the nature of the coaching relationship and to reinforce the importance of the client or student being the decision maker. Communication decisions involve both the manner by which the coach provides feedback to the client or student and the logistics of their meetings. For example, coaches might ask the following types of questions to ascertain the client or student's preferences:

- How would I know if you began to waiver from your goal?

- If you lose your train of thought during a session and start focusing on a different topic, would you like me to say anything?

- Would you like to conduct our sessions face to face, via phone calls, or through the use of e-mail?

- How often would you like to meet while you are working on this project?

A final practice shared by many coaches is their commitment to help clients make progress toward goals one step at a time. ADD and college coaches, in particular, are more likely to help clients or students identify the next specific step rather than task-analyzing all of the steps involved. This approach can minimize the procrastination that often results from a feeling of being overwhelmed by too many details. All of these beliefs and practices are designed to help clients and students achieve the dual goals of coaching: completing important goals and developing greater self-awareness in the process (Whitworth et al., 1998).

How Coaching Differs from Existing Services

When coaching is offered in a college setting, it is usually done so in addition to psychotherapy (if warranted) and the use of medications. Further, some campuses are beginning to explore differences between coaching and strategies instruction. Given the frequency with which these services are provided simultaneously, it is important to distinguish how they differ from one another. A number of authors have discussed differences between coaching and therapy. Nadeau (1995b) notes that coaches are better equipped than therapists to help clients develop daily routines through brief but frequent contacts. Griffith-Haynie and Smith (1995) present a detailed chart that contrasts the two models. A central distinction is the premise that coaches, unlike therapists, work with healthy clients who are ready and able to take action on current goals. More recently, Jaksa and Ratey (1999) reiterated this distinction by noting that therapy is based on a "pathology" model, while coaching is based on a "wellness" model. They also observed that coaching does not require face-to-face meetings and is unlikely to be paid for by health insurance programs. All three sources agreed that coaches and therapists might need to seek the client's permission to communicate with other professionals in order to coordinate services effectively.

Many service providers, particularly LD specialists, have thought that coaching is a new name for existing forms of learning strategies instruction, particularly time management techniques. After reviewing the literature, conducting interviews with private ADD coaches, and receiving training from a national coaching organization, Parker and Byron (1998b) summarized differences between a coaching model and the learning strategies model widely used with college students with LD. Table 10.1 also depicts the differences between the two models.

Table 10.1
Differences Between Coaching Services and Learning Strategies Instruction

Students Who Benefit Most from Coaching (ADHD?):	Students Who Benefit Most from Learning Strategies (LD?):
Possess effective strategies but have difficulty employing them, due to problems with organization and self-regulation.	Need to develop a repertoire for learning, due to problems with information processing.
Find it difficult to engage in temporal reasoning (e.g., prioritize most immediate goal, recall past solutions, anticipate future success).	Find it difficult to engage in metacognitive awareness (e.g., organize and monitor the effectiveness of a current approach to learning).
Find it difficult to sustain attention to a goal over time (e.g., distractions and boredom decrease focus; working memory deficits impair recall).	Find it difficult to analyze a learning activity into discrete steps and generate alternative approaches that match their strengths as learners.
Encounter difficulty regulating "on-task" behaviors despite motivation and skills.	Encounter difficulty generating various approaches to learning, despite motivation and an ability to remain on task.

When Offering Coaching, Service Providers Should:	When Offering Strategies, Service Providers Should:
Believe that students usually possess effective strategies and can identify better ways to use these strategies if they first engage in reflective thinking.	Believe that students can develop more effective ways to learn if they receive direct instruction, guided practice, and monitoring.
Use an inquiry approach, with an emphasis on asking questions.	Use a didactic approach, with an emphasis on describing and demonstrating strategies for students to practice and master.
Focus on short-term steps that the student generates and commits to carrying out.	Focus on a comprehensive sequence of steps that, in large part, they task analyze for the student.
Determine with the student, through mutual decision making, how to structure sessions and how and when to provide feedback to student.	Implicitly follow a teaching model to structure the session and, in large part, rely on the student's assessment report to decide how to individualize instruction.
Make decisions, with the student, on the frequency, length, and type of session (e.g., e-mail, phone, face to face?).	Typically suggest a weekly, 1 hour, face-to-face meeting.
Promote follow through by helping students create "in-the-moment" reminders and plans for being accountable for their progress.	Promote follow through by helping students practice a new strategy during the session, then develop self-instructions to take with them for independent practice.

Note. From *Get on the Bus: Providing Services to College Students with ADHD,* by J. Byron, D. Parker, and T. Laurie Maitland, 1998, paper presented at the AHEAD 21st Annual Conference, Las Vegas. Copyright 1998 by J. Byron. Reprinted with permission.

Why Students Seek Coaching

Compared to learning strategies instruction, coaching may be more effective with students with ADHD because it more accurately responds to the areas of impairment that can be caused by that disability. In discussing differences between LD and ADHD, Silver (1992) notes that "the treatment for a learning disability will not treat ADHD nor will the treatment for ADHD treat a learning disability" (p. 46). Richard (1995a) observes that students with ADHD may not present with skills deficits but likely would demonstrate variability in their academic performance and, "when they are faced with tasks that are routine, repetitive, and require attention to detail, they may demonstrate great difficulty voluntarily focusing and maintaining attention" (p. 19).

ADD coaches learn to pay particular attention to students' difficulties with establishing and following routines. They often help students create reminder systems to compensate for the memory impairments that are commonly reported by adults with ADHD. These prompts might take the form of Post-It notes on the student's mirror, software or a wristwatch that can be programmed to beep at certain times, or even daily calls or e-mails between the coach and the student that serve to re-identify objectives for that day. While the ultimate goal of coaching is to help the student develop independent skills for following through on important activities, Nadeau (1995a) describes an example of why some students need initial assistance with areas of weakness caused by their disability. She links prospective memory (e.g., the ability to remember that one needs to remember something) to attentional skills:

> Recall is usually initiated by an external cue, while prospective memory requires that the individual cues himself or herself. It is this self-cueing aspect of prospective memory which presents the greatest challenge for the individual with ADD. Constantly distracted by the onrushing flow of external and internal distractions, he or she is very likely to forget to self-cue at the appropriate moment. (p. 201)

Coaches help students address deficits in their executive functioning skills. These cognitive skills play a critical role in helping a person prioritize concerns, recall successful solutions from past experiences, and persist during the implementation of a current plan of action, while simultaneously monitoring his or her success at these tasks. Barkley (1998) explains the importance of providing overt assistance to some individuals with ADHD who may find it difficult to employ executive functioning skills on their own:

> By anticipating events for them, breaking future tasks down into smaller and more immediate steps, and using artificial immediate rewards . . . these

steps serve to externalize time, rules and consequences as a replacement for the weak internal forms of information, rules and motivation. . . . (p. 71)

Coaching Services in Postsecondary Settings

Today, a small but growing number of campuses offer coaching services to students with ADHD. Parker (1998), in summarizing survey responses from 21 campuses, reports that 8 offered coaching services. Until the field agrees on a common definition of coaching, however, such reports need to clarify the actual practices that are offered, note whether such services are provided to students free of charge, and identify the manner in which professionals have been trained to offer such services.

An early report ("Supporters Give ADD Coaching Credit," 1997) describes coaching services on two campuses in Pennsylvania and Ohio. At West Chester University, a TRIO grant was used to hire graduate students to provide ongoing time management and organizational support to students with both ADHD and LD (M. Patwell, personal communication, December 1997). A service provider at Kenyon College primarily relied on e-mail to help students maintain progress toward their academic goals (E. Keeney, personal communication, December 1997). Students' motivation to learn better academic coping strategies was noted to be an important prerequisite to benefiting from time management and organizational interventions. In the Boston area, service providers from Emerson College, Wellesley College, Boston College, and MIT (R. Goldhammer, personal communication, October 26, 1998) developed a coaching model that incorporated the HOPE (Help, Obligations, Plans, Encouragement) technique, an early coaching model proposed by Hallowell and Ratey (1994). In the fall 1998 survey conducted by this chapter's authors, plans at Clemson University to establish peer coaching services for students with ADHD, including a protected Internet "chat room," were identified (B. Martin, personal communication, November 5, 1998). Similarly, a recent post to the DSSHE-Listserv reported the success of a peer-coaching approach in place at Northern Illinois University (N. Kasinski, personal communication, January 8, 1999). Western New England College now offers both strategies instruction and coaching to students with LD and ADHD (B. Alpert, personal communication, November 22, 1999). This campus describes its coaching services in an undated Student Disability Services publication, which reads in part:

> Students and their coaches focus together on the areas where students need help, usually time management, organizational skills, study skills, or goal setting. Coaches keep in contact with students on a regular basis to

remind them of certain responsibilities. Coaching is about a partnership. It's about asking and helping with guided self-exploration.

In 1997, Learning Disabilities Services at UNC–Chapel Hill adapted a number of private practice ADD coaching techniques in order to assist university students with ADHD (Parker & Byron, 1998b). While private coaches helped clients with a range of concerns and goals under the general heading of "life management," the LDS staff agreed to limit its coaching services to students' academic needs. They presented the following definition of "college coaching" in a 1998 informational handout for students:

> At LDS, "coaching" is defined as a working relationship in which an LDS staff member helps you identify and reach short-term, academic goals that you are committed to working on. An LDS coach can help you act on your goals by working with you to clearly define and prioritize realistic goals, anticipate roadblocks that might stand in your way, develop ways to address these roadblocks, create a reminder system you can use in-between sessions, and check in with you about how your plans are going.

Campus professionals who would like more information about coaching may wish to contact these Web-based resources:

- The American Coaching Association, 610-825-4505, http://www.americoach.com
- The Optimal Functioning Institute, 423-524-9549, http://www.addcoach.com
- ADDA (National Attention Deficit Disorder Association), http://www.add.org
- The Coaches Training Institute, 800-691-6008, http://www.thecoaches.com
- The International Coaching Federation, http://www.coachfederation.org

Assistance with Medications Questions

College students with ADHD frequently take prescribed medications as a part of a multimodal treatment plan. It is a concern, however, when they continue to use an ineffective medication, experience uncomfortable side effects, or encounter disability-related difficulties in following the correct regimen. As the population of students with ADHD increases, a similar rise in the number of questions can be expected from students who experience such difficulties.

Service providers are wise to clarify that they do not monitor the effects of medications and that only a student's physician has the medical expertise necessary to make changes in a prescription. Nonetheless, a number of procedures may be appropriate for a disability office to implement. First, service providers may want to maintain an up-to-date and confidential record of the medications that a student uses. Because students may forget to inform service providers about changes in medications, including the decision to stop using a particular drug, service providers may need to ask for that information periodically. The second half of the intake form illustrated in Appendix 10.1 on the CD-ROM provides an example of how this information can be recorded during an intake process. Second, service providers may help students develop a strategy for recording their response to a new dosage or medication. This can be particularly important if the physician expects the student to remember and report self-observed patterns of reactions to medications after a few weeks. Barkley (1990) and others have provided examples of "titration logs" that can be adapted for this type of record keeping. Students may not be accustomed to playing an active role during medical office visits and may need to practice a proactive, information-providing role. A student with ADHD may have a greater need to refer to written records during such a meeting, rather than relying on memory alone. Third, service providers may need to help students develop effective strategies, at least initially, for remembering to take their medication at the proper time. Programmable wristwatches and pill containers that can be attached to a key chain, for example, can help students with chronic memory and organizational deficits. A fourth way in which service providers can help students improve their ability to use medications to treat their ADHD successfully is to provide a forum in which students can discuss any questions or concerns that they might have about medications. Many college students, for example, resist the idea of having to "rely" on a medication to perform satisfactorily. Similarly, college students may have questions about substance abuse issues. Again, a service provider cannot be a substitute for a physician and should encourage students to seek expert medical advice from medical professionals. A nonjudgmental forum in which students can raise these concerns, however, may precipitate a student's decision to initiate such a conversation with his or her doctor. A final way that service providers can help students with medications questions is to assist them in learning more about their options. Pharmacological treatment for adults with ADHD is relatively new; today, doctors can choose among many more options than just Ritalin. This role may include providing students with names of area physicians who specialize in treating adults with ADHD. Similarly, students may not realize that they can discuss other medication choices as well as alternative treatments with their physician. A growing number of Internet Web sites, including the two listed below, offer current information that can be helpful to students, service providers, and health care providers alike:

- http://www.mediconsult.com/add/
- http://add.tqn.com/msubmed2.htm

Effective Counseling Services

A final service that OSD professionals may be involved with, albeit indirectly, is the provision of counseling services. Some campuses find that support groups for students with ADHD offer a uniquely effective opportunity to increase disability awareness, reduce stress, and assist students in developing better coping strategies by learning from peers. Dumbauld and Daniels (1998) report a successful ADD support group for commuter students at Santa Fe Community College. This group reflected collaboration between the college's disability resource center and its counseling center. A. Stern (1997) identifies support groups as particularly helpful for adults with ADHD and delineates an 8-week series of topics that could be adapted to a college setting. White (1998) recommends that facilitators of ADHD support groups establish a balance in each session between "open" time for members' sharing of experiences and more structured time to address a previously identified topic. White also observed a high frequency of the following themes in her support groups for adults with ADHD: developing organizational strategies, dealing with distractibility and impulsivity, time management, social interaction skills, and, of particular interest to college students, completing assignments on time and increasing self-acceptance. Kelly (1995) notes the importance of providing structure and helping group members with ADHD identify and respect appropriate personal boundaries within a support group.

A growing number of authors also make recommendations for therapists who provide individualized counseling to college students (and other adults) with ADHD. Cognitive-behavioral approaches offered by a practitioner who uses clear, direct language may be especially helpful to students with this disability. Bramer (1996) notes that psychotherapists may have to employ directive language and actively help the client remain focused on a topic during a session. Hallowell (1995) discusses the limitations of therapeutic silence and interpretation in favor of redirecting a client who is apt to have difficulty following a conversational thread. Nadeau (1995a) concurs and encourages therapists to be more active when working with clients with ADHD. She notes, "Without this degree of structure, the client with ADD may tend to skip from topic to topic in the therapy session, just as in daily life, never really staying focused long enough to develop awareness and strategies" (p. 194).

The provision of coaching, assistance with medication questions, and "disability friendly" counseling services may entail a new role for campus professionals, particularly LD specialists who have not worked with significant numbers of students with co-morbid disorders. Potential limitations should be considered when developing and offering these services. Students with active and untreated psychiatric disorders, for example, may not be ready to take action or to be accountable for the behavioral changes that form the hallmark of a successful coaching relationship. Blacklock (1997) discusses the importance of clearly defined roles and boundaries when working with some students with psychiatric illnesses. Unlike learning-strategies instruction, coaching is an emerging type of intervention about which many questions still abound. Service providers who decide to offer coaching on campus, therefore, require specialized training, given its differences from the more familiar learning strategies approach. Further, it is not yet known whether students can internalize and generalize coaching techniques over time. Indeed, a small body of literature on the efficacy of self-control training in children reported varied results (Braswell, 1998). Nonetheless, a few campuses are anecdotally reporting success with this new approach to assisting students whose performance-based difficulties stem from their disability. With these challenges in mind, professionals in higher education are encouraged to draw upon the existing research and to report the results of their efforts when offering services to college students with ADHD. Research and practice continue to suggest that these students may need support services that are tailored to their needs in addition to accommodations in order to succeed in college. Further, such services may differ from those that typically benefit college students with LD.

Conclusion

In recent years, many campuses have reported a rapid increase in the number of students with ADHD. This trend has led to questions about admissions, eligibility, accommodations, and services for these students. Postsecondary personnel are beginning to find some answers, but students with ADHD continue to present new questions. Additional research is needed to refine the field's understanding of the functional impact of ADHD and to clarify what accommodations, auxiliary aids, and services are appropriate and effective for these students.

The case study that follows illustrates an approach to dealing with some of the issues discussed in this chapter.

USING DOCUMENTATION TO DETERMINE ACCOMMODATIONS AND SERVICES FOR A STUDENT WITH ADHD

Background Information

Molly is a college sophomore who was diagnosed with ADHD-Combined type in middle school. She received "consultative services" while attending a public high school. Her Section 504 plan indicated that she may need more time to complete writing assignments and that she should be allowed "unlimited" test time in a distraction-free room. Molly reports that she never felt confident about what she learned from reading her textbooks, so she developed the strategy of meeting with her teachers and certain classmates to discuss her reading assignments. She took Ritalin until her senior year in high school but found that it made her jittery and caused her to lose her appetite. She also felt embarrassed at having to take a second dose at school, during the lunch period. Molly's doctor has since switched her to 10 mg. of Adderall, which she is supposed to take at breakfast. Her mother, an executive secretary, worked closely with Molly throughout high school to help her organize her time and studying. This was extremely helpful to Molly, since she has chronic difficulty completing tasks on time and organizing projects on her own.

An intake meeting between the OSD coordinator and Molly produced additional information (see Appendix 10.1 on the CD-ROM, which depicts an intake form that can be used to collect this information). Her freshman year in college was difficult in many ways. She did not seek out accommodations or services, hoping instead to "do it on my own." Molly rarely took medication during her first year of college. She found it difficult to establish a regular morning routine, since her classes began at different times depending on the day of the week. She also said that she wished she "didn't have to take a pill to show how smart I am." Molly's mother continued to call her frequently to provide suggestions and reminders over the phone. This eventually led to a great deal of tension. Molly did not like being told what to do, but also realized she did not know how to develop effective organizational plans on her own. She had other difficulties, too. She often ran out of time during essay exams, which she attributed to "getting distracted, needing more time to think about the questions and get my thoughts organized, and dealing with how nervous this makes me feel." She reported finishing objective tests on time. Indeed, her ability to complete objective format tests on time, when distractions were minimized, was a relative strength. Distractions were a problem for Molly in several large lecture classes, particularly if instructors covered extensive amounts of information without using overhead transparencies or notes on the board. She has an "incomplete" in SOCI 10 because she was unable to finish a research project that students were supposed to work on throughout the semester.

Assessment Data

[Appendix 10.2 on the CD-ROM provides an example of a form that can be used to highlight important information from a student's ADHD report. This format, adapted from an earlier example created by Anderson and Brinckerhoff (1989), can assist with planning for accommodations and helping students to better understand their assessment reports. All reported scores are standard scores.]

Because of difficulties she encountered in her studies during her freshman year in college, Molly sought out the assistance of the Office for Students with Disabilities during the summer. Following a lengthy discussion with the OSD director as well as conversations with her mother, Molly was evaluated privately to determine her strengths and weaknesses and any impact of ADHD on her academic performance. The comprehensive assessment report noted that she was on medication (Adderall) when IQ and achievement tests were administered. Molly completed the *Wechsler Memory Scale–Third Edition* and measures of attention while off her medication. A review of her documentation provided useful information about her performance on standardized tests as well as on measures used to examine attentional functioning. Scores from the assessment report follow.

Psycho-Educational Assessment Results

WAIS–III:

Verbal IQ (103), Performance IQ (102), Full-Scale IQ (103)

Index Scores:

- Verbal Comprehension—103
- Perceptual Organization—103
- Working Memory—102
- Processing Speed—88

Woodcock–Johnson Psycho-Educational Battery–Revised Tests of Achievement:

- Broad Reading—104
- Broad Math—100
- Broad Written Language—95

Wechsler Memory Scale–Third Edition (WMS–III):

- Auditory Immediate—86
- Visual Immediate—121
- Immediate Memory—103

ADHD Assessment Results

Integrated Visual and Auditory Continuous Performance Test (IVA CPT, Sanford & Turner, 1994):

- Response Quotient—87 (this is a measure of Molly's motor modulation including impulsivity, consistency, and stamina)

- Attention Quotient—45 (this is a measure of Molly's vigilance, focus, and speed of processing)

Brown ADD Scales (BADDs) (completed by Molly and her mother):

Cluster	T-Score (* = significant problem)
• Organizing and activating to work	75*
• Sustaining attention and concentration	85*
• Sustaining energy and effort	74*
• Managing affective interference	51
• Utilizing "working memory" and accessing recall	55

Accommodations Decisions

[Appendix 10.3 on the CD-ROM provides an example of a form that can be used to synthesize information relating to accommodations decisions.]

Suggestions for accommodations were provided in Molly's documentation. Molly's diagnostician, a licensed psychologist, predicted difficulties for Molly in following lectures and completing exams (particularly essays) on time, due to processing speed and attentional issues. The report on assessment completed between her freshman and sophomore years made it clear that Molly was an emotionally stable student without any co-morbid psychiatric disorders. This testing also ruled out learning disabilities. The psychologist noted that medication could be expected to help Molly deal with tasks that call for working memory and sustained attention. The following accommodations were recommended: untimed testing for certain courses (especially essay writing), note takers, preferential seating (particularly in large lectures), a distraction-free environment in which to take tests, and instruction in the use of a daily planner. The diagnostician included a separate handout with a list of time management tips as an addendum.

In her discussions with the college service provider, Molly requested unlimited time for her American History Post-1865 (HIST 41) exams, which use an essay format, and for her Introduction to Psychology (PSYC 10) exams, which are multiple choice. She also requested a separate room for all of her exams and note takers for two of her classes: Introduction to Psychology and Painters of the Renaissance (ART 33). After hearing Molly's requests, the service provider probed the need for each of these accommodations.

Unlimited Test Time

History of Presenting Concern: Molly reports that in high school she had unlimited test time on all exams but rarely needed much additional time. She typically used an additional 30 minutes for essay exams so she would have sufficient time to organize her thoughts. Regardless of the format, however, Molly reports that a quiet test room made a significant difference in her ability to sustain her attention throughout an exam.

Information from Assessment Report:

- Slow Processing Speed from WAIS–III.

- Low Broad Written Language score in comparison to her full-scale IQ (Both aptitude and achievement were evaluated while subject was on medication.).

- The evaluator clearly stated that, even on medication, Molly will continue to have significant difficulty focusing her attention and organizing information. Since the psychologist conducted the educational testing while Molly was on medication, she was able to support such a statement.

Accommodation Decision: Provide 50% additional test time for HIST 41 essay exams and a separate test room for all exams. Additional time on the PSYC 10 exams was not supported by Molly's documentation. The service provider agreed to follow-up with Molly after the first exam in this class to evaluate the effectiveness of a separate test room as the only accommodation.

Note Taker for PSYC 10

History of Presenting Concern: Molly reports that in large lectures she has had great difficulty staying focused and remembering lecture points long enough to record them in her notes. This is most problematic in classes where the instructor presents most of the information verbally and does not use overheads or provide an outline to clarify the main points. Molly finds that her notes in classes like that are scattered, consisting mostly of incomplete fragments that make little sense to her. She feels that this difficulty contributed to her failing an introductory political science class and receiving a D in Introductory Biology last year.

Present Medication: Currently, Molly usually takes 10 mg. of Adderall daily prior to 9:00 A.M. It is important to note that her PSYC 10 class meets at 2:30 P.M., when her medication has worn off. Presently, her physician has prescribed only one dose per day.

Information from Assessment Report:

- Low processing speed coupled with weak auditory memory.
- Difficulty sustaining attention.

- Weakness in writing, particularly with organization and mechanics.
- Strong visual memory.

Clarifying Impact Issues: The service provider reviewed Molly's lecture notes and saw clear indications of what Molly reported. There were many gaps in her notes, missing words, and a disorganized attempt to abbreviate words. The service provider also called the instructor, with Molly's permission. During this conversation, the professor reported some concerns. She said that Molly tends to ask questions in class regarding material she has just covered. The instructor said that she tries to provide numerous examples to reinforce information in the textbook. She further reported that the psychology text was quite technical and that many students have found it challenging. The professor also reported that Molly does sit near the front of the class, which she thought might be helpful since the class is so large.

Accommodation Decision: Provide a note taker for PSYC 10.

Note Taker for ART 33

History of Presenting Concern: Molly wants to major in art history, and she is quite concerned that she will not do well enough in this class to be admitted into the art history curriculum. This class is a lecture format, and the professor uses slides and overheads extensively. He also provides a detailed syllabus that lists the objectives of each lecture. The class has 34 students, and the professor has a Web site that provides more detail on topics addressed in class. Molly feels that having good notes will help her make sure she has all the information she needs to prepare for exams.

Accommodation Decision: A note taker is not an appropriate accommodation in this case. Molly has a number of ways to access the important information from the lecture. Her visual processing skills are a strength and can help her use the overheads and additional copies of the artwork that are available on the Web site. In probing the need for this accommodation, the service provider and Molly recognized that Molly's actual concern was organizing the many sources of information in this class, plus the fear that she might not earn an A.

Service Provision

In addition to accommodations, Molly requested a number of services. She reported during her intake meeting that she was "ready to take another look at learning how I can handle college on my own." She requested help in developing better methods for taking essay tests and assistance in completing her SOCI 10 incomplete grade from the previous semester. When the service provider asked her about her use of Adderall, Molly expressed frustration with its effect and her ability to remember taking it. She asked for more information about how the service provider could help her address those concerns.

Taking Essay Tests

History of Presenting Concerns: Molly reports that she typically required additional time on essay tests. After reviewing two essay exams that Molly took last year without accommodations, the service provider was able to point out that she frequently lost points for failing to answer the entire question. Molly explained that she "gets lost" when reading a long essay question and typically begins to answer the question without first organizing her thoughts. She showed the service provider several comments from one professor, who observed that Molly's answers were often accurate but lacked sufficient explanation to earn a higher grade. Molly also reported that she consistently performed more poorly on essay exams taken in the afternoon, compared to the morning. Molly said that she was "really good" about taking her medication on exam days; however, the medication wore off by early afternoon.

Information from Assessment Report:

- Auditory memory low (86)—WMS–III
- Attention quotient particularly low (45)—IVACPT testing
- Sustained attention and concentration problematic—BADDS
- Visual skills a strength—WMS–III

Services Provided: Based on her observation that Molly had an organized color-coding system in place for reading textbooks, the service provider taught Molly a strategy for color-coding essay questions in order to develop a visual reminder of all the points she needed to address. They used Molly's old exams to identify the difference between "background" information in an essay question and the question itself. The service provider watched and asked questions as Molly created a color-coding system to highlight key verbs in the actual question. This allowed her to identify each aspect of the question that required an answer. Molly decided to list each verb in the margin and check it off after answering that part of the question "to help me stay focused during the test." The service provider offered to continue reviewing and practicing this new strategy with Molly over several sessions, but they both noticed in subsequent meetings that Molly could apply it without any difficulty.

The service provider reviewed with Molly the aspects of her assessment report that described difficulties with sustained attention and concentration. In discussing how this affects Molly during essay exams, they agreed that she should take a brief break after each question to get up and stretch. The service provider also asked Molly about the difference in her performance on morning exams compared to afternoon exams. Molly reported finding it much harder to focus in the afternoons but said, "My doctor said that Adderall lasts all day, so I don't really know what the problem is. I think I just get tired."

Completing an Incomplete in SOCI 10

History of Presenting Concerns: Molly received an incomplete for this class because she failed to finish a semester-long research project. The project required students to pick a topic related to families' use of community resources, conduct a literature review, complete two interviews, and then summarize all the acquired information and present a recommendation for improving the resources that had been studied. The service provider asked Molly to bring all of her materials for this project to a meeting. Molly pulled a large, disorganized stack of articles, notes, and pamphlets out of various pockets in her backpack. As they reviewed these materials, the service provider helped Molly realize that she had completed more than half of the work. Molly said, "Really? Wow! To me, it just feels overwhelming, and I don't know what's done and what's not done. So I just end up avoiding it all together!" Further probing allowed the service provider and Molly to jointly recognize that she knew how to complete the remaining work but was unsure of how to organize and carry out the process.

Information from Assessment Report and Intake Interview:

- Difficulty activating (i.e., initiating a response) to work and sustaining energy and effort (BADDS scale).

- Had received extensive external structure from her mother in high school but, more recently, expressed a strong desire to do this on her own, without being "told what to do."

Services Provided: The service provider explained "coaching" to Molly and distinguished that approach from learning-strategies instruction. Molly agreed that she needed help finishing this project, although she actually knew how to carry out the additional reading and writing tasks involved. She also expressed interest in being asked questions rather than being told how to do something. Rather than helping Molly identify and record all of the remaining incremental deadlines in her Day Planner, the service provider asked her to identify the one step that she felt confident about taking in the next 24 hours. Molly decided that she needed a better way to organize all the materials she had collected thus far. The service provider asked her to describe options she had used in the past, which led Molly to remember a specific three-ring binder system she had seen her mother use at home. Molly used her colored markers to sketch how the inside dividers would look once she organized the materials into sections. By the end of the session, she had decided to purchase the notebook that night. The service provider and Molly also agreed to begin using e-mail between sessions. Molly told the service provider that she wanted to send an e-mail the following day to describe how the notebook looked once she had organized it. They established a 3-week plan for meeting twice a week (30 minutes each time) to continue working on the SOCI 10 project.

Improving Her Ability To Benefit from Medications

History of Presenting Concerns: Molly was switched from Ritalin to Adderall to address two problems: side effects from Ritalin and her embarrassment about needing to take a second dose at school. In college, however, she has encountered problems with Adderall, too. First, she can forget to take it in the morning, since she does not have a routine for getting up and eating breakfast at the same time each morning. Second, although the dose she currently takes (10 mg.) is supposed to last all day, she finds that its effects typically wear off after 4 or 5 hours. Now that she is on campus, her doctor's office is 6 hours away, and she finds it difficult to schedule appointments there when she goes home.

Information from Relevant Sources:

- A psychiatrist at the campus Psychological Services office specializes in ADHD and follows students with medications needs.

- Molly always carries her backpack with her.

- Despite her continuing desire to not have to rely on medications, Molly has realized, after her academic difficulties last year, that she needs to use a medication to perform better.

Services Provided: Molly signed up to attend a midday showing of the videotape "ADD: The Race Inside My Head" (George Washington University, 1996). The service provider had organized a time for students with ADHD to watch this together and discuss it over pizza. Molly was struck by how much she identified with the students in the video as well as the students who watched it with her. In a subsequent meeting, the service provider referred Molly to the Psychological Services office for a medications reevaluation. The psychiatrist decided to adjust Molly's dosage to 20 mg. of Adderall in the morning and an afternoon dose of 10 mg. and arranged for follow-up appointments to monitor her response to this new regimen. Later, Molly and the service provider developed a new plan to organize how and when she took her medication. Molly now keeps a dose by her bed, with a small bottle of water. She sets her alarm clock to wake up at the same time each morning and take her medication. On some mornings, she goes back to sleep for a short time, resetting her alarm to wake her up later. At the suggestion of the service provider, she also bought a small container to add to her key chain, which she always puts in her backpack. Molly keeps her afternoon dose in the container so that she can access it if she is on campus. The service provider agreed to ask Molly about any differences in her attention level during afternoon exams that semester, in order to help her identify feedback she could share with her psychiatrist.

C H A P T E R

THE USE OF ASSISTIVE TECHNOLOGY IN POSTSECONDARY EDUCATION

Brian R. Bryant, Diane Pedrotty Bryant, and Herbert J. Rieth

It has been noted throughout this text and elsewhere that high school students with a variety of disabilities, including learning disabilities, are increasingly choosing to attend some form of postsecondary school (e.g., college or technical school). In fact, Mangrum and Strichart (1997) have cataloged over 1,000 colleges and universities that provide programs for students with LD or attention-deficit disorders. For such students, the opportunity to receive a college or technical education is a dream come true, a dream that could have been considered a pipe dream just 2 decades ago (Block et al., 1994). Although it remains a challenge for students to be sufficiently successful in grades K–12 to qualify for postsecondary education, the more formidable challenge now is to promote their success once they enter such programs (Stern & DuBois, 1994).

Assistive technology (AT) devices offer a variety of options for individuals with learning disabilities to access the postsecondary curriculum; to compensate for reading, mathematics, and writing difficulties; and to improve their quality of life across the lifespan (Bryant & Bryant, 1998). In the last decade, the field of learning disabilities has witnessed a significant increase in the availability of AT devices that enable students with learning disabilities to participate more fully in postsecondary education (Bryant & Rivera, 1995). Although AT devices have been in existence for years, historically their use was reserved for individuals with sensory or motor problems (Bryant & Seay, 1998). More

A special thanks is extended to Dr. Marshall Raskind, who helped us in the preparation of this chapter.

recently, however, it has become clear that people with any form of disability, including LD, can use AT. This became true, in part, when AT devices or adaptations focused on the person's functional strengths and limitations rather than on the name of the condition itself (e.g., visual impairment, learning disabilities). (Note: Because learning disabilities can occur concomitantly with other disabilities, AT providers have to be prepared to meet multiple needs; and because postsecondary programs must ensure equal educational access for qualified students with any type of disability, the information provided in this chapter generalizes to students with a variety of disabilities, not just LD.) By examining adaptations from a functional perspective, AT providers ensure that devices and services can be used by students with LD to help them compensate for their disability-related functional limitations by tapping into their many strengths (Raskind, 1994; Raskind & Bryant, 1996).

The purpose of this chapter is to examine challenges relating to the assurance of equal opportunity from a perspective of assistive technology service delivery and use. We do this by providing (a) a rationale for the use of AT devices; (b) an overview of the benefits of assistive technology in postsecondary education settings; (c) a brief discussion of AT service delivery systems; (d) a description of specific AT devices and their use; (e) an examination of AT assessment, selection, monitoring, and evaluation considerations; and (f) a discussion of barriers to AT use and proposed solutions.

Rationale for the Use of AT Devices

Assistive technology devices and services provide a means for students to compensate for disability-related barriers that inhibit their ability to accomplish the demands of the postsecondary setting (Raskind & Higgins, 1998). By focusing on a student's strengths, AT devices can serve to maximize abilities at a level in keeping with the person's expected performance based on general mental abilities.

Availability of AT adaptations for postsecondary students with learning disabilities is rooted in advocacy efforts to influence federal and state legislation aimed at improving the quality of life for individuals with disabilities, including learning disabilities. In this section, we provide (a) the federal definition of assistive technology and services, and (b) supporting legislation that has been influential in ensuring availability of and access to assistive technology.

AT Devices and Services Defined

According to the Technology-Related Assistance for Individuals with Disabilities Act of 1988 (Tech Act; P.L. 100-407), an AT device refers to "any item, piece of equipment, or product system, whether acquired commercially off-the-shelf, modified, or customized, that is used to increase, maintain or improve the functional capabilities of individuals with disabilities." Because the federal definition is so broad, it includes devices that are electronic (e.g., scanners and assistive listening devices) and nonelectronic (e.g., pencil grips and manual typewriters), if those devices are "used to increase, maintain or improve the functional capabilities of individuals with disabilities." It is our contention that AT devices could include remediation software (e.g., computer-aided instructional programs for reading or mathematics) and instructional technology if they fit the definition. Raskind and Bryant (1996) note that in some instances the device may assist, augment, or supplement task performance in a given area of disability; while in others, it may be used to circumvent or bypass specific deficits entirely.

Several other terms are often used synonymously with *AT devices and services*. For example, the term "auxiliary aids and services" appears as part of the Rehabilitation Act (1973) and refers to assistive technology devices. Requirements regarding auxiliary aids and services in public and private colleges, universities, and graduate and professional schools are included in the nondiscriminatory provisions of Titles II and III of the Americans with Disabilities Act of 1990. Policies in many postsecondary schools use the term *auxiliary aids*, rather than *assistive technology*. Other education synonyms for AT include *ancillary equipment* and *adaptive computer technology* (Day & Edwards, 1996). Definitions of additional key terms associated with the Tech Act are provided in Appendix 11.1 on the CD-ROM.

Rehabilitation counselors, who are often major contributors in the selection of AT devices and services for postsecondary students with disabilities, often use terms such as rehabilitation technology and adaptive technology when they discuss AT devices and services. The term durable medical equipment is often encountered when professionals in offices of students with disabilities involve Medicaid as a funding source for acquiring AT devices for their students. Whatever the term, the underlying principle remains the same: those devices and services that are instrumental in helping students with disabilities to be successful in postsecondary settings.

Legislation in Support of Assistive Technology

In the last 30 years or so, a variety of legislative measures have been passed that have facilitated the use of AT devices and services (Bryant & Seay, 1998; Raskind & Higgins, 1998). The earliest of these statutes, the Vocational Rehabilitation Act of 1973 (hereafter referred to as the Rehab Act), has been discussed at length throughout this text. Of particular interest to this chapter, however, is the portion of the law that specifically mentions the use of auxiliary aids (i.e., assistive technology devices and services) (Day & Edwards, 1996). Subpart E of the regulations for Section 504 of the Rehabilitation Act of 1973 states that postsecondary institutions that receive federal funds have to provide appropriate auxiliary aids and services to a student with a disability (Day & Edwards, 1996). By addressing the need for assistive technology, Congress specifically focused on a means to assure individuals with disabilities a chance for success in locations that previously were often not accessible (e.g., postsecondary schools receiving federal funds).

In 1988, Congress continued to recognize the value of AT devices and services when it passed the Technology-Related Assistance for Individuals with Disabilities Act (Bryant & Seay, 1998; Bryant, Seay, O'Connell, & Comstock-Galagan, 1996). During the testimony leading up to the passage of this landmark legislation, it was cogently noted that the Tech Act incorporates a fundamental concept subsequently reflected in the Americans with Disabilities Act: that people with disabilities are able to seek the "American dream" (Bryant & Seay, 1998). As Chandler, Czerlinsky, and Wehman (1993; cited in Day & Edwards, 1996) note, "This law, along with others, has directly influenced the availability and utilization of specially designed devices and accommodations meant to empower persons with disabilities" (p. 117). In the years since the Tech Act's initial passage, every state and several Canadian provinces have established statewide, consumer-responsive programs to assist with the timely acquisition and use of AT devices and services. A listing of each Tech Act project is provided in Appendix 11.2 on the CD-ROM. Readers are encouraged to contact their state's Tech Act project for information concerning its programs and services. Of particular interest to many students with disabilities and their advocates is the involvement of protection and advocacy (P&A) systems within the framework of the Tech Act. Each state's P&A system (see Appendix 11.3 on the CD-ROM) is responsible for ensuring that the AT needs of its citizenry are being met.

In 1990, Congress passed the Americans with Disabilities Act, which extended the benefits and protections of the Rehabilitation Act to people with disabilities in the private sector. Although the law does not specifically discuss AT devices and services (Day & Edwards, 1996), assistive technology is clearly an important tool in providing people with disabilities, including learning disabilities, an opportunity to be successful in all areas covered by the ADA, including postsecondary education.

Recent amendments to the Individuals with Disabilities Education Act (IDEA) also demonstrated the importance of AT devices and services to student success when it called for AT to be "considered" for all students with disabilities (Bryant & O'Connell, 1998; Carl, 1999). Although the law targets students through Grade 12, it provides evidence of the acknowledgment of AT adaptations as a viable source of support for students with disabilities of any age. It is not unreasonable to argue that students who have success using AT devices in elementary and secondary settings will generalize that success to other environments, including postsecondary institutions.

Benefits of Assistive Technology in Postsecondary Education Settings

Overall, three broad and overlapping categories of benefits have been reported (Derer, Polsgrove, & Rieth, 1996; Rieth, Bryant, & Woodward, in press). The categories are environmental, independence, and user benefits.

Environmental

Student environmental benefits associated with the use of AT devices include increased inclusion in postsecondary environments, improved instruction, and enhanced peer and teacher interactions and perceptions. With regard to inclusion, AT devices have enabled postsecondary students to access previously unavailable academic and social opportunities (Bryant & Bryant, 1998; Todis, 1996). Formerly, a host of physical, communication, and instructional barriers precluded the participation of people with disabilities in postsecondary education. However, legislation has mandated access, and the compensatory capacity of AT devices provides teachers with an extensive array of alternative tools for teaching students with disabilities (Raskind & Higgins, 1998; Vogel & Reder, 1998).

AT devices also provide students with alternative methods of responding that have proven successful in postsecondary settings (Elkind, Black, & Murray, 1996; Higgins & Raskind, 1995; Primus, 1990; Raskind & Higgins, 1998). For example, tape-recorded, Web-based lessons linked to speech synthesis devices or real audio lessons have been used to facilitate learning by students who are unable to effectively process visual information or who have memory deficits that require them to repeatedly access information to facilitate learning.

Elkind et al. (1996) report that the use of optical character recognition coupled with speech synthesis enhanced the reading rate and comprehension of college students with dyslexia. Students who have difficulty organizing and writing now have access to an array of tools such as word processors, spelling and grammar checkers, proofreading programs, outlining and brainstorming software, and speech recognition devices that help them to compensate for their disabilities (Raskind & Higgins, 1998). Pencil grips, tape recorders, alternative keyboards, speech synthesizers, word prediction software, and talking word-processing programs have also been found to help students compensate for specific learning difficulties (MacArthur & Haynes, 1995; McGregor & Pachuski, 1996). Such compensatory devices enable students to engage more effectively in school activities, increase their productivity, and develop feelings of independence and self-worth (Barton & Fuhrmann, 1994; Raskind & Shaw, 1996).

Derer et al. (1996) report that teachers had a positive perception of the competence of students with disabilities who successfully used AT devices to develop academic products. Vogel and Reder (1998) note that students who successfully used assistive technology tend to be more successful academically and are more satisfied with themselves and their performance.

Independence

In a second major category of benefits, assistive technology increases the independence of the learner by means of enhanced communication and increased motivation to learn. Derer et al. (1996) found that access to AT devices provided students with an increased capacity to independently communicate information, feelings, thoughts, and ideas. Students felt empowered, independent, and more productive as a result of access to communication devices and productivity software that enhanced their ability to complete assignments, and to share information, ideas, knowledge, thoughts, perceptions, and feelings with peers, teachers, and parents. Raskind and Higgins (1998) report that college students with disabilities who used assistive technology believe that they were more motivated to learn because of their experience with AT devices.

User Benefits

The third category of benefits relates directly to student AT device users and their increased capacity to cope with their own attitudes, feelings, and behaviors associated with their disability, their increased productivity, their enhanced self-concept through the improvement of skills, and their greater capacity for skill application.

Raskind and Higgins (1998) indicate that college students who used AT devices learned more about their strengths and weaknesses as learners as a result of the experience. They became more cognizant about the nature and magnitude of their disabilities and, perhaps more important, discovered effective ways of compensating for their disabilities. Finally, as a result of using assistive technology to accomplish tasks that they had previously been unable to do, students improved their self-concept. In fact, many students claimed that technology had transformed their lives for the better (Raskind et al., 1997).

A series of investigators have documented the use of AT devices to promote increases in student productivity (McNaughton et al., 1993; Primus, 1990; Raskind & Higgins, 1998; Vogel & Reder, 1998). For example, Primus reports that the use of word processors helped improve college students' grades. McNaughton et al. found that students made fewer mistakes when they used word processors. Higgins and Raskind (1995) concluded that students with disabilities produced better written compositions and improved their reading comprehension when they used AT devices. Overall, the benefits from using AT devices clearly underscore their important role in helping students with disabilities to be included and to succeed in postsecondary settings.

AT Service Delivery Systems

Increasingly, students with disabilities in postsecondary settings are receiving support services from a variety of resources. Raskind and Higgins (1998) note that it has been difficult to identify specific factors that led to AT use with students who have disabilities, but it is not unreasonable to assume that AT adaptations of some sort have been in existence since the first student with LD entered college. That is, some form of AT device, even if it were as "low tech" as a pencil cushion to use in writing or a ruler to help a student keep his or her place when reading, was available for students with LD when they enrolled in school. Since their inception, AT service delivery systems have evolved considerably; many schools have comprehensive service delivery systems, and others are in the initial stages of developing service delivery options. In general, services are offered by either on-campus or off-campus entities.

On-Campus Service Provision and Resources

The most convenient source of assistive technology supports to students with learning disabilities is found in on-campus Offices for Students with Disabilities. Not surprisingly, some offices provide extensive AT services, while others offer limited AT services or none at all.

An early leader in the provision of AT support services has been California State University, Northridge (CSUN). Dr. Harry Murphy and his colleagues have provided leadership and vision in how colleges and universities can take advantage of state and federal funding sources and private monies to secure AT devices for their students. As Higgins and Zvi (1995) report, CSUN established its Learning Disabilities Program in 1985 through a grant from the California State Department of Rehabilitation. What began as a program for 55 students with LD has grown to serve over 750 students with varying disabilities. In the mid-1980s, CSUN also established the Computer Access Laboratory (CAL) using grant monies provided by the Department of Rehabilitation. As Higgins and Zvi note, "The fortunate pairing of the LD Program and the CAL under the same administrative and geographic unit brought specialists in LD together for the first time with professionals, researchers, and experts in the field of assistive technology for persons with all types of disabilities" (p. 125).

In the last 25 years, research conducted at CSUN, along with its annual assistive technology conference, Technology and Persons with Disabilities, and its nationwide Assistive Technology Applications Certificate Program, has contributed extensively to our understanding of how AT devices and services can help postsecondary students with LD and other disabilities survive and prosper in college. Fortunately, CSUN's program is not alone in its efforts to serve the AT needs of postsecondary students.

Other programs, such as that offered at the University of Texas at Austin, have recently expanded their services to include AT devices. At Florida Atlantic University (FAU), where this chapter's first author was once director of the Office for Students with Disabilities, AT services were provided as the result of a combination of public and private funds. That school's experience provides the reader with a snapshot of a "catch-as-catch-can" approach to soliciting funds for student programs.

In 1992, a private donor in Florida agreed to provide seed money to each state university campus to help purchase on-campus auxiliary aids (AT devices) if the campus could raise matching funds. The director of the OSD and his students met to discuss possible funding sources that could be tapped to help raise those matching funds. The Office of Student Services, the university entity responsible for overseeing OSD operations, notified the OSD director that its shortage of funds, a typical scenario in Student Services, would not allow that office to totally match the grant; the Office for Students with Disabilities was urged to secure external funding.

The students, with one student in particular leading the way, identified Student Government as a potential funding stream. The FAU Student Government (SG) actively raises money to purchase goods and services for FAU students. It was determined that a student would make a presentation to the SG Executive Committee demonstrating the efficacy of scanning and screen-reading technologies for students with print disabilities (i.e., students who are unable to read print because of blindness or reading disabilities). The presentation was flawless, and the student leaders were so enthralled that they agreed to request that a $5,000 grant be awarded to the Office for Students with Disabilities to secure AT devices for student use.

In addition to soliciting funds from Student Government, contact was made with an alumni group of sorority members who were active volunteers in the Office for Students with Disabilities and had an avid interest in providing support services for students with visual impairments. Members met monthly to identify projects and activities on which they could work. Staff of the FAU Office for Students with Disabilities met with the group to discuss the benefits of AT services and to solicit funds in support of its AT activities. As a result of the meeting, a donation was made on behalf of students at FAU who could benefit from the use of AT devices and services. Once funds had been raised through these and other efforts, a return trip to the vice president of Student Services, the office that previously said no matching funds were available, resulted in the appropriation of the remainder of the matching funds needed for the grant.

On-Campus Service Delivery Locations

Most Offices for Students with Disabilities are provided with funds from the Division of Student Affairs, although some schools may provide disability services funding from other agencies or departments. Such monies are intended to be used for the provision of auxiliary aids and services that should include AT. Once AT devices are secured, there remains the question of where those devices should be placed. A case could be made that AT devices are best housed in locations where all students congregate (e.g., libraries, buildings that house classrooms) and where they can be used with contextual ease by students with LD. An argument also can be made that AT devices should be housed within the Office for Students with Disabilities, where students can use the devices in relative privacy. Chapter 9 delineates some of the provocative issues, such as the location of these services in the most inclusionary settings, based on the philosophical underpinnings of disability laws that embrace the concept of full inclusion. At the University of Texas at Austin, devices are placed in various locations on campus where students typically congregate (e.g., the library, in various colleges). In this way, students with disabilities have access to technology in natural settings where they learn. The Texas Assistive Technology Partnership (TATP), Texas's Tech Act project, constructed an AT lab for student use in the Learning Technology Center, housed in the College of Education. Computers in the lab were set up for screen reading, scanning, and other options that would benefit students with disabilities. Several problems emerged. All students, whether they had disabilities or not, could access the lab. Interestingly, some students without disabilities found the disability-related software to be a nuisance and disabled the programs. Daily, TATP staff would have to monitor each computer to determine if the disability software and hardware were functional. In most cases, programs had to be reinstalled, requiring an inordinate amount of valuable staff time. Efforts to have students leave the programs installed proved fruitless, and the lab was moved to a more closely supervised area. Many campuses have not had such difficulty, but the issue of where to locate AT devices remains a crucial one.

In addition to resources provided by Offices for Students with Disabilities, individual colleges, departments, or programs within a postsecondary facility can have their own AT program. At the University of Texas at Austin, for example, the College of Education has created an AT lab for use by education majors so they will gain familiarity and hands-on experience with AT devices. In addition, faculty members are encouraged to use the lab to explore how their students with disabilities can gain access to their curricula through the use of AT devices. Although it was not specifically designed for use by students with disabilities within the college, education majors who have disabilities frequently use the lab to complete assignments and other college-related tasks. Readers are referred to an article by Bryant, Erin, Lock, Allan, and Resta (1998), which describes the Department of Special Education's efforts to enhance its AT service program; it will be of interest to anyone wanting to develop a similar program at their facility.

Off-Campus Service Provision and Resources

By far, the rehabilitation counselor is the most frequent off-campus AT service provider or facilitator. Although the counselor may work with the Office for Students with Disabilities, such a relationship is not mandated. Thus, a vocational rehabilitation client may solicit and receive from his or her counselor assistive technology devices and services (Symington, 1994). Such devices for students with LD may include laptop computers, screen-reading technology, optical character recognition devices, and so forth. Because counselors have limited funds in their budgets, AT devices are sometimes not provided. When they are, we suggest that decisions regarding the appropriateness of AT adaptations are best made by members of the rehabilitation team (Lown, 1995).

We have already discussed the Tech Act state projects and their value as resources to students and professionals. An additional resource is the Alliance for Technology Access (ATA), a network of community-based resource centers that provide AT information to people with disabilities and their families. Many states have ATA centers, which are excellent resources for service providers and students to tap when asking AT questions (see Appendix 11.4 on the CD-ROM for a list of centers across the country). In addition, the ATA can provide a list of AT vendors that support its organization (see Appendix 11.5 on the CD-ROM).

Closing the Gap is another important resource for students with disabilities and their service providers. This organization hosts an annual conference at which numerous vendors provide demonstrations of their latest AT devices and workshops are held to provide up-to-date information about service delivery options. Appendix 11.6 on the CD-ROM provides a list of organizational resources located on Closing the Gap's Web site.

Assistive Technology Descriptions

In the field of learning disabilities, adaptations (e.g., alternative responding modes, modified instructional materials) have been widely used to help students compensate for specific learning difficulties associated with reading, writing, mathematics, reasoning, listening, and speaking. Moreover, in the last decade, advances in computer-based technology and the recognition of the instructional accessibility capabilities of assistive technologies have prompted an array of adaptation solutions for students with learning disabilities.

Researchers (e.g., Bryant, Carter, & Smith, 1999; Elkind, 1993; Higgins, Boone, & Lovitt, 1996; MacArthur, Schwartz, & Graham, 1991) have demonstrated the effectiveness of using assistive technology devices (e.g., word processors, "reading machines," "talking computers," electronic spell checkers) to foster academic success and independence for elementary, secondary, and postsecondary-level students who have learning disabilities. AT devices can provide a compensatory alternative that circumvents or "works around" deficits while capitalizing on a student's strengths (Mangrum & Strichart, 1997; Vogel, 1987).

Raskind and Higgins (1998) describe a number of assistive technology devices that can be used by students who have learning disabilities at the postsecondary level. In particular, postsecondary instruction assumes a level of reading, writing, and mathematical competence; that is, students are expected to possess certain skills on which postsecondary coursework is predicated. Therefore, students with learning disabilities must be cognizant of the literacy, math, listening, and study skills that are necessary to achieve at the postsecondary level. Table 11.1 provides examples of competencies that are critical for

Table 11.1
Prerequisite Skills for Postsecondary Academic Tasks

Reading

- *Word identification*: Ability to decode multisyllabic words associated with different content areas.

- *Fluency*: Ability to read text accurately and quickly.

- *Vocabulary*: Ability to understand words, concepts, and phrases associated with different content areas.

- *Comprehension*: Ability to understand information delivered orally or in writing.

Written Language

- *Writing process*: Ability to generate and organize ideas (prewriting), write an initial draft, edit it, and proofread it.

- *Mechanics*: Ability to use syntax, capitalization, and punctuation correctly.

- *Spelling*: Ability to spell content-area, multisyllabic, high-frequency, and other types of words correctly.

- *Handwriting*: Ability to express ideas quickly and legibly in written form.

Mathematics

- *Computation*: Ability to use computational algorithms.

- *Word problems*: Ability to identify word problem types and employ a method to solve equations.

Listening

- *Attending*: Ability to attend selectively to important information and to maintain on-task behavior.

- *Following directions*: Ability to attend to and follow multiple directions.

- *Vocabulary*: Ability to comprehend information presented orally.

Study Skills

- *Time management and personal organization*: Ability to manage time and organize oneself to address deadlines, maintain order of materials, and recall short- and long-term course requirements.

- *Note taking*: Ability to identify important points (orally or in writing) and record the information quickly and in an organized framework.

- *Research and reference materials*: Ability to access and use a variety of reference materials to conduct research and to complete course assignments.

- *Test taking*: Ability to read, comprehend, and answer test items successfully.

college-bound students. As mentioned in Chapter 2, effective transition planning should include a realistic discussion of a student's competencies in these areas in light of the academic expectations at the postsecondary level.

This section describes examples of assistive technology devices that can be used to address the task demands in skill areas often affected by the learning disability. These technologies are grouped together according to the area of disability the technology is intended to circumvent and/or the instructional area for which the technology can be used. Several of the technologies have more than one application and are listed under more than one heading.

Reading

Reading constitutes a significant problem area for students with LD (Hammill & Bryant, 1998). Certain AT devices and programs can be used to enhance students' abilities to access information that appears in print. Specifically discussed are devices and programs that involve speech synthesis, optical character and speech synthesis systems, and tape recorders.

Speech Synthesis

Speech synthesis systems may be used to review materials written by others, including software tutorials, help systems, letters, reports, online databases, and information banks and systems. These systems read essentially anything on a computer screen, providing it is DOS-based. Some organizations, including Recording for the Blind & Dyslexic and the American Printing House for the Blind, produce "books on disk" that make it possible for people with LD to listen to text by means of a speech synthesis system. People with LD are eligible to receive services from these organizations and others that are described in Chapters 7 and 9.

OCR/Speech Synthesis Systems

An optical character recognition (OCR) system might be thought of as a "reading machine." OCR systems provide a means of inputting print (e.g., a page in a book, a letter) into a computer and hearing the print "read" by the computer. This technology may be particularly helpful for those who exhibit no difficulty comprehending spoken language (Gough & Tunmer, 1986) yet have problems understanding language in the written form (Hughes & Smith, 1990).

Text is scanned into the computer, then read back to the user by means of a speech synthesis or screen-reading system. Text can be scanned in a variety of ways. To use a full-page flatbed scanner, a page of text is placed face down on the device (much like using a copy machine). To use a hand-held scanner, the user moves the device across a page of text (or down, depending on the system). "Book-edge" (designed for bound text) scanners and automatic document feeders also are available for several systems.

OCR systems are of two basic types: "stand-alone" and PC-based. Stand-alone (or "self-contained") systems have all components built in, including the scanner, OCR software and hardware, and the speech synthesizer. Some stand-alone systems are portable (and about the size of a briefcase), while others are desktop units. PC-based systems consist of a number of components that are hooked up to a PC. These components consist of a full-page (desktop) or hand-held scanner, an OCR board and/or software, and a speech synthesizer. Additionally, several companies (e.g., Kurzweil 3000, Arkenstone's WYNN) have designed systems with the individual with learning disabilities in mind; such systems simultaneously highlight words as they are spoken back by the system. Also, the Kurzweil 3000 can be programmed to alter the rate at which the text is read. This feature could help students develop reading fluency, a skill that contributes to comprehension. Although systems that aim to provide access to print are invaluable for students with word recognition and fluency disabilities, it should be noted that comprehension skills also must be developed to aid student understanding of course content.

In addition to these OCR/speech synthesis systems, a fully portable, pocket-sized (smaller than a TV remote control) "reading pen" recently has been introduced to the marketplace (i.e., the Quicktionary Reading Pen; see Chapter 9 for information on contacting the manufacturer). Using a "miniaturized" optical scanning system, this battery-operated device enables the user to scan single words on a page (e.g., of a textbook or magazine) and have the word read aloud by means of a built-in speech synthesizer. The product also provides definitions for scanned words, spells the words aloud, and keeps a history of scanned words.

Variable Speech Control Tape Recorders

Tape recorders can be used as playback units for listening to books on audiotape, which may help students with reading difficulties circumvent their disability by listening to prerecorded text (of books, journals, and newspapers). Prerecorded text is available from a number of sources, including the Library of Congress, Recording for the Blind & Dyslexic, and several private companies.

Although tape recorders are helpful to some students, they may present problems for those individuals with LD that have difficulty processing auditory information at standard playback rates (McCroskey & Thompson, 1973). This problem can be alleviated by the use of variable speech control (VSC) tape recorders. Unlike standard or conventional tape recorders (or units that simply have different record and playback speeds), VSC tape recorders enable the user to play back audiotaped material (e.g., books on tape) slower or faster than the rate at which it was recorded, without loss of intelligibility. Intelligible speech at varying rates is achieved by adjusting speed and pitch control levers. These devices enable the user to slow down prerecorded text by 25% of the standard rate without the loss of intelligibility.

Written Language

Many students with LD display significant problems in writing (Hammill & Bryant, 1998), which can be manifested in a variety of areas (e.g., idea generation, spelling, grammar, and handwriting). In this section, AT devices that relate to outlining and brainstorming, word processing, word prediction, spell checking, proofreading, speech recognition, and speech synthesis are described according to their functions.

Outlining and Brainstorming

Outlining programs (now included in many standard word-processing programs) may help some people generate and organize their ideas; outlining is a good tool to use during the prewriting stage of writing development. These programs enable the user to construct information electronically so that it can be placed in appropriate categories and order.

Although each outlining program has its own features, generally the user types in an idea on a specified topic without regard to overall organization. By using a few simple keystrokes (or pointing and clicking), the outlining program will create the Roman numerals for major headings and letters and numbers for subordinate headings automatically. The user need not be concerned with order, levels of importance, or categories, because text can be moved easily at a later time. Once basic ideas have been written down, those ideas that are related or that "seem to go together" provide the basis for major headings or categories. Ideas that fall under any major heading can be easily reduced to any level of subordinate heading. Moreover, if the user determines at a later time that an idea does not belong under a certain heading, that is not a problem because any piece of text can be moved easily within the outline—as many times as necessary. The program automatically reorganizes the Roman numerals, letters, and numbers designated for specific headings. Outlining programs also enable users to limit what is viewed on the computer screen to only the major headings to facilitate an overview of the document, as well as to select a single subordinate heading and view all information under it for a detailed analysis.

Programs (e.g., Inspiration, 1997) also exist that have graphic capabilities to facilitate brainstorming by enabling users to create a diagram of their ideas (semantic webs, "mind maps," cluster diagrams) prior to formulating an outline. The user types in a main or central idea, which is displayed on the screen. Related ideas are then recorded and appear in specified geometric shapes (e.g., circles, ovals, rectangles) surrounding the central idea. Lines may link ideas with the main idea (and each other). Ideas can be easily moved, rearranged, and categorized. Detailed notes also can be attached to specific ideas and hidden from view. Ultimately, the graphic representation can be converted to an outline automatically. This nonlinear, "free-form" graphic approach may be even more helpful to some students than simple text-based outlining.

Outlining or brainstorming software can be an excellent tool to help students organize ideas for writing. Additionally, both can serve as a starting point for drafting a paper by generating and sequencing paragraphs to develop ideas. Moreover, students can return to the outline during the drafting stage to add or rearrange ideas.

Word Processing

Unlike the conventional method of writing with pencil and paper or using a typewriter, word processors enable students to write without having to be overly concerned about errors. Text can be corrected on-screen prior to printing, and ideas can be shifted within text during the editing stage to reflect a more coherent composition and flow of thought. When not preoccupied with the mechanical aspects of writing, students with LD have a greater opportunity to focus on meaning. This is of particular importance for those who have developed a fear of translating their thoughts into written language as the result of a history of writing problems and the criticism that often follows. Knowing that they can simply generate language and correct errors later may reduce their anxiety, liberate their writing abilities, and facilitate written expression at a level commensurate with their understanding. Furthermore, word processing may address handwriting issues through neater and cleaner documents, which may help students foster a sense of pride in their written work and enhance the image they have of themselves as writers.

Word Prediction

Word prediction software supports word-processing programs by "predicting" the word a user is entering into the computer. Predictions are based on syntax and spelling, as well as frequency, redundancy, and recency of words. Some programs also "learn" the user's word preferences.

Typically, word prediction programs operate in the following manner: As the first letter of a word is typed, the program offers a list of words beginning with that letter. If the desired word appears in the list, the user can choose the word (by pressing a corresponding number, or pointing and clicking) and the desired word will be inserted into the sentence automatically. If the desired word is not displayed, the user enters the second letter of the word and a new list appears, of words beginning with those two letters. The user can continue this process until the desired word appears in a list. (If the word is not included in the program's database, it can be added for future use.) After a word is chosen, the next word in the sentence is predicted, even before the first letter is typed. Again, if the desired word is not present, the user continues to enter letters until it appears. Word prediction programs are available as add-on programs that work in conjunction with standard word processors. They also can be used as integrated word prediction or word-processing software packages.

Word prediction can be helpful to students with LD for several reasons. First, because it minimizes the number of keystrokes it takes to enter a word, students with poor keyboarding and handwriting skills may find such a program easier and faster to use than a standard word processor. Second, the program may act as a compensatory spelling aid, as it automatically spells the word; the user needs only to recognize the word within the list. Additionally, as these programs use grammatical rules to predict words, students with syntactical deficits may find them helpful. Finally, students who have vocabulary deficits and "word-finding" difficulties may discover that the word list acts as a prompt, cueing them to choose the appropriate word.

In some instances, however, word prediction programs may actually interfere with the writing process (Cutler, 1991). The word list may be distracting, and having to stop and choose words may slow some students down, especially those who have significant difficulty in word recognition or who are proficient typists. For those students, a word recognition program coupled with speech synthesis to pronounce unknown words or a word-processing program with only a spelling and grammar check may be a better technology solution, respectively.

Spell Checking

The use of spell checkers (generally included in word-processing programs) may help some students compensate for spelling problems because they permit the user to check for misspelled words within a document before a final copy is made. Spell checkers match the words in a document against words in the spell checker's dictionary, and, if a match is not found, the user is alerted by a visual or auditory cue and then presented with a list of words from which to choose the correctly spelled word. The user selects the correct word, and the computer automatically corrects the misspelled word in the text. Some spell checkers alert the user to spelling errors while typing (which may be disruptive to some students), while others check for mistakes after the document has been completed.

Selecting the "correct" word from a list of options can be a difficult task for many students with spelling deficits. Also, some words are misspelled to the point that the computer cannot offer alternate choices. Cross-checking the words for synonyms in the word processor's thesaurus or dictionary (if available) can assist in the selection process. It should be noted that only misspelled words will be picked up with a spell checker. The incorrect use of homonyms (e.g., *there* and *their*) that plagues many writers will not be "red flagged."

In addition to spell checkers that are part of word-processing programs, battery-operated stand-alone spell checkers are available in desktop and pocket sizes. Basic units verify and correct spelling on an LCD display, while more sophisticated devices provide dictionaries and thesauruses. Some of these units are now equipped with speech synthesizers, which enable the user to hear, as well as see, the word in question; definitions; synonyms; and help messages. These features are particularly important for students who struggle with writing vocabulary.

Proofreading Programs

These software programs (now included within some word processors) are useful for the proofing stage of writing because they scan word-processing documents and alert users to probable errors in punctuation, grammar, word usage, structure, spelling, style, and capitalization. Most of these programs can be used to either mark probable errors or mark the error along with a commentary (e.g., "Be sure you are using *is* with a singular subject."). Many programs include on-line tutorials that allow the user to study the language rules checked by the program. It is important to stress that proofreading programs are not completely accurate and may not pick up certain errors. They also may make incorrect suggestions, prompting the user to correct elements of writing that are not really incorrect. Students will need to be able to detect some of their own errors, which may not be identified by a proofreading program. Sometimes hiring a copyeditor to catch mistakes is a good alternative for a student depending on the purpose of the writing assignment (e.g., master's thesis, term paper).

Speech or Voice Recognition

Speech recognition systems are an example of an alternate input device. They operate in conjunction with personal computers (and specific laptops) and consist of speech recognition hardware (internal board), software, headphones, and a microphone. Speech recognition systems enable the user to operate the computer by speaking to it. This may be helpful for those whose oral language exceeds their written language abilities (King & Rental, 1981; Myklebust, 1973).

Used in conjunction with word processors, speech recognition systems enable the user to dictate (via a microphone) to the computer, converting oral language to written text. These systems automatically learn the phonetic characteristics of a person's voice while that person dictates to the system. The more the system is used, the better able it is to understand what the user is saying.

There are two basic types of systems: discrete speech and continuous speech. Discrete speech systems (e.g., Dragon Dictate) require a calculated pause of approximately 1/10 second between words. The word the system "thinks" the person has spoken is then placed on the screen. If the word is incorrect, the user can choose the correct word from a menu/list of similar sounding words that appear on the screen (this feature is not present in all systems). It should be noted that all keyboard editing and control commands (e.g., "delete word") can be done with the voice alone. Continuous speech systems (e.g., Dragon Naturally Speaking, IBM ViaVoice) allow the user to dictate without pausing between words. Incorrect words can be corrected by either voice or keyboard commands.

Speech Synthesis and Screen Reading

Speech synthesis refers to a synthetic or computerized voice output system usually consisting of an internal board or external hardware device. In conjunction with "screen-reading" software, a speech synthesizer will read back text displayed on a computer screen so that the user can hear, as well as see, what is displayed. Text can be read back a letter, word, line, sentence, paragraph, or "screen" at a time. The ability to hear what they have written may enable students with written language disabilities to catch errors in grammar, spelling, and punctuation that might otherwise go unrecognized. Having auditory feedback may alert the user to problems in the coherence and semantic integrity of the document.

Screen-reading programs (e.g., ULTimate Reader, TextHELP!) that are specifically designed for individuals with LD and that simultaneously (visually) highlight words as they are spoken are now available. In most cases the speed, pitch, and tone of voice can be set to accommodate individual preferences. The voice quality of speech synthesizers varies considerably from more human to more mechanical sounding. In some instances, mechanical-sounding voices may actually be more intelligible. There are also synthesizers available that provide the user with the opportunity to select a number of different voices (e.g., male, female, young, or old).

Mathematics

Students with mathematics learning disabilities have difficulties in a variety of areas including computation and word problems (Hammill & Bryant, 1998; Rivera & Bryant, 1992). The following are ideas to be used with basic computation and word problem solving.

Talking Calculators

A talking calculator can be used to help with basic calculation difficulties. A talking calculator is simply a calculator with a speech synthesizer. When number, symbol, or operation keys are pressed, they are "vocalized" or "spoken" by a built-in speech synthesizer. In that way, the user receives simultaneous auditory feedback in order to check the accuracy of visual-motor operations. Once a calculation has been made, the number can be read back via the synthesizer. This feature allows the user to double-check the answers being transferred from calculator to paper. Also, calculators come with a variety of key sizes, so that users can determine which key size is most appropriate for their needs. It is important to note that the speed at which calculations are performed could be problematic, because it takes longer to have operations spoken than displayed.

Word Problems

Solving word problems involves a number of skills, including the ability to read and comprehend the problems. Optical character recognition and speech synthesis technologies (already discussed) can assist the user in accessing word problem information when a concomitant reading disability exists.

Listening Aids

Many students with LD have listening learning disabilities. AT devices intended to help students with these problems include personal FM listening systems and tape recorders. Both are described below.

Personal FM Listening Systems

Personal FM listening systems may help some students who have difficulty auditorily focusing on a speaker. These technological aids consist of two basic components, a wireless transmitter with a microphone and a receiver with a headset or earphone. For situations in which there is only one speaker (e.g., a teacher in a classroom or lab), the speaker "wears" the transmitter unit (about 2×3 inches), while the user wears the receiver unit (about the same size). Both transmitters and receivers are easily clipped to a belt or shirt pocket. The microphone is only about 1½ inches long and is easily clipped to clothing (e.g., a tie). When there are multiple speakers (e.g., in a class discussion) an omnidirectional microphone enclosed in a small stand-alone unit is placed in the center of the conversation. Essentially, such a system carries each speaker's voice directly from the "speaker's mouth" to the "listener's ear," helping to make the speaker's voice more salient. A dial on the receiver easily controls volume.

Tape Recorders

In addition to helping compensate for reading disabilities, tape recorders can be useful to the student with listening difficulties (as well as memory problems). Tape recorders can be used to record classroom lectures as either an alternative to taking notes or an aid in verifying the accuracy of notes taken. This may be beneficial for students who have listening difficulties (either because of difficulty processing oral language or because of an attentional disorder), because they can review lectures at a later date by listening to tapes as many times as necessary to comprehend the material.

The ability to commit a lecture to a permanent record also may help students with other types of difficulties, including those who find it hard to take notes and listen simultaneously, who have fine-motor difficulties, or who have auditory memory problems. VSC tape recorders can be particularly helpful for reviewing taped material because they enable the user to increase the speech rate (generally up to 100%) to reduce the amount of time it takes to "re-listen," or as previously discussed, to reduce speech rates to more comprehensible levels.

Study Skills

Study skills include time management and personal organization, note taking, referencing materials, and test taking. The following are examples of assistive technology adaptations that can be used for those areas.

Personal Data Managers

The use of personal data managers can compensate for difficulties in remembering, organizing, and managing personal information, whether it is a question of remembering important dates or deadlines; prioritizing activities; scheduling appointments; or recording and accessing names, addresses, and phone numbers. Personal data managers are available as software programs as well as self-contained hand-held units and allow the user to easily store and retrieve vast amounts of personal information. Data input and retrieval are accomplished via a keyboard or keypad and are displayed on a computer monitor or LCD display.

Several newly released pocket-sized data managers (e.g., Voice Organizer, Voice It) allow the user to enter and retrieve data by speaking into the device. Stored data are spoken back in the user's own voice. Data managers have numerous capabilities and a diverse combination of functions. Typical features include monthly calendars, daily schedules or planners, clocks and alarms, memo files, "to do" lists, address books, telephone directories (some with electronic dialers), and bankbooks or money managers.

Free-Form Databases

Like personal data managers, free-form databases also can be valuable to people with organizational or memory problems. These software programs work with computers and might be thought of as computerized Post-It systems. Like abbreviation expanders, they are memory resistant and can be activated while in a word processor by simply pressing a "hot key." Users can create their own notes of any length, on any subject, in much the same way people use Post-It notes or a notepad to jot down important information. Unlike a manual system, free-form databases permit the user to store the notes electronically in the computer's memory, rather than on tiny pieces of paper that are misplaced easily.

Perhaps more important than how the information is stored is how it is retrieved. A note can be retrieved by typing in any piece or fragment of information contained in the note. For example, the note "Carl Stevens, Advanced Electronics, Inc., 835 West Arden, Northridge, CA 91330, 818-306-1954" could be brought up on the computer's screen by inputting any of that information, including (but not limited to) "Carl," "Advanced," "West," "North," and "818."

Abbreviation Expanders

Abbreviation expansion is a good note-taking tool and is used in conjunction with word processing. It enables users to create their own abbreviations for frequently used words, phrases, or standard pieces of text, thus saving keystrokes and, ultimately, the amount of time it takes to prepare written documents, such as taking notes in class. For example, a student in a history class who has to frequently type out "industrial revolution" in completing written assignments or taking notes might create the abbreviation "ir." In order to expand an abbreviation, the user simply types in the abbreviation, presses the spacebar on the keyboard (or points and clicks), and the abbreviation is expanded. Abbreviations are recorded easily by executing a few simple commands and can be saved from one writing session to another. Abbreviation expansion is an integral part of some word-processing programs or is available as a "memory resident add-on" program (operating simultaneously with the word-processing program).

Electronic Reference Materials

Electronic reference materials provide students with a way to access resources such as dictionaries, thesauruses, almanacs, and encyclopedias via computer. These materials can be transferred to a word-processing program to assist students with writing papers or completing other course assignments. There are several on-line electronic-text library collections that house large collections of classic works, available through the Internet. Students can interact with multisensory (e.g., music and video) materials to enhance understanding. For example, some on-line collections can be read aloud by means of a speech synthesis or screen-reader system.

Web-Based Access

Certainly, the Internet offers students a plethora of resources for conducting research and obtaining reference materials, and people who design Web pages are beginning to recognize the importance of ensuring that *all* people have an opportunity to gain information from the Web. Web site design issues include, for example, the use of tables that might be difficult to read with screen-reader software, the incompatibility of technology between Web site designers and users, and multimedia features that may not be accessible to all users. Universal design features speak to the importance of ensuring accessibility. For example, Bobby is a Web-based tool that examines pages for accessibility for people with disabilities. Questions about that free service can be directed to bobby@cast.org. Once a site has been examined and depending on the findings, its designer can receive an official seal of approval for prominent display on the site.

Access to on-line courses is another area that warrants consideration by instructors when they design their courses and means of conveying information to students. Again, Web accessibility must be addressed to ensure that all students have equal access to course content.

Finally, instructors who use electronic communication as an instructional tool also must consider Web accessibility for their students. For example, if instructors give assignments that require students to access course content, discuss content issues, or provide information to instructors and peers on the Web, all students must be able to use that instructional tool effectively.

Test Taking

Taking tests in various formats (e.g., short answers, multiple choice, essay) is a common practice in postsecondary classes. Students with learning disabilities may benefit from nonassistive technology and assistive technology adaptations to facilitate comprehension of test material and demonstration of their content knowledge. For example, the format of the test (e.g., large print, extra space for responding) can be altered, a reader can be provided, or extended time can be allocated for taking the test. Assistive technology adaptations might include the use of a calculator or recording answers into a tape recorder. Some students prefer the opportunity to use computer-based word-processing programs so that spell check and editing features can be used to write essays.

Given the array of assistive technology adaptations for various academic areas, it is important to consider how to assess an individual for the use of an AT and to select adaptations that match student needs. Moreover, ongoing monitoring of student use of the adaptation and evaluation of educational outcomes will help decision makers determine the effectiveness of adaptations and the need for reevaluation.

Assessment and Selection, Monitoring, and Evaluation Considerations

Assistive technology devices can facilitate full participation in postsecondary settings and are an integral part of an effective support system used by people with learning disabilities. Although assistive technology devices are rarely the only support needed, it could be argued that the use of AT devices can assist individuals with learning disabilities to function more independently (Bryant, Seay, & Bryant, 1999). Therefore, individuals with learning disabilities, diagnosticians and psychologists, and service providers (e.g., on-campus service providers, rehabilitation counselors) are challenged to determine appropriate assistive technology adaptations to enhance academic success. The purpose of this section is to describe a process for assessing and selecting assistive technology devices, monitoring the use of those devices, and evaluating their effect on the individual's ability to access the curriculum and be more academically successful.

Assessment and Selection

Numerous AT devices are available to students with LD. Some students may have used AT devices in their high school setting and may have some idea of their effectiveness and the need for continuing to use them. Other students may be unaware of the value of AT devices because they did not have access to them in their secondary setting or because the students are newly identified as having a learning disability and, thus, have had no need for them. Individuals at the postsecondary level who work in the identification process and disability services community should work collaboratively with students with LD to identify AT devices that could provide solutions to academic difficulties. Decision makers must be knowledgeable about assistive technology devices and services in relation to students' academic needs (Chambers, 1997). Decision makers can pose the following questions to determine the appropriateness of AT devices: (a) Is an assistive technology device necessary for the student to access the curriculum? (b) Is an assistive technology device necessary for the student to receive an education comparable to that of his or her peer group? (c) How will the assistive technology device enable the student to succeed academically? (d) Are there other adaptations that may be more appropriate than assistive technology devices?

Additionally, Bryant and Bryant (1998) have identified a process that decision makers can use to aid in the assessment and selection process. Table 11.2 provides an illustration of this process with note taking as the task. Because students with LD possess individual strengths, weaknesses, interests, and experiences, devices that are appropriate for one person and a particular setting may be inappropriate for another person or setting. It is important to assess an individual for AT devices relative to the specific setting demands and his or her individual strengths and limitations.

Demands of the Postsecondary Setting

Researchers (e.g., Bryant & Bryant, 1998; Riegel, 1988; Rieth & Evertson, 1988; Schumaker & Deshler, 1984) have documented the importance of examining the instructional demands of educational settings that students encounter daily. Setting demands include the curriculum that is taught, how information is delivered to and received by students, and how students demonstrate their understanding of the curriculum (Rivera & Smith, 1997). Setting demands also involve (a) the specific tasks students must address, and (b) the requisite abilities students need in order to perform those tasks successfully. Figure 11.1

Table 11.2
A Process for Identifying Appropriate Adaptations or Accommodations

Setting-Specific Demands		Person-Specific Characteristics		Adaptations or Accommodations	
Sample Tasks	Requisite Abilities	Functional Capabilities	Functional Limitations	Dependence-Oriented	Independence Oriented
Note taking	Listen to lecture	Listening skills	Speed of writing	Copy of professor's notes	
	Recognize pertinent ideas		Determining essential from nonessential	Note takers	Instruction in using an organizational framework for notes (e.g., the Cornell system)
	Record ideas quickly in an organized manner		Spelling		Instruction in using a tape recorder to supplement notes
					Use of a laptop

provides examples of questions decision makers can use for examining and evaluating the specific demands that students will encounter in the postsecondary setting.

Tasks

Some of the numerous tasks students encounter as part of their undergraduate- and graduate-level required and elective coursework may include comprehending textbook material (Ellis, 1996; Miller, 1996), solving complex mathematical equations, developing a speaking vocabulary in a foreign-language course,

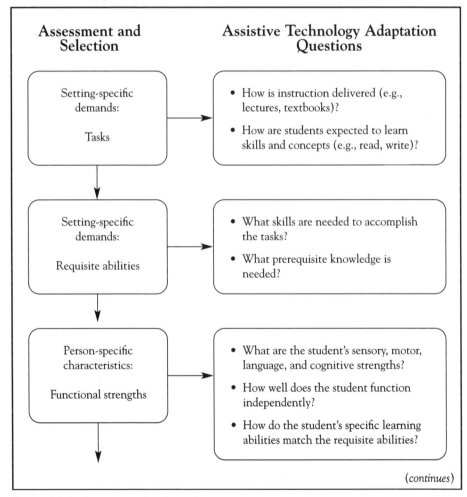

Figure 11.1. Assistive technology adaptation questions.

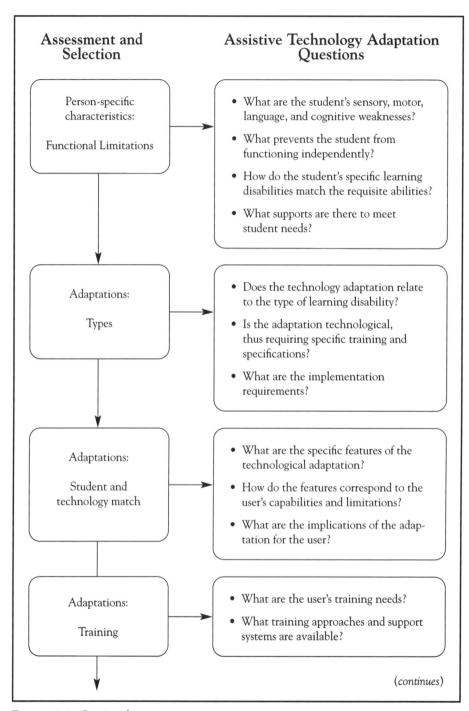

Figure 11.1. *Continued.*

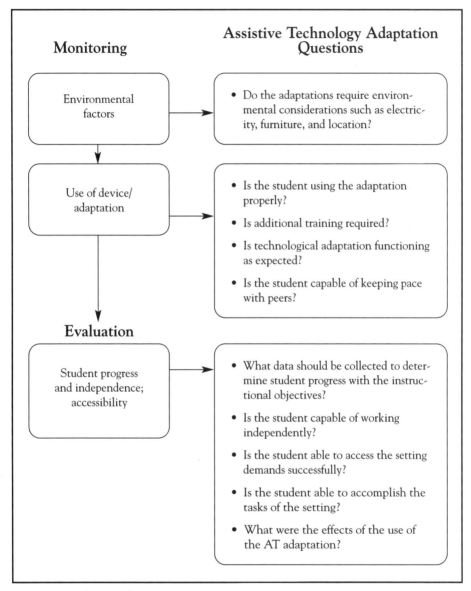

Figure 11.1. *Continued.*

demonstrating writing competency skills, and developing effective listening and note-taking skills (Suritsky & Hughes, 1996). Additionally, students may be asked to demonstrate their knowledge and understanding of subject content by taking tests (Hughes, 1996), answering questions, constructing projects, solving math problems (Miller, 1996), and writing papers.

In examining academic setting demands, Raskind and Bryant (1996) identified dozens of tasks that students must be able to perform (see Table 11.3).
Although postsecondary instructors would likely view those tasks as reasonable
for any of their students to perform, each task represents a challenge if there is a
conflict between the task demands and a student's disability-related limitations.
Such "functional dissonance" (Bryant et al., 1999) mandates that adaptations
be made so that students can successfully accomplish those tasks.

Table 11.3
Setting Demands and Requisite Abilities

Setting-Demand Tasks	Requisite Abilities for Tasks
Listening Tasks	*Listening Requisite Abilities*
• Listen to lectures.	• Differentiates relevant from irrelevant information.
• Listen to directions, instructions.	• Hears and understands the spoken word.
• Listen to and work with peers.	• Understands time concepts presented verbally.
• Listen to audiotapes, videotapes, CDs.	• Attends to speaker for a continuous period.
• Listen to announcements.	• Comprehends rapid speech.
	• Distinguishes differences among sounds, words.
Speaking Tasks	*Speaking Requisite Abilities*
• Speak to teachers, peers.	• Pronounces words correctly.
• Make class presentations, recitals.	• Speaks with appropriate vocabulary.
• Communicate during class discussions.	• Speaks with appropriate grammar.
	• Speaks well in everyday situations.
	• Speaks with appropriate tone, pitch, loudness.
Reading Tasks	*Reading Requisite Abilities*
• Read textbooks, handouts.	• Has requisite visual abilities.
• Read from chalkboard, overhead, etc.	• Reads words accurately.
• Read resource materials (e.g., dictionary, encyclopedia, and library books).	• Understands meaning of individual words.
• Read assignment sheets.	• Understands written grammatical structures.
• Read test questions.	• Understands the meaning of connected writing (i.e., phrases, sentences, paragraphs).
• Read computer text.	• Reads with speed.

(continues)

Table 11.3 *Continued.*

Setting-Demand Tasks	Requisite Abilities for Tasks

Writing Tasks

- Write test answers.
- Write term papers.
- Write stories, essays, poems.
- Write homework assignments.
- Write classroom assignments.
- Copy from blackboard, text (words, numbers).
- Take notes.
- Spell words (in isolation and in continuous text).

Writing Requisite Abilities

- Applies capitalization/punctuation rules.
- Spells correctly.
- Writes neatly with little difficulty.
- Uses appropriate grammar.
- Uses appropriate vocabulary.
- Edits, proofs well.

- Writes well conceptually.
- Applies sense of audience effectively.

Mathematics Tasks

- Compute.
- Solve story problems.
- Use math in applied settings, conditions.
- Work with manipulatives.
- Use a calculator.

Mathematics Requisite Abilities

- Understands basic number concepts.
- Calculates basic arithmetic problems.
- Knows basic math vocabulary.
- Calculates quickly.
- Applies math concepts to life situations.
- Has a sense of reasonable versus unreasonable answers (i.e., can estimate).

Memory Tasks

- Remember recently presented information that has been heard.

- Remember recently presented information that has been read.

- Remember information learned previously.
- Remember sequential information.

Memory Requisite Abilities

- Has long-term recall of previously learned information (words, objects, designs, pictures).
- Has short-term recall of recently presented information (words, objects, designs, pictures).
- Recalls objects, designs, pictures.

- Follows simple directions in sequence.
- Follows complex directions in sequence.

Organizational Tasks

- Use time management skills.
- Organize work space.
- Organize information.
- Organize assignments, projects.

Organizational Abilities

- Understands cause-effect relationships.
- Manages personal and work time.
- Manages personal and work space.
- Makes plans to accomplish task.
- Organizes ideas into a cohesive whole.
- Can understand and organize abstract concepts.

(continues)

Table 11.3 *Continued.*

Setting-Demand Tasks	Requisite Abilities for Tasks
Physical and Motor Tasks	*Physical and Motor Requisite Abilities*
• Manipulate objects, materials.	• Exhibits physical strength, endurance.
• Use pencil, pen, marker.	• Has good posture.
• Use keyboard.	• Controls objects (grasps, manipulates).
• Cut, paste, do artwork.	• Moves about freely.
• Play musical instrument.	• Has good positioning, orientation.
• Maintain good posture, positioning.	
Behavior Tasks	*Behavior Abilities*
• Attend to task.	• Stays on task.
• Work well with others.	• Can work with peers.
• Stay in place.	• Takes care of personal, school property.
• Cooperate with the teacher.	• Cooperates with people of authority.

Requisite Abilities

Requisite abilities are skills that must be possessed to accomplish the tasks of the setting demands (Bryant & Rivera, 1995). For instance, the task of reading a textbook requires the requisite abilities of decoding, comprehending text including vocabulary, and fluency skills. The task of learning from a lecture requires the requisite abilities of demonstrating selective attention, understanding words that signal main ideas, and possessing efficient and effective note-taking strategies.

Although many students have these requisite abilities, some students with learning disabilities lack the abilities that are necessary for meeting specific tasks unless adaptations are implemented. Careful consideration should be given to the skill level necessary to perform a task successfully, the profile of strengths and weaknesses of a student with LD, and adaptations including AT that can enhance the opportunity for equal access.

Person-Specific Characteristics

The examination of person-specific characteristics as part of the adaptations identification process is based on diagnostic and psycho-educational assessment information provided by individual students. Decision makers can examine reports for evidence of specific learning disabilities and make recommendations for appropriate adaptations. Diagnosticians and psychologists should be encouraged to suggest assistive technology devices as possible adaptations in addition to other types of instructional accommodations (e.g., extended time to complete assignments, alternative methods of demonstrating mastery). Decision makers should consider individual functional capabilities and limitations; Figure 11.1 provides examples of questions to pose when examining person-specific strengths and limitations.

Functional Strengths

Functional strengths refer to cognitive (e.g., reading, writing, and reasoning), sensory (e.g., visual, auditory), language (e.g., listening, speaking), and motor (e.g., fine, gross) strengths that people use to perform tasks. Assessment of a student's functional strengths is important in order to match the purpose of a device with the student's abilities. For instance, a student who has a reading disability yet has good listening skills (i.e., functional capability) may benefit from tape-recorded text to access the reading material for a course. Similarly, a student's functional capability (e.g., fine-motor skills) dictates whether a standard keyboard, touch screen, or voice recognition software should be used for accessing word-processing and computer technology.

Functional Limitations

Functional limitations are disability-related barriers that may limit a student's academic performance and impede his or her ability to meet the setting demands of postsecondary instruction. Functional limitations include difficulties with academic skills, motor skills, sensory abilities, memory, and organizational skills. Students with specific learning disabilities may have functional limitations or weaknesses (e.g., difficulty with written expression or reading) that interfere with their full participation in postsecondary courses. For instance, a student who has a writing disability (e.g., dysgraphia) may exhibit difficulty taking notes in a lecture-based course. Following assessment of the setting demands and the learning attributes of the individual, decision makers can examine possible AT adaptation solutions.

Assistive Technology Adaptations

As decisions are made about AT adaptation options, decision makers must consider the needs of the individual and the features of the adaptations; additionally, training in the use of AT devices is often necessary to ensure proper use. Examples of questions to consider when selecting adaptations are displayed in Figure 11.1.

Adaptation Types

Adaptations can be identified according to the type of disability, such as reading, writing, or mathematics, and the setting-specific demands. Adaptations can range from simple to complex (McGregor & Pachuski, 1996) depending on such variables as ease of implementation; technological features (e.g., hardware platform specifications and electronic capabilities); user training requirements; and maintenance. Adaptations also can range from nonassistive technology to assistive technology. Bryant and Rivera (1995) note that assistive technology, in most instances, is simply technology that becomes assistive when its use satisfies the criteria found in the AT definition. That is, most technology devices are "helpful technology" to most people. If a device is used by a person with a disability, it becomes assistive when it is "used to increase, maintain or improve the functional capabilities of individuals with disabilities" (P.L. 105-17, § 602[1]). For example, a tape recorder might be considered a relatively simple device because it requires only depressing a button to activate it; its technological features consist of auditory output and recording capabilities; students know how to use it; and it's a fairly durable, low-maintenance device.

Person and Technology Match

When selecting assistive technology adaptations, decision makers must decide on the types of adaptations that would enhance a particular student's academic success (Bowser & Reed, 1995) based on the setting-specific demands, the capabilities a person must have to use the adaptation, and the individual's functional limitations that should be circumvented. For instance, certain levels of reading and spelling proficiency might be necessary for using software adaptations. The features of the adaptation must be matched to individual student needs (strengths and limitations).

When matching the adaptation to a student's needs, certain criteria should be considered, including (a) ease of use (setup, operation, maintenance); (b) amount of training required for the user (student) and provider (postsecondary institution, family); (c) cost (to purchase, maintain, repair); (d) technological features (e.g., computer modifications, specialized software programs, compatibility with other devices); (e) functional assistance (e.g., a pencil grip enables some students with motor problems to grasp and hold a pencil more easily; a speech synthesizer [with appropriate software] reads text shown on the monitor, enabling students with reading problems to access the text material); (f) performance (reliable, durable, safe); (g) use across environments and tasks;

(h) promotion of student independence; and (i) user's knowledge level of how to use the device (Raskind & Bryant, 1996). Finally, decision makers must consider the viewpoint of the user when selecting assistive technology adaptations (Carney & Dix, 1992). The student's opinion about the adaptation options and the obtrusive nature of adaptations, and his or her interest in trying available options must be considered during the selection process.

Training

Once an assistive technology device or adaptation has been determined, the user must be trained on the device and its capabilities and purpose. For example, if a computer is provided, then the consumer's computer literacy and keyboarding skills must be assessed and developed (Anderson-Inman, Knox-Quinn, & Horney, 1996; Raskind & Bryant, 1996). Once the assessment and selection process is complete, monitoring the use of the adaptation occurs.

Monitoring

Once assistive technology adaptations have been chosen, students should work with university and community support systems to monitor the effectiveness of the adaptation in meeting their individual learning needs (e.g., to promote access to the curriculum, assist in circumventing the specific disability) and responding successfully to setting-specific demands. Figure 11.1 provides examples of questions that can be considered when monitoring the effectiveness of assistive technology adaptations including environmental factors and use of the adaptations.

Environmental Factors

An analysis of hardware and software features (e.g., sound, space, electrical specifications) may reveal the necessity of students working with instructors to access environmental features that maximize the use of assistive technology adaptations (Raskind & Shaw, 1996). Devices that produce sound or require electricity may necessitate student proximity to a particular area of the classroom to facilitate the use of the technology. For example, devices that produce sound (e.g., talking calculators, speech synthesizers, tape recorders, speaking spelling programs, word prediction software) may need to be used in a section of the classroom where sound distractions are minimized and devices can be used unobtrusively. Similarly, the location of classroom electrical outlets dictates environmental access to power sources for some assistive technology devices and, thus, has implications for the seating arrangement of students. Students should be advised to consult with their instructors in a timely manner about specific accommodations they may need in order to successfully use an assistive technology adaptation.

Use of Assistive Technology Adaptations

Students with learning disabilities are in the best position to identify issues regarding the use of assistive technology adaptations for course and homework requirements. Through careful monitoring, students can determine the successful implementation of the assistive technology adaptation by examining and evaluating several factors. First, they should note both how easy it is to use the adaptation and whether further training is required to use it more effectively. They should note the versatility of the device across environments, such as campus to home and class to class, to determine if it meets their needs in different settings.

Second, the performance (i.e., reliability and durability) of technological adaptations should be monitored carefully (Bowser & Reed, 1995). If the adaptation requires frequent repairs, and thus hinders student achievement, then it may need to be reconsidered. As noted by Todis (1996), devices that fail, perform sporadically, or have parts that break easily will be quickly abandoned unless repair is expedient or "loaners" are readily available. Students may need to work closely with university and community support systems to ensure quick repair or access to loaners in the event of equipment failure.

Third, students should monitor their ability to keep pace with their peers to complete assignments and to "keep up" in class. They may need practice using various types of adaptations (technological adaptations in particular) to maximize their effectiveness. For instance, Anderson-Inman et al. (1996) found that secondary school students with learning disabilities expressed a need to develop fluent keyboarding skills so that they could use specialized software for studying purposes. Finally, student fatigue in using the device should be monitored to determine if the use of the adaptation proves tiring and thus hinders productivity. Next, evaluation of the integration of assistive technology devices is discussed to determine whether the goals of mastery of instructional objectives, independence, and accessibility are being achieved.

Evaluation

Although assistive technology adaptations for students with learning disabilities have the potential to enhance access to setting demands, promote independence and productivity, and circumvent functional limitations, studies show that almost one-third of AT devices are abandoned within the first year of use (Phillips, 1991). Students report that they are not achieving independence, and that numerous equipment issues (e.g., expense, maintenance, reliability) hinder performance (Phillips, 1992). Therefore, evaluation of the effectiveness of assistive technology adaptations is crucial. Figure 11.1 provides examples of questions that can be considered when evaluating product effectiveness.

Students with learning disabilities and campus and community service providers should determine whether assistive technology adaptations are instructionally beneficial. That is, are the adaptations helping students compensate for specific difficulties (e.g., reading and writing) so they can meet the demands of the instructional settings? Students can evaluate the match between their needs and the assistive technology adaptation by determining whether they have more access to the curriculum (by circumventing the disability-related limitation), can keep pace with their peers, and have more independence. Foremost, students must determine whether the AT adaptation is helping them achieve more success in their coursework. Evaluation is an integral part of the identification process, and reevaluation of any component of the process may be necessary to determine a more appropriate adaptation to satisfy setting demands and student needs and to foster instructional success, independence, and accessibility.

Next, we discuss barriers to and solutions for using assistive technology adaptations at the postsecondary level. Like any process that involves a variety of people and decisions to be made, controversy is inevitable; however, possible solutions for the issues can lead to productive change for all involved.

Barriers to and Solutions for Using Assistive Technology

Four broad and overlapping barriers to the use of AT devices are discussed below: assessment, funding, training, and attitudinal barriers.

Assessment

The assessment used to inform the selection and use of assistive technology in postsecondary settings is a multidimensional process. It endeavors to match the individual, the task, the technology, and the context (Vogel & Reder, 1998). Problems associated with the process tend to vary. For example, although adequate instrumentation and personnel are currently available to accurately assess the learner's academic strengths and weaknesses, matching technology with the individual, task, and context is far more problematic.

There are two related barriers to matching. The first barrier is the absence of personnel with the expertise necessary to match technology with instruction. Effective matching requires combining information about the student's history with technology, including interest level and proficiency, with instructional performance, task, and contextual information. Matching requires multiple observations of the student using different AT devices to determine what device works, on what tasks, and in what context. Few instruments exist to assist the person conducting the assessment in identifying the appropriate AT device and in matching assessment information. Currently, matching is dependent on the clinical skills of observation, experimentation, and interviewing.

Clearly, these barriers need to be addressed and will require additional resources. First, additional trained staff is required. Second, appropriate instruments must be developed. The solutions require political pressure to be generated by the increased number of people with disabilities being served in postsecondary settings, coupled with information about the success of AT devices to facilitate learning. Policy makers should be pressured to develop strategies and to appropriate funds to prepare personnel to fulfill this important role and to sponsor the development of reliable and valid instruments for the use in the process of matching instruction and technology.

Funding

Many "high-tech" AT devices (e.g., Kurzweil readers) are expensive, and the cost can be a major barrier to providing needed services. In addition, while technological breakthroughs are occurring with increased frequency, they usually are the result of expensive research and development activities. In all likelihood, this will keep the prices high for AT devices that are not currently produced in large numbers. Obviously, not all AT devices are expensive, but with more students with disabilities enrolling in postsecondary education, services will have to expand. In addition, the purchase of equipment will result in customization costs and repair and maintenance costs and will also require the hiring of support and management personnel. The need for increased expenditures occurs at a time when most postsecondary institutions are experiencing diminished appropriations. Clearly, funding will remain a predominant barrier. However, options exist for identifying funding alternatives through external sources such as federal and state government, Medicare, insurance, private corporations, and philanthropic groups (Derer et al., 1996). Additional "marketing" ideas are discussed in Chapter 13.

Training and Support

Not surprisingly, the lack of training in the use of specific AT devices is one of the top-ranked barriers for successful implementation (Derer et al., 1996; Wehmeyer, 1999). Issues pertaining to training and support include identifying the needs of the target audience, determining the type of training to provide, and finding the time to deliver training.

The absence of training for personnel designated to assist in the use of AT devices is also a frequently encountered barrier (Derer et al., 1996). The absence of preservice training, coupled with the burgeoning development of new AT devices, requires an ongoing professional development program. Professional development workshop formats are challenging to those responsible for providing training because the wealth of information needed by professionals cannot be covered adequately in any one training format. Various training approaches have been used and subsequent support systems identified. Survey data suggest that hands-on training, coupled with follow-up support tailored to practical application, is essential to prepare professionals to effectively implement AT devices (Derer et al., 1996). Related barriers involve identifying persons to provide training and finding the time to deliver training. Brinckerhoff and Forer (1998) have developed an assistive technology training workshop series specifically for college students with learning disabilities at Fairleigh Dickinson University. See Appendix 11.7 on the CD-ROM for a sample course syllabus that readers can modify to suit their needs.

The solution to this barrier requires an administrative commitment to develop ongoing staff development and training. It requires planning to articulate training objectives, identify training and support personnel, create time to allow faculty to participate in training activities, and develop classroom support strategies. The absence of such commitment minimizes the effects of AT devices.

Attitudes and Acceptance

A final barrier addresses people's willingness to accept AT devices as viable options for gaining access and independence. Because the identification, implementation, and ongoing evaluation of AT devices require the collaborative work of professionals and users, attitudes and levels of acceptance can be influential factors in the ultimate success of AT. All participants must strive to gain an understanding of the various perspectives that contribute to the use of these devices. The absence of common understandings will leave professional specialists frustrated because of the improper or inadequate use of AT devices and teachers frustrated with malfunctioning devices. The result will be unused devices and students without needed support (Todis, 1996). Solutions to this barrier require staff development systems that provide opportunities for professionals to meet and to come to common understandings about respective roles and how to solve problem situations. Overall, barriers do remain to the successful use of AT devices. They require creative and viable solutions if AT adaptations are to be used effectively by students with disabilities in postsecondary education.

Conclusion

Earlier we stated that the purpose of this chapter is to examine the challenges students with LD face in postsecondary settings from a perspective of assistive technology service delivery and use. We provided readers with discussions concerning a rationale for the use of AT devices; the benefits of assistive technology in postsecondary education settings; AT service delivery systems; specific AT devices and their use; an examination of AT assessment, selection, monitoring, and evaluation considerations; and barriers to AT use. We also provided proposed solutions to those barriers. Although we do not expect all readers to immediately have sufficient knowledge to use AT adaptations with their students, we do hope that professionals will be challenged to seek out information to better assist their students, and that students will be challenged to use AT devices in their courses and, later, in the workplace.

Chapter 2 provided a detailed plan and timetable to enhance the transition of students with LD to postsecondary settings. Learning about and trying out various technological aids should occur during high school so that students enter higher education with the requisite skills in the use of AT. We also hope that instructors at the postsecondary level make sufficient adaptations to ensure that students with learning disabilities function on a level playing field and that success or failure in classes will be the result of the student's willingness and motivation to undertake the steps necessary to succeed. We also hope that students with LD will advocate for AT devices and services and that Offices for Students with Disabilities will make every effort to provide such devices and services. In short, our hope is to never again write a chapter about how AT devices and services *could* be used to meet the needs of postsecondary students with LD, but to write about how such devices and services are being used on every campus to help students succeed. We opened this chapter with a statement concerning how, not long ago, college was considered a pipe dream for students with LD and their families and that now it is a dream come true. We fully expect to write the same thing concerning AT use in the near future, when the timely acquisition and use of AT devices and services will be a reality and not an unfulfilled promise.

CHAPTER

POSTSECONDARY DISABILITY
PERSONNEL AS PROFESSIONALS

Postsecondary disability services, particularly those for students with hidden disabilities such as LD, were typically the last direct student service function included in student affairs. Blosser (1984) notes that in 1977 only 233 U.S. institutions of higher education provided services or offices for students with disabilities, but in 1999 Kravets and Wax identified 1,300 colleges and universities offering programs and services for students with learning disabilities alone. The number of postsecondary disability personnel has grown accordingly. In 1978 there were 32 members of what is now AHEAD (Madaus, 1996); now there are over 1,900 members (Dukes & Shaw, 1999).

The professional backgrounds of these practitioners are wide ranging and varied, as are the levels of preparation for careers in Offices for Students with Disabilities. In an OSD survey, respondents indicated that they were most often trained in counseling (25%), law (17%), or social work (17%). Special education (16%), higher education (14%), and rehabilitation counseling (13%) followed closely (Madaus, 1996). In a more recent study involving 563 postsecondary personnel (Dukes, 1999), most respondents identified their training as "other" (23%), with the disciplines of special education (19%) and counseling (18%) following closely. Training in rehabilitation counseling (11%), higher education (11%), elementary/secondary education (10%), and psychology (7%) was also reported.

We acknowledge the support of Lyman L. Dukes, III, from the University of Connecticut in developing material for this chapter.

It has also been noted that many OSD practitioners believe that they are inadequately prepared to effectively meet both the needs of their students and the needs of their respective institutions (Norlander, Shaw, & McGuire, 1990). Bigaj, Shaw, Cullen, McGuire, and Yost (1995) state that the diversity of educational backgrounds may reflect the fact that postsecondary disability personnel lack professional standards and certification requirements. Fortunately, recent actions have begun to create the professional underpinnings for postsecondary disability personnel (Dukes & Shaw 1999). A code of ethics (Price, 1997), professional standards (Shaw, McGuire, & Madaus, 1997), and program standards (Shaw & Dukes, in press) have recently been developed. This chapter will highlight the professionalization of postsecondary services for students with learning disabilities and will describe strategies to improve the ability of postsecondary disability personnel, as well as higher education and, specifically, student affairs administrators and faculty to effectively meet the needs of college students with learning disabilities.

The Professionalization of Postsecondary Disability Services

Legally mandated access to equal educational opportunity for college students with learning disabilities is less than 30 years old. During those two decades, postsecondary programs designed to ensure equal educational opportunity have developed rapidly, in response to both the legal mandates and an increasing student population. A growing body of literature that addresses the needs of adults with learning disabilities demonstrates that our profession is working to keep pace with the expansion of this cohort. First, Patton and Polloway (1996) note that there is a greater commitment on the part of the *Journal of Learning Disabilities* and the *Learning Disabilities Quarterly* to publish articles that explore issues related to adults with learning disabilities. There has also been growth in the number and quality of research studies submitted to the *Journal of Postsecondary Education and Disability*, with most attending to students with LD.

Perhaps most telling is the development of the AHEAD professional standards (Shaw, McGuire, & Madaus, 1997), a code of ethics (Price, 1997), and program standards (Shaw & Dukes, in press) for postsecondary disability service providers. The promulgation of these benchmarks clearly demonstrates a movement toward the assurance of professional quality among all disability service providers. Their implementation has firmly placed the postsecondary disability service provider in the arena with other student services professionals (Dukes & Shaw, 1999; Shaw, 1997a). Since the program standards were discussed in Chapter 8, this chapter will present the professional standards and code of ethics and discuss their role in professional development.

Professional Standards

The AHEAD professional standards are "those skills and knowledge that are required in the day-to-day job practice and are intended to define postsecondary personnel as professionals who are willing to establish and abide by standards relating to performance and practice" (Shaw et al., 1997, p. 26). The Council for the Advancement of Standards in Higher Education (CAS) has delineated professional standards for disability support services (Miller, 1997). It is important to note that the AHEAD professional standards, presented in Figure 12.1, are qualitatively different from the standards and guidelines set forth by CAS. The CAS standards spell out the general characteristics of a typical disability services program (Miller, 1997), while the AHEAD standards point to specific skills and responsibilities of postsecondary disability personnel. Due to the paucity of formal training available for those professionals, the development and approval of AHEAD's professional standards is considered a milestone (Shaw et al., 1997).

Jarrow (1997b) states that professional standards are necessary for a number of reasons. First, they define the responsibilities of OSD practitioners for themselves as well as for the rest of the higher education community. Their multi-faceted duties may include everything from policy development to individual student counselor to physical plant monitor. Next, professional standards can assist in the development of professional preparation programs. That is, the standards may serve as the foundation on which future service providers can be trained. Last, standards are a necessary step in the recognition of disability services as a unique and fundamental component of student services. Moreover, personnel who adhere to AHEAD's professional benchmarks should be perceived as essential components of an institution's provision of equal access for all students (Dukes & Shaw, 1999).

As previously noted, the number of postsecondary disability personnel has expanded rapidly during the past 10 years, and these people have come from a diversity of educational backgrounds. The lack of empirical data on the competencies needed for postsecondary disability positions has made appropriate job descriptions and specification of qualifications difficult. The establishment of professional standards is an effective method for addressing this dilemma. With the standards now in place, college and university administrators responsible for the development of job descriptions for disability personnel have a blueprint for meeting that obligation (Dukes & Shaw, 1999).

(text continues on p. 437)

AHEAD Professional Standards

The Association on Higher Education and Disability (AHEAD) is pleased to offer these Professional Standards as a critical milestone in the provision of services to college students with disabilities. The standards reflect the maturation of the field, recognition of the breadth of skills and knowledge required of personnel administering the Office for Students with Disabilities (OSD), and consensus among professionals in the field. It is hoped that the standards will enhance service provision for college students with disabilities by improving personnel preparation programs, focusing staff development activities, guiding the development of job descriptions for OSD personnel, and expanding the vision of disability services at the postsecondary level.

1. Administration

Responsibilities related to the administration or management of the office serving students with disabilities.

1.1   Develops program policies and procedures (e.g., required documentation, course substitutions).

1.2   Develops program services.

1.3   Maintains up-to-date knowledge of emerging issues in disability services (e.g., ADD/ADHD).

1.4   Identifies/establishes program goals.

1.5   Evaluates program services.

1.6   Communicates program activities, services, and outcomes to institutional administrators.

1.7   Supervises/trains program staff.

1.8   Develops/administers program budget.

1.9   Compiles reports on program activities/services.

1.10   Develops program brochure and handbook.

1.11   Responds to requests for interpretation of legal mandates on campus-specific issues.

1.12   Evaluates program staff.

1.13   Interprets court/government agency rulings and interpretations affecting services for students.

(continues)

Figure 12.1. AHEAD Professional Standards. *Note.* From "Standards of Professional Practice," by S. F. Shaw, J. M. McGuire, and J. W. Madaus, 1997, *Journal of Postsecondary Education and Disability, 12*(3), pp. 26–35. Copyright 1997 by *Journal of Postsecondary Education and Disability,* AHEAD. Reprinted with permission.

2. Direct Service

Providing services directly to students or acting on behalf of students with members of the campus community.

2.1 Maintains confidential student records (e.g., documentation of disability).

2.2 Serves as an advocate for students with faculty or administrators.

2.3 Determines program eligibility for services based upon documentation of a disability.

2.4 Responds to inquiries from prospective students or their parents.

2.5 Consults with students about appropriate individualized accommodations based upon documentation.

2.6 Provides information to students regarding their legal rights and responsibilities.

2.7 Communicates information regarding program activities and services to students.

2.8 Consults with faculty regarding the instructional needs of students.

2.9 Consults with institutional administrators regarding the needs of students (e.g., department directors).

2.10 Consults with other campus departments regarding the needs of students (e.g., health services, residential life, admissions, counseling services).

2.11 Communicates information regarding program services to the campus community (e.g., admissions brochure, student catalog).

2.12 Arranges auxiliary aides for students.

2.13 Arranges individualized accommodations for students (e.g., testing accommodations).

2.14 Distributes program brochure or handbook to campus departments (e.g., health services, counseling services).

2.15 Processes complaints/grievances from students.

2.16 Provides personal/individual counseling to students relating to disability issues.

2.17 Coordinates assistants for students (e.g., note takers, interpreters, readers).

2.18 Provides academic advisement to students relating to disability issues.

2.19 Provides counseling/advisement to enhance student development (e.g., self-advocacy).

2.20 Assists students in self-monitoring the effectiveness of accommodations.

(continues)

Figure 12.1. *Continued.*

3. Consultation/Collaboration

Working with campus or community personnel and agencies regarding students with disabilities or disability issues.

3.1 Consults with state, provincial, or community resources (e.g., rehabilitation services).

3.2 Collaborates with physical plant to ensure modifications to campus facilities.

3.3 Maintains up-to-date knowledge of adaptive technology.

3.4 Collaborates with campus architects to review or plan new construction and renovations.

3.5 Conducts campus-wide disability awareness activities (e.g., Disability Awareness Day).

3.6 Communicates program activities to the campus community (e.g., via campus newspapers).

3.7 Conducts outreach activities for high school students (e.g., college fairs, transition workshops).

3.8 Consults with campus personnel regarding job accommodations for faculty and campus staff with disabilities.

4. Institutional Awareness

Providing training and expertise regarding disability issues to members of the campus community.

4.1 Serves on campus committees to develop institutional policies and procedures regarding students with disabilities.

4.2 Provides training for faculty regarding awareness of disabilities.

4.3 Serves on campus committees addressing regulatory issues affecting students with disabilities.

4.4 Provides training for campus staff regarding awareness of disabilities.

4.5 Responsible for organizing training for campus personnel regarding the legal requirements of serving students with disabilities.

4.6 Provides training for faculty regarding accommodations and auxiliary aides.

4.7 Provides training for institutional administration regarding awareness of disabilities.

(continues)

Figure 12.1. *Continued.*

---

5. Professional Development

Maintaining up-to-date professional knowledge and skill.

5.1   Attends conferences and professional development workshops.

5.2   Reads professional literature related to postsecondary education and students with disabilities.

5.3   Holds membership in professional organizations.

Figure 12.1. *Continued.*

The standards not only provide a means of devising appropriate job descriptions, but also serve as an effective tool for hiring qualified disability service personnel. The standards of professional practice can and should be used by administrative bodies when examining the qualifications of potential postsecondary disability personnel. Though not intended to be used as a checklist, the standards provide a framework for determining whether applicants have a working knowledge of the practices relevant to the position for which they have interest. Without professional standards, institutions of higher education would likely continue to have difficulty identifying the candidate who is most qualified to provide "state-of-the-art" services.

Given the fiscal, administrative, and legal accountability of OSDs, it is vital that personnel responsible for ensuring equal educational access conduct a periodic assessment of their performance. Again, the professional standards can be used as a guide for managing such an evaluation. Institutional representatives or an outside consultant may assess OSD personnel with respect to each specific area of performance. The standards can serve as a guide when determining the overall quality of the services personnel are providing their students with disabilities (Dukes & Shaw, 1999).

Code of Ethics

The AHEAD code of ethics presented in Figure 12.2 stipulates guidelines for professional behavior in the performance of day-to-day responsibilities. Price (1997) clearly states the practical benefits of a code of ethics for services for students with disabilities. First, the code of professional conduct spells out what is expected of both the institution and the student. Next, it furnishes professionals with a means of assessing the appropriateness of their services for the institution

AHEAD Code of Ethics

We agree that these principles are the Code of Ethics for postsecondary disability service providers. As professionals, we are responsible for upholding, supporting, and advancing these ideas whenever possible. Members of AHEAD agree to monitor themselves and their peers in accordance with the spirit and provisions of this code, as delineated by the following principles:

1. Postsecondary disability service providers are committed to facilitating the highest levels of educational excellence and potential quality of life for postsecondary students with disabilities.

2. Postsecondary disability service providers strive to achieve and maintain the highest levels of competence and integrity in all areas of assistance to adult students with disabilities. This support is guided by the consistent use of objective, professional judgment in all areas, especially when addressing the confidential nature of the student's disability.

3. Postsecondary disability service providers continually participate in professional activities and educational opportunities designed to strengthen the personal, educational, and vocational quality of life for students with disabilities. This includes the ongoing development of strategies, skills, research, and knowledge pertinent to the highest quality of disability service delivery whenever and wherever it occurs.

4. Postsecondary disability service providers carry out their responsibilities in accordance with AHEAD professional standards and policy guidelines for adult students with disabilities. When certified, licensed, or affiliated with other professionals or organizations, they comply with those professional guidelines as well.

5. Postsecondary disability service providers are actively engaged in supporting and clarifying institutional, state, provincial, and federal laws, policies, and procedures applicable to the service delivery to students with disabilities. Compliance implies that professionals will not condone or participate in any unethical or illegal acts discussed within these guidelines.

Figure 12.2. AHEAD Code of Ethics. *Note.* From "The Development and Implementation of a Code of Ethical Behavior for Postsecondary Personnel," by L. Price, 1997, *Journal of Postsecondary Education and Disability, 12*(3), pp. 36–44. Copyright 1997 by *Journal of Postsecondary Education and Disability,* AHEAD. Reprinted with permission.

and each respective student population. That is, are the services provided benefiting both the student and the school? Like the professional standards, the code of ethics lends credibility to the work of disability personnel and defines them as professionals who are grounded in a meaningful body of standards and guidelines. Most important, the code serves as a guidepost for professionals during their daily activities and, foremost, during times of crisis.

Given the diverse challenges faced by postsecondary personnel who serve students with learning disabilities, it is imperative that the code be immediately and effectively applied. Price and Shaw (1997) have developed the mnemonic learning strategy RACES to encourage use of the code:

Remember the code.
Assess the situation.
Check the code.
Evaluate your options.
Set your plan in motion.

A worksheet using RACES is available in Figure 12.3. The responses on the worksheet relate to the following "problem situation."

▶ You receive documentation from a student about his "learning disability," along with his demand that you provide "assistance for his disability as soon as possible." However, when you examine the documentation carefully, you have the following concerns:

1. The diagnostic report is 10 years old.

2. It states only that the student has *"learning difficulties* in the areas of reading and writing."

What would you do with this situation?

Personnel Development Needs

Personnel development needs stem from three distinct concerns:

1. Until recently relatively few people had received the necessary pre-service training to work with adults with learning disabilities.

2. The multifaceted needs of adult students with learning disabilities include assessment, instruction, accommodations, and counseling across a broad range of subjects and disability severity.

3. The changing nature of the field requires professionals to constantly upgrade their skills to deal effectively with information from current research.

RACES Worksheet

Remember the code. (How will you remind yourself to use the code? Posted on your wall? Taped to your desk? Training workshops for all OSD staff?)

- A problem is defined as a professional ethical challenge.
- Check posted code.

Assess the situation. (Assess immediacy of response? Need? What is the key issue? Is there a hidden or overt agenda? What exactly is being asked of you?)

- Key issue—cannot provide services without appropriate documentation of a disability.
- Problem—author of report, parent, and student believe services should be provided based on this "documentation."

Check the code. (What guidance does the code give you? What are the key words or phases? Which principles seem to fit here?)

- Principle 2 speaks to maintaining professional integrity.
- Principle 4 requires professionals to carry out responsibilities in accordance with policy guidelines.

Evaluate your options. (Do you need to clarify this issue with anyone else? How are power politics shaping this situation? Who/what are your resources? Your allies? Your roadblocks? Who are the other stakeholders? Is there a preferred or an unacceptable outcome?)

- Do you have *approved* policies in place requiring adherence to documentation guidelines?
- Are documentation guidelines specified in institutional or program publications?
- Will your supervisor support your professional stance?
- Can you offer the student any options (testing, other forms of "assistance")?

Set your plan in motion. (What action should you take first? Next? What did you learn here that you can use next time?)

- Meet with student to discuss documentation issue, share documentation guidelines, and discuss options.
- Provide direction for student to get appropriate documentation or referral to other campus offices for assistance.
- Maintain "contemporaneous" record of these discussions.

Figure 12.3. Applying the Code of Ethics. *Note.* From "The AHEAD Code of Ethics: Principles Four and Five," by L. Price and S. Shaw, 1997, *Alert, 21*(4), pp. 16, 17. Copyright 2000 by Lynda A. Price and Stan Shaw. Reprinted with permission.

Disability Personnel

In 1998, AHEAD commissioned a study of postsecondary disability personnel to identify their levels of skills in areas of the professional standards (O'Connor, McGuire, & Madaus, 1998). Data were collected from 535 subjects regarding their self-perceived level of skill on 54 items used by Madaus for his 1996 study, which resulted in AHEAD's professional standards. Only a few of the items in O'Connor et al.'s study are irrelevant to LD (e.g., architectural and physical plant issues).

Examination of the results presented in Table 12.1 indicates that only 22 of the items received a mean score of 4.0 or higher on a 5-point Likert scale (from 1 = unimportant to 5 = very important). Only Item 16, which related to seeking external funding, was rated below 3.0. Items that had means between 3.0 and 4.0 included those related to budgeting (Item 23), program evaluation (Items 24, 41), staff supervision (Items 8, 11), training (Items 6, 35, 37, 38, 42, 49, 54), collaboration and communication (Items 1, 18, 28, 47, 52), knowledge of technology (Item 36), and policy development and implementation (Items 9, 21, 27, 29, 53). The results confirm that the diversity of training and experience of personnel serving college students with learning disabilities, combined with the paucity of programs providing preservice training in this area, leaves professionals desiring to improve their skills. Since it is unlikely that any person will have all the necessary skills, support for ongoing, intensive staff development is critical.

Faculty Training Needs

There is a long history of research on the perceptions of faculty toward college students with physical disabilities (Fonosch & Schwab, 1981; Walker, 1980). Only in the last 2 decades has the literature included studies on faculty attitudes toward, knowledge about, and willingness to accommodate college students with learning disabilities (Aksamit, Morris, & Leuenberger, 1987; Bigaj, Shaw, & McGuire, 1999; Hill, 1996; Matthews, Anderson, & Skolnick, 1987; Rose, 1993; Vogel, Leyser, Wyland, & Brulle, 1999).

As has been documented about regular classroom teachers in public schools, college faculty often have generally negative expectations of students labeled as learning disabled (Minner & Prater, 1984). However, research by Bigaj et al. (1999) and Vogel et al. (1999) indicates that faculty are generally willing to make accommodations for students with learning disabilities as long as academic standards are maintained.

The most encouraging data come from research undertaken at the University of Nebraska (Aksamit et al., 1987; Morris, Leuenberger, & Aksamit, 1987)

(*text continues on p. 445*)

Table 12.1
Training Needs

Items	Mean	SD
How skilled are you as a PDS provider in . . .		
1. Serving on campus committees to develop policies and procedures regarding students with disabilities.	3.95	.98
2. Maintaining confidential student records (e.g., documentation of disability).	4.61	.64
3. Responding to inquiries about program services from prospective students or their parents.	4.54	.69
4. Attending conferences and professional development workshops.	4.14	.92
5. Reading professional literature related to postsecondary education for students with disabilities.	4.12	.81
6. Providing training for faculty regarding awareness of disabilities.	3.76	1.01
7. Distributing program brochures or handbooks to campus departments (e.g., health services, counseling services).	4.02	.98
8. Supervising or training program staff.	3.92	1.08
9. Developing program policies and procedures (e.g., required documentation, course substitutions).	3.85	1.05
10. Providing information to students regarding their rights and legal responsibilities.	4.12	.90
11. Evaluating program staff.	3.75	1.17
12. Developing program services.	4.0	.94
13. Serving as an advocate for students with faculty or administrators.	4.40	.71
14. Arranging auxiliary aids for students.	4.01	.92
15. Providing personal, individual counseling to students relating to disability issues.	4.12	.97
16. Pursuing additional funding sources to enhance program development (e.g., grants, fund-raising).	2.76	1.26
17. Collaborating with campus architects to review or plan new construction and renovations.	3.0	1.35
18. Consulting with state, provincial, or community resources (e.g., rehabilitation services).	3.76	1.08
19. Communicating information regarding program activities and services to students.	4.31	.78

(continues)

Table 12.1 *Continued.*

Items	Mean	SD
How skilled are you as a PDS provider in . . .		
20. Holding membership in professional organizations.	4.16	.91
21. Processing complaints and grievances from students.	3.86	1.03
22. Conducting campus-wide disability awareness activities (e.g., Disability Awareness Day).	3.38	1.19
23. Developing and administering program budget.	3.46	1.37
24. Compiling reports on program activities and services.	3.86	1.06
25. Assisting students in self-monitoring the effectiveness of accommodations.	3.78	1.0
26. Arranging individualized accommodations for students (e.g., testing accommodations).	4.44	.78
27. Responding to requests for interpretations of legal mandates on campus-specific issues.	3.60	1.17
28. Serving on campus committees addressing ADA/Section 504 or Canadian Charter planning or issues.	3.78	1.21
29. Developing a program brochure or handbook.	3.89	.99
30. Coordinating assistants for students (e.g., note takers, interpreters, readers).	4.06	.97
31. Collaborating with physical plant to ensure modifications to campus facilities.	3.59	1.24
32. Consulting with other campus departments regarding the needs of students (e.g., health services, residential life, admissions, counseling services).	4.17	.87
33. Consulting with faculty regarding the instructional needs of students.	4.19	.83
34. Communicating information regarding program services to the campus community (e.g., admissions brochures, student catalog).	4.08	.92
35. Conducting outreach activities for high school students (e.g., college fairs, transition workshops).	3.46	1.32
36. Maintaining up-to-date knowledge of adaptive technology.	3.15	1.04
37. Making presentations at professional conferences.	3.28	1.36
38. Providing training for campus staff regarding awareness of disabilities.	3.75	1.06

(continues)

Table 12.1 *Continued.*

Items	Mean	SD
How skilled are you as a PDS provider in . . .		
39. Identifying and establishing program goals.	3.96	.95
40. Determining eligibility for program services based on documentation of a disability.	4.21	.90
41. Evaluating program services.	3.78	1.00
42. Conducting training for campus personnel regarding the legal requirements of serving students with disabilities.	3.65	1.14
43. Consulting with campus personnel regarding job accommodations for faculty or campus staff with disabilities.	3.31	1.38
44. Providing academic advice to students related to disability issues.	4.17	.99
45. Suggesting appropriate individual accommodations to students based on documentation.	4.36	.84
46. Consulting with campus administrators regarding the needs of students (e.g., department directors).	4.19	.84
47. Communicating program activities and services to institutional administration.	3.93	.95
48. Maintaining up-to-date knowledge of emerging issues in disability services (e.g., ADHD).	3.89	.91
49. Providing training for faculty regarding accommodations and auxiliary aids.	3.56	1.09
50. Providing counseling and advice to enhance student development (e.g., self-advocacy).	4.10	.95
51. Providing counseling and advice on managing personal assistants (e.g., personal care assistants, interpreters).	3.16	1.33
52. Communicating program activities or events to the campus community (e.g., via student newspapers).	3.41	1.14
53. Interpreting court and government agency rulings and interpretations affecting services for students.	3.51	1.12
54. Providing training for institutional administration regarding awareness of disabilities.	3.59	1.13

Note. From *Educational Training and Professional Development for Postsecondary Disability Service Providers: Honing Our Skills While We Do Our Jobs,* by M. O'Connor, J. McGuire, & J. Madaus, 1998, paper presented at the AHEAD 21st Annual Conference, Las Vegas. Copyright 1998 by M. O'Connor, J. M. McGuire, & J. Madaus. Reprinted with permission.

and the University of Connecticut (Bigaj et al., 1999) that demonstrated that *effective in-service training over time* was significantly related to faculty knowledge, attitudes, and expectations. These studies indicate that faculty training needs include:

- understanding of the institutional process for determining who has a learning disability;

- understanding of the procedures for identification and referral;

- understanding of the federal laws that apply to students and adults in postsecondary settings;

- understanding of faculty's responsibility to provide accommodations to students;

- understanding of the responsibilities of the student to the faculty and institution;

- identification of the availability and type of support services on campus;

- understanding of student "rights" versus academic freedom and maintaining academic standards;

- determining what constitutes appropriate and reasonable accommodation;

- understanding of how to provide accommodations and modifications;

- learning how to provide effective instructional strategies for students with learning disabilities and all students;

- understanding the importance of independence and self-advocacy for students with learning disabilities;

- examples and case studies of accommodations, modifications, and effective instructional techniques implemented by other faculty; and

- awareness of how textbook selection and instructional methodology relate to low-tech (e.g., RFB&D tapes) and high-tech (e.g., computers) devices.

Rather than just seeking faculty cooperation for modifications or accommodations, Scott and Gregg (2000) note that "future faculty education efforts should look more broadly at institutional and professional reinforcers for faculty and what motivates faculty to teach *any* student well" (p. 16). They go on to recommend that staff development be made available in easily accessible formats such as training over the Internet, by e-mail, or on CD-ROM. Several equal access projects funded by the Higher Education Amendments of 1998, including one at the University of Connecticut, are attempting to implement Scott and Gregg's recommendations.

Training Needs of Administrators

Higher education administrators from academic affairs (e.g., vice presidents, deans, and department chairs) and student affairs personnel from the residential life office, the office of the dean of students, admissions, and other student support services typically have limited training and little contact with students who have learning disabilities. However, they develop and implement institutional policies and procedures that often directly affect those students and, therefore, must learn more about that population. Equally important, resources for personnel and programs that serve students with learning disabilities are often allocated by these campus administrators.

A number of initiatives to provide information and technical assistance to higher education administrators regarding services for students with learning disabilities (Anderson & McGuire, 1991; Brinckerhoff, Shaw, & McGuire, 1989; Walker, Shaw, & McGuire, 1992) have resulted in identification of the following generic training needs for such personnel:

- understanding institutional obligations under federal regulations;
- developing policies and procedures for services for students with learning disabilities;
- identifying program development models and supporting service-delivery models;
- developing a staff training program for faculty awareness and delineating staff responsibilities;
- identifying admission policies and procedures; and
- implementing data collection and program evaluation initiatives.

The range of personnel classifications (e.g., teaching assistant, dormitory resident, admissions officer) at each institution also has an impact on services for students with learning disabilities. Most of these personnel require a range of training to help them meet the needs of this growing cohort of college students. The following section will describe approaches to personnel development that can enable each institution to prepare personnel who can effectively fulfill their responsibilities to students with learning disabilities.

Approaches to Personnel Development

It is clear that rounding up a large number of staff or faculty for a mandatory in-service training session on everything you need to know about college students with learning disabilities is not a very productive approach (Michaels, 1986). It is critical to begin with a thorough understanding of the many constituencies at an institution of higher education that may need training on this topic. Each group should receive a different sequence and level of training, depending on its entering knowledge and degree of involvement with students with learning disabilities. Personnel development activities should be multi-faceted to reach and motivate individuals with different levels of interest in and responsibilities to these students.

The NJCLD, in its position paper on in-service programs (National Joint Committee on Learning Disabilities, 1988), made recommendations that include the following:

- A needs assessment should be conducted prior to beginning a personnel development program.

- Trainers must have competence in the content of and the ability to complete the stated objectives of the in-service program.

- Administrative personnel should support effective staff development programs through (a) personal participation; (b) providing incentives and/or release time for participating professionals; (c) encouraging constituent involvement in planning, implementing, and evaluating the program; and (d) providing fiscal support.

Needs assessments are typically implemented through surveys or questionnaires that assess knowledge (definitions, characteristics, laws), attitudes toward disability, instructional methodologies, and willingness to make reasonable modifications (Marchant, 1990; Morris et al., 1987). Using all the program standards (Shaw & Dukes, in press), professional standards (as did O'Connor et al., 1998), or selected standards can lead to a comprehensive needs assessment. A powerful needs assessment can also come from feedback by the Office for Civil Rights that results from investigation of a complaint. Although an OCR complaint is unwelcome and time consuming, it can provide productive impetus and direction for improvement. At some colleges, consumers (students and their parents) have taken their concerns about the institution's ability or willingness to meet the needs of students with learning disabilities to the ADA coordinator, campus ombudsman, or the OSD. As students with LD have developed their self-advocacy skills, increasing numbers of peer support and disability rights groups have made their concerns known to college officials.

One of the most effective ways for an institution to determine its current ability to serve students with learning disabilities is through an on-site evaluation (Brinckerhoff et al., 1989). An external consultant with expertise in LD service delivery can review college documents (e.g., catalogs, policy statements, and admission information); talk with administrators, faculty, staff, and students; and visit campus support services. An exit interview with college officials and a written report specifying strengths and weaknesses have proved to be effective tools in identifying needs and planning staff development activities (Brinckerhoff & Anderson, 1989). AHEAD's LD Special Interest Group has developed a technical assistance team that provides this service (Fink, 1999). Evaluation data from site visits conducted through the Northeast Technical Assistance Center for Learning Disability College Programming demonstrated that 86% of recipients rated their value as very good to excellent (Brinckerhoff & Anderson, 1989).

The following sections describe an array of personnel development alternatives for direct service personnel, higher education administrators, and personnel and faculty in student affairs and related areas. Although a needs assessment will determine the specific scope and sequence of training for an individual institution, a general sequence of events is presented.

Typically, it is necessary to first address the needs of direct service personnel who work with students on a regular basis. Then higher education administrators should receive the training necessary to help them understand the rights of students with learning disabilities and to support the development of appropriate policies and procedures. Finally, academic and student affairs personnel and faculty require training regarding their roles with these students. Attempts to work with faculty before effective support services and appropriate policies are in place can create more problems than solutions.

Direct Service Personnel

Direct service personnel, whether part-time or full-time, are hired with some degree of skill in and commitment to working with students who have learning disabilities. At the onset, training is essential regarding the program's mission and service-delivery model and its particular procedures, forms, and data collection requirements. In addition, an orientation to the institution, campus, and facility will assure familiarity with the environment within which services are provided. This initial staff development can best be provided in several days of training prior to the start of service delivery at the beginning of the academic year. Major topics for this training could include:

- program philosophy, policies, and procedures;
- the roles and responsibilities of direct service personnel; and
- assessment, instructional, and counseling strategies.

Trainers for this in-service program might include program administrators, experienced direct service personnel, college faculty (e.g., faculty in special education, counseling, or school psychology), and other campus support services personnel (e.g., personnel from the counseling center or learning center).

Over time, direct service personnel will need additional training regarding new materials and approaches, current research, and, ideally, a broadening of competence across different domains. This latter area can often be dealt with through a peer-teaching approach. A special educator can share instructional methodology; a school psychologist can provide information on test interpretation; or a counselor can share approaches for developing self-advocacy skills. This training should occur through regularly scheduled weekly or monthly staff meetings. These sessions can also provide opportunities for problem-solving difficult cases, for reviewing and revising program policies and procedures, and for learning about other campus and community services.

The development or adaptation of a training manual to give to direct service personnel would be a very productive supplement to the training program. Such materials typically contain specification of institutional policies and procedures for students with learning disabilities, assessment procedures, academic and social intervention strategies, instructional resources, and program forms. A number of manuals, guides, training programs, and videotapes have been developed by exemplary projects across the country, and they are described in Appendixes 12.1 and 12.2 on the CD-ROM.

Higher Education Administrators

It is most important for college administrators to understand and be supportive of service-delivery efforts for students with learning disabilities. In addition to fiscal issues, college administrators must deal with litigation and related concerns about program modifications and instructional accommodations. As noted previously, a site visit by an expert outside consultant has often been effective in encouraging higher education administrators to adjust policies and procedures to meet the needs of students with learning disabilities (Brinckerhoff et al., 1989). The consultant can, at a later date, provide formal training on such topics as legal requirements under Section 504/ADA, alternative service-delivery models, and policies and procedures for meeting the needs of students with learning disabilities. A consultant can also implement a needs assessment and present recommendations.

A concerned administrator or the coordinator of the direct service program can also make presentations to executive councils or deans' meetings. Individual discussions with key college officials are an effective initial approach to reinforcing the reason, mission, and legal base for services to students with learning disabilities. Ongoing collaboration with the dean of students, dean of academic affairs, admissions director, and Section 504/ADA coordinator provides important opportunities to share information needed by those officials to effectively serve this population. Sharing relevant information such as articles from the *Chronicle of Higher Education*, court cases, OCR rulings, policy recommendations from newsletters (e.g., *Disability Compliance in Higher Education*) and journal articles, and brief handouts from conferences with college administrators can be very effective in keeping them aware of their responsibilities to this group. Another excellent vehicle for informing the college of the effectiveness and utility of services is an annual report with a concise executive summary that is disseminated to campus administrators (see Appendix 13.2 on the CD-ROM for an example of such a report).

Student Affairs and Related Personnel

Any campus has many offices that play important roles in retention of and quality of life for students with learning disabilities. It is important for an LD program coordinator to become attuned to administrative functions and the organizational structure, especially in light of strategic planning and reform efforts in higher education. Student affairs departments, including the dean's office, the housing and residential life office, counseling and learning centers, and the placement office, are particularly important. Other offices, such as admissions, the library, and cooperative education, are also in need of knowledge about and sensitivity to this population. Meetings with the head of each office would be helpful, but a presentation at fall orientation or at a staff meeting would provide an opportunity for interactive training and dialogue about issues of particular importance to a specific office. Identifying a contact person in each office who will facilitate opportunities for a number of staff development activities is another productive approach.

Faculty

Often consultants are called in to encourage faculty to be more supportive in providing reasonable accommodations for students with learning disabilities. Unfortunately, this approach too often tends to be the first staff development activity. This may set up expectations for faculty before the campus infrastructure organization, as a whole, is ready to be supportive. It is therefore suggested that faculty training occur only after the elements described above are in place.

Morris et al. (1987) have noted that multiple in-service contacts over time are necessary to provide sufficient information about learning disabilities to improve faculty knowledge and attitudes. Tomlan, Farrell, and Geis (1990) have developed a sequenced model for the delivery of faculty in-service training, beginning with large-group training; followed by staff development for individual departments, divisions, or committees; and ending with individual meetings with faculty who have students with learning disabilities in class.

Staff development for faculty can be implemented in a variety of ways. Typically, only smaller institutions can succeed with mandatory training sessions for faculty. In some community colleges, course credit or continuing education units have proved effective in encouraging participation (Aune & Ness, 1991a).

Information on learning disabilities can also be included in training sessions on effective instruction, dealing with diversity, or legal issues. Most departments and schools have regularly scheduled meetings where staff development activities can be planned. An advantage to this approach is that instructional techniques, accommodations, and modifications particular to specific disciplines can be discussed.

Staff development for faculty can occur in a number of ways other than presentations. A meeting with a student to review diagnostic data and plan instruction or accommodations is an ideal time to invite a faculty adviser or course instructor. In this way, faculty have the opportunity to develop an understanding of what a learning disability is, how it affects learning, and what kinds of instruction ameliorate the disability's interference. Not so incidentally, when these meetings are data based and professional, the perception of LD service-delivery efforts is greatly enhanced.

Teaching students with learning disabilities to be self-advocates, with particular emphasis on explaining the disability and needed accommodations in plain language, will improve faculty understanding and promote acceptance. At some institutions, student panels at "disability awareness day" programs have proved very effective in reaching faculty and staff. In a similar vein, the newspaper and other campus media are vehicles for pieces by or about students with learning disabilities and information on disability rights and services. An effective strategy used by politically astute professionals is to identify "friends" (i.e., administrators, faculty, or staff who have a learning disability or have loved ones with such a disability) who can formally or informally advocate for services for students with learning disabilities. Finally, Web sites that include program information, eligibility criteria, and faculty handbooks can be helpful to faculty, staff, and students.

Training Alternatives

It is not acceptable to provide services to students with learning disabilities based only on good intentions or intuition (Miller, 1997). It is imperative that disability practitioners be appropriately trained to effectively ensure equal educational access for students with disabilities while also protecting the integrity of the college or university. There are several methods through which the skills of present and future disability practitioners may be developed, including preservice training and staff development through conferences, technical assistance, publications, and technology.

Preservice Training

Though only a small number of universities offer graduate coursework specifically designed for training disability service providers, it is one avenue through which both present and future personnel can develop their skills. St. Ambrose University, located in Davenport, Iowa, presently offers a program through which candidates can earn a master's of education degree in counseling with an emphasis on postsecondary disability service provision. The curriculum of this program is closely aligned with the AHEAD professional standards. The University of Connecticut Special Education Program offers students the option of obtaining advanced graduate training in postsecondary disability service provision (Dukes & Shaw, 1998). In addition, Shaw (1998) has developed a model graduate program of study based on AHEAD's professional standards. A sequence of specific postsecondary disability courses supported by generic courses (presented in Figure 12.4) would provide a program of study covering the five areas of professional standards (administration, direct service, consultation/ collaboration, institutional awareness, and professional development).

Staff Development

Clearly, long-term university-level training programs are an option for only a small percentage of current service providers. Even in cases where personnel

Graduate Education in Postsecondary Education and Disability: Meeting Professional Standards

The Association on Higher Education and Disability has developed professional standards for postsecondary disability personnel. There are 5 categories of standards (Administration, Direct Service, Consultation/Collaboration, Institutional Awareness, and Professional Development) and 61 specific items. What follows is a sequence of specific postsecondary disability courses supported by generic courses that would provide an effective program of study.

Required Courses

- Administration of Postsecondary Services for Students with Disabilities

- The Role and Function of Postsecondary Disability Personnel

- Assessment, Documentation, and Determination of Accommodations for Students with Disabilities

- Postsecondary Personnel: Collaboration, Supervision, and Staff Development

- Seminar: Legal and Ethical Issues

- Practicum: Postsecondary Disability Services

Generic Courses (depending on job description and candidate's skills)

- Instruction and Program Planning for Students with Disabilities
- Student Affairs
- Program Evaluation
- Counseling
- Budgeting
- The Adult Learner
- Assistive Technology for Students with Disabilities
- Transition
- Understanding Educational Research

Figure 12.4. Graduate program in postsecondary disabilities services. *Note*. From *Graduate Education in Postsecondary Education and Disability: Meeting Professional Standards*, by Stan F. Shaw, 1998, unpublished material, University of Connecticut, Neag School of Education, Storrs. Copyright 1998 by Stan F. Shaw. Reprinted with permission.

have had training for a career in disability service provision, ongoing professional development is absolutely necessary in this ever changing field. To illustrate, recent court decisions have articulated fundamental questions of postsecondary institutions regarding the provision of educational access for students with disabilities (e.g., who is disabled? what is appropriate documentation? what accommodations are "reasonable"? what are essential components of a college curriculum that cannot be modified?). These issues exemplify the complex problems facing postsecondary institutions and the need to provide personnel with periodic professional development opportunities (Shaw & Dukes, in press).

Since few disability practitioners have been explicitly trained for a career in postsecondary disability service, most may not be appropriately prepared to provide "state-of-the-art" assistance to their students. In addition, practitioners are responsible for providing a broad range of services to a heterogenous population of students, and such a vast body of competencies dictates a need for professional development on a range of topics. Finally, ongoing research regarding effective service provision is now being published requiring service providers to continually upgrade their knowledge and skills.

Training for administration and direct service personnel should begin with an appraisal of the needs of each group. An assessment of this type can typically be accomplished through a survey that might query respondents regarding their knowledge of topics such as eligibility for services based on diagnostic evaluation data, the understanding of legal issues relevant to college students with disabilities, and the identification of appropriate academic adjustments and aides depending upon disability. This can most effectively be achieved by using relevant items from AHEAD's professional standards to assess staff (Dukes & Shaw, 1999).

The University of Connecticut sponsors an intensive, 4-day professional development institute, the Postsecondary Learning Disability Training Institute (PTI), each June for professionals who work with college students with hidden disabilities (for more information visit www.cped.uconn.edu). PTI sessions, which are led by experts within their respective professions, are specifically designed to provide participants with concentrated training on an array of critical topics. The California Association on Postsecondary Education and Disability (CAPED) holds an annual conference intended to enhance training of postsecondary disability personnel (www.caped.org). State chapters of AHEAD (e.g., in New Jersey and Minnesota) frequently provide staff development.

Due to the rapid expansion of the use of technology in postsecondary education, distance-learning and disability-related educational resources are now available. These, of course, also serve as worthy professional development resources. For example, the University of Georgia offers interactive satellite teleconferences facilitated by some of the foremost disability experts in the country (www.coe.uga.edu/ldcenter). With the dramatic development of the Internet has come a plethora of disability-related educational information only keystrokes away. For instance, Disability Access Information and Support (DAIS) has established a Web site (http://www.janejarrow.com) that provides information, training, and technical assistance regarding issues of disability in higher education. Roxanne Cirelli, at Northern Essex Community College in Haverhill, Massachusetts, was one of the first to use a college Web site (www.necc.mass.edu/academics/staffdevelopment-LD) as a staff development tool for learning disabilities. For institutions interested in conducting in-house training, numerous video programs cover topics whose intent is the instruction of current service providers. A list of some of the video resources may be found in Appendix 12.1 on the CD-ROM or obtained from the HEATH Resource Center (800-54-HEATH; www.acenet.edu).

Conclusion

The field of postsecondary services for students with disabilities developed and matured through the decade of the 1990s. The field now has professional standards, program standards, and a code of ethics to guide postsecondary personnel in providing access for students with LD. Few personnel preparation programs provide professionals with formalized training to work with this population. It is, therefore, incumbent upon each institution to carefully consider its mission, resources, and administrative structure in order to employ the appropriate administrative and direct service personnel. Then a comprehensive, multifaceted, ongoing personnel development program must be implemented for all college faculty and staff as well as service-delivery personnel. Only with this kind of training effort across all aspects of campus life will the institution keep up with the rapidly developing field of postsecondary programming for students with learning disabilities.

Promoting Our Products

Strategic initiatives, enrollment management, reallocation of resources, outsourcing, seamless services—these buzzwords and phrases reflect the climate in higher education as discussions abound about the need for reform. In their efforts to attract students and beat the competition in the marketplace of enrollment, many institutions of higher education have unrealistically attempted to be all things to all people. Caution is advised for consumers seeking colleges that offer LD support services since claims of assistance are sometimes misguided attempts to recruit a viable cohort of students. The call for change is clear, as suggested by Dickeson (1999): "Most institutions can no longer afford to be what they've become" (p. 29). Review of academic programs is rampant on many college campuses with a goal of rendering informed decisions about reallocation of resources. Discussions appear in the literature about the benefits of program analysis whether the focus centers on academic programs or on student affairs functions. With administrative lines of reporting for personnel of Offices for Students with Disabilities typically resting in either academic or student affairs (Vogel et al., 1998), it is unlikely that services for students with disabilities will be exempt from the institutional process of review, analysis, and prioritization.

In some settings, discussions about reorganization of services are already occurring (J. Byron and D. Parker, personal communication, June 10, 1999). Awareness of this emphasis on reform affords our profession an opportunity to engage in study about how we do the business we do, how we promote our campus visibility, and what outcomes result for students with learning disabilities who use our services. The legal responsibility of institutions to assure equal educational access for students with learning disabilities is incontestable, but it behooves disability service providers to delineate a creative agenda to promote their contributions at a time when change is in the air.

This chapter will address the following areas:

- campus "marketing" of LD program activities;
- innovative ideas for showcasing LD services beyond the campus;
- program review and evaluation; and
- performance outcomes for students with learning disabilities.

Campus Visibility

Regardless of the mission or type of postsecondary institution, creative approaches to showcasing the office that assists students with LD should be a priority. In fact, the AHEAD program standards (1998) incorporate specific activities that "will assert the credibility and unique responsibilities of campus offices that serve students with disabilities" (W. Newmeyer, personal communication, June, 1998). Research by Anderson (1998a) provides further evidence that outreach initiatives such as information dissemination are viewed as an essential component of LD program services. The National Joint Committee on Learning Disabilities recently published a position paper on issues in higher education that emphasized information dissemination and collaboration activities to build campus expertise (1999).

Disability service providers should request or negotiate a position on relevant campus committees (e.g., academic standards, enrollment management, policy development). Ways of accessing committee membership may include working with a supervisor or colleague who is familiar with the process of committee assignment and can serve in a mentoring capacity in this regard; using informal networks of campus contact personnel in key positions; and asking for committee assignment in a straightforward manner based on the relevance of the committee's work to matters of significance for students with LD.

Institutional publications and presentations (e.g., orientation information sessions, residence hall workshops) are an important vehicle for promoting disability services and eliciting the participation of students who are often the most effective spokespeople for the OSD. A personal account by a student with a learning disability of his or her goals, challenges, and successes can be powerful. Service providers must also recognize and respect the fact that students often speak candidly about their perceptions of supportive and nonsupportive personnel, however, including faculty. Sometimes a story about a celebrity with a learning disability that gets national visibility or an episode on a television show can trigger an opportunity for campus publicity about an institution's services for students with disabilities.

Opportunities to broaden campus awareness of disability services should be part of an annual agenda of "visits" or "networking for fact finding" to offices and departments integrally and peripherally related to disability services. For example, human resources personnel may not have many occasions to work with the LD office, yet a brief meeting to share information about respective office functions may add to a web of campus supporters, especially on those serendipitous occasions when the office director or assistant dean just happens to have a child with a learning disability.

Every instance of providing consultation to faculty or administrators is an occasion to promote LD services by skillfully weaving in incidental facts about students with LD and their achievements or challenges. At the University of Connecticut, a letter of appreciation is sent to faculty whom students identify as helpful in their academic pursuits following every semester (see Appendix 13.1 on the CD-ROM). This affords an opportunity for sharing information about the LD program and statistics about student performance (e.g., GPA data for students with LD who receive support services). Recognizing and acknowledging support and thanking faculty, a form of communication that is glaringly sparse in the business world (Nierenberg, 1998), which many graduates will enter, can also reinforce the reflective skills of students.

Some postsecondary LD programs have created "support groups" of faculty who are particularly sensitive and creative in working with students with LD. At the University of Massachusetts–Amherst, a Faculty and Friends Network was established in 1994 by the Office of Learning Disabilities Support Services (Silver, Bourke, & Strehorn, 1998). According to the authors, the Peer Mentoring Network, a group composed of students with disabilities, has recognized approximately 100 faculty members who provide extraordinary accommodations. A wide range of disciplines are represented, including biology, computer science, sociology, English, education, music, comparative literature, engineering, and chemistry. An annual luncheon, an event that garners widespread attention, is held to publicly recognize the contributions of the Network. Such occasions often elicit the interest of the campus community and can serve as an entree to campus publicity through student newspapers and other campus periodicals.

Since the field of postsecondary disability services has formally adopted professional standards (Shaw et al., 1997), program standards (AHEAD, 1998), and a code of ethics (Price, 1997), disability service providers now have a platform from which to promote the functions of the OSD. Reference to these standards of practice should underlie requests for administrative support, an area of institutional commitment that may undergo scrutiny in light of the review and reform movements discussed by Dickeson (1999) and others (Kelman & Lester, 1997; Stanovich, 1999). Whether it be in the process of developing written policies and procedures, especially in light of the Boston University case (*Guckenberger v. Boston University*, 1997) and rulings of the OCR, or in making the case for staffing that includes a full-time professional to coordinate LD services (Anderson, 1998a), the time has come to move beyond the infancy of the field and showcase LD programs as an essential component of institutional initiatives.

With the ever expanding array of campus Web sites about student support services, electronic links can lead consumers as well as campus constituencies to information about LD services, policies and procedures, and frequently asked questions. In creating or updating Web pages, LD service providers should use the Web to visit the multitude of sites of other colleges and universities when deciding on format, content, and links. Developers of Web pages should also use the service of the Center for Applied Special Technology (CAST), called Bobby, which will scan a Web page and determine if anything on the page is inaccessible. The Bobby "stamp of approval" can be displayed on Web pages that pass scrutiny. More information about this service is available at http://www.cast.org/bobby. Detailed Web site design specifications are also delineated by Blackhurst and his colleagues at the University of Kentucky (Council for Exceptional Children, 1999). Particularly comprehensive and informative Web sites that provide disability information include:

- www.stanford.edu
- www.salt.arizona.edu
- www.unc.edu/depts/lds/
- www.csd.uconn.edu

External "Marketing"

Ideas for promoting LD support services in the broader community are illustrative of the creativity, commitment, and collaboration of administrators and program coordinators. With the increased emphasis on transition planning incorporated in the reauthorization of the IDEA in 1997, opportunities to advertise campus LD services abound, since postsecondary education is an option to be addressed with high school students at an earlier age (i.e., 14). For example, the state of New Jersey, with the support of the New Jersey Commission on Higher Education, has developed five regional centers for college students with learning disabilities, which have widespread visibility throughout the state. These centers are located at three public, open-enrollment, community colleges (Cumberland County College, Middlesex County College, and Ocean County College), and two 4-year institutions (Fairleigh Dickinson University and New Jersey City University) (A. Suchanic, personal communication, August 10, 1999). With financial support provided by the state grant and strong institutional fiscal backing, these centers provide an array of services, including transition assistance and information dissemination; direct student support; faculty and staff development; diagnostic services encompassing matriculated regional center students and those enrolled at noncenter campuses; and technical assistance and collaboration with other postsecondary institutions within each region. Clearly, the visibility of the regional centers, program evaluation data confirming their effectiveness (McGuire, 1999), and advocacy of key administrators at the state and institutional levels have all been instrumental in the continuation of this statewide grant-funded initiative, which began in 1986.

Specific examples of creative marketing strategies to promote LD programs beyond their proverbial four walls can be tailored to unique campus profiles. At Central Regional Connections, a New Jersey regional LD center located at Middlesex County College, an annual breakfast seminar is held for area secondary guidance counselors to discuss transition planning and services offered at the college. This has been instrumental in increasing the awareness of key referral agents about the guidelines for LD documentation that have been adopted on a statewide basis (J. Ikle, personal communication, July 14, 1999). Project Academic Skills Support (PASS), another of the New Jersey regional centers, located at Ocean County College, cosponsors the High School Leadership and Self-Advocacy Conference, designed for students from surrounding high schools who come to the campus to learn more from college students with LD about the importance of self-advocacy in the transition process (M. Reustle, personal communication, July 13, 1999). This is a win–win opportunity for promoting the leadership of college students who receive support services from PASS as well as the commitment of the college in offering its facilities to outside entities because of its support of the LD program.

The New Jersey statewide collaborative approach to promoting regional postsecondary LD support services extended its marketing by sponsoring a conference held in Spring 1999, Career Directions: Which Way to the Workplace? Planned by a committee with representatives from five postsecondary institutions (J. Ikle, personal communication, March 11, 1999), the conference offered a number of workshops for consumers, college personnel, and representatives from secondary schools on topics of transition to employment. Discussions about effective career planning, rights and responsibilities of employees with disabilities, workplace accommodations, and insights of successful adults with LD on life after school offered important information about strategies to enhance transition to employment. Apprising key campus administrators about professional activities such as this can heighten awareness of the important role LD service providers play in what is a critical objective of higher education: preparing students for employment.

At St. Louis Community College in Missouri, coordinated efforts to address transition issues involve frequent interactions with secondary school personnel, another approach to promoting the visibility of LD services beyond the campus community (L. Nissenbaum, personal communication, July 26, 1999). Staff from the Office for Students with Disabilities are assigned the responsibilities of coordinating visits by secondary resource room teachers, hosting high school visits for students with disabilities, and sponsoring College Nights to share information (e.g., documentation guidelines, responsibilities of students and colleges). A transition guide developed by the college is distributed at all functions hosted by the OSD. The always challenging issue of documentation has been tackled through meetings with the administrators of the secondary schools in the immediate catchment area who are in charge of the provision of psycho-educational assessment. Not only do these activities provide valuable information to potential consumers but they also focus a spotlight on the marketing activities of the LD services office, information that should be proactively promoted among campus administrators via annual reports and periodic updates.

Conducting a Program Review and Evaluation

Now that more than 2 decades have passed since the enactment of P.L. 94-142 (Education for All Handicapped Children Act) in 1975, policy makers as well as administrators are raising provocative questions that move the focus of special education evaluation at the K–12 levels beyond compliance with P.L. 94-142 procedural requirements and on to the efficacy of special education interventions.

One area of interest is the participation of students with disabilities in higher education. Enrollment in college is typically conditional upon completion of high school, although alternative paths (e.g., earning a GED) can lead to eligibility. Recent statistics document an increase in postsecondary enrollment among students with disabilities over the past 20 years. In 1986, 29% of people 16 or older who reported a disability of any type had either attended college or completed a bachelor's degree or higher (U.S. Department of Education, 1996). By 1994, that figure had risen to 45%. Yet data from the National Longitudinal Transition Study are disturbing (Blackorby & Wagner, 1996). Among students from 10 categories of disabilities who were 3–5 years out of high school, students in only 3 categories reported enrollment in postsecondary education with less frequency than students with learning disabilities: those with serious emotional disturbance (25.6%), mental retardation (12.8%), and multiple disabilities (8.6%). Approximately 31% of students with LD indicated that they had attended some type of postsecondary education when they or their parent(s) were interviewed 3–5 years subsequent to high school graduation.

In addition to interest in the participation of students with learning disabilities in higher education, there is an emerging, yet sparse, literature on adult outcomes for students who have enrolled in college. Studies by Gerber, Ginsberg, and Reiff (1992); Greenbaum, Graham, and Scales (1996); Adelman and Vogel (1990); Witte, Philips, and Kakela (1998); and Levine and Nourse (1998) addressed various aspects of adult outcomes for college graduates, including job satisfaction, salary, areas of occupation, and attitudes toward employment. In a longitudinal study of individuals with LD over a 20-year period, Raskind, Goldberg, Higgins, and Herman (1999) attempted to search for patterns of change and variables that were related to specific life outcomes. Extensive information was gathered from 41 participants who had been identified in childhood as LD and were enrolled at the Frostig Center, a specialized program for individuals with LD. The participants were described as successful or unsuccessful based on clinical judgments of outcomes in eight domains: employment, independence, family relations, crime and/or substance abuse, education, physical health, psychological health, and community relations and interests. Of the 41, 48% had either completed college or attended between 2 and 7 years. All but 5% had taken at least 2 semesters of postsecondary academic coursework or employment training. One of the variables that significantly differentiated the successful from the unsuccessful group ($p < .0001$) was the degree of education. In the successful group, 17 of the 21 (81%) were employed at year 20 of the study. The mean level of educational attainment for adults in this group was 15.1 years. For the unsuccessful group, 4 of the 20 (20%) were employed, and the mean level of education was 12.7 years. Although the authors accurately point to the limitations of this study, it represents a valuable snapshot over a long period of time and underscores the importance of higher education as it relates to adult outcomes. Levine and Nourse (1998) cite the widening wage gap between employed people who have attained varying educational levels, noting that graduation from college may be indicative of future potential. Statistics from the Department of Labor consistently corroborate this relationship between level of education and wage-earning capacity.

To date, there has been only one comprehensive attempt to examine outcomes for students with disabilities enrolled in postsecondary education on a national level. The National Center for Education Statistics (NCES) issued a statistical analysis report, "Students with Disabilities in Postsecondary Education: A Profile of Preparation, Participation, and Outcomes" in 1999 (Horn, Berktold, & Bobbitt). Four issues were examined through analysis of four different surveys: (1) representation of students with disabilities enrolled in higher education; (2) who among high school students with disabilities attends postsecondary education; (3) how well students with disabilities enrolled in postsecondary education persist to attain a degree or certificate; and (4) among college graduates, what are the early market outcomes and graduate school enrollment rates of students with disabilities. According to the report, "While students with disabilities are less likely to persist in postsecondary education and attain a credential, those who earn a bachelor's degree appear to have relatively similar early labor market outcomes and graduate school enrollment rates as their counterparts without disabilities" (Horn et al., 1999, p. vii). The authors note, however, that college graduates with disabilities were more likely than their nondisabled counterparts to be unemployed (11% versus 4%).

Historically, emphatic encouragement to address the effectiveness of postsecondary services for students with disabilities has met with limited response, no doubt related to the time demands and methodological complexities of conducting systematic program review and evaluation. Several studies provide valuable information including the work of Adelman and Vogel, who conducted an initial follow-up study of students who participated in a comprehensive support program at a small private liberal arts college in the Midwest (1990). Questionnaires were mailed to 89 former students, and those who did not respond by mail were contacted by telephone. Of the 89 subjects, 36 (40.4%) earned an undergraduate degree; 31 of those graduates completed the questionnaire. Twenty of the 89 students were required to withdraw from college because of academic failure. The authors reported that the impact of the graduates' learning disability continued into their work experience, although most reported the ongoing effectiveness of compensatory strategies such as spending extra time on the job or asking for help.

In another study, Vogel and Adelman (1990) examined various factors to determine graduation status of college students with learning disabilities (n = 110) and a stratified, randomly selected sample of nondisabled peers (n = 153). The sample with learning disabilities had participated for at least one semester between 1980 and 1988 in a highly structured support program that included subject-matter tutoring, remediation of basic skills deficits, assistance in accessing appropriate accommodations, and instruction in individualized compensatory strategies. College performance of the two groups was compared, and results indicated that grade-point averages for the LD sample were significantly lower than those of their peers at the end of each year of study as well as upon college exit. On the other hand, the authors reported a nonsignificant difference in the graduation rate between the two groups, as well as a nearly identical failure rate. They speculated that the similarity in graduation rates was evidence of program effectiveness, since the LD sample was not equivalent to the non-LD group, as indicated by lower college entrance examination scores and poorer high school performance. Given the dearth of comparative data from other postsecondary settings, Vogel and Adelman encourage the development of research in program effectiveness in order to determine whether any generalized patterns might exist that could result in important recommendations for high school personnel as well as for students with learning disabilities in their transition to college.

More recently, Keim, McWhirter, and Bernstein (1996) investigated the relationship between academic achievement and the use of academic support services among 125 university students with learning disabilities. Academic variables that were examined included advisement (i.e., the number of times per semester a student spoke with an advisor about academic progress), computer lab use (i.e., the amount of time a student used the lab at the support service office), tutoring (i.e., the average number of hours per semester of academic tutoring from the support service), and test accommodations. The dependent variable was cumulative grade-point average. Significantly higher cumulative GPAs among students with learning disabilities were related to use of the computer lab at high levels and utilization of advisement. Although there are limitations to the generalizability of results from this study, it represents an important attempt to more fully evaluate the impact of postsecondary services on students' academic performance.

It is clear that postsecondary LD service providers can profit from evaluation studies of special education services and the movement in higher education to engage in ongoing examination of program services and outcomes. As students with LD become more aware of protections assured them under Section 504, objective evidence of institutional compliance will be critical, as illustrated in recent court cases that have centered upon statutory obligations, including provision of academic adjustments (*Bartlett v. New York State Board of Law Examiners*, 1998; *Guckenberger v. Boston University*, 1997). Furthermore, data on outcomes and anecdotal reports of adults with LD who have pursued higher education have the potential to assist service providers in effectively addressing their needs through programmatic decision making.

There are many challenges in examining the results of services for postsecondary students with disabilities. In a discussion of their review of university programs that provide academic assistance for underprepared students, Levin, Levin, and Scalia (1997) rightfully point out that the focal point of such a review should be the support program's raison d'être. This observation is aptly relevant to LD disability support services and relates to Chapter 8 on policies, procedures, and program development. Without a clear program mission statement, goals, and objectives, a review of the services provided to students with LD will lack clarity, relevance, and utility.

In conducting a review of a program and examining the effectiveness of its components, the selection of an evaluation model should be carefully considered. Adelman and Vogel (1993b) suggest two approaches: the objectives-oriented model, and the naturalistic and participant-oriented model, both of which are extensively discussed by Worthen and Sanders (1987). Demonstrating the effectiveness of program components requires rigorous research methodology to account for the many variables that impact student outcomes. Caution must be exercised to avoid mistakenly attributing student outcomes to specific program elements in a cause-effect fashion given the multiplicity of intervening variables that may be positively or negatively related to outcomes. That said, without objective data it is difficult to render decisions and set programmatic priorities. At a time of change, disability service providers must walk a taut line: representing the institution as it ensures equal educational access without lowering academic or technical standards while recognizing that legal responsibility under the ADA cannot be abrogated on the basis of student outcomes (e.g., student retention and graduation). Compliance with the ADA is mandatory regardless of student performance.

An Approach to Postsecondary LD Program Evaluation

The CIPP Model

Although there are a myriad of evaluation models, Borich and Nance (1987) point out that the process-outcome method has frequently been used in educational settings. The CIPP model—context, input, process, and product evaluation—was developed by Stufflebeam et al. (1971) as a tool to assist in decision making. Stufflebeam (1988) offers a simple yet provocative evaluation purpose that is particularly relevant to the maturing area of postsecondary LD service delivery: "The most important purpose of program evaluation is not to prove but to improve" (p. 117). Stufflebeam et al. define educational evaluation as "the process of delineating, obtaining, and providing useful information for judging decision alternatives" (p. 40).

Table 13.1 illustrates an adaptation of the CIPP model to postsecondary LD programs. This should be considered as a dynamic model since its application will vary depending on each program's stage of development. For example, in settings where comprehensive LD programs are well established, the focus may center on the process and product components of the model. If initiatives are under way to establish an LD program or consider the most effective administrative model for delivery of LD services (e.g., a generic OSD; as a component of a Learning or Academic Skills Center), the initial evaluation questions may

Table 13.1
Application of the CIPP Model to Postsecondary LD Programs

	Purpose	Method
Context evaluation	To determine whether the goals and objectives of the LD program are pertinent to the needs of students to be served as well as to the institution	Use of needs assessments, surveys, diagnostic data, institutional documents
Input evaluation	To identify the services or approaches needed to assist students to meet program goals; to assess already existing campus resources (e.g., academic skills center, career counseling, mental health services, the OSD) to determine the most efficient approach to the delivery of LD support services	Review of the literature to determine effective intervention for students with learning disabilities; site visits to other institutions with exemplary LD programs; institutional "inventories" of other student services; consideration of staffing, space, and budgetary needs
Process evaluation	To determine the extent to which LD program services are implemented, as well as the efficiency of service delivery; to gather data for use in modifying the program; to monitor student participation in LD services; to account for program expenditures (e.g., tutoring, equipment); to determine student satisfaction regarding LD services	Establishment of a systematic data collection procedure and time line; identification of LD program staff roles and responsibilities for data collection; review of program records and documents (e.g., logs, contact hours); establishment of an advisory group including students, faculty, and appropriate administrative staff; conducting interviews and administering questionnaires to student consumers as well as campus personnel (e.g., faculty)

(continues)

Table 13.1 *Continued.*

	Purpose	Method
Product	To determine the effects or outcomes of LD program services; to relate program outcomes to program objectives and procedures; to render judgments about program outcomes (both positive and negative) for the purpose of modifying the program to become more cost effective and to better serve the needs of students with learning disabilities	Student pretest and posttest performance (e.g., self-efficacy surveys, *Learning and Study Strategies Inventory* [Weinstein, Palmer, & Schulte, 1987]); grade-point average data gathered over time; retention-graduation data; case studies of program participants; follow-up surveys of program graduates; experimental research designs including students with learning disabilities who received services and control groups (e.g., non-LD peers or documented students with learning disabilities who elected not to participate in LD services)

Note. From *Postsecondary Education for Students with Learning Disabilities: A Handbook for Practitioners,* by L. C. Brinckerhoff, S. F. Shaw, and J. M. McGuire, 1993 (rev. 1999). Copyright 1993 by PRO-ED. Reprinted with permission.

include context and input variables. Regardless of the "age" of LD services, some component of the model can readily be implemented, whether for making decisions, improving services, establishing mechanisms to document compliance, or responding to the institutional process of strategic planning.

Selecting the Evaluator

Another consideration in designing a program evaluation centers around who should actually conduct it. Clearly, the director or coordinator of the LD program will be more knowledgeable about its goals, objectives, and methods than someone who has no affiliation with the program. Having an *internal* evaluator brings the benefit of an understanding of the nuances of the institutional setting, its politics, and its climate but can also raise questions about objectivity. Use of an outside or *external* evaluator offers the benefit of an objective, neutral perspective, although the cost of hiring such a consultant can be problematic. Benefits may accrue from using a team approach to evaluation since multiple perspectives can result in "richness" of observations. Selection of an evaluator may be related to the role of the evaluation. Scriven (cited in Worthen & Sanders, 1987, p. 34) differentiates evaluation roles as follows:

- *formative*, which is intended to help planners and/or staff to improve the program; and

- *summative*, which is conducted to determine the extent to which the program has been effective.

Formative evaluation is conducted throughout a program's operation, whereas summative evaluation is typically undertaken at the end of a program. Worthen and Sanders (1987) note that the audiences for these evaluation roles differ: Program personnel constitute the "users" of formative evaluation information; potential consumers, policy and financial decision makers, and program staff would be interested in summative findings. They also suggest that both types of evaluation are essential. This is particularly true in the field of postsecondary LD programming, since many colleges have only recently formalized support services or are in the process of considering the development of more comprehensive service-delivery approaches. This formative-summative distinction was addressed by Stufflebeam (1988), who concludes that the CIPP model can be tailored to both functions. The evaluator should design and conduct activities for the purpose of planning, implementing, and refining programs as well as for rendering conclusions about the program's merit and worth. Decision making and accountability are not mutually exclusive in the CIPP model.

It is reasonable to suggest that, at the very least, LD program coordinators should assume a proactive role on their campuses in articulating a commitment to planning, conducting, and sharing program evaluation information. In reality, hiring an external evaluator may be a luxury, but that should not preclude ongoing, systematic data collection by internal program staff.

Planning for Evaluation

Whether the focus of evaluation is formative or summative, several general steps should be followed for conducting the evaluation. Herman, Morris, and Fitz-Gibbon (1987, pp. 27–41) outline these stages as follows:

1. Establish the boundaries of the evaluation. This should include identification of program activities that will be assessed as well as the responsibilities of the program's staff in the data collection process.

2. Determine appropriate methods of evaluation. Specification of program goals and objectives and the means or activities by which those goals will be met should be clarified at this stage.

3. Collect and analyze data to determine program implementation and progress in attaining outcomes.

4. Report findings and suggest changes.

Stufflebeam (1988) advised evaluators to approach the task as a process, not a product. This means that evaluation goals and procedures should be clearly spelled out prior to implementation of evaluation activities, but flexibility must exist in reviewing the process, revising it, and putting it into operation. Table 13.2 provides a summary of steps that can be followed in the design and implementation of a postsecondary LD program evaluation, as well as specific questions that should be considered in the process. This sort of preplanning is important in setting priorities and weighing which aspects of a program warrant evaluation in light of limited resources (Madaus, Airasian, & Kellaghan, 1980).

An Illustration of Program Evaluation: University of Connecticut Program for College Students with Learning Disabilities

As pointed out by R. Nelson and Lignugaris/Kraft (1989), there is no one approach to LD service delivery at the postsecondary level, nor are there yet data to substantiate the efficacy of one model over another. However, since their analysis of 31 articles about LD programmatic interventions, the field has advanced to the point where empirically validated program standards exist (Anderson, 1998a) and should now be used as a blueprint for services. Although the diversity of postsecondary institutions and organizational structures necessitates flexibility in the use of these standards, they provide a common basis for program development encompassing several functional categories. With their dissemination and use, more uniform approaches to the evaluation of program activities may evolve.

The following example illustrates one institution's method for conducting ongoing activities to assist in decision making and to document accountability and compliance. The University of Connecticut Program for College Students with Learning Disabilities (UPLD) has been in existence since 1984. A comprehensive program evaluation plan has been developed and revised, and formative evaluations have been conducted regularly (see Appendix 13.2 on the

Table 13.2
Planning for a Program Evaluation

Steps	Considerations
1. Consider the audience.	• College administrators? • Potential consumers (e.g., incoming freshmen, transfer students, nontraditional students)? • Faculty? • Program staff? • Legislators? • Research community? • Governing boards?
2. Determine the purposes of the evaluation.	• Justify program needs (e.g., staff, space, equipment) and administrative lines of reporting (e.g., academic or student affairs)? • Monitor student achievement? • Document compliance with Section 504 and the ADA? • Monitor cost effectiveness? • Analyze use and effectiveness of program services? • Assist in developing institutional policy (e.g., course substitution policies)?
3. Focus the evaluation.	• Context? • Product? • Input? • Formative? • Process? • Summative?
4. Determine appropriate methods of evaluation.	• Quantitative? • Qualitative?
5. Collect and analyze data.	• Time line established? • Data collection instruments and procedures identified? • Staff responsible for data collection identified? • Data collection monitoring plan in place? • Plan for organizing, coding, storing, and retrieving data? • Data-analysis procedures identified?
6. Report and utilize data.	• Format for reporting and communicating results (e.g., formal written reports, memos, executive summaries, presentations)? • Plan in place for generating report? • Follow-up activities planned?

Note. From A Step-by-Step Approach to the Evaluation Process, by J. M. McGuire, 1992 (rev. 1999), unpublished material, University of Connecticut, Postsecondary Education Disability Unit, Storrs. Copyright 1992 by J. M. McGuire. Reprinted with permission.

CD-ROM for a complete report of an annual review). Various components of the evaluation plan illustrate that flexibility is a key in "individualizing" evaluation activities to meet institutional and setting needs.

Goals and Objectives

With an overall goal of promoting student independence and success within the context of a very competitive academic environment, 10 program objectives were developed in 1990 and revised in 1999 to reflect ongoing program review and revisions. These objectives, delineated in Table 13.3, focus on various program functions that are conducted on a day-to-day basis by the staff, which includes the director, the associate director, and graduate assistants. The program model, as portrayed in Figure 13.1, is student centered, promoting interaction among a number of existing campus resources; it operates on the assumption that it is unrealistic and inefficient in a university setting for the LD staff to be "all things to all students." If a student with a learning disability requires individual counseling, a referral may be made to the campus department of counseling services or mental health services office. This "interactive," inclusionary model requires ongoing collaboration among campus personnel (e.g., participation in staff meetings) and is reflected in objectives 5 and 9 in Table 13.3. With respect to the goal of promoting student independence, a three-step continuum of services (see Figure 13.2) serves as the foundation for assisting students to master learning strategies and study and self-advocacy skills. Throughout their enrollment at the university, students are actively involved in decision making regarding their specific needs, and they are encouraged to work toward increasing self-sufficiency. Themes that abound in the literature regarding self-determination, autonomy, and reframing the learning disabilities experience to emphasize potential for success (Gerber, Reiff, & Ginsberg, 1996; Reiff, Gerber, & Ginsberg, 1997) drive every aspect of UPLD's "model" of services.

Evaluation Plan and Methods

In operationalizing the evaluation plan, annual data collection focuses on the process or means by which services are implemented to meet program objectives. Product or outcome evaluations (e.g., retention and graduation rates) are also conducted at the end of each year. A longitudinal database is in place so that follow-up research on adult outcomes and employment data can be implemented. In fact, a study of graduates is currently in progress to examine their

Table 13.3
Program Objectives of UPLD

1. To facilitate the effective transition of incoming freshmen and transfer students with learning disabilities by assisting them in the process of gathering documentation that meets the university's *Guidelines for Documentation of a Specific Learning Disability*.

2. To provide a comprehensive packet of information about UPLD to incoming students who have self-identified in order to receive services including accommodations.

3. To serve as a referral source for unidentified full-time university students with learning difficulties.

4. To provide a continuum of services designed to increase independence and success for students with learning disabilities.

5. To promote awareness among university faculty, staff, and administration of learning disabilities, types of reasonable accommodations and academic adjustments, and the function of UPLD as a campus-wide resource.

6. To work with students in determining and documenting their eligibility for specific accommodations such as course substitution and full-time student status.

7. To serve as a training site for graduate students seeking to expand their competencies in administration, direct services, and research in programming for college students with learning disabilities.

8. To conduct a program of research and evaluation based on services offered through UPLD.

9. To disseminate information regarding UPLD to appropriate campus personnel and other professionals (e.g., high school guidance counselors).

10. To conduct outreach activities at the local, state, and national levels to promote awareness of postsecondary opportunities for people with learning disabilities.

Note. From *The University of Connecticut Program for College Students with Learning Disabilities: 1998–99 Annual Report*, by J. M. McGuire and J. W. Madaus, 1999, Storrs: University of Connecticut, Postsecondary Education Disability Unit. Copyright 1999 by J. M. McGuire and J. W. Madaus. Reprinted with permission.

employment status, salary, use of workplace accommodations, and self-efficacy regarding employment. Preliminary analyses have yielded compelling evidence of success among graduates.

In order to assure timely, comprehensive data collection, it is critical to identify staff responsibilities as well as a time line for gathering information. This relates to job functions and ongoing staff development, as discussed in Chapter 12. When tasks are laid out before the academic year begins, there is less opportunity for any misunderstanding about who is responsible for each activity. Table 13.4 presents an example of an evaluation plan that specifies the

(text continues on p. 477)

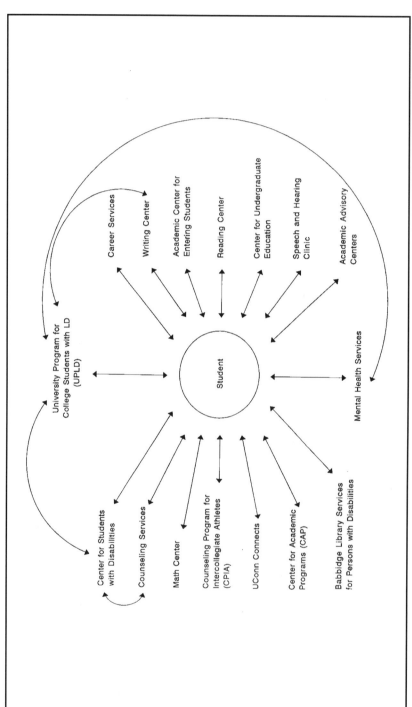

Figure 13.1. University program for college students with LD. *Note.* From *University of Connecticut Interactive Model of Support Services for Students with Learning Disabilities*, by J. M. McGuire and R. Pollack, 1988 (rev. 1999), unpublished material, University of Connecticut, Storrs. Copyright 1988 by J. McGuire. Reprinted with permission.

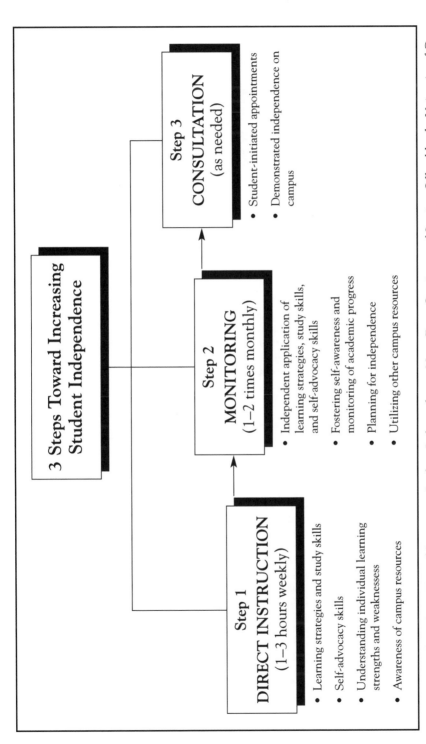

Figure 13.2. Three Steps Toward Increasing Student Independence. *Note.* From *Continuum of Services Offered by the University of Connecticut Program for College Students with Learning Disabilities (UPLD)*, by A. V. Litt and J. M. McGuire, 1989, Storrs: University of Connecticut Program for College Students with Learning Disabilities. Copyright 1989 by V. Litt and J. M. McGuire. Reprinted with permission.

Table 13.4
Comprehensive Evaluation Implementation Plan

Focus of Evaluation	Method of Data Collection	Person(s) Responsible	Date of Data Collection
Program Services	**Program Records**		
Transition planning for self-identified first-year and transfer students	Admissions database; log of discussions; documentation review sheet	Director/staff	May/June; December/January
Information dissemination to incoming students	Log of packets sent by student name and date; log of returned paperwork	Director/staff	May/June; December/January
Referral services	Referral log of students, date(s) of service, outcome	Director/staff	January; May
Continuum of direct student services	Learning specialist monthly summary sheets; semester summary reports; individual student semester goals	Associate director	Monthly; January; May
Faculty, staff, and administration awareness activities	Faculty contact log; departmental contact log; information dissemination log	Director; associate director; staff	December; May
Personnel training	Pre- and post-competency surveys; learning session logs; staff training and weekly seminar evaluation	Director; associate director	Monthly; May
Outreach activities	High school contact sheet; summary sheet for professional presentations	Director; associate director	June
Program Outcomes			
Academic performance (GPA)	Transcripts; comparative institutional data	Graduate assistant	January; June
Retention and graduation	Transcripts; comparative institutional data (source: *Annual University Fact Book*); exit interviews	Graduate assistant; director	January; June
Student independence	Project records; interviews	Associate director	April

(continues)

Table 13.4 *Continued.*

Focus of Evaluation	Method of Data Collection	Person(s) Responsible	Date of Data Collection
Program Outcomes (*continued*)			
Student's self-perceptions of learning strategies and study skills	Pre- and post-administration of *LASSI* (Weinstein, Palmer, & Schulte, 1987)	Associate director	Upon program entry and progression to consultation
Attitudes of students, staff, faculty, and administration	Questionnaires/surveys	Director; associate director	April; annually
Personnel development	Pre- and post-competency survey; staff seminar evaluations; job placement	Director; associate director	September; May; ongoing

Note. From *The University of Connecticut Program for College Students with Learning Disabilities: Administrative Procedures*, by J. M. McGuire and J. W. Madaus, 1999, unpublished materials, University of Connecticut, Postsecondary Education Disability Unit, Storrs. Copyright 1999 by J. M. McGuire and J. W. Madaus. Reprinted with permission.

focus of the evaluation (program services and program outcomes) and the method, staff, and time line for data collection.

Evaluation Results Including Performance Indicators

Comprehensive program records are examined on an annual basis to document the use of services provided by UPLD. Appendix 13.3 on the CD-ROM includes examples of data collection forms used throughout the year. For example, learning specialists, graduate students who are trained to work directly with students with LD (objective 7 in Table 13.3) who access services at any level of the UPLD continuum (objective 4 in Table 13.3), complete a log following every student session. These logs provide rich documentation of the needs of university students with LD (e.g., organizational skills to address the intense reading demands of a liberal arts curriculum; error analysis of tests to identify sources of error or incorrect responses; use of visual strategies such as mapping as a brainstorming aid in the writing task). Monthly attendance summaries are used to calculate the ratio between scheduled learning sessions and actual student attendance. This kind of information is important in monitoring trends in service delivery. For example, if the attendance of students scheduled to work with a specific staff member shows a marked decrease over the course of a semester,

it may signal a need to conduct periodic observations of the staff member working with those students to offer suggestions about style and/or relevance of the
strategy instruction.

Objective 6 (see Table 13.3) constitutes another area for evaluation. The
university has officially adopted a set of policies and procedures for students with
disabilities (see Appendix 8.1 on the CD-ROM) that include guidelines for
requesting a course substitution. UPLD is the official university agent charged
with assisting students to determine their eligibility for this accommodation in
either the foreign-language or quantitative requirement of the General Education curriculum. Through the use of program records, UPLD has documented
that since the program's initiation in 1984, 23.5% of the university undergraduates with learning disabilities have been eligible, petitioned, and been approved
for a course substitution (McGuire & Madaus, 1999). Ninety percent of the
requests for substitution were in the area of foreign language, a reflection of
the nature of the learning disability that is reflected in some students by a
severe language-processing disorder.

Annually a questionnaire is administered to student consumers to gather
their feedback about program services. The biggest challenge in this aspect of
program evaluation is response rate: it is difficult to recruit students, especially
as they become increasingly independent, to spend a few moments filling out a
survey at the end of the academic year. Despite this drawback, the ratings of
student consumers have been overwhelmingly favorable across years of service
delivery. A longitudinal table of mean student ratings for the 29-item questionnaire is updated every year as a component of the historical records UPLD
maintains. On occasion, student responses to open-ended questions have been
insightful and useful in fine-tuning the training of UPLD staff to be responsive
to specific student requests.

As indicated in objective 8 in Table 13.3, UPLD conducts an evaluation to
examine the performance indicators of retention and graduation of students
with LD. Admittedly, this is a time-consuming and methodologically complex
task, yet it is a critical one in an era of campus-wide attention on enrollment
management and student outcomes. Administrators take particular notice of
UPLD's ability to produce information such as that displayed in Figure 13.3.
Few, if any, of the other campus student support services can attest to the academic outcomes for their constituencies. A dismissal rate of 8% for academic
reasons is data of immense value, although it is important to reiterate the danger of rendering false claims about program impact without conducting an
empirically rigorous study, including a control group (Mohr, 1995). Nonetheless, when questions about student outcomes are met with information such
as that displayed in Table 13.5, administrators are hard-pressed to contest the
value of program services. It is equally impressive to consumers that program

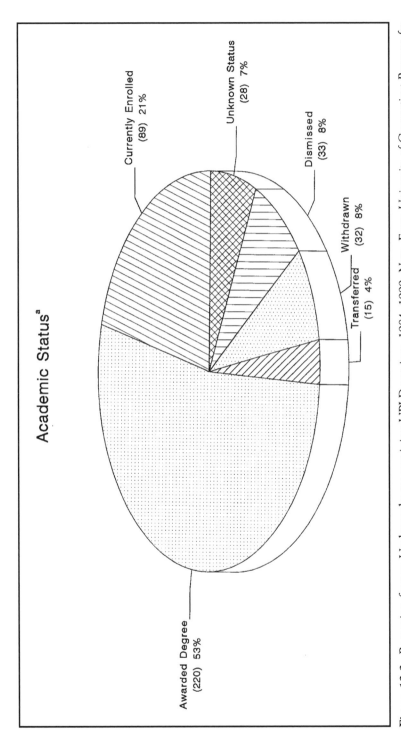

Figure 13.3. Retention figures: Undergraduates receiving UPLD services, 1984–1999. *Note.* From *University of Connecticut Program for College Students with Learning Disabilities: 1998–99 Annual Report*, by J. M. McGuire and J. W. Madaus, 1999, unpublished material, University of Connecticut, Postsecondary Education Disability Unit, Storrs. Copyright 1999 by J. M. McGuire and J. W. Madaus. Reprinted with permission.

[a]Figures total more than 100% because of rounding. Criterion for inclusion: matriculated students only (n = 417 as of 6/99).

Table 13.5

Six-Year Graduation Rates of All Freshmen and
UPLD Students with Learning Disabilities: 1983–1991

Cohort Year	All Freshmen[a]	UPLD Students with Learning Disabilities
1991	67.5%	76%
1990	67.7%	62%
1989	69.7%	80%
1988	68.4%	75%
1987	71.8%	74%
1986	68.4%	82%
1985	68.6%	72%
1984	65.6%	78%
1983	69.6%	100%
Mean	68.6%	77.3%

Note. From *The University of Connecticut Program for College Students with Learning Disabilities: 1998–99 Annual Report*, by J. M. McGuire and J. W. Madaus, 1999, unpublished materials, University of Connecticut, Postsecondary Education Disability Unit, Storrs. Copyright 1999 by J. M. McGuire and J. W. Madaus. Reprinted with permission.
[a]Comparative data provided by Office of Institutional Research.

administrators are able to directly answer their queries about how successful the LD program is by providing them with a table of comparative information about the 6-year graduation rates for LD and non-LD undergraduates.

Challenges in Examining Programs and Services

Postsecondary LD service providers should take heed of developments on a national level regarding accountability and the emphasis on outcomes. Standards-based reform constitutes the foundation for educational change in the 1990s (U.S. Department of Education, 1998). According to this annual report to Congress on the IDEA, one of the four concepts encompassed by standards-based reform is accountability, "a systematic method to assure those inside and outside the educational system that schools and students are moving toward desired goals" (Brauen, O'Reilly, & Moore, 1994, p. 2).

In addition to the concern about standards at the elementary and secondary levels, the reform and accountability activities in higher education are focusing heavily on evidence of productivity. Enrollment management and examination of retention and graduation rates are and will continue to be critical elements for study in institutions of higher education. In her survey of 131 experts in the field of postsecondary LD services who are internationally recognized researchers and service providers, Anderson (1998a) validated program evaluation as an essential service standard. The panel of experts agreed that the following components are fundamental to the evaluation process in which all LD service offices should engage: (a) data collection to monitor use of LD services; (b) student feedback to measure satisfaction with LD services; (c) data collection to measure effectiveness of LD services; and (d) dissemination of program evaluation data to administrators. Admittedly, the time demands and staff competencies required to collect, organize, and evaluate data comprise challenges, but creative solutions are available. For example, in some undergraduate and graduate courses, students are required to conduct field-based inquiry projects. The role of a program director should include responsibility to scout out such opportunities to involve other campus constituencies in the evaluation process. With a climate that focuses on institutional outcomes, offices charged with examining student progress toward degree attainment or with contacting alumni to ascertain employment status are viable "partners" to team with in these evaluation activities.

At the federal level, the Government Performance and Results Act of 1993 (GPRA) was enacted to bolster eroding public confidence and increasing concerns about governmental accountability. It is a statute that requires all federal agencies to manage their activities with attention to the consequences of those activities. In response to this regulation, the U.S. Department of Education prepared a strategic plan (U.S. Department of Education, 1997) such that every initiative it sponsors must address performance indicators. In the recent grant competition sponsored by the U.S. Department of Education's Office of Post-secondary Education, *Demonstration Projects to Ensure that Students with Disabilities Receive a Quality Higher Education Program* (U.S. Department of Education, 1999a), applicants (institutions of higher education) were required to indicate their methods of addressing the following performance indicators: increased attendance and degree attainment of students with disabilities. It is imperative that the field of postsecondary LD services remain abreast of these developments relating to student outcomes and assert its leadership in engaging in dialogues about the complexities of performance-based measurement in an area of federally mandated compliance to assure equal educational access.

In addition to the emphasis on student outcomes, the advice of Stufflebeam (1988, p. 140) about the critical role evaluation plays in program improvement should not be taken lightly:

We cannot make our programs better unless we know where they are weak and strong and unless we become aware of better means. We cannot be sure that our goals are worthy unless we can match them to the needs of the people they are intended to serve. We cannot plan effectively if we are unaware of options and their relative merits; and we cannot convince our constituents that we have done good work and deserve continued support unless we can show them evidence that we have done what we promised and produced beneficial results.

At the same time, assurances that students' rights to equal educational opportunity are guaranteed must not be tied to outcome data regarding their retention and graduation. Section 504 guarantees equal opportunities, not guaranteed outcomes, unfair advantage, equal results, or equal achievement for persons with disabilities. Postsecondary LD service providers must cautiously distinguish between the need to comply with statutory regulations requiring reasonable accommodations and academic adjustments, and the desire to provide effective, comprehensive "programs." Evaluation of the services provided for students with learning disabilities is critical in documenting institutional compliance, but evaluation of how successful programs are helping students achieve postsecondary goals is a different issue.

If the principles of scientific research are to serve as guidelines for conducting program evaluations, methodological problems must be addressed. D. T. Campbell and Stanley (1966) and Cook and Campbell (1979) discuss a number of threats caused by external variables that can jeopardize the validity of conclusions drawn from outcomes. Factors such as subject maturation and the impact of history (i.e., "specific events occurring between the first and second measurement"—D. T. Campbell & Stanley, 1966, p. 5) are particularly relevant in interpreting outcomes relating to college students with learning disabilities. The question of whether their success or lack of success in achieving goals is related to program intervention is complex and cannot be considered without careful research design.

In addition, identification of control groups may be a problem. If access to program services is determined by student self-identification, there may be a bias factor, since it is reasonable to assume that students with learning disabilities who choose to receive services and reasonable accommodations may possess characteristics (e.g., motivation, self-discipline, and persistence) that distinguish them from those students who remain anonymous. Random assignment of self-identified LD students to an experimental or control group is not feasible since withholding services is neither legal nor ethical. Random selection of a control group of nondisabled peers must address the question of group equivalency. To match students with learning disabilities with a control group drawn from the college undergraduate population, variables such as aptitude, high school performance, and achievement scores must be considered.

Conclusion

Postsecondary service providers are in a dynamic position of awareness about queries they can expect from consumers and administrators, and legislative and advocacy groups, regarding the impact of services for college students with learning disabilities. It is not surprising that discussions are occurring about compliance with Section 504 and the effectiveness and cost of disability services. As George, George, and Grosenick (1990) so aptly describe for elementary and secondary levels, service providers should expect a call for a more comprehensive approach to evaluation to "determine whether programs are designed on the basis of sound theoretical principles, operate competently . . . and impact positively on those students who are receiving services" (p. 24).

From a pragmatic perspective, the importance of developing policies and procedures attests to a need for objective data. As institutions face increasingly complex issues relating to the assurance of educational access for students with disabilities, it is imperative that disability service providers proactively project areas that are prime for challenges and systematically gather data for decision making and policy development. If a student consumer were to claim discriminatory treatment in the admissions process, for example, because of a disability, data from both admissions personnel and disability services would be required to respond to such a legal challenge. Sound institutional planning, including the development of policies, must evolve from the tenets of equal opportunity and rational information. The adage "Forewarned is forearmed" continues to be profoundly appropriate.

CHAPTER

Future Directions in Postsecondary Learning Disability Programming and Service Delivery

It is important to acknowledge and appreciate the tremendous change and development that has taken place in the postsecondary LD field during the decade of the 1990s. Only after looking at the previous decade can we fully understand the progress made and the knowledge gained, so we will be ready to meet head-on the issues posed at the beginning of the 21st century.

Where Have We Been?

As the 1990s began, it was clear that this "new" population of college students with learning disabilities was growing at a tremendous rate. Disability professionals in postsecondary institutions had to learn to serve students who needed something other than physical access. For the first time, colleges had to regularly address issues of identification, assessment, documentation, and alternative approaches to accommodation and instruction. Questions had to be answered regarding who was a qualified college student with a learning disability, and the admissions process had to be reevaluated. A new type of professional position, that of a learning disability specialist, was created to address these critical issues.

Candidates for that position were then identified, hired, and trained (often, unfortunately, on the job). Postsecondary institutions were challenged to delineate the roles and responsibilities of faculty and staff to provide access to this population of students with "hidden" disabilities in the face of limited information and almost no data on effective policies, procedures, or instructional interventions (Shaw, 1997b). These substantive matters required attention during a period of fiscal crises caused by decreased revenues that resulted from a dip in the cohort of college-age students, national economic problems that challenged the survival of many postsecondary institutions, and reduced governmental support for higher education.

The good news is that much of the "heavy lifting" in regard to the issues noted above has been accomplished. Most institutions of higher education in the United States and Canada are currently serving a population of students with so-called hidden disabilities (i.e., LD, ADHD). This population now constitutes about half the population of all identified students with disabilities. More than 1,300 colleges and universities now offer programs and services specifically for students with learning disabilities (Kravets & Wax, 1999). Learning disability specialists at these institutions are guided by the professional standards and code of ethics discussed in Chapter 12, which were called for in the first edition of this book. Similarly, the "proactive development of effective policies and procedures" (Brinckerhoff et al., 1993) has been accomplished by many postsecondary institutions; they have typically developed initial policies that help faculty and staff deal with basic issues regarding access and accommodations.

The documentation guidelines for LD and ADHD discussed in Chapter 7 have given significant direction for colleges in attempts to define, determine the eligibility of, and provide appropriate accommodations for students with learning disabilities. Although the laws affecting postsecondary education have not become more prescriptive, many of the court decisions noted in Chapter 3 have furnished the field with direction and greater understanding of issues related to the provision of equal access. The recently developed program standards for all disability programs (Shaw & Dukes, in press) and essential support services for learning disability programs (Anderson, 1998a) described in Chapter 8 provide clear benchmarks for individual institutions to determine the kinds of services they will offer that are consistent with their institutional mission.

The state-of-the-art information presented in the previous chapters gives postsecondary personnel the knowledge needed to advance to the next level of effective services for students with learning disabilities. College students with learning disabilities are no longer the "new kids on the block" but, rather, the major focus of postsecondary education for students with disabilities. The remaining sections of this chapter will identify opportunities for continued growth and change that need to be addressed if we are to fulfill our preeminent role in higher education and disability. They encompass both programmatic and professional issues, including:

- self-determination as the sine qua non of learning disability services;
- fostering transition to postsecondary education;
- faculty as collaborators;
- data-based service provision;
- professional development and training;
- the widespread need for field-based research on effective interventions and services; and
- dealing with disability backlash.

The changes that have occurred in this fast-paced field directly relate to the nature of these future developments. In the previous edition of this book, changes typically related to large, international initiatives such as the professional standards, code of ethics, program standards, and documentation guidelines discussed earlier. Most of the pressing needs today, on the other hand, are institution based. The responsibility in the new millennium is for learning disability personnel to work with their colleges and universities to operationalize and adapt the global developments of the 1990s into processes and procedures that will effectively serve students with learning disabilities in their own institutions.

Where Are We Going?

Self-Determination

This entire book has been written from the perspective that fostering self-determination is the sine qua non (i.e., the absolute prerequisite, essential condition) of postsecondary learning disability programming. Every decision, policy, instructional procedure, discussion with faculty, and interaction with students must be considered in light of the "prime directive": fostering self-determination. To put it another way, when a decision has to be made, postsecondary personnel should not ask what a judge in the 2nd Circuit would determine in relation to

Section 504 or what OCR would think, but rather how self-determination can be fostered.

What Is Self-Determination?

When the word *self-determination* is mentioned, the terms *control, goals, choice,* and *self-confidence* should come to mind. Self-determination has been defined as "one's ability to define and achieve goals based on a foundation of knowing and valuing oneself" (Field & Hoffman, 1994, p. 164) and as "the attitudes, abilities, and skills that lead people to define goals for themselves and to take the initiative to reach these goals" (Ward, 1988, p. 2). The characteristics of self-determined individuals include the following (Field & Hoffman, 1996a, b; Field, Hoffman, & Spezia, 1998):

- the ability to make decisions,
- the ability to solve problems,
- the ability to set goals and attain them,
- self-evaluation skills,
- an internal locus of control,
- positive attribution of efficacy and outcome expectancy, and
- self-knowledge.

Students with learning disabilities are often described with the opposite characteristics (e.g., learned helplessness, external locus of control, poor problem solving and planning skills). This reinforces the critical importance of self-determination and the challenge faced in teaching such skills.

Encouraging and Supporting Self-Determination

Three important characteristics of environments support self-determination and should be provided by postsecondary institutions. The most important is the availability of *self-determined role models*. This clearly begins with self-determined postsecondary learning disability professionals who demonstrate the characteristics described above. The role of postsecondary disability professionals has been debated in recent years (Shaw, 1997b, 1998). The lines have been drawn between advocate and gatekeeper, or traffic cop v. custodian. Clearly, a better approach is based on whether the professional is self-determined. A self-determined professional has established personal and professional goals, institutional policies and procedures that provide for collaborative decision making and effective problem solving, and personal and program evaluation activities that reinforce self-efficacy and positive outcomes. The role of the learning disability professional should foster self-determination in students, faculty, staff, and administration.

Over the years, many postsecondary disabilities professionals have seen dependence-provoking actions such as inappropriate labeling, provision of services without appropriate documentation, waivers and substitutions that were not substantiated by the data, and content tutoring that may have helped a student succeed without learning the material. Self-determination in students is encouraged by requiring them to self-advocate to faculty and administration, giving the student information about a process (e.g., requesting a course substitution or making an appeal) for which the student is responsible, and teaching learning strategies (test taking, note taking, metacognitive strategies, etc). Although this may initially be a time-consuming process, students in these instances are developing self-determination skills that will make them more independent and in need of fewer support services in subsequent semesters. In addition, these students can then become role models for future students seeking support services. A good rule of thumb is that if students who have received disability services for several semesters function in the same dependent way as they did when they entered, close examination of the program's philosophy and commitment to fostering independence is warranted.

Too often faculty have been considered the enemy. On listservs and at meetings of postsecondary disability personnel, talk abounds about controlling or managing uncooperative, uncaring, or ineffective faculty members. Disability service providers are touted as "the experts" with the final say about accommodations. It is time to develop a collaborative perspective that enables faculty to have the commitment, knowledge, and skills to be our allies in working with students with learning disabilities. The degree to which we have self-determined faculty who take responsibility for all their students, including those with disabilities, will be indicative of our capacity to fulfill our own responsibilities. It is certainly a productive goal to have increasing numbers of faculty seeking personnel from the disability office for help in teaching their students.

Two additional characteristics of environments that encourage self-determination are *opportunities for choice* and *availability of student supports* (Field et al., 1998). These both relate to the role that the postsecondary learning disability professional has developed. Students with learning disabilities must be afforded choices so that they can learn to take responsibility for their own lives in a supportive college setting. If the professional is the advocate, then the student can't self-advocate. The professional must be the manager and guide of the process and should provide the support necessary for the student to learn to navigate that process. The professional provides information, asks questions, and encourages student reflection as the student learns self-determination.

Fostering Transition

One of the initial challenges in encouraging self-determination relates to the transition of students from secondary to postsecondary education. Many students, parents, high school counselors, and diagnosticians have difficulty understanding the differences between secondary and postsecondary realities in light of the differences in legal mandates relating to service delivery between those levels.

In spite of the transition information and recommendations presented in Chapter 2, many students have still not experienced effective transition planning. A cause for alarm, therefore, are students seeking postsecondary education who have:

- not taken an appropriate course of study for the type of college to which they seek admission;

- received course waivers that are not justified by data and will not be continued in college;

- made a poor match between their strengths and weaknesses and their proposed major or the curricular expectations of the postsecondary institution;

- received content tutoring to get them through difficult courses and maintain their grades but have not been taught the learning strategies essential for becoming productive, independent learners in college;

- become accustomed to the prescriptive requirements and supports of the IDEA and expect them to continue in college (e.g., free diagnosis, special classes, curriculum modifications);

- poor or out-of-date documentation that they expect will be acceptable to the postsecondary institution; and

- never learned to advocate for themselves as required in postsecondary education because their parents never relinquished the advocacy role to them.

It is, therefore, necessary for professionals to be proactive in fostering collaboration and communication across secondary and postsecondary education.

Historically, personnel from many small, private postsecondary institutions have demonstrated the kind of behavior that all professionals should model. This has included participating in parent organizations (e.g., LDA, CHADD) and giving presentations at conferences for parents, high school counselors, and secondary special educators, as well as having college students with learning disabilities speak to high school students. Given the promulgation of final IDEA regulations in 1999, there is much new information about operationalizing transition to postsecondary education to focus efforts of postsecondary disability personnel for years to come. Having well-informed, self-determined applicants who have prudently selected a college and program of study based on up-to-date diagnostic data will provide an ideal starting point from which postsecondary professionals can refine and monitor effective services leading to positive student outcomes.

Faculty as Collaborators

A major initiative during this new decade centers around postsecondary disability professionals working with faculty and administration to improve the instructional environment for *all* students. Unfortunately, disability personnel have traditionally had an "unhappy alliance" with faculty. Over time, that attitude has improved to a willingness to "tolerate" professors. That has to change if we are going to truly collaborate with faculty and encourage them to be the key players for students with disabilities as they take responsibility for teaching all their students. This approach not only requires a change in attitude but also will be a major departure from the historical paradigm for dealing with students with LD in public schools: identify, label, pull out (i.e., to special services). It is also a change from the updated paradigm under the IDEA: identify, label, put back (i.e., into inclusive classrooms). Instead, we suggest that the goal should center on serving students with disabilities in universally accessible learning environments. Just as a student in a wheelchair needs no disability services in a physically accessible environment, a student with LD may need no disability services in an instructionally accessible environment.

The time is ripe for such a major change in the instructional arena. A revolution in instruction is occurring at institutions of higher education in the following ways:

- students are being seen as "consumers" who are entitled to an effective education;

- college-wide programs and offices are being created to foster effective instruction;

- there is an increased emphasis on evaluating courses and rewarding excellence in instruction; and

- the availability and use of technology offer professors many relatively easy options for meeting the needs of the diversity of students in their classes.

An instructionally accessible environment can be created if:

- professors implement effective instructional techniques (e.g., advance organizers, scaffolding, supplemental instruction);

- course syllabi, test information, alternative readings, lecture notes, and protocols of tests are available to students on line;

- a range of approaches are available to students to demonstrate mastery of the material and competence in the subject; and

- professors take responsibility for the learning of all their students.

This will not be easy to achieve, but it is an important goal. Spending time and effort on the following activities will be a most productive use of the expertise of disability professionals:

- Focus on effective instruction for all students, not just on accommodations and modifications for a few.

- Include discussions of disability access in all campus efforts to improve instruction.

- Make efforts to improve instruction a priority of your office.

- Collaborate with faculty resource labs, learning centers, faculty orientation programs, and undergraduate and academic affairs deans in committees and programs to foster instructional access for all.

These are appropriate activities for disability personnel because they will serve to increase access for students with disabilities in ways that do not directly involve the provision of services from disability offices. They are, therefore, supportive of self-determination for students with disabilities and acknowledge that faculty are valuable resources for all students. Furthermore, just as research has demonstrated that extra time on tests benefits students with LD more than students without disabilities (Runyan, 1991; Weaver, 1993), effective instruction will be shown to be significantly more beneficial for students with LD than for students without cognitive disabilities.

Developing Data-Based Services

As noted in Chapter 3, the decade of the 1990s provided considerable legal support and clarification for postsecondary disability services. While in no way meaning to denigrate past achievements and the rights protected, it is important to reinforce remarks made by the authors in 1993 regarding the role of laws in serving college students with disabilities (Brinckerhoff et al., 1993). Although Section 504 and the ADA were not developed specifically for higher education and were not intended to delineate effective postsecondary disability service-delivery practices, some postsecondary personnel seem to inappropriately see their role as no more than implementors of the law.

The issue is not whether institutions of higher education should strive to be in compliance with the law by providing equal access for students with learning disabilities. In fact, it is important for practitioners to document an institution's commitment to equal opportunity. The challenge for professionals in the field at this time is to identify "best practices" so that service delivery can be improved based upon current research. Rather than merely reacting to ongoing court cases and OCR rulings (some of which may be confusing or even lead to poor educational outcomes), professionals must be proactive in establishing the parameters of effective service delivery (Brinckerhoff et al., 1993). In Canada, services are provided without the constraints of laws. Professionals in the United States need to appreciate the protections of the law while not losing sight of what is a reasonable, professionally sound, data-based plan of action.

In the early 1990s we had little more than the law to guide us. Now, however, we have professional guidance in the form of professional and program standards, a code of ethics, and documentation guidelines. The development of program standards (Anderson, 1998a; Dukes & Shaw, 1999) has demonstrated a core of necessary services across types and competitiveness of institutions. Furthermore, the misperception that service provision should be determined by Section 504/ADA is completely undermined by data indicating that program components were consistently rated as essential across institutions in Canada and the United States that were operating under different legal standards. In addition, as demonstrated in this book, a growing body of research identifies effective practice.

In the new century, each college has a road map to follow that demonstrates what can and should be done. Although each institution will still have to determine its approach and style based on its unique mission, essential services will become more uniform in the first decade of this century. Colleges will distinguish themselves in terms of how effectively they implement the necessary services, not by whether they merely provide the services. As detailed in

Chapter 13, collecting data on outcomes and using evaluation data to market and justify programs and budgets will become increasingly important components of disability services. The section that follows discusses the training that personnel need to develop and implement these complex and multifaceted disability programs.

Professional Development and Training

As noted in Chapter 12, skilled professionals are critical to developing state-of-the-art services for college students with learning disabilities. The problem facing our field is best illustrated by a recent conversation we had with a college administrator who wanted to develop a comprehensive learning disability support program. He had questions about components to include and policies to be developed, but he had no professionals with the skills or training to implement such a program. In that case, neither the resources (i.e., fiscal resources and institutional commitment) nor the staff development plan was in place. Even if those elements were in place, neither qualified personnel nor intensive staff development opportunities were available. The lack of trained personnel is a critical dilemma facing postsecondary disability services as the new century begins. The training recommended in Chapter 12 is available only on a limited basis. With fewer than a handful of graduate training programs for postsecondary disability professionals, it is questionable whether even a college with the resources could hire someone with the skills described in the AHEAD professional standards. Short-term staff development opportunities are similarly limited and are often not data-based, comprehensive, or focused on the critical skills specified in the professional standards. For example, although the Internet has tremendous potential as a staff development vehicle, it seems that its primary use for "training" at this time is the DSSHE listserv. Postsecondary personnel use the listserv to seek advice and information from their colleagues, but it should not be viewed as a training tool. Using it may be inexpensive and quick, but that approach has the same drawbacks as seeking financial advice on line—you may get good direction, but you risk getting information that is uninformed, out of date, or self-serving. The following sections discuss professional development and training considerations for the future.

National Efforts

Given that the training of postsecondary disability personnel is such a critical need and that the development of professional standards provides a focus for training, a number of national initiatives will likely develop over the coming decade. As described in Chapter 12, those standards can lead to the development of graduate training efforts for postsecondary disability personnel. For current personnel, they should encourage the development of comprehensive training efforts that result in a certificate of mastery for those postsecondary personnel who achieve a prescribed level of competence.

The postsecondary disability field should consider the efficacy of moving to even more formal efforts. Should postsecondary disability personnel need some kind of certification based on training and experience or licensure from a professional organization? Such a move would likely enhance the skill, recognition, and remuneration of postsecondary personnel. It would also come with a price in terms of training and administrative costs.

Likewise, the development of program standards brings with it the possible consideration of some form of accreditation or program approval process. These initiatives are not being recommended at this time or being predicted to occur at any time in the future. They would have a profound effect on postsecondary disability services, and, therefore, must be carefully weighed and objectively debated.

Federal Initiatives

The Amendments to the Higher Education Act of 1998 provided millions of dollars for professional development and technical assistance for faculty and administrators to ensure that students with disabilities receive a quality postsecondary education (see www.ed.gov/offices/OPE/disabilities/grantees). Several of the projects were stipulated to focus on students with learning disabilities. This federal initiative could significantly affect the staff development issues discussed here and in Chapter 12. Projects began in September 1999 at almost two dozen institutions, including Columbia University, University of Kentucky, University of Arizona, University of Connecticut, University of Minnesota, University of Kansas, and University of Utah, with resultant products to emerge in subsequent years. Hopefully, comprehensive training opportunities and effective uses of emerging technologies will become available to faculty and disability professionals who could benefit most from these cutting-edge initiatives.

Field-Based Research

In spite of the rapid development in this field over the last decade, there is still a tremendous need for field-based research regarding postsecondary services and outcomes for students with learning disabilities. Relatively little data exist on the efficacy of various interventions and accommodations. We need to know what students with learning disabilities perceive as helpful and what instructional approaches and accommodations faculty have found most useful. Except for the comprehensive report from the National Center for Education Statistics (Horn, Berktold, & Bobbitt, 1999) and limited data from individual colleges, there are few national outcome data for college students with disabilities.

This problem is due in part to the very limited number of researchers who are in positions to pursue this area of inquiry. Postsecondary practitioners are often affiliated with student affairs rather than the academic unit of the institution of higher education. Typically, neither their role description nor their reward system fosters the implementation of research. College professors, who have a stake in research and publication, are often restrained by ties to teacher certification programs and public school supervision.

To answer any research question with confidence, we need more stringent quantitative research methodology that does the following:

- describes students with learning disabilities in a way that allows replication of the study;

- uses samples of students across several institutions or service-delivery models;

- uses a control or, at least, a contrast group;

- provides enough time for implementing the intervention to give it a reasonable opportunity to be mastered; and

- delays final data collection until enough time has passed to assess use, maintenance, and generalization.

In a similar vein, qualitative research (Berg, 1995; Bogdan & Biklen, 1992) and research involving survey methodology (Gable & Wolf, 1993) must follow established protocols.

Disability service professionals who are not themselves conducting research may want to contact researchers (e.g., faculty and doctoral students) in their institution or neighboring institutions so they can work collaboratively. The offer of a readily available sample of students and important research questions in a developing field with many outlets for publication could be very enticing. Postsecondary personnel responsible for institutional research including retention and performance outcomes constitute another resource for cooperative initiatives.

Dealing with Disability Backlash

During the past decade, it has been open season on the Americans with Disabilities Act, college students with disabilities, and, particularly, college students with learning disabilities (Cannon, 1996). Malevolent or, at least, uninformed attempts to denigrate postsecondary students with learning disabilities and those who work with them have received attention on television and in print media (e.g., *Good Morning America, New York Times, Chronicle of Higher Education*). The creation of "Somnolent Samantha" by Jon Westling, president of Boston University, was correctly condemned by the judge's decision in the *Guckenberger v. Boston University* (1997) case as representing Westling's belief "that students with learning disabilities were often fakers who undercut academic rigor" (Westling, September, 1997). Nevertheless, Westling justified his beliefs and actions, claiming victory over what he called the self-serving disability apologists.

While we appreciate the legal interpretations of Section 504 and the ADA, which guarantee equal access, some decisions are difficult to interpret and explain, but easy to ridicule. Challenging issues faced by the postsecondary learning disability community include diagnosis, definition, documentation, and *reasonable* accommodations. As we saw in the political arena at the end of the 20th century, negative advertising and the "politics of personal destruction" are easy tools for hustlers, hypocrites, and those with limited credibility themselves. Some lessons, however, can be applied to our field when such attacks occur in the future.

We can't simply hope that no one will read or believe negative articles that paint inaccurate pictures of the postsecondary disability landscape. We need to be vigilant and prepared to respond to administrators and faculty with reasoned arguments and data demonstrating that such negative claims are unfounded or premised on stereotypes. Publications that print negative material should be overwhelmed with responses documenting their errors and false charges. It is critical that these responses not be in a tone or style similar to the offending piece. Any response we write must be sound and professional (parents or students who wish to respond should, on the other hand, be encouraged to express their outrage). Even more important, we cannot expect others to write a response; we all need to respond. Copies of our responses should be sent to the supervisors and benefactors of the offending party (e.g., board of trustees; college alumni; student, faculty, and community newspapers; advertisers). This is unquestionably "playing hard ball," and the tens of thousands of students with disabilities who can be forever scarred by attacks deserve such support.

Professionals face challenging problems on a daily basis. Decisions about admission, acceptability of documentation, who is otherwise qualified, what is a significant impairment, and what is an appropriate accommodation or substitution or waiver request must be made on a regular basis. Although these are challenging and complex issues, professionals should expect to be accountable for all their decisions. In fact, we should have program evaluation and reporting mechanisms in place that allow us not only to respond to questions and challenges but also to proactively share such data with faculty, staff, and administrators.

The various standards and guidelines now in place provide the security of national benchmarks to which we can compare our performance. The code of ethics can guide professionals toward ethical decisions when faced with difficult dilemmas. The problem we have to guard against is taking the path of least resistance when faced with a challenge. If we give in to parental or administrative pressure, if we "compassionately" provide disability services to a student who is not eligible, if we accept documentation that doesn't meet established standards, if we provide or deny an accommodation in the face of contradictory data, then we are setting up disability services to be at the mercy of any critic or challenger. It would be easy to say "just do it right"—but not very helpful. The better approach, as described throughout this book, is to develop policies and procedures that clearly specify criteria and provide for collaborative, data-based decision making. In that way, decisions can be made objectively and the disability office is not defending its own decision but is helping the institution in delineating its process—two scenarios that have remarkably different dynamics. In the former case, the disability office has a problem, while in the latter case, disability professionals are in the enviable position of helping the administration solve its problem.

In order to deal with disability backlash, as well as the other challenges discussed in this chapter, the postsecondary learning disability field is going to need new leaders who are willing to take responsibility for growth and the change necessary to take us to the next level.

Who Will Lead?

Historically, the postsecondary disability field has walked softly and not carried a big stick. The belief seemed to be that the apparent needs of students with disabilities would encourage sympathetic postsecondary administrators to provide the necessary supports and accommodations. That approach seems to have worked, given the changes that have occurred in recent decades. Now that there are so many students who are seeking equal access, however—most without apparent disabilities—indifference, lack of support, and sometimes backlash are evident. Leaders are needed who are political, collaborative, and wise. As students with disabilities and support services become more visible and costly, disability professionals must be more proactive in securing the support and resources needed to effectively do our jobs.

Although this book has demonstrated the tremendous growth that has occurred in recent years, the postsecondary disability field is still young. In fact, recent developments foster a professionalism and vigor that are completely new. Professionals are needed who grasp these new realities and are ready and willing to move ahead. Although most people reading these words are probably not thinking of themselves as leaders or potential leaders, they may be underestimating themselves and missing the opportunities available for dedicated professionals. For example, we recall when current leaders in the field such as chapter authors Jane Byron, Joe Madaus, David Parker, Lynda Price, and Sally Scott were graduate students interested in college students with learning disabilities at universities around the country. They have now had a national impact by applying their skills and knowledge to training, writing, and research.

What is different today is that more leaders are needed. As noted previously, the challenge in this decade is helping each institution fulfill the challenges inherent in the national standards and guidelines that have been established. So leadership is first institutional. Once effective institutional interventions, procedures, processes, and outcomes are developed, emerging information technologies will provide easy access to a broader constituency (state or provincial, regional, national, and international). To become such a leader, an institution must apply dynamic strategies to effect change.

Principles and processes for effective leadership in higher education for students with learning disabilities (adapted from Shaw, 1994) are as follows:

1. *Set goals.* Goals that are not specified cannot be met. It is important for personnel in each program to collaboratively set short-term (e.g., 3 months or 1 year) and long-term (e.g., 3–5 years) goals.

Effective strategic planning approaches have been developed to support this process (Markides, 1997; Porter, 1996). The strategic planning process is important because it keeps program goals in line with the broader institutional goals and mission. Once goals are established, it is important to disseminate and publicize them so all staff, students (current and prospective), and personnel in relevant programs and departments throughout the institution know the philosophy and goals of the disability program. Periodically review progress, revise goals and time lines, and refocus on meeting the goals.

2. *Be data driven.* It is very easy to follow the path of least resistance, do what others are doing, or do it the way it has always been done. Leaders and state-of-the-art programs take the time to:

- review the latest research;

- collect ongoing data on programmatic procedures and evaluation data on outcomes; and

- develop and revise programs based on a and b above.

In this way professionals will have data on what has proven effective to share with others and make the modifications noted next.

3. *Monitor and adjust.* No program can claim to have implemented best practices for all elements of services. The data collection described above (and in Chapter 13) provides for an ongoing review of strengths and weaknesses and fosters revisions and changes as necessary. This commitment to correcting and adjusting encourages risk taking because problems can be quickly addressed. Taking risks is the platform for developing unique, and, possibly, nationally recognized, programs and interventions. For example, Byron and Parker (Chapter 10) at the University of North Carolina–Chapel Hill identified weaknesses in the ability of their program to meet the needs of students with ADHD. Over a period of years they made adjustments that resulted in the development of "model" ADHD services.

4. *Strive for excellence.* Managing a program that meets the letter of the law is a very limited goal. The American way is to seek to develop a "better mousetrap." Leaders strive for excellence. Professionals begin each day wanting to do the best job they can. Disability personnel need to maintain a vigilance that does not accept mediocrity or "going through the motions." The following questions and comments should permeate your program:

- Can we do it better?
- Is there a more productive approach?
- Who has a better idea?
- Let's do another draft.

Such an approach develops a team that will seek and accept nothing but the best.

5. *Collaborate.* The concept of *team* is much broader than immediate staff. An effective leader works with the entire institutional community, which can engender campus and community support. Cooperative efforts with other campus and community agencies must be carefully cultivated. Professional collaboration often evolves from a personal relationship developed over time. Involving key campus constituencies in important decisions and keeping them apprised about the mission and effectiveness (e.g., in collecting and disseminating evaluation data) of the Office for Students with Disabilities are time consuming but will lead to priceless understanding and commitment.

6. *Develop staff*. Too often disability staff have not been effectively trained for current, much less projected, roles and responsibilities. Skilled leaders encourage staff support and respect by making a commitment to provide ongoing training. Time and resources must be obtained to provide for regular staff seminars, the development of training manuals, and participation in conferences and institutes that develop skills and foster staff commitment and professionalism.

7. *Encourage self-determination for everyone*. Personnel who are empowered to contribute to decisions and trained to competently complete their responsibilities will act professionally and go the extra mile to fulfill program goals. Including staff in data collection and problem solving will lead to support for change that results from that process. As noted previously, self-determined faculty will be more supportive of program initiatives; self-determined students will represent the efficacy of your program to the entire institution; and self-determined administrative personnel who are involved in disability decision making will be allies when political or fiscal challenges occur.

8. *Get a life*. Disability personnel have chosen a demanding profession that requires a significant commitment of time, energy, and emotions. The threat of litigation; bureaucratic hassles; limited resources; and challenges from faculty, staff, and students can be exhausting. Some part of each person's life should be supportive, refreshing, and loving so that we can bring a degree of peace and strength to the professional challenges we face. Relationships with friends, spouse or partner, children, and supportive colleagues must be cultivated and honored. The oft-quoted adage "Work hard, play hard" must be a reality in each of our lives. Endeavors that are uplifting, life affirming, enjoyable, or relaxing such as hobbies, vacations, spiritual pursuits, reading, volunteering, or just plain "crashing" need to be included in our lives on a regular basis, or we will not be effective professionals for very long. Becoming a leader is not a sprint but a marathon. The degree to which we bring a complete, rested, and loving person to the office will affect the amount of productivity, joy, and collaboration in our professional lives.

In conclusion, disability personnel have the opportunity to make a tremendous difference in the lives of the students and colleagues with whom we work. We are in a field that needs our participation and offers almost unlimited challenges and opportunities. We look forward to working (and playing) collaboratively with you as we seek to achieve the personal and professional goals we have set. We would appreciate hearing your thoughts, comments, and experiences on the topics raised in this book:

- Dr. Loring Brinckerhoff, lbrincker@aol.com
- Dr. Joan McGuire, mcguire@uconn.edu
- Dr. Stan Shaw, sfshaw@uconn.edu

REFERENCES

Ackerman, T. (1995). Review of the *Wechsler Individual Achievement Test*. In J. C. Conoley & J. C. Impara (Eds.), *The twelfth mental measurements yearbook* (pp. 1125–1128). Lincoln, NE: Buros Institute.

Adelman, H. S. (1989). Toward solving the problems of misidentification and limited intervention efficacy. *Journal of Learning Disabilities, 22,* 609–612.

Adelman, P. B., & Vogel, S. A. (1990). College graduates with learning disabilities—employment attainment and career patterns. *Learning Disability Quarterly, 13,* 154–170.

Adelman, P. B., & Vogel, S. A. (1993a). Issues in the employment of adults with learning disabilities. *Learning Disability Quarterly, 16,* 219–232.

Adelman, P. B., & Vogel, S. A. (1993b). Issues in program evaluation. In S. A. Vogel & P. B. Adelman (Eds.), *Success for college students with learning disabilities* (pp. 323–343). New York: Springer-Verlag.

Adler, R. (1989). Library orientation: Intervention strategies for students with learning disabilities. *Journal of Postsecondary Education and Disability, 7*(2), 45–52.

Administrators debate: Who should pay for intern's accommodations? (1998, July). *Disability Compliance for Higher Education, 3*(12), 5.

Adults with learning disabilities: Preliminary analysis of survey data. (1994, September/October). *LDA Newsbriefs,* 3–4.

Aksamit, D., Morris, M., & Leuenberger, J. (1987). Preparation of student services professionals and faculty for serving learning disabled college students. *Journal of College Student Personnel, 28,* 53–59.

Albert J. J., & Fairweather, J. S. (1990). Effective organization of postsecondary services for students with disabilities. *Journal of College Student Development, 31,* 445–453.

Alexander, J., & Rolfe, J. (1991). "College interview preparation form." Highland Park, IL: Highland Park High School.

Alliance for Technology Access. (n.d.). *ATA resource centers.* San Rafael, CA: Author. [Online]. Available: http://www.ataccess.org/MemberDirectory/atacenters.html

Alliance for Technology Access. (n.d.). *Vendor members of the Alliance for Technology Access.* San Rafael, CA: Author. [Online]. Available: http://www.ataccess.org/MemberDirectory/atavendors.html

Alster, E. (1997). The effects of extended time on algebra test scores for college students with and without learning disabilities. *Journal of Learning Disabilities, 30*(2), 222–227.

American Coaching Association. (n.d.). *Dedicated to helping individuals with attention deficit disorder.* [Brochure]. Lafayette Hill, PA: Author.

American Council on Education. (2000). *Student issues.* [Online]. Available: www.acenet.edu/washington/distance_ed/2000/03march/distance_ed.html#top

American Psychiatric Association. (1980). *Diagnostic and statistical manual of mental disorders* (3rd ed.). Washington, DC: Author.

American Psychiatric Association. (1987). *Diagnostic and statistical manual of mental disorders* (3rd rev. ed.). Washington, DC: Author.

American Psychiatric Association. (1994). *Diagnostic and statistical manual of mental disorders* (4th ed.). Washington, DC: Author.

American Psychological Association. (1985). *Standards for educational and psychological testing*. Washington, DC: Author.

Americans with Disabilities Act of 1990, 42 U.S.C. § 12101 *et seq.*

Anderson, P. L. (1993). Issues in assessment and diagnosis. In L. C. Brinckerhoff, S. F. Shaw, & J. M. McGuire (Eds.), *Promoting postsecondary education for students with learning disabilities* (pp. 89–136). Austin, TX: PRO-ED.

Anderson, P. L. (1998a). *Essential support service components for students with learning disabilities at postsecondary institutions in North America: A consensus based determination.* Unpublished doctoral dissertation, University of Connecticut, Storrs.

Anderson, P. L. (1998b, Winter). Essential support services for postsecondary students with learning disabilities: Highlights from a Delphi study. *Postsecondary Disability Network News, 32,* 1–2, 5, 6.

Anderson, P. L., & Brinckerhoff, L. C. (1989). Interpreting LD diagnostic reports for appropriate service delivery. In J. J. Vander Putten (Ed.), *Proceedings of the 1989 AHSSPPE national conference* (pp. 92–100). Columbus, OH: Association on Handicapped Student Service Programs in Postsecondary Education.

Anderson, P. L., Halliday, K., & McGuire, J. M. (Eds.). (1997). *Resource guide of support services for students with disabilities in Connecticut colleges and universities.* Storrs: Connecticut Postsecondary Disability Technical Assistance Center, University of Connecticut.

Anderson, P. L., & McGuire, J. M. (1991). *Connecticut Postsecondary Learning Disability Technical Assistance Center: Annual report, 1990–1991.* Storrs: A.J. Pappanikou Center on Special Education and Rehabilitation: A University Affiliated Program, University of Connecticut.

Anderson-Inman, L., Knox-Quinn, C., & Horney, M. A. (1996). Computer-based study strategies for students with learning disabilities: Individual differences associated with adoption level. *Journal of Learning Disabilities, 29*(5), 461–484.

Ariel, A. (1992). *Education of children and adolescents with learning disabilities* (2nd ed.). New York: Merrill.

Arizona State University, Disability Resources for Students. (1998). *Independent contractor form* [Program Material]. Tempe: Author.

Arizona State University, Disability Resources for Students. (1999). *STA 402-1: Disability resources for students—General policy.* Tempe: Author. [Online]. Available: http://www.asu.edu/aad/manuals/sta/sta404-01.html

Arizona State University, Disability Resources for Students. (1999). *STA 402-06: Testing accommodations for students with disabilities.* Tempe: Author. [Online]. Available: http://www.asu.edu/aad/manuals/sta/sta402-06.html

Arizona State University, Disability Resources for Students. (1999). *STA 402-11: Note-taking accommodations for qualified students with disabilities.* Tempe: Author. [Online]. Available: http://www.asu.edu/aad/manuals/sta/sta402-11.html

Arizona State University, Disability Resources for Students. (1999). *STA 402-19: Variance from degree requirements—Course equivalency alternatives for students with disabilities.* Tempe: Author. [Online]. Available: http://www.asu.edu/aad/manuals/sta/sta402-19.html

Arizona State University, Disability Resources for Students. (2000). *STA 402-08: Alternative print formats, recorded textbooks, and texts for interpreter preparation.* Tempe: Author. [Online]. Available: http://www.asu.edu/aad/manuals/sta/sta402-08.html

Arizona State University, Disability Resources for Students. (n.d.). *Academic test/quiz administration authorization form* [Program Material]. Tempe: Author.

Arizona State University, Disability Resources for Students. (n.d.). *Accommodating students with disabilities: A guide for faculty and other teaching staff.* Tempe: Author. [Online]. Available: http://www.asu.edu/drs/facresources.html

Arizona State University, Disability Resources for Students. (n.d.). *Diagnostic summary and accommodation recommendations* [Program Material]. Tempe: Author.

Arizona State University, Disability Resources for Students. (n.d.). *Faculty letter regarding timely request for test administration* [Program Material]. Tempe: Author.

Arizona State University, Disability Resources for Students. (n.d.). *Foreign language petition information form* [Program Material]. Tempe: Author.

Arizona State University, Disability Resources for Students. (n.d.). *Full time enrollment equivalency verification form* [Program Material]. Tempe: Author.

Arizona State University, Disability Resources for Students. (n.d.). *Math petition information form* [Program Material]. Tempe: Author.

Arizona State University, Disability Resources for Students. (n.d.). *Note taker information* [Program Material]. Tempe: Author.

Arizona State University, Disability Resources for Students. (n.d.). *Reading policies* [Program Material]. Tempe: Author.

Arizona State University, Disability Resources for Students. (n.d.). *Reading request form* [Program Material]. Tempe: Author.

Arizona State University, Disability Resources for Students. (n.d.). *Recommended strategies, compensation techniques, technology and referrals* [Program Material]. Tempe: Author.

Arizona State University, Disability Resources for Students. (n.d.). *Test registration form* [Program Material]. Tempe: Author.

Armbruster, B., & Anderson, T. (1981). Research synthesis on study skills. *Educational Leadership, 39,* 154–156.

Assenza, A. (1994). Dyslexia: A misunderstood disability. Part I. *The Rebus Institute REPORT, 3,* 3, 4.

Assistive Technology Act of 1998, 29 U. S. C. S. § 3630 *et seq.*

Association of American Medical Colleges. (1993). *The Americans with Disabilities Act (ADA) and disabled students in medical school: Guidelines for medical schools.* Washington, DC: Author.

Association on Higher Education and Disability. (1997a). *Essential standards for the administration of postsecondary offices for students with disabilities.* Columbus, OH: Author.

Association on Higher Education and Disability. (1997b). *Guidelines for documentation of a learning disability in adolescents and adults.* Columbus, OH: Author.

Association on Higher Education and Disability. (1998). *AHEAD program standards.* Columbus, OH: Author.

Attorneys create accessibility guidelines to assure internship opportunities. (1999, May). *Disability Compliance for Higher Education, 4*(10), 1, 4.

August, G. J., & Garfinkel, B. D. (1990). Comorbidity of ADHD and reading disability among clinic-referred children. *Journal of Abnormal Child Psychology, 18,* 29–45.

Aune, E. (1991). A transition model for post-secondary-bound students with learning disabilities. *Learning Disabilities Research and Practice, 6*, 177–187.

Aune, E., & Ness, J. (1991a, July). *In service training for students with disabilities in the Minnesota Technical College system.* Paper presented at the AHSSPPE National Conference, Minneapolis, MN.

Aune, E., & Ness, J. (1991b). *Tools for transition: Preparing students with learning disabilities for postsecondary education.* Circle Pines, MN: American Guidance Service.

Aviezer, P. A. (2000). *Peterson's game plan for getting into college.* Princeton, NJ: Thompson Learning.

Ball State University, Disabled Student Development. (n.d.). *Tape-recording agreement form* [Program Material]. Muncie, IL: Author.

Ballard, J., Ramirez, D., & Zantal-Wiener, K. (1987). *Public Law 94-142, Section 504, and Public Law 99-457: Understanding what they are and are not.* Reston, VA: Council for Exceptional Children.

Banerjee, M. (1999). *Adapting traditional accommodations and services to alternate learning environments for students with disabilities.* Paper presented at the annual conference of the Association on Higher Education and Disability, Atlanta, GA.

Barkley, R. A. (1990). *Attention-deficit hyperactivity disorder: A handbook for diagnosis and treatment.* New York: Guilford Press.

Barkley, R. A. (1995). A closer look at the *DSM–IV* criteria for ADHD: Some unresolved issues. *ADHD Report, 3*(3), 1–4.

Barkley, R. A. (1997). *ADHD and the nature of self-control.* New York: Guilford Press.

Barkley, R. A. (1998, September). Attention-deficit hyperactivity disorder. *Scientific American* [Online]. Available: http://www.sciam/com/1998/0998issue/0998barkley.html

Barnett, L. (1993). *Disability support practices in community colleges: Selected examples.* Washington, DC: American Association of Community Colleges.

Barr, M., & Fried, J. (1981). Facts, feelings, and academic credit. In J. Fried (Ed.), *Education for student development: New directions for student services* (No. 15). San Francisco: Jossey-Bass.

Barr, V., Hartman, R., & Spillane, S. (1995). *Getting ready for college: Advising high school students with learning disabilities.* Washington, DC: HEATH Resource Center.

Barr, V., Hartman, R., & Spillane, S. (1998). Getting ready for college: Advising high school students with learning disabilities. *The Postsecondary LD Report.*

Bartlett v. New York State Board of Law Examiners, 156 F.3d 321 (2d Cir. 1998).

Barton, R. S., & Fuhrmann, B. S. (1994). Counseling and psychotherapy for adults with learning disabilities. In P. J. Gerber & H. B. Reiff (Eds.), *Learning disabilities in adulthood: Persisting problems and evolving issues* (pp. 82–92). Stoneham, MA: Andover Medical.

Behrens-Blake, M., & Bryant, B. (1996). Assessing students with learning disabilities in postsecondary settings. In J. R. Patton & E. A. Polloway (Eds.), *Learning disabilities: The challenges of adulthood* (pp. 93–135). Austin, TX: PRO-ED.

Bell, C. R. (1989, October). Malcolm. *Training and Development Journal, 43*, 38–43.

Benner, S. M. (1998). *Special education issues within the context of American society.* Belmont, CA: Wadsworth.

Bennett College (NC), 7 NDLR ¶26 (OCR 1995).

Berg, B. L. (1995). *Qualitative research methods for social sciences.* Needham Heights, MA: Allyn & Bacon.

Berry, C. A., Shaywitz, S. E., & Shaywitz, B. A. (1985). Girls with attention deficit disorder: A silent minority? A report on behavioral and cognitive characteristics. *Pediatrics, 76*, 801–809.

Betts v. Rector and Visitors of University of Virginia, 939 F. Supp. 461 (W.D. Va. 1996).

Biederman, J., Wilens, T., Mick, E., Spencer, T., & Faraone, S. V. (1999, August). Pharmacotherapy of attention-deficit/hyperactivity disorder reduces risk for substance use disorder. *Pediatrics* [Online]. Available: http://www.pediatrics.org/cgi/content/full/104/2/e20

Bigaj, S. J., Shaw, S. F., Cullen, J. P., McGuire, J. M., & Yost, D. S. (1995). Services for students with learning disabilities at two- and four-year colleges and universities: Are they different? *Community College Review, 23*(2), 17–36.

Bigaj, S. J., Shaw, S. F., & McGuire, J. M. (1999). Analysis of community-technical college faculty attitudes and use of accommodation strategies for students with learning disabilities. *Journal for Vocational Special Needs Education, 21*(2), 3–14.

Biggs, S. H. (1995). Neuropsychological and psychoeducational testing in the evaluation of the ADD adult. In K. G. Nadeau (Ed.), *A comprehensive guide to attention deficit disorder in adults: Research, diagnosis, and treatment* (pp. 109–131). New York: Brunner/Mazel.

Bigler, E. D. (Ed.). (1990). *Traumatic brain injury: Mechanisms of damage, assessment, intervention, and outcome.* Austin, TX: PRO-ED.

Biller, E. (1985). *Understanding and guiding the career development of adolescents and young adults with learning disabilities.* Springfield, IL: Thomas.

Bishop, B. (1995). The state-supported university libraries of Alabama: Serving the needs of patrons with disabilities. *College & Research Libraries, 56*(1), 17–28.

Blacklock, B. (1997, Winter). Perspectives from a veteran DS service provider. *Psychological Disabilities Newsletter,* 3–4.

Blackorby, J., & Wagner, M. (1996). Longitudinal postschool outcomes of youth with disabilities: Findings from the National Longitudinal Transition Study. *Exceptional Children, 62,* 399–413.

Blalock, G., & Patton, J. (1996). Transition and students with learning disabilities: Creating sound futures. *Journal of Learning Disabilities, 29,* 7–16.

Block, L. (1993). Students with learning disabilities. In S. Kroeger & J. Schuck (Eds.), *Responding to disability issues in student affairs* (pp. 69–78). San Francisco: Jossey-Bass.

Block, L. S. (1998a). The college application process: Advice from college personnel. *PostSecondary LD Report, 3,* 4–5.

Block, L. S. (1998b). *Questions to ask during the college search.* [Online]. Available: www.ldreport.com

Block, L., Brinckerhoff, L., Bird, A., Dublinske, S., Nelson, N. W., Bryant, B., Cessna, K., Gartland, D., Hammill, D., Patton, J., Butler, K. G., Bos, C., Terry, C., Gaffney, J., Cannon, L., Hagin, R., Swallwell, J., Dwyer, K. P., Howard, P., & Bashir, A. (1994). Secondary to postsecondary education transition planning for students with learning disabilities. In National Joint Committee on Learning Disabilities (Ed.), *Collective perspectives on issues affecting learning disabilities: Position papers and statements* (pp. 97–104). Austin, TX: PRO-ED.

Bloland, P. A. (1991). Key academic values and issues. In P. L. Moore (Ed.), *Managing the political dimension of student affairs* (pp. 27–41). San Francisco: Jossey-Bass.

Blosser, R. (1984). The roles and functions and the preparation of disabled student services directors in higher education. *Dissertation Abstracts International, 45,* 2396A. (University Microfilms No. 84-25, 117)

Bogdan, R. C., & Biklen, S. K. (1992). *Qualitative research for educators: An introduction to theory and methods.* Needham Heights, MA: Allyn & Bacon.

Borg, W. R., & Gall, M. D. (1989). *Educational research: An introduction* (5th ed.). New York: Longman.

Borich, G. G., & Nance, D. D. (1987). Evaluating special education programs: Shifting the professional mandate from process to outcome. *Remedial and Special Education, 8,* 7–17.

Bowers v. NCAA, 9 F. Supp. 2d 460 (D.N.H. 1998) and 974 F. Supp. 459 (D.N.J. 1997).

Bowser, G., & Reed, P. (1995). Education TECH points for assistive technology planning. *Journal of Special Education Technology, 12*(4), 325–338.

Brackett, J., & McPherson, A. (1996). Learning disabilities diagnosis in postsecondary students: A comparison of discrepancy-based diagnostic models. In N. Gregg, C. Hoy, & A. Gay (Eds.), *Adults with learning disabilities: Theoretical and practical perspectives* (pp. 68–84). New York: Guilford Press.

Bradley-Johnson, S., & Johnson, C. M. (1998). *A handbook for writing effective psychoeducational reports.* Austin, TX: PRO-ED.

Bramer, J. S. (1996). *Succeeding in college with attention deficit disorders: Issues and strategies for students, counselors, and educators.* Plantation, FL: Specialty Press.

Braswell, L. (1998). Self-regulation training for children with ADHD: Response to Harris and Schmidt. *ADHD Report, 6*(1), 1–3.

Brauen, M. L., O'Reilly, F., & Moore, M. (1994). *Issues and options in outcomes-based accountability for students with disabilities.* Rockville, MD: Westat.

Bray, M. A., Kehle, T. J., & Hintze, J. M. (1998). Profile analysis with the Wechsler scales: Why does it persist? *School Psychology International, 19*(3), 209–220.

Breimhorst v. Educational Testing Service (Case No. C-99-3387).

Brier, N. (1994). Psychological adjustment and adults with severe learning difficulties: Implications of the literature on children and adolescents with learning disabilities for research and practice. *Learning Disabilities: A Multidisciplinary Journal, 5,* 15–27.

Brinckerhoff, L. C. (1991). Establishing learning disability support services with minimal resources. *Journal of Postsecondary Education and Disability, 9,* 184–196.

Brinckerhoff, L. C. (1993). Self-advocacy: A critical skill for college students with learning disabilities. *Journal of School and Community Health, 16,* 23–33.

Brinckerhoff, L. C. (1994). Developing effective self-advocacy skills in college-bound students with learning disabilities. *Intervention in School and Clinic, 29,* 229–237.

Brinckerhoff, L. C. (1996a, Spring). LD support services at Boston University: A personal perspective. *Postsecondary Disability Network News, 27,* 1–2, 5.

Brinckerhoff, L. C. (1996b). Making the transition to higher education: Opportunities for student empowerment. *Journal of Learning Disabilities, 29,* 118–136.

Brinckerhoff, L. C. (1997). Students with learning disabilities in graduate or professional programs: Emerging issues on campus and challenges to employment. In P. J. Gerber & D. S. Brown (Eds.), *Learning disabilities and employment* (pp. 143–164). Austin, TX: PRO-ED.

Brinckerhoff, L. C. (1999). Students with learning disabilities in graduate school: Access and accommodation considerations. In T. A. Citro (Ed.), *Successful lifetime management.* Waltham, MA: LDAM.

Brinckerhoff, L. C., & Anderson, P. L. (1989). *Northeast Technical Assistance Center for Learning Disability College Programming: Progress report 1988–90.* Storrs: University of Connecticut.

Brinckerhoff, L. C., & Eaton, H. (1991). Developing a summer orientation program for college students with learning disabilities. *Postsecondary LD Network News, 12,* 1–3, 6.

Brinckerhoff, L. C., & Forer, D. (1998). *Course syllabus for assistive technology training workshop.* Unpublished material, Learning Outcomes of Greater Boston, Wayland, MA.

Brinckerhoff, L. C., & McGuire, J. M. (1999). *Factors differentiating undergraduate and graduate study.* Unpublished material, University of Connecticut, Postsecondary Education Disability Unit, Storrs.

Brinckerhoff, L. C., Shaw, S. F., & McGuire, J. M. (1989). Implementing regional consortia for post-secondary learning disability personnel. In J. J. Vander Putten (Ed.), *Proceedings of the 1989 AHSSPPE conference* (pp. 147–150). Columbus, OH: Association on Handicapped Student Service Programs in Postsecondary Education.

Brinckerhoff, L. C., Shaw, S. F., & McGuire, J. M. (1992). Promoting access, accommodations and independence for college students with learning disabilities. *Journal of Learning Disabilities, 25,* 417–429.

Brinckerhoff, L. C., Shaw, S. F., & McGuire, J. M. (1993). *Promoting postsecondary education for students with learning disabilities: A handbook for practitioners.* Austin, TX: PRO-ED.

Brinckerhoff, L. C., Shaw, S. F., McGuire, J. M., Norlander, K. A., & Anderson, P. L. (1988). Critical issues in learning disability college programs. In D. Knapke & C. Lendman (Eds.), *Celebrate in '88* (pp. 19–40). Columbus, OH: Association on Handicapped Student Service Programs in Postsecondary Education.

Brink, S. (1998, November 23). Doing Ritalin right. *U.S. News and World Report,* 76–81.

Brown v. Board of Education of Topeka, 347 U.S. 4831 (1954).

Brown, J. I., Bennett, J. M., & Hanna, G. (1981). *The Nelson-Denny Reading Test.* Itasca, IL: Riverside.

Brown, T. E. (1995a). *Brown Attention Deficit Disorder Scales.* San Antonio: Psychological Corp.

Brown, T. E. (1995b). Differential diagnosis of ADD versus ADHD in adults. In K. G. Nadeau (Ed.), *A comprehensive guide to attention deficit disorder in adults: Research, diagnosis, and treatment* (pp. 93–108). New York: Brunner/Mazel.

Brown, T. E. (1999, Fall). New understandings of attention deficit disorders in children, adolescents and adults: Assessment and treatment. *FOCUS: The Official Newsletter of ADDA, 3,* 12.

Bryan, T. H. (1989, Winter). Learning disabled adolescents' vulnerability to crime: Attitudes, anxieties, experiences. *Learning Disabilities Research, 5,* 51–60.

Bryant, B. R., & O'Connell, M. (1998). The impact of the collaboration among tech act projects and protection and advocacy systems. *Intervention in School & Clinic, 33*(5), 309–312.

Bryant, B. R., & Rivera, D. P. (1995, March). *Using assistive technology to facilitate cooperative learning.* Paper presented at the Florida Educational Technology Conference, Orlando, FL.

Bryant, B. R., & Seay, P. C. (1998). The technology-related assistance to Individuals with Disabilities Act: Relevance to individuals with learning disabilities and their advocates. *Journal of Learning Disabilities, 31*(1), 4–15.

Bryant, B. R., Seay, P. C., & Bryant, D. P. (1999). Using assistive technology to help people with mental retardation compensate for adaptive behavior deficits. In R. Schalock (Ed.), *Issues in adaptive behavior assessment* (pp. 81–98). Washington, DC: AAMR.

Bryant, B. R., Seay, P. C., O'Connell, M., & Comstock-Galagan, J. (1996). The Texas Assistive Technology Partnership and Advocacy, Incorporated: A cooperative partnership between Texas' tech act state project and its protection and advocacy system. *Technology and Disability, 5,* 275–282.

Bryant, D. P., & Bryant, B. R. (1998). Using assistive technology adaptations to include students with learning disabilities in cooperative learning activities. *Journal of Learning Disabilities, 31*(1), 41–54.

Bryant, D. P., Carter, A., & Smith, R. (1999). *The comparative effectiveness of computer-assisted instruction, flash cards, and instructional arrangements on the ability of students with learning disabilities in mathematics to compute basic mathematics facts accurately and fluently.* Manuscript submitted for publication.

Bryant, D. P., Erin, J., Lock, R., Allan, J., & Resta, P. (1998). Infusing assistive technology into a teacher training program in learning disabilities. *Journal of Learning Disabilities, 31*(1), 55–66.

BU decision a "ringing affirmation" for stringent degree requirements. (1998, July). *Disability Compliance for Higher Education, 3*(12), 1, 6.

Bureau of National Affairs. (1990). *The Americans with Disabilities Act: A practical and legal guide to impact, enforcement, and compliance.* Washington, DC: Author.

Bursuck, W. D. (1991). *Learning strategies: Module two. Specific intervention strategies.* DeKalb: Northern Illinois University.

Bursuck, W. D., & Jayanthi, M. (1993). Programming for independent study skills usage. In S. A. Vogel & P. B. Adelman (Eds.), *Success for college students with learning disabilities* (pp. 177–205). New York: Springer-Verlag.

Bursuck, W. D., & Rose, E. (1992). Community college options for students with mild disabilities. In F. R. Rusch, L. DeStefano, J. Chadsey-Rusch, L. A. Phelps, & E. Szymanski (Eds.), *Transition from school to adult life* (pp. 71–92). Sycamore, IL: Sycamore Publishing.

Bursuck, W. D., Rose, E., Cowen, S., & Yahaya, A. (1989). Nationwide survey of postsecondary education services for students with learning disabilities. *Exceptional Children, 56,* 236–245.

Butler, D. L. (1995). Promoting strategic learning by postsecondary students with learning disabilities. *Journal of Learning Disabilities, 28,* 170–190.

Byron, J., & Parker, D. (1998). *Demographic profile of students with ADHD who are eligible for services at the University of North Carolina at Chapel Hill.* Unpublished material, University of North Carolina at Chapel Hill.

Byron, J., Parker D., & Laurie Maitland, T. (1998, July). *Get on the bus: Providing services to college students with ADHD.* Presentation at AHEAD 21st annual conference, Las Vegas.

Byron, J. B., & Parker, D. R. (1997, Spring). Get on the bus: Responding to the needs of college students with AD/HD. *Postsecondary Disability Network News, 30,* 1–2, 5.

California Community Colleges. (1999, August). *Distance education: Access guidelines for students with disabilities.* [Online]. Available: http://www.rit.edu/~easi/dl/disccc.html

Campbell A. Dinsmore v. Charles C. Pugh and the Regents of the University of California. Berkeley (N.D. Cal., Sept. 23, 1990).

Campbell, D. T., & Stanley, J. C. (1966). *Experimental and quasi-experimental designs for research.* Chicago: Rand McNally.

Campbell, P., & Shaw, S. F. (1992). *Final Report: The Connecticut Symposia on Special Education in the 21st Century.* Storrs: A. J. Pappanikou Center on Special Education and Rehabilitation: A University Affiliated Program, University of Connecticut.

Cannon, L. (1996, March/April). LDA responds to report of reduction of services for students with learning disabilities at Boston University. *LDA Newsbriefs, 31*(1), 24.

Carl, D. (1999, April). *Memo concerning AT considerations.* Houston, TX: Region IV Education Service Center.

Carlton, P. M. (1998). Be sure you have appropriate documentation. *PostSecondary LD Report.*

Carney, J., & Dix, C. (1992). Integrating assistive technology in the classroom and community. In G. Church & S. Glennen, *The handbook of assistive technology* (pp. 207–240). San Diego, CA: Singular.

Carrier, C., Williams, M., & Dalgaard, B. (1988). College students' perceptions of notetaking and their relationship to selected learner characteristics and course achievement. *Research in Higher Education, 28,* 223–239.

CHADD. (1993). Not just for children anymore: ADD in adulthood. *C.H.A.D.D.er*, 19–21.

Chambers, A. C. (1997). *Has technology been considered? A guide for IEP teams*. Reston, VA: Council of Administrators of Special Education and the Technology and Media Division of the Council for Exceptional Children.

Chandler, S., Czerlinsky, T., & Wehman, P. (1993). Provisions of assistive technology: Bridging the gap of accessibility. In P. Wehman (Ed.), *The ADA mandate for special change* (pp. 117–134). Baltimore: Brookes.

Civil Rights Act of 1974, P.L. 88-352.

Civil Rights Restoration Act of 1987, 29 U.S.C. § 706(7)(8)(c).

Clark, D. M. (1990). *National assessment of handicapped student services programs in postsecondary education: Survey of programs*. Buffalo, NY: National Association for Industry-Education Cooperation.

Clark, G. M. (1996). Transition planning assessment for secondary-level students with learning disabilities. *Journal of Learning Disabilities, 29*, 79–92.

Clark, G. M., & Patton, J. R. (1997). *The transition planning inventory*. Austin, TX: PRO-ED.

Closing the Gap. (n.d.). *Other organizations*. Henderson, MN: Author. [Online]. Available: http://www.closingthegap.com/rd/otherorg.html

Cocchi, W. (1997, April/June). The community college choice. *PostSecondary LD Report, 1*(3).

Cohen, J. (1985). Learning disabilities and adolescence: Development considerations. In S. C. Feinstein (Ed.), *Adolescent psychiatry, development and clinical studies* (Vol. 12, pp. 177–195). Chicago: University of Chicago.

Cohen, L. G. (1993). Test review: *Wechsler Individual Achievement Test. Diagnostique, 18*(3), 255–268.

Cohn, P. (1998). Why does my stomach hurt? How individuals with learning disabilities can use cognitive strategies to reduce anxiety and stress at the college level. *Journal of Learning Disabilities, 31*, 514–516.

Colleges strive to give disabled students access to on-line courses. (1999, October 29). *Chronicle of Higher Education*, p. A69.

Computer labs campuswide and Web sites must be accessible. (1999, July). *Section 504 Compliance Handbook, Supplement No. 248*, 1–3.

Connecticut State Department of Education. (1999). *Guidelines for identifying children with learning disabilities* (2nd ed.). Hartford: Author.

Connell, P. (1991). *An analysis of aptitude-achievement discrepancy formulas in learning disability assessment*. Paper presented at the 20th annual meeting of the Mid-South Education Research Association, Lexington, KY.

Conners, C. K., Erhardt, D., Epstein, J. N., Parker, J. D. A., Sitarenios, G., & Sparrow, E. (1999). Self-ratings of ADHD symptoms in adults. I: Factor structure and normative data. *Journal of Attention Disorders, 3*, 3, 141–151.

Connolly, A. J. (1988). *Key Math–Revised: A diagnostic inventory of essential mathematics*. Circle Pines, MN: American Guidance Service.

Consortium on ADHD Documentation. (1998). *Guidelines for documentation of attention-deficit/hyperactivity disorder in adolescents and adults*. Boston: Author.

Contra Costa College, case no. 109-96-2104 (OCR Region IX, 1996).

Cook, T. D., & Campbell, D. T. (1979). *Quasi-experimentation: Design and analysis issues for field settings*. Chicago: Rand McNally.

Coombs, N. (n.d.). *Distance learning and students with disabilities: Easy tips for teachers.* [Online]. Available: www.csun.edu/cod/conf2000/proceedings/0199Coombs.html

Cordoni, B. (1987). *Living with a learning disability.* Carbondale: Southern Illinois University Press.

Corning Community College (NY), case no. 02-97-2045 (OCR Region II 1997).

Cosden, M. A., & McNamara, J. (1997). Self-concept and perceived social support among college students with and without learning disabilities. *Learning Disability Quarterly, 20,* 2–12.

Costenbader, V. K., & Perry, C. (1990). Test reviews. *Journal of Psychoeducational Assessment, 8,* 180–184.

Council for Exceptional Children. (1999, Fall). *Research connections in special education: Universal design (#5).* Reston, VA: Author.

Coutinho, M. J. (1996). Who will be learning disabled after the reauthorization of IDEA? Two very distinct perspectives. *Journal of Learning Disabilities, 28,* 664–668.

Cowen, S. (1988). Coping strategies of university students with learning disabilities. *Journal of Learning Disabilities, 21,* 161–164, 188.

Cowen, S. (1990). *The LINKS college transition planning guide.* Unpublished manuscript, Northern Illinois University, DeKalb.

Cowen, S. (1991). *How to choose a college: Helpful strategies for students with learning disabilities.* Unpublished manuscript.

Cowen, S. (1993). Transition planning for LD college-bound students. In S. A. Vogel & P. B. Adelman (Eds.), *Success for college students with learning disabilities* (pp. 39–56). New York: Springer-Verlag.

Cronin, M. (1996). Life skills curricula for students with learning disabilities: A review of the literature. In J. R. Patton & G. Blalock (Eds.), *Transition and students with learning disabilities* (pp. 85–112). Austin, TX: PRO-ED.

CSUN. (1999). *The creation of the center on disabilities* [Online]. Available: http://www.csun.edu/cod/wilson.html

Cummings, J. A. (1995). Review of the Woodcock–Johnson Psycho-Educational Battery–Revised. In J. C. Conoley & J. C. Impara (Eds.), *Twelfth mental measurements yearbook* (pp. 1113–1116). Lincoln, NE: Buros Institute.

Cutler, E. (1991, March). *Evaluating spell checking, abbreviation expansion and word prediction software.* Paper presented at the Sixth Annual Conference on Technology and Persons with Disabilities, Los Angeles.

Dalke, C. (1991). *Support programs in higher education for students with disabilities: Access for all.* Gaithersburg, MD: Aspen.

Dalke, C. (1993). Programming for independent study skills usage. In S. A. Vogel & P. B. Adelman (Eds.), *Success for college students with learning disabilities* (pp. 177–205). New York: Springer-Verlag.

Dalke, C., & Franzene, J. (1988). Secondary-postsecondary collaboration: A model of shared responsibility. *Learning Disabilities Focus, 4,* 38–45.

Dalke, C., & Howard, D. (1994). *Life works: A transition program for high school students.* East Moline, IL: LinguiSystems.

Dalke, C., & Schmitt, S. (1987). Meeting the transition needs of college-bound students with learning disabilities. *Journal of Learning Disabilities, 20,* 176–180.

Daly, N. F. (1980). *Andragogy: Implications for secondary and adult education programs.* (ERIC Document Reproduction Service No. ED 186627)

Darden, C. A., & Morgan, A. W. (1996). Cognitive functioning profiles of the adult population with learning disabilities. In N. Gregg, C. Hoy, & A. F. Gay (Eds.), *Adults with learning disabilities: Theoretical and practical perspectives* (pp. 184–207). New York: Guilford Press.

Davila, R. R. (1991). Clarification of policy to address the needs of children with attention deficit disorders within general and/or special education. *LDA Newsbriefs, 26*(6), 1, 6–8.

Davila, R. R., Williams, M. M., & MacDonald, J. T. (1991, September). *Clarification of policy to address the needs of children with attention deficit disorders within general and/or special education.* Washington, DC: U.S. Department of Education.

Day, N. (1994, October). Straight A's don't cut it. *Boston Magazine, 86,* 53–55, 92–95.

Day, S. L., & Edwards, B. J. (1996). Assistive technology for postsecondary students with learning disabilities. *Journal of Learning Disabilities, 29,* 486–493.

Decker, K., Spector, S., & Shaw, S. A. (1992). Teaching study skills to students with mild handicaps: The role of the classroom teacher. *Clearing House, 65,* 280–284.

DeFur, S., & Reiff, H. B. (1994). Transition of youths with learning disabilities to adulthood: The secondary education foundation. In P. J. Gerber & H. B. Reiff (Eds.), *Learning disabilities in adulthood: Persisting problems and evolving issues* (pp. 99–110). Austin, TX: PRO-ED.

Delaney, S. (1999, July). *Disability and higher education: Guidelines for Sec. 504 & ADA compliance.* Presentation at the 22nd international AHEAD conference, Atlanta, GA.

Denckla, M. (1986). The neurology of social competence. *ACLD Newsbriefs, 16,* 15, 20–21.

DePaul University, 4 NDLR 157 (OCR 1993).

Derer, K., Polsgrove, L., & Rieth, H. (1996). A survey of assistive technology applications in schools and recommendations for practice. *Journal of Special Education Technology, 13,* 62–80.

Deshler, D., Schumaker, J., Lenz, K., & Ellis, J. (1984). Academic and cognitive interventions for LD adolescents: Part II. *Journal of Learning Disabilities, 17,* 170–179.

Deshler, D., Warner, M., Schumaker, J., & Alley, G. (1983). Learning strategies intervention model: Key components and current status. In J. McKinney & L. Feagons (Eds.), *Current topics in learning disabilities* (pp. 245–283). Norwood, NJ: Ablex.

Deshler, D. D., Ellis, E. S., & Lenz, B. K. (1996). *Teaching adolescents with learning disabilities: Strategies and methods* (2nd ed.). Denver, CO: Love.

Developing study skills rather than avoiding mathematics courses. (1997, November). *Disability Compliance for Higher Education, 3*(4), 5–7.

Dexler v. Tisch, 660 F. Supp. 1418 (D. Conn. 1987).

Dickeson, R. C. (1999). *Prioritizing academic programs and services: Reallocating resources to achieve strategic balance.* San Francisco: Jossey-Bass.

Directors need to see more information for ADD documentation. (1998, January). *Disability Compliance for Higher Education, 3,* 1.

Documentation for course waivers: Details often make the difference. (1998, April). *Disability Compliance for Higher Education, 3,* 1, 4.

Don't misinterpret the court rulings. (1999, July). *Disability Compliance for Higher Education, 4,* 6.

Doris, J. L. (1993). Defining learning disabilities: A history of the search for consensus. In G. R. Lyon, D. B. Gray, J. F. Kavanagh, & N. A. Krasnegor (Eds.), *Better understanding learning disabilities: New views from research and their implications for education and public policies* (pp. 97–116). Baltimore: Brookes.

Dowdy, C. A. (1996). Vocational rehabilitation and special education: Partners in transition for individuals with learning disabilities. In J. R. Patton & G. Blalock (Eds.), *Transition and students with learning disabilities* (pp. 191–211). Austin, TX: PRO-ED.

Dowdy, C. A., & McCue, M. (1994). Crossing service systems: From special education to vocational rehabilitation. In C. A. Michaels (Ed.), *Transition strategies for persons with learning disabilities* (pp. 53–78). San Diego, CA: Singular.

Dragon Dictate [Computer software]. (1994). Newton, MA: Dragon Systems.

Dragon Naturally Speaking [Computer software]. (1997). Newton, MA: Dragon Systems.

Drover, J., McMillan, B., Owen, L., & Wilson, A. (1996). *Learning disabilities in the classroom: Handbook for postsecondary instructors.* Sackville, NB: Mount Allison University, The Meighen Centre for Learning Assistance and Research.

Dubois v. Alderson-Broaddus College, Inc., 950 F. Supp. 754 (W.D. W. Va. 1997).

DuChossois, G. (1998). Striking the match: Finding the right college for students with learning disabilities. *Their World* (pp. 76–81). New York: National Center on Learning Disabilities.

DuChossois, G., & Michaels, C. (1994). Postsecondary education. In C. A. Michaels (Ed.), *Transition strategies for persons with learning disabilities* (pp. 79–118). San Diego, CA: Singular.

DuChossois, G., & Stein, E. (1992). *Choosing the right college: A step-by-step system to aid the student with learning disabilities in selecting the suitable college setting for them.* New York: New York University.

Dukes, L. L. (1999). *The proccess: The development of the AHEAD Program Standards.* Storrs: University of Connecticut, Postsecondary Education Disability Unit.

Dukes, L. L., & Shaw, S. F. (1998). Not just CHILDREN anymore: Personnel preparation regarding postsecondary education for adults with disabilities. *Teacher Education and Special Education, 21,* 205–213.

Dukes, L. L., & Shaw, S. F. (1999). Postsecondary disability personnel: Professional standards and staff development. *Journal of Developmental Education, 23,* 26–31.

Dumbauld, J., & Daniels, D. (1998, June). Counselors team up to sponsor ADD support group. *ALERT, 22,* 17–18.

Dunn, C. (1996). A status report on transition planning for individuals with learning disabilities. In J. R. Patton & G. Blalock (Eds.), *Transition and students with learning disabilities* (pp. 19–42). Austin, TX: PRO-ED.

Dunn, L. M. (1968). Special education for the mildly retarded—Is much of it justifiable? *Exceptional Children, 35,* 5–22.

Dykman, R. A., & Ackerman, P. T. (1991). Attention deficit disorder and specific reading disability: Separate but often overlapping disorders. *Journal of Learning Disabilities, 24,* 96–103.

Eaton, H. (1996). *How students with learning disabilities can make the transition from high school to college.* Santa Barbara, CA: Excel Publishing.

Eaton, H., & Coull, L. (1998). *Transitions to postsecondary learning: Self-advocacy handbook.* Vancouver, BC: Eaton Coull Learning Group.

Eaton, H., & Coull, L. (1998). *Transitions to postsecondary learning: Video and student work guide.* Vancouver, British Columbia: Eaton Coull Learning Group.

Eaton, H., & Coull, L. (2000). *Transitions to high school: Video and instructional materials for students with learning disabilities and/or attention deficit disorder.* Vancouver, BC: Eaton Coull Learning Group.

Education for All Handicapped Children Act (EHA), P.L. 94-142, 20 U.S.C. § 1401 *et seq.* (now known as Individuals with Disabilities Education Act [IDEA], P.L. 101-476).

Educational Testing Service. (1991). *SIGI Plus*. Princeton, NJ: Author.

Educational Testing Service. (1998a, April). *Policy statement for documentation of attention-deficit/ hyperactivity disorder in adolescents and adults*. Princeton, NJ: Office of Disability Policy.

Educational Testing Service. (1998b, January). *Policy statement for documentation of a learning disability in adolescents and adults*. Princeton, NJ: Office of Disability Policy.

Educational Testing Service. (2001). *Guidelines for documentation of psychiatric disabilities in adolescents and adults*. Princeton, NJ: Office of Disability Policy.

Elkind, J. (1993). Using computer-based readers to improve reading comprehension of students with dyslexia. *Annals of Dyslexia, 43*, 238–259.

Elkind, J., Black, M. S., & Murray, C. (1996). Computer based compensation of adult reading disabilities. *Annals of Dyslexia, 46*, 159–186.

Ellis v. Morehouse University School of Medicine, 925 F. Supp. 1529 (N.D. Ga. 1996).

Ellis, E. S. (1990). What's so strategic about teaching teachers to teach strategies? *Teacher Education and Special Education, 13*, 56–62.

Ellis, E. S. (1996). Reading instruction. In D. D. Deshler, E. S. Ellis, & B. K. Lenz (Eds.), *Teaching adolescents with learning disabilities: Strategies and methods*. Denver, CO: Love.

Elswit, L., Geetter, E., & Goldberg, J. (1999). Between passion and policy: Litigating the Guckenberger case. *Journal of Learning Disabilities, 32*, 292–303, 319.

Enderle, J., & Severson, S. (1991). *Enderle-Severson transition rating scale*. Moorhead, MN: Practical Press.

Epstein, M. H., Cullinan, D., & Neiminen, G. (1984). Social behaviour problems of learning disabled and normal girls. *Journal of Learning Disabilities, 17*, 609–611.

Erikson, E. H. (1959). *Identity and the life cycle*. New York: Norton.

ETS agrees with disability groups to stop "flagging" Graduate Admissions Test. (2001, February 7). [Online]. Available: www.ets.org/aboutets/news

Evers, R. B. (1996). The positive force of vocational education: Transition outcomes for youth with learning disabilities. In J. R. Patton & G. Blalock (Eds.), *Transition and students with learning disabilities* (pp. 113–130). Austin, TX: PRO-ED.

Extra exam time: How much more time is necessary? (1995, September). *Disability Compliance for Higher Education, 1*(2), 1, 9.

Faigel, H. C. (1995). Attention deficit disorder in college students: Facts, fallacies and treatment. *Journal of American College Health, 43*, 147–155.

Faraone, S. V., Biederman, J., Keenan, K., & Tsuang, T. (1991). A family-genetic study of girls with DSM–III attention deficit disorder. *American Journal of Psychiatry, 148*, 1, 112–117.

Favorite, B. (1996). *Coaching for adults with ADD: The missing link between the desire for change and achievement of success* [Online]. Available: http://www.add-toronto.org/art_miss_link.html

Feifel, D. (1996). Attention-deficit hyperactivity disorder in adults. *Postgraduate Medicine, 100*, 207–216.

Ferrara, S. (1995). Review of the *Wechsler Individual Achievement Test*. In J. C. Conoley & J. C. Impara (Eds.), *The twelfth mental measurements yearbook* (pp. 1128–1132). Lincoln, NE: Buros Institute.

Feuer, D., & Geber, B. (1988, December). Uh-oh . . . Second thoughts about adult learning theory. *Training, 25*, 31–39.

Field, S. (1996a). Instructional strategies to promote self-determination for students with learning disabilities. *Journal of Learning Disabilities, 29*, 40–52.

Field, S. (1996b). Self-determination instructional strategies for youth with learning disabilities. In J. R. Patton & G. Blalock (Eds.), *Transition and students with learning disabilities* (pp. 61–84). Austin, TX: PRO-ED.

Field, S., & Hoffman, A. (1994). Development of a model for self-determination. *Career Development for Exceptional Individuals, 17,* 159–169.

Field, S., & Hoffman, A. (1996a). Increasing the ability of educators to support youth and self-determination. In L. E. Powers, G. H. S. Singer, & J. Sowers (Eds.), *Promoting self-competence in children and youth with disabilities: On the road to autonomy* (pp. 171–187). Baltimore: Brookes.

Field, S., & Hoffman, A. (1996b). *Steps to self-determination.* Austin, TX: PRO-ED.

Field, S., Hoffman, A., & Posch, M. (1997). Self-determination during adolescence: A developmental perspective. *Remedial and Special Education, 18,* 285–293.

Field, S., Hoffman, A., & Spezia, S. (1998). *Self-determination strategies for adolescents in transition.* Austin, TX: PRO-ED.

Field, S., Martin, J., Miller, R., Ward, M., & Wehmeyer, M. (1998). *A practical guide to teaching self-determination.* Reston, VA: Council for Exceptional Children.

Fink, R. (1998, April). Developing ADHD documentation guidelines for postsecondary institutions in the state of Colorado. *ALERT, 22,* 20–21.

Fink, R. J. (1999, April). Technical Assistance Team (TAT) update. *ALERT, 23*(2), 31, 32.

Finn, L. (1998). Students' perceptions of beneficial LD accommodations and services at the postsecondary level. *Journal of Postsecondary Education and Disability, 13*(1), 46–67.

Fisher, J. C., & Podeschi, R. L. (1989). From Lindeman to Knowles: A change of vision. *International Journal of Lifelong Education, 8,* 345–353.

Flanagan, D. P., McGrew, K. S., Abramowitz, E., Lehner, L., Untiedt, S., Berger, D., & Armstrong, H. (1997). Improvement in academic screening instruments? A concurrent validity investigation of the K-FAST, MBA, and WRAT3. *Journal of Psychoeducational Assessment, 15,* 99–112.

Flanagan, R. (1997). Test reviews. *Journal of Psychoeducational Assessment, 15,* 82–87.

Fletcher, J., Shaywitz, B., & Shaywitz, S. (1994). Attention as a process and as a disorder. In G. R. Lyon (Ed.), *Frames of reference for the assessment of learning disabilities.* Baltimore: Brookes.

Fletcher, J. M., Francis, D. J., Shaywitz, S. E., Lyon, G. R., Foorman, B. R., Staebing, K. K., & Shaywitz, B. A. (1998). Intelligent testing and the discrepancy model for children with learning disabilities. *Learning Disabilities Research and Practice, 13,* 186–203.

Fonosch, G., & Schwab, L. (1981). Attitudes of selected university faculty members toward disabled students. *Journal of College Student Personnel, 22,* 229–235.

Fox, C. L., & Forbing, S. E. (1991). Overlapping symptoms of substance abuse and learning handicaps: Implications for educators. *Journal of Learning Disabilities, 24,* 24–31, 39.

Fraenkel, J. R., & Wallen, N. E. (1996). *How to design and evaluate research in education.* New York: McGraw-Hill.

Frank-Josephson, C., & Scott, J. U. (1997, December). Accommodating medical students with learning disabilities. *Academic Medicine, 72*(12), 1032–1033.

Freils, L. (1969, June). Behavioral changes in students. *Journal of School Health, 39,* 405–408.

Gable, R. K., & Wolf, M. B. (1993). *Instrument development in the affective domain: Measuring attitudes and values in corporate and school settings* (2nd ed.). Boston: Kluwer Academic.

Gadbow, N., & Dubois, D. (1998). *Adult learners with special needs: Strategies and resources for postsecondary education and workplace training.* Malabar, FL: Krieger.

Gajar, A. H. (1992). University-based models for students with learning disabilities: The Pennsylvania State University model. In F. R. Rusch, L. DeStefano, L. Chadsey-Rusch, L. A. Phelps, & E. Szymanski (Eds.), *Transition for school to adult life: Models, linkages, and policy* (pp. 51–70). Sycamore, IL: Sycamore.

Ganschow, L., Sparks, R., & Javorsky, J. (1998). Foreign language learning difficulties: An historical perspective. *Journal of Learning Disabilities, 31*(3), 248–258.

Garber, S. W., Garber, M. D., & Spizman, R. F. (1996). *Beyond Ritalin: Facts about medication and other strategies for helping children, adolescents, and adults with attention deficit disorders.* New York: Villard Books.

Gaub, M., & Carlson, C. L. (1997). Gender differences in ADHD: A meta-analysis and critical review. *Journal of the American Academy of Child and Adolescent Psychiatry, 36,* 8, 1036–1045.

Gent v. Radford University, 976 F. Supp. 391 (W.D. Va. 1997), *aff'd,* 122 F.3d 1061 (4th Cir. 1997).

George, M. P., George, N. L., & Grosenick, J. K. (1990). Features of program evaluation in special education. *Remedial and Special Education, 11*(5), 23–30.

George Washington University (Producer). (1996). *ADD: The race inside my head* [Videotape]. (Available from the Association on Higher Education and Disability, University of Massachussetts–Boston, 100 Morrisey Boulevard, Boston, MA 02125-3393)

Gephart, D. (Ed.). (1998). *Testing accommodations in higher education.* Horsham, PA: LRP.

Gerber, P. J., Ginsberg, R., & Reiff, H. B. (1992). Identifying alterable patterns in employment success for highly successful adults with learning disabilities. *Journal of Learning Disabilities, 25,* 475–487.

Gerber, P. J., & Reiff, H. B. (1991). *Speaking for themselves: Ethnographic interviews with adults with learning disabilities.* Ann Arbor: University of Michigan Press.

Gerber, P. J., Reiff, H. B., & Ginsberg, R. (1996). Reframing the learning disabilities experience. *Journal of Learning Disabilities, 29,* 97, 98–101.

Gersh, F. (1994). Treatment of ADD in college students. *Conduit, 10,* 1–3.

Gersten, R. (1998). Recent advances in instructional research for students with learning disabilities: An overview. *Learning Disabilities Research & Practice, 13*(3), 162–170.

Goggin, M. L. (1987). *Policy design and the politics of implementation: The case of child health care in the American states.* Knoxville: University of Tennessee Press.

Goldhammer, R., & Brinckerhoff, L. C. (1992). Self-advocacy for college students. *Their World,* 94–97.

Gonzalez v. National Board of Medical Examiners, F. Supp. 2nd, 1999 WL 613434 (E. D. Mich., August 10, 1999).

Gordon, M., & Keiser, S. (1998). *Accommodations in higher education under the Americans with Disabilities Act (ADA).* New York: Guilford Press.

Gordon, M., & Murphy, K. (1998). Attention-deficit/hyperactivity disorder (ADHD). In M. Gordon & S. Keiser (Eds.), *Accommodations in higher education under the Americans with Disabilities Act (ADA)* (pp. 98–129). New York: Guilford Press.

Gough, P. B., & Tunmer, W. E. (1986). Decoding reading and reading disability. *Remedial and Special Education, 7*(1), 6–10.

Government Performance and Results Act of 1993, 31 U.S.C. § 1101 *et seq.*

Green, R. (1999). *Assistive technologies for print disabilities in academic libraries.* Unpublished doctoral dissertation, Virginia Polytechnic Institute, Blacksburg.

Greenbaum, B., Graham, S., & Scales, W. (1996). Adults with learning disabilities: Occupational and social status after college. *Journal of Learning Disabilities, 29,* 167–173.

Greenspan, S., Apthorp, H., & Williams, P. (1991). Social competence and work success of college students with learning disabilities. *Journal of Postsecondary Education and Disability, 9,* 227–234.

Gregg, N., & Ferri, B. (1996). Paradigms: A need for radical reform. In N. Gregg, C. Hoy, & A. F. Gay (Eds.), *Adults with learning disabilities: Theoretical and practical perspectives* (pp. 21–54). New York: Guilford Press.

Gregg, N., & Ferri, B. A. (1998). Hearing voices and witnessing pain: In response to "Why does my stomach hurt? How individuals with learning disabilities can use cognitive strategies to reduce anxiety and stress at the college level." *Journal of Learning Disabilities, 31,* 517–519.

Gregg, N., & Hoy, C. (1990). Identifying the learning disabled. *Journal of College Admissions, 129,* 30–33.

Griffith-Haynie, M., & Smith, L. (1995, Fall). Differences between the therapist and the coach. *Coaching Matters: The Newsletter of the American Coaching Association, 3,* 2–3.

Groth-Marnat, G. (Ed.). (1997). *Handbook of psychological assessment* (3rd ed.). New York: Wiley.

Groundbreaking study may have found a scientific test to diagnose ADHD. (1999, January). *Disability Compliance for Higher Education, 4,* 1, 6.

Guckenberger v. Boston University, 974 F. Supp. 106 (D. Mass. 1997).

Guidelines for LD documentation. (1996, October). *Disability Compliance for Higher Education, 2*(3), 9.

Haight v. Hawaii Pacific University, 116 F.3d 484 (9th Cir. 1997).

Hall, C. W., & Haws, D. (1989). Depressive symptomatology in learning-disabled and nonlearning-disabled students. *Psychology in the Schools, 26,* 359–364.

Hall, F. (1995, January). *Students with learning disabilities in medical school.* Presentation at Boston University School of Medicine conference, Boston, MA.

Hallahan, D. P., & Kauffman, J. M. (1997). *Exceptional learners: Introduction to special education.* Needham Heights, MA: Allyn & Bacon.

Hallahan, D. P., & Reeve, R. E. (1980). Selective attention and distractibility. In B. K. Keough (Ed.), *Advances in special education* (Vol. 1, pp. 141–181). Greenwich, CT: JAI Press.

Hallowell, E. M. (1995). Psychotherapy of adult attention deficit disorder. In K. G. Nadeau (Ed.), *A comprehensive guide to attention deficit disorder in adults: Research, diagnosis, and treatment* (pp. 144–167). New York: Brunner/Mazel.

Hallowell, E. M., & Ratey, J. J. (1994). *Driven to distraction.* New York: Pantheon.

Halpern, A. S. (1994). The transition of youth with disabilities to adult life: A position statement of the Division on Career Development and Transition, Council for Exceptional Children. *Career Development for Exceptional Individuals, 17,* 115–124.

Hammill, D. D. (1990). On defining learning disabilities: An emerging consensus. *Journal of Learning Disabilities, 23,* 74–84.

Hammill, D. D. (1993). A brief look at the learning disabilities movement in the United States. *Journal of Learning Disabilities, 26,* 295–310.

Hammill, D. D., Brown, L., & Bryant, B. R. (1992). *A consumer's guide to tests in print* (2nd ed.). Austin, TX: PRO-ED.

Hammill, D. D., & Bryant, B. R. (1998). *Learning disabilities diagnostic inventory.* Austin, TX: PRO-ED.

Handicapped Children's Protection Act of 1987, 20 U.S.C. § 1400 *et seq.*

Handicapped requirements handbook. (1993, January). Washington, DC: Thompson Publishing Group.

Hartlage, L. C., & Golden, C. J. (1990). Neuropsychological assessment techniques. In T. B. Gutkin & C. R. Reynolds (Eds.), *The handbook of school psychology* (2nd ed., pp. 431–486). New York: Wiley.

Hartman, R., & Redden, M. R. (1985). *Measuring student progress in the classroom: A guide to testing and evaluating progress of students with disabilities*. Washington, DC: HEATH Resource Center.

Hartman, R. C. (1993). Transition to higher education. In S. Kroeger & J. Schuck (Eds.), *Responding to disability issues in student affairs* (pp. 31–43). San Francisco: Jossey-Bass.

Hartman, R. C. (1997). Foreword. In C. T. Mangrum & S. S. Strichart (Eds.), *Peterson's guide to colleges with programs for students with learning disabilities* (pp. iv–v). Princeton, NJ: Peterson's Guides.

Hasazi, S., Furney, K., & Destefano, L. (1999). Implementing the IDEA transition mandates. *Exceptional Children, 65*, 555–566.

Hawks, R. (1996). Assessing adults with learning disabilities. In N. Gregg, C. Hoy, & A. F. Gay (Eds.), *Adults with learning disabilities: Theoretical and practical perspectives* (pp. 144–161). New York: Guilford Press.

Hayes, M. L. (1993). *You don't outgrow it: Living with learning disabilities*. Novato, CA: Academic Therapy Publications. (ERIC Document Reproduction Service No. ED 354 668)

Hayes, M. L., & Sloat, R. S. (1988). Learning disability and suicide. *Academic Therapy, 23*, 469–475.

HEATH Resource Center. (1997). *Make the most of your opportunities: A guide to postsecondary education for adults with disabilities*. Washington, DC: American Council on Education.

Henderson, C. (Ed.). (1999). *College freshmen with disabilities: A statistical profile*. Washington, DC: American Council on Education.

Herman, J. L., Morris, L. L., & Fitz-Gibbon, C. T. (1987). *Evaluator's handbook*. Newbury Park, CA: Sage.

Heumann, J. (1998). *Judith Heumann Speaks on Individuals with Disabilities Education Act to the U.S. Senate Committee on Labor and Human Resources* [Online]. Available: www.ed.gov/speeches/01-1997

Heyward, Lawton & Associates (Eds.). (1991a). Compliance with both the Education of the Handicapped Act (EHA) and Section 504: Mission impossible? *Disability Accommodation Digest, 1*(1), 5, 7.

Heyward, Lawton & Associates (Eds.). (1991b). Documenting the need for academic adjustments. *Disability Accommodation Digest, 1*(3), 1–3.

Heyward, Lawton & Associates. (1991c). Significant court cases and OCR findings. *Disability Accommodation Digest, 1*(1), 6.

Heyward, Lawton, & Associates. (Eds.). (1992). Significant court cases. *Disability Accommodation Digest, 2*(3), 7.

Heyward, Lawton & Associates. (1995a). Faculty members and service providers: The unhappy alliance. *Disability Accommodation Digest, 4*(3 & 4), 1–4.

Heyward, Lawton & Associates. (1995b). Readers' digest, continued: Your questions answered. *Disability Accommodation Digest, 5*, 6–7.

Heyward, S. (1998). *Disability and higher education: Guidance for Section 504 and ADA compliance*. Horsham, PA: LRP Publications.

Higgins, E. L., & Raskind, M. H. (1995). An investigation of the compensatory effectiveness of speech recognition on the written composition performance of postsecondary students with learning disabilities. *Learning Disability Quarterly, 18*, 159–174.

Higgins, E. L., & Zvi, J. C. (1995). Assistive technology for postsecondary students with learning disabilities: From research to practice. *Annals of Dyslexia, 45*, 123–142.

Higgins, K., Boone, R., & Lovitt, T. C. (1996). Hypertext support for remedial students and students with learning disabilities. *Journal of Learning Disabilities, 29*(4), 402–412.

Hill, J. L. (1996). Speaking out: Perceptions of students with disabilities regarding adequacy of services and willingness of faculty to make accommodations. *Journal of Postsecondary Education and Disability, 12,* 22–43.

Hill Top Preparatory School. (1988). Learning disabled adolescents viewed at risk for drug and alcohol abuse. *Hill Top Spectrum* (Rosemont, PA), 3. (ERIC Document Reproduction Service No. ED 309 602)

Hilton-Chalfen, D. (1992). Information technology, campus libraries, and patrons with disabilities: Emerging issues and access strategies. *EDUCOM Review, 27*(6), 47–49.

Hishinuma, E. (1999). An update of NCAA college freshman academic requirements: The impacts on students with LD. *Journal of Learning Disabilities, 32*(4), 362–371.

Hishinuma, E. S., & Tadaki, S. (1997). The problem with grade and age equivalents: WIAT as a case in point. *Journal of Psychoeducational Assessment, 15,* 214–225.

Holland, J. (1971). *The self-directed search.* Odessa, FL: Consulting Psychologists Press.

Horn, L., Berktold, J., & Bobbitt, L. (1999, June). *Students with disabilities in postsecondary education: A profile of preparation, participation, and outcomes.* Washington, DC: U.S. Department of Education, Office of Educational Research and Improvement, National Center for Education Statistics.

Hoy, C., Gregg, N., Wisenbaker, J., Manglitz, E., King, M., & Moreland, C. (1997). Depression and anxiety in two groups of adults with learning disabilities. *Learning Disability Quarterly, 20,* 278–292.

Hoy, C., Gregg, N., Wisenbaker, J., Siglais Bonham, S., King, M., & Moreland, C. (1996). Clinical model versus discrepancy model in determining eligibility for learning disabilities services at a rehabilitation setting. In N. Gregg, C. Hoy, & A. F. Gay (Eds.), *Adults with learning disabilities: Theoretical and practical perspectives* (pp. 55–67). New York: Guilford Press.

Hughes, C. A. (1996). Memory and test-taking strategies. In D. D. Deshler, E. S. Ellis, & B. K. Lenz, *Teaching adolescents with learning disabilities: Strategies and methods* (2nd ed., pp. 209–266). Denver, CO: Love.

Hughes, C. A., & Smith, J. D. (1990). Cognitive and academic performance of college students with learning disabilities. *Learning Disability Quarterly, 13,* 66–79.

Hynd, G. W., Hern, K. L., Novey, E. S., Eliopulos, D., Marshall, R., Gonzalez, J. J., & Voeller, K. K. (1993). Attention-deficit hyperactivity disorder and asymmetry of the caudate nucleus. *Journal of Child Neurology, 8,* 339–347.

Hynd, G. W., Marshall, R., & Gonzalez, J. (1991). Learning disabilities and presumed central nervous system dysfunction. *Learning Disability Quarterly, 14,* 283–296.

IBM ViaVoice [Computer software]. (1997). Austin, TX: International Business Machines Corp. Special Needs Systems.

Illinois Online Network. (2000). *Online education resources* [Online]. Available: http://illinois.online. uillinois.edu/IONresources/index.html

Impara, J. C., & Plake, B. S. (Eds.). (1998). *The thirteenth mental measurements yearbook.* Lincoln, NE: Buros Institute.

Individuals with Disabilities Education Act of 1990, 20 U.S.C. § 1400 *et seq.*

Individuals with Disabilities Education Act Amendments of 1997, 20 U.S.C. § 1400 *et seq.*

Inspiration [Computer software]. (1997). Portland, OR: Inspiration.

Interagency Committee on Learning Disabilities. (1987). *Learning disabilities: A report to the U.S. Congress.* Bethesda, MD: National Institutes of Health.

Interview with an ADD coach. (1998, Fall). *FOCUS: The Official Newsletter of the National Attention Deficit Disorder Association,* 12–13.

Jackson, S. C., Enright, R. D., & Murdock, J. Y. (1987). Social perception problems in learning disabled youth: Developmental lag versus perceptual deficit. *Journal of Learning Disabilities, 20,* 361–364.

Jaksa, P., & Ratey, N. (1999, Summer). Therapy & ADD coaching: Similarities, differences and collaboration. *FOCUS: The Official Newsletter of the National Attention Deficit Disorder Association,* 3, 10.

Jarrow, J. (1998). *Guidelines for documentation* [Online]. Available: http://www.janejarrow.com/study/samplepolicy/index.html

Jarrow, J. (1999a, May). Handling requests for campus housing accommodations. *Section 504 Compliance Handbook, Supplement No. 246,* 5–7.

Jarrow, J. (1999b, January). Institutional politics: "The game is afoot." *DAIS,* 3, 2–3.

Jarrow, J. E. (1986). *Integration of individuals with disabilities in higher education.* Washington, DC: ATA Institute, Catholic University of America.

Jarrow, J. E. (1991, Winter). Disability issues on campus and the road to ADA. *Educational Record, 72,* 26–31.

Jarrow, J. E. (1992a, June). *Legal issues.* Paper presented at the University of Connecticut Fourth Annual Postsecondary Training Institute, Farmington, CT.

Jarrow, J. E. (1992b). *Title by title: The ADA's impact on postsecondary education.* Columbus, OH: Association on Higher Education and Disability.

Jarrow, J. E. (1997a). *Higher education and the ADA: Issues and perspectives.* Columbus, OH: Disability Access Information and Support.

Jarrow, J. E. (1997b). Why we need professional standards. *Journal of Postsecondary Education and Disability, 12*(3), 5–7.

Jaschik, S. (1990, May 30). U.S. court rules that requiring multiple-choice tests may violate the rights of learning disabled students. *Chronicle of Higher Education,* pp. A17, A20.

Jastak, S. R., & Wilkinson, G. S. (1984). *Wide Range Achievement Test–Revised.* Wilmington, DE: Jastak.

Javorsky, J., & Gussin, B. (1994). College students with attention deficit hyperactivity disorder: An overview and description of services. *Journal of College Student Development, 35,* 170–177.

Jax, J., & Muraski, T. (1993). Library services for students with disabilities at the University of Wisconsin–Stout. *Journal of Academic Librarianship, 19*(3), 166–168.

Johnson, D. J. (1987). Principles of assessment and diagnosis. In D. J. Johnson & J. W. Blalock (Eds.), *Adults with learning disabilities: Clinical studies* (pp. 9–30). Orlando, FL: Grune & Stratton.

Johnson, G. O. (1962). Special education for the mentally handicapped—A paradox. *Exceptional Children, 29,* 62–69.

Johnson, J. (1989). *The LD academic support group manual.* Columbus, OH: Association on Handicapped Student Service Programs in Postsecondary Education.

Jordan, C. (1995, September). *Learning disabilities at the graduate or professional school level: Identification, acceptance and accommodation.* Paper presented at Higher Education and Students with Learning Disabilities Conference, Curry College, Milton, MA.

Jordan, C. (1998, June). Personal perspectives on the use of documentation guidelines. *ALERT, 22,* 12–14.

Jordan, C. (2000, June). *Potential, possibilities, programs, pandemonium and Prozac: Working with students with disabilities.* Keynote address at the 12th annual Postsecondary Learning Disability Training Institute, sponsored by the Postsecondary Education Disability Education Unit of the University of Connecticut, Saratoga Springs, NY.

Jordan, C. (2000). Using documentation guidelines: Applications for clinical service. *Learning Disabilities: A Multidisciplinary Journal, 10,* 37–42.

Kaltenberger v. Ohio College of Podiatric Medicine, 162 F.3d 432 (6th Cir. 1998).

Katz, L. J. (1998, March/April). Transitioning into college for the student with ADHD. *ADHD Challenge, 12,* 3–4.

Kaufman, A. S. (1994). *Intelligent testing with the WISC-III.* New York: Wiley.

Kaufman, A. S., & Lichtenberger, E. O. (1999). *Essentials of WAIS-III assessment.* New York: Wiley.

Kauffman, J. M. (1989). The Regular Education Initiative as Reagan-Bush education policy: A trickledown theory of education of the hard-to-teach. *Journal of Special Education, 23*(2), 256–277.

Kavale, K. A. (1988). The long-term consequences of learning disabilities. In M. C. Wang, M. C. Reynolds, & H. J. Walberg (Eds.), *Handbook of special education research and practice* (Vol. 2, pp. 304–344). New York: Pergamon Press.

Kavale, K. A., Forness, S. R., & Lorsbach, T. C. (1991). Definition for definition of learning disabilities. *Learning Disability Quarterly, 14,* 257–266.

Keim, J., McWhirter, J. J., & Bernstein, B. L. (1996). Academic success and university accommodations for learning disabilities: Is there a relationship? *Journal of College Student Development, 37,* 502–509.

Keiser, S. (1998). Test accommodations: An administrator's view. In M. Gordon & S. Keiser (Eds.), *Accommodations in higher education under the Americans with Disabilities Act (ADA)* (pp. 46–69). New York: Guilford Press.

Kelly, K. M. (1995). Adult ADD support groups. In K. G. Nadeau (Ed.), *A comprehensive guide to attention deficit disorder in adults: Research, diagnosis, and treatment* (pp. 352–374). New York: Brunner/Mazel.

Kelman, M., & Lester, G. (1997). *Jumping the queue: An inquiry into the legal treatment of students with learning disabilities.* Cambridge, MA: Harvard University Press.

Kilcarr, P. (1998). Additional risks facing college students with AD/HD. In P. Quinn & A. McCormick (Eds.), *Re-thinking AD/HD: A guide to fostering success in students with AD/HD at the college level* (pp. 67–75). Bethesda, MD: Advantage Books.

Kincaid, J. (1998, January). What should I do if . . . *Disability Compliance for Higher Education, 3,* 1, 8–9.

Kincaid, J. (1999a, October). OCR rules on admission, documentation and test accommodation issues. *Disability Compliance for Higher Education, 5*(3), 1, 6.

Kincaid, J. (1999b, July). Supreme Court rulings pose more questions for service providers. *Disability Compliance for Higher Education, 1,* 6.

Kincaid, J. M. (1997a, July). Don't cry for me: I'm in compliance. Paper presented at the annual conference of the Association on Higher Education and Disability, Boston, MA.

Kincaid, J. M. (1997b, September). Provost's uninformed stereotypes discriminated against students with learning disabilities. *ALERT, 21,* 5–9.

King, M. L., & Rental, V. M. (1981). Research update: Conveying meaning in written texts. *Language Arts, 58,* 721–728.

King, W., & Jarrow, J. (1990). *Testing accommodations for students with disabilities.* Columbus, OH: AHEAD.

King, W., & Jarrow, J. E. (1991). *Testing accommodations for students with disabilities: A guide for licensure, certification, and credentialing.* Columbus, OH: Association on Handicapped Student Service Programs in Postsecondary Education.

Kirk, S. A. (1962). *Educating exceptional children.* Boston: Houghton Mifflin.

Knowles, M. (1970). *The modern practice of adult education*. New York: Association Press.

Knowles, M. (1978). *The adult learner: A neglected species* (2nd ed.). Houston, TX: Gulf.

Knowles, M. (1984). *Andragogy in action: Applying modern principles of adult education*. San Francisco: Jossey-Bass.

Koehler, M., & Kravets, M. (1998). *Counseling secondary students with learning disabilities*. Paramas, NJ: Prentice-Hall.

Kolligian, J., & Sternberg, R. J. (1987). Intelligence, information processing, and specific learning disabilities: A triarchic synthesis. *Journal of Learning Disabilities, 20*, 8–17.

Konecky, J., & Wolinsky, S. (2000). Through the maze: Legal issues and disability rights. *Learning Disabilities: A Multidisciplinary Journal, 10*, 73–83.

Koppitz, E. M. (1963). *The Bender Gestalt Test for Young Children*. New York: Grune & Stratton.

Koppitz, E. M. (1975). *The Bender Gestalt Test for Young Children: Volume 2. Research and application, 1963–1973*. New York: Grune & Stratton.

Kravets, M. (Winter/1999). Pertinent facts about the college selection process. *PostSecondary LD Report, 3*, 2–3, 7.

Kravets, M., & Wax, I. F. (1999). *The K&W guide to colleges for the learning disabled* (5th ed.). New York: Random House.

Kroll, L. G. (1984). LD's—What happens to them when they are no longer children? *Academic Therapy, 20*, 133–148.

Kuperstein, J. S., & Kessler, J. M. (1991). *Building bridges: A guide to making the high school–college transition for students with learning disabilities*. Edison, NJ: Middlesex Co. College.

Kurzweil 3000 [Computer software]. (1997). Waltham, MA: Kurzweil Educational Systems.

Latham, P. (1997). ADD and test accommodations under the ADA, Attention! *CHADD, 4*, 41–43, 46.

Latham, P. H. (1998, July/August). Learning disabilities and the law. After high school: An overview for students. *LDA Newsbriefs, 33*(4), 3–4.

Latham, P. H., & Latham, P. S. (1993). *Learning disabilities and the law*. Washington, DC: JKL Communications.

Latham, P. S., & Latham, P. H. (1994). Legal rights of students with ADD. In P. Quinn (Ed.), *ADD and the college student: A guide for high school and college students with attention deficit disorder* (pp. 85–96). New York: Magination Press.

Latham, P. S., & Latham, P. H. (1998). Legal issues regarding AD/HD at the postsecondary level: Implications for service providers. In P. Quinn & A. McCormick (Eds.), *Re-thinking AD/HD: A guide to fostering success in students with AD/HD at the college level* (pp. 102–107). Bethesda, MD: Advantage Books.

Lavenstein, B. (1995). Neurological comorbidity patterns/differential diagnosis in adult attention deficit disorder. In K. G. Nadeau (Ed.), *A comprehensive guide to attention deficit disorder in adults: Research, diagnosis, and treatment* (pp. 74–92). New York: Brunner/Mazel.

LD–On line guide to postsecondary education information [Online]. Available: http://www.ldonline. org/ld_indepth/postsecondary/index.html

Leacock v. Temple University School of Medicine, 14 NDLR 30 (E.D. Pa. 1998).

Learning Disabilities Association of America. (1990, May). LDA position paper: Eligibility for services for persons with specific learning disabilities. *LDA Newsbriefs*, 1a–8a.

Learning Disabilities Services, University of North Carolina at Chapel Hill. (1998). *Coaching services for students with ADHD* [Brochure]. Chapel Hill, NC: Author.

Lee, S. W., & Flory Stefany, E. (1995). Review of the *Woodcock–Johnson Psycho-Educational Battery–Revised*. In J. C. Conoley & J. C. Impara (Eds.), *The twelfth mental measurements yearbook* (pp. 1116–1117). Lincoln, NE: Buros Institute.

Lendman, C. (1991). *Volunteer reader/taping service handbook* (2nd ed.). Columbus, OH: Association on Handicapped Student Service Programs in Postsecondary Education.

Lenn, K. (1996). Library services to disabled students: Outreach and education. *Reference Librarian, 53*, 13–25.

Lerner, J. (1997). *Learning disabilities: Theories, diagnosis, and teaching strategies*. Boston: Houghton Mifflin.

Lesley University, Disability Services. (n.d.). *Determining accommodations for students with learning disabilities for on-line courses* [Program Material]. Cambridge, MA: Author.

Levin, M. E., Levin, J. R., & Scalia, P. A. (1997). What claims can a comprehensive college program of academic support support? *Equity and Excellence in Education, 30*, 71–89.

Levine, P., & Nourse, S. W. (1998). What follow-up studies say about postschool life for young men and women with learning disabilities: A critical look at the literature. *Journal of Learning Disabilities, 31*, 212–233.

Levinson, D. J. (1986). A conception of adult development. *American Psychologist, 41*, 3–13.

Lewin, T. (1998, September 20). Shaky crutch for the learning-disabled. *New York Times*, pp. 1, 5.

Lewin, T. (2001, February 8). Disabled win halt to notations of special arrangements on tests. *New York Times*, pp. 1, 20.

Lewis, E. (1996). *Help yourself: Advice for college-bound students with learning disabilities*. New York: Random House.

Lewis, L., & Farris, E. (1999). *An institutional perspective on students with disabilities in postsecondary education* (NCES 1999-046). Washington, DC: U.S. Department of Education, Office of Educational Research and Improvement.

Library resources and computers must be accessible for students with visual impairments, OCR determines. (1998, June). *Section 504 Compliance Handbook, Supplement No. 235*, 7–8. Washington, DC: Thompson.

Link, T. (1989, May 5). Dyslexic student sues UC for denying extra exam time. *Oakland Tribune*, p. B-2.

Lipkin, M. (1993). *Guide to colleges with programs or services for students with learning disabilities*. Belmont, MA: Schoolsearch Press.

Lissner, S. (Winter/1999). Choosing a college. *PostSecondary LD Report, 3*, 4–5.

Litt, A. V., & McGuire, J. M. (1989). *Continuum of services*. Unpublished material, University of Connecticut, A. J. Pappanikou Center on Special Education and Rehabilitation, Storrs, CT.

Lombana, J. H. (1992). Learning disabled students and their families: Implications and strategies for counselors. *Journal of Humanistic Education and Development, 31*, 33–40.

Lorry, B. J. (1998). Language-based learning disabilities. In M. Gordon & S. Keiser (Eds.), *Accommodations in higher education under the Americans with Disabilities Act* (ADA) (pp. 130–153). New York: Guilford Press.

Lown, N. F. (1995). *The rehabilitation team: A systematic approach for use of technology in vocational rehabilitation services*. (ERIC Document Reproduction Service No. ED 404 831)

Lyon, G. R. (1996). Learning disabilities. *The future of children: Special education for students with disabilities, 6*, 54–76.

Lyon, G. R., & Moats, L. C. (1993). An examination of research in learning disabilities: Past practices and future directions. In G. R. Lyon, D. B. Gray, J. F. Kavanagh, & N. A. Krasnegor (Eds.), *Better understanding learning disabilities: New views from research and their implications for education and public policies* (pp. 1–13). Baltimore: Brookes.

MacArthur, C. A., & Haynes, J. A. (1995). Student assistant for learning from text (SALT): A hypermedia reading aid. *Journal of Learning Disabilities, 28*(3), 150–159.

MacArthur, C. A., Schwartz, S. S., & Graham, S. (1991). A model for writing instruction: Integrating word processing and strategy instruction into a process approach to writing. *Learning Disabilities Research and Practice, 6*, 230–236.

MacMillan, D. L., Gresham, F. M., & Bocian, K. M. (1998). Discrepancy between definitions of learning disabilities and school practices: An empirical investigation. *Journal of Learning Disabilities, 31*, 314–326.

Madaus, G. F., Airasian, P., & Kellaghan, T. (1980). *School effectiveness.* New York: McGraw-Hill.

Madaus, J. W. (1996). *Administration of postsecondary offices for students with disabilities: Perceptions of essential job functions.* Unpublished doctoral dissertation, University of Connecticut, Storrs.

Madaus, J. W. (1997). The process: Development of AHEAD professional standards. *Journal of Postsecondary Education and Disability, 12*, 8–25.

Madaus, J. W. (1998). Screening college students for potential learning disabilities. *Learning Disabilities: A Multidisciplinary Journal, 9*(1), 13–16.

Madaus, J. W. (1999). *The University of Connecticut Program for College Students with Learning Disabilities: Administrative procedures* (Rev. ed.). Unpublished material, University of Connecticut, Storrs.

Madaus, J. W., & Madaus, M. M. R. (1998). *"Johnny has a learning altercation" and other dubious documentation: An illustrative case.* Unpublished material, University of Connecticut, Storrs.

Majone, G. (1989). *Evidence, argument, and persuasion in the policy process.* New Haven, CT: Yale University Press.

Maller, S. J., & McDermott, P. A. (1997). WAIS–R profile analysis for college students with learning disabilities. *School Psychology Review, 26*, 575–585.

Mamarchev, H. L., & Williamson, M. L. (1991). Women and African Americans: Stories told and lessons learned—A case study. In P. L. Moore (Ed.), *Managing the political dimensions of student affairs* (pp. 67–79). San Francisco: Jossey-Bass.

Mangrum, C. T., & Strichart, S. (1997). *Peterson's colleges with programs for students with learning disabilities or attention-deficit disorders.* Princeton, NJ: Peterson's.

Mangrum, C. T., & Strichart, S. S. (1988). *College and the learning disabled student* (2nd ed.). Orlando, FL: Grune & Stratton.

Mapou, R. L. (1998, June). Attention deficit hyperactivity disorder and comorbid conditions: Research, assessment and documentation. *ALERT, 22*, 19–23.

Mapou, R. L. (2000). *Learning disabilities.* Manuscript submitted for publication.

Marby, L. (1995). Review of the *Wide Range Achievement Test 3.* In J. C. Conoley & J. C. Impara (Eds.), *The twelfth mental measurements yearbook* (pp. 1108–1110). Lincoln, NE: Buros Institute.

Marchant, G. J. (1990, November). Faculty questionnaires: A useful resource for LD support services. *Intervention in School and Clinic, 26*(2), 106–109.

Margalit, M. (1998). Loneliness and coherence among preschool children. *Journal of Learning Disabilities, 31*, 173–180.

Markides, C. (1997). Strategic innovation. *Sloan Management Review, 39*, 9–23.

Maroldo, R. (Ed.). (1991). *Individuals with Disabilities Education Act of 1990 (IDEA)*. Horsham, PA: LRP Publications.

Marshall, R. M., Hynd, G. W., Handwerk, M. J., & Hall, J. (1997). Academic underachievement in ADHD subtypes. *Journal of Learning Disabilities, 30*, 635–642.

Martin, J. E., Huber-Marshall, L. H., Maxson, L., & Jerman, P. (1996). *Self-directed IEP*. Longmont, CO: Sopris West.

Martin, J. E., & Marshall, L. H. (1996). Choice maker: Infusing self-determination into the IEP and transition process. In D. J. Sands & M. L. Wehmeyer (Eds.), *Self-determination across the life span* (pp. 215–236). Baltimore: Brookes.

Math class offers an alternative to waivers and substitutions. (1998, October). *Disability Compliance for Higher Education, 4*(3), 1, 8.

Mather, N., & Healey, W. C. (1990). Deposing aptitude-achievement discrepancy as the imperial criterion for learning disabilities. *Learning Disabilities: A Multidisciplinary Journal, 1*, 40–48.

Mather, N., & Roberts, R. (1994). Learning disabilities: A field in danger of extinction. *Learning Disabilities Research and Practice, 9*, 49–58.

Mather, N. & Woodcock, R. W. (2001a). *Woodcock–Johnson III Tests of Achievement: Examiner's manual*. Itasca, IL: Riverside.

Mather, N. & Woodcock, R. W. (2001b). *Woodcock–Johnson III Tests of Cognitive Abilities: Examiner's manual*. Itasca, IL: Riverside.

Matthews, P., Hameister, B., & Hosley, N. (1998). Attitudes of college students toward study abroad: Implications for disability service providers. *Journal of Postsecondary Education and Disability, 13*(2), 67–77.

Matthews, P. R., Anderson, D. W., & Skolnick, B. D. (1987). Faculty attitude toward accommodations for college students with learning disabilities. *Learning Disabilities Focus, 3*, 46–52.

McCormick, A. (1998). Retention interventions for college students with AD/HD. In P. Quinn & A. McCormick (Eds.), *Re-thinking AD/HD: A guide to fostering success in students with AD/HD at the college level* (pp. 85–89). Bethesda, MD: Advantage Books.

McCormick, A., & Leonard, F. (1994). Learning accommodations for ADD students. In P. Quinn (Ed.), *ADD and the college student: A guide for high school and college students with attention deficit disorder* (pp. 75–83). New York: Magination Press.

McCroskey, R., & Thompson, N. (1973). Comprehension of rate controlled speech by children with specific learning disabilities. *Journal of Learning Disabilities, 6*, 29–35.

McGill University, Office for Students with Disabilities. (1995). *Policy concerning the rights of students with disabilities*. Montreal, Quebec: Author. [Online]. Available: http://www.mcgill.ca/stuserv/osd/rights.html

McGill University, Office for Students with Disabilities. (2000). *Information for McGill University professors: Students with attention deficit or attention deficit hyperactivity disorder* [Program Material]. Montreal, Quebec: Author.

McGill University, Office for Students with Disabilities. (2000). *Information for McGill University professors: Students with learning disabilities* [Program Material]. Montreal, Quebec: Author.

McGill University, Office for Students with Disabilities. (2000). *Notetaking*. Montreal, Quebec: Author. [Online]. Available: http://ww2.mcgill.ca/stuserv/osd/services.htm#notetaking

McGill University, Office for Students with Disabilities. (2000). *OSD computing facilities* [Program Material]. Montreal, Quebec: Author. [Online]. Available: http://ww2.mcgill.ca/stuserv/osd/services.htm#computing

McGill University, Office for Students with Disabilities. (2000). *Receiving services at McGill*. Montreal, Quebec: Author. [Online]. Available: http://ww2.mcgill.ca/stuserv/osd/services.htm#services

McGill University, Office for Students with Disabilities. (2000). *Tutoring*. Montreal, Quebec: Author. [Online]. Available: http://ww2.mcgill.ca/stuserv/osd/services.htm#tutoring

McGill University, Office for Students with Disabilities. (2000). *Writing final exams at OSD*. Montreal, Quebec: Author. [Online]. Available: http://ww2.mcgill.ca/stuserv/osd/services.htm#exams

McGill University, Office for Students with Disabilities. (n.d.). *Reading services*. Montreal, Quebec: Author. [Online]. Available: http://ww2.mcgill.ca/stuserv/osd/services.htm#reading

McGill University, Office for Students with Disabilities. (n.d.). *Student file: Information summary form* [Program Material]. Montreal, Quebec: Author.

McGregor, G., & Pachuski, P. (1996). Assistive technology in schools: Are teachers ready, able, and supported? *Journal of Special Education Technology, 13*(1), 4–15.

McGrew, K. S., & Woodcock, R. W. (2001). *Woodcock–Johnson III technical manual*. Itasca, IL: Riverside.

McGuinness v. University of New Mexico School of Medicine, 170 F.3d 974 (10th Cir. 1998).

McGuire, J. M. (1992a). *Academic affairs or student affairs: Pros and cons*. Unpublished material, University of Connecticut, A. J. Pappanikou Center on Special Education and Rehabilitation, Storrs, CT.

McGuire, J. M. (1992b). *A step by step approach to questions to be asked in planning a program evaluation*. Unpublished material, University of Connecticut, A. J. Pappanikou Center on Special Education and Rehabilitation, Storrs, CT.

McGuire, J. M. (1992c). *The University of Connecticut Program for College Students with Learning Disabilities: Administrative procedures*. Unpublished material, University of Connecticut, Storrs.

McGuire, J. M. (Winter/1997). Documenting a need . . . for dialogue about documentation. *Postsecondary Disability Network News, 1–2*, 5.

McGuire, J. M. (1998). Educational accommodations: A university administrator's view. In M. Gordon & S. Keiser (Eds.), *Accommodations in higher education under the Americans with Disabilities Act (ADA)* (pp. 20–45). New York: Guilford Press.

McGuire, J. M. (1999). *Program evaluation of Central Regional Connections*. Storrs, CT: McGuire & Associates.

McGuire, J. M., Anderson, P. L., & Shaw, S. F. (1998). *Guidelines for documentation of a specific learning disability*. Storrs: University of Connecticut.

McGuire, J. M., & Brinckerhoff, L. C. (1997, June). *Crafting campus policies: Facing ongoing challenges to access and equity*. Strand presentation at the 9th annual Postsecondary Learning Disability Training Institute, sponsored by the Postsecondary Education Disability Education Unit of the University of Connecticut, Saratoga Springs, NY.

McGuire, J. M., & Brinckerhoff, L. C. (1998, April). Independent consortium issues new ADHD documentation guidelines. *ALERT, 22*, 19–20.

McGuire, J. M., Fresco, K. M., Foley, T. E., Madaus, J. W., & Owen, S. V. (1999). *Documentation of learning disabilities at the postsecondary level: Good news . . . but not enough!* Unpublished material, Storrs, CT.

McGuire, J. M., Hall, D., & Litt, A. V. (1991). A field based study of the direct service needs of college students with learning disabilities. *Journal of College Student Development, 32*, 101–108.

McGuire, J. M., Harris, M. W., & Bieber, N. (1989). Evaluating college programs for learning disabled students: An approach for adaptation. In *Support services for LD students in postsecondary education:*

A compendium of readings (Vol. 2, pp. 131–136). Columbus, OH: Association on Handicapped Student Service Programs in Postsecondary Education.

McGuire, J. M., & Madaus, J. W. (1999a). *The University of Connecticut Program for College Students with Learning Disabilities: Administrative procedures.* Unpublished material, University of Connecticut, Storrs.

McGuire, J. M., & Madaus, J. W. (1999b). *The University of Connecticut Program for College Students with Learning Disabilities (UPLD): 1998–99 annual report.* Storrs, CT: Postsecondary Education Disability Unit, Neag School of Education.

McGuire, J. M., & Madaus, J. W. (1999). *Faculty letter of appreciation* [Program Material]. Storrs: University of Connecticut, University Program for College Students with Learning Disabilities.

McGuire, J. M., Madaus, J. W., Litt, A. V., & Ramirez, M. O. (1996). An investigation of documentation submitted by university students to verify their learning disabilities. *Journal of Learning Disabilities, 29,* 297–304.

McGuire, J. M., Madaus, J. W., & Plaia, K. (Eds.). (1998). *Learning specialist training manual* (2nd ed.). Storrs: University Program for College Students with Learning Disabilities, Postsecondary Education Disability Unit, University of Connecticut.

McGuire, J. M., Norlander, K. A., & Shaw, S. F. (1990). Postsecondary education for students with learning disabilities: Forecasting challenges for the future. *Learning Disabilities Focus, 5,* 69–74.

McGuire, J. M., & Pollack, R. (1988; rev. 1999). *University of Connecticut interactive model of support services for students with learning disabilities.* Unpublished material, University of Connecticut, A. J. Pappanikou Center on Special Education and Rehabilitation, Storrs, CT.

McGuire, J. M., & Shaw, S. F. (1986). *McGuire-Shaw postsecondary selection guide and manual for learning disabled college students.* Storrs: University of Connecticut.

McGuire, J. M., & Shaw, S. F. (Eds.). (1989; rev. 1996, 1999). *Resource guide of support services for students with learning disabilities in Connecticut colleges and universities.* Storrs, CT: University of Connecticut, A. J. Pappanikou Center on Special Education and Rehabilitation.

McLoughlin, J. A., & Lewis, R. B. (1994). *Assessing special students* (4th ed.). Upper Saddle River, NJ: Merrill.

McNaughton, D., Hughes, C., & Clark, K. (1993). *An investigation of the effect of five writing conditions on the spelling performance of college students with disabilities.* Paper presented at the 30th international conference of the Learning Disability Association of America, San Francisco.

Mellard, D. F. (1990). The eligibility process: Identifying students with learning disabilities in California's community colleges. *Learning Disabilities Focus, 5,* 75–91.

Meltzer, L. (1994). Assessment of learning disabilities: The challenge of evaluating the cognitive strategies and processes underlying learning. In G. R. Lyon (Ed.), *Frames of reference for the assessment of learning disabilities: New views on measurement issues* (pp. 571–606). Baltimore: Brookes.

Mendle, J. (1995). Library services for persons with disabilities. *Reference Librarian, 49–50,* 105–121.

Mercer, C. (1991). *Students with learning disabilities* (4th ed.). New York: Merrill.

Mercer, C. D., Hughes, C., & Mercer, A. R. (1985). Learning disabilities definitions used by state education departments. *Learning Disability Quarterly, 8,* 45–55.

Miami University, Bernard B. Rinella Jr. Learning Assistance Center. (n.d.). *Foreign language course substitution information packet* [Program Material]. Oxford, OH: Author.

Michael, R. (1988). Library services for LD college students. *Academic Therapy, 23*(5), 529–532.

Michaels, C. (1986). Increasing faculty awareness and cooperation: Procedures for assisting college students with learning disabilities. In J. J. Vander Putten (Ed.), *Proceedings of the 1989 AHSSPPE*

Conference (pp. 78–87). Columbus, OH: Association on Handicapped Student Service Programs in Postsecondary Education.

Michaels, C. (1997). Preparing for employment: Counseling practices for promoting personal competency. In P. J. Gerber & D. S. Brown (Eds.), *Learning disabilities and employment* (pp. 187–215). Austin, TX: PRO-ED.

Michaels, C. A. (1994). Curriculum ideology in the secondary special education transition planning process. In C. A. Michaels (Ed.), *Transition strategies for persons with learning disabilities* (pp. 23–52). San Diego, CA: Singular.

Michaels, C. A.,Thaler, R., Zwerlein, R., Gioglio, M., & Apostoli, B. (1988). *From high school to college: Keys to success for students with learning disabilities*. Albertson, NY: Human Resources Center.

Middlesex County College. (1997). *Middlesex County College catalog*. Edison, NJ: Author.

Milani, A. (1996). Disabled students in higher education: Administrative and judicial enforcement of disability law. *Journal of College and University Law, 22,* 989–1043.

Miller, S. P. (1996). Perspectives on mathematics instruction. In D. D. Deshler, E. S. Ellis, & B. K. Lenz (Eds.), *Teaching adolescents with learning disabilities: Strategies and methods* (2nd ed., pp. 313–368). Denver, CO: Love.

Miller, T. K. (Ed.). (1997). *The book of professional standards for higher education*. Washington, DC: Council for the Advancement of Standards in Higher Education.

Mills v. The Board of Education of the District of Columbia, 348 F. Supp. 866 (D.D.C. 1972).

Minner, S., & Prater, G. (1984). College teachers' expectations of LD students. *Academic Therapy, 20,* 225–229.

Mohr, L. B. (1995). *Impact analysis for program evaluation*. Thousand Oaks, CA: SAGE.

Morris, M., Leuenberger, J., & Aksamit, D. (1987). Faculty in-service training: Impact on the postsecondary climate for learning disabled students. *Journal of Postsecondary Education and Disability, 5,* 58–66.

Morris, R. (1993). Issues in empirical versus clinical identification of learning disabilities. In G. R. Lyon, D. B. Gray, J. F. Kavanagh, & N. A. Krasnegor (Eds.), *Better understanding learning disabilities: New views from research and their implications for education and public policies* (pp. 73–94). Baltimore: Brookes.

Morris, R. (1994). A review of critical concepts and issues in the measurement of learning disabilities. In G. R. Lyon (Ed.), *Frames of reference for the assessment of learning disabilities: New views on measurement issues* (pp. 615–626). Baltimore: Brookes.

Murphy, K. R. (1995). Empowering the adult with ADD. In K. G. Nadeau (Ed.), *A comprehensive guide to attention deficit disorder in adults: Research, diagnosis, and treatment* (pp. 135–145). New York: Brunner/Mazel.

Murphy, K., & Gordon, M. (1996, December). ADHD as a basis for test accommodations: A primer for clinicians. *ADHD Report, 4*(6), 10–11.

Murphy, S. (1992). *On being LD: Perspectives and strategies of young adults*. New York: Teachers College Press.

Muskingum College, Center for Advancement of Learning. (2000). *Parent contact sheet* [Program Material]. New Concord, OH: Author.

Muskingum College, Center for Advancement of Learning. (2000). *PLUS program philosophy statement* [Program Material]. New Concord, OH: Author.

Muskingum College, Center for Advancement of Learning. (2000). *Responsibility contract—Full services* [Program Material]. New Concord, OH: Author.

Muskingum College, Center for Advancement of Learning. (2000). *Responsibility contract—Maintenance level services* [Program Material]. New Concord, OH: Author.

Myers, P. I., & Hammill, D. D. (1990). *Learning disabilities: Basic concepts, assessment practices, and instructional strategies* (4th ed.). Austin, TX: PRO-ED.

Myklebust, H. R. (1973). *Development and disorders of written language: Studies of normal and exceptional children* (Vol. 2). New York: Grune & Stratton.

Nadeau, K. G. (Ed.). (1995a). *A comprehensive guide to attention deficit disorder in adults: Research, diagnosis, and treatment*. New York: Brunner/Mazel.

Nadeau, K. G. (1995b). Diagnosis and assessment of ADD in postsecondary students. *Journal of Postsecondary Education and Disability, 11*, 3–15.

Nadeau, K. G. (1995c). An introduction to the special issue on attention deficit disorder. *Journal of Postsecondary Education and Disability, 11*, 1–2.

National Information Center for Children and Youth with Disabilities. (1997, August). *The IDEA amendments of 1997* (Vol. 26). Washington, DC: Author.

National Institutes of Health. (1998, November). *Diagnosis and treatment of attention deficit disorder* [Online]. Available: odp.od.nih.gov/consensus/cons/110/110_statement.htm

National Joint Committee on Learning Disabilities. (1987, September). *Issues in learning disabilities: Assessment and Diagnosis*. Austin, TX: PRO-ED.

National Joint Committee on Learning Disabilities. (1988). In-service programs in learning disabilities. *Journal of Learning Disabilities, 21*, 53–55.

National Joint Committee on Learning Disabilities. (1994a). *Collective perspectives on issues affecting learning disabilities: Position papers and statements*. Austin, TX: PRO-ED.

National Joint Committee on Learning Disabilities. (1994b). Issues in learning disabilities: Assessment and diagnosis. *Collective perspectives on issues affecting learning disabilities: Position papers and statements* (pp. 49–55). Austin, TX: PRO-ED.

National Joint Committee on Learning Disabilities. (1994c). Secondary to postsecondary education transition planning for students with learning disabilities. *Collective perspectives on issues affecting learning disabilities: Position papers and statements* (pp. 97–104). Austin, TX: PRO-ED.

National Joint Committee on Learning Disabilities. (1999, January). Learning disabilities: Issues in higher education. *ASHA Desk Reference, 1999 edition*.

Navicky, J. (1998, Winter). A match made by design not accident. *PostSecondary LD Report*. Columbus, OH: Block Educational Consulting.

Navicky, J. (2000, Spring). Understanding the differences between secondary and postsecondary education: The key to success. *PostSecondary LD Report, 4*(3).

NCAA alters policy: Students with learning disabilities can play college sports under Justice Department agreement. (1998). *LDA Newsbriefs, 33*(4), 1.

Nelson, R., & Lignugaris/Kraft, B. (1989). Postsecondary education for students with learning disabilities. *Exceptional Children, 56*, 246–265.

New Jersey Special Needs Regional Centers for Learning Disabilities. (1998, November). *Policy of the New Jersey Special Needs Regional Centers on diagnosing a learning disability at the postsecondary level*. Trenton, NJ: Author.

Newman, A. P. (1994). Adult literacy programs: An overview. *Learning Disabilities: A Multidisciplinary Journal, 5*, 51–61.

Nierenberg, A. (1998, Fall). Take note: 10 ways to say "thank you." *Workforce Diversity for Engineering and IT Professionals, 5*, 60–61.

Norlander, K. A., Shaw, S. F., & McGuire, J. M. (1988). Competencies needed by college personnel serving students with learning disabilities: Issues in preparing and hiring. In D. Knapke & C. Lendman (Eds.), *Proceedings of the 1988 AHSSPPE conference* (pp. 248–263). Columbus, OH: Association on Handicapped Student Service Programs in Postsecondary Education.

Norlander, K. A., Shaw, S. F., & McGuire, J. M. (1990). Competencies of postsecondary education personnel serving students with learning disabilities. *Journal of Learning Disabilities, 23,* 426–432.

Notes from the LD–ADHD SIG meetings in Las Vegas. (1998, August/September). *ALERT, 22,* 38–41.

Nussbaum, N. L., Grant, M. L., Roman, M. J., Poole, J. H., & Bigler, E. D. (1990). Attention deficit disorder and the mediating effect of age on academic and behavioral variables. *Developmental and Behavioral Pediatrics, 11,* 22–26.

O'Connor, M. L., McGuire, J. M., & Madaus, J. W. (1998, July). *Educational training and professional development for postsecondary disability service providers: Honing our skills while we do our jobs.* Paper presented at the international conference of the Association on Higher Education and Disability, Las Vegas.

Offering campus LD testing can be helpful, but also risky. (1996, July). *Disability Compliance for Higher Education, 1*(12), 9.

Office for Civil Rights. (n.d.). *Contact OCR.* Washington, DC: Author. [Online]. Available: http://nle2.ed.gov/CFAPPS/OCR/contactus.cfm

O'Leary, E. (1998, February). *Transition: Terms and concepts.* Des Moines, IA: Mountain Lakes Regional Resource Center.

Overton, T. (2000). *Assessment in special education: An applied approach* (3rd ed.). Upper Saddle River, NJ: Merrill.

Parker, D., & Byron, J. (1998a). *College students with ADHD.* Unpublished material, University of North Carolina at Chapel Hill.

Parker, D., & Byron, J. (1998b). Differences between college students with LD and AD/HD: Practical implications for service providers. In P. Quinn & A. McCormick (Eds.), *Re-thinking AD/HD: A guide to fostering success in students with AD/HD at the college level* (pp. 14–30). Bethesda, MD: Advantage Books.

Parker, D. R. (1998, August/September). Campuses report trends in college students with ADHD. *ALERT, 22,* 42–44.

Patton, J., & Dunn, C. (1998). *Transition from school to young adulthood.* Austin, TX: PRO-ED.

Patton, J. R., & Polloway, E. A. (1992). Learning disabilities: The challenges of adulthood. *Journal of Learning Disabilities, 25*(7), 410–415.

Patton, J. R., & Polloway, E. A. (1996). Adults with learning disabilities: An emerging area of professional interest and public attention. In J. R. Patton & E. A. Polloway (Eds.), *Learning disabilities: The challenge of adulthood* (pp. 1–10). Austin, TX: PRO-ED.

Payne, M. (1993). *Distance learning and adults with disabilities.* Washington, DC: HEATH Resource Center.

Payne, N. (1997). Job accommodations: What works and why. In P. J. Gerber & D. S. Brown (Eds.), *Learning disabilities and employment* (pp. 255–275). Austin, TX: PRO-ED.

Pennsylvania Association for Retarded Citizens (PARC) v. Commonwealth of Pennsylvania, 334 F. Supp. 1257 (E.D. Pa. 1972).

Perkins, D., Bailey, M., Repetto, J., & Schwartz, S. (1995). *Dare to dream: A guide to planning your future.* Tallahassee: Florida Department of Education.

Perreira, D., & Richards, A. (2000). The role of undergraduate programs in preparing students with learning disabilities for professional school enrollment. *Learning Disabilities: A Multidisciplinary Journal, 10,* 57–64.

Phillips, B. (1991). *Technology abandonment: From the consumer point of view.* Washington, DC: Request Publications.

Phillips, B. (1992). *Perspectives on assistive technology services in vocational rehabilitation: Clients and counselors.* Washington, DC: National Rehabilitation Hospital, Assistive Technology/Rehabilitation Engineering Program.

Phipps, R., & Merisotis, S. J. (1999). *What's the difference? A review of contemporary research on the effectiveness of distance learning in higher education.* Washington, DC: Institute for Higher Education Policy. Available on-line: www.ihep.com/difference.pdf

Porter, M. E. (1996). What is strategy? *Harvard Business Review, 74,* 61–78.

Powers, L. E., Sowers, J., Turner, A., Nesbitt, M., Knowles, E., & Ellison, R. (1996). TAKECHARGE: A model for promoting self-determination among adolescents with challenges. In L. E. Powers, G. H. S. Singer, & J. Sowers (Eds.), *Promoting self-competence in children and youth with disabilities: On the road to autonomy* (pp. 291–322). Baltimore: Brookes.

Price v. The National Board of Medical Examiners, 966 F. Supp. 419 (S.D.W.Va. 1997).

Price, L. (1988). Support groups work! *Journal of Counseling and Human Services Professions, 2,* 35–46.

Price, L. (1993). Psychosocial characteristics and issues of adults with learning disabilities. In L. Brinckerhoff, S. Shaw, & J. McGuire (Eds.), *Promoting postsecondary education for students with learning disabilities: A handbook for practitioners* (pp. 137–167). Austin, TX: PRO-ED.

Price, L., & Shaw, S. (1997). The AHEAD Code of Ethics: Principles Four and Five. *Alert, 21*(4), 16, 17.

Price, L. A. (1997). The development and implementation of a code of ethical behavior for postsecondary personnel. *Journal of Postsecondary Education and Disability, 12*(3), 36–44.

Primus, C. (1990). *Computer assistance model for learning disabled.* Washington, DC: Office of Special Education and Rehabilitation Services, U.S. Department of Education.

Protection and Advocacy. (1999). *Direct links to P&As/CAPs websites.* Washington, DC: Author. [Online]. Available: http://www.protectionandadvocacy.com/demofile.htm

Psychological Corporation. (1992). *The Wechsler Individual Achievement Test.* San Antonio, TX: Harcourt Brace.

Quinn, P. O. (Ed.). (1994). *ADD and the college student: A guide for high school and college students with attention deficit disorder.* New York: Magination Press.

Quinn, P. O. (1998). The issue of medication for college students with AD/HD and related disorders. In P. Quinn & A. McCormick (Eds.), *Re-thinking AD/HD: A guide to fostering success in students with AD/HD at the college level* (pp. 90–96). Bethesda, MD: Advantage Books.

Rada, H. (1980). An interview with Malcolm Knowles. *Journal of Developmental and Remedial Education, 4,* 2–4.

Rapp, R. (1998, July). *Distance education and students with disabilities.* Paper presented at the annual conference of the Association on Higher Education and Disability, Las Vegas, NV.

Raskind, M. (1994). Assistive technology for adults with learning disabilities: A rationale for use. In P. J. Gerber & H. B. Reiff (Eds.), *Adults with learning disabilities* (pp. 152–162). Austin, TX: PRO-ED.

Raskind, M. (1998). Literacy for adults with learning disabilities through assistive technology. In S. A. Vogel & S. Reder (Eds.), *Bridging the gap: Learning disabilities, literacy, and adult education.* Baltimore: Brookes.

Raskind, M., & Bryant, B. R. (1996, November). *Assistive technology evaluation for persons with learning disabilities*. Paper presented at the Council for Learning Disabilities International Conference, Nashville, TN.

Raskind, M., & Higgins, E. (1998). Assistive technology for postsecondary students with learning disabilities: An overview. *Journal of Learning Disabilities, 31*(1), 27–40.

Raskind, M., & Scott, N. (1993). Technology for postsecondary students with learning disabilities. In S. A. Vogel & P. B. Adelman (Eds.), *Success for college students with learning disabilities* (pp. 240–279). New York: Spring-Verlag.

Raskind, M., & Shaw, T. (1996, March). *An overview: Assistive technology for students with learning disabilities*. Council for Learning Disabilities Assistive Technology Symposium, Las Vegas, NV.

Raskind, M. H., Goldberg, R. J., Higgins, E. L., & Herman, K. L. (1999). Patterns of change and predictors of success in individuals with learning disabilities: Results from a twenty-year longitudinal study. *Learning Disabilities Research and Practice, 14*, 35–49.

Raskind, M. H., Higgins, E., & Herman, K. L. (1997). The compensatory effectiveness of optical character recognition speech syntheses on reading comprehension of postsecondary students with learning disabilities. *Learning Disabilities: A Multidisciplinary Journal, 8*, 75–87.

Ratey, J. J., Miller, A. C., & Nadeau, K. G. (1995). Special diagnostic and treatment considerations in women with attention deficit disorder. In K. G. Nadeau (Ed.), *A comprehensive guide to attention deficit disorder in adults: Research, diagnosis, and treatment* (pp. 260–283). New York: Brunner/Mazel.

Recruit volunteer staff for disability office by focusing on rewards other than money. (1999, August). *Disability Compliance for Higher Education, 5*(1), 1, 4–5.

Reed, J., & Woodruff, M. (1995). *Using compressed video for distance learning* [Online]. Available: www.kn.pacbell.com/wired/vidconf/using.html

Reeve, R. E. (1990). ADHD: Facts and fallacies. *Intervention in School and Clinic, 26*, 70–78.

Rehabilitation Act of 1973, Section 504, P.L. 93-112, 29 U.S.C. § 794 (1977).

Rehabilitation Act Regulations, 34 C.F.R. part 104 (1977).

Rehabilitation Engineering and Assistive Technology Society of North America. (1999). *State contact list*. Arlington, VA: Author. [Online]. Available: http://www.resna.org/taproject/at/statecontacts.html

Reid, J. (2000, June). *Weakness of online programs* [Online]. Available: http://illinois.online.uillinois.edu/lonresources/onlineoverview/weakness.html

Reiff, H. B., Gerber, P. J., & Ginsberg, R. (1997). *Exceeding expectations: Successful adults with learning disabilities*. Austin, TX: PRO-ED.

Renick, M. J., & Harter, S. (1989, December). Impact of social comparisons on the developing self-perceptions of learning disabled students. *Journal of Educational Psychology, 81*, 631–638.

Reynolds, C. R. (1981). The fallacy of "two years below grade level for age" as a diagnostic criterion for reading disorders. *Journal of School Psychology, 19*, 350–358.

Reynolds, C. R. (1985). Critical issues in the measurement of learning disabilities. *Journal of Special Education, 18*, 451–476.

Reynolds, M. C. (1984). Classification of students with handicaps. In E. W. Gordon (Ed.), *Review of research in education* (Vol. 11, pp. 63–92). Washington, DC: American Educational Research Association.

Richard, M. (1994, December). College and university students with ADHD. *ADHD Report, 2*(6), 4–6.

Richard, M. M. (1995a). Pathways to success for the college student with ADD: Accommodations and preferred practices. *Journal of Postsecondary Education and Disability, 11*, 16–30.

Richard, M. M. (1995b). Students with attention deficit disorders in postsecondary education: Issues in identification and accommodation. In K. G. Nadeau (Ed.), *A comprehensive guide to attention deficit disorder in adults: Research, diagnosis, and treatment* (pp. 284–307). New York: Brunner/Mazel.

Riegel, R. H. (1988). *A guide to cooperative consultation.* Jason Court, MI: RHR Consultation Services.

Rieth, H. J., Bryant, D. P., & Woodward, J. (in press). Technology applications for persons with disabilities: Benefits, barriers, and solutions. In I. Pervova (Ed.), *People, time, and society.*

Rieth, H. J., & Evertson, C. (1988). Variables related to the effective instruction of difficult-to-teach children. *Focus on Exceptional Children, 20*(5), 1–8.

Rivera, D., & Smith, D. D. (1997). *Teaching students with learning and behavior problems* (3rd ed.). Needham Heights, MA: Allyn & Bacon.

Rivera, D. M., & Bryant, B. R. (1992). Mathematics instruction for students with special needs. *Intervention in School and Clinic, 28*(2), 71–86.

Rock, E. E., Fessler, M. A., & Church, R. P. (1997). The concomitance of learning disabilities and emotional/behavioral disorders: A conceptual model. *Journal of Learning Disabilities, 30*, 245–263.

Rose, E., & Bursuck, W. D. (1989). A survey of college transition planning for students with learning disabilities. In *Support services for LD students in postsecondary education: A compendium of readings* (Vol. 2). Columbus, OH: Association on Handicapped Student Service Programs in Postsecondary Education.

Rose, R. (1993). Faculty development: Changing attitudes and enhancing knowledge about learning disabilities. In S. A. Vogel & P. B. Adelman (Eds.), *Success for college students with learning disabilities* (pp. 131–150). New York: Springer-Verlag.

Rosenberg, M. S. (1997). Learning disabilities occurring concomitantly with other disability and exceptional conditions: Introduction to the special series. *Journal of Learning Disabilities, 30*, 242–244.

Rothstein, L. F. (1986). Section 504 of the Rehabilitation Act: Emerging issues for colleges and universities. *Journal of College and University Law, 13*, 229–265.

Rothstein, L. F. (1991, September). Campuses and the disabled. *Chronicle of Higher Education*, B3, B10.

Rothstein, L. F. (1997). *Disabilities and the law.* St. Paul, MN: West Group.

Rothstein, L. R. (1998, April 24). Guidelines emerge for accommodating students who have learning disabilities. *Chronicle of Higher Education*, p. B6.

Rourke, B. P. (1989). A childhood learning disability that predisposes those afflicted to adolescent and adult depression and suicide risk. *Journal of Learning Disabilities, 22*, 169–174.

Rubenstone, S., & Dalby, S. (1994). *College admissions: A crash course for panicked parents.* New York: Macmillan.

Ruhl, K. (1996). Does nature of student activity during lecture pauses affect notes and immediate recall of college students with learning disabilities. *Journal of Postsecondary Education and Disability, 12*(2), 16–27.

Ruhl, K., & Suritsky, S. (1995). The pause procedures and/or an outline: Effect on immediate free recall and lecture notes taken by college students with learning disabilities. *Learning Disability Quarterly, 18*(1), 2–12.

Runyan, M. K. (1991). The effect of extra time on reading comprehension scores for university students with and without learning disabilities. *Journal of Learning Disabilities, 24*, 104–108.

Ryan, A., & Price, L. (1992). Adults with LD in the 1990s: Addressing the needs of students with learning disabilities. *Intervention in School and Clinic, 28,* 6–20.

Salvador v. Bell, 800 F.2d 97 (7th Cir. 1986).

Salvia, J., & Ysseldyke, J. E. (1998). *Assessment* (7th ed.). Boston: Houghton Mifflin.

Salvia, J., & Ysseldyke, J. E. (2001). *Assessment* (8th ed.). Boston: Houghton Mifflin.

Sandeen, A. (1989). Issues influencing the organization of student affairs. In U. Delworth, G. R. Hanson, & Associates (Eds.), *Student services: A handbook for the profession* (2nd ed., pp. 445–460). San Francisco: Jossey-Bass.

Sanford, J., & Turner, A. (1994). *Integrated Visual and Auditory Continuous Performance Test.* Richmond, VA: Braintrain.

Sattler, J. M. (1992). *Assessment of children: Revised and updated third edition.* San Diego, CA: Jerome M. Sattler.

Sattler, J. M., & Ryan, J. J. (1999). *Assessment of children: Revised and updated third edition* WAIS–III *supplement.* San Diego, CA: Jerome M. Sattler.

Schrank, F. A., McGrew, K. S., & Woodcock, R. W. (2001). *Technical abstract* (Assessment Service Bulletin No. 2). Itasca, IL: Riverside.

Schrank, F. A., & Woodcock, R. W. (2001). *WJ III Compuscore and Profiles Program.* Itasca, IL: Riverside.

Schuerholz, L. J., Harris, E. L., Baumgardner, T. L., Reiss, A. L., Freund, L. S., Church, R. P., Mohr, J., & Bridge Denckla, M. (1995). An analysis of two discrepancy-based models and a processing-deficit approach in identifying learning disabilities. *Journal of Learning Disabilities, 28,* 18–29.

Schumaker, J. B., & Deshler, D. D. (1984). Setting demand variables: A major factor in program planning for the LD adolescent. *Topics in Language Disorders, 4*(2), 22–40.

Scott, S. (2000, June). *Strategies for faculty development.* Strand presentation at the 12th annual Postsecondary Learning Disability Training Institute, sponsored by the Postsecondary Education Disability Education Unit of the University of Connecticut, Saratoga Springs, NY.

Scott, S. (2001). *Study strategies web sites.* Unpublished material. Storrs: University of Connecticut.

Scott, S. (2001). *Web sites for e-text.* Unpublished material. Storrs: University of Connecticut.

Scott, S., & Gregg, N. (2000). Meeting the evolving education needs of faculty in providing access for college students with LD. *Journal of Learning Disabilities, 33*(2), 158–167.

Scott, S., Gregg, N., & Davis, M. (1998, April). Making accommodations decisions pertaining to students with ADHD: The documentation dilemma. *ALERT, 22,* 22–23.

Scott, S., & Manglitz, E. (2000). Foreign language learning: A process for broadening access for students with learning disabilities. *Journal of Postsecondary Education and Disability, 14*(1), 23–37.

Scott, S. S. (1991). A change in legal status: An overlooked dimension in the transition to higher education. *Journal of Learning Disabilities, 24,* 459–466.

Scott, S. S., McGuire, J. M., & Foley, T. E. (2000). *Universal design for instruction: An exploration of principles for anticipating and responding to student diversity in the classroom.* Manuscript submitted for publication.

Scruggs, T., & Wong, B. (1990). *Intervention research in learning disabilities.* New York: Springer-Verlag.

Section 504 compliance handbook. (1999). Washington, DC: Thompson.

Section 504 of the Rehabilitation Act of 1973: Old problems and emerging issues for public schools. (1991, October). *Liaison Bulletin* (National Association of State Directors of Special Education, Alexandria, VA), *17*(8), 1–3.

Seidenberg, P. (1986, April). *Curriculum-based assessment procedures for secondary learning disabled students: Student centered and programmatic implications* (Doc. No. 4). Long Island University.

Semmel, M. I. (1986). *Special education in the year 2000 and beyond: A proposed action agenda for addressing selected issues.* Proceedings of the CEC Invitational Symposium on the Future of Special Education, Council for Exceptional Children.

Semrud-Clikeman, M., Biederman, J., Sprich-Buckminster, S., Lehman, B. K., Faraone, S. V., & Norman, D. (1992). Comorbidity between ADHD and learning disability: A review and report in a clinically referred sample. *Journal of the American Academy of Child and Adolescent Psychiatry, 31,* 439–448.

Semrud-Clikeman, M., Filipek, P. A., Biederman, J., Steingard, R., Kennedy, D., Renshaw, P., & Bekken, K. (1994). Attention-deficit hyperactivity disorder: Magnetic resonance imaging morphometric analysis of the corpus callosum. *Journal of the American Academy of Child and Adolescent Psychiatry, 33,* 875–881.

Shalit, R. (1997, August 25). Defining disability down. *New Republic,* 16–22.

Shaw, R. (1999). The case for course substitutions as a reasonable accommodation for students with foreign language learning difficulties. *Journal of Learning Disabilities, 32*(4), 320–328, 349.

Shaw, S. F. (1994, Fall). Change agentry at the institutional level. *Latest Developments,* 2–3.

Shaw, S. F. (1997a). Professional standards and a code of ethics for postsecondary disability personnel. *Journal of Postsecondary Education and Disability, 12,* 3–4.

Shaw, S. F. (1997b, Fall). The role of postsecondary disability service personnel: Not advocate or institutional gatekeeper but professional. *Postsecondary Disability Network News, 31,* 1–2, 9.

Shaw, S. F. (1998a). *Graduate education in postsecondary education and disability: Meeting professional standards.* Unpublished material, University of Connecticut, Neag School of Education, Storrs, CT.

Shaw, S. F. (1998b, February). What is our role? *ALERT, 22,* 1.

Shaw, S. F., Brinckerhoff, L. C., Kistler, J. K., & McGuire, J. M. (1991). Preparing students with learning disabilities for postsecondary education: Issues and future needs. *Learning Disabilities: A Multidisciplinary Journal, 2,* 21–26.

Shaw, S. F., Cullen, J. P., McGuire, J. M., & Brinckerhoff, L. C. (1995). Operationalizing a definition of learning disabilities. *Journal of Learning Disabilities, 28,* 586–597.

Shaw, S. F., & Dukes, L. L. (in press). Program standards for disability services in higher education. *Journal of Postsecondary Education and Disability.*

Shaw, S. F., & McGuire, J. M. (1996, Spring). What can we learn from the "Boston University Experience"? *Latest Developments,* 1–3.

Shaw, S. F., McGuire, J. M., & Brinckerhoff, L. C. (1994). College and university programming. In P. J. Gerber & H. B. Reiff (Eds.), *Learning disabilities in adulthood: Persisting problems and evolving issues* (pp. 141–151). Stoneham, MA: Butterworth-Heinemann.

Shaw, S. F., McGuire, J. M., & Madaus, J. W. (1997). Standards of professional practice. *Journal of Postsecondary Education and Disability, 12*(3), 26–35.

Shea, L. (1998). Gender and comorbidity issues: Considerations for service providers. In P. Quinn & A. McCormick (Eds.), *Re-thinking AD/HD: A guide to fostering success in students with AD/HD at the college level* (pp. 57–66). Bethesda, MD: Advantage Books.

Siegel, L. (1999). Issues in the definition and diagnosis of learning disabilities: A perspective on *Guckenberger v. Boston University. Journal of Learning Disabilities, 32*(4), 304–319.

Silver, A. A. (1984). Children in classes for the severely emotionally handicapped. *Developmental and Behavioral Pediatrics, 5,* 49–54.

Silver, L. B. (1992). *Attention-deficit hyperactivity disorder: A clinical guide to diagnosis and treatment.* Washington, DC: American Psychiatric Press.

Silver, P., Bourke, A., & Strehorn, K. C. (1998). Universal instructional design in higher education: An approach for inclusion. *Equity and Excellence in Education, 31,* 47–51.

Simon, J. (1998, November). Ground-breaking decision in Bartlett case. *ALERT, 22*(5), 1, 8–9.

Simon, J. (1999, August). Avoid assumptions, be prepared to explain impact of disability. *Disability Compliance for Higher Education, 5,* 1, 8.

Siperstein, G. N. (1988). Students with learning disabilities in college: The need for a programmatic approach to critical transitions. *Journal of Learning Disabilities, 21,* 431–436.

Sitlington, P. L., & Frank, A. (1990). Are adolescents with learning disabilities successful crossing the bridge to adult life? *Learning Disability Quarterly, 13,* 97–111.

Small, W. (1996). Choosing a college for students with learning disabilities [Online]. Available: www.ldonline.org

Smith, B. K. (1986). *The wilted flower syndrome.* Paper presented at the meeting of the Association for Children and Adults with Learning Disabilities, New York. (ERIC Document Reproduction Service No. ED 270 913)

Smith, T. E. C. (1997). Adolescence: A continuing challenge for special education. *Remedial and Special Education, 18,* 258–260.

Smith, T. E. C., Dowdy, C. A., Polloway, E. A., & Blalock, G. E. (1997). *Children and adults with learning disabilities.* Needham Heights, MA: Allyn & Bacon.

Solden, S. (1995). *Women with attention deficit disorder: Embracing disorganization at home and in the workplace.* Grass Valley, CA: Underwood Books.

Southeastern Community College v. Davis, 442 U.S. 397 (1979).

Spector, S., Decker, K., & Shaw, S. F. (1991). Independence and responsibility: An LD resource room at South Windsor High School. *Intervention in School and Clinic, 26,* 159–167.

Stanovich, K. E. (1999). The sociopsychometrics of learning disabilities. *Journal of Learning Disabilities, 32,* 350–361.

Steinberg, H. (1998). Moving along the program continuum: From LD to AD/HD. In P. Quinn & A. McCormick (Eds.), *Re-thinking AD/HD: A guide to fostering success in students with AD/HD at the college level* (pp. 8–13). Bethesda, MD: Advantage Books.

Steinberg, P. (1998). Meeting the health care needs of students with AD/HD on campus. In P. Quinn & A. McCormick (Eds.), *Re-thinking AD/HD: A guide to fostering success in students with AD/HD at the college level* (pp. 97–101). Bethesda, MD: Advantage Books.

Stern, A. (1997). Assessment and treatment of adult attention-deficit/ hyperactivity disorder. In L. Vandercreek, S. Knapp, & T. Jackson (Eds.), *Innovations in clinical practice: A source book* (Vol. 15, pp. 25–40). Sarasota, FL: Professional Resource Exchange.

Stern, L. (1997). Paying the bills. *How to get into college.* Livingston, NJ: Newsweek, Inc. and Kaplan Educational Centers.

Stern, V., & DuBois, P. (1994). *You're in charge: A career-planning guide in science, mathematics, and engineering for college students with disabilities and advocates and advisors who work with them* (2nd ed.). Princeton, NJ: Recording for the Blind & Dyslexic.

Sternberg, R. J. (1999). Ability and expertise: It's time to replace the current model of intelligence. *American Educator, 23*(1), 10–13, 50–51.

Sternberg, R. J., & Spear-Swerling, L. (Eds.). (1999). *Perspectives on learning disabilities.* Boulder, CO: Westview Press.

Stewart, D. W. (1994). Distinguishing "yearning disabilities" from learning disabilities in postsecondary settings. *Guidance and Counseling, 9*(5), 11–13.

Stone, D. (1996). The impact of the Americans with Disabilities Act on legal education and academic modifications for disabled law students: An empirical study. *University of Kansas Law Review, 44,* 567–595.

Stracher, D. A. (1996). Learning disabilities, language deficits, and WISC's: The tale of a preventable misdiagnosis. *Research and Teaching in Developmental Education, 12*(2), 51–60.

Strauss, A. A., & Lehtinen, L. (1947). *Psychopathology and education of the brain-injured child* (Vol. 1). New York: Grune & Stratton.

Students with attention deficit disorder may not be entitled to private rooms. (1998, December). *Disability Compliance for Higher Education, 4*(5), 1, 8.

Study abroad creates accessibility barriers. (1998, April). *Disability Compliance for Higher Education, 3*(9), 1, 6–7.

Stufflebeam, D. L. (1988). The CIPP model for program evaluation. In G. F. Madaus, M. S. Scriven, & D. L. Stufflebeam (Eds.), *Evaluation models: Viewpoints on educational and human services evaluation* (pp. 117–141). Boston: Kluwer-Nijhoff.

Stufflebeam, D. L., Foley, W. J., Gephart, W. J., Guba, E. G., Hammond, R. L., Merriman, H. O., & Provus, M. M. (1971). *Educational evaluation and decision making.* Itasca, IL: F. E. Peacock.

Supporters give ADD coaching credit for low attrition rates, improved grades. (1997, December). *Disability Compliance for Higher Education, 3,* 1, 8.

Supreme Court rulings pose more questions for service providers. (1999, July). *Disability Compliance for Higher Education, 4*(12), 1, 6.

Suritsky, S. (1992). Notetaking difficulties and approaches reported by university students with learning disabilities. *Journal of Postsecondary Education and Disability, 10*(2), 3–10.

Suritsky, S. K., & Hughes, C. A. (1996). Notetaking strategy instruction. In D. D. Deshler, E. S. Ellis, & B. K. Lenz (Eds.), *Teaching adolescents with learning disabilities: Strategies and methods* (2nd ed., pp. 267–312). Denver, CO: Love.

Sutton v. United Airlines, 119 S. Ct. 2139 (1999).

Swanson, H. L. (1987). Information processing and learning disabilities: An overview. *Journal of Learning Disabilities, 20,* 3–7.

Swanson, H. L. (Ed.). (1991a). *Learning Disability Quarterly, 14*(4) [Special Issue].

Swanson, H. L. (1991b). Operational definitions and learning disabilities: An overview. *Learning Disability Quarterly, 14,* 242–254.

Swanson, H. L. (1993). Learning disabilities from the perspective of cognitive psychology. In G. R. Lyon, D. B. Gray, J. F. Kavanaugh, & N. A. Krasnegor (Eds.), *Better understanding learning disabilities: New views from research and their implications for education and public policies* (pp. 199–228). Baltimore: Brookes.

Swanson, H. L., & Christie, L. (1994). Implicit notions of learning disabilities: Some directions for definitions. *Learning Disabilities Research and Practice, 9,* 244–254.

Swanson, H. L., & Cooney, J. B. (1991). Learning disabilities and memory. In B.Y.L. Wong (Ed.), *Learning about learning disabilities* (pp. 103–127). San Diego, CA: Academic Press.

Swanson, H. L., & Hoskyn, M. (1998). Experimental intervention research on students with learning disabilities: A meta-analysis of treatment outcomes. *Review of Educational Research, 68,* 277–321.

Swanson, H. L., & Watson, B. (1982). *Educational and psychological assessment of exceptional children.* St. Louis, MO: Mosby.

Sydnor-Greenberg, J. (1998). The neuropsychological profile of the student with ADHD. In P. Quinn & A. McCormick (Eds.), *Re-thinking AD/HD: A guide to fostering success in students with AD/HD at the college level* (pp. 48–56). Bethesda, MD: Advantage Books.

Symington, D. C. (1994). Megatrends in rehabilitation: A Canadian perspective. *International Journal of Rehabilitation Research, 17*(1), 1–14.

Takakuwa, K. M. (1998, January 7). Coping with a learning disability in medical school. *Journal of the American Medical Association.*

Technology-related assistance for Individuals with Disabilities Act of 1988. Catalogue No. 850. (Senate Rpt. 100–438). Washington, DC: U.S. Government Printing Office.

Telander, J. E. (1994). *The adjustment of learning disabled adults: A review of the current literature.* Unpublished doctoral dissertation, Biola University, La Mirada, CA. (Also see ERIC Document Reproduction Service No. ED 372 586)

Tennant, M. (1986). An evaluation of Knowle's theory of adult learning. *International Journal of Lifelong Education, 5,* 113–122.

Tessler, L. (1997, September/October). How college students with learning disabilities can advocate for themselves. *LDA Newsbriefs.*

Testing accommodations for students with ADD is not eliminated by Ritalin. (1998, October). *Disability Compliance for Higher Education, 4,* 5.

TextHELP! [Computer software]. (1997). County Antrim, N. Ireland: Lorien Systems.

Thoma, C. (1999). Supporting student voice in transition planning. *Teaching Exceptional Children, 31,* 4–9.

Tips v. Regents of Texas Tech University, 921 F. Supp. 1515 (N.D. Tex. 1996).

Todis, B. (1996). Tools for the task? Perspectives on assistive technology in educational settings. *Journal of Special Education Technology, 13*(2), 49–61.

Tomlan, P., Farrell, M., & Geis, J. (1990). The 3 S's of staff development: Scope, sequence, and structure. In J. J. Vander Putten (Ed.), *Proceedings of the 1989 AHSSPPE Conference* (pp. 23–32). Columbus, OH: Association on Handicapped Student Service Programs in Postsecondary Education.

Tomlan, P. S., & Mather, N. (1996). Back on track: A response to Shaw, Cullen, McGuire, and Brinckerhoff. *Journal of Learning Disabilities, 29,* 220–224.

Torgesen, J. K. (1994). Issues in the assessment of executive function: An information processing perspective. In G. R. Lyon (Ed.), *Frames of reference for the assessment of learning disabilities: New views on measurement issues* (pp. 143–162). Baltimore: Brookes.

Trueba, C. M. (1991, Spring). LD assessment within a disabled student service office: One campus's dilemma and response. *Latest Developments,* 5–6.

Tucker, B. P. (1996). Application of the Americans with Disabilities Act (ADA) and Section 504 to colleges and universities: An overview and discussion of special issues relating to students. *Journal of College and University Law, 23,* 1–41.

Tucker, J., Stevens, L. J., & Ysseldyke, J. E. (1983). Learning disabilities: The experts speak out. *Journal of Learning Disabilities, 16,* 6–14.

Turnock, P. (1998). Academic coping strategies in college students with AD/HD symptoms. In P. Quinn & A. McCormick (Eds.), *Re-thinking AD/HD: A guide to fostering success in students with AD/HD at the college level* (pp. 76–84). Bethesda, MD: Advantage Books.

Tzelepis, A., Schubiner, H., & Warbasse, L. H., III. (1995). Differential diagnosis and psychiatric comorbidity patterns in adult attention deficit disorder. In K. G. Nadeau (Ed.), *A comprehensive guide to attention deficit disorder in adults: Research, diagnosis, and treatment* (pp. 35–57). New York: Brunner/Mazel.

ULTimate Reader [Computer software]. (1997). Peabody, MA: Universal Learning Technology.

Unger, K. (1991, Summer). Providing services to students with psychological disabilities: Clarifying campus roles. Columbus, OH: Association on Higher Education and Disability.

United States v. Board of Trustees for University of Alabama, 908 F.2d 740 (11th Cir. 1990).

United States v. National Collegiate Athletic Association. (1998). [Online]. Available: http://www.usdoj.gov/crt/ada.ncaafact.htm

University of Arizona, The SALT Center. (n.d.). *Authorization for release of information* [Program Material]. Tucson: Author.

University of Arizona, The SALT Center. (n.d.). *SALT center consent for release of information* [Program Material]. Tucson: Author.

University of Arizona, The SALT Center. (n.d.). *SALT center grade monitor for semester* [Program Material]. Tucson: Author.

University of Arizona, The SALT Center. (n.d.). *SALT interview evaluation* [Program Material]. Tucson: Author.

University of Arizona, The SALT Center. (n.d.). *SALT interview protocol* [Program Material]. Tucson: Author.

University of Arizona, The SALT Center. (n.d.). *SALT student study plan for semester* [Program Material]. Tucson: Author.

University of Arizona, The SALT Center. (n.d.). *You can balance your academic career and college life! A freshman survival guide for SALT students* [Program Material]. Tucson: Author.

University of California, Disabled Students' Program. (1999). *Berkeley campus policy for accommodating the academic needs of students with disabilities*. Berkeley: Author. [Online]. Available: http://dsp.berkeley.edu/berkacompolicy.html

University of California, Disabled Students' Program. (n.d.). *Berkeley campus plan for funding reasonable accommodations for individuals with disabilities* [Program Material]. Berkeley: Author.

University of Connecticut, Center for Students with Disabilities. (n.d.). *Policies and procedures regarding students with disabilities*. Storrs: Author. [Online]. Available: http://www.csd.uconn.edu/policies.html

University of Connecticut, Connecticut Postsecondary Disability Technical Assistance Center. (1999). *Resource list: Adults with disabilities* [Brochure]. Storrs: Author.

University of Connecticut, Connecticut Postsecondary Disability Technical Assistance Center. (1999). *Resource list of videotapes: Adults with disabilities* [Brochure]. Storrs: Author.

University of Connecticut, University Program for College Students with Learning Disabilities. (n.d.). *Student report questionnaire* [Program Material]. Storrs: Author.

University of Connecticut, University Program for College Students with Learning Disabilities. (n.d.). *Student semester data sheet* [Program Material]. Storrs: Author.

University of Connecticut, University Program for College Students with Learning Disabilities. (n.d.). *UPLD learning session log* [Program Material]. Storrs: Author.

University of Connecticut, University Program for College Students with Learning Disabilities. (n.d.). *UPLD monthly staff summary* [Program Material]. Storrs: Author.

University of Connecticut, University Program for College Students with Learning Disabilities. (n.d.). *UPLD testing accommodation form* [Program Material]. Storrs: Author.

University of Georgia, Learning Disabilities Center. (2000). *Policy memorandum* [Program Material]. Athens: Author.

University of Georgia, Learning Disabilities Center. (n.d.). *LDC student accommodation review form* [Program Material]. Athens: Author.

University of Idaho. (1995). *Strategies for teaching at a distance. Guide #2.* Moscow: University of Idaho, College of Engineering. Available on-line: www.uidaho.edu/evo/dist2.html

University of Massachusetts, 5 NDLR 483 (September 1994).

University of Massachusetts, Learning Disabilities Support Services. (n.d.). *Contact form* [Program Material]. Amherst: Author.

University of Massachusetts, Learning Disabilities Support Services. (n.d.). *Faculty and friends network: Letter of invitation* [Program Material]. Amherst: Author.

University of Massachusetts, Learning Disabilities Support Services. (n.d.). *Helping students with note taking: Suggestions for instructors* [Program Material]. Amherst: Author.

University of Massachusetts, Learning Disabilities Support Services. (n.d.). *Recommended accommodations* [Program Material]. Amherst: Author.

University of Minnesota, 6 NDLR § 296 (OCR 1995).

University of Minnesota, Disability Services. (n.d.). *Access assessment.* Twin Cities: Author. [Online]. Available: http://umrtv.cee.umn.edu/aa/proinfo/survey.htm

University of Minnesota, Disability Services. (n.d.). *Accommodations checklist for study abroad.* Twin Cities: Author. [Online]. Available: http://umrtv.cee.umn.edu/aa/proinfo/accomchk.htm

University of North Carolina, Disability Services. (n.d.). *Accommodation approval* [Program Material]. Greensboro: Author.

University of North Carolina, Disability Services. (n.d.). *Testing accommodations request* [Program Material]. Greensboro: Author.

University of North Carolina, Learning Disability Services. (1998). *ADHD student profile* [Program Material]. Chapel Hill: Author.

University of North Carolina, Learning Disability Services. (1998). *Course description checklist* [Program Material]. Chapel Hill: Author.

U.S. Department of Education. (1977). Definition and criteria for defining students as learning disabled. *Federal Register, 45*(250), 65083. Washington, DC: U.S. Government Printing Office.

U.S. Department of Education. (1990). *Twelfth annual report to Congress on the implementation of the Education of the Handicapped Act.* Washington, DC: U.S. Government Printing Office.

U.S. Department of Education. (1991). *Auxiliary aids and services for postsecondary students with handicaps: Higher education's obligations under Section 504.* Washington, DC: U.S. Government Printing Office.

U.S. Department of Education. (1994). *Sixteenth annual report to Congress on the implementation of the Education of the Handicapped Act.* Washington, DC: U.S. Government Printing Office.

U.S. Department of Education. (1996). *Eighteenth annual report to Congress on the implementation of the Individuals with Disabilities Education Act.* Washington, DC: Office of Special Education and Rehabilitative Services.

U.S. Department of Education. (1997). *U.S. Department of Education strategic plan: 1998–2002.* Washington, DC: Author. Available online: www.ed/gov/pubs/StratPln97

U.S. Department of Education. (1998). *Twentieth annual report to Congress on the implementation of the Individuals with Disabilities Education Act.* Washington, DC: Office of Special Education and Rehabilitative Services.

U.S. Department of Education. (1999a). *Demonstration projects to ensure students with disabilities receive a quality higher education program* (Catalog of Federal Domestic Assistance #84.333). Washington, DC: Office of Postsecondary Education, Higher Education Programs.

U.S. Department of Education. (1999b). *Distance education at postsecondary institutions: 1997–1998* (Report # NCES 2000-013). Washington, DC: National Center for Education Statistics. Available online: http://nces.ed.gov/pubs2000/2000013.pdf

U.S. Department of Justice. (1991). *ADA requirements handbook*. Washington, DC: Author.

Vandercook, T., & York, J. (1989). The McGill Action Planning System (M.A.P.S.): A strategy for building vision. *Journal of the Association for the Severely Handicapped, 14*, 205–215.

Vogel, S. (1997). *College students with learning disabilities: A handbook*. (Available from LDA Bookstore, 4156 Library Road, Pittsburgh, PA, 15234, 412/341-1515)

Vogel, S. A. (1982). On developing LD college programs. *Journal of Learning Disabilities, 15*, 518–528.

Vogel, S. A. (1987). Issues and concerns in LD college programming. In D. J. Johnson & J. W. Blalock (Eds.), *Adults with learning disabilities: Clinical studies* (pp. 239–276). Orlando, FL: Grune & Stratton.

Vogel, S. A. (1993). The continuum of university responses to Section 504 for students with learning disabilities. In S. A. Vogel & P. B. Adelman (Eds.), *Success for college students with learning disabilities* (pp. 83–113). New York: Springer-Verlag.

Vogel, S. A., & Adelman, P. B. (1990). Extrinsic and intrinsic factors in graduation and academic failure among LD college students. *Annals of Dyslexia, 40*, 119–137.

Vogel, S. A., & Adelman, P. B. (Eds.). (1993). *Success for college students with learning disabilities*. New York: Springer-Verlag.

Vogel, S. A., Leonard, F., Scales, W., Hayeslip, P., Hermansen, J., & Donnells, L. (1998). The national learning disabilities postsecondary data bank: An overview. *Journal of Learning Disabilities, 31*, 234–247.

Vogel, S. A., Leyser, Y., Wyland, S., & Brulle, A. (1999). Students with learning disabilities in higher education: Faculty attitudes and practice. *Learning Disabilities Research and Practice, 14*, 173–186.

Vogel, S. A., & Reder, S. (1998). *Learning disabilities, literacy, and adult education*. Baltimore: Brookes.

Volunteer notetakers provide services at little cost to colleges. (1999). *Disability Compliance for Higher Education, 4*(6), 7.

VSA Educational Services. (1991). *An overview of alcohol and other drug abuse prevention and disability*. Washington, DC: VSA Educational Services, Resource Center on Substance Abuse Prevention and Disability. (ERIC Document Reproduction Service No. ED 346 643)

Wade, S. E., & Reynolds, R. E. (1989). Developing student's metacognitive awareness may be essential to effective strategy instruction. *Journal of Reading, 33*, 6–15.

Walker, J. K., Shaw, S. F., & McGuire, J. M. (1992). Concerns of professionals and consumers regarding postsecondary education for students with learning disabilities. *Learning Disabilities, 3*, 11–16.

Walker, M. L. (1980). The role of faculty in working with handicapped students. In H. Z. Sprandel & M. R. Schmidt (Eds.), *Serving handicapped students*. San Francisco: Jossey-Bass.

Wang, M. C., & Palincsar, A. S. (1989). Teaching students to assume an active role in their learning. In M. C. Reynolds (Ed.), *Knowledge base for the beginning teacher* (pp. 71–84). Elmsford, NY: Pergamon.

Ward, A. W. (1995). Review of the *Wide Range Achievement Test 3*. In J. C. Conoley & J. C. Impara (Eds.), *The twelfth mental measurements yearbook* (pp. 1110–1111). Lincoln, NE: Buros Institute.

Ward, M. J. (1988). The many facets of self-determination. *Transition Summary, 5*, 2–3.

Ward, M. J. (1992). OSERS initiative on self-determination. *Interchange, 12*, 1–7.

Ward, M. J., & Kohler, P. D. (1996). Teaching self-determination: Content and process. In L. E. Powers, G. H. S. Singer, & J. Sowers (Eds.), *Promoting self-competence in children and youth with disabilities: On the road to autonomy* (pp. 275–322). Baltimore: Brookes.

Weaver, S. M. (1993). *The validity of the use of extended and untimed testing for postsecondary students with learning disabilities.* Ontario, Canada: University of Toronto.

Wechsler, D. (1974). *Wechsler Intelligence Scale for Children–Revised.* San Antonio, TX: Psychological Corp.

Wechsler, D. (1981). *Wechsler Adult Intelligence Scale–Revised.* San Antonio, TX: Psychological Corp.

Wechsler, D. (1989). *Wechsler Preschool and Primary Scale of Intelligence–Revised.* San Antonio, TX: Psychological Corp.

Wechsler, D. (1991). *Wechsler Intelligence Scale for Children–Third Edition.* San Antonio, TX: Psychological Corp.

Wechsler, D. (1997a). *Wechsler Adult Intelligence Scale–Third Edition.* San Antonio, TX: Psychological Corp.

Wechsler, D. (1997b). *Wechsler Memory Scale–Third Edition.* San Antonio, TX: Psychological Corp.

Wehman, P. (1992). *Life beyond the classroom: Transition strategies for young people with disabilities.* Baltimore: Brookes.

Wehman, P. (1998). *Developing transition plans.* Austin, TX: PRO-ED.

Wehmeyer, M. L. (1999). Assistive technology and students with mental retardation: Utilization and barriers. *Journal of Special Education Technology, 14*(1), 48–58.

Weiner, J. (1998). The psychiatric morbidity hypothesis: A response to San Miguel, Forness, and Kavale. *Learning Disability Quarterly, 21*, 195–201.

Weingand, D. (1990). The invisible client: Meeting the needs of persons with learning disabilities. *Reference Librarian, 31*, 77–88.

Weinstein, C. E., Palmer, D. R., & Schulte, A. C. (1987). *Learning and Study Strategies Inventory.* Clearwater, FL: H&H Publishing.

Weiss, G., & Hechtman, L. (1993). *Hyperactive children grown up* (2nd ed.). New York: Guilford Press.

Weiss, K. E., & Repetto, J. B. (1998). *Finding academic success: Variables influencing academic success of students with learning disabilities.* Manuscript submitted for publication.

Wells, S., & Hanebrink, S. (1998). Auxiliary aids, academic adjustments, and reasonable accommodations. In S. Scott, S. Wells, & S. Hanebrink (Eds.), *Educating college students with disabilities: What academic and fieldwork educators need to know* (pp. 37–49). Bethesda, MD: American Occupational Therapy Association.

Wender, P. (1987). *The hyperactive child, adolescent, and adult.* New York: Oxford University Press.

Wender, P. H. (1995). *Attention-deficit hyperactivity disorder in adults.* New York: Oxford University Press.

West, L., Corbey, S., Boyer-Stephens, A., Jones, B., Miller, R., & Sarkees-Wircenksi, M. (1992). *Integrating transition planning into the IEP process.* Reston, VA: Council for Exceptional Children.

Westling, J. (1997, September 3). One university defeats disability extremists. *Wall Street Journal*, A21.

White, M. (1998, November/December). Support/therapy groups for adults with ADHD. *ADHD Challenge, 12*, 5–6.

White, W. J. (1992). The postschool adjustment of persons with learning disabilities: Current status and future projections. *Journal of Learning Disabilities, 25*, 448–456.

Whitworth, L., Kimsey-House, H., & Sandahl, P. (1998). *Co-active coaching: New skills for coaching people toward success in work and life*. Palo Alto, CA: Davies-Black Publishing.

William Rainey Harper College. (n.d.). *Sign-in tutoring record* [Program Material]. Palatine, IL: Author.

Whole language does not work for LD. (1996, Winter/Spring). *CACLD Crossroads, 32*(1), 1.

Wilchesky, M., & Minden, H. A. (1988). *A comparison of learning and non-learning disabled university students on selected measures*. Proceedings of the 1988 Association on Handicapped Student Service Programs in Postsecondary Education Conference, Columbus, OH.

Wilens, T. E., Spencer, T. J., & Biederman, J. (1995). Pharmacotherapy of adult ADHD. In K. G. Nadeau (Ed.), *A comprehensive guide to attention deficit disorder in adults: Research, diagnosis, and treatment* (pp. 168–188). New York: Brunner/Mazel.

Wilkinson, G. S. (1993). *The Wide Range Achievement Test–3: Administration manual*. Wilmington, DE: Jastak Associates/Wide Range.

Williams, W. M., & Ceci, S. J. (1999, August). Accommodating learning disabilities can bestow unfair advantages. *Chronicle of Higher Education*, B4. Available: http://www.chronicle.com/colloquy/99/disabled/background.htm

Willis, B. (1995). *Distance education at a glance. Guide #10*. Moscow: University of Idaho, College of Engineering, Engineering Outreach. Available online: www.uidaho.edu/evo/dist10/html

Willis, C., Hoben, S., & Myette, P. (1995). Devising a supportive climate based on clinical vignettes of college students with attention deficit disorder. *Journal of Postsecondary Education and Disability, 11*, 31–43.

Wilson, G. L. (1994). Self-advocacy skills. In C. A. Michaels (Ed.), *Transition strategies for persons with learning disabilities* (pp. 153–184). San Diego, CA: Singular.

Witte, R. H., Philips, L., & Kakela, M. (1998). Job satisfaction of college graduates with learning disabilities. *Journal of Learning Disabilities, 31*, 259–265.

Wolinsky, S., & Whelan, A. (1999). Federal law and the accommodation of students with LD: The lawyers' look at the BU decision. *Journal of Learning Disabilities, 32*(4), 286–291.

Wong v. The Regents of the University of California, 192 F.3d 807,16 NDLR 93 (9th Cir. 1999).

Wong, B. Y. (1991). *Learning about learning disabilities*. San Diego, CA: Academic Press.

Wong, B. Y., & Jones, W. (1992). Increasing metacomprehension in learning disabled and normally achieving students through self-questioning training. *Learning Disability Quarterly, 5*, 228–238.

Wong, B. Y. L., Butler, D. L., Ficzere, S. A., & Kuperis, S. (1997). Teaching adolescents with learning disabilities and low achievers to plan, write, and revise compare and contrast essays. *Learning Disabilities Research and Practice, 12*, 2–15.

Woodcock, R. W. (1994). *Woodcock Reading Mastery Tests–Revised*. Circle Pines, MN: American Guidance Service.

Woodcock, R. W., & Johnson, M. B. (1989a). *Woodcock–Johnson Psycho-Educational Battery–Revised*. Itasca, IL: Riverside.

Woodcock, R. W., & Johnson, M. B. (1989b). *WJ–R Tests of Achievement: Examiner's manual*. Itasca, IL: Riverside.

Woodcock, R. W., & Johnson, M. B. (1989c). *WJ–R Tests of Cognitive Ability: Examiner's manual*. Itasca, IL: Riverside.

Woodcock, R. W., McGrew, K. S., & Mather, N. (2001a). *Woodcock–Johnson III Tests of Achievement*. Itasca, IL: Riverside.

Woodcock, R. W., McGrew, K. S., & Mather, N. (2001b). *Woodcock–Johnson III Tests of Cognitive Abilities*. Itasca, IL: Riverside.

Woods, P. A., Sedlacek, W., & Boyer, S. P. (1990). Learning disability programs in large universities. *NASPA Journal, 27,* 248–256.

Worthen, B. R., & Sanders, J. R. (1987). *Educational evaluation: Alternative approaches and practical guidelines.* New York: Longman.

WYNN [Computer software]. (1998). Sunnyvale, CA: Arkenstone.

Wynne v. Tufts University School of Medicine, 932 F.2d 19 (1st Cir. 1991).

Yost, D., Shaw, S., Cullen, J., & Bigaj, S. (1994). Practices and attitudes of postsecondary LD service providers in North America. *Journal of Learning Disabilities, 27,* 631–640.

Ysseldyke, J. E. (1987). Classification of handicapped students. In M. C. Wang, M. D. Reynolds, & H. J. Walberg (Eds.), *The handbook of special education: Research and practice* (Vol. 1, pp. 253–271). Oxford, England: Pergamon.

Zametkin, A. J., Nordahl, T. E., Gross, M., King, A. C., Semple, W. E., Rumsey, J., Hamburger, S., & Cohen, R. M. (1990). Cerebral glucose metabolism in adults with hyperactivity of childhood onset. *New England Journal of Medicine, 323,* 1361–1366.

Zentall, S. (1993). Research on the educational implications of attention deficit hyperactivity disorder. *Exceptional Children, 60,* 143–153.

Zirkel, P. (2000, December). Sorting out which students have learning disabilities. *Chronicle of Higher Education,* B15–16.

Zukle v. Regents of University of California, 166 F.3d 1041 (9th Cir. 1999).

GUIDE TO THE CD-ROM
APPENDIXES

Chapter 9: Providing Accommodations

Chapter 10: Students with ADHD

Chapter 11: Assistive Technology

Chapter 12: Postsecondary Disability Personnel as Professionals

Chapter 13: Promoting Our Products

Chapter 14: Future Directions

No Appendix Items

Author Index

Subject Index

About the Authors
and Contributors

Loring C. Brinckerhoff, PhD, is the disability accommodations specialist for Educational Testing Service and a disability and education consultant to Recording for the Blind & Dyslexic and Harvard Medical School. He is also an adjunct instructor of special education at Tufts University. He has been active in the field of higher education and learning disabilities since 1983. He received his doctorate in learning disabilities from the University of Wisconsin–Madison. He is past president of the Association on Higher Education and Disability. He specializes in transition planning for high school students, legal rights of adults with learning disabilities, and programming for students with learning disabilities and ADHD, at the undergraduate and graduate levels.

Brian R. Bryant, PhD, lives and works in Austin, Texas. His professional interests, which cross a variety of disabilities, are in literacy, assessment, and technology. He is currently retired but teaches occasionally in the Department of Special Education at the University of Texas at Austin.

Diane Pedrotty Bryant is an associate professor in the Department of Special Education at the University of Texas at Austin. She serves as the faculty coordinator for the Assistive and Instructional Technology Lab and chairs the college's Faculty Computer Committee. Her research interests include instructional interventions for literacy, mathematics, and technology for students with learning disabilities. She is the author of several books and book chapters and numerous journal articles related to instructional methodology.

Jane Byron, MA, is the director of Learning Disabilities Services at the University of North Carolina at Chapel Hill. She is responsible for the operation of a comprehensive college program for UNC students with LD and ADHD. In addition, she serves on four university committees that address issues pertaining to students with disabilities. She is also a board member of several private schools and nonprofit organizations. Her special interest is program development for college students with LD and ADHD.

Joseph W. Madaus, PhD, is the director of the University Program for Students with Learning Disabilities and an assistant professor in residence in the Department of Educational Psychology at the University of Connecticut. He is responsible for the evaluation of the 3-year U.S. Department of Education Grant on Universal Design for Instruction, including the field testing and dissemination of products. His professional interests include the transition of students with LD from high school to college, assessment of learning disabilities, and student athletes with learning disabilities.

Joan M. McGuire, PhD, is a professor of special education in the Department of Educational Psychology in the Neag School of Education at the University of Connecticut and co-director of the Center on Postsecondary Education and Disability. She has worked in the field of postsecondary learning disabilities since 1977 and was the director of the University of Connecticut Program for College Students with Learning Disabilities from 1986 to 2000. She specializes in postsecondary disability program development, administration, and evaluation; professional development and training; assessment and documentation of learning disabilities in adults; and Universal Design for Instruction (UDI), a paradigm for designing college-level instruction that is responsive to student diversity. Dr. McGuire also served as co-editor of AHEAD's *Journal of Postsecondary Education and Disability*, and has published and presented extensively in the field of postsecondary education for students with disabilities.

David R. Parker is the assistant director of Learning Disabilities Services at the University of North Carolina at Chapel Hill. His previous professional roles include teaching students with LD, ADHD, and other disabilities in private and public schools, co-coordinating an overseas student teaching project, and serving as director of a private school for students with dyslexia. He recently served for 2 years as a co-chair of AHEAD's LD-ADHD Special Interest Group (SIG). Currently, his interest areas include psychosocial interventions for adults with LD and ADHD, staff training and supervision, and effective programming for college students with ADHD.

Lynda Price, PhD, is an assistant professor of special education at Temple University in Philadelphia, Pennsylvania, where she teaches both graduate and undergraduate courses in educational psychology and special education. She is also the co-principal investigator of a new National Science Foundation project called Daughters with Disabilities. She has been actively involved in the area of transition and psychosocial issues for adolescents and adults with learning disabilities for over 13 years.

Herbert J. Rieth is a professor of special education and department chair at the University of Texas at Austin. He has a doctoral degree in special education (learning disabilities) from the University of Kansas. He has published extensively regarding the effect of technology on the classroom ecology, the role and effect of technology in teacher education training programs, and the use of multimedia and anchored instruction with students with disabilities.

Laura F. Rothstein is the dean and a professor of law at the University of Louisville, Louis D. Brandeis School of Law. She received her BA from the University of Kansas and her JD from Georgetown University Law Center. She has published eight books, many book chapters, and articles on disability issues, focusing much of her work on disability issues in higher education. She has served on many national boards and committees addressing these issues and is a frequent lecturer at national conferences on disability discrimination. She has worked closely with the Association of American Law Schools, the American Bar Association Section on Legal Education and Admission to the Bar, the Law School Admission Council, and the American Council on Education HEATH project on disability issues in higher education.

Sally S. Scott is the project coordinator of a 3-year U.S. Department of Education grant at the University of Connecticut focusing on Universal Design for Instruction. She has been involved in service delivery for college students with learning disabilities since 1985. Previously, she served as the head of services at the University of Georgia Learning Disabilities Center and as the state coordinator of higher education for the Virginia Department on Rehabilitative Services. She is currently the editor of the *Journal of Postsecondary Education Disability*. Her research interests include program development and evaluation, accommodations, self-advocacy, reflective practice, and instructional strategies.

Stan F. Shaw is co-director of the Center on Postsecondary Education and Disability in the Department of Educational Psychology at the University of Connecticut (UConn). His responsibilities with the center include co-principal investigator for the grant implementing Universal Design for Instruction to improve access for college students with learning disabilities and serving as coordinator for the Annual Postsecondary Learning Disability Training Institute. He has taught for 30 years at UConn, where he is a professor and coordinator of the Special Education Program. Dr. Shaw was co-editor of the *Journal of Postsecondary Education and Disability* and is now a member of its editorial board. He has recently published articles in *Career Development for Exceptional Individuals*, *Journal of Vocational Special Needs Education*, *Journal of Developmental*

Education, Teacher Education and Special Education, and *Journal of Postsecondary Education and Disability.* His primary areas of interest are professional development for postsecondary disability personnel, services for college students with disabilities, transition from secondary to postsecondary settings, disability policy and law, and teacher education.